INDIA

SECOND EDITION

Development and Participation

INDIA

SECOND EDITION

Development and Participation

JEAN DRÈZE
and
AMARTYA SEN

OXFORD
UNIVERSITY PRESS

OXFORD
UNIVERSITY PRESS

Great Clarendon Street, Oxford OX2 6DP

Oxford University Press is a department of the University of Oxford.
It furthers the University's objective of excellence in research, scholarship,
and education by publishing worldwide in

Oxford New York

Auckland Bangkok Buenos Aires Cape Town Chennai
Dar es Salaam Delhi Hong Kong Istanbul Karachi Kolkata
Kuala Lumpur Madrid Melbourne Mexico City Mumbai Nairobi
São Paulo Shanghai Singapore Taipei Tokyo Toronto
with an associated company in Berlin

Oxford is a registered trade mark of Oxford University Press
in the UK and in certain other countries

Published in the United States
by Oxford University Press Inc., New York

British Library Cataloguing in Publication Data
Data available

Library of Congress Cataloging in Publication Data
Data available

ISBN 0-19-925748-5 (Hbk.)
ISBN 0-19-925749-3 (Pbk.)

1 3 5 7 9 10 8 6 4 2

Typeset in Galliard
by Eleven Arts, Keshav Puram, Delhi 110035
Printed in Great Britain
on acid-free paper by
Biddles Ltd., Guildford and King's Lynn

Preface

'The Moving Finger writes,' said Edward Fitzgerald, in approximate translation of Omar Khayyam, adding the reassurance, 'and, having writ, Moves on.' Well, we did move on after the first edition of this book was published in 1995, under the title *India: Economic Development and Social Opportunity*. But the Indian economy and society have also moved on, and it seems right, seven years after the last manuscript went to print, to look back and take stock. Not only is it right to assess what has been happening in India, but also to reexamine and reassess our own analyses, expectations and concerns. How does India look to us today, with added experience and observations (even without, we fear, any profound accumulation of wisdom)? What should we alter, amend, add or emphasize as we reexamine this immensely complex and vibrant country? And what— this has been consistently our major concern—are the priorities of public action in India today, interpreting public action to include policy and governance, on the one side, and cooperation, disagreement and public protest, on the other?[1]

First some reassurance, at least for those who saw any merit in our previous edition: we do not think we were wildly mistaken in 1995. In fact, we would claim that the general analyses presented in the first edition have been so far vindicated and even reinforced. But since our general optimism was also combined with intense apprehensions in certain respects, the confirmation of our previous analyses is not substantively such good

---

[1] The diverse aspects and roles of public action (collaborative as well as adversarial) were discussed in our earlier joint book, *Hunger and Public Action* (Oxford: Clarendon Press, 1989).

news. We would have much preferred it had we been proved totally wrong in having entertained some serious fears. However, on the other side, we did combine our diagnoses of problems with suggestions about ways and means of tackling them, mainly through public action. We would argue that those ways and means still remain relevant and available, and in this sense, this book too, like the previous edition, is aimed at engagement and hope.

During the 1990s, the Indian economy has done reasonably well in terms of economic growth and related macroeconomic indicators. This is especially so in the light of the fact that the nineties have been a decade of relatively slow economic growth in most parts of the world. The quickening of the tempo of growth that had occurred in India in the 1980s went with faster growth rates all around us. In the 1990s, the tempo in India has been marginally higher than in the 1980s, but in a world that had slowed remarkably. India now ranks among the ten fastest-growing economies in the world, much in contrast with its earlier image of a laggard economy. The nature of this growth and its basis and content call for close scrutiny (and this we do try to provide in this book, along with broader social and political assessments), but judged in terms of aggregate growth, things have indeed moved on fast.

On the other hand, high growth in the nineties has coexisted with the continuation and sometimes even intensification of deep social failures. In particular, India's success in reducing poverty and deprivation has been very moderate (as we discuss and scrutinize in some detail). In fact, in some important respects the progress of social indicators has been rather slower in the 1990s than in the 1980s. As India enters the twenty-first century, the lives of a majority of its citizens continue to be blighted by endemic poverty, undernutrition, ill health, educational deprivation, environmental degradation and wide-ranging social inequalities.

In the last edition of the book we put particular emphasis on a set of jointly relevant concerns, which included the following:

1. the recognition and realization of the strong growth potential of the Indian economy;
2. the importance of achieving equitable and participatory growth, in contrast with the divisive patterns that prevailed;
3. the urgent need for a broader programme of economic reform, which takes due note of the requirements of equitable and participatory growth, including the need for major initiatives in fields such as basic education, health care, and social security, *along with* reducing the hold of red tape and the 'license Raj'; and
4. the role of civil and political activism in bringing about the required changes in public policy.

In the light of the experience of the 1990s (and our reading of the situation today), we see reason for emphasizing each of these claims even more firmly. There has been, as we shall discuss, some progress in a few of these spheres, but much more remains to be done. The urgency is no less today. While still affirming our familiar ground, we did also think that the book must have a considerably broader focus, if only because things have moved on. In particular, it is now possible to look back at the 1990s, rather than to speculate about the likely impact of economic reforms, as we had to do in the first edition of this book. Many other recent developments are pertinent to the concerns of this book. These include, on the positive side, constructive developments such as the remarkable success of information technology and software production and services in India, and on the other, the bewildering accumulation of gigantic, uncoordinated and 'underpurposed' food stocks, amidst continuation of the severest incidence of undernourishment in the world. There are also major developments of a more political nature such as the nuclear tests of May 1998 and the consolidation of authoritarian and communal tendencies. While this book is not primarily a political commentary, a serious engagement with Indian development cannot ignore these issues.

The focus of this new edition is thus broader in several ways, and these further investigations have added to the corpus of the book. In particular, we have included three entirely new chapters, dealing respectively with (1) population, health and the environment (chapter 6), (2) the social costs of military expansion, particularly in a nuclear India (chapter 8), and (3) the challenges of democracy (chapter 10). The first of these three new chapters deals with issues that already figured prominently in our earlier work, but called for consolidation in the light of recent research and discussions. In particular, the much-publicized official birth of India's billionth citizen in the spring of 2000 has triggered a revival of interest in demographic issues, and also renewed the old fears of a 'population explosion' in India. Given the potential damage caused by misguided population and health policies, it is particularly important to approach and investigate these issues with adequate objectivity and reach. The complementarity between development and the environment, already presumed in the previous edition, also needed more explicit discussion, particularly in view of the often-repeated argument that there is an inescapable opposition between the two. We put emphasis on exploring the different ways in which environmental issues can be more adequately addressed in a democratic polity.

The inclusion, in this new edition, of a chapter on 'security and democracy in a nuclear India' (chapter 8) may appear to some readers to be a 'diversion'. These issues certainly do not belong to the standard territory of development economics. And yet the costs and risks of military expansion cannot but deeply influence the nature and prospects of Indian development, whether in the form of rising insecurity, or of diversion of scarce resources, or of the consolidation of anti-democratic tendencies in a climate of preoccupation with 'national security'. Also, the ravages caused by armed conflict in many countries across the world in the twentieth century give good reason to regard peace as an important ingredient of sustainable development. There is indeed a general need for better recognition of these issues in development economics in general (not just in the analysis of Indian development), and even that more ambitious concern did seem to us to argue for the inclusion of this subject as one of the focal issues in this book.

The concluding chapter discusses 'the practice of democracy', and there is a sense in which this may indeed be considered as the main theme of the book as a whole. It is through democratic practice that there is some hope of addressing the prevailing biases of public policy and development patterns, whether they relate to the neglect of basic education, or to the tolerance of environmental plunder, or to the squandering of scarce resources on military hardware. In this context, it is important to take note of some significant limitations of Indian democracy (without denying its remarkable success in other respects), particularly related to unequal opportunities to participate in democratic institutions. Further, we have to acknowledge the failure of Indian democracy to remedy, at adequate speed or depth, the antecedent economic and social disparities that make the country so deeply unequal. On the other hand, the practice of democracy, with wider participation and with a focus on social disparities between haves and have-nots (rather than sectarian divisions of narrow kinds), offers some real prospect of overcoming these hardened inequalities. The future of Indian development will depend a great deal on the extent to which the opportunities of democratic practice are utilized and adapted to address the massive inequalities that make India such a bastion of disparity.

The older chapters have also undergone very substantial revision and extension. In some cases, this has been linked with the emergence, or clearer recognition, of particular issues, such as the magnitude and sweep of undernourishment in India (chapters 3 and 9), or the changing nature of gender inequality in India (chapter 7). These problems call, in almost all cases, for a firmer engagement with public action, principally of a supportive kind. As a result, the major role of public participation has been investigated in this book in a variety of different fields, along with examining the complementarities involved and their combined reach.

Participation was a central theme in the previous edition as well, but its extensive role receives greater recognition in this edition. Indeed, this characteristic of the present study gave us reason enough to modify the subtitle of the book, from the more specialized theme of 'economic development and social opportunity' highlighted in the last edition to the more general idea of 'development and participation' in the present version.

The updated and expanded Statistical Appendix incorporates a fair amount of new material derived from the recent rounds of the National Sample Survey, the National Family Health Survey, the Sample Registration System, and related sources. India is a statistician's paradise, but the wealth of data is not always matched by easy availability or comparability, nor invariably by the clarity of presentation. We hope that the compendium presented in this book will prove helpful to those who lack the interest to find their own way through the maze.

As before, we have made considerable use of development indicators published by the Government of India as well as by international agencies such as the World Bank and the United Nations Development Programme (UNDP). In handling these sources, we have paid sustained attention to the quality of the data, which varies a great deal. For instance, literacy rates from India's decennial censuses are fairly reliable, but the school enrolment rates published by the Department of Education are not worth the paper on which they are written. Accordingly, we have used the former, but shunned the latter. Similarly, the World Bank's annual *World Development Report* contains much valuable information on a wide range of development indicators, yet some numbers contained in it are best ignored. The same can be said of the UNDP's useful *Human Development Reports*. As far as possible, we have restricted ourselves to figures that have some minimal credibility. The nitty-gritty statistical issues are discussed in the 'explanatory note' included in the Statistical Appendix.

The draft of this book was revised and updated in the summer of 2001. We have tried, at that stage, to incorporate early results of the 2001 census, although detailed census data (e.g. age-specific literacy rates) are still awaited. Another important event that occurred as this book approached completion is the formation of three new Indian states: Chattisgarh, Jharkhand, and Uttaranchal, made up of districts that used to belong respectively to Madhya Pradesh, Bihar, and Uttar Pradesh. These boundary changes made things more difficult, since the use of time series data is hard when the units of division change radically. Also, in some cases the older classification had merits that we did not want to lose altogether. We have chosen to retain the pre-2001 classification, if only to reduce the hopeless search for retrospective data for the newly-formed states.

Thus, unless stated otherwise the terms 'Bihar', 'Madhya Pradesh' and 'Uttar Pradesh' should be understood to refer to these states as they existed in the nineties, i.e. *inclusive* of the districts that are now part of Jharkhand, Chattisgarh and Uttaranchal. Selected indicators for the three new states are presented in the Statistical Appendix.

In handling Indian statistical sources, we have benefited from the expert advice of many helpful civil servants including N.C. Saxena and Pronab Sen (Planning Commission), Subhash Chander and Amarjeet Sinha (Department of Education), R.P. Singh and S.K. Sinha (Office of the Registrar General), K.V. Rao (Ministry of Health and Family Welfare), T.K. Roy (International Institute for Population Sciences, Mumbai), Rajeev Lochan (Central Statistical Organisation), and also the Registrar General, J.K. Banthia.

Chapter 5 of this book draws heavily on the recently-published *Public Report on Basic Education in India* (also known as the 'PROBE report'), with which one of us (Jean Drèze) has been closely associated.[2] Much credit is due to other members of the 'PROBE team': Anuradha De, Claire Noronha, Pushpendra, Anita Rampal, Meera Samson, A.K. Shiva Kumar, and Amarjeet Sinha. In other parts of the book, especially chapter 3, we have also drawn on three case studies of specific Indian states, presented in a collection of essays (Drèze and Sen, 1996) published along with the first edition of this book. The case studies consist of essays on Kerala by V.K. Ramachandran, on West Bengal by Sunil Sengupta and Haris Gazdar, and on Uttar Pradesh by Jean Drèze and Haris Gazdar. We have benefited a great deal not only from these case studies but also from the collaborative work involved in the preparation of that 'companion volume'.

For helpful advice and suggestions, we are grateful to Bina Agarwal, P. Arokiasamy, M.D. Asthana, Amiya Bagchi, Pranab Bardhan, Sajitha Bashir, Bela Bhatia, Kiran Bhatty, Praful Bidwai, Hans Blomkvist, Robin Burgess, Robert Cassen, Gurcharan Das, Monica Das Gupta, Ashim Dasgupta, Gaurav Datt, Angus Deaton, Bibek Debroy, Ravi Duggal, Tim Dyson, Deon Filmer, R. Gopalakrishnan, Haris Gazdar, John Harriss, Stephen Howes, Athar Hussain, Usha Jayachandran, T. Jayaraman, Rajan Katoch, Geeta Gandhi Kingdon, Stephan Klasen, Valerie Kozel, Peter Lanjouw, Arup Maharatna, Manabi Majumdar, James Manor, Harsh Mander, P.N. Mari Bhat, Harinder Mehrotra, Nidhi Mehrotra, Rani Mullen, Mamta Murthi, Siddiq Osmani, Lant Pritchett, N. Ram, V.K.

---

[2] The PROBE Team (1999), *Public Report on Basic Education in India* (New Delhi: Oxford University Press).

Ramachandran, Sujatha Rao, Martin Ravallion, Rammanohar Reddy, Tom Rawksi, Carl Riskin, Ben Rogaly, Emma Rothschild, Rinki Sarkar, Sasanka Sarma, Abhijit Sen, Somnath Sen, Sunil Sengupta, A.L. Sharada, A.K. Shiva Kumar, Farooque Siddiqui, P.V. Srinivasan, K. Subrahmanyam, S.V. Subramanian, Alessandro Tarozzi, Rosie Vaughan, Achin Vanaik, Pravin Visaria, Limin Wang, Lehar Zaidi and Salman Zaidi. We have also benefited from useful editorial advice from Arunima Hoskote, Claire Noronha and the editors at Oxford University Press. Last—and perhaps foremost—we wish to thank Reetika Khera for extremely skilful research assistance.

Jean Drèze   Amartya Sen
Santiniketan, August 2001

Preface 1995

We have tried, in this monograph, to analyse the task of economic development in India in a broad perspective, in which social as well as economic opportunities have central roles. We consider, therefore, not only the facilities offered—important as they are—by well-functioning markets and beneficial exchanges, but also the fundamental role of human capabilities, and their dependence on basic education, health services, ownership patterns, social stratification, gender relations, and the opportunities of social cooperation as well as political protest and opposition. Variations in social opportunities not only lead to diverse achievements in the quality of life, but also influence economic performance, and in particular, the extent to which the facilities offered by functioning markets can be used by the citizens in general.

This general approach is explored fairly extensively, drawing on empirical findings from different parts of India, and also on international comparisons. We outline in particular what can be learned from the experiences of other countries—successful as well as unsuccessful ones—and also from the varieties of experiences *within* India. Special attention is paid to the role of basic education in social transformation as well as economic expansion. The importance of women's agency in bringing about major changes is another central area of investigation in this work. There is also considerable discussion of the role of political and social movements, particularly in confronting deep-seated inequalities.

At the end of the monograph we present a substantial Statistical Appendix, partly as a supplement to the empirical arguments presented here, but also as general information which might be of interest to the reader. Since we do discuss in reasonable detail the nature of the economic challenge faced in India at this time, there is some possibility of treating this book also as an introduction to aspects of the Indian economy (usable even by those readers—those dreadful ones!—who are uninterested in the main theses of this monograph).

The broad perspective presented here, we believe, has some relevance in understanding the obstacles to economic development in India and the basic failure of public policies to remove them. Even though the expansion of social opportunities was very much the central theme in the vision that the leaders of the Indian independence movement had presented to the country at the time the British left, rather little attempt has, in fact, been made to turn that vision into any kind of reality. An opportunity for a break from the past, in this respect, could have been seized when economic reforms were initiated in 1991, but the focus of attention in that programme has been almost exclusively on the opening up of the Indian economy and on broadening the reach of the markets. Those are certainly worthy goals, and the need for reform had been strong for a long time in the over-regulated Indian economy, but the lack of any initiative towards a radical change in social policies, including those in basic education and elementary health care, is a major failure, with deeply negative implications on the prospects of improving living conditions and even on the chances of success of the market reforms themselves. While this book is not primarily a commentary or a critique of contemporary economic policies in India, that subject receives some attention in the general context of diagnosing the roots of India's economic and social backwardness.

The study draws on comparisons of India's achievements with those of other countries, including the ones that have skilfully used market opportunities and international economic integration, such as South Korea and other economies of east Asia and south-east Asia, and more recently post-reform China. In terms of social opportunities, each of these countries had done much more *already* at the time when they were initiating their major economic changes than India has achieved even by *now* (for example, each of them had a much higher level of literacy, already then, than India—still half illiterate—has now). India is in some danger of emulating the divisive pattern of economic growth experienced in countries such as Brazil, with much social inequality, rather than the more participatory development seen in, say, South Korea.

Expansions of basic human capabilities, including such freedoms as the ability to live long, to read and write, to escape preventable illnesses, to work outside the family irrespective of gender, and to participate in collaborative as well as adversarial politics, not only influence the quality of life that the Indian people can enjoy, but also affect the real opportunities they have to participate in economic expansion. An illustration of the compartmentalized nature of official Indian thinking on this subject is provided by the statement made on behalf of the Government of India to the 'Group of 77' in its meeting at the United Nations in New York last September, asserting that 'the concepts of sustainable human development and of human security' involve a 'conceptual derailment of our basic purpose of development cooperation'. The statement was made precisely at a time when the mini-epidemic of plague in India was frightening foreign tourists and businessmen away from India, and the consequences of neglecting 'sustainable human development and human security' were painfully apparent not only in living conditions in India but also in its impact on India's putative attempt at integration with the world economy.

The policy limitations relate not only to governmental decisions, but also to the nature of public discussion, particularly the potential for criticizing these decisions. So much energy and wrath have been spent on attacking or defending liberalization and deregulation that the monumental neglect of social inequalities and deprivations in public policy has received astonishingly little attention in these debates. The issues underlying liberalization are not, of course, trivial, but engagement on these matters—in opposition or in defence—cannot justify the conformist tranquillity on the neglected provisions of public education, health care, and other direct means of promoting basic human capabilities. In fact, sometimes contentious regulational matters seem to get astonishing priority in political discussions over more foundational concerns related directly to the well-being and freedom of the mass of Indian citizens. Debates on such questions as the details of tax concessions to be given to multinationals, or whether Indians should drink Coca Cola, or whether the private sector should be allowed to operate city buses, tend to 'crowd out' the time that is left to discuss the abysmal situation of basic education and elementary health care, or the persistence of debilitating social inequalities, or other issues that have a crucial bearing on the well-being and freedom of the population. In a multi-party democracy, there is scope for influencing the agenda of the government through systematic opposition, and the need to examine the priorities of public criticism is as strong as is the necessity that the government should scrutinize its own relative weights and concerns.

The interstate comparisons presented in this monograph draw on more comprehensive studies of the Indian development experience, focusing in particular on three Indian states (Kerala, West Bengal, and

Uttar Pradesh), presented in a companion volume, edited by us, and prepared for the World Institute for Development Economics Research.[1] The Kerala study has been prepared by V.K. Ramachandran, the West Bengal study by Sunil Sengupta and Haris Gazdar, and the Uttar Pradesh study by Jean Drèze and Haris Gazdar. We are extremely grateful to Ramachandran, Sengupta, and Gazdar for their contributions. Parts of Chapter 7 of this book also draw on recent research undertaken by Jean Drèze in collaboration with Mamta Murthi and Anne–Catherine Guio.

The work for the present monograph was done at the Delhi School of Economics, at STICERD (London School of Economics), and at Harvard University (particularly the Center for Population and Development Studies), and we would like to acknowledge the facilities offered by these institutions. We would also like to thank the International Development Research Centre (IDRC, Canada) for supporting our collaborative work.

For commenting on parts of the manuscript and for extensive discussions, we are most grateful to Sudhir Anand, Robin Burgess, Robert Cassen, Bhaskar Dutta, Haris Gazdar, Athar Hussain, A.K. Shiva Kumar, Peter Lanjouw, Mamta Murthi, Jenny Olson Lanjouw, V.K. Ramachandran, Carl Riskin, Meera Samson, Sunil Sengupta, Amrit Singh, and Limin Wang. We have been greatly helped by the information and analyses provided to us by the Registrar General, Amulya Nanda, and his colleagues Madan Mohan Jha and K.S. Natarajan. We have also benefited from helpful discussions with Bina Agarwal, Satish Agnihotri, Sanjay Ambatkar, David Archer, Roli Asthana, R.V. Vaidyanatha Ayyar, Amiya Bagchi, Kaushik Basu, Bela Bhatia, Bipul Chattopadhyay, Lincoln Chen, Marty Chen, Ansley Coale, Max Corden, Monica Das Gupta, Gaurav Datt, Angus Deaton, S. Mahendra Dev, Tim Dyson, Fang Jianqun, Michel Garenne, Arun Ghosh, Debasish Ghosh, Anne–Catherine Guio, Stephen Howes, Praveen Jha, Shikha Jha, Inge Kaul, Stuti Khemani, Sunita Kishor, Stephan Klasen, Atul Kohli, John Kurian, Chris Langford, James Manor, George Mathew, S.S. Meenakshisundaram, Nidhi Mehrotra, Aditi Mehta, Ajay Mehta, Sumati Mehta, Kaivan Munshi, Nirmala Murthy, Sarmistha Pal, S.S. Parmar, Xizhe Peng, Ritu Priya, Ajit Ranade, Sharad Ranjan, Nina Rao, Jon Rohde, Paul Romer, Emma Rothschild, Denzil Saldanha, Sudipta Sarangi, S.K. Shetty, Amarjeet Sinha, E. Somanathan, Rohini Somanathan, P.V. Srinivasan, T.N. Srinivasan, K. Sundaram, Suresh Tendulkar, Sarojini Thakur, J.B.G. Tilak, and John Williamson. For research

---

[1]Jean Drèze and Amartya Sen, eds. (1996), *Indian Development: Selected Regional Perspectives*, Oxford University Press, WIDER Studies in Development Economics Series.

assistance at different stages of this work, we are indebted to Jason Furman, Jackie Loh, Pia Malaney, Shanti Rabindran, and Snigdha Srivastava. We would also like to thank Meera Samson and Anomita Goswami for invaluable editorial advice. Jackie Jennings kept track of the organizational tasks at the London School of Economics, as did Anna Marie Svedrofsky at Harvard, and to both of them we are most grateful.

J.D.
A.K.S.

Contents

List of Tables   xxiii

List of Figures   xxvii

1. INTRODUCTION AND APPROACH   1
    1.1   The Perspective of Freedom   1
    1.2   Inequality and Participation   8
    1.3   Comparative Perspectives   11
    1.4   Women's Agency and Social Change   17
    1.5   Institutions and Opportunities   20
    1.6   Democracy, Environment and Militarism   23
    1.7   Voice, Assertion and Solidarity   28
    1.8   A Concluding Remark   32

2. ECONOMIC DEVELOPMENT AND SOCIAL OPPORTUNITY   34
    2.1   Development, Freedom and Opportunities   34
    2.2   On Education and Health   38
    2.3   The Social Dimension of Health and Education   41
    2.4   The Government, the State and the Market   44
    2.5   Interdependence between Markets and Governance   46
    2.6   Market-excluding and Market-complementary
          Interventions   49
    2.7   Market Mania and Market Phobia   53

2.8   Cooperative Action and Social Context   56
2.9   A Positive Focus   61

3. INDIA IN COMPARATIVE PERSPECTIVE   64
3.1   India and the World   64
3.2   Lessons from Other Countries   70
3.3   East Asia and Growth-mediated Progress   73
3.4   Human Capital and More Basic Values   81
3.5   India's Internal Diversities   83
3.6   Selected Regional Perspectives   89
3.7   Political Action and Rural Development in
       West Bengal   94
3.8   Kerala: Scrutiny and Significance   97
3.9   Social Opportunities in Himachal Pradesh   101
3.10   Concluding Remark   110

4. INDIA AND CHINA   112
4.1   Perceptions of China   112
4.2   Conditions of Life and Death   114
4.3   Contrasts in Basic Education   116
4.4   Pre-reform Achievements   120
4.5   Post-reform Records   122
4.6   Health Care in the Post-reform Period   128
4.7   Pre-reform and Post-reform Connections   130
4.8   Authoritarianism, Famines and Vulnerability   132
4.9   Coercion, Population and Fertility   134
4.10   The Real Lessons for India from China   140

5. BASIC EDUCATION AS A POLITICAL ISSUE   143
5.1   Basic Education and Social Change   143
5.2   The State of School Education   146
5.3   Educational Hopes and the Discouragement Effect 154
5.4   On Female Education   160
5.5   The Shifting Goalpost of Universal Elementary
       Education   164
5.6   Public Expenditure and Education Policy   168
5.7   School Quality and the Need for Accountability   172
5.8   The Schooling Revolution in Himachal Pradesh   177

5.9   Compulsory Schooling and the Right to Education   184
5.10   Education and Political Action   186

6. POPULATION, HEALTH AND THE ENVIRONMENT   189
   6.1   India's Population: Concerns and Scrutiny   189
   6.2   Malthusian Fears and the Real Issues   196
   6.3   Gender Equity and the Demographic Transition   198
   6.4   Health Care as a Social Responsibility   201
   6.5   Reproductive Health and Beyond   208
   6.6   Achievements of Tamil Nadu   213
   6.7   Environment and Development   218
   6.8   Consequences of Environmental Plunder   222
   6.9   Environment and the Constructive Perspective   226

7. GENDER INEQUALITY AND WOMEN'S AGENCY   229
   7.1   Female Deprivation and Missing Women   229
   7.2   On the Female-Male Ratio   231
   7.3   Women's Agency and Child Survival   245
   7.4   Fertility and Women's Emancipation   253
   7.5   Gender Bias in Natality   257
   7.6   Widowhood and Gender Relations   262
   7.7   Criminal Violence: Poverty vs Patriarchy   266
   7.8   Gender Equality and Social Progress   271

8. SECURITY AND DEMOCRACY IN A NUCLEAR INDIA   275
   8.1   The Wages of War   275
   8.2   The Moral and the Pragmatic   278
   8.3   Sources of Strength and Dangers of Underestimation 280
   8.4   Deterrence and Security   283
   8.5   The Nuclear Debate   286
   8.6   The Social Costs of Militarism   289
   8.7   Defence Expenditure and Social Needs   292
   8.8   Escalation: Costs and Risks   294
   8.9   Militarism and Democracy   299

9. WELL BEYOND LIBERALIZATION   306
   9.1   What is the Cage?   306
   9.2   Radical Needs and Moderate Reforms   310

9.3   Growth and Development in the Nineties   315
9.4   Economic Reform and Social Policy   333
9.5   Hunger Amidst Plenty   336
9.6   Globalization and Inequality   340
9.7   A Concluding Remark   345

10. THE PRACTICE OF DEMOCRACY   347

10.1   Ideals, Institutions and Practice   347
10.2   Inequality and Empowerment   352
10.3   Decentralization and Local Democracy   358
10.4   Transparency and Corruption   363
10.5   Accountability and Countervailing Power   368
10.6   Human Rights and Democracy   371
10.7   Democracy and Participation   375

Statistical Appendix   381

References   415

Subject Index   479

Name Index   500

Tables

3.1 India and sub-Saharan Africa: Selected Development
Indicators, 1999   68
3.2 Adult Literacy Rates (age 15+) in Selected Asian Countries   76
3.3 Selected Indicators for Major Indian States   84
3.4 India, Uttar Pradesh and Kerala: Contrasts in Access to
Public Services, 1998–9   92
3.5 Political Participation in Kerala and Uttar Pradesh   93
3.6 Himachal Pradesh: Selected Indicators of Social
Development, 1998–9   103
3.7 Himachal Pradesh and Haryana   104
3.8 Himachal Pradesh: Gender-related Indicators   106

4.1 India, China and Kerala: Selected Comparisons   115
4.2 Literacy Rates in India, China and Kerala   117
4.3 Mortality Decline in China and Selected Countries   125
4.4 India and China: Economic Growth and
Population Growth   135
4.5 Fertility Rates in China, Kerala and Tamil Nadu   139

5.1 School Education in India (Parts 1 and 2)   147–8
5.2 School Facilities in North India, 1996   167
5.3 Trends in Public Expenditure on Elementary
Education in the 1990s   169
5.4 Social Disparities in Basic Education, 1993–4   180

6.1   Health Expenditure: Selected Indicators   204
6.2   State of Health Centres in Rajasthan, 1999   207
6.3   Selected Health-related Indicators, 1998–9   215
6.4   Quality of Family Planning Services in Tamil Nadu,
      1993   216
6.5   Selected Indicators of India's Urban Environment   224

7.1   Female-Male Ratio and Caste in Uttar Pradesh,
      1901 and 1981   243
7.2   Basic Results of a Cross-section Analysis of the
      Determinants of Child Mortality, Fertility and
      Gender Bias in Indian Districts (1981)   248
7.3   Effects of Selected Independent Variables
      (Female Literacy, Male Literacy and Poverty) on
      Child Mortality (Q5), Female Disadvantage (FD)
      and Fertility (TFR)   252

8.1   Defence vs Development in the Media: Front-page
      Coverage in *The Hindu*   301
8.2   Subject-wise Number of Opinion Articles Published on
      the Editorial page of *The Hindu*, January–June 2000   302

9.1   Economic Growth in Recent Decades   316
9.2   State-specific Growth Rates of Per-capita
      'Gross Domestic Product'   319
9.3   India: Development Trends in the 1980s and 1990s   328

A.1   Economic and Social Indicators in India and Selected
      Asian Countries, 1999   390
A.2   India in Comparative Perspective, 1999   393
A.3   Selected Indicators for Indian States   394
      Part 1:   Per-capita Income and Related Indicators   394
      Part 2:   Mortality and Fertility   395
      Part 3:   Literacy and Education   396
      Part 4:   School Attendance   397
      Part 5:   Other Gender-related Indicators   398
      Part 6:   Reproductive Health and Related Matters   399

Part 7:   Health Care and Related Matters   400
Part 8:   Nutrition-related Indicators   401
Part 9:   Other Public Services   402
Part 10: Media and Politics   403
Part 11: Other Indicators   404

A.4 Selected Development Indicators for the North-
     Eastern States   405–6

A.5 Development Indicators for the 'New' States   407

A.6 India: Trends over Time   408

Figures

3.1 Indian States: Poverty and Child Mortality, 1994   88

4.1 Adult Literacy Rates in Indian States and Chinese
     Provinces (1981–2)   118
4.2 Adult Literacy Rates in Indian States and Chinese
     Provinces (1990–1)   119
4.3 Infant Mortality in China and Selected Asian Economies 126
4.4 Life Expectancy in India, China and Kerala   127

5.1 Social Disparities in Educational Attainments (India),
     1992–3   150
5.2 Declining Illiteracy in Himachal Pradesh   178

6.1 India's Population, 1901 to 2001   192
6.2 India's Total Fertility Rate, 1971–98   193
6.3 State-specific Fertility Rates, 1996–8   195

7.1 Ratio of Female to Male Child Mortality Among
     Hindus and Muslims in Different States, 1981–91   235
7.2 Ratio of Female to Male Age-specific Mortality Rates
     (India), 1970–2 and 1996–8   239
7.3 Ratio of Female to Male Mortality in the 0–4 and
     5–9 Age Groups (India), 1971 to 1996   240

7.4 Female-Male Ratio in 0–6 Age Group, 2001   260

8.1 Military Expenditure in India and Pakistan   297

9.1 Gini Coefficient of Inter-state Economic Inequality,
    1980–1 to 1997–8   321
9.2 Head Count Index of Poverty (India), 1973–4 to
    1999–2000   325
9.3 India: Development Trends in the 1980s and 1990s
    (Parts 1 and 2)   330–1

1

Introduction and Approach

1.1. THE PERSPECTIVE OF FREEDOM

The first edition of this book, which was published in 1995, began by invoking Jawaharlal Nehru's inspiring speech on the eve of independence. On 14 August 1947, Nehru had declared: 'Long years ago we made a tryst with destiny, and now the time comes when we shall redeem our pledge'. 'The achievement we celebrate today', Nehru went on, 'is but a step, an opening of opportunity, to the great triumphs and achievements that await us'. He reminded the country that the tasks ahead included 'the ending of poverty and ignorance and disease and inequality of opportunity'.[1]

Despite Nehru's insightful leadership of a multireligious and multicultural country committed to pluralism and tolerance, perhaps most notably illustrated by his insistence that democracy could work even in a poor country (a commitment that firmly separated out India from most developing countries), many of the economic and social policies his— and successive —governments chose to pursue were not ideally suited to the fulfilment of the momentous tasks that he identified on the eve of independence. Nevertheless, he had set up an agenda for independent India and had identified visionary criteria by which its successes and failures could be plausibly judged. The reach of the basic agenda and the depth of the perspicuous criteria were not compromised by the limitations of Nehru's practical policies.

---

[1] Jawaharlal Nehru's speech at the Constituent Assembly, New Delhi, on 14 August 1947; reprinted in Gopal (1983), pp. 76–7.

The Unfinished Tasks

By the first half of the 1990s, when we were working on the first edition of the book, we noted some evidence of progress in the tasks that Nehru had identified, but we also had to record that the achievements were quite limited, and that much remained to be done. Much still remains to be done. The ambitious goals that Nehru had boldly—and rightly— placed before the country remain largely unaccomplished. Poverty is still rampant in India, and so are widespread illiteracy, avoidable morbidity, premature mortality, and deep-seated inequality of opportunity. Economists of different schools can debate whether poverty has actually diminished or not in the last decade (more on that in chapter 9), but it would be hard to dispute seriously that the absolute level of deprivation in India is still extraordinarily high. Indeed, the gap between hope and realization looks formidable as we reexamine India's achievements and failures in the summer of 2000 while preparing this enlarged edition.

The enquiries that must be added to the ones that were pursued in the first edition include the direction and magnitude of the changes that have been recently occurring. Is India moving in the right direction, and adequately fast? In what fields is progress particularly slow, and how can that be modified? Is there even some regression in particular areas? If so, how may we halt and reverse that? With these issues, which require detailed information as well as sustained scrutiny, we shall be much concerned in this enlarged edition, while retaining what was already investigated in the earlier edition.

Things are certainly happening all around us. The changes have varied from the country's rapid economic expansion in specific fields (such as computer software production and the use of information technology) to India's sluggish progress in elementary education, health care, land reform and environmental protection. We must also take note of the imposition of new burdens on government expenditure, including the expansion of military spending and the development of nuclear weapons, and we have to consider, furthermore, the associated insecurities that have recently escalated in the subcontinent. How these developments have influenced the lives of the Indian people in general and the Indian poor in particular must be examined. These issues relate closely to questions that were already asked in the earlier edition. Our basic approach is not, ultimately, different, but a changing India requires that we must organize new facts and fresh evidence.

Freedom as an End and as Means

The publication of a new edition also gives us an opportunity to discuss, perhaps with somewhat greater clarity and focus, the basic approach we have followed in this book (in the earlier as well as the present edition).[2] It should be clear that we have tended to judge development by the expansion of substantive human freedoms—not just by economic growth (for example, of the gross national product), or technical progress, or social modernization. This is not to deny, in any way, that advances in the latter fields can be very important, depending on circumstances, as 'instruments' for the enhancement of human freedom. But they have to be appraised precisely in that light—in terms of their actual effectiveness in enriching the lives and liberties of people—rather than taking them to be valuable in themselves.[3]

We are, of course, much concerned with economic development in particular. However, we cannot interpret economic development merely as expansion in the production of inanimate objects of convenience—the goods and services that are (as Aristotle put it) 'merely useful and for the sake of something else'.[4] We have to see what these goods and services do to the actual opportunities and freedoms of people, categorized according to class, gender, location, social status, and other relevant distinctions. This view of development is further explored in the next chapter.

The emphasis on the significance of freedoms as ends of development does not, of course, require us to deny their importance also as means of development. The connection between freedom as an end and freedom as means would be immediate—indeed trivial—had there been only one kind of freedom. But freedoms are of different types, and the claim here is that freedoms of distinct kinds tend to help the enhancement and consolidation of one another. This is because freedoms of different kinds interrelate, we argue, in mutually supportive ways.

[2] We have also used this basic approach in our earlier work on 'hunger and public action' (Drèze and Sen, 1989), where many of the concerns of this book are pursued in world-wide perspective.

[3] The distinctions as well as interconnections are more fully discussed in Sen (1985a, 1999a).

[4] Aristotle, *The Nicomachean Ethics*, translated by D. Ross (Oxford: Oxford University Press, 1980), book I, section 5, p. 7. On the relation between Aristotelian ethics and contemporary work on 'commodities and capabilities', see Nussbaum and Sen (1993).

This important connection is, of course, primarily empirical in content, but at the root of these interlinkages lies the human ability to make use of one kind of freedom to boost freedoms of other kinds. The integral nature of human lives leads to inescapable interrelations between the different domains of living.[5] For example, lack of freedom in the form of illiteracy can severely restrict a person's economic opportunities. School education, thus, not only advances social and cultural freedoms, it also enhances economic opportunities (for example, to get a job and to earn an income). Similarly, income poverty can also make it harder for a person to pursue social goals and even to participate adequately in the exercise of political rights.

Again, democratic and civil rights give a person the opportunity to demand and insist on the fulfilment of economic rights. In the absence of a political voice of the deprived, a government may be immune to public pressure when a policy failure occurs, and it is not surprising that famines, which typically result in one way or another from policy failures, continue to occur only in countries that lack democratic freedoms. This connection, which was discussed in the first edition of the book, can be further illustrated not only by the continued occurrence of famines in despotic regimes (for example, in Sudan or North Korea, even as we write), but also by the difficulty of safeguarding basic economic security when the recent Asian economic crisis hit some economically successful but politically authoritarian countries, such as Indonesia and South Korea. Not surprisingly, democracy has become much more of a fighting issue in east and south-east Asia since that economic crisis. At the practical level there has also been much progress in that direction, well illustrated by the great strides towards the establishment or enhancement of democratic institutions in a number of countries in east and south-east Asia. The championing of democratic values has a much stronger presence now in Indonesia, South Korea, Thailand, and several other Asian and African countries.

Tryst with Destiny

Freedoms are, thus, among the principal means as well as the primary ends of development. How does this freedom-centred view, with its conceptual underpinnings, relate to Jawaharlal Nehru's stirring public speech on the eve of independence, on an intensely political occasion?

As it happens, they relate very closely indeed. Consider Nehru's

---

[5] The connections are discussed in Sen (1999a).

identification of the task of 'the ending of poverty and ignorance and disease and inequality of opportunity'. Economic poverty in the form of low income limits the lives of people and curbs their freedom to do even the very basic things which they have reason to want to do (like eating adequately or being comfortably clothed and sheltered). The motivation underlying our concern for eliminating poverty clearly relates to the unfreedoms it imposes.

Similarly, illiteracy and what Nehru called, more generally, 'ignorance', involve not only a negation of the freedom to read and write, but also an impairment of the opportunity to understand and communicate, to take informed personal decisions, and to participate in social choice. Illiteracy is, in fact, a type of 'social unfreedom' and supplements and often intensifies the burden of economic unfreedom in the form of income poverty. Similarly, limitations in health care may be immediately associated with a lack of adequate public or private health facilities (or the inability to afford what is available), but its real rub lies in the lack of freedom to live healthy lives, free from preventable ailments and untimely death.

In effect, by formulating the demands of India's 'tryst with destiny' in the way he did, Nehru pointed to the basic need for the removal of some central constraints that made human lives limited, insecure and unfree. By ambitiously affirming the importance of eliminating these unfreedoms, he was outlining a freedom-oriented commitment to development. Nehru was not, of course, the first person to focus on these issues, even though his emphasis on them in his watershed public speech contributed to the wider use of this type of conceptual approach in practical discussions. The basic importance of freedoms and opportunities had often been invoked earlier, and had been critically defended, directly or indirectly, by such diverse authors as Aristotle, Voltaire, Adam Smith, Condorcet, Karl Marx, John Stuart Mill, Frank Knight, and Friedrich Hayek, to mention just a few leading theorists who belonged, in other respects, to very different schools of thought.[6]

Furthermore, interest in the freedom-centred view of human predicament and challenge is not confined only to the so called Western heritage. Many non-Western thinkers have argued in that direction as well. Even two and a half millennia ago, when Gautama Buddha felt moved to leave his princely home in pursuit of enlightenment, he was directly influenced by the sight of three concrete illustrations of unfreedom, related respectively to old age, illness, and death. He sought his solution for the

---

[6] The connection between contemporary arguments and older literatures have been discussed in Sen (1987a, 1999a).

human predicament in a way and at a level that can hardly be compared with the more mundane policies of social change. Indeed, 'nirvana', which can also be seen as a freedom of a sort, takes us in a very different direction from 'human development'. But Gautama Buddha's focus on the loss involved in unfreedom did provide plentiful inspiration for his followers to address in an immediate way the deprivations that people suffer here and now. Indeed, Emperor Ashoka, perhaps Buddha's greatest disciple (who was largely responsible for the beginning of the spread of Buddhism from India to the rest of the world), extended the identification of significant deprivation to include, inter alia, the unfreedom that resulted from intolerance and bigotry. His stone inscriptions on good governance as well as acceptable behaviour covered that issue among others, in a statement that must count as one of the earliest and most eloquent defences of the liberty of thought and belief.[7]

Focusing on different types of unfreedoms provides an enlightening perspective on the challenges facing any society, including India. Nehru had reason enough to choose that focus in articulating India's 'tryst with destiny'. This perspective remains deeply relevant in the formulation of the ends and means of development in contemporary India.

Social Opportunity and Human Agency

The approach used in this study is much concerned with the opportunities that people have to improve the quality of their lives. It is essentially a 'people-centred' approach, which puts human agency (rather than organizations such as markets or governments) at the centre of the stage. The crucial role of social opportunities is to expand the realm of human agency and freedom, both as an end in itself and as a means of further expansion of freedom.

The word 'social' in the expression 'social opportunity' (extensively used in the first edition of this book), is a useful reminder not to view individuals and their opportunities in isolated terms. The options that a person has depend greatly on relations with others and on what the state and other institutions do. We shall be particularly concerned with those opportunities that are strongly influenced by social circumstances and public policy, especially those relating to education, health, nutrition, social equity, civil liberties, and other basic aspects of the quality of life.

The use of the term 'social' is not intended as a contrast with 'economic'. Indeed, it will be argued that various economic arrangements (including

---

[7] On this see Sen (1999a), chapter 10, and the references cited there.

the market mechanism) are of central importance to the presence or absence of 'social opportunities', and there is, thus, a deep-seated complementarity here. To illustrate, the opportunities offered by a well-functioning market may be difficult to use when a person is handicapped by, say, illiteracy or ill health. Conversely, a person with some education and fine health may still be unable to use his or her abilities because of the limitation of economic opportunities, which in turn can be related to the absence of markets, or inadequate public facilities, or some other restraint that limits economic initiatives. There are also, in many circumstances, important complementarities between economic advancement and political participation—another social opportunity that will receive sustained attention in this book. In focusing on social opportunities, we propose a perspective that is substantially *broader* than (though not inconsistent with) more standard economic analyses of development.

There is also an issue of ends and means, for freedoms, as discussed earlier, are valuable in both respects. The elimination of illiteracy, ill health and other avoidable deprivations are valuable for their own sake, and this must be recognized even as we acknowledge the far-reaching instrumental role of these achievements. In that sense, it is perhaps a mistake to see the development of education, health care and other basic achievements *only* or *primarily* as expansions of 'human resources'—the accumulation of 'human capital' (the language that is often chosen in the professional economic literature). The bettering of human life does not have to be justified by showing that a person with a better life is also a better producer. As Kant had noted, there is a categorical need to 'treat humanity, whether in their own person or in that of any other, in every case as an end withal, never as means only'. In arguing for a people-centred view of economic development that focuses on human agency and social opportunities, we are not just arguing for giving importance to so-called 'human capital'.

However, after noting this basic point, and getting our ends and means sorted out, we have every reason to pay full attention to the importance of human capabilities *also as instruments* for economic and social performance. A quality that is of intrinsic importance can, in addition, also be instrumentally momentous, without compromising its intrinsic value. Basic education, good health, and other human attainments are not only directly valuable as constituent elements of the quality of life, these abilities can also help in generating economic success of more standard kinds, which in turn can contribute to enhancing human freedoms in other ways.

The instrumental analysis has to be integrated with the intrinsic importance of human freedoms. There are, thus, two distinct elements in this view of economic development: (1) the intrinsic and inalienable eminence of human freedoms and the quality of life, and (2) the contingent but significant practical importance of many of these freedoms (especially those related to education, health, and political liberties) in promoting participatory development and, through it, further advancing the quality of life that people can enjoy. It is this dual concern that has largely motivated the approach we have tried to present in this work.

1.2. INEQUALITY AND PARTICIPATION

One of the deprivations to which Nehru made an explicit reference is 'inequality of opportunity'. The connection between opportunity and freedom is, of course, extremely close, but the pointer specifically to *inequality* of opportunity enriches the investigation in three distinct ways. First, it emphasizes the need not only to promote freedoms in general (no matter who the beneficiary is), but also to recognize the distributional aspects of freedoms in a society. Since there is, in economics, a tradition of identifying inequality with income distribution, it is important to acknowledge the case for being involved also with inequality of freedoms and opportunities. Indeed, in so far as freedom provides a better perspective on individual advantage than does the mere size of one's income, the interest in inequality of freedom has, it can be argued, a greater claim to our attention than income inequality could command. For example, a disabled person, or someone living in an epidemiologically vulnerable location (due, for example, to the prevalence of communicable diseases), can be seen to be particularly disadvantaged vis-à-vis others who have similar income levels but are free from that disability or those epidemiological surroundings.[8]

There is a second reason why the focus on inequality of opportunity can be particularly illuminating in the context of development. In any society, most types of opportunities are enjoyed by some people, but not by others. The unfreedom of a section of the people contrasts with what others can do without any difficulty whatever. Extending freedom widely across the society typically involves countering this division between haves and have-nots. For example, the expansion of elementary schooling would reduce not only the overall extent of illiteracy, but also the inequality of educational achievements.[9] The goal of inequality reduction, thus, fits

---

[8] The importance of equality in the freedom-based perspective has been discussed in Sen (1980, 1992a).

[9] While it can be argued that the idea of inequality, interpreted mechanically, can suggest a different way of reducing inequality of literacy, to wit, make everyone illiterate,

in well, in general, with that of removing the deprivation of those bereft of basic opportunities.

There is also a third reason for focusing particularly on the issue of inequality of opportunities. This concerns the importance of participation in social change. The ability of people to participate in social decisions has been seen, particularly since the French Revolution, as a valuable characteristic of a good society. Indeed, the subject of 'social choice theory', with its focus on the participation of members of the society in the making of social decisions, emerged as a discipline in the late eighteenth century, and that development was, to a great extent, inspired by the participatory focus of contemporary revolutionary thought. For example, one of the principal theorists of the French Revolution, Marquis de Condorcet, was also the main founder of the discipline of social choice theory.[10]

Participation is intimately connected with demands of equality. At the most immediate level, democratic participation requires the sharing and symmetry of basic political rights—to vote, to propagate and to criticize. Actual participation in political movements and public action can make a major difference to the agenda of governments and influence its priorities.[11]

Going beyond that elementary and fundamental association, another important causal connection is that political participation can be more effective and more equally enjoyed if there is some equity in the sharing of economic resources as well. Indeed, economic inequality can seriously compromise the quality of democracy, for example through the influence of money on electoral processes, on public decision-making, and on the content of the media. Overcoming the inequalities of power associated with economic privilege is an important aspect of democracy in the full sense of the term.

This integrating claim should not be confused with the very different claim that democracy is worthless or unimportant in the presence of sharp economic disparities. That reactionary argument with an apparently progressive veneer has supposedly provided intellectual justifications of much tyranny and arbitrary authoritarianism in the world. The sharing of political power need not be postponed until economic power is widely generated and equitably shared. We have to acknowledge that many democratic countries have achieved much success in the practice of sharing

---

the importance of the freedom in question militates against that 'simple' route to an egalitarian society. On this see also Dworkin (1978), particularly his distinction between 'being treated equally' and 'treatment as equals'.

[10] That history and its contemporary relevance are discussed in Arrow (1963a) and Sen (1999b). See also Arrow, Sen and Suzumura (1996–7).

[11] We discussed the evidence in that direction across the world in Drèze and Sen (1989).

political power despite the economic divisions between the rich and the poor. But in the same spirit, we must avoid taking what has been achieved as just fine, and acknowledge inter alia the adverse effects of economic inequality on effective political participation.

Social inequalities too can seriously interfere with equality of political participation. Divisions of power and influence related to caste, gender and even education can, in many situations, make the socially underprivileged also politically marginalized. Here again, it is important to recognize the adverse effects of inequality on political participation, and also the possibility of countering this by promoting greater social equality as well as by overcoming the association between social privilege and political power. We shall have more to say on these issues later on in this volume.

Participation and equality are extremely important also in extending the use of economic and social facilities that a nation can offer. For example, those who are solicitous of the idea that opportunities of market transaction should be open rather than restricted have good reason to consider not only the liberty of the rich to participate in market activities, but also the opportunity of the poor to join in what the market can offer. This is one reason, among others, why initiatives geared to the economic participation of disadvantaged groups (e.g. through asset redistribution, or the creation of microcredit facilities, or the diffusion of skills) can be very significant. Similarly, the ability of the underprivileged to make use of public services such as health centres, government offices and the courts is often undermined by the social distance that separates them from those who run these services. This type of participation, too, can be promoted through means such as educational advancement and political organization.

Participation also plays a crucial role in the formation of values and in generating social understanding. An analogy may be useful here. Aside from their role in modifying or countering existing policies and practices, 'public interest litigations' (or 'class actions suits') also provide an opportunity for wider hearing of the problems of the underdogs, and this can be very important in shaping public understanding and even lead to some reexamination of values. Similarly, participatory discussion about traditional disparities in the media and in political platforms can lead to more social attention being paid to these inequalities. So can collective agitations against specific inequities and deprivations—they influence not only actions and rules but also thought and perceptions. For example, in fostering a greater awareness of the existence and perniciousness of gender-based inequality (one of the more positive developments that have been occurring in recent years in India is an expansion of this awareness), participatory processes of public discussion as well as 'agitprop' have been portentous, in spreading a different outlook, with greater recognition of the need for questioning inherited tolerance of inequality.

Issues of inequality and participation are particularly crucial in India, where social divisions (based on class, caste and gender among other sources of disparity) are pervasive and have tended to take a heavy toll on both economic development and social opportunities. While social disparities in India are often assumed to be extremely rigid, if not immutable, there is in fact enormous scope for countering the inequalities that happen to prevail today. The potential for change has already been demonstrated, to some extent, in recent decades (e.g. through social movements for the emancipation of 'backward' castes, advances in the political representation of women, and fairly radical changes in power structures at the village level). The future course of development and democracy in India will depend a great deal on the extent to which further possibilities in this domain are realized.

1.3. Comparative Perspectives

It is not hard to notice that the task of eliminating basic deprivations in India remains, alas, largely unaccomplished. This is not to deny that progress has been made in particular fields. One example is the elimination of substantial famines that continued to wreck the country right up to independence (the last major famine was the Bengal famine in 1943, which killed between 2 and 3 million people). That achievement is far from negligible since many other countries in Asia and Africa have had large famines in recent decades. There are also other achievements to which one can point, varying from the successful functioning of a multiparty democratic system to the emergence of a large scientific community and the development of information-technology based industries.

However, India's overall success in promoting social opportunities since independence has been quite limited. The intensities of many basic deprivations have been considerably reduced, but there is nevertheless a long way to go in ensuring anything like acceptable living conditions for all citizens. To illustrate, while infant mortality in India today (about 70 per 1,000 live births) is certainly much lower than at the time of independence (around 180 per 1,000), many other developing countries that were in a comparable position to India not so long ago are now doing much better in that respect—with infant mortality rates well below 20 in many cases.[12] Similar remarks can be made about other aspects of living conditions,

---

[12] For further information, see the Statistical Appendix of this book, which also presents other development indicators and discusses the statistical sources.

dealing for instance with life expectancy, elementary education, nutritional well-being, protection from illness, social security, and consumption levels. India's progress over the decades, while far from the worst, has been substantially and systematically outclassed by many other developing countries.

One important point to note here is that the more successful countries, which have left India behind, have pursued very diverse economic policies, from market-oriented capitalism (South Korea, Taiwan, Thailand) to communist-party-led socialism (Cuba, Vietnam, pre-reform China), and also various mixed systems (Costa Rica, Jamaica, Sri Lanka). As far as economic growth is concerned, their records have also been extremely diverse. And yet all of them have been able to achieve a radical reduction in human deprivation and insecurity. Despite major differences in economic policy and growth performance, these countries have had much in common in terms of social policies, particularly those relating to the expansion of basic education and health care, and India contrasts with all of them in this fundamental respect. There is much to learn from these diverse countries and the commonality of their social policies, even though we would have good reason to shun emulating them in other respects. We shall have more to say on this general contrast in this monograph, which retains and consolidates the comparative perspective that informed the first edition.

There is one field in which India has done worse than *even* the average of the poorest countries in the world, and that is elementary education. In 1999, India's adult female literacy rate (age 15 and above) was only 44 per cent, which is low not only in comparison with China's 75 per cent, but even compared with the estimated average of 59 per cent for all 'low-income economies' excluding China as well as India.[13] India has been left way behind in the field of basic education even by countries which have not done better than India in many other developmental achievements, such as Ghana, Indonesia, Kenya, Myanmar (Burma), Philippines, Zimbabwe, and Zambia. Even Bangladesh, which remains far behind India in many other respects (and has a much lower per-capita income), is rapidly catching up in terms of educational achievements in the younger age groups.[14]

[13] *World Development Indicators 2001*, Table 2.14, and *World Development Indicators 2000*, Table 2.12. The pattern is similar for adult male literacy (72, 91 and 78 per cent, respectively). For further discussion of literacy estimates for India, see the 'explanatory note' in the Statistical Appendix.

[14] Recent demographic surveys suggest that average school attendance rates are now quite similar in Bangladesh and India, even though they used to be much lower in Bangladesh. Further, a remarkable feature of school attendance rates in Bangladesh

This particular issue will receive considerable attention in this monograph, both because education is a crucial social achievement, and also because it plays an important instrumental role in facilitating other achievements. These international comparisons also raise an important general question about the complementarity between the opening up of economic opportunities and the social conditions that facilitate the use of those opportunities (e.g. widespread literacy). There is, in fact, some empirical evidence suggesting that the economic returns to educational expansion tend to increase with the expansion of market opportunities, and such a complementarity is natural to expect on the basis of general economic reasoning. Education has done much for the quality of life in, say, Sri Lanka, without doing quite so much yet for economic growth.

Similarly, Kerala's growth performance, which was very poor until recently despite high educational and social achievements, indicates that something more than just education and other social inputs may be needed to accomplish rapid growth of the kind that countries such as South Korea, Thailand or China have been experiencing. Kerala's human resources have found plentiful markets outside India, as migrants from Kerala have seized remunerative work in the Gulf and elsewhere. The scope for using these human resources at home as well can certainly be increased to a great extent by expanding economic opportunities within the borders of India.

However, there is also the other side of the complementarity between economic opportunities and social conditions. The effectiveness of opening up new economic opportunities and expanding the productive uses of labour and skill may depend greatly on basic educational facilities and related circumstances. This is where a fuller reading of the experiences of the rapidly growing countries in Asia is crucially important. As will be presently discussed (in chapter 3), India's current literacy rates are not only much lower than those of South Korea, Thailand or China *today*, but also lower than what these and other newly industrializing Asian countries had already achieved when they moved ahead with their rapid economic growth (say, by 1960). Since broad-based economic growth in these countries involved using a range of modern industries, and made considerable demand on widely shared skills and education, the instrumental role of basic education in these development experiences can hardly be overlooked. A similar point can be made about China's recent experience of market-based rapid economic growth, since China too was starting, at the time of its economic reforms, from a much higher base of elementary education than India

---

today is that they are as high for girls as for boys, in sharp contrast with India where a large gender gap remains. On these matters, see the data presented in Filmer (1999).

has achieved so far. To understand what happened in these countries, it is necessary to take a reasonably comprehensive view of their economic and social conditions, rather than just proposing to imitate one particular aspect of their performance, namely, their use of market-based incentives. *Learning* from an integrated experience has to be distinguished from simply *copying* some particular features of it.

India and China

Special attention will be paid in this monograph to the contrast between India and China, not only because of the obvious relevance of the Chinese experience for India, but also because of the sustained influence of that particular comparison in Indian political debates. In interpreting China's experience (particularly involving a much more radical elimination of endemic deprivations than India has been able to achieve so far), there are good reasons to focus on the complementarities between the *pre-reform* achievements and the *post-reform* success in promoting rapid and widely-shared economic expansion.[15] When China adopted its programme of market-oriented economic reforms in the late seventies, it had already gone a long way towards achieving the conditions that facilitate broad-based involvement of people in the process of economic expansion. The relevant achievements, in this case, include (1) land reform, (2) near-universal literacy in the younger age groups, (3) a radical reduction of endemic morbidity and undernutrition, (4) wide-ranging social security arrangements, (5) a functioning system of local governance, and (6) a major expansion of the participation of women in the labour force. India still has a long way to go in achieving these solid foundations of broad-based economic expansion, and the challenges of economic and social reform in India have to be seen in that light.

Having said this, we are not advocating imitative emulation of the Chinese approach. China's experience of expanding social opportunities, while most impressive in many respects, has included some failures of monumental proportions. As discussed in chapter 4, many of these failures reflect China's authoritarian system of governance, which keeps government policies beyond the reach of public scrutiny and popular challenge. The famines of 1958–61, the excesses of the Cultural Revolution, the abrupt dismantling of public health care services in the post-reform period, the widespread and continuing violation of elementary freedoms, and the devastating human consequences of coercive population policies,

[15] See chapter 4.

are telling illustrations of that pattern. Just as China's achievements provide a powerful illustration of the scope for positive government activity in economic development, its failures clearly point to the dangers of authoritarian governance.

Regional Contrasts

One of the most interesting aspects of India's development record is its remarkable regional diversity in the elimination of basic deprivations. For example, while India's life expectancy figure of around 63 years compares quite unfavourably with China's 70 years, Kerala's life expectancy—about 74 years—appears on the other side of China's achievement. Similarly, the infant mortality rate of 71 per thousand live births in India is much higher than China's 30, but Kerala's rate of 14 is less than half that of China.[16] Again, while India's literacy rate is much lower than that of China, Kerala's is substantially higher than China's. In fact, Kerala's female literacy rate is higher than that of *every individual province* in China (see chapter 4). On the other side, some of the Indian states (for example, Uttar Pradesh, Rajasthan, Madhya Pradesh, Bihar) have much lower achievements than even the low Indian average.[17]

These contrasts *within* India are important to study for their own interest. But there is also much to be learned, we argue, from the light that is thrown by these comparative experiences on what can or cannot be achieved elsewhere in the country. This applies to learning from high achievements in some fields (as in Kerala) as well as from low ones in those very fields (as in Uttar Pradesh), and also from the rather mixed cases (as in West Bengal).[18] One of the main themes of this work is the importance of the lessons to be learned *by* India *from* India, and this can be just as important as learning from the achievements of other countries. In many respects, the lessons arising from international comparisons

[16] See Table 4.1 in chapter 4. The reference year is 1999.

[17] As mentioned in the preface, the 'Indian states' considered in this book are those that existed prior to the formation of three new states (Jharkhand, Chattisgarh and Uttaranchal) in late 2000. Throughout the book, the terms 'Bihar', 'Madhya Pradesh' and 'Uttar Pradesh' refer to these states as they existed in the nineties, i.e. *inclusive* of the districts that now form the new states of Jharkhand, Chattisgarh, and Uttaranchal, respectively.

[18] A companion volume of essays (Drèze and Sen, 1996), published along with the first edition of this book, includes case studies of these three states, authored respectively by V.K. Ramachandran (Kerala), Jean Drèze and Haris Gazdar (Uttar Pradesh), and Sunil Sengupta and Haris Gazdar (West Bengal).

are reinforced by a consideration of regional diversities within India. Indeed, the regional contrasts within India relate especially to the varieties of public policies pursued in the respective states, and, in particular, to dissimilar uses of public action to enhance the quality of life and expand social opportunities.

Kerala's experience is particularly instructive in that respect, and receives sustained attention in this book. There is, indeed, much evidence of the extensive links between Kerala's outstanding social achievements (including a life expectancy of 74 years, near-universal literacy in the younger age groups, a fertility rate that is now well below the replacement level, a virtual absence of child labour, and relatively low levels of gender inequality) and its rich history of public action (involving early state initatives and social movements for the promotion of literacy, the implementation of land reforms, the elimination of traditional discriminations, the provision of wide-ranging public services, and related goals).[19] Kerala's experience of early promotion of social opportunities based on public action is of far-reaching significance for other Indian states (and indeed for other countries also).

Kerala's record includes some failures as well, and we have noted in particular how Kerala's performance in generating economic growth has been quite moderate. While the social opportunities of living long, healthy, and literate lives have been radically enhanced in an exemplary manner, the opportunities that depend on economic success (including high levels of employment) have been more stagnant. The roots of this failure include the continuation of overregulated economic governance that has blighted the prospects of economic expansion all over India for many decades, the removal of which has met more resistance in Kerala than in most other Indian states. Kerala, it would appear, has to learn as well as teach. But while Kerala's *learning* can be easily integrated into the fairly standard reformist focus on incentives, economic growth, and deregulation, what it has to *teach* takes us well beyond these straightforward concerns.

Even though Kerala stands out in having achieved decisive progress in social development at an early stage, illustrations of that possibility are no longer confined to Kerala. Many recent experiences in other states of India also indicate that substantial results can be obtained from serious public efforts to promote social opportunities. West Bengal provides a good example of the possibility and rewards of land reform programmes

---

[19] See the study by V.K. Ramachandran (1996) in the companion volume, and also the literature cited there and in chapter 3 of this book.

(enhancing equity as well as the efficiency of local agriculture).[20] Tamil Nadu is an outstanding case of rapid demographic transition based on a combination of positive state initiatives and comparatively favourable social background (relating in particular to the agency of women in society). Himachal Pradesh has made exceptional progress in the field of basic education, even catching up with Kerala within forty years for the younger age groups (starting from a state of extreme educational backwardness). In Gujarat, sustained commitment to economic growth and active infrastructural development have fostered remarkable economic dynamism, to the extent that the state's per-capita GDP has apparently grown at more than 6 per cent per year or so during the 1990s.[21] Early signs of these successes had already been noted in the first edition of this book, and have been significantly consolidated in recent years.

On the other side, the penalties of neglect of social opportunities are well illustrated by a number of other states, such as Uttar Pradesh, where basic deprivations remain endemic. In fact, as will be discussed in chapter 3, there is a significant complementarity between the lessons emerging from positive and negative experiences. Just as Kerala's achievements richly illustrate the enabling roles of widespread literacy, public services, women's agency, cooperative action, adversarial politics, and related factors of social progress, the failures of (say) Uttar Pradesh illustrate the stifling of social opportunities that results from neglecting these enabling factors.

Even in some of India's 'problem' states, however, there have been interesting developments in recent years, such as the 'education guarantee scheme' in Madhya Pradesh and the 'right to information' movement in Rajasthan. While the practical results of these initiatives are not yet absolutely clear, these developments are particularly significant as a pointer to the changing orientation of democratic politics in India. We shall have more to say on these issues later on in this book.

1.4. WOMEN'S AGENCY AND SOCIAL CHANGE

In the course of different arguments in this monograph, we shall have the occasion to comment on the importance of women's agency for social progress. The focus on women's agency has to be distinguished from the more usual concentration on women's well-being. There are good reasons to pay particular attention to each in examining the requirements

[20] See the paper by Sunil Sengupta and Haris Gazdar (1996) in the companion volume; also chapter 3, and the literature cited there.
[21] See Statistical Appendix, Table A3, Part 1.

of economic development and social change in India. The persistence of sharp gender inequalities in many different forms is one of the most striking aspects of Indian society, and it yields disparities in well-being as well as differences in power and decision-making authority.

Perhaps the most telling expression of inequality of well-being is to be found in the low female-male ratio in India, and the high proportion of 'missing women' whose absence can be attributed to differential care, including medical attention.[22] Unequal sharing within the family is another prominent feature of gender relations in India. In remedying these inequalities, the activities of women's organizations and other forms of agency can be of crucial importance, and in several different contexts, the effectiveness of such activities has already been well demonstrated.[23]

The first reason for the importance of women's agency is, thus, the persistence of gender-based inequalities of well-being, given the relevance of women's actions and movements in bringing about a change in this field. The need for women's own agency in securing gender justice arises partly from the fact that gender inequality does not decline automatically with the process of economic growth. In fact, as will be seen in chapter 7, in some cases economic progress can even lead to a relative deterioration in the position of women in society. In so far as economic expansion does reduce gender inequality, this happens mainly through other variables that relate more closely to women's agency, such as female labour-force participation and female literacy. Broad-based economic growth, for instance, can positively influence the status of women through expanding opportunities for remunerative female employment, which often results in an improvement in the 'deal' that a woman receives within the family. But even these influences, though fairly extensive in some cases, can be slow, and in great need of supplementation by more direct public action in pursuit of gender equity, focusing for instance on educational transformation, women's ownership rights, and political participation.

Second, women's empowerment can positively influence the lives not only of women themselves but also of men, and of course those of children. There is much evidence, for instance, that women's education tends to reduce child mortality rates, for both boys and girls.[24] In fact,

---

[22] See chapter 7, where the empirical evidence relating to other issues discussed in this section is also reviewed.

[23] See Omvedt (1980, 1989, 1993), K. Bardhan (1985), Poitevin and Rairkar (1985), Desai (1988), Duvvury (1989), Stree Shakti Sanghatana (1989), Kishwar and Vanita (1991), I. Sen (1990), Dietrich (1992), Rose (1992), D.K.S. Roy (1992), Chaudhuri (1993), Ray and Basu (1999), among others.

[24] See section 7.3, and the studies cited there. It is worth emphasizing that the

there is good reason to relate the remarkably high life-expectancy levels in Kerala to its educational achievements, particularly of women, and on the other side, to relate the low life-expectancies of some of the northern states to backwardness in female education. The subordination of women in Indian society tends to impair their effectiveness in reducing deprivation in general, and it is not only the well-being of female children or adult women which is improved by the enhanced agency of women.

Third, women's emancipation (through basic education, economic independence, political organization and related means) tends to have quite a strong impact on fertility rates. This linkage has been widely observed in international comparisons, but it is consistent also with recent experiences of remarkably rapid fertility reduction in several Indian states, including Kerala, Tamil Nadu and Himachal Pradesh. On the other side, the subordination of women in the 'northern heartland' clearly does contribute not a little to the high fertility rates that are found in such states as Uttar Pradesh, Madhya Pradesh, Rajasthan, and Bihar. Through this connection with demographic change, the role of women's agency extends well beyond the interest of today's women, and even beyond the interests of all living people today, and has a significant impact on the lives of future generations.

Fourth, aside from specialized roles, women's agency is important as a part of the agency of all people. Women's decisions and actions can have a profound impact on the policies the government decides to pursue and the lives that people can lead. Women have often been very active in demanding and working for basic social change, and our general emphasis on the importance of human agency and participation in development applies particularly to women. In much of India, women tend to be rather homebound and politically unassertive, but given the critical importance of political action and pressure, a real difference can be made by women taking an active role in these activities. The effectiveness of public action and the expansion of social opportunities depend a great deal on the effective freedom of women to exercise their reasoned agency.

Since the first edition of this book was published, further evidence has

---

positive link between female education and child survival is likely to relate not only to the agency of women *within* the family, but also to their role in politics and public life. In particular, a more active and informed public role of women in society tends to be associated with greater pressure in the direction of expanding health care and related public services. This link has been observed in contexts as diverse as the Total Literacy Campaign (Ghosh et al., 1994, p. 38), collective action by self-employed women (Rose, 1992, p. 249), and the participation of women in village panchayats (Chattopadhyay and Duflo, 2001).

emerged both of the potential for wider participation of women in Indian society and politics, and of the importance of such participation for social change. In Himachal Pradesh, for instance, women's agency has played a crucial part in the 'schooling revolution' that has recently swept through that state, as well as in other forms of social progress associated with educational advancement (including a rapid demographic transition).[25] Wherever the Total Literacy Campaign has been a success (if not in terms of achieving 'full literacy', at least in terms of social mobilization around issues of literacy and education), it has owed a great deal to women's active participation in the programme.[26] In Andhra Pradesh, the anti-arrack campaign (and its subsequent offshoots) has provided a dramatic example of effective political mobilization of women.[27] There have been many other examples of this kind, from the formation of all-women panchayats in Maharashtra to the national campaign for more equitable political representation of women. Further expansion of women's agency, and the gradual transformation of gender relations associated with it, are emerging as one of the most powerful forces of social change in contemporary India.

1.5. INSTITUTIONS AND OPPORTUNITIES

Our focus on participation relates to the crucial recognition that development calls for the use of many different institutions—the market, the public services, the judiciary, the political parties, the media, and so on. These institutions can often supplement and also complement each other. Since freedoms of different kinds contribute to one another, a freedom-centred view calls for an institutionally integrated approach.

The need for thinking in terms of a multi-institution format was emphasized in the earlier edition of this book, and that need is no less acute now. We were then concerned that the debates surrounding 'liberalization' had tended to divide the protagonists into simply 'pro-market' and 'anti-market' camps, rather than addressing the issues with adequate breadth. Reform of market arrangements, we had argued, had to be embedded in a wider and much more radical programme of social and economic change, involving a variety of institutions.

[25] See chapters 3 and 5; also Drèze (1999) and Probe Team (1999).
[26] See Ghosh et al. (1994), who observe that 'women have invariably been the large majority of the participants' (p. 22). The authors also note that the campaign has led to 'greater and more vociferous demand for [education and] other services to meet [the participants'] basic needs in regard to employment, housing, health, etc.' (p. 38). On these matters, see also Sundararaman (1996).
[27] See e.g. Anveshi (1993).

The liberalization agenda is largely inspired by the assumption that India's past failures are due to the insufficient development of market incentives. We have suggested that while there is some truth in this diagnosis, it is quite inadequate as an analysis of what has gone wrong in this country. There are many failures, particularly in the development of public education facilities, health care provisions, social security arrangements, local democracy, environmental protection, and so on, and the stifling of markets is only one part of the larger picture. The failures can, thus, be scarcely seen simply as the result of an 'overactive' government. What can be justifiably seen as overactivity in some fields has been inseparably accompanied by thoroughgoing *underactivity* in others.

It is, thus, not a simple matter of 'more' or 'less' government. Rather, it is a question of the *type* of governance to have, and of seeing the role of public policies in promoting as well as repressing social opportunities. Indeed, the interrelations between the state, the public and the market have to be seen in a larger framework, with influences operating in different directions. That broader framework does not lend itself to the derivation of simple formulae used by different sides in the contemporary debates (selling liberalization over all else, or—on the other side—rubbishing it forcefully). But this loss of simplicity is a gain as well.

We argued, in short, for taking the debates on contemporary India's political economy *beyond* the familiar battle-lines around the issue of liberalization. There are, of course, things to be discussed there and pros and cons to be assessed, but the main problem with focusing on that question is the resulting neglect of other public policy matters, dealing for instance with education, health, and social security. Both the vigorous defences of liberalization and the spirited attacks on it contribute to hiding other—basic and urgent—issues. If the central challenge of economic development in India is understood in terms of the need to expand social opportunities, then liberalization must be seen as occupying only one part of that large stage. By spotlighting that one part, the rest of the stage is left obscure.

The central questions, as we had tried to identify them, were:
1. What should be the content of economic reform (liberalization was only one issue among many others, including employment promotion, land reforms, and building of economic infrastructure)?
2. What changes are needed in social and other not-purely-economic fields in addition to economic reform (particularly in promoting social opportunities related to elementary education, basic health care, effective political participation and related matters)?

We would argue that the need for focusing on these issues has not diminished despite the changes—some of them positive and promising—that have occurred over the last decade. This is both because economic reforms, while badly needed, have been inadequate, and because the creation of social opportunities, no less strongly needed, has been painfully slow.

It is not that nothing has happened in the 1990s. There have been removal of some counterproductive controls and opening up of economic opportunities. These changes have often been particularly helpful to the middle classes, who have had the opportunity to be more gainfully active than before. These gains, which have often been very substantial, should not be dismissed, since India's middle classes are large, and there have been benefits for some others as well, who have been involved in the newly prospering sectors of the economy. Further reform, with fuller use of trade opportunities and technology development, can potentially be combined with a greater sharing of the economic opportunities among the Indian labour force. That, however, requires much greater emphasis on policies and initiatives that facilitate broad-based economic participation, such as employment programmes, educational expansion, health care, land reform, microcredit facilities and social security arrangements.

Compared with clearly articulated policies of economic reform, originally initiated in 1991, there has been relatively little departure in expanding social facilities of this type. In particular, social policies in the 1990s have been confined, in most states, to a timid continuation of earlier approaches.[28] While there have been new initiatives in some states (particularly in the field of elementary education), the general condition of basic public services in India remains abysmal. In some cases, there has even been an erosion of government commitment in this respect. For instance, while every major political party is now, in theory, committed to raising public expenditure on education to 6 per cent of GDP, the share of education expenditure in GDP actually *fell* in the 1990s, from a peak of 4.4 per cent in 1989 to 3.6 per cent or so towards the end of the decade (see p. 166). This is a significant reversal of earlier trends, involving a slow but steady increase in public expenditure on education as a share of GDP in earlier decades.[29] A similar pattern applies to public expenditure on health, which is now below one per cent of GDP, an astonishingly low

---

[28] For further discussion, see chapters 5, 6 and 9.
[29] See Government of India (2000d), p.ii. The share of public expenditure on education in GDP increased from less than one per cent in the early 1950s to 1.5 per cent or so in the early 1960s, 2.5 per cent or so in the early 1970s, 3 per cent or so in the 1980s, and a little over 4 per cent in the early 1990s, when it started declining.

figure in international perspective (see p. 204). Also alarming is growing evidence of a qualitative deterioration of public health services, which started before the 1990s but appears to have continued (if not intensified) in many states during that decade. As discussed in chapters 5 and 6, there are many other grounds for concern about the continuing inadequacy of education and health facilities in India.

The absence of any breakthrough in this field is one reason why India's handicap in terms of of social opportunities (on which we had commented extensively in the earlier edition of the book) remains large, and also why the pace of change in overcoming that handicap is far from satisfactory. As will be seen in chapter 9, the pace of improvement has even slowed down in some important respects in the 1990s. Clearly, much remains to be done both (1) in making economic reform adequately broad, and (2) in ensuring that social opportunities expand with acceptable rapidity.[30]

1.6. DEMOCRACY, ENVIRONMENT AND MILITARISM

Even though the enlarged edition of this book is mainly an extension of what was presented in the earlier edition, we have paid additional attention to three particular subjects: (1) democracy, (2) the environment, and (3) militarism. Each of them were discussed in the previous edition as well, though to variable extents—democracy the most and militarism perhaps the least. But each of these calls for more attention, partly because the situation has worsened in some fields (particularly in the form of environmental destruction and military expansionism), but also because the interconnections between them require more exploration than we had provided in the last edition.

A fuller understanding of these interconnections calls for a firmer grasp of the role and reach of democracy, since the protection of the environment and sanity in military decisions depend ultimately on the practice of democracy, given the nature of India's polity. No one other than the people of India can save India from its deteriorating environment, or from the wastefulness of—and indeed from the insecurity generated by its military policies. Democracy is, thus, a crucial link in the chain of these social choices.

---

[30] The improved performance of the Indian economy in the 1990s may create an impression that these concerns are redundant, given the powerful effects of economic growth. This claim requires close scrutiny, which will be undertaken in chapter 9. As discussed there, India's recent development experience actually gives further reason to emphasize the need for achieving participatory growth, as well as the crucial role of public action in promoting social opportunities.

The Practice of Democracy

In emphasizing the role of non-market institutions in successful development, it is extremely important to see the different institutions in an integrated way, and here the practice of democracy—in the fullest sense—can be critically important. The analysis presented in the first edition of this book was, of course, very committed to the importance of democracy for India in particular and for the world in general, and this focus remains unchanged in this enlarged edition as well. But this is also an occasion for asking some probing questions both about the content of democracy and about the nature and reach of its practice. The connection with the environment and with militarism is part of a general structure of interrelations in which the more traditional development issues (such as raising living standards, reducing poverty and inequality, countering gender-based disparities, ensuring human security, etc.) also belong. In this book, we have tried to integrate these development issues with a sustained concern for participatory democracy.

Democracy must not be confused merely with the establishment of the formality of majority rule. Democracy has complex demands, which certainly include free and fair elections, but also involve the protection of human rights and political liberties, respect for legal entitlements, the guaranteeing of free discussions and uncensored distribution of news and fair comment, and—last but not least—widespread actual participation of people, including the most disadvantaged. Indeed, even elections can be deeply defective if they occur without giving the different sides adequate opportunity to present their respective cases, or without giving the electorate the opportunity to explore the pros and cons of the proposals, or without drawing the underdogs of society into active engagement with electoral issues. The need to take the practice of democracy well beyond the observance of electoral rules is a recurrent theme of this work.

We can distinguish between three different ways in which democracy enriches the lives of citizens.[31] First, political freedom is a part of human freedom in general, and civil and political rights are crucial for good living of individuals as social beings. Thus, political and social participation has *intrinsic value* as an aspect of the quality of life. Second, democracy has an important *instrumental role* in enhancing the hearing that people get in response to their claims to political attention (including the claims of economic needs). The instrumental role of democracy extends from the elementary function of preventing drastic deprivations (such as famines)

---

[31] For further discussion, see Sen (1999a, 1999c).

to more radical changes in social priorities, and its reach depends on the extent to which the opportunities offered by democratic institutions are seized and utilized. Third, the practice of democracy gives the citizens an opportunity to learn from each other, and can also profoundly influence the values and priorities of the society. Even the idea of 'needs' (including the understanding of 'economic needs'), which is often taken to be fixed and well-defined, can respond to public discussion and exchange of information, views and analyses. In this sense, democracy has a *constructive importance*, in addition to the intrinsic value it has in the lives of the citizens and its instrumental role in political decisions. Value formation is as much a democratic activity as is the use of social values in the determination of public policy and social response.

The success of a democracy has to be judged by taking into account the fulfilment or otherwise of these distinct functions. This requires a more probing look at democratic practices—and their successes and failures—in India, and to this we have devoted some additional attention (in chapter 10). The connection with environmental as well as military concerns, discussed more fully in chapters 6 and 8, may deserve some early pointers here.

Environmental Problems

Belief in the robustness of nature has been a long-standing conviction of humanity. 'Though you drive Nature out with a pitchfork', Horace had assured us, 'she will still find her way back'. That comforting belief was nice and reassuring. But environmental smugness is difficult to sustain given the scientific evidence that is now available, and it has given way, in recent decades, to the increasing recognition that the environment in which we live is, in many ways, quite fragile. We can not only rapidly deplete our exhaustible resources and drive many species to extinction, we can also heat up the globe, decimate the ozone layer, and foul up our rivers in ways that are not easy to reverse.

India's environmental record has many alarming features. Even if we leave out the contribution that India increasingly makes to global atmospheric damage (this is still comparatively small, but can expand rapidly through the growing consumption level of a large population), the local environment shows many signs of being under stress, and in some cases, thoroughly ravaged. This applies to the air that we breathe in Indian cities (and often even in small towns), the water that people are forced to drink in the absence of any alternative, the barrenness of vegetation and the decimation of plants that impoverish rural life, and a variety of other phenomena. Environmental decline can be a major shrinkage of social opportunities, no matter how these opportunities may be enhanced in other ways.

If changes are to occur in India's environmental management—or mismanagement—the 'constructive' as well as 'instrumental' roles of democracy must have a vital role. It is through public discussion that the precariousness of the environmental situation can be brought more fully into recognition. This appreciation can be particularly apt in influencing values and behaviour patterns of individuals and groups, and also of course of governments and local authorities. In the determination of official policy (at different levels of governance), the instrumental role of democracy can be critically influential in turning environmental concerns into electoral issues and giving them political significance. It is this combination of constructive and instrumental roles of democracy on which much of the future of Indian environmental health must ultimately depend. By taking the environmental questions within the broader framework of development and democracy, we can see constructive possibilities that might be missed otherwise. We shall go further into these questions in the text of the book.

The Waste and Dangers of Militarism

While environmental deterioration is a loss of social opportunity, so—in a different way—is the diversion of resources into military expenditure. Those resources are not available for positive use in furthering the economic development of the country, or for enhancing the well-being or freedom of the individuals that make up the nation. In principle, of course, the purpose of military expenditure is to make the nation— and presumably the citizens—more secure. When, however, military escalation goes hand in hand with greater tension, and involves tit-for-tat response from 'hostile' countries (Pakistan's blasting of six nuclear bombs in response to India's five blasts in the summer of 1998 can certainly be seen in that light), it is doubtful that security is, in fact, augmented. The fact that Pokhran-II in May 1998 was followed not only by these matching blasts, but also by border incursions in which Pakistan was directly involved, also generates little confidence that defence policies are achieving the purpose for which they were apparently aimed. Indeed, the few years since these blasts have been a period of heightened insecurity in the region. The sharp rise in India's military expenditure and broadening of its fields of operation (including expansion of nuclear programmes, missile systems and related arrangements) can hardly be seen as positive moves in the direction of economic development and prosperity.

During the first half of the nineties, India's defence budget increased at a modest rate of about 1.5 per cent per year in real terms. Since 1996–7, however, the defence budget has doubled in nominal terms, which corresponds to an annual increase of about 10 per cent per year in real terms.[32] This pattern of accelerated increase stands in sharp contrast with the world-wide *decline* in military expenditure in the nineties.[33] In fact, India's military spending has also accelerated compared with Pakistan's. India spent somewhat more than twice as much as Pakistan on defence at the beginning of the nineties. The ratio now is closer to four times as much (see p. 297).

We shall have more to say on this deflection of resources, as well as on other social costs of military expansion, in the text of the book (chapter 8), but we should note here the need to have more public discussion of India's military policies and priorities. We are very aware that many commentators on this subject, whose expertise we respect, have taken a very different view on the increasing burden of military expenditure as well as on what we would argue is the resulting increase in *insecurity*, rather than greater security. But there should be agreement at least on the need to discuss and debate these subjects more fully. It is not adequate to be told that there are 'compelling' reasons for Indian official policy to go in one direction or another. It is also far from reassuring to find that the vocal advocates of higher spending on military research or combat preparations are often experts whose own career and bounty are heavily dependent on those same resources. Military matters call not only for more discussion in the public domain but also for more objective scrutiny.

Ultimately, in democratic India, there is a basic necessity to bring the 'constructive' as well as 'instrumental' roles of democracy to bear on these questions, as on any other matter of public policy (especially one that involves such heavy public expenditure and which has such strong implications— one way or the other—for India's peace and security). The constructive role relates to understanding more clearly what the options are and what

---

[32] See chapter 8. The current budget allocation for 'defence' is Rs 62,000 crores per year, or about three times as much as public expenditure on health.

[33] Between 1990 and 1999, world-wide military expenditure declined by nearly 30 per cent in real terms (from over US$ 1,000 billion to US$ 719 billion, at 1995 prices). The decline was particularly sharp in eastern Europe and the former Soviet Union, but also occurred in most other regions except Asia, e.g. 16 per cent in western Europe, 27 per cent in north America, and 30 per cent in sub-Saharan Africa. In Asia, military expenditure increased by 21 per cent in real terms. See *SIPRI Yearbook 2000*, p. 234. There are, however, signs of an impending reversal of this broad-based decline in world military expenditure, led by big increases in defence spending in the United States.

values most compel our loyalty and determination. The instrumental role carries the fruits of public discussion and scrutiny into policy decisions. Both are essential for the integrity of India's democratic polity.

1.7. Voice, Assertion and Solidarity

As discussed earlier, the quality of democracy can be seriously compromised by economic and social inequality. The latter often prevents the underprivileged from participating effectively in democratic institutions, and gives disproportionate power to those who command crucial resources such as income, education and influential connections. This problem applies to varying extents in every democracy, but it is particularly serious in India, where sharp economic and social inequalities (related inter alia to class, caste and gender) have led to a significant marginalization of many disadvantaged groups from democratic institutions. We shall return to this important issue in the concluding chapter of this book, which focuses on 'the practice of democracy'.

One aspect of this problem is the lack of 'voice' of disadvantaged groups in Indian society and politics. The concerns of the rich and powerful tend to command disproportionate attention from the media, the parliament, the courts, and other democratic institutions, while those of the underprivileged get little hearing. Parliamentary proceedings, for instance, include relatively little discussion of basic social issues such as elementary education, health care, rural employment, social security, and human rights. By contrast, the concerns of corporate chambers, the defence establishment and other influential groups are handsomely represented. Similar biases apply in the media, as discussed in chapter 8.

For the most disadvantaged groups, 'voicelessness' can take an extreme form. For instance, the interests of the so-called 'scheduled tribes' (which represent 8 per cent of India's total population) have received extraordinarily little attention in Indian politics. This is one reason why it has been possible for large development projects to displace millions of them over the years, without any compensation worth the name, and without anyone taking much interest in them in the corridors of power.[34] The situation is, of course, significantly changing in this respect, as tribal communities in different parts of the country have gradually learned to defend their rights. But the basic problem of voicelessness remains in

---

[34] On this issue, see e.g. Fernandes and Thukral (1989), Drèze, Samson and Singh (1997), Roy (1999).

substantial measure. Some sections of the population (beggars, widows, migrant labourers, disabled persons, undertrial prisoners) are even more disadvantaged and voiceless.[35]

In principle, this problem of voicelessness can be overcome in two distinct ways. One is *assertion* (or, more precisely, self-assertion) of the underprivileged through political organization. The other is *solidarity* with the underprivileged on the part of other members of the society, whose interests and commitments are broadly linked, and who are often better placed to advance the cause of the disadvantaged by virtue of their own privileges (e.g. formal education, access to the media, economic resources, political connections). Both self-assertion and solidarity may be regarded as important parts of the creation of social opportunities, with intrinsic as well as instrumental value.

Some underprivileged sections of Indian society have been able to acquire considerable 'voice' on the basis of self-assertion. Women's interests, for instance, find much stronger expression today than before, through various organizations led by women themselves. This has significantly re duced women's marginalization in Indian politics, with strong prospects of further progress in that direction in the future. On the whole, however, the potential for assertion of the underprivileged remains vastly underutilized in India. Large sections of the population have very limited opportunities to speak for themselves. The daily struggle for survival leaves them with little leisure to engage in political activity, and efforts to do so sometimes invite physical repression. Lack of formal education and access to information restricts their ability to intervene in public discussions and electoral debates, or to make effective use of the media, the courts, and other democratic institutions. Lack of adequate collective organizations further enhances this political marginalization.

Because of the limited (though growing) extent of 'assertion' on the part of the underprivileged groups, 'solidarity' is often the main route through which their voices are heard. India has a rich tradition of solidarity-based social movements and political activism, which has found further expression in recent years in diverse contexts, ranging from literacy and human rights to the environmental movement. These movements are often 'led', initially at least, by persons who are not themselves among the primary victims of deprivation or inequality, but stand in solidarity with them. To some extent this applies also to many movements with a strong

---

[35] For an enlightening attempt to give expression to some of these 'unheard voices', see Mander (2001).

commitment to assertion-based action, such as the trade union movements or even the Naxalite movement.[36]

There is nothing wrong, of course, in the fact that solidarity is a crucial ingredient of many social movements in India. Quite the contrary, since it relates to the far-reaching role of social cooperation (one of the recurrent themes of this book). Ultimately, both assertion and solidarity are needed for effective political action. However, there is also a danger of over-reliance on the solidarity element, when the assertion element itself is relatively weak. One specific issue is that solidarity, on its own, is a somewhat undependable basis of authentic representation of the interests of the underprivileged. Indeed, solidarity can have diverse roots (e.g. empathy, class or caste consciousness, sharing a common 'enemy'), and typically coexists with significant differences of perspective among the concerned parties. Those who lead solidarity-based social movements often have their own perspectives, motivations and ideologies, which need not be entirely congruent with the interests of those whom they seek to represent. While the victims of hunger, illiteracy, unemployment, ill health, violence and other basic deprivations tend to feel the pinch when their interests are misrepresented, this does not always apply to those who speak or act on their behalf.

A related issue is that some groups are often better placed than others to attract solidarity, based for instance on how their 'cause' fits with particular ideologies, or on the extent to which they offer a potential 'power base' to political leaders and social activists. The most disadvantaged social groups are often unattractive partners for solidarity-based movements. This tends to perpetuate their political marginalization, while more articulate and resourceful constituencies are able to mobilize widespread support.

To illustrate these issues, consider the predicament of the vast majority of Indian workers who belong to the so-called 'informal sector' (agricultural labourers, sharecroppers, small farmers, artisans, vendors, casual industrial labourers, etc.).[37] For reasons discussed earlier, political assertion on the part of informal-sector workers in India has been an uphill task, with relatively

---

[36] On this feature of the Naxalite movement, see Ray (1992) and Bhatia (2000).

[37] In rural areas (and to some extent even in urban areas), there is a case for regarding this section of the labour force as belonging to one combined class of underprivileged workers, without attaching too much importance to finer distinctions within that class (e.g. based on land ownership, tenancy status, or terms of employment). The common predicament of the working class can be far more significant, in many contexts, than differences of interest associated with those distinctions. For an insightful discussion of the common features of the underprivileged class in rural areas, see Rudra (1988).

limited results so far. These workers have also gained little from solidarity-based movements, as trade unions and related organizations (e.g. the main communist parties) have focused most of their activities on the 'formal' sector, especially employees of the public sector and major industries. As a result, the 'voice' of the informal sector has tended to be comprehensively muted in Indian politics. The interests of casual workers, whether at the work place (e.g. in the form of more humane work conditions, protection from health hazards, entitlements to minimum wages, social security arrangements, or participation in management) or in the economy and society at large (e.g. in the form of employment-oriented macroeconomic policies) tend to remain, by and large, poorly articulated and inadequately represented.

In assessing this situation, it is important to recognize that the over-concentration of left-wing parties and organizations on the formal sector has not only contributed to the voicelessness of the informal sector but also, in some respects, *undermined* social opportunities for informal-sector workers. To illustrate, consider the record of public-sector trade unions. On the one hand, public-sector trade unions deserve much credit for enhancing the security and dignity of their own members and for standing up for them. On the other, they have contributed to the steady erosion of public sector accountability over the years, wrecking a wide range of social opportunities for informal-sector workers and indeed for the public at large (we shall return to this issue in chapter 5, with reference to the teaching profession). Recent hikes in public-sector salaries (well beyond the recommendations of independent commissions) have also made a major contribution to the bankruptcy of state governments, again deeply compromising what other groups might have gained from state activities. It is hard to escape the impression that well-intended activists who saw themselves as the champions of the 'working class' have often misread the wider interests of Indian workers.

To take another example, consider the bewildering accumulation of gigantic foodgrain stocks (60 million tonnes—and growing—as this book goes to press) by the Indian government, against a background of wide spread undernutrition across the country. The basic root of this problem lies in unsustainably high 'minimum support prices' for foodgrains, fixed by the government under pressure from influential farmers' lobbies. Clearly, the underprivileged have a strong stake in these stocks being used (e.g. for income-generation programmes or an expansion of the public distribution system). Yet political parties, almost across the board, have supported the policy of high support prices, for fear of antagonizing farmers' organizations (representing the rich as well as not so rich farmers). Here again, many activists and analysts who intend to stand in solidarity with the underprivileged have hesitated to speak up, and even added their influential voice to the chorus on the other side.[38]

These biases call for fresh thinking about class divisions and other aspects of India's political economy. Indeed, public debates on economic policy and development issues in India have often been heavily influenced by fossilized slogans and misleading analytical categories. In some quarters, for instance, a 'subsidy' is typically viewed in a favourable light, no matter how inequitable or wasteful it might be. In other quarters, 'privatization' is always applauded, even when the consequences are patently disastrous.[39] The first edition of this book already commented on these tendencies, with specific reference to the rather sterile 'liberalization debate'. The syndrome has not disappeared, and has even spread to new territories, such as the more recent debate on 'globalization' (see chapters 2 and 9). A clearer understanding of the real issues is an essential requirement of more effective solidarity-based action.

Overcoming voicelessness is not just a question of more enlightened 'solidarity', but also, ultimately, of much further 'assertion' on the part of underprivileged sections of the society. There have been important developments in that respect in recent years, including the spread of working-class organizations in the much neglected informal sector.[40] This particular field of political activism is crucial for the future of Indian development and democracy.

1.8. A CONCLUDING REMARK

This work is dedicated to examining and scrutinizing the tasks of development in India. The interpretation of development in terms of enhancement of freedom connects the different fields of enquiry with one another. They also direct our attention to the interrelated roles of different institutions.

Rather than seeing the policy debates in terms of narrowly defined 'opposites' (pro-market versus anti-market, pro-state versus anti-state, etc.), we had tried, in the first edition, to apply this broader approach to the developmental challenges faced in India. In this book, we have expanded

---

[38] For further discussion, see chapter 9; also Drèze (2001a).

[39] For an insightful critique of conceptual categories in Indian political debates, see Pranab Bardhan and Ashok Rudra's discussion of the 'taboos and totems of left mythology' in India (Bardhan and Rudra, 1975).

[40] For interesting examples, see I. Sen (1990), Anveshi (1993), Deshpande (1999), Dey and Roy (2000), Kothari (2000), Datta (2001), among others.

that analysis, applied it over a wider domain, and tried to analyse the recent developments and their implications in this light.

There are, we have argued, rich lessons here, which cannot be seized without taking an interest in the ends and means of development in general and in the intrinsic value, constructive role and instrumental importance of public participation in particular. The basic approach involves an overarching interest in the role of human beings—on their own and in cooperation with each other—in running their lives and in using and expanding their freedoms. The integrated nature of human living suggests the need for a correspondingly consolidated approach. We have attempted to investigate the nature, promise and reach of such an approach.

2

Economic Development and Social Opportunity

2.1. DEVELOPMENT, FREEDOM AND OPPORTUNITIES

Shortly after the second world war, when development economics emerged as a distinct field of study, the subject had the appearance of being a bastard child of growth economics. Some influence other than growth economics was clearly involved in the origin of development economics, but it was not altogether clear what form this influence had taken. In one respect at least, the offspring did not differ from what could be expected from a genuine 'son of growth economics', namely an overarching preoccupation with the growth of real income per head.

Ian Little reflected this understanding very well in his depiction of 'development economics' (in *The Fontana Dictionary of Modern Thought*) as a field that 'in a broad sense comprises all work on *the growth of incomes per head*, including that of the classical economic theorists from Smith to Mill'.[1] The focus of development economics is seen here as uncompromisingly on the growth of incomes. However, while the two classical authors cited by Little, namely Smith and Mill, did indeed write a great deal on the growth of real income per head, they saw income as one of several means to important ends, and they discussed extensively the nature of these ends—very different as they are from income.

These classical authors were deeply concerned with the recognition that we have reasons to value many things other than income and wealth,

---

[1] Little (1977), p. 222. See, however, Little's much broader treatment of development economics in his own major treatise on this subject: Little (1982).

which relate to the real opportunities to lead the kind of life we would value living. In the writings of Smith, Mill and other classical political economists, there is much interest in the foundational importance of our ability to do the things we value, so that they saw the freedom to lead valuable lives as intrinsically important—not merely instrumentally so. They did comment fairly extensively on the connection between these matters, on the one hand, and income, wealth, and other economic circumstances, on the other, and they had much to say on economic policies that promote the more basic ends.[2] Neither Smith nor Mill would have had any quarrel with taking a much broader view of the changes that are involved in the process we now call economic development—even with putting into that category Nehru's list of things to do.

In recent years, the profession of development economics has also moved increasingly in that direction, taking a much more inclusive view of the nature of economic development.[3] One way of seeing development is in terms of the expansion of the real freedoms that the citizens enjoy to pursue the objectives they have reason to value, and in this sense the expansion of human capability can be, broadly, seen as the central feature of the process of development.[4]

The 'capability' of a person is a concept that has distinctly Aristotelian roots.[5] The life of a person can be seen as a sequence of things the person does, or states of being he or she achieves, and these constitute a collection of 'functionings'—doings and beings the person achieves. 'Capability' refers to the alternative combinations of functionings from which a person can choose. Thus, the notion of capability is essentially one of freedom—the range of options a person has in deciding what

---

[2] In the case of Smith, see both *The Wealth of Nations* and *The Theory of Moral Sentiments* (Smith, 1776, 1790), and in the case of Mill, *Principles of Political Economy, Utilitarianism, On Liberty*, and also *The Subjection of Women* (Mill, 1848, 1859, 1861, 1869).

[3] See, for example, Adelman and Morris (1973), Sen (1973, 1984), Grant (1978), Morris (1979), Streeten et al. (1981), Stewart (1985), Chenery and Srinivasan (1988), Desai (1991), Dasgupta (1993), Anand and Ravallion (1993), Kakwani (1993), Toye (1993), Thirlwall (1994), Deaton (1997); also the *Human Development Reports*, published by UNDP from 1990 onwards.

[4] See Sen (1980, 1985a, 1985b, 1999a), Desai (1989, 1994), Drèze and Sen (1989, 1990), Griffin and Knight (1990), UNDP (1990, 1994), Crocker (1991, 1992), Nussbaum (1992, 1993), Lane (1994), Atkinson (1995).

[5] Discussed by Aristotle in *The Nicomachean Ethics* in particular, but also in his *Politics*. On this and on the connection between the Aristotelian focus and the recent analyses of capabilities, see Nussbaum (1993) and the other articles included in Nussbaum and Sen (1993).

kind of life to lead. Poverty of a life, in this view, lies not merely in the impoverished state in which the person actually lives, but also in the lack of real opportunity—given by social constraints as well as personal circumstances—to choose other types of living. Even the relevance of low incomes, meagre possessions, and other aspects of what are standardly seen as economic poverty relates ultimately to their role in curtailing capabilities (that is, their role in severely restricting the choices people have to lead valuable and valued lives). Poverty is, thus, ultimately a matter of 'capability deprivation', and note has to be taken of that basic connection not just at the conceptual level, but also in economic investigations or in social or political analyses.[6] This broader and more foundational view of poverty has to be kept in view while concentrating, as we often would in this monograph, on the deprivation of such basic capabilities as the freedom to lead normal spans of life (undiminished by premature mortality), or the freedom to read or write (without being constrained by illiteracy). While the term 'poverty' will typically not be explicitly invoked in such contexts, the underlying concern is one of deprivation and impoverished lives. Even when we focus on economic poverty in the more conventional sense (that is, as having an insufficient income), the basic motivation will be its relevance as a substantial influence on capability deprivation.

The basic objective of development as the expansion of human capabilities was never completely overlooked in the modern development literature, but the focus has been mainly on the generation of economic growth, in the sense of expanding gross national product and related variables.[7] The expansion of human capabilities can clearly be enhanced

[6] On this see Sen (1984, 1985a, 1992a). There is an enormous literature on 'poverty in India', which addresses many of the issues taken up in this book, although the general orientation of that literature has been somewhat different, with a more concentrated focus on the specific problem of low incomes or expenditure. Important contributions to this literature include Dandekar and Rath (1971), Srinivasan and Bardhan (1974), Ahluwalia (1978), Bardhan (1984a), Ghate (1984), Agarwal (1986), Jain et al. (1988), Srinivasan and Bardhan (1988), Kurian (1989), Kakwani and Subbarao (1990), Krishnaswamy (1990), Saith (1990), I. Singh (1990), Minhas et al. (1991), Nayyar (1991), Osmani (1991), Krishnaji (1992), Harriss, Guhan and Cassen (1992), Ravallion and Subbarao (1992), EPW Research Foundation (1993), Gaiha (1993), Parikh and Sudarshan (1993), Tendulkar et al. (1993), Vyas and Bhargava (1995), Beck (1994), Dutta (1994), Lipton and Ravallion (1994), Ninan (1994), Datt and Ravallion (1995, 1998), Dutta et al. (1997), World Bank (1997a, 2000b), Datt and Ravallion (1998), Datt (1999a, 1999b), among others. See also the more recent literature cited in chapter 9.

[7] W.A. Lewis, one of the pioneers of development economics, emphasized that the appropriate objective of development is increasing 'the range of human choice',

by economic growth (even in the limited sense of growth of real income per head), but (1) there are many influences other than economic growth that work in that direction, and (2) the impact of economic growth on human capabilities can be extremely variable, depending on the nature of that growth (for example, how equitable and employment-intensive it is, and whether the economic gains from growth are used to address the deprivations of the most needy).

What is crucial in all this is the need to judge the different policies, ultimately, by their impact on the enhancement of the capabilities that the citizens enjoy (whether or not this comes about through the growth of real incomes). This differs sharply from the more standard practice of judging economic policies by their contribution to the growth of real incomes—seen as a merit in itself. To dispute that practice must not be seen as an invitation to ignore the important instrumental role of economic growth in enhancing basic objectives such as human capabilities; it is mainly a matter of being clear about our ends and our means.

The recent attempts, in India and elsewhere, to open up market opportunities without being thwarted by bureaucratic barriers has been justified primarily in terms of the expected impact of this change on economic expansion, enhancing outputs and incomes in the economy. To quote the semi-official and distinctly authoritative report by Bhagwati and Srinivasan (1993), commissioned by the Government of India, 'these structural reforms were necessary because we had evidently failed to generate adequate rates of growth of income and of per capita income' (p. 2).[8] This is indeed a significant direction of causal analysis. On the other side, the justification for focusing on outputs and incomes lies ultimately in the impact that their augmentation may have on the freedoms that people actually enjoy to lead the kind of lives they have reason to value. The analysis of economic development must take note of both the causal connections, and also of other policies and institutional changes that contribute to the enhancement of human capabilities. The success of development programmes cannot be judged merely in terms of their effects on incomes and outputs, and must, at a basic level, focus on the

---

but nevertheless he decided to concentrate specifically on 'the growth of output per head', since that 'gives man greater control over his environment and thereby increases his freedom' (Lewis, 1955: pp. 9–10, 420–1).

[8] For other recent evaluations of the performance of the Indian economy, and analyses of different approaches to economic policy, see Jalan (1991, 1992), Bhagwati (1993), Desai (1994), Joshi and Little (1994, 1996), Bhaduri and Nayyar (1996), Cassen and Joshi (1995), Lewis (1995), Sachs et al. (1999), Srinivasan (2000), among others, and also the literature cited in chapter 9.

lives that people can lead. This applies as much to the assessment of economic reforms and current economic policies in India today as it does to evaluations of development programmes anywhere else in the world.

2.2. ON EDUCATION AND HEALTH

Importance has to be attached to the distinct influences that promote or constrain the freedoms that individuals have, including their ability to make use of economic opportunities. As was discussed in the last chapter, education and health can be important 'enabling' factors. The role of these so-called 'social' variables in the fostering of economic progress has recently received much attention in the development literature. But, of course, the subject is of some antiquity, and classical political economists such as Smith or Turgot or Condorcet or Mill or Marx would have seen the recognition of this role as quite non-controversial.[9]

The remarkable neglect of elementary education in India is all the more striking given the widespread recognition, in the contemporary world, of the importance of basic education for economic development. Somehow the educational aspects of economic development have continued to be out of the main focus, and this relative neglect has persisted despite the recent radical changes in economic policy. Similar remarks apply to health care. Even Bhagwati and Srinivasan's (1993) lucid discussion of the challenge of economic reforms is entirely silent on the subject of education and health, and their possible roles in promoting the use of the economic opportunities that may be created by the reforms. An opportunity is missed here to question an old imbalance in Indian planning efforts. The issue relates to the tendency to see the economic reforms as standing on their own,[10] without linking the case for reform inter alia to the failures in social policies (demanding radical changes in social programmes, particularly basic education, *along with* more narrowly economic changes).

Education and health can be seen to be valuable to the freedom of a person in at least five distinct ways.[11]

---

[9] Theodore Schultz (1962, 1963, 1971, 1980) has made outstanding contributions in clarifying and emphasizing the importance of the connection between education and economic progress. See also T. Paul Schultz (1988), who provides an illuminating account and critique of the literature on the subject.

[10] Cf. 'Prime Minister Nehru's vision of a strong, independent India, with a sound economy generating rapid growth and reduction of the poverty afflicting many among us, is within our grasp if only the economic reforms are sustained and intensified' (Bhagwati and Srinivasan, 1993, p. 1).

[11] On the personal and social roles of basic education, with specific reference to India, see also Probe Team (1999), chapter 1.

1. *Intrinsic importance:* Being educated and healthy are valuable achievements in themselves, and the opportunity to have them can be of *direct* importance to a person's effective freedom. In the case of education, the act of learning itself may have much intrinsic value, e.g. in terms of fulfilling aspirations for enlightenment, self-improvement and social interaction.

2. *Instrumental personal roles:* A person's education and health can help him or her to do many things—*other* than just being educated and healthy—that are also valuable. They can, for instance, be important for getting a job and more generally for being able to make use of economic opportunities. Education and health also facilitate a wide range of other valuable activities, from playing soccer to reading newspapers or participating in local politics.

3. *Instrumental social roles:* Greater literacy and basic education can facilitate public discussion of social needs and encourage informed collective demands (e.g., for health care and social security); these in turn can help expand the facilities that the public enjoys, and contribute to the better utilization of the available services. Widespread education also helps to hold political leaders accountable, and to address social issues (such as environmental degradation, population growth and the threat of AIDS) in a cooperative and non-authoritarian way. Widespread education is indeed essential to the practice of democracy.

4. *Instrumental process roles:* The process of schooling can have benefits even aside from its explicitly aimed objectives, namely formal education. For example, the incidence of child labour is intimately connected with non-schooling of children, and the expansion of schooling can reduce the distressing phenomenon of child labour so prevalent in India.[12] Schooling also brings young people in touch with others and thereby broadens their horizons, and this can be particularly important for young girls.[13]

5. *Empowerment and distributive roles:* Greater literacy and educational achievements of disadvantaged groups can enhance their ability to resist oppression, to organize politically, and to get a fairer deal. The redistributive effects can be important not only between different social groups or households, but also *within* the family, since there is evidence that better education (particularly female education) contributes to the reduction of gender-based inequalities (see chapter 7 below).

These influences need not work only for the person who receives

[12] This issue has been extensively discussed by Myron Weiner (1991); see also chapter 5, and the literature cited there.

[13] See e.g. Karuna Chanana (1988).

education or health care. They can also involve important interpersonal effects. For example, one person's educational ability can be of use to another (e.g. to get a pamphlet read, or to have a public announcement explained).[14] The interpersonal connections can be of political significance as well; for example, a community may benefit generally from the civic attention it receives through the educated activism of a particular group within that community. Also, the use of economic opportunity by one person can, in many circumstances, open up further opportunities for others. To evaluate the contributions of education in an adequately inclusive way, we have to use a broad 'social choice' approach (as Tapas Majumdar has shown).[15] There are similar interconnections in matters of health because of the obvious importance of externalities in morbidity, preventive care, and curative treatment.[16] Expansion of health and education can have influences that go much beyond the immediate personal effects.

Through these various interconnections, education and health can be variables of great strategic importance in the process of economic development.[17] India's failure to have an adequate public policy in educational and health matters can be, thus, of profound significance in assessing the limited success of Indian development efforts over the last half a century. A policy reform that concentrates just on liberalization and deregulation cannot deal with this part of the dismal failure of past planning.

The removal of counter-productive government controls may indeed expand social opportunities for many people. However, to change the circumstances (such as illiteracy and ill health) that severely constrain the actual social opportunities of a large part of the population, these permissive reforms have to be supplemented by a radical shift in public policy in education and health. If we see economic development in the perspective of social opportunities in general, both for their intrinsic

[14] There are typically significant 'externalities' in the contribution of education to the adoption of innovation, as for example in agriculture, so that one family can benefit from the knowledge and experiences of neighbouring families; on this and related issues, see Chaudhri (1979).

[15] See Tapas Majumdar (1983).

[16] This characteristic affects, in many different ways, the nature of 'the health economy' (see Fuchs, 1986).

[17] On various aspects of the relationship between education, health, and economic development, see Behrman and Deolalikar (1988), Psacharopoulos (1988, 1994), Osmani (1990, 1992), Summers (1992), Colclough (1993), Dasgupta (1993), among others, and the literature cited in these studies. See also Robert Lane's (1994) discussion of governmental responsibility in developing 'qualities of persons'.

importance and for their instrumental value, we cannot afford to miss this crucial linkage.

2.3. THE SOCIAL DIMENSION OF HEALTH AND EDUCATION

The interpersonal influences mentioned in the preceding section constitute only one aspect of the social dimension of health and education. The latter pertains not only to the *outcomes* of health and education programmes, but also to the *process* of improving health and education levels. The case for social intervention in the provision of health and education is strong from several viewpoints. First, the interdependence of outcomes itself calls for social intervention (if only in the form of subsidies), since private decisions often overlook the positive externalities associated with improved health and education. This issue is particularly crucial in matters such as public health, especially the eradication of communicable diseases.

Second, social intervention is often required to overcome various 'market failures' that have been extensively analysed in public economics. For instance, the asymmetry of information between users and providers of health services often undermines the efficiency of the market mechanism in this field, and may even lead to the disappearance of market-based arrangements.[18] The pervasive uncertainties involved in health matters, together with the inherent limitations of market-based insurance arrangements, have similar consequences.

Third, there is a strong case for public involvement in health and education matters from the viewpoint of equity and rights. This is not an issue of market failure, even in the broadest sense of the term, since ensuring equity or protecting rights is nowhere within the province of the market mechanism. The inequitable nature of private health and education arrangements in India is evident enough. So is their inability to guarantee basic entitlements such as 'free and compulsory education for all children until they complete the age of fourteen years' (Indian Constitution, Directive Principles, article 45). Entitlements of this type are important not only because they consolidate the bargaining power of those who are deprived of basic health and education services, but

---

[18] See Arrow (1963b), Akerlof (1970), Rothschild and Stiglitz (1976). See also Zweifel and Breyer (1997) for an enlightening discussion of the literature, and the readings cited there.

also because they shape broader notions of solidarity and citizenship. There is, thus, a strong case for thinking about education and health in terms of fundamental rights, and this calls for social arrangements that go well beyond the market mechanism.

Last but not least, one crucial aspect of interpersonal influences in matters such as health and education relates to *motivation*. One parent's inclination to send his or her child to school, for instance, tends to be strongly influenced by the corresponding attitude of *other* parents in the neighbourhood, village, caste or reference group. The motivation of children, too, is likely to vary depending on the behaviour of their peers. This feature also applies to personal attitudes towards family planning, dietary habits, and work patterns, to cite a few other examples. The work culture in schools and hospitals is another important context where interpersonal effects have a paramount influence on individual motivation. The interdependence of personal decisions is, in fact, a pervasive feature of social life, which influences many aspects of everyday behaviour even outside the field of health and education, from relatively trivial ones such as the decision to wear a seat belt to more momentous matters such as occupational and matrimonial choices.

In recent years, the discipline of economics has seen a revival of interest in the role of 'social norms' in individual decisions, which has also influenced development economics.[19] The main focus of this strand of research has been on how social norms can emerge, or sustain themselves, in a framework (e.g. that of repeated games) where individual decisions remain driven by well-defined, exogenous 'preferences'. What has received less attention is the possibility of influencing social norms through public discussion and social intervention. Indeed, social norms are as much a matter of explicit discussion and reflection as one of equilibrium behaviour in a world of decentralized individual decisions.

The possibility of influencing social norms is well understood in the world of advertisement and propaganda. In drawing attention to this possibility, we are not just suggesting the extension of these techniques to health and education matters. That can indeed be done, as India's recent Total Literacy Campaign and polio vaccination programme illustrate. More importantly, however, what is at issue here is the possibility of health and education becoming matters of broad-based public discussion and concern. Achieving this transformation of the politics of

[19] See e.g. Frank (1984), Banerjee (1992), Sethi and Somanathan (1996), Akerlof (1997), Basu (2000), Munshi (2000), among many others; also Elster (1989), Dasgupta (1993), and Bowles (1998), and the literature cited there.

health and education is one part of the broader agenda of democratic practice in India, discussed in chapter 10.

These arguments for social intervention in health and education matters have to be considered together with the equally real fact that the standards of public services in India are abysmally low. We are not making a case here for public provision of every aspect of health and education, or denying that private provision has a role. Rather, we are arguing for seeing the promotion of health and education as irreducibly social concerns, *even* when particular services are effectively provided through private channels. In every modern economy, health and education is divided to a varying extent between public provision and private supply. However, this does not detract from the overarching importance of public discussion and social planning in these sectors.

The social dimension of health and education is evident even in the so-called market economies of western Europe and north America. It is often forgotten that in these 'market economies', public expenditure standardly accounts for 35 to 45 per cent of GDP (rising to 50 per cent or so in countries like the Netherlands, which are not bad achievers, to say the least).[20] Further, the share of health, education and social security in total government expenditure in these economies tends to range between one half and three quarters.[21] These are, in other words, fundamental areas of state involvement, which also account for a major share of overall economic activity. Health, education and social security also have a high *political* visibility in western societies, as can be seen for instance in the attention they receive in electoral campaigns. Even outside electoral campaigns, education and health issues (from abortion and AIDS to the school curriculum) are the object of a great deal of public attention and media coverage. All these patterns, incidentally, persisted (and indeed, in many respects, intensified) through the Reagan and Thatcher years. These years, for instance, were a period of sustained *increase* in public expenditure on 'social services' in many western countries, notwithstanding the free-market rhetoric. The universalization of basic entitlements to health care, elementary education and social security is perhaps the most significant social achievement of western 'market economies' in the twentieth century.

The achievement is not confined to western economies. Cuba and pre-reform China, for instance, also made impressive progress in the direction of universal entitlements to basic education, health care and

[20] See *World Development Indicators 2000*, Table 4.13, pp. 228–30 (1997 figures). The average for countries belonging to the European Monetary Union is 41 per cent.
[21] *World Development Report 1997*, Tables A.3 (pp. 200–1) and 14 (pp. 240–1).

social security. China's post-reform experience, for its part, illustrates the dangers of social abdication in these fields.[22] As reforms were ushered in through the floodgates in 1979–80, the market principles were suddenly extended to health and education, leading to a major decline in the accessibility and affordability of public services. The results give room for thought. For instance, while infant mortality in China fell by 75 per cent or so during the 1960s and 1970s (a period of extensive public involvement in health matters), further progress during the 1980s and 1990s has been quite small—almost negligible. What is important to recognize here is not just the adverse effect of state abdication in health and education, but also how the lack of opportunity for public debate and criticism on these matters has enabled the Chinese government to go much further in drastically privatizing health and education services than might have been possible in a more democratic country. While public opinion in Britain compelled Margaret Thatcher to moderate her designs on the National Health Service, Deng Xiao Ping was able to privatize health services in China almost overnight without much opposition.

2.4. THE GOVERNMENT, THE STATE AND THE MARKET

The competing virtues of the market mechanism and governmental action have been much discussed in the literature. But the comparative merits of the two forms of economic decision are so thoroughly context-dependent that it makes little sense to espouse a *general* 'pro state' or 'pro market' view. To illustrate the point at the most obvious level, we could note the simple fact that what a government can do, and will in fact do, must depend on the *nature* of that government. Unfortunately, the history of the modern world is no less full of tales of tyrannies and tortures than the medieval chronicles of barbarity of those times. The terrifying success that the Khmer Rouge had in Cambodia in quickly disposing off a million people on extraordinary ideological grounds is an obvious example. Idi Amin's Uganda provides an illustration of brutality of another kind—less ideological but not much less vicious. That this is not a simple 'third world' phenomenon is easily illustrated by the enormity of the Nazi atrocities and genocide in the twentieth-century Germany. The implicit belief, expressed in some writings, that government interventions are, by and large, guided by the demands of social progress is surely a folly.

[22] See chapter 4.

Even when the government's objectives are not as vicious as they were in Pol Pot's Cambodia, or in Amin's Uganda, or in Nazi Germany, there is still a question as to who is trying to achieve what through the mechanism of governmental activities. The implicit faith in the goodness and the good sense of the government that underlies much reasoning in favour of government-led economic development cannot, frequently, stand up to scrutiny.

The distinction between the state and the government may be of some significance in this context. The state is, in many ways, a broader concept, which includes the government, but also the legislature that votes on public rules, the political system that regulates elections, the role that is given to opposition parties, and the basic political rights that are upheld by the judiciary. A democratic state makes it that much harder for the ruling government to be unresponsive to the needs and values of the population at large. The nastiness of the Khmer Rouge's governance was sustainable because Pol Pot did not have to face elections or cater to opposition parties, and it is the militarist, undemocratic state that made the genocidal policy of the Khmer Rouge politically feasible.[23] So we have to ask questions not merely about the nature of the actual government in office, but, going beyond that, also about the nature of the state of which the ruling government is only one part.

There is a similar question about the context-dependence of the role of the market mechanism.[24] What kinds of markets are we talking about? Most of the theory of efficiency or effectiveness of the market mechanism relates to competitive markets in equilibrium. It is not unreasonable to assume that small violations of those competitive conditions need not alter the results violently (some kind of Leibnizian belief in the 'continuity of nature' is clearly involved in this implicit faith), but actual markets can take very different forms indeed. For example, the cornering by a few operators of goods in short supply—leading to a massive accentuation of shortage and suffering—has happened too often to be dismissed as

[23] While state repression of insurgencies and rebellions is often brutal enough even in democratic countries (including India, especially in Kashmir), it rarely involves civilian massacres of the kind that have taken place under authoritarian regimes in Cambodia, East Timor, Guatemala, Iraq, Rwanda, Sudan, Uganda, and the Soviet Union, to cite a few cases. In fact, in almost all cases where governments have perpetrated large-scale massacres of their own citizens in the twentieth century, an authoritarian regime was in place; see Rummel (1994, 1998).

[24] The market mechanism also has social influences in the formation of attitudes and ideas, which too can be critically evaluated from alternative perspectives; see e.g. Hirschman (1992), and also Lindblom (1982) and Lane (1991).

imaginary nightmares. The recent history of Asia and Africa provides plentiful examples of market exchanges being used to make profits out of the miseries of millions.

There are also cases where the market manages to misjudge the extent of a shortage quite badly, and causes suffering—even chaos—as a result, without this being the result of much wilful manipulation. This happened, for example, in the Bangladesh famine of 1974, when misguided speculation on the part of traders contributed to an enormous hiking of rice prices, followed later by a sharp fall towards pre-hike prices (meanwhile the famine had taken its toll).[25] The periodic havoc caused by under-regulated financial markets in different parts of the world is another illustration. To take a general 'pro market' view without conditions attached is no less problematic than taking a general 'pro government' view.

The contrast between market-based and government-based economic decisions, thus, requires a clearer understanding of the nature of the markets and the governments involved. These are not, of course, all-or-none questions. There are variations in market forms, in the extent of competition, in the openness of entry, in the actual scope for manipulability, and so on. And there are diversities in the nature of governments, depending on the political system underlying the state, the legal system that sustains political freedom, the power of ruling political groups, the treatment of opposition and dissent, and so on. The assessment of the respective merits of market-based and governmental decisions cannot but be thoroughly dependent on the reading of the markets and of the governments involved.

2.5. INTERDEPENDENCE BETWEEN MARKETS AND GOVERNANCE

In assessing the relative merits of the market and the government, note has to be taken of their thoroughgoing interdependence. In particular, the operation and successes of the market mechanism can be deeply influenced by the nature of governmental arrangements and actions that go with it. This is so for various reasons—some more obvious than others.

First, it is fairly straightforward to recognize that markets can hardly function in the absence of legal provisions and justiciable rights (to

---

[25] See particularly Ravallion (1987) for an econometric study of this process; see also Alamgir (1980). Coles and Hammond (1995) have discussed the operation of markets in the development of famines in general.

property and contractual entitlements, for example). While some of these obligations are carried out automatically (and business ethics can play an important part in the fulfilment of contractual market exchanges), the possibility of legal action in the absence of such compliance is an important background condition for the smooth operation of systems of exchange and production. It is not surprising that the development of the market mechanism during the industrial revolution in Europe closely followed the establishment of law and order that could provide security to business and economic operations. To take a different type of example, it is impossible to understand why the market mechanism is so weak in, say, contemporary Somalia without seeing it in the context of the breakdown of law and order—the form that the 'comeuppance' of the militarist regime has taken in that country. Indeed, the Somalian famine of 1992 was, in part, the result of the breakdown of the market mechanism which in turn had resulted from the breakdown of governance. The disastrous results of indiscriminate liberalization and wholesale privatization in Russia in the 1990s illustrate the penalities of ignoring the basic recognition that the effective functioning of the market mechanism is highly contingent on adequate institutional foundations.

Second, the government may have a major role in initiating and facilitating market-reliant economic growth. This has been studied a great deal in the history of such successful capitalist countries as Germany and Japan. More recently, the role of the government has received much attention in interpreting the so-called 'East Asian miracle'—the remarkable economic success of the newly industrializing countries in east Asia (in particular South Korea, Taiwan, Hong Kong, Singapore, and more recently China and Thailand).[26] This role is easy to understand in the light of economic theory—particularly related to difficulties of initiation, connected with such factors as difficulties of 'tâtonnement' (pre-exchange negotiations about market prices, leading to simultaneous production decisions), economies of large scale, importance of technological externalities, and the integral nature of skill formation. The nurturing of an early market mechanism by an active state does not, of course, preclude a more self-sufficient role of the market *later on*.

Third, even the formal theory of achievements of the market mechanism

---

[26] For different perspectives on the role of the state in the east Asian experience, see White (1988), Amsden (1989), Wade (1990), Balassa (1991), Corden (1993), Johansen (1993), Lucas (1993), World Bank (1993c), Fallows (1994), Fishlow et al. (1994), Rodrik (1994), Birdsall, Ross and Sabot (1995), Stiglitz (1996), Bello (1998), Hayami (1997), Hayami and Aoki (1998), among others.

is, implicitly, much dependent on governmental action. Consider the so-called fundamental theorems of welfare economics.[27] The first theorem, which shows that—given some standard conditions—any competitive equilibrium is Pareto efficient, is thought to be less interesting than the second, since a Pareto efficient allocation can be terribly unequal and thoroughly revolting. The second theorem, on the other hand, shows that under some—rather more stringent—assumptions (including the absence of significant economies of large scale), any Pareto efficient allocation is a competitive equilibrium for some set of prices and some initial distribution of resources. If Pareto efficiency is regarded as a necessary condition for overall social optimality, this entails that a socially optimum allocation can be—given the assumed framework—sustained through a competitive equilibrium *provided* the initial distribution of resources is appropriately fixed.

The question is: *who* would fix the initial distribution of resources in this way? Here again, the agency of the government would generally be required. Thus, the significance of the second 'fundamental theorem of welfare economics' is deeply dependent on governmental action. There may be good reasons for scepticism regarding the political scope, in many societies, for redistributing initial endowments in this way—certainly to the extent that would be needed for social optimality with an equity-sensitive social welfare function. But what can be made achievable by the market in the direction of equity (via the second theorem) would be entirely conditional on appropriate governmental activism.

The interdependence between market and government works, in fact, in the other direction also. It is hard to think of a government achieving anything like an acceptable social arrangement if citizens are prohibited from exchanging commodities, or producing goods and service, on their own initiative. These activities—involving transactions and compacts—form integral parts of the market mechanism, no matter how rudimentary that mechanism might be.

Recent developments in economic theory focusing on the importance of economies of large scale, and of endogenous growth, have done much to clarify the role of markets and trade.[28] Indeed, as Adam Smith (1776) had argued, markets provide great opportunities for acquiring benefits

---

[27] See Arrow (1951), Debreu (1959), McKenzie (1959), Arrow and Hahn (1971). For a helpful non-technical introduction, see Koopmans (1957).

[28] See particularly Paul Krugman (1979, 1986, 1987) and Paul Romer (1986, 1987a, 1987b, 1990, 1993). On related issues, in the context of international trade, see also Helpman and Krugman (1990), Grossman and Helpman (1990, 1991a, 1991b), and the collection of contributions in Buchanan and Yoon (1994).

from trade based on specialization and division of labour, and the recent departures in growth theory and trade theory have involved what Buchanan and Yoon (1994) have aptly called 'the return to increasing returns'.

On the other hand, this line of analysis has also brought out the extent to which the pattern of international division of labour is not given simply by natural blessings and comparative advantages, but is also substantially influenced by the actual history of past experiences and specializations. Thus public policy can have a lasting role in the way the markets are used. The issue of interdependence is, indeed, of even greater significance than a history-free analysis might suggest. While markets might be, in this analysis, an essential vehicle of realizing economic potentials, the long-run influence of active public policy, for example in initiating particular industries and in providing a wide base of public education (as occurred, say, in Japan or South Korea), can be more easily interpreted and understood in this light.

The wider interdependences discussed here call for a clearer understanding of the relation between government policy and market operations. In particular, it is important to distinguish between market-excluding and market-complementary government interventions.

2.6. MARKET-EXCLUDING AND MARKET-COMPLEMENTARY INTERVENTIONS

The contributions and failures of any social arrangement involve both commission (what it does) and omission (what it fails to do). A 'failure' can arise from *either* positively doing something that would have harmful consequences, *or* from not doing something that would have to be done for good results. To illustrate from a different field of ethical judgement, murdering would be an example of harmful commission, whereas failing to stop a preventable murder would be seen as a case of omission. There are, of course, plenty of philosophical difficulties in pressing this distinction very far. However, it does have some relevance in assessing the achievements and failures of the market mechanism.[29]

The market, like other institutions, does certain things, and abstains from doing others. There is a real asymmetry here which is hidden by unclear contrasts between the market mechanism and 'non-market' systems. An economic arrangement can be 'non-market' in the sense that markets are not allowed to operate freely or even to operate at all. This can be called a 'market-excluding' arrangement. Or it can be 'non-market'

---

[29] For further discussion, see Sen (1993a, 1993b).

in the sense that many things are done, say, by the state, that the market would not do. Such supplementary operations do not have to prohibit markets and exchanges. This can be called a 'market-complementary' arrangement.

Obviously, it is possible for a system to have a mixture of market-excluding and market-complementary interventions. The respective implications of the two types of 'non-market' arrangements may be very different indeed. The nature of the issue can be usefully illustrated with concrete examples from a particular area of contemporary concern, namely the terrible phenomenon of famine, which continues to plague the modern world. Famines have, of course, occurred in non-market socialist economies as well as in market-based systems. But looking for the moment at famines in market economies, we can ask: why has the market system not been able to avoid them?

It has often been argued that the markets can and do distort food trade. Certainly, examples of markets being manipulated by organized traders are not hard to find. These manipulations have sometimes heightened the suffering and misery associated with famines. On the other hand, it is hard to find evidence to suggest that active trade distortion has been a *primary* cause of famines in market economies. The most obvious failure of the market mechanism lies, in this context, in the things that the market leaves *undone*. If some groups lose their purchasing power and their entitlement to food, say, due to employment loss as a result of a drought or a flood, the market may not do much to regenerate incomes or to recreate their lost command over food. That is a problem of *omission*, which has to be distinguished from any positively bad thing that the market might do. The remedy in this case need not be sought in 'market-excluding' interventions.

It is not being argued here that *all* the problems associated with the market mechanism in the context of a famine are invariably of the 'omission' type, that is, the result of what the markets do *not* do, rather than of their active presence. In some circumstances, the working of the market can positively worsen the situation of particular groups of people. An example is the role of the market in the decimation of pastoralists when the price of animals and animal products falls in relation to the cost of cheaper staple food, as is common in many famines (for reasons which have been discussed elsewhere; see Sen, 1981, chapters 7 and 8). Pastoralists suffer in this way because their economic existence has come to depend on the way the market functions, due to commercialization.

Even when there is a problem of market-driven commission, however, the threat of famine cannot be eliminated by outlawing the market, that is, by adopting any *general* 'market-excluding' intervention.[30] Indeed, what typically happens is that the benefits individuals receive from participating in the market (e.g., by selling labour-power and buying food with one's wage, or by selling animal products and buying cheap food) are suddenly compromised by changed economic circumstances. The process, thus, works through a *reduction of the advantages* of market transaction—advantages that may be vital for survival, and on which people may have come to rely. The process of destitution is sustained by the failure of the market mechanism to provide security of these exchange arrangements and terms of trade.

Lack of clarity about the distinction between market-excluding and market-complementary interventions has been responsible for some misanalysis and misinterpretation. For example, Adam Smith's (1776) defence of private trade in food grains and criticism of prohibitory restrictions by the state have often been interpreted as a proposition that state interference can only make a famine worse. But Smith's defence of private trade took the form of disputing the belief that food trades produce serious errors of *commission*. That disputation does not deny in any way the need for state action, in tackling a threatening famine, to supplement the operations of the market by creating incomes (e.g. through work programmes) because the market *omits* to do this. Smith's is a rejection of market-excluding systems, but not of public intervention for market-complementary arrangements.

Indeed, Smith's famine analysis is consistent with arguing for a discriminatingly activist government that would create incomes and purchasing power for the disentitled population, and then leave the supply of food to respond to the newly created demand through private trade. There is evidence—both from south Asia and from sub-Saharan Africa— that this combination of (1) undertaking state action to generate incomes and purchasing power of the potential famine victims, and (2) letting

---

[30] In some specific famine situations, stopping the market from functioning can have a limited but useful role, for example in preventing 'food countermovements' (see Sen, 1981, Chichilnisky, 1983). Sometimes food can move out from famine-stricken areas to more prosperous regions where people have greater ability to pay for food (for example, from famished Ireland to relatively opulent England during the Irish famines of the 1840s). In such situations, selective restrictions on the market can actually help (in the case of food countermovement, by preventing price increases in the famine-affected food-exporting country or region). But such cases are, on the whole, rather rare.

private markets to respond then to those incomes and demands, often works remarkably well in preventing famines.[31] That combination was explicitly discussed by Smith's friend Condorcet, and Smith's own analysis is entirely consistent with taking that route.[32]

Smith did provide a strong defence of the commissioning aspects of the market mechanism. His famous statement about gains from trade between the butcher, the brewer, and the baker, on the one hand, and the consumer, on the other, points to the advantages that the market positively produces for all the parties involved in the exchange. It does not deny that if we lack the *means* to buy meat, beer, or bread, the butcher, the brewer, and the baker won't do much for us. Stifling that trade would, he argued, be an active mistake, but waiting with hopeful passivity for incomes to be generated that would set the baker et al. to supply the needy can also be a costly error.

The distinction between omission and commission is important in understanding the division between the respective roles of the market and of non-market institutions in modern economies. In fact, it is possible to argue at the same time both (1) for *more* market institutions, and (2) for going *more beyond* the market. Indeed, in the context of the challenges of Indian planning, such a combination may be exactly what is needed. The fact that the form of the Indian political debates has tended to be quite traditional ('pro' or 'against' the market) has certainly contributed to confounding the nature of the issues. The need for more active use of the market in, say, industrial production and trade does not do away with the need for more state activity in raising India's abysmal level of basic education, health care and social security. Similarly, on the other side, the recognition of the latter need does nothing to reduce the importance of reforming the over-bureaucratized Indian economy.

The market-complementary arrangements needed to eliminate famines have, on the whole, worked quite well in post-independent India.[33] However, the problem of omission remains a central one in the context of the contemporary Indian economy—not in terms of vulnerability to famine, but in the form of regular undernourishment, widespread illiteracy, and high rates of morbidity and mortality. These are denials of basic freedoms that human beings have reasons to value. Furthermore, these deprivations can also be instrumentally significant by severely constraining

---

[31] On the circumstantial and strategic aspects of this combined policy, see Drèze (1990a, 1990b) and Drèze and Sen (1989).

[32] See Rothschild (2001).

[33] See Drèze and Sen (1989), chapter 8, Drèze (1990a), and the literature cited there.

the opportunity to participate in the process of economic expansion and social change. In trying to guarantee these freedoms, combining the functionings of markets and those of governments can be critically important. In these circumstances, market-complementary interventions can achieve positive results of a kind that neither market-excluding intervention, nor non-intervention, can deliver.

2.7. MARKET MANIA AND MARKET PHOBIA

The arguments developed so far in this chapter are not particularly novel. If they are worth spelling out, it is because public debates—in India as well as elsewhere—are often dominated by one-sided presentations, reflecting either uncritical faith in the market or blind opposition to it. Indeed, there are signs of both 'market mania' and 'market phobia' in the sharp exchanges that characterize debates on this subject.

Market mania involves an underexamined faith in the efficiency and other virtues of the market, regardless of context. It is reflected, for instance, in calls for indiscriminate deregulation and privatization, as well as in intuitively upbeat expectations about the effects of such policies. Market mania played a role in Russia's rush towards a market economy in the nineties. The catastrophic results of this rush are one indication that something may be deeply wrong in this enthusiastic unreason.

In India, a common form of market mania is the notion that radical deregulation is all it would take to 'kick-start the economy' (to use one of the favourite expressions of Indian financial journals). This belief is naïve in several ways. First, it is based on a narrow reading of the impediments that are holding the Indian economy. The relevant failures go much beyond a lack of market incentives, and also include widespread illiteracy and undernourishment, inadequate infrastructure, the paralysis of the legal system, endemic corruption, dismal public services, to cite a few concerns. Market mania overlooks the lack of preconditions in the Indian economy for the kind of take-off that has followed market-oriented reforms in countries such as China and Vietnam. The notion that deregulation on its own could lift the Indian economy out of its present predicament (let alone usher a rapid reduction of poverty) requires supplementing the recognition of the possible contributions of the market economy with a good blast of underreasoned optimism.

Second, the deregulation recipe overlooks the deep complementarities between market efficiency and state action. As discussed earlier in this chapter, the performance of the market is highly contingent on various forms of state action, from the provision of an adequate legal framework to redistributive policies. One implication of these complementarities is that liberalization does not necessarily diminish the importance of state action. This applies even to regulation itself, in so far as a relaxation of one type of rules often calls for developing new rules of a different type. For instance, allowing private entry into new sectors (such as medical insurance or electricity distribution), which may be considered as a form of deregulation, calls for an adequate overseeing framework, especially if these sectors have features (e.g. economies of scale, information asymmetries, pervasive externalities) that interfere with the efficiency of the market mechanism. Even in western 'market economies', including the United States, this necessity is well recognized.

Third, concentrating exclusively on deregulation can amount to taking a somewhat exaggerated view of the role of bureaucratic controls in shackling the Indian economy. This applies particularly to the rural economy, which has given ample room to market forces for a long time. In this respect, some Indian villages even resemble a Chicago economist's paradise, with an effectively unregulated market for most commodities.[34]

Further, in sectors where bureaucratic regulations do have a sharp edge, a question remains as to how the concerns that motivate such regulations are to be addressed in the event of deregulation. Not all regulations are based on bureaucratic arbitrariness or pernicious lobbying. Some also reflect pertinent concerns such as environmental destruction, hazardous labour conditions or monopolistic practices. While it is certainly true that the controls in question have often become excessively stifling, wholesale deregulation would be substituting one basic mistake for another.[35]

None of this detracts from the importance of reducing the burden of over-regulation in India. It can be argued, however, that India combines a massive excess of regulations with a serious lack of effective regulation in many fields, ranging from environmental protection and labour safety to public transport and the medical profession. This contrast arises from the fact that the regulations in question are often misguided, or not applied, or arbitrarily applied, or used as a means of harassment. Both problems (excessive regulations and ineffective regulation) need to be addressed, and this calls for a very different approach from that advocated by market fundamentalists.

Turning to market phobia (in the sense of uncritical opposition to market-based arrangements), the most common basis of this fear is the notion that giving greater room to the market mechanism invariably

---

[34] For further discussion, see Drèze, Lanjouw and Sharma (1998), pp. 224–7.

[35] The pitfalls of unregulated markets are well understood by the business community, which often lobbies for its own version of an appropriate regulatory framework, involving e.g. legal safeguards, arbitration procedures, quality standards and the protection of 'intellectual property rights'. On this point see e.g. Cable (1995).

exacerbates economic inequalities. This is a pertinent concern, and there are indeed many examples of market-driven increases in economic disparities. There is a strong case, in many situations, for interfering with the market mechanism on distributional grounds, e.g. through minimum wage legislation or positive discrimination in employment policies. This does not, however, imply that stifling the market mechanism typically has egalitarian effects. In many cases, state regulation in India has had exactly the opposite effect, consolidating privileged interests and the concentration of power.[36] Even more frequently perhaps, bureaucratic controls have led to colossal inefficiencies (the costs of which are borne by the public at large) without doing anything much for the underprivileged.

Further, the relation between markets and inequality has to be seen in a broad perspective, which focuses not only on economic inequality (as captured, for instance, in the distribution of incomes), but also on other dimensions of social inequality, such as gender or caste discrimination as well as inequalities of political power. In that broader perspective, market exchange sometimes emerges as a factor of liberation for disadvantaged sections of the population. It is by taking advantage of new opportunities for selling their labour, for instance, that many agricultural labourers in India have managed to free themselves from traditional bonds and feudal oppression.[37] In so far as market opportunities enable people to go about their economic activities without being dependent on the goodwill of officials and bureaucrats, they also represent a potential source of liberation from official harassment and arbitrariness.[38] It is, of course, also possible

[36] For some examples (among many), see Bhatia (1992) on groundwater management in Gujarat, Kapadia (1995) on tenancy legislation in Tamil Nadu, Parikh (1994) and Tarozzi (2000) on the public distribution system, Drèze (2001a) on agricultural pricing, Kishwar (2001a, 2001b) and Nayar (2001a) on the regulation of hawking and rickshaw-pulling in Delhi; also Saxena (1996), for a range of further illustrations.

[37] For reviews of the evidence, see Pal (1994) and Platteau (1995). For some case studies, see Breman (1974), Ramachandran (1990), and the literature cited in Drèze and Mukherjee (1989). That the replacement of tied labour by wage labour may to some extent serve as an instrument of liberation from traditional inequities was discussed by Karl Marx, among others; see e.g. Marx (1887), p. 240.

[38] Hinton (1990) notes this liberating aspect of market exchange in the context of post-reform China, despite his own aversion to the reforms (p. 147): 'Functionaries in China just assume that they have a right to run everything, down to the smallest details of people's lives. This tradition is really feudal. It is deeply resented down below and that is one of the reasons for the extraordinary attraction that a free market economy such as the one now appearing in Shenjen has for ordinary Chinese citizens. For people suffering under feudal restraints the cash nexus seems to promise a radical liberation where ability and not influence derived from social connections count.'

to give examples where market forces consolidate rather than reduce social disparities. The point is that there is no simple relation between markets and social inequality, broadly understood.

In cases where market processes do exacerbate economic or social inequality, it remains important to consider this problem together with other social consequences of the market economy. To illustrate, consider the recent expansion of software-related industries in India. Although government intervention has contributed to this expansion, market incentives have been its main driving force. It is quite possible that this process has led to some increase in economic inequality. Yet, it has also generated a great deal of employment, not only for programming wizards and other highly skilled personnel but also (through various backward and forward linkages) for many other people in the areas (e.g. around Bangalore and Hyderabad) where software-related services have flourished. In assessing these developments, it would be quite wrong to concentrate only on the inequality-enhancing effects of market incentives and ignore the employment-generation aspects. There are many other cases where the market process has diverse social consequences, which cannot be adequately evaluated on the basis of either 'market phobia' or 'market mania'.

2.8. COOPERATIVE ACTION AND SOCIAL CONTEXT

State intervention and the market mechanism may be seen as two alternative ways of coordinating economic activity. A third is cooperative action. India has a rich history of economic institutions based on cooperation: exchange labour, chit funds, traditional irrigation systems and arrangements for the protection of village commons are some examples. Cooperative action need not, of course, be confined to economic activity. It may also be important for matters such as conflict resolution, cultural life or political organization. The role of cooperative action in social life is so pervasive that it is easy to lose sight of it.

It is often argued that economic development fosters an individualistic culture and undermines the cooperative spirit. This reading, however, overestimates the cooperative features of 'traditional communities', just as it underestimates the role of cooperation in modern—even market-oriented—societies. In fact, an expansion of the scope of social cooperation may be regarded as a central feature of the development process, which arises from mutually reinforcing connections between the two. On the one hand, social cooperation plays a crucial *enabling role* in the process of development, by helping to translate economic prosperity into social opportunities. Some of the treasured activities in life, such as playing games or celebrating a festival, are intimately associated with cooperation. More significantly perhaps, social progress in fields such as public health, environmental protection and conflict prevention also depends a great deal on various forms of social cooperation. Even achieving economic prosperity is often facilitated by cooperative action, e.g. in the form of community activities to maintain irrigation structures or civic initiatives for the promotion of education.

On the other hand, development itself opens up new opportunities for social cooperation. At an early stage of development, the main focus of human activity has to be, almost by necessity, on satisfying basic needs associated with relatively simple commodities (e.g. food, clothing, shelter). As the horizon of human concerns and social interdependence expands, so does the realm of cooperative action.[39] Technological progress also paves the way to more complex forms of cooperative action, involving large numbers of persons instead of the relatively small social units (e.g. family, village, caste) typically involved in early forms of cooperation. The recent expansion of cooperative action on a global scale (involving concerns such as environmental protection, the debt crisis and world peace) is one example of this process. This is not to deny that some traditional forms of cooperation may well decline with economic development. But economic development also provides new *opportunities for cooperative action*, which are pursued to varying extents, depending on circumstances (for instance, on the quality of democratic institutions).

The notion that the expansion of cooperative action is an integral part of development can also be understood in a normative way. In so far as cooperative activity has intrinsic value and contributes to the quality of life, an expansion of social cooperation may be regarded as one of the central goals of development. It is in this perspective, among others, that the prevention of armed conflicts (both within and across borders) is also an integral part of development, in so far as peace makes it possible for citizens to engage in a wide range of cooperative activities instead of fighting each other. A similar comment applies to democracy (a quintessentially

---

[39] A recent opinion survey provides interesting evidence of the broad reach of personal concerns in contemporary India. The respondents were asked to state whether they agreed with the statement 'I am not very concerned about what happens in other parts of the country as long as nothing changes for me'. A majority of respondents disagreed (*Times of India*, 15 August 1997). The recent country-wide (indeed world-wide) wave of solidarity with earthquake victims in Gujarat is another interesting example.

contemporary form of political organization), which can further enlarge the realm of cooperative action.

Just as the state and the market are highly complementary institutions (even though they are often seen in antagonistic terms), a similar relation holds between cooperative action on the one hand and the state or the market on the other. There are, in particular, extensive complementarities between state intervention and cooperative action. In a democratic society, the priorities and actions of the state depend on organized public demands, and other aspects of a broad political process in which cooperative action plays a crucial part. Conversely, what cooperative action can achieve depends to a considerable extent on the opportunities created through state action, e.g. the level of education in the community, the accountability of government institutions, and the legal framework of civic association.

Similar remarks apply to the relation between cooperative action and market institutions. Markets and cooperative action are often taken to be antagonistic because the operating principle of the former is competition as opposed to cooperation. This interpretation is misleading because competition and cooperation themselves are, in many situations, complementary. For instance, cooperation within a cricket team or political party is sustained by the pressure of competition with the rival team or party. Even *between* competing teams or parties, a certain amount of cooperation is often at work, if only in the form of mutual observance of the 'rules of the game'.[40] In these and other ways, an element of cooperation is also involved in the operation of the market mechanism (along with the competitive principle), just as an element of competition often stimulates civic cooperation.

Thus, cooperative action and market institutions are often compatible or even complementary. For instance, the efficiency of the market mechanism can be greatly enhanced by cooperative social norms that reduce so-called 'transaction costs'. Indeed, markets can flourish more easily

---

[40] Even in situations of ruthless armed conflict, many interesting forms of cooperation between 'enemies' have been observed (aside from extensive cooperation *within* the respective camps). These include (1) mutual observance of fighting conventions (van Creveld, 1991), (2) cooperation between enemy leaders to prolong a conflict that suits their economic or other interests (Keen, 1998), and (3) reciprocal restraint on the part of soldiers on opposite sides (Andreski, 1992). A striking illustration of the latter is the 'live and let live' system that prevailed in many frontline trenches during the first world war, when soldiers on opposite sides cooperated in avoiding lethal clashes (sometimes even shaking hands or exchanging cigarettes when they accidentally found themselves in the same hole); for an insightful account of this arrangement, see Ashworth (1980).

when contracts are not typically broken and do not have to be rescued by litigation. Similarly, the economic freedom associated with the market mechanism often facilitates voluntary association and cooperative endeavours. Even global action against capitalism in recent years, oddly enough, has benefited a great deal from various facilities made available by the market mechanism, from swift communication (e.g. through the internet) to media publicity.

The subject of schooling provides many illustrations of the diverse interconnections (positive as well as negative) between state intervention, the market mechanism, and cooperative action.[41] The complementarity of these institutions is well exemplified in both Kerala and Himachal Pradesh—two 'success stories' in this field. In both cases, state action (e.g. provision of free schooling facilities) and cooperative action (e.g. missionary schools in Kerala) have been important. They have also tended to complement each other. In Himachal Pradesh, for instance, it is common for village communities to cooperate in building extra rooms for the local school, or in raising funds for extra-curricular activities. In both states, community monitoring has played an important part in sustaining the accountability of the schooling system. In Kerala, market incentives have also played a part, notably in the growth of 'private-aided schools' (involving a combination of private initiative and state support). Private-aided schools in Kerala provide an important example of a successful blend of state intervention, market incentives and cooperative action.

At the other extreme, the problems and failures of schooling policy in Uttar Pradesh illustrate the potentially antagonistic aspects of state intervention, cooperative action and the market mechanism. Soon after independence, massive centralization of education management in Uttar Pradesh throttled the autonomy of local authorities, and thereby undermined the role of cooperative action in schooling matters.[42] The deterioriation of teaching standards in government schools paved the way for the rapid growth of private (*unaided*) schools, and the latter, in turn, contributed to further deterioration of government schools as privileged classes (the main clients of unaided private schools) opted out of the public facilities and lost interest in them. This is a case where state intervention, cooperative action and the market mechanism have bypassed or even undermined each other. Today, there is much talk of restoring accountability in government schools through 'community participation'. However, this

---

[41] For further details, see chapter 5; also Probe Team (1999).
[42] See Kingdon and Muzammil (2001) and Muzammil and Kingdon (2001).

is unlikely to work unless community participation is integrated with more responsible management of the schooling system. For instance, there is little point in forming a 'village education committee' unless the educational administration—a quintessential bureaucracy—is responsive to their demands.

The case of schooling also illustrates the fact that cooperative action has to be seen in its social context. This recognition is important for a balanced assessment of what can be achieved, in different circumstances, through cooperative action. Just as the market and the state have their devotees, cooperative action is sometimes advocated as a simple remedy for a wide range of problems, and the claims in question call for critical scrutiny.[43]

To illustrate, consider the issue of pervasive environmental degradation in India. It is often argued that the best solution is to leave the management of environmental resources to 'local communities'. There are, indeed, many situations where this would be the right thing to do, and there are also plenty of examples of earlier success based on this approach.[44] But this does not imply that community management is invariably an effective general formula for environmental protection. How environmental concerns would play themselves out in, say, a village community must depend to a considerable extent on the local social structure, the distribution of power, cultural norms and related factors. The anthropological literature on this subject clearly brings out the diversity of possible outcomes, ranging from astonishingly sophisticated community institutions for environmental protection to the wanton destruction of environmental resources in other communities.[45] Also, most environmental resources involve public interests that extend well beyond local communities (for instance, aquifers are connected over large areas), and may take the concerns beyond the immediate domain of local decision-making. There is little evidence to support the belief that environmental

[43] For a helpful critique of 'anarcho-communitarian' discourse in India, see Bardhan (1997b).

[44] For some striking examples of community protection of environmental resources in India, see Somanathan (1991) and Chakravarty-Kaul (1996). See also Agarwal and Narain (1989), Gadgil and Guha (1995), and various contributions in Centre for Science and Environment (1999) and The Hindu (1999, 2000).

[45] See Baland and Platteau (1996), especially the review of anthropological literature in chapter 10. For various assessments of the reach of local cooperation in India, see Wade (1988), Agarwal and Narain (1989), Bardhan (1997b), Drèze, Lanjouw and Sharma (1998), Jayal (1999b), Blomkvist (2000a, 2000b), among others.

resources would automatically be managed in an efficient and equitable manner if only they were 'left to local communities', irrespective of the social context.

A particularly important contextual feature is the extent of antecedent social inequalities. It has been observed, for instance, that where the social structure is relatively egalitarian, traditional institutions for cooperative environmental protection are themselves comparatively equitable.[46] In highly unequal social settings, by contrast, these institutions tend to be manipulated by privileged groups.[47] These examples are also important pointers to the general role of social equality in facilitating cooperative action. Indeed, cooperative arrangements often break down when they fail to meet basic standards of equity and fairness. These issues will feature again in the chapters that follow.

2.9. A POSITIVE FOCUS

The literature on freedom in political philosophy is full of discussions that turn on the distinction between 'negative' and 'positive' liberties. That distinction can be interpreted in many different ways, but one way of seeing the contrast is to identify 'negative' liberty with *not being prevented* from doing certain things, while 'positive' liberty also includes those *supportive influences* which actually help a person to do the things that she wants to do.[48] While libertarians have been inclined to stress negative liberty, advocates of public support have tended to concentrate on positive versions of it.

A similar—though not identical—distinction can be made about the readings of the government's 'duties' vis-à-vis the citizens. The *negative* roles include preventing what are taken to be bad developments (for example, monopolistic arrangements), whereas *positive* roles encompass supporting constructively the efforts of the citizens to help themselves (for example, by arranging public education, by redistributing land, by protecting the legal rights of disadvantaged groups). Leaving out extremist

---

[46] See e.g. Somanathan (1991) on community management of local forests in the hill region of Uttar Pradesh. For further examples, see also Swamy (1991) and Jayal (1999b).

[47] See e.g. Sengupta (2000) on the management of irrigation tanks in Orissa.

[48] For different ways of characterizing the distinction between positive and negative liberty, see Berlin (1969), Nozick (1974), Dworkin (1978, 1981), Sen (1980, 1985b), Roemer (1982), Hamlin and Pettit (1989), Raz (1986), Arneson (1989), Cohen (1990, 1993), Dasgupta (1993), among other contributions.

advocacies, most political theories tend to provide room for both positive and negative roles of the government, but the relative importance that is given to the respective spheres can vary greatly.

Much of the debate on liberalization and deregulation is concerned with removing what is diagnosed to be the counterproductive nature of negative operations of the government. This position has been forcefully presented by the central government and the supporters of the new policies. On the other hand, the opposition to these types of reforms tends to come from those who see beneficial consequences of these negative governmental functions. The debate on current policy in India has been to a considerable extent preoccupied with this battle.

There are certainly issues of importance within the 'negative' sphere, but what that perspective neglects altogether is the importance of positive functions, such as provision of public education, health services, and arrangements for social security. There is scope for debate in this field as well (for example, on how much, and how soon, and exactly how), but nothing is sorted out in these matters by concentrating almost completely on the pros and cons of negative roles of the government (and the corresponding advantages and disadvantages of liberalization and deregulation). What is needed most of all is an adequately broad focus.

The tendency to concentrate on the negative roles of government has contributed to another bias in the liberalization debate, namely, the neglect of what can be achieved through cooperative action. This neglect is particularly serious if we acknowledge the wide-ranging nature of the reforms that are required in India, not only in economic matters but also in the social and political domains. There is urgent need not only for more efficient and equitable economic institutions, but also for uprooting corruption, protecting the environment, eradicating caste inequalities, preventing human rights violations, restoring the credibility of the legal system, halting the criminalization of politics (to cite a few major concerns). These different fields of reforms are no less important than the kinds of 'economic reforms' that have captured most of the attention in the 1990s. They are indeed best seen in an integrated perspective, where the promotion of human freedoms (rather than just the acceleration of economic growth) is the overarching goal. In that perspective, cooperative action acquires a new importance, in so far as it has a major bearing on many of these broader fields of economic and social life where reform is needed. To illustrate, eradicating corruption or protecting the environment (two goals that have much intrinsic as well as instrumental importance) are not just matters of sound government policy; they also involve cooperative action of various kinds, e.g. public vigilance against bribery and community management of local environmental resources.

In short, the liberalization debate in its present form is too narrow in at least three respects: (1) over-concentration on the negative roles of government, (2) over-preoccupation with narrowly 'economic' reforms, and (3) neglect of the role of cooperative action in economic and social reform. The perspective presented in this book is partly aimed at correcting these biases, without denying the need to address the issues that already figure prominently in this debate.

3

India in Comparative Perspective

3.1. INDIA AND THE WORLD

In historical terms, the improvement of living conditions that has taken place in the developing world during the last few decades has been quite remarkable. To illustrate, it is estimated that, between 1960 and 1999, life expectancy at birth in developing countries has expanded from 46 to 65 years, infant mortality has declined by 60 per cent, and real per-capita income has more than trebled.[1] These global *trends* are quite at variance with the gloomy predictions of famine and chaos that have been regularly made over the same period, even if absolute levels of deprivation remain intolerably high in large parts of the world.[2]

The pace of improvement has, of course, been quite uneven between different countries and regions, and recent decades have also seen the emergence of striking diversities within the developing world. In fact, the leading countries in the developing world are now, in many ways, much closer to industrialized market economies than to the poorer developing countries. It is not just that real per-capita income is now as high in (say) Singapore or Hong Kong as in Sweden or the United Kingdom. Even

---

[1] *Human Development Report 2001*, pp. 144 and 169, and *Human Development Report 1998*, p. 149. Social progress in the 1990s has been slower than in earlier decades, and even reversed in some countries of Africa and the former Soviet Union.

[2] For examples of these predictions, see Ehrlich (1968), Paddock and Paddock (1968), Brown and Eckholm (1974), Ehrlich and Ehrlich (1990), Hardin (1993), Kaplan (1994), Brown and Halweil (1999). India has held centre-stage in many of the gloomy prophecies in question, particularly during the 1960s (see chapter 6). To

countries such as South Korea and Argentina seem to have more in common with Greece or Portugal, which have comparable levels of real per-capita income, than with Nepal or Kenya, where real per-capita income is about ten times as low. Similarly, adult literacy rates are not very different in Uruguay and Italy (about 98 per cent each), but only 16 per cent in Niger and 36 per cent in Afghanistan. And the expectation of life at birth is about the same in Costa Rica as in Denmark (76 years each), or in Cuba as in the United States (77 years each), while a person born in Sierra Leone or Malawi has a life expectancy of less than 40 years.[3] While the common division of the world between 'North' and 'South' may have political interest and historical relevance, it is quite misleading in terms of many of the central features of development.

An important aspect of this diverse picture is that elementary deprivation in the world is now heavily concentrated in two specific regions: south Asia and sub-Saharan Africa.[4] Consider, for instance, the set of all countries where the infant mortality rate (IMR) is above 60 per 1,000 live births. According to recent estimates, there are 51 such countries, with a combined population of two billion.[5] Only seven of these countries (Afghanistan, Cambodia, Haiti, Iraq, Lao, Myanmar, and Yemen) are outside South Asia and sub-Saharan Africa; their combined population is 135 million, or less than seven per cent of the total population of this set of countries. The remaining 44 countries consist of the whole of south

---

illustrate: 'In thirteen years India is going to add two hundred million more people to their population. In my opinion, as an old India hand, I don't see how they can possibly feed two hundred million more people by 1980. They could if they had the time, say until year 2000. Maybe they could even do it by 1990, but they can't do it by 1980' (Dr. Raymond Ewell, in Ehrlich, 1968, pp. 39–40).

[3] The figures mentioned in this paragraph (which apply to 1999) are taken from *World Development Indicators 2001* (the 'real per-capita income' comparisons are based on purchasing-power-parity estimates of GDP per capita). Some of the figures presented in that report, as well as in *Human Development Report 2001* (also used in this chapter), involve substantial margins of error. This has to be borne in mind when comparing India's reasonably firm estimates with the corresponding—often less reliable—figures for other developing countries. The comparisons presented in this section give a rough idea of where India stands vis-à-vis the rest of the developing world, but the detailed inter-country comparisons would, in many cases, call for more scrutiny. For further discussion of the data sources used in this book, see the Statistical Appendix.

[4] The recent decline of living standards in parts of eastern Europe and the former Soviet Union is another crucial aspect of this picture. As things stand, however, living standards in that region remain considerably higher, in most respects, than in south Asia or sub-Saharan Africa.

[5] The figures cited in this paragraph are calculated from *World Development Indicators 2001* (CD-ROM). The reference year is 1999.

Asia except Sri Lanka and the whole of sub-Saharan Africa except Botswana, Ghana and Mauritius. Of course, even in countries where the infant mortality rate is below 60 on the *average*, it can be well above that figure for particular sections of the population (just as the IMR can be much below 60 for the more privileged sections of the population in the poorer countries). But it is clear that there are few regions where elementary deprivation is as endemic as in south Asia and sub-Saharan Africa.

India alone accounts for more than half of the combined population of these 51 deprived countries. It is not the worst case by any means (India's infant mortality rate is around 70 per 1,000 live births), but this observation has to be interpreted bearing in mind that there are large regional variations in living conditions *within* India. While India is doing significantly better than, say, Ethiopia or Congo in terms of most development indicators, there are large areas within India where living conditions are not very different from those prevailing in these countries. Even entire states such as Uttar Pradesh (which has a larger population than Russia) are not doing much better than the least developed among sub-Saharan African countries in terms of basic development indicators.[6]

Considering India and sub-Saharan Africa as a whole, infant mortality rates appear to be of a similar order of magnitude in the two regions (71 and 92 per 1,000 live births, respectively). This is not to say that both regions are generally in the same boat as far as development is concerned. In many respects, living standards are now distinctly higher in India than in sub-Saharan Africa. Life expectancy, for instance, is around 63 years in India, while in sub-Saharan Africa it is as low as 47 years (this is partly due to the spread of AIDS, which has led to a sharp decline of life expectancy in many African countries in recent years, but the gap was large even before this). Also, since independence, India has been relatively free of the problems of famine and large-scale civil war that periodically wreck various countries of sub-Saharan Africa. And many countries of sub-Saharan Africa have had a specific problem of economic *decline*—partly related to these tragedies—which makes it particularly hard to improve living standards.

[6] For further discussion, see Drèze and Sen (1995a), pp. 29–31. Shiva Kumar's (1991) estimates of UNDP's 'human development index' (HDI) for Indian states put Uttar Pradesh near the bottom of the international scale, between Ethiopia and Zaire (now Congo). Uttar Pradesh's performance is even worse in terms of some indicators not included in that index, such as the female-male ratio and other indicators of basic gender inequality. On this and related issues, see also the case study of Uttar Pradesh by Drèze and Gazdar (1996) in the companion volume (Drèze and Sen, 1996).

Having said this, the comparison between India and sub-Saharan Africa is not entirely to India's advantage—far from it. In at least three crucial respects, living conditions in India are no better than in sub-Saharan Africa (see Table 3.1). First, the two regions share a common problem of endemic illiteracy and low educational achievements. Available estimates suggest that adult literacy rates are quite similar in the two regions. If anything, India comes out worse in the comparison, mainly because of low female literacy rates. As Table 3.1 indicates, India is entering the twenty-first century with a *majority* of adult women unable to read and write.

It is rather striking that India turns out to be doing no better than sub-Saharan Africa in this respect. Unlike many countries of sub-Saharan Africa, India has been relatively protected from the calamities of political instability, military rule, divisive wars, and recurring famines for a period of more than fifty years, but it has failed to take advantage of these favourable circumstances to achieve a breakthrough in the field of basic education. This failure, which stands in sharp contrast with a relatively good record in higher education and scientific research, is one of the most deplorable aspects of India's contemporary development experience.

Second, there is much evidence that the incidence of undernutrition is considerably higher in India (and south Asia) than in sub-Saharan Africa.[7] Whether we look at the estimated incidence of child undernourishment, or of low birthweights, or of anaemia among pregnant women, India does consistently worse (*much* worse) than sub-Saharan Africa. In fact, among all countries for which estimates are available, *none* does worse than India in any of these respects, with the possible exception of Bangladesh.[8] As Table 3.1 indicates, more than half of all Indian children are undernourished (in terms of standard 'weight-for-age' criteria), and the incidence of anaemia among pregnant women is estimated to be as high as 88 per cent. These are catastrophic failures, with wide-ranging implications not only for the people of India today but also for the generations to be born in the near future.

There does exist a school of thought that argues that growth retardation in children does not matter much (that 'small' may even be 'healthy', or at least not very harmful), but recent medical research suggests quite the

[7] On south Asia's nutritional disadvantage vis-à-vis sub-Saharan Africa, see also Scrimshaw (1997) and Svedberg (2000).

[8] The comparative levels of undernutrition in India and Bangladesh are not very clear from available data, and depend on the choice of indicators and sources. Based on the indicators and sources used in Table 3.1, the situation appears to be much the same in the two countries, though India fares even worse than Bangladesh in terms of the incidence of anaemia among pregnant women.

TABLE 3.1 *India and sub-Saharan Africa:*
Selected Development Indicators, 1999

	India	Sub-Saharan Africa
Estimated per-capita income (purchasing power parity $)	2,230	1,500
Health-related indicators		
Infant mortality rate (per 1,000 live births)	71	92
Life expectancy at birth (years)	63	47
Nutrition-related indicators		
Proportion (%) of undernourished children, 1995–2000[a] ('weight-for-age' criterion, age below 5)	53	30
Proportion (%) of low-birthweight babies, 1995–9[a]	34	15[b]
Proportion (%) of pregnant women with anaemia, 1985–99[a]	88	45
Literacy-related indicators		
Adult literacy rate (age 15+) (%)		
Female	44[c]	53
Male	68[c]	69
Youth literacy rate (age 15-24) (%)		
Female	64	73
Male	79	82
Gender-related indicators		
Female-male ratio in the population (women per 1,000 men)	933	1,015
Ratio of female to male child mortality rates, 1988–99[a] (age 1–4)	1.5	0.9
Female participation in gainful employment (women's share in the labour force)	0.32	0.42

Notes: [a] Latest year for which data are available within the specified period.

[b] Population-weighted average based on the 35 sub-Saharan countries for which estimates are available; this figure should be taken as indicative.

[c] The corresponding estimates from the National Family Health Survey 1998–9 are 44 and 72 respectively (see Statistical Appendix).

Sources: World Development Indicators 2001, Tables 1.1, 1.2, 2.2, 2.14, 2.18, 2.19, and *Human Development Report 2001*, Table 7. The female-male ratios are from Government of India (2001b) and United Nations Population Division (1999). Unless stated otherwise, the reference year is 1999.

contrary: growth retardation does make a big difference to health, morbidity, and even cognitive skills.[9] There is also growing evidence that low birthweights lead to serious health impairment, not only in childhood but also in adult life.[10] Given that low birthweights are themselves closely related to the poor nutritional status of adult women, there is a resilient trap of undernourishment here from which India is yet to escape.

Third, in some respects at least, economic and social inequalities are sharper in India than in sub-Saharan Africa. This applies in particular to many dimensions of gender inequality.[11] One symptom of basic gender inequality in India is the low female-male ratio in the population (933 women per 1,000 men, according to the preliminary results of the 2001 census), mainly reflecting excess female mortality in the younger age groups, itself related to gender discrimination within the family. In this respect, again, India is at the rock bottom of the international scale, together with Pakistan.[12] There is a good deal of further evidence of extreme gender inequality and female deprivation in India, relating for instance to women's participation in gainful employment, schooling opportunities, patterns of property rights, and decision-making within the family.[13] This is not to say that the social disadvantages of women are uniformly more pronounced in India than in sub-Saharan Africa. Fertility rates, for instance, are much higher in sub-Saharan Africa than in India (5.3 and 3.1 children per woman, respectively). In so far as the strains of repeated child-bearing can be seen as an important restriction of freedom for women

[9] See the literature reviewed in Scrimshaw (1997); see also Dasgupta and Ray (1990) and Osmani (1990, 1992).

[10] On these and other consequences of low birthweights, see Gopalan (1994), Barker (1998), Osmani and Sen (2001), and various contributions to the First World Congress on the Fetal Origins of Adult Disease (summarized in a forthcoming issue of *Pediatric Research*); also Pojda and Kelley (2000), and the literature cited in that survey.

[11] For further discussion of this particular contrast between India and sub-Saharan Africa, see Sen (1988). Caste-based discrimination is another aspect of social inequality in India that has only limited counterparts in sub-Saharan Africa. There is also some evidence of economic inequalities being larger in India than in most African countries.

[12] The female-male ratio is, in fact, even lower than India and Pakistan's 0.93 in a few oil-exporting countries of west Asia (*World Development Indicators 2001*, Table 1.3), but this is mainly due to large-scale immigration of male labourers from abroad. On the significance of the female-male ratio as an indicator of basic gender inequality, see chapter 7.

[13] To illustrate, according to *Human Development Report 1998* (pp. 131–3), only five countries in the world have a larger female-male literacy gap than India: Bhutan, Syria, Togo, Malawi, and Mozambique. Rajasthan alone has as large a population as these five countries combined, and no country in the world has a wider female-male literacy gap than Rajasthan.

(which is also closely related to other aspects of gender inequality and female disadvantage), this issue appears to be particularly serious in sub-Saharan Africa.[14] The fact remains that India stands out as a country of exceptional gender inequality in many crucial fields.

It is worth noting that there are wide-ranging interconnections between these three aspects of human deprivation in India (low literacy, endemic undernutrition, and social inequality). For instance, gender inequality plays a major part in the persistence of widespread illiteracy, not only by fostering a deep neglect of female education, but also by suppressing women's agency roles in bringing about educational advancement (for girls *and* boys).[15] Similarly, both gender inequality and educational backwardness are crucial causal antecedents of endemic undernutrition. Indeed, women's education has emerged in many empirical investigations as one of the most powerful determinants of child health. Also, low birthweights partly reflect the poor nutritional status of adult women, related in turn to gender discrimination within the family.[16] Again, poor nutrition undermines many children's schooling opportunities, e.g. by affecting their cognitive abilities and making it harder for them to attend school on a regular basis. Going beyond these elementary interconnections, illiteracy, undernutrition and social inequality (including gender inequality) also have far-reaching effects on a wide range of human freedoms. The fact that India is especially deprived in these respects imposes a heavy burden on many aspects of Indian development.

3.2. LESSONS FROM OTHER COUNTRIES

The cases of successful economic development in other developing countries are often cited in Indian policy debates. It is, in general, appropriate to do this: many countries have done much better than India, and it is natural to learn from the accomplishments of these countries. The countries frequently selected for comparison (such as South Korea and the other three of the so-called 'four tigers', as well as Thailand and post-reform China) are indeed among the countries from which India can expect to learn greatly, since they have, in different ways, done so very well. To claim that 'India is unique' would be true enough in itself but thoroughly misleading as an alleged ground for refusing to try to learn from other countries.

[14] The relation between fertility, gender inequality and women's empowerment is discussed at greater length in chapters 6 and 7.
[15] For further discussion, see chapter 5.
[16] On this and related issues, see Osmani (1997) and Osmani and Sen (2001).

However, in learning from the experiences of other countries, we have to be careful to avoid taking an over-simple view of what it is that the 'others' have done, or identifying the relevant 'others' from an over-narrow perspective. First, it would be a great mistake to assume—as is often done—that all that the successful experiences of, say, the four so-called 'tigers' (South Korea, Hong Kong, Singapore, Taiwan) teach us is the importance of 'freeing' the markets. Much else happened in these countries other than freeing the markets, such as educational expansion, public health programmes, extensive land reforms, determined governmental leadership in promoting economic growth, and so on.[17] These countries—and also post-reform China—have all been well ahead of India in many 'social' respects that have helped them to make use of the economic opportunities offered by the expansion of markets, and they were, in fact, in that 'better prepared' position even at the inception of their market-based leap forward. To overlook these differences on some imagined ground of separating out alleged 'essentials' from other—'ancillary'—features would be both mistaken and quite counterproductive in learning from these experiences. We shall examine these issues in the next section.

Second, the 'others' to learn from are not just the countries that have experienced high economic growth (such as the four 'tigers', or Thailand, or post-reform China), but also those that have managed to raise the quality of life through other means (even in the absence of fast economic growth), such as public support for health care and basic education. It is worth remembering that life expectancy is higher in, say, Sri Lanka than in Thailand, or in Jamaica than South Korea, despite large income differences in the opposite direction, while 'lower middle-income' Costa Rica is in the same league as Singapore (one of the richest countries in the world) in this respect.[18] China's remarkable success in transforming many aspects of the quality of life during the pre-reform period, at a time of relatively slow economic growth, is also relevant here (we shall have more to say on this, as well as on some of China's failures, in the next chapter). These and other experiences of rapid improvement in living conditions despite slow economic growth are full of important lessons—about the feasibility of

---

[17] Some of these countries—South Korea in particular—have also benefited from low levels of antecedent economic inequality, which helped to make the process of economic expansion more participatory, and possibly also enhanced economic growth itself. Alesina and Rodrik (1994) have investigated the contribution of lesser inequality to economic growth and development; see also Persson and Tabellini (1994), Fishlow et al. (1994), Rodrik (1994), and the literature cited in Bardhan, Bowles and Gintis (2000).

[18] See *World Development Indicators 2001*, Tables 1.1 and 2.19. The life expectancy estimates are: Thailand (69 years), Sri Lanka (73), South Korea (73), Jamaica (75), Costa Rica (77), Singapore (78).

achieving radical social progress at an early stage of economic development, about the powerful effects of well-devised public programmes in the fields of health and education, about the relatively inexpensive nature of labour-intensive public provisions such as primary education in a low-wage economy, about the collaborative and adversarial roles of public action, and so on.[19] It is just as important to identify these lessons as to learn from countries that have achieved rapid economic growth, and succeeded in using rapid growth as a basis for improving the quality of life.

Third, it must be remembered that not all countries with high growth rates have succeeded in translating an expanded command over material resources into a corresponding transformation of living conditions for broad sections of the population. In fact, the development experience of some fast-growing countries during the last few decades has resembled one of 'unaimed opulence', combining high rates of economic growth with the persistence of widespread poverty, illiteracy, ill health, child labour, criminal violence and related social failures.[20] Brazil is one conspicuous example. In many cases (including Brazil itself), the roots of this failure to use economic growth as a basis for transforming the quality of life include high levels of economic and social inequality as well as a lack of public involvement in the protection of basic entitlements. The dangers of unaimed opulence, which may be particularly real for India, form an integral part of the lessons to be learnt from discriminating analyses of the experiences of fast-growing countries.

Fourth, as was argued earlier, given India's heterogeneity, lessons from other countries have to be integrated with the possibility of learning from India itself. We cannot, for example, altogether ignore the fact that Kerala, despite its low income level and poor record in generating economic growth, has as high a life expectancy at birth (about 74 years) as South Korea (73 years), despite per-capita income being many times larger in South Korea than in Kerala. Similarly, Himachal Pradesh's experience of rapid improvement in the quality of life during the last fifty years is of no less interest to other Indian states than that of east Asia. We have to learn

---

[19] We have tried to discuss some of these lessons in Drèze and Sen (1989). For insightful studies of specific country experiences, see also Castaneda (1985), Halstead et al. (1985), Caldwell (1986), Riskin (1987, 1990), Mata and Rosero (1988), Anand and Kanbur (1990), Bruton et al. (1993), Alailima and Sanderatne (1997), Mehrotra and Jolly (1997), among others.

[20] On this phenomenon of 'unaimed opulence', see Drèze and Sen (1989), chapter 10. On the specific case of Brazil, see Sachs (1990) and Birdsall and Sabot (1993). Even east and south-east Asia's overall success in terms of participatory growth has had its shortcomings and setbacks, as the recent financial crisis and its social consequences illustrate; we shall return to this.

from the experiences *within* India itself, and this applies to failures as well as successes. The relevant failures include not only the continued social backwardness of many states (such as Uttar Pradesh), but also Kerala's failure to achieve rapid economic growth, despite a remarkably high performance in terms of many aspects of the quality of life.

In an earlier study, we found that, among ten developing countries that had achieved the largest reductions in child mortality between 1960 and 1985, five were cases of what we called 'growth-mediated' success, while the other five succeeded in reducing mortality on the basis of organized programmes of public support for health, education, and social security, without fast economic growth.[21] The latter approach—what we called 'support-led' success—proved to be feasible largely because the costs of elementary health care and education tend to be comparatively low in low-wage economies (because of the labour-intensive nature of these activities), so that a poorer economy is not as disadvantaged in providing these services as might appear on the basis of its lower ability to pay. In drawing lessons for India from recent development experiences elsewhere in the world, it is important to pay attention to both types of progress, based respectively on economic growth and public support. It is also important to be aware of the possibility of 'unaimed opulence', and to take note of the fact that India could go the way of Brazil rather than of South Korea. We have to discriminate, rather than assume some 'stylized model' of liberalization.

3.3. EAST ASIA AND GROWTH–MEDIATED PROGRESS

In learning from the experiences of other countries, it is also essential to integrate our 'theory' of what is causing what with an understanding of the facts of the case. The importance of markets and trade in generating economic expansion has been a part of mainstream economic principles for a very long time. Even Adam Smith's (1776) classic analysis of the 'causes' of the wealth of nations dealt precisely with this question, among others. The recent revival of growth oriented trade theory has done much to bring out the importance of two issues on which Adam Smith himself had much to say, to wit, (1) the importance of economics of large scale, and (2) the influence of skill formation and human qualities in causing prosperity.[22]

---

[21] Drèze and Sen (1989), chapter 10.
[22] See Krugman (1979, 1986, 1987), Romer (1986, 1987b, 1990), Lucas (1988, 1993), Grossman and Helpman (1990, 1991a, 1991b). On different aspects of the lessons to be learned from recent experiences of rapid growth and trade expansion, see also Lucas (1988), Stokey (1988), Helpman and Krugman (1990), Helpman and

The shift in emphasis from seeing the gains from trade primarily in terms of 'comparative advantages' (the traditional 'Ricardian' focus) is important in interpreting east Asia's sucess and its relevance to India and other countries.

The growing recognition of the role and importance of economies of large scale has also changed one of the intellectual bases of closed-economy planning that was so fashionable—in India as well as elsewhere—from the 1960s onwards.[23] Underlying that acceptance of economic autarchy was a sense of export pessimism that made planners in India and elsewhere look for more internally-oriented economic development, aimed at producing within the borders whatever the country needed. The concentration, then common, on 'comparative advantage' as the real source of gainful trade (dependent on differences of factor ratios, natural endowments, etc.) did not persuade those analysts who tended to be sceptical of the possibility of trade expansion, and who underestimated the real gains from trade. Autarchy was, often enough, not so much a policy of jubilant rejection of trade, but the result of a pessimistic perception that the opportunities for trade were severely limited.[24]

With the shifting focus in trade theory, from Ricardo's comparative advantage to Adam Smith's economies of scale, the limits of trade expansion have been substantially reformulated and the grounds for export pessimism have been largely debunked. The limits of trade are not to be seen as being constrained simply by differences in factor ratios and endowments, and what a country loses from autarchy includes the efficiency advantages of a division of labour that makes use, inter alia, of scale advantages and gains from specialization. The need for a radical departure in this respect in Indian economic planning is brought out both by reasoning based on modern growth theory, and by the actual experience of the economies—

Razin (1991), Helleiner (1992), Ethier, Helpman and Neary (1993), Findlay (1993), Krugman and Smith (1994), among other contributions.

[23] For a fine account of the rationale behind planning approaches used in India, see Chakravarty (1987).

[24] One of the authors of this monograph was, in fact, involved in constructing a model, jointly with K.N. Raj, explicitly assuming this pessimism, entitled 'Alternative Patterns of Growth under Conditions of Stagnant Export Earnings' (Raj and Sen, 1961). While the main interest in that analysis was not with trade, but with the relations between different sectors in a growth model with constant returns to scale (on this see Atkinson, 1969, and Cooper, 1983), it was the sense—mistaken as it happens—of export pessimism that made models of this kind look particularly relevant to Indian planning. Even when export pessimism was not explicitly assumed, it tended to colour the growth scenarios that were explored in development models in that period (see for, example, Chakravarty, 1969).

such as those in east Asia—that have made such excellent use of trade-using patterns of economic growth. India's own recent experience, especially the export-led boom in the software industry (a sector where economies of scale are paramount), is consistent with this reappraisal of trade opportunities.

Recent work on economic growth has also brought out sharply the role of labour and (so-called) 'human capital'. The economic roles of school education, learning by doing, technical progress, and even economies of large scale can all be seen as contributing—in different ways—to the centrality of human agency in generating economic expansion. In terms of economic theory, this focus on human capital has provided one way of filling the large 'residual' that was identified in the basic neo-classical model of economic growth of Solow (1956), and this programme of investigation has done much to bring out the function of human agency in economic growth, over and above the contribution made through the accumulation of physical capital.[25] Attempts to learn from the 'East Asian miracle' and other cases of growth-mediated progress cannot ignore the wealth of insights that these analyses have provided.[26]

The crucial role of human capital makes it all the more essential to pay attention to the close relation between sensible public action and economic progress, since public policy has much to contribute to the expansion of education and the promotion of skill formation. The role of widespread basic education in these countries with successful growth-mediated progress cannot be overemphasized.[27] The modern industries in which these countries have particularly excelled demand many basic skills for which elementary education is essential and secondary education most helpful. While some studies have emphasized the productivity contribution of learning by doing and on-the-job training, rather than

[25] There is a vast literature in this field, beginning with Solow's own works that followed his 1956 model (see particularly Solow, 1957). For aspects of the recent revival of the subject, involving 'new' growth theory as well as further exploration of older neo-classical models, see Romer (1986, 1987a, 1987b), Krugman (1987), Barro (1990a, 1990b), Matsuyama (1991), Stokey (1991), Young (1992), Mankiw, Romer and Weil (1992), Barro and Lee (1993, 1994), Lucas (1993), among other contributions. For a critical assessment, see Bardhan (1995).

[26] See Rodrik (1994) for a different reading of the 'East Asian miracle', with more focus on the investment boom in South Korea and Taiwan; see also Fishlow et al. (1994) and Malinvaud et al. (1997).

[27] On different aspects and interpretations of this role, see Behrman (1987), Behrman and Schneider (1994), Stevenson and Stigler (1992), Barro and Lee (1993, 1994), Easterly et al. (1993), World Bank (1993c), Birdsall, Ross and Sabot (1995), among many other contributions.

TABLE 3.2 *Adult Literacy Rates (age 15+) in Selected Asian Countries*

	1960	1980	1990	1999
India	28	36	49	56[a]
South Korea	71	93	96	98
Hong Kong	70	90	90	93
Thailand	68	86	92	95
China	n/a	69	77	83

Notes: [a]The National Family Health Survey 1998–9 suggests a slightly higher figure—around 58 per cent. For details, see Statistical Appendix.
Sources: World Development Report 1980, Table 23, for 1960; *World Development Report 1983*, Table 1, for 1980; *World Development Indicators 2000* (CD-ROM) for 1990. The 1999 literacy rates were calculated from sex-specific literacy rates given in *World Development Indicators 2001*, Table 2.14, using the relevant female-male ratios.

the direct impact of formal education, the ability to achieve such training and learning is certainly helped greatly by basic education in schools prior to taking up jobs.[28]

The development of basic education was significantly more advanced in all these countries with successful growth-mediated progress at the time of their economic breakthrough compared with India—not just at that time but even today. Table 3.2 presents some comparative information on this subject. The point to notice is not so much that India's literacy rate *is* far lower than in these countries *today*, nor that India *was* way behind in that respect at the time when these countries jumped forward economically, but that India *today* still remains behind where these countries *were* when they initiated their rapid economic expansion. The really instructive comparison is between India now and, say, South Korea in 1960 or China in 1980. Despite the passage of time, India's literacy rate remains below what these countries had achieved many years ago when they began their market-based economic transformation.

Age-specific literacy rates, if available, would convey this contrast even more sharply. From the fact that adult literacy in South Korea, Hong Kong

---

[28] The World Bank (1993c) study of 'the East Asian miracle', which draws on a wide range of empirical works, has particularly emphasized the importance of this linkage: 'We have shown that the broad base of human capital was critically important to rapid growth in the HPAEs [high-performing Asian economies]. Because the HPAEs attained universal primary education early, literacy was high and cognitive skill levels were substantially above those in other developing economies. Firms therefore had an easier time upgrading the skills of their workers and mastering new technology' (World Bank, 1993c, p. 349).

and Thailand was virtually universal in 1990, we can infer that literacy rates in the younger age groups were already close to 100 per cent in those countries in 1960.[29] In India, by contrast, about a quarter of all children in the 15–19 age group are illiterate today. And barely one half of all children in that age group have achieved the norm of eight years of schooling corresponding to the constitutional directive on universal elementary education.[30]

In the educational expansion of the high-performing Asian economies, the state has played a major part in every case. An essential goal of public policy has been to ensure that the bulk of the young population had the capability to read, write, communicate and interact in a way that prepared them to participate in a modern economy. In India, by contrast, there has been a remarkable apathy towards expanding elementary and secondary education, and certainly 'too little' government action—rather than 'too much'—is the basic failure of Indian planning in this field.[31]

India does, of course, have a large body of people with higher education, and there is certainly an opportunity to use their proficiency to develop skill-centred industries, as has begun to happen to a considerable extent (for example, in and around Bangalore or Hyderabad, involving computer software and related industries). These achievements are important and are certainly good signs for the Indian economy. But the abysmal inequalities in India's education system represent a real barrier against widely sharing the fruits of economic progress, in general, and of industrialization, in particular, in the way it has happened in economies like South Korea and China—economies which have succeeded in flooding the world market with goods the making of which requires no great university training, but is helped by widespread basic education. In contrast, the software boom in India is doing relatively little for the poor, illiterate masses, despite some important spillover effects. It may be much less glamorous to make simple toys, pocket knives or alarm clocks than to design state-of-the-art computer programmes, but the former gives the Chinese poor a source of income that the latter does not provide—at least not directly—to the Indian poor. It is in the making of

---

[29] This inference is based on the plausible assumption that most people learn to read and write at a young age (if at all), rather than, say, through adult literacy programmes.

[30] See chapter 5, especially Table 5.1; also Statistical Appendix, Table A.3.

[31] As argued in chapter 5, this failure reflects not only the low priority given by the state to educational expansion, but also a serious lack of concern for education in social and political movements.

these unglamorous products, the market for which is very large across the world, that widespread education is a major asset for China—and for many other high-growth economies of east and south-east Asia.[32]

Despite impressive booms in specific high-skill industries, the overall growth rate of the Indian economy and that for the industrial sector *as a whole* remain far from spectacular. In fact, in both respects the performance of the Indian economy has been much the same in the 1990s as in the 1980s (see chapter 9). This is not to deny that India can quite possibly achieve higher rates of growth of GDP or industrial output even with present levels of massive illiteracy. The absolute number of Indians with good education is very large. But the low coverage and poor quality of basic education in India make it harder to move from the conspicuous dynamism of a limited range of industries and services (the expansion of which has been so eulogized in financial journals) to a really broad-based economic advance of a sweeping, shared and participatory kind that has often happened further east. It is ultimately a question of the strength and the nature of the economic expansion that can occur in India today, and the extent to which the growth in question can be widely participatory. For reasons presented earlier on in this monograph, the social opportunities offered by market-based economic growth are severely limited in a society in which very large numbers (even majorities in large parts of the country) cannot read or write or count, cannot follow printed or hand-written instructions, cannot operate comfortably in a modern industry, and so on.[33] Inequality in basic education thus translates into inefficiency as well as in further inequality in the use of new economic opportunities. The *distributive* failure supplements the effect of educational backwardness in restricting the *overall* scale of expansion of skill-related modern production.

The relationship between education and inequality applies also to gender-based disparities. Again, the high-performing Asian economies have been able to reduce the gender gap in basic education much more rapidly than happened elsewhere, and this achievement has certainly played an important part in reducing the relative disadvantage of women in social opportunities, including economic participation. The growth-

---

[32] While China has impressive achievements in expanding the production and export of simple industrial products (with their massive employment and income effects), it must also be recognized that China has, by now, also acquired a great production base of more sophisticated industrial goods, such as computer hardware, in which China is a leading producer in the world.

[33] As noted in chapter 1, there is also considerable evidence that the rate of return to basic education tends to be higher in countries that are more 'open', with less restriction on trade. On this and related issues, see Birdsall, Ross and Sabot (1995).

mediated success of the east Asian economies has drawn particularly on the expansion of employment options and other opportunities for women. The contrast with India is extremely sharp. In fact, in this respect, south Asia—including India—lags behind every other region of the world except 'Middle East and North Africa'.[34]

While the contrast in the field of education is perhaps the most radical difference between India and the high-growth countries in east Asia, there are also other areas in which supportive public policies in social fields have helped these successful Asian economies in a way that has not happened in India. These countries have typically had much better levels of health care even before their period of rapid economic growth. Greater provision of medical facilities in the east Asian countries, particularly in terms of public health and preventive health care, is an important factor in explaining this contrast. In the case of China, the expansion of rural health care has been one of the most remarkable achievements of the *pre-reform* period.[35] It has proved to be an asset of great value in the economic reforms. This is an important issue not only for the quality of life, but also for economic performance, since morbidity and undernourishment can be serious barriers to productive work and economic performance.[36]

Another area in which many of the great practitioners of growth-mediated progress have done much better than India is that of land reform. Extensive land reforms were carried out in many east Asian countries, including Japan, South Korea, Taiwan, and of course China. The advantages of the abolition of landlordism from the point of view of equity are obvious enough, but it also has much to contribute to the general incentive to expand production, and to making it easier for agricultural producers to respond to the opportunities offered by a freer market.[37] Significantly

---

[34] See *World Development Indicators 2001*, Tables 1.3 and 2.2. In 1999, women accounted for one third of the labour force in India and south Asia, compared with 45 per cent or so in China and east Asia.

[35] On this see Drèze and Sen (1989), chapter 11, and the studies cited there; also chapter 4 of this book.

[36] See Bliss and Stern (1978), Sahn and Alderman (1988), Dasgupta and Ray (1986, 1987, 1990), Osmani (1990, 1992), Dasgupta (1993), among other contributions. The east Asian achievements in this field are reviewed in World Bank (1993c).

[37] On the historical experiences of land reform in some of these east Asian countries (such as Taiwan and South Korea), and their extensive consequences, see Galenson (1979), Kuo (1983), Kim and Leipziger (1997), World Bank (1993c). It has been argued that sharecropping need not be inefficient when certain conditions (relating for instance to the flexibility of relative shares and the monitorability of inputs) are met, but the assumptions needed tend to be quite strong and seem to be at variance with empirical observation. On the theory of resource allocation under share tenancy, see Bliss and Stern (1982), Binswanger and Rosenzweig (1984), Quibria and Rashid

enough, one of the least successful growth performers among the east Asian economies, namely the Philippines, is also an example of deep failure to carry out adequate land reforms.[38] The Indian record is even worse than the general situation in the Philippines; some success in land reforms has been achieved in West Bengal and Kerala, but the overall achievements in most Indian states are quite dismal.

The lessons of successful growth-mediated progress in east Asia include the importance of various areas of state action, including basic education, general—particularly preventive—health care, and land reform. In understanding and interpreting east Asia's achievements, these roles of public action have to be viewed along with the part played by governments in directly promoting and guiding industrial expansion and export growth. These directly interventionist functions have been brought out sharply by some—so-called 'revisionist'—studies of the east Asian experience, which have interpreted the economic achievements as integrally related to productive public intervention.[39] While other studies have had somewhat different emphases,[40] there is much evidence that the government did play a significant role in directly promoting industrialization in east Asia, inter alia through systematic intervention (for example, through variable financial terms) in advancing particular industries, and in giving priority to chosen directions of international trade (in particular, selective export promotion). The special contributions of governmental initiative in educational expansion, health care, land reforms, etc., can be seen as important examples of this general state activism. It would be quite bizarre to read the east Asian success stories as simple results of liberalization and of the 'freeing' of markets.

The recent economic crisis in east Asia further highlights the inadequacy of that particular interpretation. Two issues in particular stand out as lessons of that event. First, the crisis underlines the potential danger of *indiscriminate liberalization*, especially of capital markets.[41] Second,

---

(1984), Otsuka and Hayami (1988), Otsuka et al. (1992), Hayami and Otsuka (1993), and the earlier literature cited in these surveys.

[38] See World Bank (1993c), p. 169.

[39] On this see White (1988), Amsden (1989), Datta-Chaudhuri (1990), Wade (1990), Kim and Leipziger (1997), Hayami (1997), Mehrotra and Jolly (1997).

[40] See World Bank (1993c) and the large literature, cited there, on which it has drawn. See also the critical reviews of Amsden (1994) and Rodrik (1994), and other contributions to the special section of *World Development*, 22(4), edited by Alice Amsden.

[41] On this and other lessons of the recent economic crisis in east Asia, see e.g. Stiglitz (1998), Wade (1999), and various contributions in Griffith-Jones and Kimmis (1999).

it also points to areas of government activity that remain underdeveloped in east Asian countries, especially that of social security. The absence of strong social security systems in these countries has both exacerbated the crisis (by suppressing the elements of counter-cyclical spending inherent in such systems), and forced vulnerable sections of the society to bear a large part of the burden of recession.

This crisis does not detract from the long-term achievements of these countries. Indeed, even at the height of the crisis, living standards in east Asia remained much above those found in, say, south Asia. The short-lived nature of the worst of the crisis also confirms the resilience and strong base of these economies. Nevertheless, the crisis of the late 1990s was a sobering reminder of extant weaknesses in the east Asian 'model'.[42] It also injected a note of realism in earlier, uncritical readings of the so-called 'East Asian miracle'. Miracles in the field of development are few, but there are many lessons to learn from the experience of east Asia, both on what to do and on what may be best avoided.

3.4. HUMAN CAPITAL AND MORE BASIC VALUES

While we have occasionally used the language of 'human capital' in this book, as a concession to general practice, that term is somewhat misleading in general, and particularly so in the context of one of the issues on which we want to put some emphasis. This concerns the intrinsic importance of the quality of human life—not seeing it *just* as an instrument for promoting economic growth and success. There is a real asymmetry between what is called 'human capital' (such as education, skill, good health, etc.) and physical capital, in that the items covered by the former have importance of their own (aside from being instrumentally important in production) in a way that does not apply to a piece of machinery. To put it another way, if a machinery did nothing to raise production, it would be quite eccentric to value its existence nevertheless, whereas being educated or being in good health could be valued *even if* it were to do nothing to increase the production of commodities. The constituents of human capital, which are parts of human lives, are valuable for their own sake—above and beyond their instrumental importance as factors of production. Indeed, being a 'component of human capital' cannot be the most fulfilling achievement to which a human being can aspire.

While the distinction between the intrinsic and instrumental importance

---

[42] On related limitations of the east Asian experiences, see Bello and Rosenfeld (1991) and Bello (1998).

of human capabilities is of some significance for clarity about means and ends, we should not make heavy weather of this dichotomy. It is important to bear in mind: (1) that health, education, and other features of a good quality of life are important on their own (and not just as 'human capital', geared to commodity production), (2) they can also be, in many circumstances, extremely good for promoting commodity production, and (3) they can also have other important personal and social roles (as discussed in chapter 2). There is no particular difficulty in using the language of 'human capital' if it is also recognized that there are other—more direct— rewards of human health, knowledge, and skill.

While human capabilities have both intrinsic and instrumental value, growth of GNP per head must be seen, primarily and directly, as just having instrumental importance. As discussed earlier, success in economic growth must ultimately be judged by what it does to our lives—the quality of life we can enjoy and the liberties we can exercise. In general, economic success cannot be dissociated from the 'end' of promoting human capabilities and of enhancing well-being and freedom. The tradition of judging success by the growth of GNP per head, or by some distribution-corrected value of GNP per head, is quite well established in economics. There is no great harm in this so long as the purely instrumental role of real incomes and commodities is borne in mind—not confusing instrumental effectiveness with intrinsic importance. In this connection, it has been noted that variations in real income per head have considerable explanatory power in accounting for differences in life expectancy, child mortality, literacy, and related indicators of well-being. For example, Anand and Ravallion (1993) find, in regressing proportionate shortfalls of life expectancy from the postulated maximum of 80 years against the logarithm of per capita GNP, that nearly half the variations in life expectancy can be attributed to differences in GNP per head.[43]

There can be little doubt about the value of higher real income in opening up possibilities of living worthwhile lives that are not available at lower levels of income. On the other hand, it is also interesting to note that the main impact of higher GNP per head on life expectancy seems to work via factors in which public policies play a significant part. Anand and Ravallion (1993) also report that when they relate life expectancy to public health spending per person, the proportion of people below the poverty line (defined in terms of per-capita expenditure), and GNP per head, the significantly positive relationship between GNP and life expectancy entirely

[43] On related matters, see also Anand (1993), Anand and Kanbur (1993), Pritchett and Summers (1996).

vanishes.[44] This need not entail that GNP does not contribute to the raising of longevity. Rather, it would appear that in so far as GNP does contribute to expanding life expectancy, it does this largely through making it possible to reduce the incidence of poverty and to have higher public spending (particularly on health care). The Anand-Ravallion findings are not a denial of the effectiveness of 'growth-mediated' progress, but an argument for seeing the role of growth-mediation through its connection with public services and poverty removal as routes to the expansion of living standards in general.

This is one illustration of the important interrelations between economic growth, sensible governmental action, and the enhancement of social and economic opportunities. These interrelations are particularly crucial in the task of transforming the Indian economy.

3.5. India's Internal Diversities

As was mentioned in chapter 1, India is characterized by enormous variations in regional experiences and achievements. These regional variations are a rich source of insights on the interconnections between economic development, public action and social progress.

Table 3.3 presents a sample of development indicators for India's major states.[45] It should be noted that the state-level indicators presented in this table remain highly aggregative. The internal diversities within, say, Uttar Pradesh (which has a population of 175 million) are of much interest in themselves, and cannot be fully captured in these broad interstate comparisons.[46] At finer levels of disaggregation, the contrasts are even sharper, with, for instance, district-level female literacy rates in 1991 varying from 8 per cent to 94 per cent. Further, inter-regional contrasts are only one aspect of the internal diversities that characterize India's

---

[44] Anand and Ravallion's (1993) analysis is based on all the developing countries for which they could find reasonably reliable data on these variables—22 countries in all. Obviously, all such studies need more corroboration and scrutiny, but these results seem to be broadly in line with economic arguments that have been presented elsewhere (see Drèze and Sen, 1989). For further evidence, see also Bidani and Ravallion (1997).

[45] In this book, the term 'major states' refers to the 17 Indian states with a population of at least 5 million in 1991. More detailed development indicators for different states can be found in the Statistical Appendix; see also Dutta et al. (1997), Shariff (1999), Debroy et al. (2000).

[46] Some of these internal diversities within Uttar Pradesh are discussed in the chapter on this state's experience, authored by Drèze and Gazdar (1996), in the companion volume.

Table 3.3 Selected Indicators for Major Indian States

State	Population, 2001 (millions)	Life expectancy at birth, 1993–7 (years) Female	Male	Death rate age 0–4, 1996–8	Total fertility rate 1996–8	Female-male ratio, 2001	Literacy rate (age 7+), 2001 Female	Male	Proportion of children aged 6–14 attending school, 1998–9 (%) Female	Male	Head-count index of poverty 1993–4 (%) Rural	Urban
Kerala	32	75.9	70.4	3.5	1.8	1,058	88	94	97	97	19.5	13.9
Himachal Pradesh	6	65.2	64.6	16.6	2.4	970	68	86	97	99	17.1	3.6
Maharashtra	97	66.6	64.1	12.7	2.7	922	68	86	87	90	42.9	18.2
Tamil Nadu	62	65.1	63.2	13.0	2.0	986	65	82	89	91	38.5	20.9
Punjab	24	68.8	66.7	15.6	2.7	874	64	76	90	92	6.2	7.8
West Bengal	80	63.6	62.2	16.6	2.5	934	60	78	77	80	25.1	15.5
Gujarat	51	62.9	60.9	20.3	3.0	921	59	81	73	84	32.5	14.7
Karnataka	53	64.9	61.6	16.6	2.5	964	57	76	78	82	37.9	21.4
Haryana	21	64.6	63.7	22.7	3.4	861	56	79	86	91	17.0	10.6
Assam	27	57.1	56.6	26.1	3.2	932	56	72	75	80	35.4	13.0
Madhya Pradesh	81	55.2	55.6	32.8	4.0	937	51	77	71	81	36.6	18.5
Orissa	37	57.0	57.1	29.2	3.0	972	51	76	75	83	43.5	15.2
Andhra Pradesh	76	63.5	61.2	17.6	2.5	978	51	71	71	81	29.2	17.8
Rajasthan	56	60.1	59.1	29.5	4.2	922	44	76	63	86	23.0	18.3
Uttar Pradesh	175	56.9	58.1	30.7	4.8	902	44	71	69	83	28.7	21.7
Jammu and K ashmir	10	n/a	n/a	n/a	n/a	900	42	66	78	90	10.1	3.1
Bihar	110	58.4	60.4	25.6	4.4	926	35	62	54	71	48.6	26.7
INDIA	1,027	61.8	60.4	23.2	3.3	933	54	76	74	83	32.9	18.1

Sources: See Statistical Appendix, which also presents more detailed information on different aspects of living conditions in Indian states. This table includes all states with a population of at least 5 million in 1991. The states have been ranked in descending order of female literacy.

literacy achievements. A detailed analysis of the literacy situation would also have to take note of other types of disparities, e.g. related to gender and caste. In 1991, for instance, 94 per cent of males in Kerala were literate, while literacy rates were still well below 10 per cent (even as low as 2 or 3 per cent in some districts) among scheduled-caste women in Bihar or Rajasthan.[47]

Even broad state-level contrasts, however, have much interest in so far as the state is a crucial political, administrative and cultural unit. As Table 3.3 indicates, there are striking contrasts between different states in terms of various indicators of well-being. Life expectancy at birth varies from 55 to 73 years between different states; female school attendance ranges from just about 50 per cent in Bihar to nearly universal in Kerala and Himachal Pradesh; the child death rate is nearly ten times as high in Madhya Pradesh as in Kerala; the proportion of the rural population below the poverty line is close to 50 per cent in Bihar, but only 6 per cent in Punjab; the number of women per 1,000 men varies from 861 in Haryana (a level lower than that of any country in the world) to 1,058 in Kerala (a level typical of advanced industrial economies);[48] and so on. There is almost as much diversity within India, in terms of these indicators, as in the rest of the developing world.

While Kerala is an exceptional case of outstanding achievement in the social field, which broadens the range of regional contrasts within India, it would be a mistake to think that the rest of the country—after taking out Kerala—is mainly homogeneous. The variations within India are enormous whether or not Kerala is included in these comparisons. For example, variations in school attendance are the same with or without Kerala, since school participation rates are now just as high in Himachal Pradesh. Similarly, while Kerala's fertility rate of 1.8 contrasts powerfully with the rate of 4.8 for Uttar Pradesh, the contrast between Uttar Pradesh and Tamil Nadu is also sharp enough, since the latter's fertility rate of 2.0 (just below the 'replacement level') is only marginally higher than Kerala's, and much less than half that of Uttar Pradesh. To look at these numbers in another way, Tamil Nadu's fertility rate of 2.0 is similar to that of the United States (2.1) or high-income European countries (1.7);

---

[47] Government of India (2000d), Tables 25 and 26. See also chapter 5.

[48] A few countries of west Asia (e.g. Saudi Arabia and the United Arab Emirates) have even lower female-male ratios than Haryana (*World Development Indicators 2001*, Table 1.3). As mentioned earlier, however, this is mainly due to male immigration; the same explanation would not apply to Haryana or Uttar Pradesh (see e.g. Agnihotri, 2000).

among low-income countries, only four (Armenia, Georgia, Moldova, Ukraine) have a lower fertility rate. The fertility rate of 4.8 in Uttar Pradesh, for its part, is not much below the average for sub-Saharan Africa (5.3), and is higher than that of all but five countries in the world outside that region.[49] When we include Kerala in the inter-state comparisons, the contrasts are made sharper, but the divergences are not lost even when Kerala is excluded. Even though we shall often concentrate specifically on Kerala, since there is so much to learn from this striking example of internal diversity within India, we must nevertheless resist the temptation to see it all as 'Kerala versus the rest'.

In interpreting the picture of internal diversities within India, it is also important to remember that human deprivation has different aspects, involving failures of different kinds of capabilities (see chapter 2). Further, different indicators of deprivation need not be closely correlated with each other, as Table 3.3 brings out clearly enough with respect to the different regions within India. Thus, the relative intensity of deprivation in different parts of the country depends on which aspect of deprivation we are particularly concerned with. The incidence of rural poverty as measured by the conventional head-count ratio, for instance, is highest in the eastern states of Bihar and Orissa.[50] But child death rates follow quite a different regional pattern, with the central and northern states of Uttar Pradesh, Madhya Pradesh, and Rajasthan doing worse than all other states (including Bihar and Orissa) in this respect. And the female-male ratio figures suggest that gender discrimination is particularly pronounced in the north-western region, including the relatively prosperous states of Punjab and Haryana—a finding on which there is a good deal of independent evidence.[51] There is, thus, no single 'problem region' within India, and public policy has to be alive to the different kinds of challenges that arise in different parts of the country. In so far as any broad pattern can be identified, it is mainly one of deprivation being endemic in most of north India (except in Punjab and Haryana, where there is a specific problem of gender inequality despite other indicators being relatively favourable), with the south Indian states doing significantly better in most

---

[49] The international figures are taken from *World Development Indicators 2001*, Table 2.17. 'Low income countries' are defined here, as in that report, as countries with 'gross national income per capita' of $ 755 or less in 1999.

[50] The head-count index of rural poverty also used to be extremely high in West Bengal, the third major state of the eastern region. As discussed further on, however, the incidence of rural poverty appears to have declined quite rapidly in that state in recent years.

[51] See chapter 7, and the references cited there.

respects, especially in matters of mortality, fertility, literacy, and gender equity.

A related issue concerns the connection between well-being indicators and standard 'poverty' indices such as the head-count ratio (i.e. the proportion of the population below some pre-defined poverty line, drawn in the space of per-capita expenditure). There is, of course, a general association between expenditure-based poverty indicators and many aspects of well-being, including health and education levels. For instance, it is mainly on the basis of higher incomes and lower poverty that Punjab and Haryana (with head-count ratios as low as 6 and 17 per cent, respectively) have achieved much better levels of health and education than most other states in the northern region. Similarly, Bihar's low life expectancy (below 60 years) and high levels of illiteracy (the highest in India) clearly have something to do with the low level of income in that state, where half of the population lives below the poverty line.

Having said this, differences in well-being between different states are not a matter of income poverty alone. This point is illustrated in Figure 3.1, which plots the child mortality rate against the head-count ratio in different states.[52] A broad association can be observed between the two variables: child mortality tends to be higher in states with higher levels of poverty. However, the association is far from tight, to say the least. Some aspects of this weakness of association are indeed rather striking. For instance, Tamil Nadu and Madhya Pradesh respectively have the lowest and highest child mortality rates among all major states (Kerala excepted), despite being quite similar in terms of the incidence of poverty. The contrast between Tamil Nadu and Uttar Pradesh is no less striking: child mortality is more than twice as high in Uttar Pradesh as in Tamil Nadu, despite poverty (in terms of the head-count index) being lower in Uttar Pradesh. This does not imply that income or expenditure have no effect on child mortality and related indicators of well-being. As noted earlier, there is plenty of evidence that health achievements in different countries improve with higher incomes, and this pattern applies within India as well. The point is that many *other* factors are involved, some of which may be no less important than income in improving longevity and health.

One such factor is basic education. In fact, female literacy is a much

---

[52] The poverty estimates presented in Table 3.3 and Figure 3.1 are due to Deaton and Tarozzi (2000), and involve careful adjustments for differences in prices between states. Other estimates are also available (e.g. Datt, 1998), and there are significant differences between the various sources for specific states. The broad patterns emerging from Figure 3.1, however, are fairly robust.

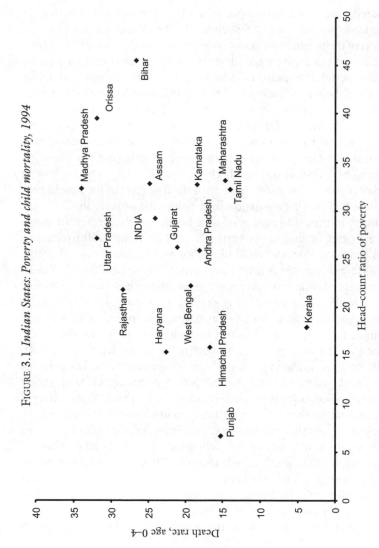

FIGURE 3.1 *Indian States: Poverty and child mortality, 1994*

Sources: Deaton and Tarozzi (2000), based on National Sample Survey data, for poverty estimates (see also Statistical Appendix, Table A.3); Sample Registration System data presented in Government of India (1997f) and Government of India (1998d), for death rates. The precise reference years are 1993–4 for poverty and 1994–5 for death rates.

better 'predictor' of child mortality in different states than per-capita expenditure.[53] The provision of health services is another influential factor. In the present case, differences in child mortality between (say) Tamil Nadu on the one hand, and Uttar Pradesh and Madhya Pradesh on the other, reflect not only higher levels of education in Tamil Nadu (especially in the younger age groups), but also better access to maternal and child health services. Tamil Nadu, for instance, has India's highest levels of child immunization: in 1998–9, about 90 per cent of children aged 12–23 months in Tamil Nadu were 'fully immunized', compared with barely 20 per cent in Madhya Pradesh and Uttar Pradesh. In the same year, 99 per cent of recent births in Tamil Nadu had been preceded by an antenatal check-up, compared with only 61 per cent in Uttar Pradesh and an abysmal 35 per cent in Madhya Pradesh.[54]

Behind these specific examples is a general lesson about the important roles played by particular types of public action in the process of development, especially those geared to the widespread and equitable provision of basic services. The contrast between Kerala and Uttar Pradesh, pursued in the next section, provides another useful illustration of this point.

3.6. SELECTED REGIONAL PERSPECTIVES

As discussed earlier, there is much to learn from the diversity of development experiences among different Indian states. In a companion volume of essays (Drèze and Sen, 1996) published along with the first edition of this book, some of the lessons to be drawn are pursued, based on case studies of Kerala (by V.K. Ramachandran), Uttar Pradesh (by Jean Drèze and Haris Gazdar) and West Bengal (by Sunil Sengupta and Haris Gazdar). In subsequent chapters of this book, we shall make frequent use of the insights arising from these case studies.[55]

---

[53] The correlation coefficient between child mortality and female literacy is 0.8 (in absolute value), compared with only 0.4 for the correlation coefficient between child mortality and per-capita expenditure. After controlling for female literacy, per-capita expenditure bears no significant association with child mortality at the state level. Even in more detailed analyses of child mortality based on district-level data, expenditure-based indicators have little predictive power after controlling for female literacy (Murthi, Guio and Drèze, 1995). In international data, too, female literacy is a much stronger predictor of child survival than per-capita income, as observed by Caldwell (1986), and confirmed by many subsequent studies.

[54] See Statistical Appendix, Table A.3, Parts 6 and 7, based on the National Family Health Survey 1998–9. For further discussion of the demographic transition in Tamil Nadu, see also chapter 6.

[55] This section itself draws extensively on these case studies.

The contrast between Kerala and Uttar Pradesh is of particular interest, and we shall have the occasion to refer to it in various contexts. These two states are poles apart in terms of many indicators of well-being, as Table 3.3 clearly indicates; to cite just one indicator, women born in Kerala can expect to live almost 20 years longer than their counterparts in Uttar Pradesh. As it happens, per-capita expenditure levels are also higher in Kerala, and the incidence of poverty is lower. However, this is a relatively recent pattern, reflecting Kerala's outstanding rates of poverty reduction in recent decades. Kerala's lead in terms of social development, on the other hand, was already considerable in the 1950s and 1960s, when the incidence of poverty in Kerala (in terms of conventional measures) was among the highest in India.[56] As V.K. Ramachandran's case study investigates in some detail, Kerala's success in improving living conditions at an early stage of economic development can be traced to the role of public action in promoting a range of social opportunities relating inter alia to elementary education, the role of women in society, and the widespread and equitable provision of health care and other public services.[57] Interestingly, Uttar Pradesh's *failures* can be plausibly attributed to the public *neglect* of the very same opportunities.[58] The fact that both case studies identify much the same factors of success (in Kerala) and failure (in Uttar Pradesh) is of considerable significance in understanding the diversity of social achievements in different parts of India. Among the identified determinants of social achievements, the following deserve strong emphasis.[59]

First, the role of basic education (and particularly of female literacy) in promoting basic capabilities emerges forcefully in both case studies. One of the distinguishing features of Kerala's development experience

---

[56] See section 3.8 below.

[57] On these and related aspects of Kerala's development experience, see also Krishnan (1976, 1991, 1997), Mencher (1980), Nair (1981), Nag (1983, 1989), Raj and Tharakan (1983), Panikar and Soman (1984, 1985), Robin Jeffrey (1987, 1992), Franke and Chasin (1989), Mari Bhat and Rajan (1990, 1992), Kannan et al. (1991), Oommen (1999), Mahendra Dev (1994), Prakash (1999), Zachariah et al. (1994), Kannan (1995), Kabir and Krishnan (1996), Zachariah and Rajan (1997), Heller (1999), Mathew (1999), Parayil (2000), Vijaychandran (2001), among others, and also the extensive collection of papers summarized in AKG Centre for Research and Studies (1994).

[58] See the case study of Uttar Pradesh by Drèze and Gazdar (1996) in the companion volume.

[59] There are, of course, close interconnections between these different social influences. For instance, the expansion of literacy in Kerala has been both an *outcome* of extensive state involvement in the provision of basic services and a *determinant* of further expansion of social provisions. Public provisioning and widespread literacy have developed together.

is the early promotion of basic education, and this feature has led to important social achievements later on, based on the diverse social and personal roles of education (discussed in chapter 2). In Uttar Pradesh, by contrast, the adult female literacy rate is still as low as 35 per cent or so, and as recently as 1992–3, about half of all adolescent girls in rural areas had *never* been to school. This educational backwardness has wide-ranging penalties, including high mortality and fertility rates.[60]

Second, another element in social success that clearly emerges from both experiences is the agency of women. Uttar Pradesh has a long history of oppressive gender relations, and even now inequalities between men and women in that part of the country are extraordinarily sharp (as we noted earlier, for instance, very few countries in the world have as low a female-male ratio as Uttar Pradesh). As with illiteracy, the suppression of women's active and liberated participation in the economy and the society has been a cause of much social backwardness in Uttar Pradesh. In Kerala, by contrast, the position of women in society has been relatively favourable for a long time, and the informed agency of women has played a crucial role in a wide range of social achievements.[61] The expansion of literacy itself owes a great deal to that agency, reflected even in the fact that more than 70 per cent of primary-school teachers in Kerala are women (compared with 25 per cent in Uttar Pradesh).[62]

Third, the contrast between Uttar Pradesh and Kerala brings out the essential role of well-functioning public services in improving living conditions. As we noted earlier in this chapter, the widely divergent levels of well-being in the two states cannot be explained primarily in terms of higher incomes and lower levels of poverty in Kerala (since Kerala's outstanding social achievements pre-date the lead it subsequently achieved vis-à-vis Uttar Pradesh in terms of per-capita income and related indicators). If entitlements to basic commodities and services differ so sharply between the two states, it is also because of a marked difference in the scope, quality and equity of a wide range of public services such as schooling facilities, basic health care, child immunization, social security arrangements, and public food distribution. In Uttar Pradesh, these public services are comprehensively neglected, sometimes even non-existent, especially in rural areas. Table 3.4 presents some illustrative indications of this particular contrast between Uttar Pradesh and Kerala.

Fourth, both case studies highlight the social influence of public action

---

[60] On the role of literacy (especially female literacy) in reducing mortality and fertility rates, see chapter 7.

[61] On this, see particularly Robin Jeffrey (1992).

[62] Calculated from Government of India (2000d), p. 47.

TABLE 3.4 *India, Uttar Pradesh and Kerala:*
Contrasts in Access to Public Services, 1998–9

	India	Uttar Pradesh	Kerala
Proportion (%) of children aged 10–12 who have never been enrolled in a school, 1992–3			
female	33	44	1
male	16	19	1
Proportion (%) of primary schools with:[a]			
at most two teachers	58	63	1
no female teacher	61	67	1
pupil/teacher ratio above 60	26	61	1
pupil/classroom ratio above 90	17	26	1
Proportion (%) of children aged 12–23 months who have not received any vaccination	14	30	2
Proportion (%) of recent births			
preceded by an antenatal check-up	65	35	99
attended by health professional	42	22	94
Proportion (%) of villages with medical facilities, 1981[b]	14	10	96
Proportion (%) of households receiving subsidized foodgrains from the public distribution system, 1993–4	27	4	78

Notes: [a] These figures apply to districts covered by the 'District Information System for Education' (14 districts in Uttar Pradesh and 6 districts in Kerala), with 1999–2000 as the reference year.
[b] Calculated from *District Census Handbooks*, 1981.
Sources: International Institute for Population Sciences (2000a), Tables 6.11, 8.7, 8.13; Tarozzi (2000); Filmer (1999); Aggarwal (2000), pp. 40, 72, 79, 83. Unless stated otherwise, the reference year is 1998–9. For further details, see Statistical Appendix.

in a wide sense, going beyond the initiative of the state and involving the public at large. The early promotion of literacy in Kerala has enabled the public to play an active role in state politics and social affairs in a way that has not happened in Uttar Pradesh. Public action in Kerala has been particularly important in orienting the priorities of the state in the direction of a strong commitment to the promotion of social opportunities. The expansion of public services in general—going well beyond school education—has often taken place in response to the organized demands of a well-educated public. The vigilance of the public has also been essential to ensure the adequate *functioning* of public services such as health centres and primary schools in Kerala.[63]

[63] On this issue, see Mencher (1980), Nag (1989), Majumdar (1993); also chapters 5, 6 and 10 of this book.

TABLE 3.5 *Political Participation in Kerala and Uttar Pradesh*

	Kerala	Uttar Pradesh
Proportion (%) of respondents who actively participate in at least one association	50	4
Proportion (%) of respondents who took part in the following political activities during the preceding five years:		
voting in state elections	87	87
participating in campaign	39	12
contacting elected representative	55	3
joining protest march	45	10
using force or violent methods	8	23
Proportion (%) of respondents who agree that:		
'the state government is interested in the needs of people like yourself'	52	23
'democracy is always best'	76	41
Proportion (%) of respondents who feel that they:		
'understand issues'	79	28
'have enough information about politics'	64	22
'are well-prepared to participate'	42	26

Source: Blomkvist (2000a, 2000b), based on a household survey undertaken in 1998 in seven localities of each state (100 randomly-selected households in each locality). In both states, about one third of the respondents were women. We are grateful to Hans Blomkvist for helpful clarifications.

Finally, the contrast between Uttar Pradesh and Kerala also points to the special importance of a particular type of public action: the political organization of deprived sections of the society. In Kerala, informed political activism, building partly on the achievement of mass literacy, has played a crucial role in the reduction of social inequalities based on caste, gender, and (to some extent) class.[64] Political organization has also been important in enabling disadvantaged groups to take an active part in the general processes of economic development, public action, and social change. In Uttar Pradesh, traditional inequalities and social divisions remain extremely powerful, and their persistence hinders many social endeavours.[65] It is still possible, for instance, to find villages in Uttar Pradesh where a powerful landlord has deliberately obstructed the creation of a village school by the government.[66] More generally, the concentration of political power in the

[64] The reduction of social and economic inequalities in Kerala is extensively discussed by V.K. Ramachandran (1996); see also Heller (1999). In tackling class inequalities, land reforms and social security arrangements have played an important part.

[65] On inequality as an obstacle to social progress, see chapters 1 and 10.

[66] For an example, see Drèze and Gazdar (1996). This phenomenon of landlord

hands of privileged sections of the society has contributed, perhaps more than anything else, to a severe neglect of the basic needs of disadvantaged groups in state and local politics. The contrasting nature of political participation in Kerala and Uttar Pradesh is illustrated in Table 3.5.

Underlying many of these contrasts is the general importance of politics in the development process. Kerala does, of course, possess some special cultural and historical characteristics which may have helped its social transformation. But the political process itself has played an extremely important role in Kerala's development experience, supplementing or supplanting these inherited characteristics.[67] This issue has a strong bearing on the 'replicability' of Kerala's sucess. Given the role of political movements, there is no reason why Uttar Pradesh—and other states of India where basic deprivations remain endemic—should not be able to emulate many of Kerala's achievements, based on determined and reasoned political activism.

3.7. POLITICAL ACTION AND RURAL DEVELOPMENT IN WEST BENGAL

A good illustration of the feasibility of political change in India comes from West Bengal.[68] This is a state where political organization of disadvantaged classes has significantly altered the balance of political power, especially in rural areas. Changes were rapid after the Left Front coalition came to office at the state level in 1977. The main electoral base of the Left Front, which has retained office since then through successive elections, consists of landless labourers, sharecroppers, slum dwellers, and other disadvantaged groups. This change in the balance of power has made it possible to implement a number of far-reaching social programmes that are often considered 'politically infeasible' in many other states. Two notable examples are land reform and the revitalization of democratic institutions at the village level.[69]

---

resistance to the spread of elementary education has also been noted elsewhere in north India; see e.g. Wadley and Derr (1989), p. 111, and Banerjee (1994).

[67] One important indication of this comes from the comparative experiences of Kerala's three different regions—Travancore, Cochin, and Malabar. We will return to this in section 3.8.

[68] For further discussion, see the case study of West Bengal by Sunil Sengupta and Haris Gazdar (1996) in the companion volume.

[69] See Sengupta and Gazdar (1996), Gazdar and Sengupta (1999), and the literature cited there. A number of other public programmes also appear to have been more successful in West Bengal than in most other states, due to the political commitments

The Left Front's commitments and initiatives appear to have achieved some important results. In particular, there has been a comparatively rapid decline of rural poverty in West Bengal since 1977.[70] Indeed, in the 1970s, West Bengal was one of the highest-poverty states in India, together with Bihar and Orissa (also in the eastern region). Today, Bihar and Orissa continue to have exceptionally high levels of rural poverty, but West Bengal's ranking has radically improved, and recent estimates even suggest that the incidence of rural poverty in West Bengal is now a little *lower* than in India as a whole.[71] Among all major Indian states, West Bengal has also achieved the fastest growth in calorie consumption between 1972–3 and 1993–4.[72] There has been some debate about the extent to which these improvements reflect redistributive measures on the one hand, and the rapid growth of the agricultural sector on the other.[73] But it is worth noting that even the latter may not be unrelated to the initiatives of the Left Front government, including its efforts to improve the rural infrastructure as well as the institutional basis of local governance.[74]

There is also some evidence of far-reaching social change in rural West Bengal during the last twenty-five years. Many observers have argued, for instance, that the political empowerment of disadvantaged groups has not only helped them in economic terms but also enhanced their dignity and self-confidence.[75] As Arild Ruud (1999) points out, the fact that political action has 'raised the social standing of formerly low-ranking groups' is an important achievement.[76] Indeed, liberation from indignity,

---

of the government and the improved scope for collective action at the local level. Examples include public programmes relating to poverty alleviation (see Drèze, 1990d, Lieten, 1996a, and Swaminathan, 1990), rural infrastructure (Saha and Swaminathan, 1994, Sengupta and Gazdar, 1996), and participatory management of environmental resources (Shah, 1987, S.B. Roy, 1992, Gadgil and Guha, 1995).

[70] On this issue, see also Gazdar and Sengupta (1999).

[71] See Table 3.3 above. According to the Planning Commission's provisional poverty estimates for 1999–2000 (Government of India, 2001d), the incidence of rural poverty in West Bengal is still a little higher than the all-India average, but nevertheless much lower than it used to be (and also radically lower than in Bihar and Orissa).

[72] See Hanchate and Dyson (2000); also Ramachandran and Swaminathan (1999).

[73] During the 1980s and 1990s, West Bengal's agricultural sector grew at about 6 per cent per year, on average, outperforming all other major states in this respect (calculated from unpublished data supplied by the Central Statistical Organization).

[74] On these matters, see J. Harriss (1993), Saha and Swaminathan (1994), Rawal and Swaminathan (1998), Gazdar and Sengupta (1999), Rogaly, Harriss-White, and Bose (1999), Banerjee, Gertler and Ghatak (forthcoming).

[75] See Beck (1994), Ruud (1994), Lieten (1996a), among others.

[76] Ruud (1999), p. 275.

oppression and exploitation is among the basic freedoms and social opportunities with which this book is concerned. Note should also be made of the lower level of violence in rural West Bengal, particularly so in the field of communal tensions, in which West Bengal's record of peace and solidarity is quite exceptional.

Having said this, the government of West Bengal has been notably less active in promoting some other types of social opportunities. The opportunities of industrial employment and economic participation are still severely restrained by the inability of the West Bengal government to change the industrial trends in the state. Part of the problem lies undoubtedly in the memory of persistent industrial strifes in the days of confrontational politics, but the necessary shift in the climate of industrial enterprise and initiative has not yet occurred. There is an important need here to take more positive initiatives in expanding industrial employment and economic opportunities in West Bengal.

Even in rural areas, West Bengal's record in promoting social opportunities is quite mixed. While issues such as land reform and minimum wages have received high priority in the programme of the Left Front coalition (partly because of the importance of these issues in the political battles that led this coalition to office), public policies concerned with health, education, and related matters have been comparatively neglected. Correspondingly, West Bengal's achievements in these fields remain relatively modest.

This applies inter alia to school education. Indeed, West Bengal's comparative position vis-à-vis other states, in terms of basic educational achievements, has deteriorated over a long period, and this trend has continued after 1977. In 1998–9, according to the second National Family Health Survey, only Bihar and Andhra Pradesh had lower levels of male school attendance than West Bengal among all major states.[77] Further, the Left Front government has a long way to go in addressing this problem with adequate resolve (despite some important initiatives in recent years). In fact, the nineties have been a period of spiralling decline in per-capita expenditure on elementary education in West Bengal (see Table 5.3, p. 169). Recent field studies also suggest that the state of the schooling system in West Bengal is not fundamentally different from what it is

---

[77] See Statistical Appendix, Table A.3, Part 4. For females, West Bengal's ranking is somewhat better, reflecting the fact that the male-female gender gap is much smaller in West Bengal than in many north Indian states. Even for females, however, school attendance rates in West Bengal are not significantly higher than the national average (77 and 74 per cent, respectively, for the 6–14 age group).

elsewhere in north India (in terms of, say, infrastructural facilities, pupil-teacher ratios and work culture).[78] These studies also highlight some specific problems of the education system in West Bengal, notably the adverse effects of political interference with teacher appointments and school management.

An important opportunity has been missed here, since the skills of popular mobilization of the West Bengal government (amply demonstrated in other fields) could have been used with good effect to achieve a real transformation in the fields of education and health. These are serious failures of the West Bengal experience, but they do not detract from the importance of the positive achievements, nor from the general value of that experience as an example of the possibility of radical political change in India today.

3.8. KERALA: SCRUTINY AND SIGNIFICANCE

The significance of Kerala's experience is often underestimated in international discussions. One reason for this is that Kerala, not being an independent country, is often missed in policy analyses based on international comparisons. Yet Kerala, with its 32 million people, has a larger population than most countries in the world (even Canada), including many from which comparative lessons are often drawn for India, such as Sri Lanka (19 million) or Malaysia (23 million), not to speak of tiny Costa Rica or Singapore (less than 4 million each). Even South Korea, which receives a great deal of attention in the development literature, had about the same population size in the early sixties (when its rapid transformation began) as Kerala has today. To achieve as much as Kerala has done for a population of its size is no mean record in world history.

Leaving aside the issue of population size, there have been other sources of resistance to attaching much significance to Kerala's experience. Some rejoinders take the form of a wholesale dismissal of the basic approach underlying that experience. This often consists of highlighting some particular aspect of development in terms of which Kerala does not fare particularly well, and presenting this as evidence of the 'failure' of Kerala's approach. One common version of this line of reasoning turns on the fact that Kerala has a high suicide rate. This feature of Malayali

---

[78] This is, for instance, the picture that is beginning to emerge from a study of schooling facilities in 18 villages of West Bengal, sponsored by the Pratichi Trust (Rana et al., 2001). See also Acharya (1996).

society is indeed a pertinent concern. However, the relevance of the suicide rate as a basic development indicator is far from clear. Indeed, many countries with high suicide rates (e.g. the Scandinavian countries) are doing extremely well in terms of overall social opportunities, and it would be quite odd to take their high suicide rates as a severe indictment of their development record. Suicide rates do correlate with specific social problems such as high rates of unemployment or divorce, and it is quite possible that social problems of this kind (especially educated unemployment) contribute to the high rate of suicide in Kerala.[79] But these problems, such as they are, do not detract from Kerala's achievements in other, more fundamental fields such as health and education, just as—say—Finland's high suicide rate does not detract from its success in guaranteeing extensive social opportunities to its citizens.[80]

Kerala's approach is sometimes also called a model, viz., the so-called 'Kerala model'. It is, however, quite misleading to view Kerala as a 'model', implying (1) that Kerala's experience is an all-round success, and (2) that this experience can somehow be copied elsewhere irrespective of historical and social conditions. Indeed, the rhetoric of 'Kerala model' is more convenient for 'debunking' purposes than for identifying what there is to learn from Kerala's experience. It does little to foster a balanced interpretation of Kerala's experience, which must integrate lessons from Kerala's successes with those of other states or countries, and also with development *failures* in Kerala and elsewhere.

An integrated perspective is also important in interpreting another limitation of Kerala's development experience, namely, its relatively low

[79] For an insightful discussion of the evidence, see Halliburton (1998). It is also possible that higher *reporting rates* account for Kerala's high number of recorded suicides, reflecting better recording practices in general as well as a lower tolerance for supressed distress. Quite likely, a significant proportion of suicides in states such as Bihar or Madhya Pradesh (where administration is poor and extreme distress is an accepted feature of everyday life) remain unrecorded.

[80] It may be tempting to view the suicide rate as an index of 'unhappiness', and, following on that, to treat it as a crucial indicator of well-being. This would be misleading for two distinct reasons. First, international data suggest that there is no significant correlation between suicide rates and self-reported happiness; if anything, the correlation may well be positive (David Blanchflower, Dartmouth College, personal communication based on work in progress). Indeed, some countries combine high suicide rates with high levels of self-reported happiness (Denmark and Finland are two examples). Second, it can be argued that focusing on self-reported 'happiness' is itself a misleading approach to the evaluation of human well-being; for further discussion, see Sen (1995a, 1999a).

rates of domestic economic growth.[81] This failure, which is real enough, has also been widely cited (like Kerala's high suicide rate) as proof of the failure of the so-called 'Kerala model'. It is important, however, not to view the low growth of the domestic economy in isolation from related economic trends. In particular, it has to be seen together with the fact that Kerala has achieved the fastest rate of poverty reduction among all major states during the last fifty years.[82] One major reason for this contrast is that while *domestic production* has grown rather slowly, *per-capita incomes* have risen quite fast, mainly due to substantial remittances from abroad (principally the Gulf states) as well as from other parts of India. This does not detract from the importance of addressing the causes of slow domestic growth in Kerala. However, it does mean that the stagnation of the domestic economy has had an important counterpart in the form of economic success outside the state's own boundaries, building on Kerala's early investment in education and related human skills. Kerala's overall success in reducing poverty is a far more significant feature of its recent development experience than the slow growth of its domestic economy, even though the latter does have important social penalties, especially in the form of high unemployment.

There is a different kind of objection that could be a more legitimate reason for questioning the significance of Kerala's experience, and doubting that it can be emulated. Kerala has been fortunate with its past. For one thing, the bulk of what is now Kerala used to consist of two 'native states'— Travancore and Cochin—formally outside British India. They were not subjected to the general lack of interest of Whitehall officialdom in Indian elementary education (as opposed to higher education). When Rani Gouri Parvathi Bai, the young queen of Travancore, made her pioneering statement in 1817 on the importance of basic education, there was no need to bring that policy initiative in line with what was happening in the rest of India, under the Raj.[83]

---

[81] There has been much discussion of this issue in the recent literature on Kerala's development; see particularly Tharamangalam (1998), and further comments on that study published in *Bulletin of Concerned Asian Scholars*, vol. 30.

[82] See Datt and Ravallion (1998). According to the authors' poverty estimates (see Datt, 1998, 1999b), Kerala had the highest head-count ratio among all major states in the late 1950s; today, it has the lowest head-count ratio outside the northwestern region (consisting of Punjab, Haryana, Himachal Pradesh, and Jammu and Kashmir). The last point is corroborated by Deaton and Tarozzi's poverty estimates for 1993–4, reported in Table 3.3.

[83] The independence from general British Indian policy applied not only to the

Kerala has also been fortunate in having strong social movements that concentrated on educational advancement—along with general emancipation—of the lower castes, and this has been a special feature of left-wing and radical political movements in Kerala. It has also profited from a tradition of openness to the world, which has included welcoming early Christians (at least from the fourth century), Jews (from shortly after the fall of Jerusalem), and Muslims (from the days of early Arab trading, with settlers coming as economic participants rather than as military conquerors). Into this rather open and receptive environment, the extensive educational efforts of Christian missionaries, particularly in the nineteenth century, fitted comfortably. Kerala has also benefited from the matrilineal tradition of property inheritance for an important part of the community (the Nairs), which has enhanced the social status of Nair women, even in the past. While the Nairs constitute about 20 per cent of the total population, and the practice has changed a good deal in recent years, nevertheless the social and political influence of a long tradition of this kind, which goes against the conventional Indian norms, must not be underestimated.

Having good luck in one's history is not, however, a policy parameter that one can command. Those who see a unique and unrepeatable pattern in Kerala's remarkable record of social progress can point to the very special nature of its past, and suggest that other states can learn rather little from it. This, however, would be quite the wrong conclusion to draw from Kerala's heterogeneous history. When the state of Kerala was created in independent India, it included not only the erstwhile native states of Travancore and Cochin, but also—on linguistic grounds—the region of Malabar from the old province of Madras in British India (later Tamil Nadu). The Malabar region, transferred from the Raj, was at that time very much behind Travancore and Cochin in terms of literacy, life expectancy, and other achievements that make Kerala so special. But by the eighties, Malabar had 'caught up' with the rest of Kerala to such an extent that it could no longer be seen in divergent terms.[84] The initiatives that the state governments of Kerala took, under different 'managements'

---

princely rulers of these states, but also to the British 'Residents' in Trivandrum. The Residents could consider independent initiatives, and indeed in the big move in Travancore in the direction of elementary education in the early nineteenth century, the Resident Mr. Munro played an extremely supportive—and possibly even catalytic—role. There is some evidence that he drafted Parvathi Bai's 1817 statement, whether or not the initiative was also his (see Ramachandran, 1996).

[84] On this see George (1994), Kabir and Krishnan (1996), Krishnan (1997), Ramachandran (1996), Salim and Nair (1997).

(led by the Communist Party as well as by the Congress), succeeded in bringing Malabar rather at par with the rest of Kerala over a short period of time. So there is a lesson here that is not imprisoned in the fixity of history. Other parts of India can indeed learn a lot from Kerala's experience on what can be done here and now by determined public action.

It is also worth noting that while Kerala was already quite advanced compared with British India at the time of independence, much of the great achievements of Kerala that are so admired now are the results of post-independence public policies. In fact, in the fifties Kerala's adult literacy rate was around 50 per cent compared with over 90 per cent now, its life expectancy at birth was 44 years vis-à-vis 74 now, and its birth rate was 32 as opposed to 18 now.[85] Kerala did have a good start, but the policies that have made its achievements so extraordinary today are, to a great extent, the products of post-independence political decisions and public action.

3.9. SOCIAL OPPORTUNITIES IN HIMACHAL PRADESH

An interesting feature of development experiences in India is that large parts of the Himalayan region (more precisely, the hill region of north and north-east India) are doing quite well in many important respects.[86] These include relatively low poverty rates, high levels of school attendance, and a rapid demographic transition. There is an interesting contrast here with the situation in China, and indeed in much of the rest of the world, where mountain areas typically have *high* levels of poverty and deprivation. The current situation in India also contrasts with that found fifty years ago, when the hill districts were widely considered as 'backward' areas.

Himachal Pradesh provides a remarkable illustration of this phenomenon of development in the Himalayan region. In the fifties and sixties, the region known today as Himachal Pradesh was widely considered as 'one of the most underdeveloped areas of the country' (Sharma, 1987, p. 45), and its people were commonly described as 'extremely poor and conservative in outlook' (M.G. Singh, 1985, p. 102). Even the Report of the States Reorganization Commission referred to the inhabitants of that region as 'extremely backward and exploited people', and considered Himachal Pradesh's apparent lack of potential for independent

---

[85] On Kerala's social achievements at the time of independence, and the general history that they represent, see Ramachandran (1996).

[86] One major qualification is that many parts of that region (including several states of the north-east as well as Kashmir) have been afflicted with high levels of violence, related inter alia to separatist movements. This has taken its toll, both in terms of human tragedies and by discouraging economic investment in the region.

development as a major argument against it becoming a separate state.[87] Fifty years or so down the line, living conditions in Himachal Pradesh seem to have been radically transformed for the better.

The transition is perhaps most striking in the field of basic education. In 1951, less than 20 per cent of children aged 10–14 in Himachal Pradesh were literate.[88] In this respect, Himachal Pradesh did not differ at that time from states such as Bihar, Madhya Pradesh or Uttar Pradesh. Today, according to the National Family Health Survey 1998–9, school participation rates among 6–14 years-old in Himachal Pradesh are as high as 99 per cent for boys and 97 per cent for girls (see Table 3.3). In this respect, Himachal Pradesh is at par with Kerala, and well ahead of all other states.

Hand in hand with this spectacular schooling transition, there has been impressive progress in many other fields. For instance, Himachal Pradesh is now going through a rapid 'demographic transition' from high to low mortality and fertility rates. In the early 1970s, birth and death rates in Himachal Pradesh were comparable to those of Orissa and Madhya Pradesh. Since then, Himachal Pradesh has achieved a remarkable decline in death rate of nearly 50 per cent and also in birth rate (almost 40 per cent). No other state has achieved a proportionate reduction of more than 35 per cent on *both* counts over this period.[89] Today, Himachal Pradesh has the highest contraceptive prevalence rate, the second-highest child immunization rate, and the third-lowest fertility rate among all major states, and it is also doing better than most other states in many other aspects of social development (see Table 3.6, and also the Statistical Appendix). The 'extremely backward and exploited people' of this region also now enjoy relatively high wages and low poverty rates.[90] Finally, those who judge progress by low suicide rates (one of the common lines of

---

[87] Government of India (1955). In a prophetic note of dissent, the chairperson of the Commission, Fazl Ali, argued that 'in small states, the administration will be more accessible to people and there will be a livelier sense of local needs' (quoted in Singh, 1985, p. 78).

[88] See Figure 5.2, p. 184. For further discussion of the 'schooling revolution in Himachal Pradesh', see also Probe Team (1999), chapter 9.

[89] Calculated from Government of India (1999a), Tables 1 and 2, and *Sample Registration Bulletin*, October 1999, Table 1. Taking birth and death rates separately, Himachal Pradesh's rank in the 'league' of major Indian states is third for each (in terms of proportionate reduction since the early 1970s). However, no other state has a better *combined* record of reduction in birth and death rates.

[90] By 1993–4, the head-count ratio of poverty in Himachal Pradesh was about the same as in Haryana (around 15 per cent), with only two states (Punjab, and Jammu and Kashmir) achieving lower rates of rural poverty. See Statistical Appendix, Table A.3, Part 1.

TABLE 3.6 *Himachal Pradesh:*
Selected Indicators of Social Development, 1998–9

	Himachal Pradesh	India	Himachal Pradesh's rank among 17 major states	States doing 'better' than Himachal Pradesh (if any)[a]
School attendance in 6–14 age group (%)				
female	97	74	1	None
male	99	83	1	None
Under-five mortality rate, 1994–8 (per 1,000 live births)	42	95	2	Kerala (19)
Total fertility rate, 1996–8	2.4	3.3	3	Kerala (1.8), Tamil Nadu (2.0)
Proportion (%) of young children who have received				
all vaccinations	83	42	2	Tamil Nadu (89)
at least one dose of vitamin A	71	30	1	None
Proportion (%) of households using adequately iodized salt	91	49	1	None
Murder rate, 1998 (murders per million)	21	40	2	Kerala (14)

Notes: [a] 'Better' means a higher indicator, except for the under-five mortality rate, fertility rate, and murder rate (where the reverse applies). In brackets, the relevant figures for the states outdoing Himachal Pradesh.

Sources: International Institute for Population Sciences (2000a), pp. 440–3; International Institute for Population Sciences (forthcoming); Government of India (1999a, 2000g, 2000h); Government of India (1999a), Tables 1 and 10; Government of India (2000g), p. 49; Government of India (2000b), p. 44. Unless stated otherwise, the reference year is 1998–9. For further details, see Statistical Appendix.

criticism of Kerala's experience, discussed earlier) may wish to note that Himachal Pradesh has one of the lowest suicide rates in India.[91]

Attempts to explain Himachal Pradesh's success often focus on a few relatively well-known features of the state, such as its fairly prosperous rural economy (best known for its flourishing apple orchards), high levels of per-capita government expenditure (made affordable by substantial transfers from the central government), and high proportion of persons employed in the public sector (including the army). These features are indeed pertinent in explaining why living conditions in Himachal Pradesh are so much better than in, say, Uttar Pradesh or Bihar. There is, however, much more than this to Himachal's story. One way of appreciating this

[91] See Statistical Appendix, Table A.3, Part 11.

TABLE 3.7 *Himachal Pradesh and Haryana*

	Himachal Pradesh	Haryana
INCOME AND EXPENDITURE		
Per-capita household expenditure, 1999–2000 (Rs/month)[a]	740	771
Head-count index of poverty, 1993–4[a]	16	15
Per-capita government expenditure, 1993–4 (Rs)		
Total	3,252	2,490
Education, sports etc.	498	280
PUBLIC SERVICES		
Proportion of children aged 12–23 months fully immunized, 1998-9 (%)	83	63
Teacher-pupil ratio in primary schools, 1998–9 (teachers per 1,000 pupils)	40	20
Proportion (%) of households receiving subsidized foodgrains from the public distribution system, 1993–4	44	5
Proportion (%) of households with electricity, 1998–9	97	89
EDUCATIONAL ACHIEVEMENTS		
Literacy rate, age 15–19, 1998–9	96	88
Proportion of rural women aged 15–19 who have attained grade 8, 1992–3 (%)	48	28
MORTALITY AND FERTILITY		
Death rate, age 0–4, 1996–8	17	23
Total fertility rate, 1996–8	2.4	3.4

Notes: [a] Population-weighted average of the rural and urban estimates.
Sources: Calculated from International Institute for Population Sciences (1995b, 1999, forthcoming); Government of India (1999a, 2000h); Tarozzi (2000); Aggarwal (2000), p. 71; Deaton and Tarozzi (2000), Table 10; Centre for Monitoring the Indian Economy (1999), pp. 442–6. For further details, see Statistical Appendix.

is to compare Himachal Pradesh with the state of Haryana, where each of the above-mentioned favourable features also apply. As Table 3.7 illustrates, the two states have similar levels of per-capita household expenditure, per-capita government expenditure, and poverty incidence. Yet, Himachal Pradesh is doing substantially better in terms of basic social indicators. The contrast is all the more striking bearing in mind Himachal Pradesh's historical 'backwardness'.

Why, then, has Himachal Pradesh done so well, especially in terms of creating social opportunities, even in comparison with states such as Haryana, which are no less prosperous in terms of per-capita income? An adequate explanation must include at least the following distinguishing features of Himachal Pradesh, which are, as it happens, closely related to the enabling factors discussed earlier in this chapter with reference to

Kerala and Uttar Pradesh. These are, respectively, (1) well-directed public intervention in support of social opportunities, (2) active agency of women, and (3) local democracy and social cooperation.[92] First, Himachal Pradesh has benefited from a strong state commitment to development, particularly focused on the social infrastructure in rural areas. Roads and schools, in particular, have been among the government's highest priorities. In spite of the adverse topography and settlement pattern (with small hamlets scattered over wide areas in a difficult terrain), enormous progress has been made in the provision of basic amenities at the village level. To illustrate, Himachal Pradesh comes first among all major Indian states in terms of the proportion of households having an electricity connection (88 per cent) and access to piped water (71 per cent).[93]

One indication of the positive impact of development planning in Himachal Pradesh is the gradual reduction of regional inequalities. There is an interesting parallel here with the case of Kerala, discussed earlier. Within-state, inter-regional inequalities used to be large in both states, but have sharply declined in each through sustained public support in favour of disadvantaged areas.[94] In particular, the remote tribal areas of Himachal Pradesh (e.g. in Kinnaur, Lahaul and Spiti) have benefited from considerable support, making it possible for these regions to participate more fully in the state's broader experience of agricultural diversification, infrastructural expansion and educational progress.

The second enabling factor relates to the agency of women. In many respects, gender relations are distinctly less patriarchal in Himachal Pradesh than in, say, Haryana (indeed for that matter most states of the northern and western regions). One indication of this, conveyed in Table 3.8, is the absence of any bias against girls in child survival. Correspondingly, Himachal Pradesh has a high female-male ratio by Indian standards.[95] In comparison with their counterparts in Haryana, Himachali women also

[92] These enabling factors have been comparatively unimportant in Haryana, where rapid economic growth has tended to be the main driving force behind improvements in living standards; on Haryana's development experience, see Sheila Bhalla (1995).

[93] Shariff (1999), p. 59, based on the NCAER/HDI survey, 1994. By 1998–9, access to electricity had further risen to an astonishing 97 per cent (see Statistical Appendix, Table A.3, Part 9).

[94] The same cannot be said of Haryana. For instance, anyone who has visited Mewat is bound to wonder how this pocket of extreme deprivation has been allowed to persist in the heart of Gurgaon (adjacent to Delhi), one of Haryana's most prosperous districts. As Zarina Bhatty aptly comments, '"Two hours to the Middle Ages" would be a fitting sign on the road from Delhi to Mewat' (Bhatty, 1999, p. 49).

[95] There are, however, disquieting signs of recent change in this respect, especially the spread of sex-selective abortion, reflected in a significant decline in the female-

TABLE 3.8 *Himachal Pradesh: Gender-related Indicators*

	Himachal Pradesh	Haryana	India	Himachal Pradesh's rank among 17 major states[a]
Female-male ratio, 2001	970	861	933	5
Ratio of female to male death rate, age 0–4, 1996–8	1.00[b]	1.31	1.14	5
Female school attendance in the 6–17 age group, 1998–9 (%)	93	78	66	1
Female labour force participation rate, 1991 (%)	35	11	22	1
Proportion (%) of women aged 20–24 married before age 18, 1998–9	11	42	50	1
Proportion (%) of recent births preceded by antenatal checkup, 1998–9	87	58	65	6
Proportion (%) of adult women, 1998–9, who are:[c]				
exposed to any media	84	67	60	2
involved in decisions about own health care	81	67	52	1
using any contraceptive method	68	62	48	1
aware of oral rehydration therapy	93	72	62	1
having access to money	80	71	60	1

Notes: [a] A higher value of the relevant indicator is interpreted as a higher achievement, except for 'ratio of female to male death rates' and 'proportion of women married before age 18' (where the reverse applies). The states doing better than Himachal Pradesh in terms of at least one of the indicators listed here are: Kerala, Tamil Nadu, Andhra Pradesh, Orissa, West Bengal, Maharashtra.

[b] 1991–8.

[c] Base: women aged 15–49 who are ever-married (currently-married, in the case of contraceptive use).

Sources: Calculated from International Institute for Population Sciences (2000a), pp. 33, 70, 223, 440–3 and Government of India (1999a, 2000h, 2001b, 2001c). For further details, see Statistical Appendix.

marry much later, retain closer bonds with their parents and siblings after marriage, and have a greater sense of independent decision-making.[96] Finally, Himachal Pradesh has the highest female labour-force participation among all major states (in terms of the proportion of women counted as

male ratio in the 0–6 age group in Himachal Pradesh between 1991 and 2001 (from 951 to 897). For further discussion of the recent spread of sex-selective abortion in India, see chapter 7.

[96] On these aspects of gender relations in Himachal Pradesh and Haryana, see Bondroit (1998, 1999), Drèze (1999), and Bhatty (forthcoming).

'workers' by the 1991 census). This last feature is likely to have played a major role in influencing other aspects of gender relations in Himachal Pradesh. There is, for instance, much evidence that high levels of female labour force participation are typically associated with a lower female disadvantage in child survival and a higher status of women in society (on this general issue, see chapter 7). The genesis of lower gender inequality in Himachal Pradesh may, thus, have economic as well as social aspects.

These features of gender relations are crucial in understanding the contrast between Himachal Pradesh and Haryana. Himachal Pradesh's lead in elementary education, for instance, largely reflects a narrower gender gap in school attendance. The latter, in turn, has much to do with the less rigid nature of patriarchal norms in Himachal Pradesh.[97] Similarly, the fact that gender relations in Himachal Pradesh are relatively favourable to women's agency and employment has greatly facilitated the demographic transition. Indeed, in a society which gives more room to valuing women's abilities, and where women have some freedom of movement and decision-making, it is easier for mothers to send their daughters to school, to get their children immunized, to make informed family-planning decisions, and so on. This feature of Himachal Pradesh fits well into the general causal connections we have tried to investigate, but it comes out with special clarity in this particular case.

The third enabling factor relates to local democracy and cooperation. Hill villages are far from 'egalitarian', but nevertheless the divisions of class, caste and gender that have been so pernicious elsewhere in north India are not so sharp in this region.[98] Among all major Indian states, Himachal Pradesh has the lowest incidence of landlessness (this is, in turn, due in part to post-independence land reforms), and the lowest proportion of agricultural labourers in the rural population.[99] Also, common property resources such as forests and pastures play a major role in the rural economy, further enhancing the comparative equity of access to productive resources. Similarly, while caste distinctions certainly do exist in Himachal Pradesh, they tend to take a relatively less hierarchical and divisive form than in many other regions. These features of the social structure in Himachal Pradesh, together with relatively progressive gender relations, have created favourable conditions for cooperative action and

[97] The relation between patriarchal norms and female education is discussed at greater length in chapter 5.

[98] As Chetan Singh (1998) observes in his scholary account of Himachal society: 'If indeed there was a characteristic that made hill society different from that of the plains it was the relative lack of social stratification' (C. Singh, 1998, p. 207).

[99] See Statistical Appendix, Table A.3, Part 11; also Shariff (1999), pp. 48–50, and Nanda (1992), pp. 106–42.

local democracy.[100] Indeed, the region has a rich tradition of lively collective institutions at the village level, geared for instance to the protection of common access resources, the maintenance of local irrigation systems, the management of village festivals and the settlement of disputes.[101]

As discussed in chapter 5 with reference to schooling, this aspect of village communities in Himachal Pradesh makes wide-ranging contributions to the successful functioning of local public services. Teacher accountability, for instance, is much easier to ensure when disgruntled parents are able to get together and demand better teaching standards. Teacher-parent cooperation, too, is easier to achieve when parents are relatively united. The sense of village community in Himachal Pradesh has also facilitated the emergence of consensual social norms on schooling matters, such as the notion that education is an essential part of every child's upbringing. Similar remarks apply to other local public services and institutions, from health centres and fair-price shops to village panchayats and mahila mandals.[102]

It is worth noting that these enabling factors help to explain not only Himachal Pradesh's rapid progress in 'social' fields such as health and education, but also its *economic* progress. As many authors have noted, for instance, the state's post-independence economic take-off has been

---

[100] On these aspects of village communities in Himachal Pradesh (and the neighbouring hill districts of Uttar Pradesh), see Berreman (1972), Parmar (1979), Guha (1989), Saraswat and Sikka (1990), Sax (1991), Somanathan (1991), Sikka and Singh (1992), Moller (1993), Gaul (1994), Keith-Krelik (1995), C. Singh (1998), Jayal (1999b), among others. These studies are best read along with similar studies for other regions, since the point being made here is not that local social inequalities in Himachal Pradesh are unimportant, but rather that they are *less* pervasive than in many other parts of India.

[101] See the literature cited in the preceding footnote. Some examples of local cooperative action reported in these studies are fairly striking. Sarkar (1999), for instance, reports a case where the local *mahila mandal* (women's association) decided to ban video games in the village, as those were felt to interfere with children's studies. Similarly, Jayal (1999b) describes a village where there are moral sanctions and even fines against people who take their disputes to the police or the courts rather than to the village elders.

[102] These observations have something in common with recent analyses of the role of 'social capital' in development. The notion of social capital, however, lends itself to many different interpretations, and has tended to be used as an all-purpose device to explain otherwise puzzling economic phenomena ranging from slow growth in Africa to the recent economic collapse in Russia. The general concern with social capital can be extended, in this case, to more precise links between cooperative action and development and also to the historical and material roots of social cooperation.

closely related to the transition from conservative feudal regimes to a 'developmental state'. In particular, the growing prosperity of the rural economy (including the 'apple boom') owes much to the state's bold infrastructural investments and active promotion of marketing arrangements, producer cooperatives, credit facilities, technological innovation, extension services and storage networks.[103] As L.R. Sharma has pointed out, Himachal Pradesh's 'relatively egalitarian socio-economic structure' also appears to have contributed to the state's rapid economic progress, by enabling most people to 'participate in the development process' and fostering 'growth with equity'.[104] Even the gender factor may be relevant here. There is indeed some evidence that, in India, economic growth and poverty reduction have tended to be more rapid in regions with relatively high levels of female labour force participation.[105]

Aside from the individual significance of these enabling factors, the complementarities between them have played a major role in Himachal Pradesh's success. In particular, the synergy between state initiative and cooperative action has been one of the cornerstones of the schooling revolution—and it is hardly less than that—in Himachal Pradesh (Probe Team, 1999). When either of these elements is missing, the results can be very disappointing. For instance, the social structure of tribal communities in central India has much in common with that of hill villages, including the absence of severe class, caste and gender inequalities. However, due to political marginalization and official neglect, these communities have had little opportunity to take advantage of these favourable social factors. Similarly, the derailing of positive state initiatives by social divisions and privileged interests at the local level is a pervasive problem in many Indian states.[106] It is when state initiatives complement the efforts of local communities to help themselves that the prospects of success are highest. The schooling revolution in Himachal Pradesh is an instructive illustration of this point, as is the demographic transition in Tamil Nadu, discussed in chapter 6.

The comparative development experiences of Himachal Pradesh and Haryana reinforce the lessons derived earlier from the comparison

---

[103] On this and related aspects of Himachal Pradesh's economy, see e.g. Singh (1985, 1992), Sharma (1987), Azad, Swarup and Sikka (1988).
[104] Sharma (1987), pp. 68 and 158.
[105] See Drèze and Srinivasan (1996).
[106] For a case study, see Drèze and Gazdar (1996) in the companion volume; also Drèze, Lanjouw and Sharma (1998).

between Kerala and Uttar Pradesh. There is also an interesting contrast between Himachal Pradesh and Kerala when it comes to the politics of development. In both regions, overcoming social inequalities has been an important precondition of widely-shared development. This precondition, however, has been achieved through rather different routes in the two cases. Himachal Pradesh, we have argued, has benefited from favourable social conditions, particularly in the form of a relatively egalitarian social structure and a strong tradition of cooperative action at the village level. Kerala, on the other hand, started off with a highly inegalitarian and oppressive social structure, and it is political action in combating these inequalities that has made it possible to overcome that initial obstacle. In this sense, Kerala's progress has more dialectical features than Himachal Pradesh's more straightforward advancement. But they do share the common asset of supportive public intervention, active agency of women, and vibrant local democracy and social cooperation.

We end by noting that, like Kerala, Himachal Pradesh is no 'model', if model is understood in the sense of a flawless, replicable success. As in Kerala, the other side of the coin of mass schooling in Himachal Pradesh is a high level of educated unemployment. Similarly, women's greater economic freedom has a counterpart in a heavy burden of work, as many Himachali women continue to shoulder most household responsibilities even when they work outside the household. Other major concerns include environmental destruction and the dependence of the government of Himachal Pradesh on central government transfers.[107] These reservations, however, do not detract from the significance of Himachal Pradesh's achievements. There are things to learn from Himachal Pradesh's experience (as from Kerala's), but there are things also for Himachal Pradesh (like Kerala) to learn from the achievements of other Indian states in other fields. The social 'preparedness' of Himachal Pradesh is likely to facilitate future progress in the domains where the state's achievements are quite limited as things stand.

3.10. CONCLUDING REMARK

The experience of Himachal Pradesh illustrates an important feature of contemporary development patterns in India, namely, that examples of positive achievements are not confined to the well-known case of Kerala. Further examples can be cited, relating for instance to rapid demographic

---

[107] Environmental degradation is a major issue throughout the Himalayan region; on this see Somanathan (1991), Chand (1996), Pathak (1997), United Nations Development Programme (forthcoming), among others.

transitions (e.g. in Tamil Nadu and Andhra Pradesh), land reforms (in West Bengal, Himachal Pradesh and Kashmir), the empowerment of disadvantaged castes (e.g. in Maharashtra), democratic decentralization (in Karnataka, West Bengal and Madhya Pradesh), rapid economic growth (e.g. in Gujarat), and innovative education programmes (in Madhya Pradesh, Tamil Nadu and Rajasthan). While India's overall development record leaves much to be desired, there are positive lessons of one sort or another to learn from the different states.

This applies also to the 'smaller' states, which are often out of focus in discussions of India's development (even Himachal Pradesh did not receive much attention until recently). To illustrate, Goa has excellent social indicators compared with most other states, and the fact that Goa has a small population (a little over one million) does not diminish the interest of this experience. Similar remarks apply to the northeastern states, which are doing quite well in terms of many aspects of social development.[108] These smaller states are often assumed to be 'special cases', with limited relevance for other states, but there is in fact much to learn from them, too.[109]

Some states are also conspicuous for their comprehensive failure to expand social opportunities. This applies, for instance, to Uttar Pradesh, discussed earlier in this chapter. Another telling example is Bihar, where there are few signs of any major improvement in living conditions in recent decades. In fact, the social environment in Bihar (and to some extent in Uttar Pradesh as well) has significantly *deteriorated* in some important respects, e.g. in the form of rising crime, environmental degradation, flourishing corruption, and the breakdown of many civic amenities. If anything, these two states have fallen further behind other states in the nineties (see chapter 9). And it is quite possible that the disparities will continue to grow for some time, especially as other states reap the benefits of demographic transition while Uttar Pradesh and Bihar struggle with high fertility rates and high dependency ratios. These are not trivial matters, considering the enormous sizes of these states. There is a strong case for giving them much greater attention in public policy and debate, instead of dismissing them as 'basket cases' as tends to happen today.

---

[108] For some relevant indicators, see Statistical Appendix, Table A.4. See also Kumar (1992, 1994) for a case study of Manipur.

[109] Indeed, the fact that small states seem to be doing comparatively well (while the large states, e.g. Uttar Pradesh and Bihar, are among the most problem-ridden) is itself of some interest, and there may be an important message here about the impediments associated with large administrative and political units.

4

India and China

4.1 PERCEPTIONS OF CHINA

"An' the dawn comes up like thunder outer China 'crost the Bay!" This isn't politics, but Kipling on nature, on the road to Mandalay. However, following the establishment of the People's Republic of China in 1949, the *political* perceptions of many activists in India began to match this arresting description of the coming dawn from China. Comparison with China and the lessons to be learned from its experience became staple concerns in activist Indian politics.

Indeed, it is natural to judge Indian successes and failures in comparative terms with China. Some of these comparisons have been academic and scholarly, even distant.[1] Others have been used to precipitate particular political debates in India, with considerable practical impact—in some cases linked to specific revolutionary causes (particularly in giving shape to Maoist political parties). Even non-revolutionary parties of the 'left', which are well integrated in India's parliamentary system of governance, have paid sustained attention to the perceived economic and social achievements of China—looking for lessons and guidance on how to make things move faster in India.

Since the economic reforms introduced around 1979, China's example has been increasingly quoted by quite a different group of political com-

[1] Fine examples of academic attempts at comparison can be found in Malenbaum (1956, 1959, 1982), S.J. Patel (1985), Bhalla (1992), Howes (1992), Matson and Selden (1992), Rosen (1992), Srinivasan (1994), Lal (1995), Wood and Calandrino (2000), among others.

mentators and advocates, to wit, those keen on promoting liberalization—
and integration of India into the world economy. China's successful
liberalization programmes and its massive entry into international trade
have been increasingly projected as a great model for India to act on.
The pro-market new 'dawn' may be quite a different event from what the
Naxalites dreamed about in their grim struggle, but it too looked to many
"like thunder outer China 'crost the Bay!'"

The People's Republic of China was established in October 1949, just
a few months before the constitution of the federal Republic of India
came into force in January 1950. The Indian leadership—at that stage on
good terms with China—tended to underplay the competing importance
of China's example, treating the respective efforts at economic development
and political emancipation as similar in spirit. As Jawaharlal Nehru put it
in a speech in 1954, 'these new and revolutionary changes in China and
India, even though they differ in content, symbolize the new spirit of Asia
and new vitality which is finding expression in the countries in Asia'.[2]

The sense that there is much to learn from China's experience was
immediate and powerful. The radicalism of Chinese politics seemed to
many to be deeply relevant to India, given the enormity of its poverty and
economic misery. China was the only country in the world comparable
with India in terms of population size, and it had similar levels of
impoverishment and distress. The fact that as a solution China sought a
revolutionary transformation of society had a profound impact on political
perceptions in the subcontinent. Similarly, later on, China's move towards
market-oriented reform and integration with the world economy has given
those policies a much wider hearing in India than they could have
conceivably had on the basis of what had happened in countries that are
much smaller and perceived to be quite dissimilar to India: Hong Kong,
Taiwan, Singapore, even South Korea. From revolutionary inspiration to
reformist passion, China has got India's ear again and again.

We shall presently argue that there is indeed a great deal to learn from
China. For that to happen, however, it is crucial to have a clear view of the
roots of Chinese triumphs and successes, and also of the sources of its
troubles and failures. It is, of course, first of all necessary to distinguish
between—and contrast—the different phases of the Chinese experience,
in particular, *before* and *after* the economic reforms initiated in 1979. But
going beyond that, it is also important to take note of the *interdependence*
between the achievements in the different periods. We argue, in particular,
that the accomplishments relating to education, health care, land reforms,

2 Speech made on 23 October 1954, reproduced in Gopal (1983), pp. 371–3.

and social change in the pre-reform period made significant contributions to the achievements of the post-reform period. This is so in terms of their role not only in sustaining high life expectancy and related achievements, but also in providing firm support for economic expansion based on market reforms.

It may have been very far from Mao's own intentions to develop literacy and basic health care in ways that would help to promote market-based, internationally-oriented enterprises (though that dialectical contrariness must have some interest for a Marxist theorist). But these structural achievements in the pre-reform period have certainly served as direct and valuable inputs in fostering economic performance in post-reform China. In drawing lessons from China, these apparently contrary interconnections can be particularly important.

This chapter is much concerned with understanding Chinese political and economic developments (both before and after the reforms of 1979), the interdependence between them, and the lessons that India might draw from what China has or has not done. But we should begin with taking stock of the relative positions of China and India as they are now.

4.2. Conditions of Life and Death

Living conditions in China at the time of the political transformation in 1949 were probably not radically different from those in India at that time. Both countries were among the poorest in the world and had high levels of mortality, undernutrition, and illiteracy. While generalizations about living standards in India or China of those times are subject to wide margins of error, the available evidence makes it hard to support the idea that a large gap between the two countries already existed in the late forties.[3]

Since then, however, a striking contrast has emerged between the two countries, in terms of the incidence of basic deprivations. This applies even in terms of income-based indicators. For instance, the proportion of the population below the World Bank's 'international poverty line' is estimated to be less than half as high in China as in India (Table 4.1). If China and India were comparably poor in the late 1940s, they now stand quite far apart.

The contrasting achievements of India and China can be seen no less

[3] *Human Development Report 1994*, Table 4, gives the following estimates for 1960: real GDP per capita: India 617, China 723; life expectancy at birth: India 44, China 47; infant mortality rate: India 165, China 150. These are, of course, just estimates, rather than hard information, but there is also other evidence to suggest that the sharp contrasts in development indicators between the two countries are of relatively recent origin; see Drèze and Sen (1989), chapter 11, and the literature cited there.

TABLE 4.1 *India, China and Kerala: Selected Comparisons*

	India	China	Kerala
Estimated proportion of the population living below the 'international poverty line', 1997–8[a] (%)	44.2	18.5	n/a
Gross national income per capita, based on purchasing power parities, 1999 (USA = 100)	7.0	11.1[b]	n/a
Annual growth rate of per-capita GDP (%)			
1980–90	3.7	8.6	2.3[c]
1990–99	4.1	9.6	5.1[c]
Life expectancy at birth, 1999 (years)	63	70	74[d]
Infant mortality rate, 1999 (per 1,000 live births)	71	30	14[d]
Total fertility rate, 1999	3.1	1.9	1.8[d]
Estimated proportion of low-birthweight babies, 1995–99 (%)	33	6	n/a
Literacy rates, 1999			
Age 15+			
Female	44	75	83
Male	72	91	93
Age 15–19			
Female	68	96[e]	98
Male	85	99[e]	99

Notes: [a] 1998 for China and 1997 for India. This is based on the World Bank's international poverty line of 'a dollar a day' (at constant 1985 prices, adjusted for purchasing power parity).
[b] Subject to a wide margin of error, most likely, an underestimate (see 'explanatory note' in the Statistical Appendix).
[c] Annual growth rate of per-capita 'state domestic product' (at constant prices).
[d] Reference years: 1997–9 for infant mortality; 1996–8 for fertility; the life expectancy figure is an interpolation between the actual figure for 1993–7 (73 years) and the projected figure for 2001 (75 years).
[e] Age 15–24.
Sources: For China and India: *World Development Indicators 2001*, Tables 1.1, 2.6, 2.14, 2.17, 2.19, 4.1 (growth rates of GDP have been converted into per-capita terms using population growth rates from 2000–1 census data) and *Human Development Report 2001*, pp. 163–4. For Kerala: Government of India (1999a, 2000h, 2001c) and production data supplied by the Central Statistical Organisation. The literacy rates for India and Kerala are from International Institute for Population Sciences (2000a, forthcoming). For further details, see Statistical Appendix.

forcefully in terms of direct indicators of living standards. Particular aspects of this contrast are summarized in Table 4.1 (Kerala is also included for later reference). While life expectancy at birth in India is still around 63 years, the Chinese figure is much higher—70 years, not very far behind life expectancies in much richer South Korea or in the more advanced countries in Latin America. Infant mortality is more than twice as high in India (71 per thousand live births in comparison with China's 30), and the proportion of low birthweight babies is more than five times as high (33 per cent compared with China's 6). Further evidence based on child anthropometry, disease patterns, food intakes and related information support the notion that China is well ahead of India as far as the elimination of health deprivation is concerned.[4]

Another important area in which the contrast is extremely sharp is basic education and literacy. In the next section China and India are compared in this field.

4.3. CONTRASTS IN BASIC EDUCATION[5]

As Table 4.1 shows, literacy rates are a good deal higher in China than in India. Further examination of this particular contrast is possible, based on census data. Both China and India conducted careful censuses in the early eighties and nineties—in 1981 and 1991 in the case of India, and 1982 and 1990 in the case of China. Each of these four censuses includes detailed information on literacy, which provides a useful basis of comparison.

Table 4.2 presents some relevant figures, derived from these censuses. For convenience, we shall take the reference year '1981–2' to mean 1981 for India and 1982 for China, and '1990–1' to stand for 1991 for India and 1990 for China. In Figures 4.1 and 4.2, we plot male and female literacy rates in 1981–2 and 1990–1 for each province of China and each state of India. The following observations emerge from these basic comparisons.[6]

First, census data unambiguously show that India is well behind China in the field of basic education. Adult literacy rates in India were as low as 34 per cent for women and 62 per cent for men in 1990–1, compared with 68 per cent for Chinese women and 87 per cent for Chinese men.

Second, age-specific literacy rates bring out a crucial feature of the Chinese advantage. In 1991, 25 per cent of adolescent boys in India, and

---

[4] See Bumgarner (1992), *World Development Report 1993* (particularly on morbidity), *Human Development Report 1999*, United Nations Development Programme (1999), and also the literature cited in Drèze and Sen (1989), chapter 11.

[5] This section is based on literacy data from the 1982 and 1990 Chinese censuses, and 1981 and 1991 Indian censuses. The corresponding details of more recent censuses (2000 and 2001 for China and India, respectively) are not available at the time of writing. Early results of the 2000 and 2001 censuses in China and India suggest that there has been significant progress in both countries during the nineties, with no fundamental change in the broad comparative patterns discussed in this section; see also Table 4.1.

[6] For a more detailed discussion, see Drèze and Loh (1995).

TABLE 4.2 *Literacy Rates in India, China and Kerala*

	1981–2		1990–1	
	Female	Male	Female	Male
Adults (age 15+)				
India	26	55	34	62
China	51	79	68	87
Kerala	71	86	84	93
Adolescents (age 15–19)				
India	43	66	55	75
China	85	96	92	97
Kerala	92	95	98	98

Sources: For India and Kerala: Government of India (2000d), based on census data. For China: Drèze and Loh (1995), based on census data.

45 per cent of adolescent girls, were found to be *illiterate*. The corresponding figures for China in 1990 are only 3 per cent for boys and 8 per cent for girls (Table 4.2). In other words, China is now quite close to universal literacy in the younger age groups. In India, by contrast, there is still a massive problem of illiteracy among young boys and—especially—girls. As the latest data on age-specific literacy rates indicate (see Table 4.1), this basic problem persists as India enters the twenty-first century.

Third, the 1981–2 census data show that China's lead over India was achieved *before* China embarked on a wide-ranging programme of economic reforms at the end of the seventies. During the eighties and nineties, there has been progress in both countries, with no major change in their comparative positions. The Chinese relative advantage over India is, thus, a product of its pre-reform groundwork, rather than its post-reform redirection.

Fourth, female literacy rates are well below male literacy rates in both countries. The gender gap is particularly large in India, where only a little more than half of all adolescent girls were able to read and write in 1991. In China, the gender gap in literacy is narrowing quite rapidly, as the country approaches universal literacy in the younger age groups.

Fifth, there are wide inter-regional disparities in literacy rates in both countries. The regional contrasts are, to a large extent, driven by differences in female literacy. The persistence of high levels of female illiteracy in particular states or provinces is a matter of concern in both countries, but especially so in India.

Sixth, in spite of sharp regional contrasts within each country, most Chinese provinces have much higher adult literacy rates than every Indian state except Kerala. The state of Kerala in India stands in sharp contrast

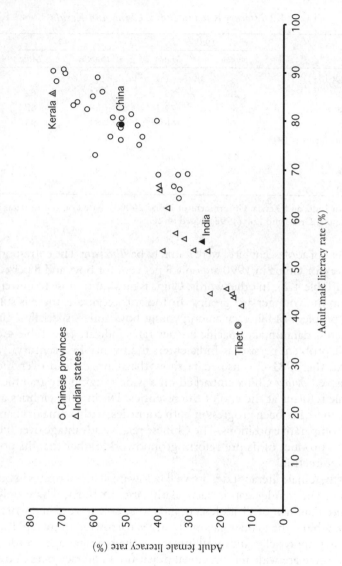

FIGURE 4.1 *Adult Literacy Rates in Indian States and Chinese Provinces (1981–2)*

Sources: Loh (1993) and Drèze and Loh (1995), based on census data. The literacy rates apply to persons aged 15 and above.

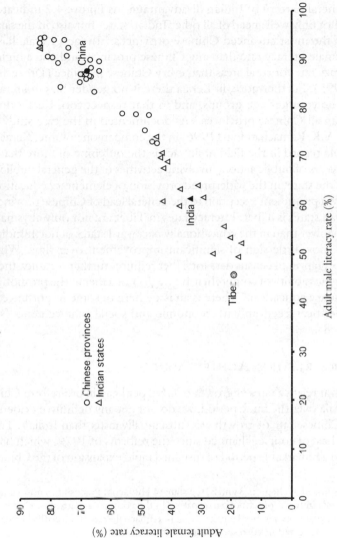

FIGURE 4.2 *Adult Literacy Rates in Indian States and Chinese Provinces (1990–1)*

Sources: Loh (1993), Drèze and Loh (1995), Government of India (2000d), based on census data. The literacy rates apply to persons aged 15 and above.

to the general pattern of Indian disadvantage. As Figure 4.2 indicates, Kerala is not only well ahead of all other Indian states but also in the same league as the most advanced Chinese provinces.[7] In fact, Kerala has a higher female literacy rate than any Chinese province, and also a higher male literacy rate for rural areas than every Chinese province (Drèze and Saran, 1995). Furthermore, in Kerala there is no gender bias in literacy rates in the younger age groups, and in that respect too, Kerala does better than all Chinese provinces.[8] As documented in the case study of Kerala by V.K. Ramachandran (1996) in the companion volume, Kerala's remarkable record in the field of literacy is the outcome of more than a hundred years of public action, involving activities of the general public as well as of the state, in the widespread provision of elementary education.

Finally, a prominent exception to the general lead of Chinese provinces over Indian states is Tibet. Literacy rates in Tibet are not only abysmally low (even lower than in the educationally backward states of north India), they also show little sign of significant improvement over time. While the interpretation of census data for Tibet requires further scrutiny, there is a strong possibility of comprehensive neglect of Tibet in the promotion of elementary education.[9] There is an issue here of some importance in linking political freedom with economic and social achievements (see section 4.8).

4.4. PRE-REFORM ACHIEVEMENTS

If we look at relative rates of growth of GNP per head in pre-reform China and in India over the same period, we do not get any definitive evidence that the Chinese rate of growth was substantially faster than India's. That situation has, of course, changed since the reforms of 1979, which have ushered in a remarkable period of sustained rapid expansion of the Chinese

[7] As discussed in chapters 3 and 5, the state of Himachal Pradesh has now caught up with Kerala in terms of school participation in the younger age groups. However, because the expansion of school participation in Himachal Pradesh is relatively recent, this is not yet reflected in correspondingly high *adult* literacy rates.

[8] Further evidence on school participation and educational attainments from the National Family Health Survey (1998–9) confirms the absence of any gender bias in Kerala, among the younger age groups. See Table 3.3 and Statistical Appendix, Table A.3.

[9] It should be mentioned that the Chinese censuses count persons who are able to read and write in any local language or script as literate (Dr Peng Xizhe, Institute of Population Research, Shanghai, personal communication). This suggests that census evidence on high levels of illiteracy in Tibet cannot be dismissed as an artificial result of misdefining literacy in terms of command over Chinese.

economy. We shall comment on the post-reform experience in the next section, but as far as the pre-reform period is concerned, it is hard to claim that China was really marching ahead in terms of GNP per head, or the related measures of real national income or gross domestic product.

To be sure, the Chinese official statistics claimed high rates of GNP growth over the pre-reform period as well, and organizations such as the World Bank—not to mention the United Nations—went on faithfully reflecting these claims in the statistics distributed in such documents as *World Development Reports*. For example, in the tables included in the Annexe in *World Development Report 1979*, an annual growth rate of 5.1 per cent in GNP per head is attributed to China over 1960–77, compared with India's 1.3 per cent over the same period. But these claims do not square with other statistics that are also available, some of which are, in fact, presented in the same documents (on this, see Drèze and Sen, 1989, chapter 11). There is much evidence that if the per-capita growth rate of GNP in China was higher than that in India in the period up to the reforms of 1979, the gap was not especially large.[10]

China's real achievement in this period lies in what it managed to do *despite* poor economic growth, rather than in what it could do *through* high economic growth. For example, the remarkable reduction in chronic undernourishment took place despite the fact that there had been relatively little increase in food availability per person; as Judith Banister (1987) notes, 'annual per capita grain production through 1977 was about the same as in the late 1950's: it averaged 301 kilograms in 1955–57 and 305 kilograms in 1975–77' (p. 354). The causal processes through which the reduction of undernutrition was achieved involved extensive state action including public redistributive policies, nutritional support, and of course health care (since undernourishment is frequently caused by parasitic diseases and other illnesses).[11]

China's achievements in the field of health during the pre-reform period include a dramatic reduction of infant and child mortality and a remarkable expansion of longevity. By 1981, the expectation of life at birth was estimated to be already as high as 68 years (compared with 54 years in

---

[10] In a careful reappraisal of Chinese economic performance, Angus Maddison (1998) estimates that the annual growth rate of per-capita GDP in China in 1952–78 was 2.3 per cent, compared with 1.7 per cent for India. This is broadly consistent with other independent assessments; see e.g. Perkins (1983), World Bank (1983), Meng and Wang (2000).

[11] On this see Riskin (1987, 1990). On the connection between disease and undernutrition, see also Drèze and Sen (1989, 1990), Tomkins and Watson (1989), Dasgupta and Ray (1990), Osmani (1990).

India), and infant mortality as low as 37 deaths per 1,000 live births (compared with 110 in India).[12] During the eighties and nineties, there has been some further progress in these fields, but at a much slower rate.

As was noted earlier, China's breakthrough in the field of elementary education had also taken place before the process of economic reform was initiated at the end of the 1970s. Census data indicate, for instance, that literacy rates in 1982 for the 15–19 age group were already as high as 96 per cent for males and 85 per cent for females (the corresponding figures for India at that time were 66 per cent and 43 per cent—see Table 4.2). The 1980s continued that progress and consolidated China's lead, but the relative standings had been decisively established *before* the Chinese reforms.

4.5. POST-REFORM RECORDS

The developments that have taken place in China since the reforms of 1979 have been quite remarkable. The rates of economic growth have been outstandingly high. During the 1980s and 1990s, per-capita GDP in China seems to have grown at an astonishing 8.6 and 9.6 per cent, respectively (Table 4.1).[13] Industrial production has grown at more than 10 per cent per year in both decades, and even agricultural production— traditionally much more sluggish than industry—has experienced respectable annual growth rates of 5.9 and 4.3 per cent in the 1980s and 1990s, respectively.[14]

The high rates of growth of output and real income have permitted the use of economic means to reduce poverty and to improve living

[12] The figures are from Coale (1993), Tables 1 and 2, and Government of India (1994a), p. 147; see Table 4.3 below.

[13] Two qualifications are due. First, there is some evidence of upward bias in the post-reform Chinese growth statistics. Independent studies, however, suggest that the bias is relatively small. A recent review of the evidence, for instance, concludes that official Chinese statistics overestimate the annual growth rate of GDP by about 1 percentage point for the 1978–97 period, and 2.2 percentage points for the 1992–7 period (Meng and Wang, 2000, Table 7.1; see also Wu, 2000). Second, the growth rate of the Chinese economy has slowed down after 1998, partly due to the adverse effects of the 'East Asian crisis'; on this, see e.g. Rawski (2001).

[14] *World Development Indicators 2001*, Table 4.1. On these and other aspects of economic reform in China, see also Perkins (1988), Hussain (1989), Byrd and Lin (1990), Wood (1991), Bhalla (1992), Chen et al. (1992), Lin (1992), Rosen (1992), Rawski (1999), United Nations Development Programme (1999), Khan and Riskin (2001), among others; also various contributions in Garnaut and Yiping Huang (2001).

conditions. The scope for removing poverty is obviously much greater in an economy where per-capita income *doubles every seven years*, as China's annual growth rate of 10 per cent or so in the 1990s implies, than in a country where it limps along at 2 or 3 per cent per year, as has been the case in India for much of the last five decades. For China, it is estimated that the proportion of the rural population below the national poverty line fell by two thirds in the 1980s.[15] Today, the estimated proportion of the population below the World Bank's international poverty line of one dollar per person per day is 18.5 per cent in China, compared with 44.2 per cent in India (see Table 4.1). There can be little doubt that China has done much better than India in this particular respect, and in explaining this difference, the much higher growth rate of the Chinese economy must receive the bulk of the credit. Indeed, the post-reform period in China has not been one of substantial redistributive efforts, and there is much evidence that income inequality has in fact increased rather than decreased since the reforms were initiated.[16] It is participatory growth, rather than radical redistribution, that accounts for the rapid decline of poverty in China in the post-reform period. In India, the eighties and nineties have witnessed some acceleration of economic growth, but the decline of poverty has remained comparatively modest.

This way of evaluating poverty relies on what has been called the head-count index, defined as the proportion of the population with per-capita income (or expenditure) below a specified 'poverty line'. It is based on the notion of poverty as insufficient income or expenditure, and this can be quite inadequate since human deprivation can take many different forms and reflect a range of enabling influences (such as public services, personal characteristics, and environmental conditions) other than private incomes.[17] Further, even within that income-centred perspective,

---

[15] World Bank (1992). This finding is consistent with independent evidence of major improvement in dietary patterns in China during the 1980s; see e.g. Garnaut and Ma (1993), Table 4.

[16] See Khan et al. (1992), Bramall and Jones (1993), Griffin and Zhao Renwei (1993), Knight and Song (1993), Riskin (1993), Howes and Hussain (1994), Naughton (1999), Yao Shujie (1999), Khan and Riskin (2001), among others.

[17] See chapter 2, pp. 35–6; also Sen (1984, 1992a). The notion of poverty as capability inadequacy relates to Adam Smith's (1776) treatment of 'necessities', and it treats the lowness of income (such as income levels being below a specified 'poverty line') as being only instrumentally and contingently relevant (with the appropriate poverty line varying between different societies and with diverse individual and social conditions).

the head-count index is insensitive to the levels and inequalities of incomes below the poverty line, and a more distribution-sensitive evaluation of poverty may be necessary for a fuller understanding of even income deprivation.[18]

Trends in the head-count ratio have obvious informational value, even when we adopt a broader approach to poverty.[19] The reduction in income poverty in China in the post-reform period is an achievement of great importance, given that lack of income often drastically constrains the lives that people can lead. But this finding needs to be supplemented with further information about what has been happening in matters of living conditions, e.g. based on mortality rates and related indicators. While the improvements of living conditions during the pre-reform period have been consolidated and extended in the post-reform period, the rate of progress in these fields since 1979 has been, in some important respects, rather moderate in comparison with (1) the radical transformations of the *pre-reform* period, (2) what has been achieved during the post-reform period in terms of raising *income levels* and reducing head-count measures of poverty, (3) what many *other countries* at a comparable stage of development have achieved since the late seventies. This is especially true of health-related indicators, which have improved only marginally during the post-reform period.

The last point is illustrated in Table 4.3 with reference to life expectancy and infant mortality (see also Figures 4.3 and 4.4). It can be seen that while China achieved outstanding progress during the sixties and seventies (starting with levels of infant mortality and life expectancy similar to India's, but catching up with Kerala, Sri Lanka and South Korea within two decades), the pace of improvement during the post-reform period has been very slow in comparison.[20] In comparative international terms, China has not fared well during this period. Life expectancy, for instance, has expanded by only 1.8 years between 1981 and 1991 in China, compared

[18] See Sen (1976b), Blackorby and Donaldson (1980), Foster (1984), Foster, Greer and Thorbecke (1984), Kakwani (1986), Atkinson (1989), and Ravallion (1994).

[19] In the literature on poverty in India, the head-count index has been far more used than any other indicator of poverty, and the rationale for this arises not from any intrinsic importance of this indicator, but rather from the likelihood of its correlation with other—more significant—characterizations of deprivation. On the relationship between different indicators of poverty in the Indian economy, see Tendulkar, Sundaram, and Jain (1993), Dutta et al. (1997), Dubey and Gangopadhyay (1998).

[20] Some early mortality statistics derived from official sources even suggest a recorded *increase* in mortality rates in the immediate post-reform years (as discussed in Drèze and Sen, 1989, pp. 215–18). But there are reasons to doubt the accuracy of these statistics. Table 4.3 is based on more recent and comparatively reliable sources, including life tables derived from 1982 and 1990 census data (Coale, 1993).

TABLE 4.3 *Mortality Decline in China and Selected Countries*

	Infant mortality rate (per 1,000 live births)				Annual rate of decline (%)			Life expectancy at birth (years)				Pace of improvement (years per decade)		
	1960	1981	1991[a]	1999	1960–81	1981–91	1991–99	1960	1981	1991[a]	1999	1960–81	1981–91	1991–99
China	150	57	31	30	6.7	2.0	0.0	47.1	67.7	69.3	70	9.8	1.8	0.8
India	165	110	80	71	1.9	3.2	1.5	44.0	53.9[b]	59.0[d]	63	4.7	5.1	5.0
Kerala	93[c]	37	16	14	4.4	8.4	1.7	50.3[c]	66.9[b]	71.2[d]	74	7.9	4.3	3.5
South Korea	85	33	23	8	4.5	3.6	13.2	53.9	66	70	73	5.8	4.0	3.8
Sri Lanka	71	43	26	15	2.4	5.0	6.9	62.0	69	71	73	3.3	2.0	2.5

Notes: [a] 1990, for China.

[b] Unweighted average of SRS-based estimates for 1976–80 and 1981–5.

[c] Unweighted average of census-based estimates for 1951–60 and 1961–70.

[d] Unweighted average of SRS-based estimates for 1986–90 and 1991–5.

Sources: All countries, 1960: *Human Development Report 1994*, Table 4 (pp. 136–7). Kerala, 1960: calculated from Ramachandran (1996), based on census and Sample Registration System data. Sri Lanka and South Korea, 1981 and 1991: *World Development Report 1983*, pp. 148–9 and 192–3, and *World Development Report 1993*, pp. 238–9 and 292–3. China, 1981 and 1990: Coale (1993), Tables 1–4. India and Kerala, 1981 and 1991: Government of India (1999a), based on SRS data. All countries, 1999: *World Development Indicators 2001*, Table 2.19. Kerala, 1999: see Table 4.1. The 1960 figures for China are 'trend' figures, which ignore excess mortality associated with the 1958–61 famine.

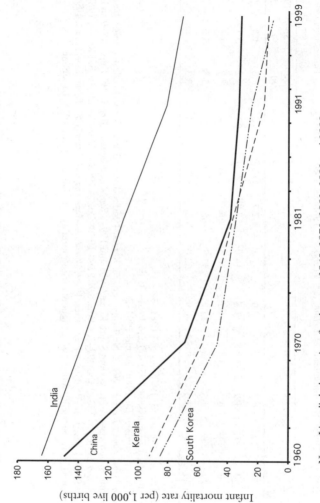

FIGURE 4.3 *Infant Mortality in China and Selected Asian Economies*

Note: Lines link data points for the years 1960, 1970, 1981, 1991 and 1999.

Sources: See Table 4.3. As mentioned there, the 1960 figure for China is a trend figure, which ignores excess mortality associated with the 1958–61 famine. The figures for 1970 are from *World Development Indicators 2001* (CD-ROM) and (for Kerala) Government of India (1999a).

FIGURE 4.4 *Life expectancy in India, China and Kerala*

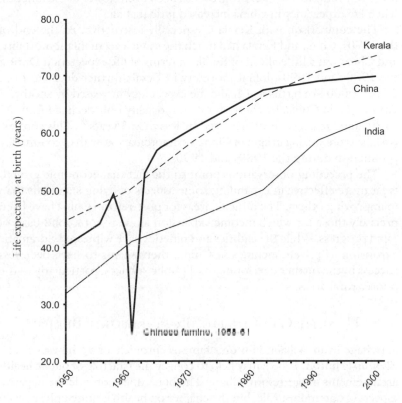

Sources: China: Banister (1984), Coale (1993), and *World Development·
Indicators 2001.* India: Government of India (2001c), p. S-1,
and *World Development Indicators 2001* (see also Statistical
Appendix). Kerala: See Tables 4.1 and 4.3.

with about 2 years in Sri Lanka, 4 years in South Korea and Kerala, and 5 years in India as a whole. Progress has been even slower in the nineties, when life expectancy in China increased little if at all.

The comparison with Kerala is especially instructive. At the end of the 1970s, China and Kerala had much the same level of infant mortality, and China was a little ahead of Kerala in terms of life expectancy. During the 1980s and 1990s, infant mortality in Kerala further declined from 37 per 1,000 live births to 14, and life expectancy increased by another 7 years or so; in China, by contrast, infant mortality only declined from 37 to 30, and life expectancy increased by less than 3 years.[21] This contrast is all the more striking in light of China's extraordinary growth of commodity production during the 1980s and 1990s.

The preceding observations point to the fact that economic growth is far more effective in expanding some aspects of living standards than in improving others. The difficult areas for post-reform China have been precisely those for which income expansion alone is not a solid basis of rapid progress. While the eighties and nineties have witnessed a dramatic expansion of private incomes in China, there seems to have been less success in the further development of public services, particularly in the poorer rural areas.

4.6. HEALTH CARE IN THE POST-REFORM PERIOD

A passage from William Hinton's famous chronicle of a Chinese village, *Shenfan* (Hinton, 1983), may help to convey the vital role of public health arrangements in pre-reform China. The book does not hide the negative aspects of communist rule, but the chapter on health is quite upbeat, even concluding that 'if there had been progress in no other field, the progress here would have justified the revolution' (p.267). The chapter begins with the following account of a 'medical emergency' in the study village, Long Bow:

On September 14, 1971, the loudspeaker burst in upon our sleep earlier than usual, but instead of 'The East is Red' we heard the voice of the brigade doctor,

---

[21] It is plausible that the slowing down of infant mortality decline in China during the 1980s and 1990s is partly a reflection of the effects of the 'one-child policy' (see section 4.8). But the same explanation cannot be invoked for the slowing down of mortality decline in other age groups. Even if infant mortality had declined as fast in China as in Kerala during the 1980s and 1990s, the expansion of life expectancy in China would have been only just over 3 years (taking as given the pace of mortality decline in the *other* age groups), compared with 7 years in Kerala.

Three Gingers Chi, announcing an emergency. 'Attention, everyone! Everyone pay attention! Two Long Bow children have been stricken with encephalitis. We sent them to the hospital last night. This disease is spread by mosquitoes. We are launching a massive campaign to kill mosquitoes, clean up all mosquito breeding spots, and innoculate all children. We want everybody out. Kill every mosquito you see. We will spray every house with DDT, treat every toilet cistern, put chlorine in the pond, sweep up and carry off all trash, and dry out and fill in every puddle. Please bring all children under six to the brigade clinic. And please report any suspicious symptoms to me immediately.[22]

The author proceeds to describe how these simple measures succeeded in preventing the spread of encephalitis in Long Bow. Anyone familiar with the state of health services in rural India is bound to be impressed with this episode of social mobilization for public health.

Preventive health campaigns were part of a larger system of public health facilities in pre-reform China. Other aspects included an extensive network of health workers, a major expansion of medical infrastructure, and well-developed collective health insurance arrangements. In sharp contrast with India, these arrangements reached deep into rural areas, even in the poorer counties. By the end of the 1970s, 'almost the entire rural population had access to essential health services at a reasonable cost'.[23]

The institutional and financial basis of collective health arrangements in China, however, has drastically changed with the economic reforms initiated in the late 1970s, with some serious setbacks in the less privileged areas. There have been several reasons for this.[24] First, the post-reform period has seen a transition from a system where the collective had the first claim on the products of economic activity (as in the pre-reform commune system) to one where local public services have to be financed by taxing private incomes (a method which raises standard problems of incentives and administrative barriers). This has eroded the financial basis of local public services in some areas, particularly those which have experienced relatively slow economic growth. Second, the rapid expansion of the private economy has tended to drain human resources away from the public sector, where income-earning opportunities (eg. for teachers and doctors) are

[22] Hinton (1983), p. 262.
[23] Bloom and Gu Xingyuan (1997b), p. 351.
[24] For further discussion of these diverse developments, see Drèze and Sen (1989), World Bank (1992), Yu Dezhi (1992), De Geyndt et al. (1992), Wong (1994), Bloom et al. (1995), Drèze and Saran (1995), Hillier and Shen (1996), Bloom and Gu Xingyuan (1997a, 1997b), Bloom (1998), White (1998), United Nations Development Programme (1999), and various contributions in Bloom and Wilkes (1997).

less attractive. Third, there is also some evidence of a reduced state commitment to the widespread and equitable provision of public services. One symptom of this is the extension of the 'enterprise responsibility' model of public-sector management to social services, leading to widespread introduction of user fees as a means of ensuring cost recovery.

For these and other reasons, public services in large parts of rural China have come under severe strain during the post-reform period. For instance, the proportion of the rural population covered by the 'cooperative medical system' dropped from around 90 per cent in the late 1970s to less than 10 per cent ten years later.[25] Village health services have been comprehensively privatized, and 'China no longer organises mass public health campaigns'.[26] The adverse effects of these developments on health achievements in the post-reform period have clearly been outweighed by the favourable impact of rapid growth of private incomes, and the overall progress of living conditions has continued. But the result of this tension has been to moderate China's rate of progress in health and related fields, just when it has done so very well in stimulating economic growth.

This line of reasoning does not dispute the importance of what has been achieved in China in the post-reform period, but it suggests that China's progress on the income front has been diluted in the social field by its changed approach to public services, which could have got more from the expanded resources made available by rapid economic growth. These observations also guard us against 'rubbishing' what China had already done before the reforms. That general conclusion receives further support from the need to consider and scrutinize the factors underlying China's rapid economic growth in the post-reform period.

4.7. PRE-REFORM AND POST-REFORM CONNECTIONS

The spread of basic education across the country is particularly relevant in interpreting the nature of the Chinese economic expansion in the post-reform period. The role of mass education in facilitating fast and widely-shared growth has been much analysed in the recent development literature, particularly in the context of the performance of east Asian economies.[27] In China, the big step in that direction was taken in the pre-reform period. The fact, noted earlier, that by 1982 literacy rates in China were already as

[25] United Nations Development Programme (1999), p. 37.
[26] Bloom (1998), p. 240.
[27] See chapters 2 and 3, and also the works cited there.

high as 96 per cent for males in the 15–19 age group, and 85 per cent even for females in that age group, made participatory economic expansion possible in a way it would not have been in India *then*—and is quite difficult in India even *now*.

Another area in which the post-reform expansions benefited from pre-reform achievements is that of land reforms, which has been identified as an important factor of economic development in east Asia in general.[28] In China, things went, of course, much further than land reforms, and the development of communal agriculture certainly was a considerable handicap for agricultural expansion in the pre-reform period, and indeed had a direct role in precipitating the great famines of 1958–61 (on which more presently). But that process of collectivization had also, inter alia, abolished landlordism in China (in ways that had often been quite brutal) and ensured fairly equitable access to land in rural areas. When the Chinese government opted for the 'responsibility system' in the late 1970s, the country had a land-tenure pattern that could readily support individual farming without the social problems and economic inefficiencies of highly unequal land ownership and widespread landlessness, in sharp contrast with India.

It is interesting that the institutional developments that have favoured participatory economic growth throughout east Asia (in particular, the spread of basic education and health care, and the abolition of landlordism) had come to different countries in the region in quite different ways. In some cases, even foreign occupation had helped, for example, in the land reforms of Taiwan and South Korea. In the case of China, the pre-reform regime, with its own goals and commitments, carried out some changes that turned out to be immensely useful in the market-based economic expansion of the post-reform period. That connection is extremely important to note for an adequately informed interpretation of the Chinese successes of recent years. If India has to emulate China in market success, it is not adequate just to liberalize economic controls in the way the Chinese have done, without creating the social opportunities that post-reform China inherited from the pre-reform transformation. The reach of China's market rests on the solid foundations of social changes that had occurred earlier, and India cannot simply hope for that reach, without making the enabling social changes—in education, health care, land reforms, etc.—that help make the market function in the way it has in China.

---

[28] See, for example, Amsden (1989), Wade (1990), World Bank (1993c), and the literature cited there; see also chapter 3.

4.8. AUTHORITARIANISM, FAMINES AND VULNERABILITY

In learning from China, it is not enough to look only at positive lessons— what can be fruitfully emulated; it is important to examine the 'non-lessons' as well—what may be best avoided. An obvious instance is the Chinese experience of famine compared with India's better record in that field. The famine of 1958–61 killed, it appears, between 15 and 30 million people.[29] India's performance in famine prevention since independence has been much more successful, and even when a natural calamity like a drought has led to a potential famine situation, the occurrence of an actual famine has been averted through timely government action.[30]

The causation of the Chinese famine of 1958–61 can be analysed from different perspectives. First, the disastrous experience of the Great Leap Forward and the related programme of rapid collectivization of agriculture are important elements in this story. The incentive system crashed badly and the organizational base of the Chinese agricultural economy collapsed.

Second, the problem was made worse by the arbitrary nature of some of the distributional policies, including features of communal feeding.[31] There was also an important question of distribution between town and country. The proportion of procurement for the urban areas actually went up precisely when the food output had plummeted.[32]

Third, the Chinese government did not wake up to the nature and magnitude of the calamity for quite a long time, and the disastrous policies were not substantially revised for three years, while the famine raged on. The informational failure was linked to a controlled press, which duped the public in suppressing information about the famine, but in the process deluded the government as well. The local leaders competed with each other to send rosy reports of their alleged success, out-doing their regional

[29] Official Chinese mortality statistics suggest some 15 million extra deaths (State Statistical Bureau of the People's Republic of China, 1999, p. 360); Peng's (1987) estimates is 23 million, whereas that of Ashton et al. (1984) is close to 30 million. See also Kane (1988) and Riskin (1990, 1998).

[30] See Drèze and Sen (1989) and Drèze (1990a). For case studies of famine prevention in post-independence India, see also Ramlingaswami et al. (1971), Choudhary and Bapat (1975), Mathur and Bhattacharya (1975), K.S. Singh (1975), Subramaniam (1975), Desai et al. (1979), Hubbard (1988), Government of India (1989b), Chen (1991), Currie (2000), among others.

[31] On this see Peng (1987), who argues that communal kitchens led to over-consumption in some areas while starvation was widespread in others; see also Yang and Su (1998).

[32] See Riskin (1987, 1990).

rivals, and at one stage the Chinese government was convinced that it had a 100 million more metric tons of foodgrains than it actually had.[33] Fourth, the government was immune to public pressure, because no opposition party or political dissent was tolerated. There was, thus, no organized demand for the government to resign despite evidence of starvation and mortality, and the political leaders could hang on to the disastrous policies for an incredibly long time. This particular aspect of the Chinese famine—its linkage with the lack of democracy in China— fits into a more general pattern of association between democracy and successful prevention of famines, or—seen the other way—between the absence of democracy and the lack of any guarantee that serious attempts to avert famines will be undertaken.[34]

Indeed, it is a remarkable fact that no substantial famine has ever occurred in a democratic country where the government tolerates opposition, accepts the electoral process, and can be publicly criticized. A government which has to deal with opposition parties, to answer probing questions in the parliament, to face condemnation from the public media, and to go to the polls on a regular basis, simply cannot afford *not* to take prompt action to avert a threatening famine. In a non-democratic country, there is no such guarantee against famines.

In some ways, even the *other* causal factors in the above interpretation of the Chinese famine relate ultimately to the lack of democracy. A policy as disruptive and drastic as the Great Leap Forward could not have been initiated in a pluralist democracy without its being debated extensively. Similarly, government decisions relating to food distribution—between individuals and between town and country—could not have been placed above criticism and public scrutiny. And of course the controlling of news and information would not have been possible in a multiparty democracy in the way it happened routinely in China when it experienced that gigantic famine. In the multi-faceted causal account of the great famine in China, the absence of democracy must be seen as quite central, with influences on the other elements in the string of causation.

India's democratic system has many flaws (more on this in chapter 10), but it certainly is radically more suited to deal with famines. Underlying that specialized point about famines and famine prevention, there is a more general issue which is worth considering in this context. The successes of the Chinese economic and social policies have depended crucially on the concerns and commitments of the leadership. Because of its radical

---

[33] See Bernstein (1984) and Riskin (1987, 1998).
[34] On this see Sen (1982, 1983a) and Drèze and Sen (1989).

commitment to the elimination of poverty and to improving living conditions—a commitment in which Maoist as well as Marxist ideas and ideals played an important part—China did achieve many things that the Indian leadership failed to press for and pursue with any vigour. The elimination of widespread hunger, illiteracy, and ill health falls solidly in this category. When state action operates in the right direction, the results can be quite remarkable, as is illustrated by the social achievements of the pre-reform period.

The fragility of this way of doing things turns on the extreme dependence of the process on the values and politics of the leadership. If and when there is no commitment on the part of the leadership to pursue some particular cause, that cause can be very badly neglected. Also, whenever the leadership is deluded into getting the causal relations wrong, the whole system might still operate as if those mistaken presumptions were just right and in no need of exacting scrutiny. When the political leaders, for one reason or another, fail to address a problem, or refuse to even recognize it, there is little scope for public pressure to challenge their inertia or to expose their mistakes. The famine of 1958–61 represents a clear example of this pattern, but there are many others, including the acceptance of endemic illiteracy in Tibet (see section 4.3), the drastic privatization of health services in the post-reform period (see section 4.6) the imposition of a draconian one-child policy (discussed in the next section), the excesses of the Cultural Revolution, and the frequent violation of basic human rights. Authoritarianism is an unreliable route to social progress.

4.9. COERCION, POPULATION AND FERTILITY

One particular field in which the operation of the authoritarianism of contemporary China can be seen in a very clear form is that of population policy, and it is often suggested, particularly in activist neo-Malthusian circles, that India should emulate China in this important area. China has adopted fairly draconian measures to force the birth rate down, and its success in this respect has been widely studied and admired, given the alarmist views of the 'world population problem' that are currently shared by many international leaders. The fear of an impending crisis makes many policy advocates seek forceful measures in the third world for coercing people to have fewer children, and despite criticism from diverse quarters including women's groups, China's attempts in that direction have received much attention and praise.

How alarming the 'population crisis' actually is in a country such as China (or for that matter India) is a debatable question. The case for

TABLE 4.4 *India and China: Economic Growth and Population Growth*

Country	Annual growth rate of population (1990–99)	Annual growth rate of GDP (1990–99)	Annual growth rate of GDP per capita, assuming the population growth rate of:[a]	
			India	China
India	1.9	6.0	4.1	4.9
China	1.1	10.7	8.8	9.6

Notes: [a] Calculated by subtracting the population growth rate of the country mentioned in the column heading from the GDP growth rate of the country mentioned in the row heading.

Source: Calculated from *World Development Indicators 2001*, Table 4.1, and recent census data on population growth rates.

concern about rapid population has, in fact, involved a combination of excellent arguments with rather misleading interpretations of the nature of the problem. One of these misinterpretations relates to the connection between population growth and economic growth. It is sometimes thought that restraining population growth is an essential means of raising the rate of growth of per-capita GNP (or of preventing its decline). In fact, however, for countries such as India and China, population policies— important as they may in general be—are likely to make relatively little difference to the rate of per-capita economic growth.

This point is illustrated in Table 4.4. If China had a population growth rate similar to India's (i.e. 1.9 per cent instead of 1.1 per cent), its growth of per-capita GDP—assuming no change in the growth rate of *total* GDP— would only decline from 9.6 per cent per year to 8.8 per cent.[35] Similarly, should India succeed in cutting down the rate of population growth to 1.1 per cent (as in China), its growth rate of per-capita GDP would only increase from 4.1 to 4.9 per cent. The contrast in growth rates of per-capita income between India and China are primarily due to China's much faster growth rate of total income, with differences in population growth rates playing relatively little role in that contrast.

This remark is not intended to dismiss the need for concern about rapid population growth. There are good reasons for such concern, related for instance to the adverse effects of population pressure on public infra-structure and the local environment, as well as to the burden of frequent

---

[35] The decline would be even smaller under the alternative assumption that a higher rate of population growth raises the growth rate of total GDP. This alternative assumption is rather more plausible than the assumption of unchanged growth of total GDP, which implies that the additional population is totally unproductive.

pregnancies for women.[36] The point is to recognize that the nature of the problem is quite different from what is usually stressed in the much-publicized fears about 'the population problem' as a cause of low or negative economic growth.

Coercive methods such as the 'one child policy' have been tried in large parts of China since the reforms of 1979. Also, the government often refuses to offer housing and related benefits to families with several children—thus penalizing the children as well as the unconforming adults. China's total fertility rate (a measure of the average number of children born per woman) is now 1.9, a little below the 'replacement level' (conventionally set at 2.1), and much below India's 3.1 and the weighted average of 4.3 for low-income countries other than China and India.[37] This has been seen—understandably—as a story of much success.

The difficulties with this 'solution' of the population problem arise from different sides.[38] First, the lack of freedom associated with this approach is a major social loss in itself. Human rights groups and women's organizations in particular have been especially concerned with the lack of reproductive freedom involved in any coercive system.[39]

Second, apart from the fundamental issue of individual freedom, there are specific consequences to consider in evaluating compulsory birth control. Coercion works by making people do things they would not freely choose to do. The social consequences of such compulsion, including the ways in which an unwilling population tends to react when it is coerced, can be appalling. For example, the demands of a 'one child family' can lead to the neglect—or worse—of infants, thereby increasing the infant mortality rate. Also, in a country with a strong preference for male children—a characteristic shared by China with India and many other countries in Asia and north Africa—a policy of allowing only one child per family can easily be particularly detrimental for girls, e.g. in the form of fatal neglect of female children. This, it appears, is exactly what has happened on a fairly large scale in China.[40]

---

[36] See e.g. Dasgupta (1993) and Cassen (2000); also chapter 6.

[37] *World Development Indicators 2001*, Table 2.17, and *World Development Indicators 2000*, Table 2.16.

[38] On coercive and collaborative approaches to family planning, see Sen (1994a, 1994b).

[39] On the general subject of reproductive freedom and its relation to the population problem, see Sen, Germain and Chen (1994). This issue is also discussed in chapters 6 and 7 of this book, with reference to India.

[40] These and related consequences of the one-child policy in China (such as the sharp decline in the female-male ratio at birth, primarily reflecting widespread abortion

Third, it is not at all clear how much additional reduction in the birth rate has actually been achieved through these coercive methods. Many of China's longstanding social and economic programmes have been valuable in reducing fertility, including those that have expanded education (for women as well as men), made health care more generally available, provided more job opportunities for women, and raised income levels. These factors would themselves have reduced the birth rate, and it is not clear how much 'extra lowering' of fertility rates has been achieved in China through compulsion. To illustrate the point, consider the following question: among all the countries that match (or surpass) China in terms of life expectancy, female literacy, and female participation in the labour force, how many have a *higher* fertility rate than China's 1.9? The answer is 'only three': Jamaica, Uzbekistan, and the United States, with fertility rates of 2.6, 2.7 and 2.0 respectively.[41] The *extra* contribution of coercion in reducing fertility in China is, thus, far from obvious.

Despite all these problems, many commentators point out that China has nevertheless achieved something in its birth control programme that India has not been able to do. This is indeed the case, and in terms of national averages, it is easy to see that China with its low fertility rate of 1.9 has got population growth under control in a way that India, with its average fertility of 3.1, has not achieved. However, what is far from clear is the extent to which this contrast can be attributed to the effectiveness of the coercive policies used in China, since we would expect the fertility rate to be much lower in China given its much higher levels of female literacy, life expectancy, female labour force participation, and so on.

In order to sort out this issue, it is useful to look at those parts of India which have relatively high literacy rates, and other social features that are associated with voluntary reduction of fertility rates. The state of Kerala does provide an interesting comparison with China, since it too enjoys high levels of basic education, health care, and so on. Kerala's

---

of female foetuses) have been discussed by Hull (1990), Johansson and Nygren (1991), Banister (1992), Greenhalgh et al. (1995), Zeng Yi et al. (1993), Coale and Banister (1994), Zhang (1998), Peng and Huang (1999), among others. In 1981, the infant mortality rate in China was estimated to be a little lower for females than for males (Coale, 1993). Today, according to official Chinese statistics, the female infant mortality rate is 30 per cent higher than the corresponding figure for males (State Statistical Bureau, 1999, p. 60). The female-male ratio at birth, for its part, has been falling steadily from the late 1970s onwards, reaching 86 in 1994 (Zhang, 1998); this compares with a world-wide norm of 94 or so, which also applied in China in the 1960s and 1970s (Zeng Yi et al., 1993).

[41] *World Development Indicators 2001*, Tables 2.2, 2.14, 2.17, and 2.19.

fertility rate of 1.8 is just below China's 1.9, and this has been achieved without any compulsion by the state. This is in line with what we could expect through progress in factors that help voluntary reduction in birth rates. As we saw earlier, Kerala has higher literacy rates than China (see Tables 4.1 and 4.2). In fact, the female literacy rate is higher in Kerala than in *every* province in China. Also, in comparison with male and female life expectancies at birth in China of 68 and 72 years in 1999, the corresponding estimates for Kerala in 1993–7 are 70 and 76 years, respectively. Further, women have played an important role in Kerala's economic and political life, and to some extent in property relations and educational movements.[42]

Kerala's success in reducing the birth rate, based on these and other positive achievements, disputes the necessity of coercion for cutting down fertility in poor economies. And since this low fertility has been achieved voluntarily, there is no sign of the adverse effects that were noted in the case of China, e.g. heightened female infant mortality and widespread abortion of female foetuses. As was discussed earlier, Kerala's infant mortality rate (14 per 1,000 live births) is now much lower than China's (30 per 1,000), even though both regions had the same infant mortality rate around the time of the introduction of the one-child policy in China. Further, while in China the infant mortality rate is about 30 per cent higher for females than for males, in Kerala the male and female figures are virtually identical.[43]

It is sometimes argued that what makes compulsory birth control important and necessary is the speed with which birth rates can be cut down through coercive means, in a way that cannot happen with voluntary processes. However, Kerala's birth rate has fallen from 44 per thousand in the 1950s to 18 by 1991—a decline no less fast than that in China. It could, of course, be argued that looking at this long period does not do justice to the effectiveness of one-child family and other coercive policies that were introduced in 1979, and that we ought really to compare what has happened since then.

Table 4.5 presents the comparative pictures of fertility rates in China and Kerala in 1979 (when the 'one child policy' was introduced) and after.

[42] See Robin Jeffrey (1992), and also V.K. Ramachandran's (1996) paper on Kerala in the companion volume.

[43] See State Statistical Bureau of the People's Republic of China (1999), p. 60, and Government of India (1999a), p. 129. As mentioned earlier (footnote 40), the survival disadvantage of infant females vis-à-vis males in China apparently did not exist in the 1970s (*before* the introduction of the one-child policy).

TABLE 4.5 *Fertility Rates in China, Kerala and Tamil Nadu*

	1979	1991	1998
China	2.8	2.0	1.9
Kerala[a]	3.0	1.8	1.8
Tamil Nadu[a]	3.5	2.2	2.0

Notes: [a] Three-year averages (the last figure applies to 1996–8).
Sources: For China: Peng (1991), Li Chengrui (1992), *World Development Report 1994*, and *World Development Indicators 2000*. For India: Government of India (1999a), pp. 117 and 213, and Government of India (2000h), p. 44.

The figures for Tamil Nadu are also presented here, since Tamil Nadu has an active family planning programme, one of the highest literacy rates among the major Indian states, and also relatively high female participation in gainful employment and low infant mortality (third among major states in both respects), all of which have contributed to a steady reduction of fertility.[44] It turns out that both Kerala and Tamil Nadu have achieved bigger declines in fertility than China has since 1979. Kerala began with a *higher* fertility rate than China in 1979, but the positions were reversed by the end of the 1980s. In Tamil Nadu, the absolute reduction of fertility since 1979 (from 3.5 to 2.0) has been much larger than the corresponding reduction in China (from 2.8 to 1.9). Despite the added 'advantage' of the one-child policy and other coercive measures, the Chinese fertility rate seems to have fallen much less sharply.

Contrasts between the records of Indian states offer some further insights on this subject. While Kerala and Tamil Nadu have radically reduced fertility rates, other states in the so-called 'northern heartland' (such as Uttar Pradesh, Bihar, Madhya Pradesh, Rajasthan) have much lower levels of education, especially female education, and of general health care. These states all have high fertility rates—between 4 and 5 in each case (see Table 3.3 in chapter 3). This is in spite of a persistent tendency to use heavy-handed methods of family planning in those states (see sections 6.5 and 7.4), in contrast with the more 'collaborative' approach used in Kerala and Tamil Nadu.[45] The regional contrasts within India strongly argue for

---

[44] See chapter 6, and the literature cited there.

[45] There are also other cases of fast progress in fertility reduction through non-coercive methods elsewhere in India. Himachal Pradesh, for instance, is going through a rapid demographic transition, building inter alia on the oustanding expansion of education (especially female education) in recent decades, as well as on comparatively effective and equitable health care services; see chapters 3, 5 and 6.

collaboration (based inter alia on the active and educated participation of women), as opposed to coercion.

India has many lessons to learn from China, but the need for coercion and for the violation of democracy is not one of them. India's democracy is faulty in many ways, but the faults are not reduced by making the system *less* democratic. It is possible to admire China's various achievements and to learn from them, *without* emulating its non-democratic features.

4.10. THE REAL LESSONS FOR INDIA FROM CHINA

The 'dawn' may or may not come up 'like thunder outer China,' but there is, in fact, much to learn from China's experience, if we take a discriminating approach. First, there is the important demonstration of the possibility of bringing market forces to bear on the pursuit of economic development and the elimination of mass deprivation. People moved by the intensity of poverty in India often remain sceptical of what the market mechanism can do. To some extent that scepticism is justified, and indeed we have argued that the market mechanism *on its own* may not take us very far in eliminating deprivation in India, if liberalization goes hand in hand with a continued neglect of other conditions of social progress. But the Chinese experience convincingly demonstrates that, properly supplemented, a thriving market economy can help a great deal to lift the masses out of poverty and transform their living conditions. People who have admired China for its other achievements over the decades cannot sensibly shut their eyes to this rather large message.

Second, China's experience also brings out the complementarity between two essential bases of expansion of social opportunity, namely (1) *supportive public intervention*, especially in fields such as education, health care, social security, and land reforms, and (2) *the market mechanism*—an essential part of effective trade and production arrangements. We discussed how the achievements of the pre-reform period in the former area have helped China to sustain and promote the market-based opportunities in the post-reform period.

Third, China's liberalization programme has certain pragmatic features that distinguish it from some other attempts at surging towards a market economy. The market mechanism has been used in China to create additional channels of social and economic opportunities, without attempting to rely on the market itself as a surrogate social system on its own. There has been no breathless attempt at privatization of state enterprises, and no abdication of governance; instead the focus has been on opening up new possibilities for the private sector together with reforming management practices in collectively-owned enterprises. While the privatization attempts in the former Soviet Union and eastern Europe could not but threaten a large section of the established labour force with deep insecurity, the operative mode of the Chinese reforms has been based on a more positive combination of public-sector reform with expansion of private enterprises.[46] Similarly, in carrying out the rural reforms (based on a new stress on 'household responsibility'), land has been kept under collective ownership, with each adult person in a village—male or female— being entitled to cultivate a given amount of land.[47] This has largely prevented the emergence of a class of dispossessed landless households, and has provided some protection against destitution to the rural population. This combination of collective ownership and individual use rights has been a special feature of Chinese economic reforms.[48] There is a great deal to learn from these and other examples of pragmatic combination of market incentives and state action in China.

Fourth, even with that pragmatism, China's market-oriented reforms have been much more successful in raising income levels and in reducing income poverty than in expanding social services (notably in the field of health care) and the social opportunities that depend on these services. While real incomes have galloped forward, life expectancies have moved upwards rather slowly. Oddly enough, China'a lead over India in life

[46] Even then, China's social security arrangements in urban areas have come under some strain in recent years. These arrangements used to be based on guaranteed employment for urban residents and the social responsibilities of the enterprise. The lifting of restrictions on rural-urban migration in the post-reform period, however, has led to the emergence of a large 'floating population' of unofficial migrants, who do not enjoy the social protection measures that used to be available to registered urban residents. Widespread deprivation among this floating population is a major social concern in China today.

[47] For evidence of the effectiveness, equity and also continued popularity of this combination of collective land ownership with individual use rights in rural China, see Kung and Liu (1997) and Burgess (2000). It is worth noting that this land tenure system also has the positive feature of being gender-symmetric, in the sense that adult women and men have similar entitlements. This contrasts sharply with land rights in India, which are overwhelmingly patrilineal. This is not a trivial matter, considering that patrilineal land rights are a major source of gender inequality and female disadvantage (Agarwal, 1994).

[48] The combination of collective ownership with enterprise responsibility is also a feature of the spectacularly successful 'township and village enterprises' (TVEs). For a good discussion of this aspect of China's TVEs, see Weitzman and Chenggang Xu (1993). See also Byrd and Lin (1990), and the literature cited there.

expectancy has narrowed rather than widened since the reforms began (see Figure 4.4), and despite its massively faster economic growth, China has actually fallen behind Kerala in this field exactly over this period of economic dynamism. In international perspective, post-reform China is a startling example of slow progress in the field of health in spite of very rapid economic growth for more than twenty years.

Finally, while India has much to learn from China in the field of economic and social policy, the lessons do not include any overwhelming merit of China's more authoritarian system. This is not to deny that the larger success of the Chinese efforts at social progress has been, to a great extent, the result of the stronger political commitment of its leadership to eliminating poverty and deprivation. But the less challenged powers of the leaders have also left the Chinese economy and society more vulnerable to the kind of crises and disasters of which the famine of 1958–61 is an extreme example. The general problem of lack of democratic control remains, and has manifested itself in different forms. It has also had implications on such subjects as coercive family planning and the loss of reproductive and political freedoms. The fact that India's record is terrible in many fields where China has done quite well does not provide a good reason to be tempted by political authoritarianism.

In learning from China what is needed is neither *piecemeal emulation* (involving liberalization without the supportive social policies), nor indeed *wholesale emulation* (including the loss of democratic features). There is much to learn from causal analyses relating Chinese policies in different periods to the corresponding achievements. The relationships between the accomplishments in China before and after the economic reforms are particularly important to study. There is much for India to learn from China on a *discriminating* basis.

5

Basic Education as a Political Issue

5.1. BASIC EDUCATION AND SOCIAL CHANGE

The far-reaching personal and social roles of education were discussed in general terms in chapter 2 of this book. In connection with issues of social inequality and political action, which are among the integrating themes of this book, it is important to pursue further the empowerment and redistributive effects of basic education. Literacy is an essential tool of self-defence in a society where social interactions include the written media. An illiterate person is significantly less equipped to defend herself in court, to obtain a bank loan, to enforce her inheritance rights, to take advantage of new technology, to compete for secure employment, to get on the right bus, to take part in political activity—in short, to participate successfully in the modern economy and society. Similar things can be said about numeracy and other skills acquired in the process of basic education.

Basic education is also a catalyst of social change. The contrasts between different states of India, on which we have already commented in chapter 3, provide ample illustration of this elementary fact. For instance, Kerala's historical experience powerfully brings out the dialectical relationship between educational progress and social change: the spread of education helps to overcome the traditional inequalities of caste, class, and gender, just as the removal of these inequalities contributes to the spread of education. Kerala made an early start down that road, in the nineteenth century, leading to wide-ranging social achievements later on. At the other extreme, the educationally backward states of north India have made comparatively little progress in eradicating traditional inequalities, particularly those of caste and gender. There is an intimate connection here. The value of basic education as a tool of social affirmation appears to be well seized by the people. In fact, a common finding of village studies and household surveys is that education is widely perceived by members of socially or economically disadvantaged groups as the most promising means of upward mobility for their children.[1] The empowerment role of basic education was also well understood by many social leaders during the independence movement. Gokhale, for instance, was a strong advocate of the promotion of basic education, and, as soon as the Indian Councils Act of 1909 made it possible for Indians to propose legislative reforms, he formulated a pioneering Elementary Education Bill (later rejected by the British administration) which would have enabled local authorities to introduce compulsory education. Dr Ambedkar, whose own scholarship helped him to overcome the disadvantage and stigma of low caste (indeed 'untouchability'), saw education as a cornerstone of his strategy for the liberation of oppressed castes—a strategy which has been put to good effect in some parts of India, notably Maharashtra. Education was also of paramount concern to Rammohan Roy, Maharshi Karve, Pandita Ramabai, Swami Vivekananda, Jotirao Phule, Rabindranath Tagore, Mahatma Gandhi, Abdul Ghaffar Khan, Jayaprakash Narayan, and numerous other social reformers of the pre-independence period.

The empowerment value of basic education is so obvious that there is something puzzling in the fact that the promotion of education has received so little attention from social and political leaders in the post-independence period. One aspect of this neglect is the flagrant inadequacy of government policy in the field of elementary education; we will return to that.[2] But lack of attention to education has not been confined to government circles. There has also been much neglect of it on the part

[1] For some relevant empirical studies, see Vlassoff (1980, 1996), Nair et al. (1984), J.C. Caldwell et al. (1985), Bara et al. (1991), Chanana (1988, 1996), Drèze and Saran (1995), Probe Team (1999), Lieten (2000), Vasavi (2000), among others. On the relationship between education and social change, see also Nair (1981), A. Basu (1988), Karlekar (1988), Nag (1989), Nautiyal (1989), Verma (1989), Raza (1990), Jeffrey (1992), Lieten (1993), Majumdar (1993), Ghosh et al. (1994).

[2] In India, the term 'elementary education' usually refers to the first eight years of schooling, corresponding to the constitutional goal of universal education until the age of 14, and divided in most states into primary and upper-primary cycles (e.g. classes 1–5 and 6–8).

of political parties, trade unions, revolutionary organizations, and other social movements.[3] Doubts about the empowerment value of education often arise from the conservative nature of the school curriculum. It has been argued, for instance, that education is unlikely to contribute to the emancipation of women, considering that school textbooks and classroom processes often impart patriarchal values.[4] There is, indeed, much scope (in India as elsewhere) for making the schooling process more liberating. The fact remains, however, that an educated person is better equipped to overcome vulnerability and marginalization in modern society, and it is in that sense that education has considerable empowerment value despite all the shortcomings of the present schooling system. The patriarchal orientation of school textbooks, for instance, does not detract from the fact that an educated woman is better placed to liberate herself from the economic dependence on men that shackles so many Indian women, to gain independent access to information, and to make her voice heard within the family. Similarly, an educated labourer is comparatively better placed to avoid exploitative work conditions, or to demand the legal minimum wage, even if he or she has never heard of Marx at school.[5]

Even the act of going to school, in itself, is often an important challenge to traditional inequalities. This applies in particular to the schooling of girls, considering the long history of scepticism towards female education in large parts of the country. Similarly, school participation on the part of children from disadvantaged castes is a major challenge to the conservative upper-caste notion that knowledge is not important or appropriate for members of the lower orders.[6]

---

[3] This feature of social movements in India stands in sharp contrast with the Latin American experience, where basic education has often been a cornerstone of popular mobilization and a major focus of radical politics; see e.g. Archer and Costello (1990).

[4] On this important concern, see e.g. Jeffery and Jeffery (1997, 1998).

[5] As Anand Chakravarti (2001) notes in a recent study of class relations in Bihar, 'lack of education was an overwhelmingly significant factor that emasculated the capacity of labourers to cope with the conditions of existence imposed upon them' (p. 264). For similar observations, see also Bhatia (1998b, 2000).

[6] The influence exercised by this traditional view over a long period is evident in a large number of historical documents, from the second-century *Manusmriti* (which forbids the reading of the Vedas to the lower castes) to the writings of the eleventh century Arab traveller Alberuni (who commented on 'those castes who are not allowed to occupy themselves with science'). There are similar traditional attitudes towards the education of women (see e.g. Chanana 1988), including 'the prevalent view [in the early nineteenth century] that widowhood would result if women were educated' (Karlekar, 1988, p.136).

Even though these traditional attitudes have lost much of their force, the notion that school education is not important or appropriate for the underprivileged continues to have much influence in India.[7] Various ideological convictions have contributed to this mindset, ranging from caste prejudice to distorted interpretations of Gandhi's view that 'literacy in itself is no education'.[8] It is hard to overstate the need for unequivocal rejection of these and other dismissive views of the value of education. A firm commitment to the widespread and equitable provision of basic education is the first requirement of rapid progress in eradicating educational deprivation in India.

5.2. THE STATE OF SCHOOL EDUCATION

The limited reach of basic education in India has been mentioned on several occasions earlier in this book. Before examining some reasons for these low educational achievements, it may be helpful to recapitulate some essential features of the educational situation in India.

Table 5.1 presents a set of relevant indicators.[9] Aside from reporting the figures for India as a whole, we have added some comparative information for Uttar Pradesh and Kerala. This is partly to give an idea of the extent of regional contrasts within India, and partly because the contrast between Uttar Pradesh and Kerala has wider significance, as discussed elsewhere in this book (particularly chapter 3). The figures presented in Table 5.1 are based on two independent and reasonably reliable sources: the decennial censuses and the National Family Health Survey.

We should mention that Table 5.1 makes no use of official data on 'school enrolment', and related statistics published by the Department of Education. Official school enrolment figures are known to be grossly inflated, partly due to the incentives that government employees at different levels have to report exaggerated figures.[10] According to these

---

[7] On this point, see particularly Weiner (1991).

[8] Mahatma Gandhi, cited in Kurrien (1983), p.45. Gandhi's main concern was that education should go *beyond* literacy, but his emphasis on productive handicraft as the foremost school activity, and the related insistence on the financial self-sufficiency of individual schools, have contributed to some confusion in educational policy in the post-independence period, as Kurrien aptly argues.

[9] See Statistical Appendix for further details, including some early results of the 2001 census. The latter are consistent with the corresponding findings of the second National Family Health Survey (1998–9), used in Table 5.1.

[10] For further discussion, see Probe Team (1999), pp. 91–3; also Sen (1970a), Prasad (1987), Drèze and Gazdar (1996), Kingdon and Drèze (1998).

TABLE 5.1 *School Education in India*
Part 1: *Achievements and Diversities, 1991*

	India	Uttar Pradesh	Kerala
Literacy rates (age 7+) for selected groups (%)			
Total population:			
Female	39	25	86
Male	64	56	94
Rural scheduled castes:			
Female	19	8	73
Male	46	39	84
Literacy rates for the 15–19 age group (%)			
Female	55	39	98
Male	75	68	98
School attendance among children aged 6–14[a] (%)			
Rural			
Female	52	43	94
Male	72	72	95
Urban			
Female	79	70	96
Male	85	77	95
Proportion of never-enrolled children in the 10–12 age group[a] (%)			
Female	33	44	0.6
Male	16	19	0.9
Proportion of persons who have completed grade 8[a] (%)			
Age 15+			
Female	20	16	45
Male	41	43	51
Age 15–19			
Female	36	30	77
Male	54	55	73

Note: [a]1992–3 (based on the National Family Health Survey).
Sources: (1) Government of India (2000d), Tables 12, 26, 43 and Sub-table 21, based on 1991 census data. (2) International Institute for Population Sciences (1995a), Tables 3.8 and 3.10, and International Institute for Population Sciences (1995b), Tables 3.6 and 3.7, based on National Family Health Survey data. (3) The figures on proportion of 'never-enrolled' children are calculated from unpublished National Family Health Survey data given in Filmer (1999). For further details, see Statistical Appendix.

TABLE 5.1 *School Education in India*
Part 2: *Progress in the 1990s*

	1992–3		1998–9	
	female	*male*	*female*	*male*
Literacy rates (%)				
Age 15+	34[a]	62[a]	44	72
Age 15–19	55[a]	75[a]	68	85
School attendance, age 6–14 (%)				
Rural	52	72	70	81
Urban	79	85	86	89
Combined	59	75.5	74	83
Proportion of persons aged 15–19 who have completed (%)				
Grade 5	51	73	61	77
Grade 8	36	54	43	56

Note: [a] 1991 (based on census data).
Sources: Calculated from National Family Health Survey (1992–3 and 1998–9) data, as reported in International Institute for Population Sciences (1995a), Tables 3.8 and 3.10, and International Institute for Population Sciences (2000a), Tables 2.7, 2.8 and 2.9. For further details, see Statistical Appendix.

figures, for instance, in 1995–6 the gross enrolment ratio at the primary level (number of children enrolled in primary school as a proportion of the relevant age group) was a heart-warming—if somewhat baffling— 104 per cent, rising to 112 per cent among scheduled castes. State-specific patterns were no less surprising, with the gross enrolment ratio rising to (say) 127 in Nagaland and 131 in Gujarat, while Kerala managed 'only' 97 per cent.[11] These official enrolment figures are impossible to reconcile with the survey-based evidence (see Table 5.1). In contrast, the broad consistency between independent survey data and the official census data gives additional reason to accept these combined sources as being more reliable (certainly much more so than the official enrolment figures).

Coming back to the state of school education in India, it may be helpful to begin by taking note of the situation at the beginning of the nineties (Table 5.1, part 1). The general picture emerging from 1991 census data

[11] Government of India (1997e), pp. 262–4. It is possible, in principle, for the gross enrolment ratio to exceed 100 per cent, due to the enrolment in primary classes of girls or boys outside the standard age group. But this can hardly explain the enormous discrepancy between official enrolment figures and survey-based data on school enrolment and attendance. Indeed, even official figures on 'net enrolment' (proportion of children attending school in a given age group) are much higher than the corresponding survey-based estimates (Kingdon and Drèze, 1998).

is one of dismal educational achievements, with, for instance, about half of the adult population unable to read and write at that time. We have already commented, in earlier chapters, on this general issue of low educational achievements in India. We have noted, for instance, how literacy rates in India are much lower than in China (chapter 4), lower than literacy rates in many east and south-east Asian countries 30 years ago (section 3.3), lower than the average literacy rates for 'low-income countries' other than China and India (section 1.3), and also no higher than estimated literacy rates in sub-Saharan Africa (section 3.1).

This problem of low average literacy rates is exacerbated by enormous *inequalities* in educational achievements. One aspect of these inequalities, already mentioned in chapter 3, concerns the existence of large disparities between different states. In 1991, for instance, the female literacy rate varied from 20 per cent in Rajasthan and 25 per cent in Uttar Pradesh to 86 per cent in Kerala, reflecting highly uneven efforts to expand basic education in different states.[12] There are also large inequalities in educational achievements between urban and rural areas, between different social groups, and of course between men and women. These diverse inequalities, combined with low average literacy rates, entail abysmally low levels of education for disadvantaged sections of the population. To illustrate, the rural female literacy rate in 1991 was only 19 per cent among scheduled castes (which represent 16 per cent of the Indian population); 16 per cent among scheduled tribes (representing 8 per cent of the population); and below 10 per cent (for *all* women aged 7 and above) in many educationally backward districts of Bihar, Madhya Pradesh, Orissa, Rajasthan, and Uttar Pradesh. When different sources of disadvantage are combined (e.g. the handicap of being female is added to that of belonging to a scheduled caste and living in a backward region), the literacy rates for the most disadvantaged groups come down to minuscule figures. For instance, in 1991 the literacy rate among rural scheduled-caste women was below 5 per cent in a majority of districts of Rajasthan; for scheduled-tribe women, it was even below *one* per cent in some districts (e.g. Barmer, Jalor and Jodhpur).

The cumulative effects of different types of social disadvantages on educational achievements are illustrated in Figure 5.1. As the figure indicates, a boy coming from a 'non-poor' upper-caste family is almost certain to enter the schooling system, and even has a very high chance (about 75 per cent) of attaining grade 8. By contrast, a girl from (say) a poor scheduled-caste family has only one chance in five of ever entering

---

[12] The literacy rates cited in this paragraph refer to the age group of 7 years and above, and are based on 1991 census data presented in Government of India (2000d).

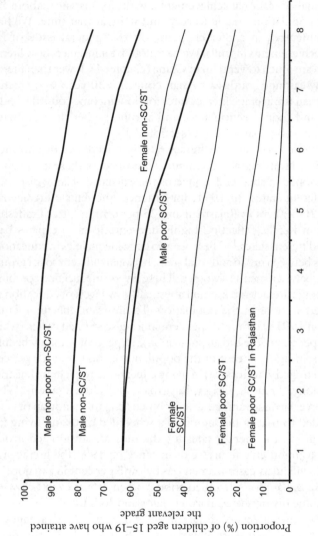

FIGURE 5.1 *Social Disparities in Educational Attainments (India), 1992–3*

Proportion (%) of children aged 15–19 who have attained the relevant grade

Grade attained

Male non-poor non-SC/ST

Male non-SC/ST

Female non-SC/ST

Male poor SC/ST

Female SC/ST

Female poor SC/ST

Female poor SC/ST in Rajasthan

Note: SC Scheduled Castes; ST Scheduled Tribes.
Source: Calculated from National Family Health Survey data given in Filmer (1999).

the schooling system, and is virtually certain never to attain grade 5 (let alone grade 8).

As these figures suggest, another crucial feature of the educational situation in India is that illiteracy is widespread not only in the older age groups (as would apply even in, say, China), but also among young boys and girls, particularly in rural areas. In 1991, for instance, about half of all women in the 15–19 age group were unable to read and write (Table 5.1). In the states of Bihar, Madhya Pradesh, Rajasthan and Uttar Pradesh (which account for about 40 per cent of India's total population), illiteracy among women aged 15–19 was still the rule rather than the exception. Similar failures are apparent from school attendance data: in 1992–3, for instance, about half of all girls aged 6–14 were out of school in rural areas. The persistence of endemic illiteracy and schooling deprivation in the younger age groups is the most shocking aspect of the educational situation in contemporary India.

Turning to more recent developments, there has been significant progress in all these respects in the nineties. This is mainly a continuation of earlier trends, but there are also signs of a perceptible *acceleration* in the progress of literacy and school attendance in the younger age groups in the nineties, compared with earlier decades. Fairly convincing evidence in that direction is available from the National Sample Survey as well as from the second round of the National Family Health Survey, 1998–9 (hereafter NFHS-II).[13] It is encouraging, for instance, to find that school attendance in the 6–14 age group has risen to nearly 80 per cent, according to NFHS-II data (see Table 5.1, part 2). Also noteworthy is the narrowing of gender gaps in school attendance, driven by a comparatively rapid increase in female school participation (e.g. from 59 to 74 per cent between 1992–3 and 1998–9, in the 6–14 age group).[14] The fact that this narrowing reflects, first and foremost, a major increase in female school participation in the educationally backward states is another positive development. Data on age-specific literacy rates also suggest a significant acceleration in the progress of literacy in India in the nineties.

[13] Early results of the 2001 census further corroborate this pattern; see Statistical Appendix.

[14] The NFHS-II school attendance rates are best compared with the corresponding NFHS-I figures (as in Table 5.1), rather than with the 1991 census figures, as there is a substantial discrepancy between census and NFHS-I data for the 6–10 age group. The broad consistency between NFHS-I, NFHS-II and National Sample Survey (1995–6) data on school attendance suggests that these sources are more credible in this respect than the 1991 census data. The NSS figures are given in Government of India (2000d), Tables 51–3.

There are, thus, important signs of faster progress in the field of elementary education, at least in terms of the basic literacy and school attendance indicators. This trend is consistent with independent evidence of a broad-based surge in educational aspirations in recent years.[15] It may also reflect the positive effects of recent initiatives to bring marginalized children into the schooling system, notably in the context of the Total Literacy Campaign, the District Primary Education Programme, the National Programme of Nutritional Support to Primary Education, and various state-specific initiatives under government as well as non-government auspices.

Having said this, it would be a serious mistake to conclude from these indications of accelerated improvement that the constitutional goal of universal education until the age of 14 is about to be reached, and that no major initiatives are required in this regard. There are, indeed, several reasons for continued concern about the schooling situation in India. First, school attendance rates are still quite low in many states. In the large north Indian states (Bihar, Madhya Pradesh, Rajasthan and Uttar Pradesh), about one third to one half of all girls in the 6–14 age group are still out of school. Even in other states, a significant proportion of children who are reported to be 'attending school' in terms of standard survey criteria may not spend many days at school over the year.[16] If the goal of universal school attendance is understood to refer to *regular attendance*, and not just to school enrolment or occasional attendance, much remains to be done in most Indian states.

Second, school attendance figures are a little deceptive for another reason, namely that many children who are 'attending school' make little progress towards the completion of the upper-primary cycle due to ineffective teaching and persistent failure (reflected in high 'repetition' rates). As many studies have noted, it is not uncommon to find children aged 9 or 10 who are still enrolled, say, in class 1 or class 2 because they have learnt very little over the years.[17] If the constitutional goal is interpreted

[15] See Probe Team (1999), particularly chapter 3; also Minturn (1993), Sundararaman (1996), Vyasulu (1998), Lieten (2000), Vasavi (2000), among many others.

[16] There is some evidence that recent drives to boost school enrolment have sometimes resulted in 'nominal' enrolment of children, not matched by regular attendance. The recent increase in school attendance figures has to be interpreted in that light. A similar issue arises with literacy data: literacy figures from NFHS-II, and even from the 2001 census, may be swelled by the inclusion of many semi-literate persons who learnt very basic skills (e.g. writing their names) during recent 'literacy campaigns', without really achieving functional literacy.

[17] One recent study of school enrolment patterns in ten states even finds that, among children enrolled in class 1 in 1992–3, 17 per cent were still in class 1 or 2 six years later (Operations Research Group, 1999, p. IV.20). This finding calls for further

to mean that every child should complete the upper-primary cycle (8 years of education in most states), that goal is still quite distant in every major state, Kerala included. At the all-India level, *less than half* of all children aged 15–19 had completed the upper-primary cycle in 1998–9.[18]

Third, even the completion of the upper-primary cycle is not a momentous achievement on its own, independently of the *quality* of schooling. It is one thing to boost school enrolment, and quite another to ensure that children receive education of acceptable quality, whether in terms of basic learning achievements (e.g. the three Rs) or in terms of broader pedagogical criteria. As things stand, average pupil achievements in Indian schools (particularly government schools) are extremely low, due to overcrowded classrooms, lack of teaching aids, absence of classroom activity, poor teaching standards, and related deficiencies of the schooling system.[19] Much remains to be done to enhance the quality of schooling, even if the quantitative goal of universal 'attendance' is getting closer.

Fourth, the problem of sharp *inequalities* of educational opportunities persists, in spite of the ongoing improvement in school participation. It is even possible that in some respects these social disparities have increased in recent years, due inter alia to the expansion of private schooling opportunities for privileged children, and also, in some areas, to the declining quality of government schools.[20] The egalitarian goal of integrating all children in a 'common schooling system' (as recommended by the Kothari Commission in the 1960s) is as distant as ever.

For these reasons, among others, the improvement of school education (both quantitative and qualitative) continues to demand greater attention as a matter of urgent priority. This is all the more so as exclusion from the schooling system is now overwhelmingly concentrated among girls, disadvantaged communities, and deprived regions. Given the wide-ranging personal and social roles of basic education, discussed earlier, improving educational opportunities for the underprivileged is an essential precondition of social equity. The universalization of elementary education in India is, more than ever, a matter of social justice.

---

scrutiny, based as it is on official enrolment data; nevertheless, there is an alarming indication here of the possible magnitude of the problem of high repetition rates in Indian schools.

[18] Calculated from NFHS-II data presented in International Institute for Population Sciences (2000a), p. 28. See also Table 5.1, and Statistical Appendix, Table A.3.

[19] See Probe Team (1999), p. 28, and other studies cited there, especially Govinda and Varghese (1993).

[20] On the phenomenon of growing 'school differentiation' in India, see Vasavi (2000); also De et al. (2000) and Sanshodhan (2000).

5.3 EDUCATIONAL HOPES AND THE DISCOURAGEMENT EFFECT[21]

The reasons why so many Indian children are out of school have been helpfully elucidated in a number of recent studies.[22] In particular, these studies help to dispel two resilient myths that have tended to cloud official thinking and public debates on this subject. Both myths take the form of oversimplified, single-focus 'explanations' of the problem of educational deprivation in India.

One myth is that Indian parents have little interest in education. This view has been particularly influential in official circles, where it provides a convenient rationalization of the state's failure to achieve universal elementary education in a reasonable time frame. The myth of parental indifference, however, does not survive close scrutiny. Indeed, there is much evidence that an overwhelming majority of Indian parents today, even among deprived sections of the population, attach great importance to the education of their children.[23] To illustrate, the PROBE survey found that, in India's most educationally backward states, the proportion of parents who considered it 'important' for a child to be educated was as high as 98 per cent for boys and 89 per cent for girls.[24] Further, educational aspirations were highly consistent with the constitutional goal of universal elementary education: only a small minority of respondents, for instance, aspired to fewer than 8 years of education for their sons or daughters. Only 3 per cent of parents were opposed to compulsory education at

[21] This section draws extensively on Probe Team (1999), chapter 3, even though the term 'discouragement effect' is used in a somewhat broader sense here. For a similar diagnosis, see Lokshala Team (1996), Lieten (2000), and also various contributions in Vaidyanathan and Nair (2000).

[22] See Caldwell et al. (1985), Prasad (1987), Chanana (1988), Govinda and Varghese (1993), Labenne (1995), Sinha and Sinha (1995), Chaudhri (1996), Drèze and Gazdar (1996), Nambissan (1996, 1997), Banerji (1997), Jayachandran (1997), Maharatna (1997), Majumdar (1997), Senapaty (1997), Srivastava (1997), Bhatty (1998), Bondroit (1998), Sipahimalani (1998), Mehrotra (1999), De et al. (2000), Lieten (2000), Vasavi (2000), Drèze and Kingdon (2001), Kabeer (2001), Leclercq (2001a, 2001b), Ota (forthcoming), among others; also Probe Team (1999) and Vaidyanathan and Nair (forthcoming), and further studies cited there.

[23] This is one fairly consistent finding emerging from the literature cited in the preceding footnote.

[24] Probe Team (1999), p. 14; see also pp. 19–28. The PROBE survey (which took place in late 1996) is based on an investigation of schooling facilities in 188 randomly-selected villages of Bihar, Madhya Pradesh, Rajasthan and Uttar Pradesh, also involving interviews with 1,221 randomly-selected households from these villages. Similar investigations were also carried out in 48 villages of Himachal Pradesh.

the primary level.[25] Similar patterns emerge from NFHS-II data, which indicate, if anything, even stronger parental motivation for education.[26]

This is not to deny that lack of parental motivation (even parental irresponsibility in some cases) may be an issue in specific contexts. Parental commitment to female education, in particular, is still rather inadequate in many areas (we shall return to this in the next section). And even parents who state that education is 'important' may not always translate that interest into practical efforts to send their children to school on a regular basis. Yet, it is important to take note of the generally positive disposition of most parents towards elementary education (indeed universal elementary education), and in particular, of the consistency between parental aspirations and the constitutional goal of eight years of education for all children. As we shall presently discuss, the reasons why that goal remains quite distant today are often 'external' (connected with the accessibility, affordability and quality of schools) rather than 'internal' (reflecting a motivational reluctance).

It is also important to recognize that parental attitudes towards education are far from immutable, and can be positively influenced through various means. For one thing, educational *aspirations* are not independent of the *opportunities* that people have (or perceive that they have). Attitudes towards education, especially female education, are also strongly influenced by cultural norms, role models, public discussions, and related factors. Indeed, as discussed in chapter 2, educational aspirations and schooling decisions have a significant 'social' dimension. For instance, educational aspirations among parents and children of disadvantaged castes are bound to be influenced by *other* people's perceptions of the importance of education for the 'lower castes'. Ultimately, the task to be faced is not just to consolidate the motivation of individual parents, seen as isolated decision-makers, but also to build a social consensus about the centrality of elementary education for every child's upbringing. The possibility of making rapid progress in that direction has been well illustrated in recent years in the context of the Total Literacy Campaign and related initiatives.[27]

A second myth is that the economic dependence of poor families on child labour is the primary reason why so many children are still out of

[25] Another 17 per cent were 'undecided', often for understandable reasons (relating, for instance, to the perceived futility of compelling children to attend non-functional schools). For further discussion, see Probe Team (1999), pp. 14 and 24.

[26] See International Institute for Population Sciences (2000a), pp. 69–72.

[27] See particularly Ghosh et al. (1994), who report that 'tremendous enhancement of demand for primary education and enrolment of children in primary schools have been noticed in many literacy campaign districts' (p.23).

school.[28] Contrary to this presumption, recent studies of the time utilization of Indian children reveal that a large majority of out-of-school children do relatively little work.[29] Most of them are so-called 'nowhere children' (to borrow a term coined by D.P. Chaudhri), i.e. children who are neither going to school nor doing enough work to be counted as members of the labour force even on the basis of fairly broad labour-force participation criteria.

Further, in cases where out-of-school children do work, the direction of causation need not run from child labour to non-attendance. In many cases, it is the other way round: children who are excluded from the schooling system take up productive work (of their own choice or through parental pressure) as a 'default occupation'. One recent case study of working children in Calcutta, for instance, finds that two thirds of these children 'work as they have nothing else to do as the schools are not very attractive and teaching conditions are poor'.[30]

Even among children whose income-earning activities are essential for the family, the time spent in these activities is often relatively small. For many of them, there is also some flexibility of work hours, given that most of the work performed by children consists of family labour at home or in the fields. Bearing in mind that school hours in India are— in practice—quite short (about 4 to 6 hours a day for about half of the days in the year), the proportion of children for whom schooling is ruled out due to rigid work requirements is likely to be small.

The preceding arguments apply especially to young children. As children grow older, work opportunities expand, and so do labour-force participation rates. It is interesting to note, however, that most working children seem to be children who have *never* been to school. This, again, suggests that school deprivation is often a causal antecedent of child

[28] This myth, like that of parental indifference, serves a useful ideological purpose. As Shanta Sinha (1995) points out (pp. 32–3): 'It should be clearly understood that acceptance of the premise that poverty compels parents to send their children to work is extremely convenient to those charged with the responsibility of reducing if not eliminating child labour because in such a case, improving the economic status of the parents becomes the focal point of attention. This is neither the responsibility of the labour or the education department and the buck can be passed elsewhere.'

[29] See especially Chaudhri (1996) and Probe Team (1999), pp. 14–16 and 28–31; also Rustagi (1996), Banerji (1997), Maharatna (1997), Nagarajan (1997), National Council of Applied Economic Research (1996, 1997), National Sample Survey Organisation (1997), Bhatty (1998), Majumdar (1998), Drèze, Lanjouw and Sharma (1998), Duraisamy (2000), Lieten (2000), Leclercq (2001a).

[30] CINI-ASHA (1996), p. 169. For similar observations in Tamil Nadu and Uttar Pradesh, see Kapadia (1997) and Lieten (2000), respectively.

labour, rather than the other way round, since the pressure to work is unlikely to account for a child's failure to be enrolled in class 1 (at a young age, when work opportunities tend to be limited).[31]

To recognize these facts is not, of course, to dismiss the social problems connected with child labour in India, or to deny that child labour may contribute to the persistence of educational deprivation.[32] In localities with a high concentration of industries that, for technological or other reasons, make intensive use of child labour (e.g. match-making in Sivakasi, carpet-weaving in Mirzapur, bangle manufactures in Firozabad, the brassware industry in Moradabad), child labour is both a crucial issue in its own right (especially in light of the hazardous nature of many of these occupations) and a major obstacle to the universalization of elementary education. Even in other areas, household chores and other work responsibilities are a significant obstacle to regular school attendance for specific categories of children. This applies, for instance, to eldest daughters in poor families, who are often expected to look after younger siblings, and also to the children of widowed mothers.[33] It would be quite wrong, however, to view the average out-of-school child as a victim of rigid work responsibilities. There is some overlap between the two problems—child labour and school exclusion—but no congruence. Indeed, child labour and school exclusion are not, as is sometimes claimed, two sides of the same coin: the latter problem is much more extensive than the former, important though both are.

If parents are interested in education, and if most children have enough spare time to attend school, why are so many Indian children out of school? In answering this question, the first point to note is that sending a child to school on a regular basis demands a great deal of effort. To start with, schooling is expensive: even though government schools charge only nominal fees (if any), the costs of textbooks, uniforms, slates, pencils and related items are far from negligible.[34] In addition to the financial costs, sending a child to school demands a good deal of

[31] On this point, see particularly Leclerq (2001a, 2001b).

[32] On various aspects of this problem, see Government of India (1979), Khatu et al. (1983), Burra (1988, 1995), Kanbargi (1991), Weiner (1991), Nieuwenhuys (1994), Chaujar and Ateeq (2000), among many others.

[33] For further discussion (and other examples), see Probe Team (1999), pp. 30–1. It is interesting to note that while low birth-order is a disadvantage (for girls) in this particular respect, the reverse applies in the case of mortality rates, which tend to increase sharply with birth order among girls (see chapter 7).

[34] For various estimates of the private costs of schooling in India, see Probe Team (1999), p. 17, and other studies cited there; also Tilak (1996, 2000a, 2000b).

time and attention, e.g. to prepare the child for school in the morning, stimulate his or her interest, help him or her with homework, and establish a rapport with the teachers. In many respects, these efforts are much more demanding for underprivileged families, especially when the children are first-generation school-goers.

The abysmal quality of Indian schools (on which more below) often discourages parents from making that effort. Indeed, many parents have a dim view of the *schooling system*, even though they are interested in *education* for their children.[35] Survey data confirm that their reservations are far from baseless. To illustrate, the PROBE survey found that there was no teaching activity whatsoever in half of the sample schools at the time of the investigators' (unannounced) visit. Overcrowded classrooms, a crumbling infrastructure, absence of teaching aids and dull teaching methods also undermined the quality of schooling. Pupil achievements were abysmally low, with, for instance, many children unable to read or write even after several years of schooling. In light of these survey findings, it is not surprising that parents often lose patience with government schools, even when they have a genuine interest in education.

The 'discouragement effect' applies not only to parents but also to children. As many observers have noted, the initial disposition of children towards school education tends to be very positive. If the school environment is lively and supportive, children enjoy going to school and learn with enthusiasm.[36] Quite often, unfortunately, the stifling nature of the school environment saps this initial enthusiasm. It is not uncommon, for instance, for children to drop out of school after traumatizing experiences of physical punishment. Even when the discouragement effect does not take that brutal form, children are often gradually put off by the school's alienating curriculum, inactive classrooms and indifferent teachers. Social discrimination in the classroom is another common cause of child discouragement.[37] Recent NFHS-II data support the notion that the school environment often saps the motivation of children: 'lack of interest in studies' on the part of the child is the most important

---

[35] Lieten (2000) makes a similar observation (based on intensive fieldwork in Uttar Pradesh): 'Ambivalence in the attitude of poor parents is the outcome of the conviction that the child, in any case the son, should go to school, and the realisation, on the other hand, that "hardly any teaching is being done"' (p. 2175).

[36] As one parent nicely puts it, '*roti khate khate bhi school bhag jata hai*'— sometimes the child rushes to school in the middle of his breakfast (Sanshodhan, 2000, p. 16). On this point, see also Probe Team (1999), pp. 27–8.

[37] On the latter, see e.g. Drèze and Gazdar (1996), Nambissan (1996), Talib (1999), Vasavi (2000), Sainath (2001c); also Probe Team (1999), pp. 49–51 and 75.

cause of non-attendance among drop-out children, especially among boys.[38]

Focusing on the discouragement effect helps both to dispel the myths discussed earlier, *and* to integrate the underlying concerns (parental indifference and child labour, respectively) with a broader analysis of educational deprivation where the *accessibility, affordability* and *quality* of schooling are centre-stage. The possible dependence of poor families on child labour, for instance, can be seen as a further reinforcement of the discouragement effect since it does make it harder for poor parents to send their children to school. Similarly, weak parental motivation, when it applies, can also be a barrier—a *further* barrier—reinforcing the social environment that makes parents less active in sending their children to school.

Seeing social discouragement as a crucial factor in low school atten-dance also helps to recognise the vast possibilities for public action (both state-based and community-based) in this field. If it were the case that parents are not interested in education, or that children from poor families are too busy to go to school, there might be good reason for concern about the possibility of universalizing elementary education in a reason-able time frame. Contrary to that diagnosis, there is every reason to expect parents and children to respond positively to public initiatives aimed at facilitating their involvement in the schooling system. That expectation is amply confirmed by recent experiences, from the striking popularity of many schools run by non-government organizations among disadvan-taged communities to the overwhelming public response to (say) Madhya Pradesh's 'education guarantee scheme'. The effectiveness of these initia-tives reflects the fact that much can be done without delay to overcome the 'discouragement effect': improving the accessibility of schools, organizing enrolment drives, providing school meals, upgrading the infrastructure, raising teacher-pupil ratios, supplying free textbooks, improving teacher supervision, making the curriculum and classroom processes more child-friendly, to cite a few examples. There is, in short, enormous scope for rapid progress towards universal elementary education. Indeed, one of the crucial lessons of the nineties is the *possibility* of rapid progress in this field—a possibility that remains to be seized in full.

[38] International Institute for Population Sciences (2000a), Table 2.10, p. 35. Parental responses to questions about the reasons why children are not going to school vary significantly between different surveys, possibly because they are sensitive to the manner in which the questions are posed. For further findings on this, see Minhas (1992), Probe Team (1999), International Institute for Population Sciences (2000a), Pradhan and Subramanian (2000).

5.4. ON FEMALE EDUCATION

As mentioned in the preceding section, the PROBE survey found that close to 90 per cent of parents in the sample states (Bihar, Madhya Pradesh, Rajasthan and Uttar Pradesh) considered it 'important' for a girl to be educated.[39] Viewed against a historical background of resilient indifference (and even active opposition) to female education in those states, this finding is highly encouraging. And yet, the fact that about 10 per cent of the respondents considered female education to be of no importance whatsoever is a matter of serious concern. It also suggests that, even among those who did consider it important for a girl to be educated, practical commitment to female education may not be very strong. The social roots of these attitudes deserve closer examination.

The recognition of female education as a social issue is quite recent in India. An influential strand of the conservative traditions of India reserves the study of the Vedas to men of the twice-born castes, and tends to consider female education as a threat to the social order. While it is certainly true that female scholars and writers make spectacular appearances in Indian history (there are indeed many examples of remarkable female intellectuals, such as Maitreyi and Gargee, in the ancient scriptures), nevertheless widespread female literacy is a very recent phenomenon.[40] In fact, at the beginning of the twentieth century, the female literacy rate was below *one* per cent in every province of British India and every 'native state', with a few exceptions such as Coorg, the Andaman and Nicobar Islands, and the native states of Travancore and Cochin in what is now Kerala.[41] Even in Travancore and Cochin, the female literacy rate was below one per cent as late as 1875, and remained as low as 3 per cent in 1901.

Against this historical background, the expansion of female literacy in the twentieth century (and particularly after independence) can be seen as a positive development. In comparative international terms, however, India's record in this respect remains dismal. For instance, as we saw in chapter 3, the available estimates suggest that adult female literacy is higher even in sub-Saharan Africa than in India. A comparison with China

---

[39] The respondents included both women and men, and the responses were quite similar in both cases (Probe Team, 1999, p. 20).

[40] Tharu and Lalita (1991) present a useful anthology of women's writings in Indian history.

[41] Census of India, 1901 (also Ramachandran, 1996, for Travancore and Cochin). The female literacy rate was also above one per cent in what is now Myanmar (Burma), where it was around 4 per cent.

(let alone south-east Asia) is even more gripping: in 1991, when almost half of all Indian women in the 15–19 age group were illiterate, the corresponding figure in China was below 10 per cent (see chapter 4).

The poor functioning of India's schooling system is one reason for the persistence of endemic female illiteracy. In this connection, it is important to stress that the failure of government primary schools in large parts of the country is not gender-neutral, especially in rural areas. As discussed in the case study of Uttar Pradesh in the companion volume (see Drèze and Gazdar, 1996), a common response of parents to the poor functioning or non-functioning of a government-run village school is to send their sons to study in other villages, or in private schools. But the same response is less common in the case of girls, because parents are often reluctant to allow their daughters to wander outside the village, or to pay the fees that would be necessary to secure their admission in a private school. The underdevelopment or breakdown of a government village school typically affects female children much more severely than male children.[42]

This is not to say that low levels of female education in India are exclusively due to the poor functioning of the schooling system. Indeed, even when local teaching standards are relatively good, male participation in education is usually much higher than female participation.[43] The problem of low parental motivation for female education needs attention on its own, in addition to the issue of poor functioning of the schooling system.

The low value attached to female education in much of India links with some deep-rooted features of gender relations. Three of these links have been widely observed.[44]

First, the gender division of labour (combined with patrilineal property rights) tends to reduce the perceived benefits of female education. In rural India, a vast majority of girls are expected to spend most of their adult life in domestic work and child-rearing (and possibly some family labour in agriculture). It is in the light of these social expectations about the adult life of women that female education appears to many parents

[42] Another aspect of the poor quality of the schooling system which may also discourage female education more than male education is the low number of female teachers in many states. While the proportion of female teachers among primary-school teachers is above 70 per cent in Kerala, the corresponding figure is only 35 per cent for India as a whole and 25 per cent in Uttar Pradesh (Government of India, 2000d, p. 47). On the importance of female teachers, see Probe Team (1999), p. 55.

[43] See e.g. Caldwell et al. (1985).

[44] For further discussion, see Drèze and Saran (1995); also Probe Team (1999), pp. 21–5. The focus of the present discussion is primarily on rural areas.

to be of somewhat uncertain value, if not quite 'pointless'. Of course, female education can bring immense benefits even within the limited field of domestic work and child-rearing, but these benefits do not always receive adequate recognition.[45]

Second, the norm of patrilocal exogamy (requiring a woman to settle in her husband's village at the time of marriage and to sever most links with her own family), prevalent in large parts of India, has the effect of further undermining the economic incentives which parents might have to send their daughters to school. Since 'an Indian girl is but a sojourner in her own family', as Sudhir Kakar (1979) aptly puts it, the investments that parents make in the education of a daughter primarily 'benefit' other, distant households. This can strongly reduce the perceived value of female education, at least from the point of view of parental self-interest. The perception is neatly summed up in such popular sayings as 'bringing up a daughter is like watering a plant in another's courtyard.'[46]

Third, the practice of dowry and the ideology of hypergamous marriage (it being thought best that a woman should marry 'up' in the social scale), also influential in large parts of India, can turn female education into a liability. In communities with low levels of *male* education, parents are often apprehensive about educating a daughter, for fear of being unable to find (or to 'afford') a suitably educated groom. Even in communities where basic education is considered to improve a daughter's marriage prospects (because young men expect their brides to have at least some education), 'over-educating' a daughter may make her more difficult—and more expensive—to marry. There is much evidence that these preoccupations are quite real for many parents.[47]

Given these and other links between female education and gender relations, it is not surprising that the twentieth-century progress of female

---

[45] This lack of recognition derives partly from an observational bias (the benefits of female education in household-based activities are less easy to observe than, say, differences in salaries between educated and uneducated men), and partly from the general undervaluation of female activities in a patriarchal society.

[46] Quoted by Leela Dube (1988), p.168. Interestingly, this is a Telugu proverb, confirming the notion that the social influence of patrilocal exogamy is not confined to north India (as Dube herself observes), even though it may be stronger there. For a fine empirical investigation of the relationship between exogamy and the relative neglect of female children, see Kishor (1993).

[47] For further discussion, see Drèze (1998a), Probe Team (1999), p.23, and the studies cited there. Here again, the problem is not confined to north India. In rural Karnataka, for instance, some parents are reported to be worried that education 'would make daughters unmarriageable', because a woman 'must be married to a male with at least as much education' (Caldwell et al., 1985, pp.39, 41).

education has been particularly slow in areas of India (such as the large north Indian states) where the gender division of labour, patrilineal inheritance, patrilocal residence, village exogamy, hypergamous marriage, and related patriarchal norms tend to be particularly influential.[48] The positive side of the same coin is that the expansion of female literacy has been comparatively rapid in areas where gender relations are less patriarchal. Kerala is the most obvious example, but the same observation also applies to varying extents in a number of other states. For instance, in Meghalaya (an overwhelmingly tribal state with a strong matrilineal tradition), there is no gender bias in school attendance. Female school attendance also tends to be comparatively high (with little gender bias if any) in many other parts of the Himalayan region in north and north-east India, including Himachal Pradesh, Uttarakhand, Mizoram, Sikkim and Manipur.[49] As several studies have noted, the patriarchal norms discussed in this section tend to be less rigid in those regions than elsewhere in north India.[50] Himachal Pradesh is a particularly striking example, discussed in section 5.8 below.

In regions with rigid patriarchal norms, it is clear that the considerations involved in educational decisions are radically different for boys and girls. In the case of male education, the economic incentives are strong, because improved education enhances employment prospects, and parents have a strong stake in the economic advancement of their sons (including— but not exclusively—for reasons of old age security). The influence of these economic motives on educational decisions relating to male children emerges clearly in many studies.[51] Economic returns and parental self-interest, on the other hand, provide very weak incentives for female education, given the prevailing gender division of labour, marriage practices, and

---

[48] Punjab and Haryana might seem like exceptions to this pattern. But in fact, the record of these two states in the field of female literacy is quite poor, if one controls for their high income levels. While Punjab and Haryana come first and second in the income scale, they only come sixth and ninth, respectively, in the scale of female literacy (see Table 3.3 in chapter 3). Punjab, however, provides a good example of how attitudes to female education can, in some circumstances, change quite rapidly.

[49] See Statistical Appendix, Tables A.3 (Part 4) and A.4.

[50] See Berreman (1962, 1993), Sharma (1980), Sopher (1980b), Miller (1981), A.K. Shiva Kumar (1992), B. Agarwal (1996), Agnihotri (2000), among others; also section 5.8 below.

[51] See e.g. J.C. Caldwell et al. (1985), Raza and Ramachandran (1990), Drèze and Saran (1995), Sanshodhan (2000), Srivastava (2001b). This pattern is also evident from the PROBE survey: 87 per cent of parents mentioned 'improved employment and income opportunities' as a major reason for educating boys; for girls, only 40 per cent did so (Probe Team, 1999, p. 19).

property rights. Parental concern for the well-being of a daughter in her own right, and recognition of the contribution which education can make to the quality of her life (and that of others), are more important motivations.

Having said this, it would be a mistake to conclude that female education is bound to trail well behind male education (and to rise mainly in response to the 'demand' of educated boys for educated brides). In fact, one major lesson of the 1990s is that parental commitment to female education can change very substantially over a short period of time under the impact of economic change, public action, and social movements. For instance, the provision of a mid-day meal in the local school has been found to reduce the proportion of out-of-school girls by as much as 50 per cent.[52] Parental attitudes have also been strongly influenced by well-planned campaigns, e.g. under the umbrella of the Total Literacy Campaign.[53] Even in states such as Rajasthan, where gender bias in education and related gender inequalities are extremely large, there have been effective initiatives in this respect in recent years, leading to a major rise in female school attendance (from 41 to 63 per cent between 1992–3 and 1998–9, according to the National Family Health Survey). Bearing in mind the 'social dimension' of educational decisions, discussed earlier, these achievements are perhaps not entirely surprising, but they are nevertheless remarkable enough. There is every reason to expect positive achievements based on further public activism in that direction.

5.5. THE SHIFTING GOALPOST OF UNIVERSAL ELEMENTARY EDUCATION

Education policy in India since independence has been characterized by a deep inconsistency between ends and means.[54] One of the directive principles of the Constitution (Article 45) urges the state to provide free and compulsory education up to the age of 14 by 1960. This was an

[52] Drèze and Kingdon (2001). On the effectiveness of school meals and related 'incentives' in enhancing school attendance, see also Rajan and Jayakumar (1992) and Sipahimalani (1998), among others.

[53] On the high involvement of women in this campaign (both as learners and as instructors), and the diverse achievements linked with this positive response, see Ghosh et al. (1994); also Agnihotri and Sivaswamy (1993), Rao (1993), Saldanha (1994), Athreya and Chunkath (1996), Sundararaman (1996).

[54] Various aspects of this problem have been noted in a number of distinguished analyses of educational policy in India, including Naik (1975a, 1975b, 1982), Kurrien (1983), K. Kumar (1991), Weiner (1991, 1994), Tilak (1995).

ambitious goal, and the practical measures that were taken to implement it have fallen far short of what was required. To this day, the provision of educational facilities remains completely out of line with the stated goal of universal school education until the age of fourteen.

This basic inconsistency of ends and means is also reflected in a series of commission reports and policy statements that have appeared since 1947. The elusive goal of providing free and compulsory education until the age of 14 within a few years has been regularly reiterated, without any corresponding improvement of schooling facilities. In 1986–7, nearly half of all rural children in the 6–11 age group had never been enrolled in any school.[55] This did not prevent the National Policy on Education of 1986 from declaring with blind optimism that 'by 1995 all children will be provided free and compulsory education up to 14 years of age' (Singha, 1992, p.12), without giving any sense of the radical policy changes that would be needed to achieve this goal. Not surprisingly, the cheerful expectations of instant success did not materialize.

The revised National Policy on Education, 1992, is in line with the earlier tradition.[56] Despite stressing that it was 'imperative for the Government to formulate and implement a new Education Policy for the country' (p.4), the Policy did little more than to repeat the old credo with a different time frame: 'it shall be ensured that free and compulsory education of satisfactory quality is provided to all children up to 14 years of age before we enter the twenty-first century' (p.20). Once again, the Policy gave little hint of the practical steps that would make this so-called 'resolve' a reality. Instead it enunciated a remarkable collection of platitudes such as 'all teachers should teach and all students should study' (p. 34), 'the New Education Policy ... will adopt an array of meticulously formulated strategies based on micro-planning to ensure children's retention at school' (p.20), and 'a warm, welcoming and encouraging approach, in which all concerned share a solicitude for the needs of the child, is the best motivation for the child to attend school and learn' (p.18). Nevertheless, the authors felt able to conclude with an upbeat note:

The future shape of education in India is too complex to envision with precision. Yet, given our tradition which has almost always put high premium on intellectual and spiritual attainment, we are bound to succeed in achieving our objectives.

[55] P. Visaria et al. (1993), p.53.
[56] All the quotes in this paragraph are from Government of India (1992c). This document spells out the policy of the central government, and leaves room for wide differences in state-level policies, which have indeed varied a great deal in content and effectiveness.

The main task is to strengthen the base of the pyramid, which might come close to a billion people at the turn of the century. Equally, it is important to ensure that those at the top of the pyramid are among the best in the world. Our cultural well springs had taken good care of both ends in the past; the skew set in with foreign domination and influence. It should now be possible to further intensify the nation-wide effort in Human Resource Development, with Education playing its multifaceted role.[57]

The inconsistency between ends and means has continued in the nineties. To illustrate, consider recent trends in public expenditure on education. Judging from election manifestoes, every major political party today is committed to raising public expenditure on education to 6 per cent of GDP.[58] Yet, the ratio of public education expenditure to GDP has actually *declined* in the nineties under successive governments, from a peak of 4.4 per cent in 1989 to 3.6 per cent or so towards the end of the decade.[59]

Due to this persistent neglect of elementary education in official policy, schooling facilities in India remain grossly inadequate in relation to the constitutional goal of free and universal education until the age of 14. Some progress has of course been made, particularly in terms of the physical accessibility of primary schools: in 1993, about 94 per cent of the rural population lived within one kilometre of a primary school.[60] However, basic infrastructural requirements are still far from being met in most states. Indeed, the recent PROBE survey found gross inadequacies in this respect in four sample states (Bihar, Madhya Pradesh, Rajasthan, Uttar Pradesh), involving for instance large pupil-teacher and pupil-classroom ratios, endemic shortages of basic teaching aids, dilapidated buildings, and lack of essential facilities such as drinking water. These deficiencies, and related problems mentioned earlier (e.g. low levels of classroom activity) are illustrated in Table 5.2. At the upper-primary level, even physical accessibility was still a serious problem: only 29 per cent of the sample villages had an upper-primary school.

There has been improvement in some of these respects since 1996 (the reference year for this survey). Yet, more recent data indicate that the basic inadequacies continue. To illustrate, according to 1999–2000

[57] Government of India (1992c), p. 50.
[58] This was one of the recommendations of the Kothari Commission report, submitted in 1966.
[59] Government of India (2000d), p. ii. The figure of 3.6 per cent applies to 1997, the latest year for which data are available in that publication. On patterns of education expenditure in India, see also Tilak (1995) and Bashir (2000).
[60] Aggarwal (2000), p. 25, based on the Sixth All-India Educational Survey.

TABLE 5.2 *School Facilities in North India, 1996*

Average pupil-teacher ratio in primary schools	50
Average number of pupils per classroom	83
Proportion (%) of primary schools with at least two classrooms and a non-leaking roof	26
Proportion (%) of primary schools with	
blackboard in every classroom	74
lockable building	61
playground	48
drinking-water facility	41
maps and charts	41
toys	25
toilet	11
Proportion (%) of primary schools where there had been no inspection during the preceding 12 months	26
Proportion (%) of primary schools where the headteacher was absent when the investigators arrived	33
Proportion (%) of primary schools where there was no teaching activity when the investigators arrived	48

Source: Probe Team (1999), pp. 40–4, 47, 87, 89, 103, based on a detailed survey of school facilities in 188 randomly selected villages of Bihar, Madhya Pradesh, Rajasthan and Uttar Pradesh. This table refers to government schools only (these account for 80 per cent of all primary schools in the sample villages).

data from the 'District Information System for Education' initiated under the District Primary Education Programme (DPEP): (1) 58 per cent of India's primary schools have at most two teachers (20 per cent have a single teacher); (2) 61 per cent of primary schools have no female teacher; (3) 26 per cent have a pupil-teacher ratio above 60; (4) 35 per cent have a pupil-classroom ratio above 60.[61] The DPEP data also indicate that these and related inadequacies are not confined to the 'problem states' covered by the PROBE survey—they apply to a varying extent in all the major states, with the notable exception of Kerala.

The lack of preparedness of the schooling system for universal elementary education is one reason for the government's reluctance to recognise elementary education as a 'fundamental right', despite recent electoral promises to do so on the part of every major political party. This is yet another example of the glaring contrast between rhetoric and action in this field. We shall return to this issue in section 5.9.

[61] Aggarwal (2000), pp. 40, 72, 79 and 83. The figures pertain to 127 DPEP districts in 13 major states.

5.6. PUBLIC EXPENDITURE AND EDUCATION POLICY[62]

The basic inconsistency between ends and means in education policy persists to this day. In some respects, the inconsistency has even grown in recent years under the pressure of fiscal austerity.

On the positive side, the nineties have seen a surge of popular interest in elementary education, as discussed earlier. The subject has also received increasing attention in media discussions, public debates and parliamentary proceedings. The central government, in particular, has been under much pressure to play a more active role in this field. On the other side, both central and state governments have been coping with growing budgetary imbalances and forceful calls for fiscal discipline. The 'discipline' has often been highly selective, with the financial axe falling on the relatively 'soft' sectors while largesse continued in other domains, where attempts to restrain public expenditure came up against well-organized lobbies.

These contrasting demands (for an expansion of schooling facilities on the one hand, and fiscal discipline on the other) have led to different responses from the central and state governments, respectively. The central government has considerably expanded its activities in the field of elementary education in the 1990s, with a little help from foreign funds (e.g. under the umbrella of the District Primary Education Programme).[63] The state governments, for their part, have tended to refrain from major expansions of public expenditure on education. In fact, as a proportion of the 'state domestic product', public expenditure on elementary education has *declined* in a majority of states in the 1990s (see Table 5.3). In Uttar Pradesh and West Bengal, real per-capita expenditure on elementary education has even declined in *absolute* terms during that period.

The reference period in Table 5.2 ends in 1997–8, the latest year for which adequately detailed data are available. Budgetary pressures on education sharply intensified in recent years, due to the combined effects of (1) bankruptcy of state governments, and (2) large increases in teacher salaries (based on the recommendations of the 'Fifth Pay Commission', amplified by the central government under trade-union pressure).[64] State-level education policies have tended to adapt to this budgetary squeeze

---

[62] We are grateful to Amarjeet Sinha (former Director, Elementary Education, Ministry of Human Resource Development) for helpful clarifications relating to the issues discussed in this section.

[63] On the District Primary Education Programme, see e.g. World Bank (1997b). For a spirited critique, see Kumar, Priyam and Saxena (2001).

[64] Salary expenditure accounts for about 95 per cent of public expenditure on

TABLE 5.3 *Trends in Public Expenditure on Elementary Education in the 1990s*

	Growth rate of real per-capita expenditure on elementary education, 1990–1 to 1997–8[a] (% per year)	Share of elementary education expenditure in net state domestic product	
		1990–1	1997–8
Maharashtra	5.9	1.2	1.3
Orissa	4.9	2.5	2.8
Assam	4.6	2.6	3.7
Karnataka	4.3	2.0	1.9
Himachal Pradesh	3.3	4.1	n/a
Rajasthan	3.3	2.4	2.5
Haryana	2.8	1.2	1.1
Gujarat	2.7	1.9	1.6
Tamil Nadu	1.5	2.3	1.8
Madhya Pradesh	0.9	2.0	1.9
Andhra Pradesh	0.7	1.5	1.2
Kerala	0.7	3.3	2.1
Bihar	0.4	3.3	3.6
Uttar Pradesh	−1.8	2.5	2.0
West Bengal	−2.5	1.5	1.0
15 states combined [b]	1.4	2.0	1.8

Notes: [a] Using WPI deflator (see Bashir 2000, pp. 26–7, for discussion).
[b] Weighted average of the state-specific figures, using the relevant weights.
Source: Calculated from Bashir (2000), Tables 2.4, 2.5, 2.9, 2.10 and Annex Table 2.9. We are grateful to Sajitha Bashir for helpful advice and clarifications. The states are listed in decreasing order of the growth rate of real per-capita expenditure on elementary education.

in two ways. First, there has been growing reliance on 'centrally-sponsored schemes', notably the foreign-funded District Primary Education Programme and the National Programme of Nutritional Support to Primary Education. Second, and more importantly, the expansion of schooling facilities has increasingly taken the form of low-cost, 'second-track' arrangements. These involve, for instance, the creation of non-formal education centres in areas where no schooling facilities existed earlier, or the appointment of *shiksha karmis* (literally 'education workers'—in effect,

---

elementary education. Salary increases therefore tend to have a high opportunity cost in terms of non-salary expenditure (or new teacher appointments). On related issues, see Drèze and Sen (1995a), pp. 120–3; also Mehrotra and Buckland (2001).

para-teachers) in such centres as well as in under-staffed schools. Some states, notably Madhya Pradesh, have developed low-cost facilities on a large scale, and this 'formula' is increasingly considered as the way forward in other states as well. In fact, during the last few years, appointments of regular teachers have been 'frozen' in many states, with new appointments being confined to low-cost para-teachers. Since 1997–8, the number of regular teachers posted in primary schools has declined in absolute terms in most states.[65]

While the development of low-cost schooling facilities has helped to expand the reach of elementary education in spite of widespread budgetary crises at the state level, gaping inadequacies remain (both in quantitative and qualitative terms) in the schooling infrastructure, as the findings mentioned in the preceding section indicate. Further, the trend towards increasing reliance on second-track education facilities has some troubling features.[66] At least three serious issues arise in this context, related respectively to *quality, equity* and *sustainability.*

The quality issue is concerned with the fact that teacher qualifications and infrastructural facilities are often poorer in second-track schooling facilities than in regular schools. In some cases there are also compensating features, especially greater accountability (e.g. due to better work incentives or closer community involvement), but the question remains whether these facilities can really be expected to deliver education of acceptable quality.

The equity issue follows from that concern: if 'second-track' means 'second-rate', the expansion of alternative schooling facilities involves a real danger of diluting the right of underprivileged children to quality education. While these facilities might help them in the short term, this might be done at the risk of perpetuating the deep inequities of India's schooling system, whereby children of different social backgrounds have vastly different educational opportunities (not only in terms of the divide between government and private schools but now also within the framework of government schools).

Even in cases where quality and equity issues are somehow resolved, an important question remains about the sustainability of second-track schooling facilities. These arrangements tend to be somewhat *ad hoc* and essentially fragile; a change of government, for instance, can undermine the political backing on which non-formal education schemes often depend.

[65] Government of India, *Selected Educational Statistics,* various years. For a useful review of para-teacher programmes in different states, see Dayaram (2001).

[66] For further discussion, see Probe Team (1999), pp. 97–101; also Drèze (1998b) and Leclercq (2001c).

Also, the effectiveness of second-track schooling facilities often hinges on strong accountability mechanisms, in which the insecure terms of employment of instructors play an important role. Continual use of 'double standards' of employment between regular teachers and informal instructors is often difficult politically, ethically and legally.[67]

These respective issues (quality, equity and sustainability) need to be addressed in context, and it would be inappropriate to 'applaud' or 'dismiss' low-cost schooling independently of that context. There have, indeed, been successes as well as failures in this field. For instance, the first wave of 'non-formal education centres' initiated by the central government in the 1980s was a resounding failure.[68] By contrast, preliminary evaluations of Madhya Pradesh's 'education guarantee scheme' suggest significant achievements, particularly in terms of bringing schooling facilities within reach of the underprivileged.[69] This does not provide the basis of an unconditional endorsement of the second-track formula, but it does indicate the possibility of making good use of that approach, with adequate political commitment. The overall achievements and potential of this approach remain somewhat uncertain at this time, in the absence of detailed, independent evaluations of its diverse applications.

Much depends also on whether second-track schooling facilities are intended as a *temporary supplement* to regular schools, or as a *permanent substitute* for them. If the provision of such facilities is integrated with a coherent plan for the universalization of elementary education in a non-discriminatory schooling system, they may have something important to contribute in the short-term. Providing special learning facilities for drop-out children, for instance, is certainly a useful move, as is posting a para-teacher in a provisionally under-staffed school. On the other hand, if second-track schooling facilities are treated as a permanent substitute for formal schools in underprivileged areas, they may end up institutional-

---

[67] Legal petitions demanding 'equal pay for equal work' have been submitted by para-teachers in several states, notably Madhya Pradesh. In the latter case, the Supreme Court ruled that the panchayats were entitled to define the service conditions of their own employees, independently of those of state government employees. Thus, para-teachers (who are, formally, employees of the panchayats in Madhya Pradesh) lost the case.

[68] For further discussion, see Probe Team (1999), chapter 8; also Shariff (1999), pp. 127–8. The latter study indicates that, in 1993–4, only 1.5 per cent of children not enrolled in school were studying in a 'non-formal education centre' (officially, there is one such centre in every other village or so), and that only 1.7 per cent of children studying in a non-formal education centre could 'read and write fluently'.

[69] See e.g. Vyasulu (1998), Jha (2000), Leclercq (2001c), Srivastava (2000).

izing—instead of eliminating—the prevailing disparities of educational opportunities. There are worrying signs that this is the direction in which the schooling system is moving in some parts of the country.

The 'compartmentalization' of the schooling system in the nineties has been further enhanced by the rapid growth of private schooling, itself closely related to the inadequacies of government schools. With government schools increasingly falling short of parental expectations, private schools have tended to fill the gap for those who can afford it. In rural India, the proportion of children aged 6–14 enrolled in private schools was already above 30 per cent in 1994.[70] There are indications of a further acceleration in effective privatization in the late nineties, especially in areas where government schools are in bad shape. A similar trend applies in urban areas, where the corresponding proportion is estimated to have risen to 80 per cent or more in some cases.[71]

In short, there are grounds for serious concern about the growing social differentiation of schooling opportunities in India, both within the government schooling system and between government and private schools. This differentiation, in turn, could lead to further decay of government schools, as public pressure to improve them is undermined by the growing reliance of influential groups on private schools.[72] Reversing these tendencies calls for a radical upgrading of schooling facilities, backed by a renewed commitment to the universalization of elementary education on a non-discriminatory basis.

5.7. SCHOOL QUALITY AND THE NEED FOR ACCOUNTABILITY

As was argued earlier, overcoming the 'discouragement effect' depends crucially on improving the accessibility, affordability and quality of schooling in India. Much can be done without delay in that respect: opening more schools, improving the infrastructure, appointing more teachers, simplifying

[70] Shariff (1999), Table 6.8, p. 120, based on National Council of Applied Economic Research data ('government-aided' private schools are included in this figure). On private schooling in India, see also Kingdon (1996), De, Majumdar, Samson and Noronha (2000), Tilak and Sudarshan (2000).

[71] See e.g. Kingdon (1994) and De, Majumdar, Samson and Noronha (2000).

[72] As Krishna Kumar, a distinguished educationist, warned many years ago: 'the state supported part of the school education system is crumbling everywhere because proliferation of private schooling has siphoned off the concern of the educated and vocal middle class' (Kumar, 1986, p. 566). This issue is not specific to India, and was indeed discussed in general terms by Albert Hirschman (1970) in his insightful analysis of the relation between 'exit' and 'voice' as accountability devices.

the curriculum, organizing enrolment drives, providing free textbooks, to cite a few examples. The effectiveness of such initiatives has been well demonstrated in states where elementary education has received comparatively high political priority, e.g. Tamil Nadu and Himachal Pradesh (both of which have made rapid progress towards universal elementary education in recent years). Even in Rajasthan, sustained efforts to improve schooling opportunities in the nineties have achieved significant results, as can be seen from the comparatively rapid progress of school attendance (especially female attendance) in that state.[73]

The primary challenge, however, is to improve teaching standards in the classroom. As was mentioned earlier, the PROBE survey found that there was no teaching activity in half of the sample schools at the time of the investigators' visit. Even in the 'active' schools, teaching methods were far from engaging. Slow educational progress of pupils and the unstimulating nature of the school environment are major causes of parental and child discouragement.

Low teaching standards, in turn, have two distinct roots. First, the disempowering environment in which many teachers have to work often saps their motivation. A teacher trapped in a ramshackle school, surrounded by disgruntled parents, irregular pupils and corrupt inspectors can hardly be expected to work with enthusiasm. Second, low teaching standards reflect an endemic lack of accountability in the schooling system. As the PROBE report notes, for instance, low levels of classroom activity have become a 'way of life in the profession', even when the work environment is relatively supportive.[74]

Low teaching standards are not the only reason to be concerned about the lack of accountability in the schooling system. Accountability failures also tend to erode many other aspects of the quality of schooling, from the timely arrival of free textbooks to the proper maintenance of school premises and honest conduct of examinations. As these examples suggest, the issue is not just teacher accountability, but the erosion of accountability in the schooling system as a whole. The two are indeed

---

[73] See Statistical Appendix, Table A.3, Part 4. Recent initiatives in Rajasthan include the Lok Jumbish programme (initiated in 1992), substantial pupil incentives (e.g. free textbooks), widespread provision of teaching aids, and a major expansion of second-track education facilities. Signs of positive change in Rajasthan were already noted in the PROBE report (Probe Team, 1999, pp. 93–4).

[74] Probe Team (1999), p. 63. See also pp. 62–7, for further discussion of accountability issues. A third cause of low teaching standards is the growing 'social distance' between teachers and pupils in government schools; we shall return to that.

closely related. Teacher absenteeism, for instance, has much to do with the corruption of inspection procedures.[75] Also, one reason why teachers' organizations have resisted the introduction of stronger accountability mechanisms, and even worked to dismantle existing ones, is that these accountability mechanisms have a tendency to become instruments of arbitrary harassment. Teacher promotions, for instance, have been widely used for political purposes (rather than as an incentive device), reinforcing the determination of teachers' unions to press for automatic promotion based on seniority rather than professional record. Similarly, when the Government of Madhya Pradesh introduced a rule whereby teachers could not draw their monthly salary without a signature of approval from the village head, the new-found power of village heads over schoolteachers was often misused.[76]

Restoring accountability in the schooling system is a major political challenge. The first step is to recognize the problem and bring it within the scope of public debate. There has, indeed, been great reluctance to address this issue, because of its political sensitivity and the strong interests involved in a continuation of the status quo. There are interests on the other side, too, but the victims of the status quo (underprivileged children and their families) tend be much less organized and influential. This asymmetry of power and influence (between teachers and administrators on the one hand, and underprivileged parents on the other) is a crucial feature of the political economy of schooling in India. However, this situation is not immutable, and there are many possibilities for building countervailing power on the latter side through political action.

As far as practical means of restoring accountability are concerned, there is scope for action both 'from above' and 'from below'. Examples of top-down accountability mechanisms include school inspections, promotion rules, and answerability to 'superiors' in the bureaucratic hierarchy. Using these procedures in a fair and restrained manner is a difficult task. On the one hand, over-emphasis on top-down accountability procedures carries a danger of these procedures being abused by those who control them (as has happened, for instance, in the field of family planning—see chapter 6). On the other hand, over-relaxing these procedures

---

[75] For a good case study of the ineffectiveness of official school inspection procedures, see Prasad (1987), pp. 75–81; see also Probe Team (1999), pp. 89–91.

[76] The rule was later modified: *two* different members of the 'village education committee' (including the village head) are now authorized to sign. This reduces the power of the village head while preserving some accountability of teachers to the community (Farooque Siddiqui, Rajiv Gandhi Shiksha Mission, personal communication).

opens the door to the corruption of the work culture in the schooling system. While public policy needs to be alive to both dangers, it is arguable that the second one is more serious at this time, as far as the schooling system is concerned.

Accountability from below relies first and foremost on the vigilance of parents. Unlike government inspectors, who often prosper by extorting bribes from errant teachers, parents have a strong personal interest in an improved performance of schoolteachers. The problem is that, as things stand, they have no easy means of taking action. In most states, teachers are accountable to the Education Department, not to the village community. Official complaints have to go through complicated bureaucratic channels, which are particularly forbidding for underprivileged or uneducated parents. Reforming the chain of accountability, and bringing the levers of control closer to the village community, are important means of improving teaching standards. In fact, this route has already been used with good effect in some parts of the country. In Karnataka, for instance, it is reported that the panchayati raj experiment initiated in the late 1980s considerably reduced absenteeism and shirking among teachers, health workers and other government employees in rural areas. As one study puts it, 'all manner of government employees were now made to work because they were for the first time under the supervision of the questioning public mind'.[77] In Tamil Nadu, too, it has been observed that 'close monitoring by a politically conscious parent community' has been an essential factor in the success of pre-school education and school meal programmes (Swaminathan, 1991, p. 2989). As many observers have noted, accountability to the village community is also an important reason why para-teachers (who, unlike regular teachers, are often directly answerable to the local *panchayat*) have done reasonably well in many states, in spite of limited formal qualifications and difficult work conditions.

Accountability from below depends on achieving a measure of 'democratization' of the education system, in the sense of an active involvement of parents and other concerned citizens in the management of schools. Democratization must not be confused with decentralization, in the sense of a formal delegation of responsibilities to local bodies. Decentralization can certainly contribute to democratization, but the former does not guarantee the latter (we shall have more to say on this in chapter 10). To illustrate, in many villages the top-down formation

---

[77] Crook and Manor (1998), p.60. Similar observations are reported in Aziz (1994), p.26, Seetharamu (1994), p.45, Vyasulu (1995). Karnataka's decentralization experiment, however, was substantially reversed after a change of government in 1989.

of a 'village education committees' (VEC) in response to government directives has failed to foster genuine popular participation in schooling matters.[78] The possibility of going beyond those token gestures of decentralization, and of fostering genuine popular participation in school management, is one important lesson of recent experiences such as the Lok Jumbish programme in Rajasthan and Madhya Pradesh's 'education guarantee scheme'. In both cases, this has involved a much broader programme of social mobilization than the bureaucratic formation of village education committees.

These recent experiences also highlight the crucial complementarity between accountability from above and from below. Just as accountability from above has important limitations when it is used on its own, accountability from below may achieve little in the absence of state support. To illustrate, it has been observed that school inspectors in north India rarely take the trouble of talking with parents.[79] This reduces the effectiveness not only of the inspection system (accountability from above), but also of parental vigilance (accountability from below). Indeed, parents have little reason to take active interest in school management issues if their complaints and suggestions fall on deaf ears. For their role to be effective, it has to receive a positive response from higher levels of the education administration (not necessarily via school inspectors). It is the *combination* of more responsible management with greater democratization that may hold the best promise of restoring accountability in the schooling system.

This observation is one example of the general complementarity, discussed in chapter 2, between state initiative and cooperative action. In the context of education, this complementarity comes into play at many different levels, not just in relation to the issue of accountability. For instance, while the state bears the main responsibility for providing school facilities and appointing teachers, cooperative action has much to contribute in ensuring that all parents are able to send their children to school (e.g. through 'enrolment drives' organized under the auspices of a village panchayat). This complementarity between state initiative and cooperative action has played a major role in the 'schooling revolution' in Himachal Pradesh, examined in the next section.

[78] See Probe Team (1999), p. 66. As one teacher put it to the investigators: '*VEC bolo, PTA bolo, jo sarkar ka hukum hai, vo hum karte hain*' (call it the Village Education Committee, call it the Parent-Teacher Association, we follow whatever orders the government gives us). On this issue, see also Mehrotra (2001b).

[79] Probe Team (1999), p. 90.

5.8. THE SCHOOLING REVOLUTION IN HIMACHAL PRADESH

As recently as 1961, literacy rates in Himachal Pradesh were lower than the corresponding all-India averages in every age group. In fact, at that time, Himachal Pradesh was in the same league as India's most educationally backward states. Since then, the state has made spectacular progress towards universal elementary education (see Figure 5.2). The literacy rate among girls aged 15–19, for instance, shot up from 11 per cent in 1961 to 86 per cent in 1991.[80] Further rapid progress has been achieved in the 1990s: in 1998–9, school attendance in the 6–14 age group was an astonishing 97 per cent for boys and even higher for girls (see Statistical Appendix, Table A.3). In this respect Himachal Pradesh had caught up with Kerala, and was well ahead of all other states.[81]

In some respects, Himachal Pradesh's transition from mass illiteracy to near-universal elementary education has been even more impressive than Kerala's. First, this transition has taken place over a much shorter period of time in Himachal Pradesh than in Kerala, where sustained educational expansion began in the 19th century. Second, educational expansion in Himachal Pradesh has been based almost entirely on government schools, with relatively little contribution from private schools, missionary organizations and related institutions.[82] Third, Himachal Pradesh's topography and settlement pattern (with small villages scattered over large and often inaccessible areas) is not favourable to the expansion of public services in rural areas, in sharp contrast with Kerala where rural settlements are highly accessible. Fourth, child labour used to play an important role in Himachal Pradesh's economy, partly due to the dependence of many households on environmental resources and also (in the case of girls) to the fact that a high proportion of adult women work outside the household.

The foundations of the 'schooling revolution' in Himachal Pradesh await detailed investigation, but meanwhile, recent studies shed some

[80] Government of India (2000d), Tables 40 and 43, based on census data.

[81] In fact, for the 6–17 age group, Himachal Pradesh was doing *even better* than Kerala: 94 per cent school attendance (with virtually no gender bias), compared with 91 per cent in Kerala. See International Institute for Population Sciences (2000a), Table 2.9.

[82] In 1994, 95 per cent of children aged 6–14 in rural Himachal Pradesh were enrolled in government schools—a higher figure than in any other Indian state (Shariff, 1999, p. 120).

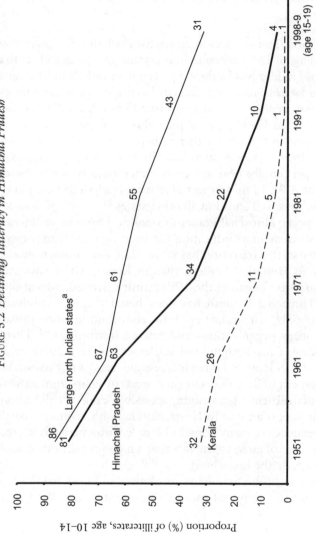

FIGURE 5.2 *Declining Illiteracy in Himachal Pradesh*

Notes: [a] Bihar, Madhya Pradesh, Rajasthan, Uttar Pradesh.

Sources: Calculated from census data presented in Government of India (2000d), pp. 147–86, and (for 1951) Probe Team (1999), p. 116. The 1998–9 figures pertain to the 15–19 (rather than 10–14) age group, and are based on National Family Health Survey data (International Institute for Population Sciences, forthcoming).

useful light on this subject.[83] The relatively low level of poverty in Himachal Pradesh is one relevant consideration. This factor alone, however, does not explain why Himachal Pradesh is much closer to universal elementary education than (say) Punjab and Haryana, which are even better off economically.[84] The hypothesis that Himachal Pradesh's success is primarily income-driven would also be difficult to reconcile with recent studies of the determinants of school attendance in rural India.[85] Some of Himachal Pradesh's most striking achievements, e.g. the virtual elimination of gender bias in schooling opportunities, would be particularly hard to explain in those terms. Similar remarks apply to other single-focus explanations Himachal Pradesh's success, e.g. the notion that it is based on the demonstration effects of public-sector recruitment. These and other factors have certainly played a role, but a convincing account of the dramatic changes that have taken place there in recent years (not only in the field of elementary education, but also in terms of many other areas of social development) requires a broader canvas.

Broadly speaking, the schooling revolution in Himachal Pradesh can be plausibly interpreted in terms of a virtuous circle of state initiative (involving a massive expansion of schooling facilities) and public response (leading to active utilization of these facilities and further pressure for state investment).

As discussed in chapter 3, social development in Himachal Pradesh (and also, to varying extents, in other parts of the Himalayan region) has been facilitated by a relatively favourable social context, which includes the comparative lack of sharp social disparities in village communities and a strong tradition of local cooperative action. It may be worth spelling out why this particular feature of Himachal Pradesh's social structure has facilitated the spread of education. This happens in at least four different ways. First, social equality facilitates the emergence of consensual social norms on educational matters. Indeed, a striking feature of parental motivation for education in Himachal Pradesh is that it cuts across the barriers of caste, class and gender that have been so pernicious elsewhere

[83] See especially Probe Team (1999), chapter 9; also Bondroit (1998), Drèze (1999), Mehrotra (1999), Chakrabarti and Banerjea (2000), De, Noronha and Samson (2000), and Bhatty (forthcoming).

[84] It is also worth noting that Himachal Pradesh's economic take-off in recent decades is partly an *outcome* of the educational breakthrough. Indeed, the latter began in the 1960s, and appears to have largely preceded rather than followed the rapid growth of per-capita incomes (on the latter, see Anon, 2001).

[85] See Drèze and Kingdon (2001), and other studies cited there.

TABLE 5.4 *Social Disparities in Basic Education, 1993–4*

	Proportion of children aged 6–14 who have been to school		
	Himachal Pradesh	Haryana	India
By income group			
Low income	91	69	65
Lower-middle income	96	79	75
Upper-middle income	95	86	81
High income	90	86	87
By social group			
Caste Hindu	93	81	72
Scheduled caste/tribe	88	69	62
Muslim	80	41	62
By gender			
Female	90	72	65
Male	96	84	77

Source: Shariff (1999), pp. 105 and 270–1, based on the NCAER/HDI survey, 1994.

in India. In Himachal Pradesh, the notion that schooling is an essential part of *every* child's upbringing has acquired the character of a widely-shared social norm. This contrasts with the socially fragmented nature of educational opportunities and aspirations in other north Indian states, where it is not uncommon, say, for most children of one caste to go to school while most children of another caste in the same village are out of school (or for boys to go to school while girls stay at home). The comparatively equitable nature of school participation patterns in Himachal Pradesh is illustrated in Table 5.4.

Second, social equality facilitates cooperative action for the provision of local public services, including schooling facilities. A successful schooling system depends a great deal on cooperative public action, including cooperation between parents and teachers (e.g. in ensuring regular pupil attendance), cooperation between parents (e.g. in keeping the teachers on their toes), and cooperation between teachers and the management (e.g. in implementing pupil incentive schemes). The PROBE survey suggests that cooperative efforts of this type are much more common in Himachal Pradesh than elsewhere in north India. For instance, in many of the sample villages in Himachal Pradesh, parents had collaborated to build an extra room for the local school, or to help in other ways (e.g. by supplying wood in the winter or levelling the playground). The rapport between teachers and parents was also more cooperative than in other states, where parent-teacher relations are often undermined by mutual indifference or even antagonism.

Third, social equality helps to generate undivided public pressure for the improvement of schools (and local public services in general). In most Himachali villages, the local school is a 'common school' where children of all social backgrounds study together. The entire village community has a stake in the good functioning of this common school, and this joint interest can play a crucial role in preserving the integrity of the schooling system. In Himachal Pradesh, village communities rarely put up with a non-functional school. All this contrasts with the situation, extremely common elsewhere in north India, where children from privileged families are sent to private schools while children from poor families are stranded in a non-functional government school.

Finally, schools also tend to function better when the 'social distance' between teachers and parents is not too large, as appears to be the case in Himachal Pradesh. The problem of social distance arises from the fact that, compared with the pupils and their parents, teachers in government schools often come from a relatively privileged social background in terms of class, caste and gender. The alienation of many teachers from the parental community, especially in deprived neighbourhoods, tends to have an adverse effect on their motivation, and also on the rapport between teachers and parents.[86] These problems, widely observed elsewhere in India, appear to be less pronounced in Himachal Pradesh, where differences of social background between parents and teachers (and the social distance associated with these differences) are not particularly large.

Another enabling aspect of the social structure in Himachal Pradesh (closely related to the absence of sharp social disparities in general) concerns gender relations, which tend to be less patriarchal than in other states of north India.[87] As noted in chapter 3, this derives in part from the fact that female labour participation rates in Himachal Pradesh are quite high. This tends to reduce the economic dependence of women on men, give them substantial freedom of movement outside the house, and enhance their bargaining power and social recognition.

As far as education is concerned, there are many positive connections between women's work opportunities and female school participation. First, a high level of female labour-force participation raises the economic returns to female education. In Himachal Pradesh, parents tend to have relatively high hopes as far as their daughters' future employment

---

[86] On this issue, see Probe Team (1999), pp. 54–6; also Majumdar (2000) and Srivastava (2001a). An interesting illustration of the problem comes from a recent study of residential schools in tribal areas of Orissa, which reports that 61 per cent of the teachers (a majority of whom are described as 'upper caste Hindus') 'consider time spent in teaching as a waste of time' (Sikshasandhan, 2000, pp. 5 and 7).

[87] For further discussion, see Drèze (1999).

opportunities are concerned, and young girls themselves have ambitious aspirations.[88] Second, in so far as women's labour-force participation boosts their influence in the family, schooling decisions are likely to be less male-centred. Third, a similar connection may also operate at the level of the society as a whole, with girls' schooling receiving more attention (not only from parents but also, say, in public policy) where women are more involved in the public sphere. Fourth, if women are used to participating in a wide range of economic activities, it is that much easier to involve them in the teaching profession, too. The proportion of female teachers in Himachal Pradesh (above 40 per cent at the primary level, in rural areas) is indeed much higher than in other north Indian states (about 20 per cent, on average). This, in turn, is likely to facilitate school participation among girls. Fifth, social acceptance of the presence of women in the public sphere makes it easier for adolescent girls to attend school outside their own village, if need be. Elsewhere in north India, parental reluctance to allow daughters to leave the village (often for objective reasons of physical insecurity) is a common problem. Last but not least, in so far as women's labour-force participation reduces gender inequality in general, it is also likely to promote positive attitudes towards girls' schooling.[89]

Similar remarks apply to several other aspects of gender relations in Himachal Pradesh. Marriage practices, in particular, tend to be less restrictive in Himachal Pradesh than elsewhere in north India, again facilitating the spread of female education in various ways. For instance, the norm of patrilocal residence is comparatively flexible (e.g. women often marry within the village), and married women retain close bonds with their parents. This fosters parental concern for the well-being of a daughter after her marriage, and a sense that education contributes to it (instead of a daughter's education being seen as 'watering a plant in someone else's courtyard'). Similarly, late marriage is socially acceptable in Himachal Pradesh (only 10 per cent or so of Himachali women marry

[88] Probe Team (1999), pp. 117–9.

[89] Note that these positive links between women's work and girls' schooling operate mainly through the 'social dimension' of schooling decisions. At the household level, there are also negative links to consider, notably the burden of domestic work on elder daughters in families where both parents work outside the household. How this particular obstacle has been overcome in Himachal Pradesh (where the incidence of child labour used to be high) is an issue of much interest. It has not been overcome in Andhra Pradesh, where high rates of female labour force participation coexist with a high incidence of child labour (the highest in India) and relatively low school attendance rates. For some interesting econometric evidence of the overall positive association between adult female labour-force participation and girls' schooling in India, based on district-level data, see Jayachandran (2001).

before the age of 18, compared with more than 40 per cent in Haryana), making it easier for girls to continue studying beyond adolescence. It is also socially acceptable for a married woman to be better educated than her husband, so that parents need not fear that a well-educated daughter may be difficult to marry.[90]

Having said this, the favourable nature of the social context in Himachal Pradesh would not have gone far on its own in the absence of bold state initiatives to promote the universalization of elementary education. While 1951 age-specific literacy data suggest that Himachal Pradesh was slowly 'catching up' with other states in the first half of the twentieth century, the real breakthrough occurred from the 1960s onwards, with the gradual formation of Himachal Pradesh as a separate state and the adoption of independent economic and social policies. As mentioned in chapter 3, these policies included a major emphasis on developing the rural infrastructure, especially roads and schools. The promotion of elementary education was a paramount concern of S.S. Parmar, Himachal Pradesh's first Chief Minister, and this commitment (sorely lacking in most other states) has been sustained by successive governments. One symptom of this commitment is the high level of per-capita expenditure on education in Himachal Pradesh—about twice the all-India average. Correspondingly, the teacher-child ratio is much higher in Himachal Pradesh than in India as a whole.[91]

The combination of state commitment and community involvement has succeeded in preserving some accountability in the schooling system, and in preventing the kind of deterioration of work culture in the teaching profession that has taken place in many other states. This can be seen in the relatively good functioning of primary schools. To illustrate, the PROBE survey brings out that the following have become accepted norms of the teaching profession in Himachal Pradesh: the enrolment register is accurate; pupil attendance is carefully recorded; enquiries are made about non-attending children; formal tests are held at regular intervals, and there is a Board examination at the end of class 5; and, last but not least, school hours are spent in active teaching. None of this applies in the typical rural school of Bihar or Uttar Pradesh, where apathy and disorder reign supreme.

The schooling revolution in Himachal Pradesh has done a great deal to make it a better place to live in. In the wake of this transition to near-universal elementary education, the region has witnessed a dramatic

[90] On these and related perceptions, and contrasting attitudes in neighbouring Haryana, see particularly Bondroit (1998, 1999); also Bhatty (forthcoming).

[91] For a useful review of government initiatives for the promotion of schooling in Himachal Pradesh, see A. Ram (2000).

reduction of poverty, mortality, illness, undernutrition and related deprivations (see chapter 3). This positive experience, which stands in sharp contrast with the dismal overall picture of elementary education in India, deserves greater attention than it has received so far, and is full of important lessons for other states. The historical and social conditions that have made this success possible cannot be blindly copied elsewhere, but they do point to useful areas of public action.

5.9. COMPULSORY SCHOOLING AND THE RIGHT TO EDUCATION

There has been much debate, in recent years, about the possibility of introducing compulsory schooling in India. The idea used to have relatively few supporters (on this, see Weiner, 1991), and this scepticism is reflected in the fact that to this day compulsory education has not been implemented in any Indian state. However, public perceptions on this issue have changed a good deal in the 1990s, with, for instance, most political parties including the introduction of compulsory schooling in their manifestoes. Over time, there has also been a healthy change of focus, from 'compulsory schooling' to 'the right to education'. The relation between these two notions, however, is often confused, and there is still much resistance to both. This lack of clarity and commitment is one reason why an important proposal to make elementary education a fundamental right (the 83rd constitutional amendment bill) has been gathering dust for nearly four years.[92] A few remarks on this subject are in order.

The right to elementary education is best seen as a right of the child vis-à-vis society. The responsibility for enforcing this right need not rest with a single person or institution. It is a *shared* responsibility. First and foremost, it is a responsibility of the state, which has to provide the necessary facilities, outline the curriculum, make sure that teachers are qualified and accountable, and so on. But parents also have a responsibility to send the children to school, teachers to impart learning, and employers not to employ children in ways that conflict with their education. Thus, the overall responsibility of guaranteeing the right to education is shared between different persons and institutions (parents, teachers, employers, the state, etc.), though not in equal parts.

This feature does not imply that the right to education is unenforceable and therefore useless, as some commentators have argued.[93] When a child

---

[92] Confusion was particularly evident in the first draft of the amendment, which spoke of the 'right to compulsory education'—who wants a right to be compelled?

[93] For a cogent argument along those lines, see Béteille (1999), who concludes:

is deprived of education, it is possible, in many cases, to take concrete action. If school facilities are not available at a reasonable distance, they can be provided. If a teacher is chronically absent, he or she can be replaced. If parents are too poor to send their children to school, suitable incentives (e.g. free textbooks or school meals) can often be arranged. These steps are more likely to be taken if education is recognized as a fundamental right of the child. Indeed, educational planning is part of a democratic process in which social perceptions of who is entitled to what can play a major role.

It is true that some aspects of the right to education may be difficult to enforce. This is particularly the case if we consider that children have a right to *quality* education of some kind. To some extent, the quality aspect can be translated into enforceable norms such as a minimum teacher-pupil ratio. But other requirements of quality education, such as teacher motivation, would be much harder to enforce. This limitation, however, does not detract from the value of reducing educational deprivation, where possible, by invoking the fundamental right to education.

Compulsory education, for its part, is *one of the means* that can be used to make the child's right to education a reality. Essentially, compulsory education sends a clear message to parents, to the effect that it is not up to them to decide whether or not to send a child to school—they have a duty to do so.[94] This message is important, in so far as many children (particularly girls) are victims of parental irresponsibility. It also facilitates the emergence of a social consensus about the need for every child to go to school—a crucial step in the journey towards universal elementary education. And while compulsory education may seem to restrict the freedom of parents, most of them (according to the PROBE survey) actually support this measure. One reason for this has to do with the social dimension of schooling decisions (discussed in chapter 2): parents know that it is easier for them to send their children to school when *other* members of the community do so, too.

Having said this, the right to education should not be *reduced* to compulsory education, as has often been done in the context of this debate (and as some state governments may be tempted to do when they design

---

'Good laws certainly help to change customs, but the creation of laws that cannot be enforced, that are disparaged and disregarded does more harm than good to society'.

[94] Strictly speaking, a distinction should be made between compulsory *education* and compulsory *schooling*; indeed, many countries have the former without the latter (i.e. the law allows for education outside the schooling system). In India, however, the priority at this time is to integrate all children in the schooling system rather than to introduce special provisions for a small minority of children who might have the privilege of receiving adequate education at home.

practical legislative measures to implement the right to education). Compulsory education makes sense only if it is *conditional* on adequate facilities being available at a convenient distance, and also on education being free. The primary challenge is to create these enabling conditions. Introducing compulsory education before these conditions are met would be putting the cart before the horse. Even when the required facilities are in place, care should be taken to avoid authoritarian sanctions and parental harassment.

The government's reluctance to recognize elementary education as a fundamental right appears to be based on two fears. One is that this step will trigger a spate of wasteful court cases. The danger is real, as illustrated by recent attempts to invoke the right to education to compel the government to pay the fees of children enrolled in private schools. In strict legal terms, however, elementary education is already a fundamental right (Unnikrishnan vs State of Andhra Pradesh, 1993). It would be wiser for the government to take the initiative of defining and promoting the entitlements that flow from this right rather than to wait for the courts to do so.

The other fear is that implementing the fundamental right to elementary education would be very expensive. The financial requirements of universal elementary education, however, are well within the official target of 6 per cent of GDP for public expenditure on education. The main reason why this target remains so elusive is not that it is unreasonable, but rather that the bulk of the government's resources is cornered by powerful lobbies. By contrast, there is no vocal lobby for elementary education. Seen in this light, the fact that schooling facilities are expensive is an argument *for* rather than against making elementary education a fundamental right: this will force the government to reconsider its distorted spending priorities.

Universal elementary education is a realizable goal. If this goal is to be reached in good time, elementary education has to become a more lively political issue. In this respect, the notion that elementary education is a fundamental right could make a major difference. Even the process of demanding that this right should be enshrined in the constitution has much political value.

5.10. EDUCATION AND POLITICAL ACTION

In this chapter, we have had occasion to present brief comments on a number of shortcomings of government activity in the field of basic education, including the biases of official statistics (section 5.2), the neglect of female education (section 5.4), the inconsistencies of education policy (section 5.5), the inadequacy of education expenditure (section 5.6), the lack of accountability in the schooling system (section 5.7), and the dilution of the right to education (section 5.9), among others. We have also argued that a deep lack of real commitment to the widespread and equitable provision of basic education lies at the root of these diverse failures (section 5.1).

What is perhaps most striking of all is that the failures of government policy over an extended period have provoked so little political challenge. Had the government shown similar apathy and inconsistency in dealing with, say, the demands of the urban population for basic amenities, or of farmers' organizations for adequately high crop prices, or of the military establishment for modern hardware, or of the World Bank for structural adjustment measures, it is safe to predict that a major political battle would have followed. The fact that the government was able to get away with so much in the field of elementary education relates to the lack of political power of the illiterate masses (we have commented on this issue in section 5.1). It also reflects the fact, discussed at the beginning of this chapter, that the social value of basic education has been neglected not only by government authorities but also in social and political movements.

Much the same remarks also apply at the local level. The case study of Uttar Pradesh by Drèze and Gazdar (1996) in the companion volume, for instance, shows how it is quite possible for a village school to be non-functional for as long as ten years without any action being taken and any collective protest being organized.[95] There is a crucial contrast to be found here between Uttar Pradesh and Kerala, where a comparable state of affairs would not be passively tolerated.[96]

It is, of course, also the case that public expenditure on education is higher in Kerala than in Uttar Pradesh, and this factor is undoubtedly important in Kerala's higher educational achievements. But this difference in expenditure levels is much less striking than the difference relating to the politics of education. In fact, Uttar Pradesh is notorious for chronic *underutilization* of grants made available by the central government and international agencies for enhanced investment in the social sectors, including elementary education. Similarly, in Uttar Pradesh, very little interest has been taken in the recent Total Literacy Campaign, and, as a

[95] Similar observations have been made for other states of north India. Narain (1972), for instance, notes that in Rajasthan 'all the villagers may be dissatisfied with a school teacher, yet if he is in the good books of the *sarpanch* and *pradhan* he is not transferred' (p.152).

[96] The same point applies with reference to health services; see chapter 6, p. 213.

result, almost nothing has been gained from it.[97] The main constraint on educational expansion in Uttar Pradesh is not basically a financial one—it is the low importance attached to basic education in public policy. The responsibility for this failure lies not only with the government, but also with the political movements in this part of India.

Ultimately, the expansion of basic education in India depends a great deal on these political factors. There is no question that, even in a country as poor as India, means can be found to ensure universal attainment of literacy and other basic educational achievements. There are important strategic questions to consider in implementing that social commitment, but the primary challenge is to make it a more compelling political issue.

[97] See Ghosh et al. (1994), who attribute this poor response in Uttar Pradesh to a 'low political commitment to the eradication of illiteracy' in that state (p.39).

6

Population, Health and the Environment

6.1. INDIA'S POPULATION: CONCERNS AND SCRUTINY

In the summer of 1999, there was some excited discussion in the newspapers centred on the belief that India's population was about to reach the mark of one billion just around the independence day of the country: the 15th of August. It would have been an interesting coincidence, if two independent events had really been congruent in this way. The Office of the Registrar General of India poured cold water on the thrill of that coincidence by insisting that the crossing of the billion mark would occur later—around May 2000. This did not prevent an avalanche of discussion on the size of the Indian population in August 1999, but it did leave a later occasion also for a further round of discussions on the same topic. This duly occurred, in the spring of 2000, and was accompanied by some revelry at the gala event of the one billionth Indian being born.[1]

The size of the Indian population has been a subject of much concern for quite some time now—both inside India and outside it. Given the size of the country and its already large population, the absolute numbers of additions to the Indian population per year are often cited as dreadful evidence of alarming problems in the making. This is certainly serious enough statistics, but it is important to place it in the historical context to avoid being mesmerized by the force of total numbers.

[1] It would, however, appear from the provisional results of the 2001 census that, interestingly enough, India's billionth baby was in fact born very close to 15 August 1999, or at any rate much closer to that date than to the official May 2000.

India has been a country with a relatively large population for a very long time, based to a great extent on its relatively tolerant climate and, most importantly, its early development of settled agriculture which could historically support large concentrations of people in towns and villages. Looking at Asia as a whole, the proportion of total world population that lived there in 1650 or 1750 was much higher than the proportion of the world population that belonged to Asia in 1950, or for that matter, belongs to it right now.[2] The big rise in population that went with the industrial revolution in the West (led by a sharp fall in the death rate well ahead of the subsequent sharp fall in birth rate) is having its parallel in other parts of the world in recent times (with east Asia in the lead in this transition). As it happens, the projected ratio of the Asian and African population in the world population in 2050 A.D. is roughly comparable to the corresponding ratio in 1750 A.D., and India's own population ratio fits into this picture closely enough.

This historical perspective is no reason at all to be complacent about the population-related problems in India. Nor is it a reason to be unconcerned about the size of the world population and the pressures in the respective countries and regions. The environmental challenges, in particular, are very different now from what they were before the industrial revolution. However, since it is quite customary to cause panic by quoting India's large numbers and to attribute its manifold problems to population growth (Winston Churchill even attributed the Bengal famine of 1943 during the British Raj to the alleged tendency of Indians to 'breed like rabbits'), it is important not to lose sight of history altogether. Even in assessing the causal roots of the pressure of world population, it is relevant to note that this pressure is to a considerable extent the result of the large increase in the Western population over the last two hundred years or so. Not only has this increase added massively to the population base of the world, it has also made the status quo today quite different from anything that can be related to the historical division of world population prior to the industrial revolution. While India's population problems must be seen as challenges that require attention in contemporary terms (historical ratios do not make those problems any less intense), it is also important not to be diverted from critical scrutiny by the elocutionary force of the large numbers that are so frequently quoted to generate a sense of panic before scientific scrutiny can begin.

In absolute terms, the growth rate of India's population, despite some

[2] See Philip Moris Hauser's estimates presented in National Academy of Sciences (1971).

decline, is now around 1.8 per cent per year.[3] As Figure 6.1 illustrates, there is a firm upward trend in the total size of the Indian population that has not yet slackened adequately. Furthermore, demographic projections suggest that around the middle of the present century, India will overtake China, and India will then become the most populous country in the world.[4] Even though some would no doubt see this prospect as evidence of India's awesome importance in the committee of nations, it cannot but cause considerable worry for a country where there is already much pressure on environmental resources and the social infrastructure. Certainly, Figure 6.1 gives us rather little cause for joy in analysing the demographic situation in India, and there is even some temptation to read it as evidence of the much talked about 'population bomb' that may, sooner or later, tear India asunder.

And yet there is also quite a different, fuller story. Even though the 'total fertility rate' (roughly understandable as the average number of births per couple) for India as a whole is still well above the 'replacement level' (around 2.1), fertility in India has fallen quite sharply in recent decades, from around 6 in 1961 to just above 3 today.[5] Figure 6.2 portrays the declining trend.

In order to interpret these contrasting trends (continuing rapid population growth on the one hand, and declining fertility rates on the other), population growth has to be placed in the context of the 'demographic transition' from high to low fertility *and* mortality rates. In the initial phases of this transition, death rates typically fall faster than birth rates (indeed the demographic transition is usually *led* by falling mortality), so that the rate of population growth increases: in India, for instance, it increased from virtually zero at the beginning of the twentieth century to 2.2 per cent per year in the 1960s and 1970s. As the transition progresses, the rate of decline of birth rates gradually overtakes that of death rates, leading to a decline in population growth, as began to happen in India about twenty years ago (much earlier in some individual states).

---

[3] This growth rate roughly corresponds to crude birth and death rates of 26.5 and 9 per thousand, respectively (1998 data from Government of India, 2000h). Early results of the 2001 census indicate that the average annual growth rate of India's population for the decade of the 1990s as a whole was 1.9 per cent (Government of India, 2001b), and this is consistent with a current growth rate of 1.8 per cent per year.

[4] See e.g. United Nations Population Division (forthcoming).

[5] See Statistical Appendix, Tables A.3 and A.6, and Mari Bhat (1989), Table 8. The 'total fertility rate' measures, in fact, the number of births per woman, but in terms of getting an intuitive idea of 'balance', it is useful—and not grossly misleading—to think of it as the number of children per couple.

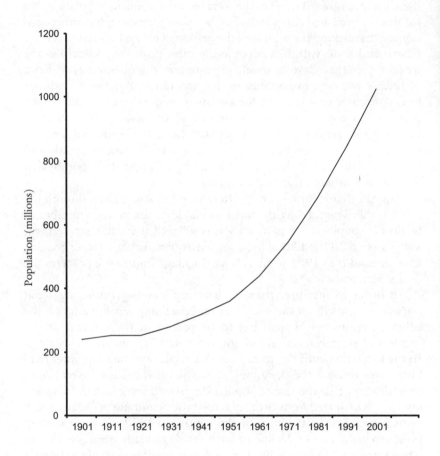

FIGURE 6.1 *India's Population, 1901 to 2001*

Source: Government of India (2001b), p. 34; the 2001 figure is the provisional 2001 census total.

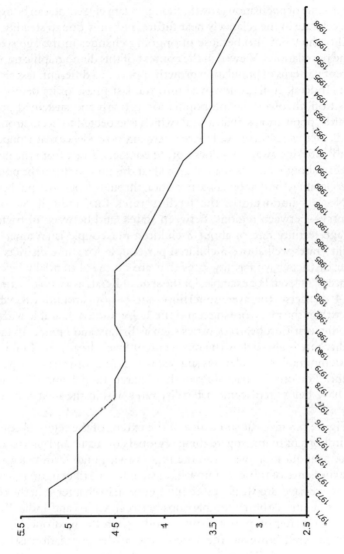

FIGURE 6.2 India's Total Fertility Rate, 1971–1998

Sources: Government of India (1999a), Table 1, and Government of India (2000h), p. 46.

The decline of population growth, though relatively recent, can be expected to accelerate in the relatively near future, not only due to steadily falling fertility rates but also because of ongoing changes in the age structure of the population.[6] Viewed in the context of this demographic transition, current patterns of population growth appear in a different, less alarming light. Indeed, India is now well into the last phase of its demographic transition, involving falling population growth and sustained progress towards 'population stabilization' (which is expected to occur around the middle of this century). And there is certainly no evidence that a 'population bomb' is ticking away. This does not, of course, detract from the need for concern about rapid population growth at this time, or from the possibility of accelerating the demographic transition through supportive public policy.

No less importantly, the fertility rates vary radically across the country—between regions, between states, and between districts. The average fertility rate of about 3 children per couple is an amalgam of fertility rates well above 5 children per couple for some districts, while other districts have fertility rates that are quite substantially below the replacement level. For example, for the state of Kerala as a whole—consisting of 14 districts—the average fertility rate is now around 1.8, which is lower than the rates for China and the USA, and comparable with those of some west European countries such as Britain and France. In fact, the fertility rate is also below the replacement level already for Tamil Nadu, and demographic calculations suggest that several other states (including Andhra Pradesh, Himachal Pradesh, Gujarat, Punjab and West Bengal) will have below-replacement fertility rates within the next five years or so.[7]

Figure 6.3 gives us some idea of the extent of the regional contrasts. It is important to investigate these regional contrasts, and also to address the crucial question: what can the regions with high fertility learn from the experience of those that now have such low fertility figures? To some extent, we have already discussed this question in chapter 4, in the context of related inter-country comparisons between China and India. We shall return to it later on in this chapter, and also in the next one.

In general, however, the seriousness of the population issue must not be dismissed. There is no case for the crude alarmism that often

---

[6] In fact, it is interesting to note that *absolute* population numbers are already declining in some younger age groups (e.g. the 0–9 age group), according to recent demographic estimates (see Government of India, 1996, p. 91).

[7] See Natarajan and Jayachandran (2001), Table 2.

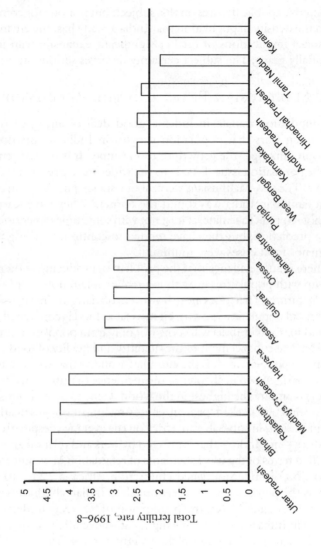

FIGURE. 6.3 *State-specific Fertility Rates, 1996–8*

Source: See Statistical Appendix, Table A.3, Part 2. The horizontal line is drawn at 2.1, which approximately corresponds to the 'replacement level' of fertility.

characterizes public debates on this subject, but nor one for complacency. Given the density of population that India already has, the environmental and social implications of further significant expansion can indeed be potentially grave. The subject certainly deserves serious attention.

6.2. MALTHUSIAN FEARS AND THE REAL ISSUES

The population debate includes a good deal of airing of traditional Malthusian fears that population growth in India is outstripping—or will soon outstrip—the growth of food supply. It is indeed tempting to link the population issue directly to the widespread prevalence of hunger in India. The neo-Malthusians were, at one stage, quite keen on predicting that a famine in India was round the corner.[8] They have learned since then not to predict a famine, at least not with some time dimension attached to the prediction, but they have tended to continue warning the world that major food crises were imminent.

There is little evidence that the problem of producing enough food to keep up with population growth is a real problem now—or in the foreseeable future. That does not, however, obviate the need for concern about rapid population growth. First, as far as food is concerned, the extra demand for food in India will come not only from population growth, but also from the enhancement of the quantity and quality of food consumed per unit of population. It is the cumulative effects that we have to look at.

As was discussed in chapter 3, the incidence of nutritional deprivation in India is among the highest in the world. General undernourishment— what is sometimes called 'protein-energy malnutrition'—is nearly twice as high in India as in sub-Saharan Africa on the average (despite the fact that it is Africa—not India—that is ravaged by wars and turmoil and famines). Judged in terms of the usual standards of retardation in weight for age, the proportion of undernourished children in Africa is 20 to 40 per cent, whereas the percentage of undernourished Indian children is a gigantic 40 to 60 per cent.[9] Even the proportion of 'severely undernourished' children in India is astonishingly high, e.g. above 20 per cent in the larger north Indian states (based on the weight-for-age criterion).[10]

As Indians acquire greater purchasing power, and as the biases against

[8] See chapter 3, p. 70–1.

[9] See Scrimshaw (1997); also Table 3.1 in chapter 3, and International Institute for Population Sciences (2000a). On the comparison with sub-Saharan Africa, see also Peter Svedberg's (2000) investigation, which brings out just how nutritionally deprived the Indian population is compared even with other poor regions of the world.

[10] See Statistical Appendix, Table A.3.

particular groups (such as young girls) diminish, the size and composition of food consumption per head will have to change. The challenges of food production and food availability in India have to be seen in that light, rather than in terms of the old Malthusian comparison between the growth of total population and that of aggregate food production (on this see also Hopper, 1999). The Malthusian fear of a falling ratio of food to population is easy enough to counter in the case of India, since there is no evidence that such a decline has occurred or is about to occur. But the actual challenge is substantially tougher than to avert a decline, since the consumption of nutrients—calories among them but other nutrients as well—has to go up per unit of population.

Second, the pressure on environmental resources is strong in many different ways that go well beyond the perspective of food production and consumption. There is much evidence of rapid deterioration of the local environment across the country (in addition to India's contribution to global environmental degradation), with a wide range of adversities, varying from overcrowding of habitat and increases in man-made pollution to the denuding of forests and vegetation. We shall come back to the environmental problems more fully later on in this chapter.[11]

Third, rapid population growth leads to heightened pressure not only on the environment but also on the social infrastructure, including sewage systems, hospital facilities, railway networks, power grids, garbage-processing plants, and many other components of the 'stock' of public amenities. When public authorities are constantly racing to bring this stock in line with a larger population, there is that much less room for *qualitative* improvements in public facilities. This phenomenon is clearly visible in some urban agglomerations, the rapid growth of which has gone hand in hand with a qualitative deterioration of the social infrastructure.

Fourth, there is a *compounding* of the impact of population growth and economic growth to which we have to pay attention. Even when the impact of population growth today happens to be small, if we consider the long-run effects of today's population expansion in the light of prospective prosperity in the future, we have to take into account compounded aggregate effects that can be quite large and are likely to grow over time (even when population growth itself slows down, or stops altogether). In all the spheres of concern to which we have already referred (food and nutritional adequacy, environmental degradation, infrastructural pressure,

[11] The recognition of population growth as *one* source of pressure on environmental resources should not be confused with the possible claim (common in neo-Malthusian circles) that it is the *main* source of environmental degradation. The latter phenomenon, in fact, also has many other economic, social and political roots.

etc.), we have to look at the cumulative effects of growth in population size and increase in economic activity.

To summarize, concern about population growth must not be simply dismissed as groundless. The size of the Indian population is already large, and its continued rapid expansion can certainly be a source of anxiety for the environment, in addition to the problems it raises for improving the living standards and economic and social well-being of the people. And yet the population situation is not as terrifying as it is sometimes made to look, based on the citation of selectively chosen statistics (or non-statistics). First, food supply has not been falling behind population—quite firmly to the contrary. The possibility of accommodating considerable increases in food consumption per head—both quantitative and qualitative—is still quite favourable. Second, the fertility rate is falling quite rapidly, and may decline faster still with sensible policies, especially related to child health and women's empowerment. Third, the fertility rate varies widely between different regions in India, and there is much to learn from those that have already achieved low fertility rates, and also much evidence that these achievements are indeed spreading to other regions as well. This last issue receives further attention in the next section.

6.3. GENDER EQUITY AND THE DEMOGRAPHIC TRANSITION

The regional contrasts within India call for detailed statistical scrutiny of possible causal factors that can explain the differences, but at the same time they also demand some kind of an integrated understanding of the process of fertility decisions in the family. This understanding requires the significant recognition that the most immediate adversity caused by a high rate of population growth lies in the loss of freedom that women suffer when they are shackled to a life of persistent bearing and rearing of children. This connection is important in itself because of its direct and immediate relevance to the well-being and freedom of women. But going beyond that, since the interests of young women are so closely involved, it would also be natural to expect that anything that increases the voice and power of young women in family decisions will tend to have the effect of sharply reducing fertility rates. This expected connection has received substantial statistical confirmation from inter-country comparisons across the world as well as from analyses of inter-state and inter-district contrasts within India.[12] In the light of this evidence, it is clear that women's empowerment and agency cannot but be central to an effective resolution of the so-called population problem.

---

[12] See chapter 7, and the literature cited there.

Why, then, do women have low decisional power in some societies, and how can that be remedied? There are various distinct influences to be considered here. First, social and economic handicaps (such as female illiteracy, lack of paid employment and other income-earning opportunities, deprivation of property rights, non-availability of credit facilities) contribute greatly to muffling the voice of women in society and even within the family. Second, lack of contraceptive knowledge or absence of family planning facilities can also be an importance source of helplessness. Lack of access to family planning is, in fact, a part of women's deprivation. Third, there are also cultural, even religious, factors that give a subservient position to young women, making them accept the burden of constant bearing and rearing of children (as desired by the husband or the parents-in-law). These inequities may not even have to be physically enforced, since women's subservient role as well as frequent child-bearing may appear 'natural' when these practices have been sanctified by a long history that generates uncritical acceptance—no injustice being seen there.

The promotion of female literacy, women's employment opportunities, family planning facilities, as well as open and informed public discussion can enhance the voice and decisional role of women in family affairs and also bring about radical changes in the understanding of justice and injustice. Indeed, in terms of policy analysis, there is much evidence now, based on inter-country comparisons as well as inter-regional contrasts within India, that women's empowerment (through employment, education, property rights, etc.) can have a very strong effect in reducing fertility rates. Speedy fertility declines in the states of Kerala, Tamil Nadu or Himachal Pradesh in India can be firmly linked to the rapid enhancement of female education and other sources of empowerment of young women. Indeed, the principal variables that seem to account for inter-district variations in fertility rates in India are directly linked to women's empowerment, in particular female literacy and women's participation in gainful employment.[13]

These opportunities not only enhance women's voice in family decisions (thereby contributing directly to lowering fertility), they also have other favourable social effects (some of which also indirectly lower fertility). The wide-ranging personal and social roles of female education were discussed in chapters 2 and 5, and some of these roles can also be seen as powerful influences on fertility decline. For example, female literacy has a strong impact in reducing child mortality rates, which is a great result

[13] See Murthi, Guio and Drèze (1995) and Drèze and Murthi (2001). On the connections between fertility and various 'dimensions of patriarchy' in India, see also Malhotra, Vanneman and Kishor (1995).

in itself, and additionally also contributes to reducing fertility. Similarly, the promotion of women's employment opportunities and related sources of empowerment contribute to their security in old age, and offer some protection from the adversities of widowhood. These, again, are important achievements in themselves, and also make a further contribution to fertility decline, in so far as the fear of old-age insecurity often slows down the adoption of small-family norms.

The central importance of gender equity and women's empowerment for fertility decline is reinforced by the fact, discussed earlier, that fertility decline is best seen in the context of the 'demographic transition' from high to low levels of fertility *and* mortality. Given the gender division of responsibilities in many Indian households, the reduction of mortality—especially child mortality—depends a great deal on the informed agency of women (see chapter 7). The recognition that mortality reduction is an essential requirement of sustained fertility decline thus gives us further reason to put women's agency at the centre of the analysis.

It must, of course, be recognized that many different influences operate on fertility rates, and it would be a mistake to look for a single 'magic instrument' that would work uniformly well in reducing high fertility. What is needed instead is a unified approach that places different variables within a general framework of family decisions on fertility. The advantage of bringing gender equity and women's empowerment to the centre of the stage is that they provide a broad perspective of this type, within which many specific influences on fertility decisions can be accommodated. This includes acknowledging the role of educational development (including the schooling of girls), economic arrangements (including female job opportunities), social concerns (including the status of women), cultural factors (including the value of equity in family decisions), health care (including reproductive health), as well as the more traditional variables that can assist family planning (such as the availability of contraceptive facilities and access to medical attention). For example, seen on its own, the expansion of family planning facilities may appear to be just a demographic intervention, but the importance of improved family-planning opportunities can also be seen in the broader light of the decisional freedom of families in general and of vulnerable women in particular. The way forward is through more freedom and justice, not through more coercion and intimidation. Nothing is, it would seem, as important in dealing with the population problem as to reverse the various social and economic handicaps that make women voiceless and powerless.

6.4. HEALTH CARE AS A SOCIAL RESPONSIBILITY

Few subject   more important than health as a constitutive element
of the well-   nation. And yet health care has been
one of the   in India. Despite stirring
statement   and health
care, the   policy in
general a   , many of
the prol   preceding
chapter   nifestations
are diff

A   ealth matters
is that   gh incidence
of co   ommunicable
dise   the 'burden of
dise   cclined in large
par   etanus, measles,
pn   e a few) continue
to   orldwide leprosy
c   cussed earlier, the
incidence of   ailments in India
is also very high by interna
It is also worth noting that the burden   falls very unevenly
on different sections of the population. Indeed, health *inequalities* are
very sharp in India, in comparison with many other countries, even poor
ones.[16] Class differences in health achievements, in particular, are large by
international standards. The same applies to gender-based inequalities in
health.

These features of the health situation in India relate closely to the state
of health services, and, going beyond that, to the persistent neglect of

[14] Murray and Lopez (1996). The 'burden of disease' is not easy to assess, and
information on morbidity patterns in India is extremely scarce (this is one symptom,
among others, of the low priority assigned to health matters in public policy).
Nevertheless, a number of recent studies throw useful light on disease patterns in
India. See particularly Murray and Lopez (1996), Vaidyanathan (1997), Shariff (1999),
Duraisamy (2000), International Institute for Population Sciences (2000a); also World
Bank (2001a), and the studies summarized in that report.

[15] World Bank (2001a), p. 28. This proportion is much larger than India's share
of the world population, which is about 17 per cent.

[16] See World Bank (2001a), pp. 32–9 and 81–9, and *World Development Indicators
2001*, Table 2.7.

health matters in public policy. One sympton of this neglect is the abysmally low level of public expenditure on health—around 0.8 per cent of GDP. Among 142 countries for which the relevant data are available, only six (Burundi, Cambodia, Georgia, Indonesia, Myanmar, and Sudan) have a lower figure for public expenditure on health as a proportion of GDP.[17] The low level of public expenditure on health in India is aggravated by (1) a highly inefficient use of available resources, and (2) sharp inequalities in access to health care based on region, class, caste, and gender.[18]

Critical analyses of India's health care system have been dominated by two very special diagnoses, which deserve comment, given their hold. According to one school of thought, India made the cardinal mistake of following the 'western model' of health care, instead of promoting indigenous approaches.[19] Another view holds that health care in India has been undermined by the chronic inefficiencies of public services, and that greater reliance on the private sector would be, thus, by far the best answer.

In assessing both the theses, it is important to take note of the basic fact that India's health care system, as things stand, is essentially a market-based system where diagnoses and drugs are treated much like any other commodity. Many patients, in fact, buy powerful drugs (e.g. broad-spectrum antibiotics or steroids) over the counter from chemist shops—the most thriving business in many small towns. Even in public health centres and hospitals, financial inducements are often required for basic services that are supposed to be available free of cost.

To describe this dominant system as the 'western model' is not only dubious description, it is also exceedingly unfair to the history of health care in western countries. That tradition has, in many cases, involved diametrically opposite principles such as long-term relations between doctor and patient, widespread health education, emphasis on preventive

---

[17] *World Development Indicators 2001*, Table 2.15. The figure of 0.8 per cent given there for India is consistent with central and state government budget data presented in Government of India (2000a, 2000e, 2000f). We are grateful to Ravi Duggal for his advice on these matters.

[18] For detailed evidence, and further discussion, see e.g. Banerji (1996), Deolalikar and Vashishta (1996), National Council of Applied Economic Research (2000). The last study suggests that three rupees of public expenditure on curative health services reach the richest 20 per cent of the population for every rupee that reaches the poorest 20 per cent.

[19] Even the 'national health policy' of 1983, in its valuable effort to re-focus public policy on public health and primary health care, attributes existing biases to 'the almost wholesale adoption of health manpower development policies and the establishment of curative centres based on the Western models, which are inappropriate and irrelevant to the real needs of our people' (Government of India, 1985, p.35).

medicine and public health, extensive involvement of voluntary institutions, close supervision of the medical profession, and—last but not least—a large degree of socialization of health services, especially in Europe. It would, of course, also be a mistake to consider these features as exclusively 'Western'. Indeed, countries such as Cuba and China have taken radically new steps in the development of preventive medicine, public health and socialized services, with much success. Also, there have been major differences of approach *among* western countries, with some (notably the United States) following more market-based patterns than others. In short, analysing the predicament of health care in India today through the prism of some undifferentiated 'western model' (seen in either negative or positive terms) is not particularly helpful.[20]

Similar misperceptions are involved in the second view, which holds that India's health care system has been paralysed by excessive state intervention and that greater reliance on private initiative may be the answer to this problem. This view is associated with a growing mood of abdication about public medical services in some official circles, buttressed by the growing influence of the corporate sector in policy advice. Sometimes the criticism of 'bureaucracy'—fair enough in its own right—gets mixed up with downplaying the importance of public health care, in favour of private or voluntary organizations. The amalgamation of two quite distinct concerns is reflected in an oddly combined statement attributed to the Union Minister of Health, arguing that we should 'do away with the bureaucracy and entrust the job to genuinely voluntary organizations'.[21] To argue for state withdrawal from the health sector not only overlooks the basic fact that the state has rather little presence in the country's health system (health care in India is *already* highly privatized), but also neglects the reasoned need for state involvement in this field, forcefully brought out by the experiences of different countries across the world (in Europe and America as well as in Asia and Africa).

Indeed, international comparisons make interesting reading in this field as well. In India's economy—allegedly committed to 'socialism'— the share of public expenditure in total health expenditure is only around

---

[20] A more pertinent point is that health care in India has come to rely too heavily on western medical *technology.* Better use can certainly be made of local knowledge and indigenous systems such as ayurvedic medicine. Even with reference to technology, however, the 'western' label is often misleading. For instance, while homeopathy is often contrasted with 'Western' allopathy, homeopathy actually originated in Germany.

[21] *Indian Express* (Kochi edition), 8 August 1992 (also reported in Zachariah, 1997, p. 111).

Table 6.1: *Health Expenditure: Selected Indicators*

	Public expenditure on health, 1990–98[a]		
	In absolute terms (PPP$ per capita)	*As a share of total health expenditure (%)*	*As a share of GDP (%)*
India	14	15	0.8
South Asia	16	18	0.9
Sub-Saharan Africa[b]	36	40	1.7
East Asia & Pacific[b]	60	40	1.7
Middle East & North Africa[b]	114	50	2.3
Latin America & Caribbean[b]	221	49	3.2
Europe & Central Asia[b]	251	77	4.0
High-income countries			
Europe EMU	1,485	75	6.7
All	1,604	62	6.0

Notes: [a] Latest year for which the relevant data are available.
[b] Low- and middle-income countries only.
Source: Calculated from *World Development Indicators 2001*, Table 2.15.

15 per cent, compared with 75 per cent in western Europe's 'market economies', rising to 84 per cent in Thatcherism-ravaged Britain. In fact, the share of public expenditure in total health expenditure is lower in India than in any other major region of the world (Table 6.1).

The case for public involvement in health matters was discussed in chapter 2. The arguments are particularly strong when it comes to preventive medicine and public health, since private practitioners have little incentive to get involved in such matters. Even though there are, clearly, many public spirited and socially dedicated doctors, not many have found the time and commitment to lead public health initiatives such as disinfecting the local well, lobbying for better garbage removal, or diffusing information on healthy diets. This is a field where concerted action, and the allocation of adequate public resources, are badly needed.[22] The arguments for public involvement in preventive medicine and public health are particularly strong in India, where the incidence of basic communicable diseases and related illnesses is still extremely high.

The possibility of making rapid progress in this field, even at an early stage of development, has been demonstrated not only by international

---

[22] The vast possibilities of low-cost public intervention in the fields of basic health and child nutrition have been highlighted for many years by UNICEF. See e.g. the annual UNICEF report on *The State of the World's Children*, and also similar reports published by UNICEF's India office.

experience but also in several Indian states, including of course Kerala but also Tamil Nadu (discussed in section 6.6) and, more recently, Himachal Pradesh. It would be a mistake, however, to think that the effectiveness of public health measures is confined to a few 'model' states where the social or political context happens to be favourable. Indeed, despite the low standards of government activity in most Indian states, there are many other examples of rewarding initiatives in this field. For instance, the installation of simple, well-designed public handpumps in most Indian villages has dramatically enhanced people's access to safe water at a convenient distance.[23] Child vaccination rates have increased at an impressive rate since the Universal Immunisation Programme was initiated in 1985. Oral rehydration therapy has protected millions of children from diarrhoea at very low cost.[24] Salt iodization has successfully reduced iodine deficiency in several states, notably Himachal Pradesh.[25] The latest success story is the all-India polio immunization programme, which involved unprecedented feats such as the vaccination of about 100 million children in a single day. While the overall record of public health initiatives in India is quite dismal in general, there is no ground for pessimism about what *can* be done, in the light of the experiences of successes that have already occurred.

The preceding examples relate mainly to specific campaigns or pro-grammes that involve a high concentration of resources and attention on focused goals. Successfully implementing such campaigns is not quite the same as running an efficient, comprehensive health care system on a day to day basis (indeed, sometimes ad hoc campaigns mobilize the health infra-structure at the expense of other services). As far as the overall performance of health services is concerned, the picture is far from encouraging in most states. While health services have steadily expanded in quantitative terms, there is much evidence that their *quality* has deteriorated. In many states, health centres are dilapidated, medicines are not available, doctors are

[23] These ingenious Indian handpumps are adapted from a simple design originally due to a self-taught mechanic, and are now exported world-wide (UNICEF, 1996). In 1998-9, 78 per cent of Indian households had access to 'drinking water that is piped or from a handpump' (International Institute for Population Sciences, 2000a, p. 38).

[24] According to the National Family Health Survey 1998-9, about half of all young children who had diarrhoea during the two weeks preceding the survey were treated with oral rehydration therapy ('ORS packets' in a majority of cases); see Statistical Appendix, Table A.3, Part 7. ORS packets are usually obtained from government sources (Shariff, 1999, p. 365).

[25] One medical expert even takes the view that the reduction of iodine deficiency in Himachal Pradesh paved the way for the 'schooling revolution' there, by improving children's learning abilities (Dr. Kochupillai, All-India Institute of Medical Sciences, personal communication).

chronically absent, and patients are routinely charged for services that are meant to be free (when they are treated at all).[26] Recent 'health facility surveys' by the Indian Institute of Health Management Research provide chilling evidence of this state of affairs, illustrated in Table 6.2 with reference to Rajasthan. The dismal state of public health services is the main reason why most patients turn to private providers, however unreliable or expensive.

Private provision of health care poses its own problems, which are often no less serious than those of public health facilities, depending on the context and the type of health care being considered. We have already noted, for instance, that private practitioners have little incentive to get involved in preventive medicine and public-health initiatives. Even for curative services, the private provision of health care poses well-known difficulties, relating in particular to informational asymmetries between user and provider: when patients are unable to assess the quality of services being provided to them, competition by itself is a poor efficiency-enhancing device. In principle, these problems can often be addressed through well-aimed regulation. Indeed, in many countries (including the so-called 'market economies'), private provision of health care is highly regulated, not only by the state but also by sophisticated professional associations. Similar regulatory mechanisms also exist in India, but their effectiveness has been extensively undermined for a number of reasons, ranging from the informal nature of a large part of the health-care sector to widespread corruption.[27] The outcome is a highly differentiated 'market' for health services, which combines reliable but expensive facilities (e.g. elite hospitals in major cities) with a large informal sector where patients are exposed to the hazards of unregulated, uncoordinated and exploitative marketing of 'cures'.[28]

[26] See e.g. Khan et al. (1980, 1986, 1987, 1988, 1989), Khan and Prasad (1983), Indian Institute of Management (1985), Indian Council of Medical Research (1989), Voluntary Health Association of India (1997), Koenig and Khan (1999); also the special issue of *Seminar* on the state of India's public health system (May 2000), and the literature cited there. That the quality of health services (especially those relating to public health and preventive care) has deteriorated over time from the 1970s or so onwards has been noted by many experts; see e.g. Banerji (1997), Mukhopadhyay (1997), Misra (2001).

[27] On the 'unethical and irrational practices' that have proliferated in India's private health sector as a result of the 'most unregulated and unmonitored manner' in which it effectively operates, see Nandraj (1994, 1997); also Duggal (2000a, 2000b).

[28] Health facilities managed by charitable trusts, NGOs and other non-profit organizations provide a useful alternative in some cases, but their reach is obviously limited. There is, in fact, much scope for greater activism in this field, not least on the part of trade unions and workers' organizations. For interesting cases of recent experiments of this type, see e.g. Chaudhuri et al. (1996), Mukhopadhyay (1998), Antia et al. (2000), Menon (2000), Shukla and Phadke (2000), and B. Sen (2001).

TABLE 6.2 *State of Health Centres in Rajasthan, 1999*

Proportion (%) of 'primary health centres' (PHC) with: [a]	
toilet	75
continuous w ater supply	64
at least one basic laboratory service	59
infant w eighing machine	56
labour room	52
para-medical staff trained in checking blood pressure	43
regular building maintenance [b]	10
telephone	5
X-ray machine	3
female medical officer [c]	3
Proportion (%) of 'community health centres' (CHCs) with: [a]	
white-w ashing at least once in three y ears	44
telephone	44
generator	36
clean operation theatre [d]	12
facility for sterilizing instruments	11
priv acy during gynaecological examination	9
clean w ards	7
clean toilets	4
sew erage facility	4
regular blood supply	4

Notes: [a] In this sample, each PHC serves 21 villages on average. A 'community health centre' is a middle-level health facility, between the PHC and the district hospital. In this sample, an average CHC covered a population of about 360,000 and conducted about one delivery per day.
[b] More than 70% of PHCs have 'no building maintenance at all'.
[c] Most PHCs have at least one 'medical officer'.
[d] Most CHCs have at least one operation theatre.
Source: Calculated from Indian Institute of Health Management Research (1999), based on a survey of 484 primary health centres and 55 community health centres in 12 districts of Rajasthan.

India's public health services, for their part, are not uniformly dismal. Some health facilities, in fact, appear to provide useful services, not only in the states that are acknowledged to have comparatively effective and equitable public services in general (say Kerala, Tamil Nadu, Gujarat and Maharashtra), but to varying extents elsewhere as well. This applies in particular to family planning and child immunization. The achievements and limitations of public health services in India call for further scrutiny.

6.5. REPRODUCTIVE HEALTH AND BEYOND

In contrast to the general pattern of overwhelming reliance on private health care, public facilities are the main source of contraception and vaccination services in India. The use of these services has grown steadily over time, though much scope remains for expanding them. Further, recent surveys indicate reasonably high levels of user satisfaction in most states, in contrast to widespread public discontent with health services in general.[29] This is not to say that all is well with family planning and immunization services—far from it. In 1998–9, less than half of all Indian children aged 12–23 months were fully vaccinated, a telling indication that much remains to be done.[30] Qualitative achievements have also been much less impressive than quantitative progress. Nevertheless, the general trend in this field is one of steady progress towards free and universal access to reasonably convenient contraception and immunization services. In several states (Tamil Nadu, Himachal Pradesh, Goa, Kerala), the proportion of 'fully immunized' children ranges between 80 and 90 per cent, with rapid progress towards similar levels in many other states.[31] This is a major step forward compared to the situation that prevailed, say, twenty years ago.

The reasons why the accomplishments of India's health services, such as they are, have been concentrated in these specific fields (combined with severe neglect of other aspects of primary health care) are worth scrutinizing. To some extent it is natural for the public sector to focus heavily on services such as immunization and family planning, since private provision of such services is unlikely to work without additional incentives as well as skilful regulation. To illustrate, consider the case of child vaccination. A mother who takes her child to a public hospital for vaccination knows that (1) the government doctors and nurses have at least basic qualifications and training, (2) they have no obvious reason to give her misleading information about her child's vaccination requirements, and (3) they will be using standard quality-controlled vaccines. If she goes to a cheap private clinic, on the other hand, there are likely to be doubts

[29] For empirical evidence of these patterns, see International Institute for Population Sciences (1995a, 1995b, 1999, 2000a) and Koenig and Khan (1999). According to the second National Family Health Survey (1998–9), 76 and 82 per cent of contraception and vaccination services (respectively) are obtained from the public sector (see Statistical Appendix, Table A.3, Part 7).

[30] See International Institute for Population Sciences (2000a), p. 209, where 'full immunization' is understood to cover BCG, measles, and three doses each of DPT and polio vaccines. For further details, see Statistical Appendix, Table A.3.

[31] See Statistical Appendix, Table A.3, Part 7.

on each count, with no way of telling, for instance, whether the doctor's injection is actually a vaccine or plain water. Further, private doctors who are willing to settle for plain water (or, say, outdated vaccines) have a competitive edge in terms of profitability over honest doctors, so that the market mechanism, instead of weeding out dishonest doctors, can actually give them a comparative advantage in this case, given the asymmetry of information.

This argument, however, is not specific to child vaccination or family planning, and also applies to many other types of health services. A more direct reason for the concentration of public health services in these specific fields is the simple fact that these activities have received very considerable— indeed overwhelming—priority in the values governing public health policy. Family planning, in particular, has been the primary focus of the entire health infrastructure for many years now. From the mid-1980s onwards, child immunization also became a major concern. Even though this is partly because of the recognition—the belated recognition—that reducing child mortality is a necessary precondition of fertility decline, there is now evidence of a strong interest in spreading immunization as widely as possible.

The preoccupation with family planning arises partly from widespread recognition of a real need, but also reflects an obsessive fear of the 'population bomb' among political leaders, policy makers and health administrators. The climate of feverish urgency associated with this fear has had some remarkable results in terms of galvanizing the health system into action. It is interesting, for instance, that in contrast with the general pattern of apathy and neglect in public health institutions, close supervision and exacting incentives have ensured high levels of activity among the 'auxiliary nurse midwives' (ANMs) who are the foot soldiers of this battle against population growth. Unlike many other government employees with peripatetic duties in rural areas, ANMs in most states do spend much time in the villages, going from house to house to promote family planning and child vaccination. Some of them are even constrained to catch up with administrative work on Sundays.[32]

---

[32] See e.g. Coutinho et al. (2000) and Visaria (2000b). Household surveys confirm that a majority of households in rural India are regularly visited by ANMs; see e.g. Roy and Verma (1999), who report that in 1993 a large majority of women aged 15–49 in each of four sample states (Bihar, Karnataka, Tamil Nadu and West Bengal) had been 'visited by ANM in the last three months' (p. 23). Most ANM 'visits', however, seem to be confined to advice, registration and related matters (not including health care itself), judging from the fact that 'only 24 per cent of births in rural areas... received antenatal care through home visits' in 1992–3 (International Institute for Population Sciences, 1995a, p. 232).

The 'family planning fever' has not been an unmixed blessing. It has led, in particular, to a massive displacement—sometimes verging on destruction—of other health care activities. Field-based reports on health services in rural areas are replete with observations such as the following.

From Rajasthan: '[family planning] targets have become the hallmark of all government activity in the name of health' (Gupta et al., 1992, p. 2330).

From Uttar Pradesh: 'preoccupation with attaining the family planning targets has had devastating effects on the other health activities' (Budakoti, 1988, pp. 153–4).

From Andhra Pradesh: 'family planning was taken as the priority function at all levels of health organization' (Raghunandan et al., 1987).

From Gujarat: 'the primary health care machinery, village, taluka and district level machinery including teachers, officials, non-officials, etc., were geared to work for achieving the [family planning] targets' (Iyengar and Bhargava, 1987, p. 1087).

From Maharashtra: 'the extremely high priority assigned to [family planning] targets has worked to the detriment of the public health system as a whole' (Iyer and Jesani, 1999, p. 235).

There are other reports from these and other areas that can arouse the greatest of concerns.[33] As a leading expert on health care in India aptly puts it, India's family planning programme 'has been like a ferocious bull in the China shop of the health services' (D. Banerji, 1997).

The progress made with contraception and immunization services also raises the question of *how* so much energy has been mobilized for these purposes. As the preceding testimonies illustrate, the extensive use of quantitative targets and target-based incentives (e.g. linking salary bonuses with pre-specified numbers of sterilizations or IUD insertions) is a large part of that story. In the case of family planning, the process of target-driven mobilization is well documented, as is the associated propensity to use heavy-handed methods to persuade eligible couples to 'cooperate'.[34] In

---

[33] For further evidence in the same direction, see Khan, Prasad and Qaiser (1987), Priya (1987, 1990), Jeffery (1988), Banerji (1989), Jeffery et al. (1989), Maurya (1989), Prakasamma (1989), Shah (1989), World Bank (1989), Jesani (1990), Rose (1992), Sundari (1993), Ramasundaram (1995a), Shiva (1996), Coutinho et al. (2000), among others. For a useful overview of the functioning of health services in India prior to the introduction of a 'target-free approach' in 1996, see the collection of papers in Koenig and Khan (1999).

[34] To give just one example, many observers have noted the practice of surreptitious postpartum sterilization or IUD insertion (without the consent or even

the 1990s, the target approach was extended to child immunization (which also lends itself to convenient quantitative benchmarks) in the context of the Universal Immunisation Programme.[35] Aside from contributing to the displacement of other health services, the target-based approach has raised a number of serious concerns, relating for instance to (1) infringements of human rights, (2) the potentially counter-productive effects of authoritarian measures, and (3) the adverse effects of quantitative targets on the quality of reproductive and child health services.

Target-based programming was officially abandoned in April 1996, in the context of a broader effort to improve the current approach to 'reproductive and child health'.[36] Interestingly, the removal of targets does not appear to have led to any significant setback in family planning or child immunization. The results of the second National Family Health Survey, for instance, suggest continued progress in this field, as do recent field evaluations of the impact of the removal of targets.[37] To some extent, the persistence of earlier trends is attributable to the fact that there has been more continuity than change in the system itself. Indeed, field evaluations suggest that the so-called 'target culture' is alive and well in many states, as is the preoccupation with 'population control' among health administrators. The 'paradigm shift' advocated by reproductive rights activists (and trumpeted in some official documents) is often hard to find. Nevertheless, there has been a significant change, in most states, in the way targets are devised and used. For one thing, targets are now set by local health staff on the basis of household surveys, instead of being imposed from the top. For another, they are no longer linked with draconian incentives and punishments. That, at any rate, is the picture that emerges from early evaluations of the so-called 'target-free approach'.[38]

---

knowledge of the patient). It is hard to think of a better way of scaring women away from health clinics. This is a telling illustration of the potentially counter-productive effects of heavy-handed methods.

[35] On the use of targets in child immunization programmes, see particularly Coutinho, Bisht and Raje (2000).

[36] The reforms have been much influenced by the consultation processes associated with the International Conference on Population and Development in Cairo in 1994 and its aftermath, and also with the framing of a new 'population policy' (Government of India, 2000c).

[37] To illustrate, National Family Health Survey data indicate that the proportion of children without any immunization declined from 30 to 14 per cent between 1992–3 and 1998–9; see International Institute for Population Sciences (1995a, 2000a). The steady decline of fertility rates has also continued after 1996 (see Figure 6.2).

[38] See Ramachandran and Visaria (1997), Visaria and Visaria (1998), Pachauri and Subramanian (1999), HealthWatch Trust (1999), Sangwan and Maru (1999), Coutinho et al. (2000), Mavalankar (2000), Visaria (2000a, 2000b), among others.

The apparent effectiveness of this approach suggests that the real driving force behind the comparative dynamism of reproductive and child health services in India is the sustained interest of political leaders and health administrators in this particular aspect of health services. With or without target-based harassment, they seem to be able to translate this interest into concrete results. As we noted, the preoccupation with population control has caused serious damage to the health system as a whole. Yet there is also a positive lesson in this experience, namely that strong commitment to particular health goals produces results, even without authoritarian means. A similar lesson emerges from the programme-specific achievements mentioned earlier, varying from India's initial success with malaria control (rather diluted later on) to the recent pulse polio programme.

Extending this commitment to other aspects of basic health care (especially preventive action and public health) is one of the central challenges involved in transforming health services in India. If ANMs can go from house to house promoting family planning, there is no good reason why health workers should not make similar enquiries about tuberculosis, malaria or diarrhoea. If primary health centres are well supplied with contraceptives and delivery kits, there is no reason why they should be short of basic drugs. If the public can be bombarded with family planning messages, it should also be possible to promote widespread public understanding of, say, communicable diseases and basic hygiene. Some progress is being made in this respect within the field of 'reproductive and child health' (going well beyond the usual emphasis on contraception and vaccination), reflecting sustained pressure on the part of reproductive rights activists and women's organizations. But the dominant pattern is one of continued neglect of health issues in public policy. In some respects, the neglect may have intensified in the nineties. Public expenditure on health as a proportion of GDP, for instance, has marginally *declined* during that period.[39] Another issue of much concern in this connection is the slowdown of infant mortality decline in the 1990s, compared with the 1980s (see chapters 1 and 9).

There is, thus, an urgent need for radical reform in this field. Here again, as with elementary education, one of the main tasks is to elevate the political visibility of health matters. Indeed, this is one crucial lesson

---

[39] World Bank (2001a), p. 52. As in the case of education, discussed in the preceding chapter, salaries account for an overwhelming share of public expenditure on health, and the combination of a 'budgetary squeeze' with rapid salary increases has been particularly detrimental to non-salary expenditure, making it that much harder to improve basic facilities as well as the supply of drugs.

emerging from the history of health care in Kerala, where health has been a lively political issue for a long time.[40] A similar message seems to be strongly suggested by the experience of Tamil Nadu, discussed in the next section.

6.6. ACHIEVEMENTS OF TAMIL NADU

As was mentioned earlier, examples of impressive progress in health care and related matters are not confined to Kerala, the trailblazer in this field. Substantial parts of the southern and western regions in India are now moving rapidly in the same direction. This tendency is particularly visible in Tamil Nadu.

Since the mid-1970s, when its child mortality rate was not much below the all-India average, Tamil Nadu has achieved the largest proportionate reduction in child mortality among all major Indian states other than Kerala. Today, Tamil Nadu has the third-lowest child mortality rate among major Indian states and the second-lowest maternal mortality rate.[41] Over the same period, Tamil Nadu also achieved the largest proportionate reduction in total fertility rate (about 50 per cent). Today, it is the only major state other than Kerala where the total fertility rate is below the 'replacement level' (see Figure 6.3, p. 195). These achievements are all the more remarkable in view of the fact that Tamil Nadu has no less income poverty than the Indian average. In fact, the head-count index of poverty is a little higher in Tamil Nadu than in India as a whole (see Table 6.3 below).

Recent studies point to a number of enabling factors that have facilitated Tamil Nadu's rapid demographic transition.[42] Commonly-cited factors include a good infrastructure, a rich history of social reform movements,

---

[40] See Mencher (1980), Nag (1989) and Ramachandran (1996). Mencher, in particular, stresses the role of 'political awareness' in ensuring the effective functioning of health services in Kerala: 'In Kerala, if a PHC was unmanned for a few days, there would be a massive demonstration at the nearest collectorate led by local leftists, who would demand to be given what they knew they were entitled to. This had the effect of making health care much more readily available for the poor in Kerala' (p.1782). This account is in sharp contrast with the corresponding state of affairs in north India, where widespread absenteeism of government doctors is passively accepted as a normal state of affairs (see e.g. Khan et al., 1986).

[41] See Statistical Appendix, Table A.3, Part 2. On mortality and fertility decline in different states, see Government of India (1999a), Tables 1 and 10.

[42] For different perspectives on the demographic transition in Tamil Nadu, see Antony (1992), Kishor (1994b), Srinivasan (1995), Ramasundaram (1995a, 1995b), Krishnamoorthy et al. (1996), Ramasundaram et al. (1997), and Visaria (2000a); also Kulkarni et al. (1996), for an enlightening review.

high literacy rates in the younger age groups, wide popular exposure to mass media, and strong 'political will'. Less widely discussed is the relatively liberated status of women in contemporary Tamil society. Tamil Nadu has a high female-male ratio, little gender bias in school attendance, and high levels of female labour force participation. Also interesting is some recent information from the second round of the National Family Health Survey (1998–9) relating to different aspects of 'female autonomy'.[43] Whether we look at the proportion of adult women who work outside the household (43 per cent), or who have independent access to money (79 per cent), or who are able to go to the market 'without permission' from other family members (79 per cent again), Tamil Nadu is ahead of all other major states (with one exception—Himachal Pradesh—in the case of 'independent access to money'). Bearing in mind the role of women's agency in the demographic transition, discussed earlier in this chapter, this feature of gender relations is crucial to our understanding of what has happened in Tamil Nadu.

Extensive state initiatives in the fields of child nutrition, health care and social security have also made an important contribution to mortality and fertility decline in Tamil Nadu. The state's pioneering school-meal programme has simultaneously boosted school attendance and reduced child undernutrition. In the 1980s, Tamil Nadu also introduced innovative social security programmes such as old-age pensions and social support for widows. Last but not least, as Leela Visaria (2000a) points out, the demographic transition in Tamil Nadu has been facilitated by 'widespread accessibility of reasonably good quality health care'. Today, 89 per cent of children in Tamil Nadu are fully immunized (a higher proportion than in any other state including Kerala), and 84 per cent of births are attended by a health professional. In these respects, the contrast between Tamil Nadu and the large north Indian states is extremely sharp, as Table 6.3 illustrates.[44]

Leela Visaria's study (2000a) also contains a wealth of insights into the practical, day-to-day measures that have helped to enhance the quality of health services in Tamil Nadu. To illustrate: (1) primary health centres in

---

[43] See Statistical Appendix, Table A.3, Part 5.

[44] On Tamil Nadu's health, nutrition and social security programmes, see Babu and Hallam (1989), Rajivan (1991, 2001), Swaminathan (1991), Guhan (1992b, 1993), Rajan and Jayakumar (1992), Mahendra Dev (1994), Visaria and Visaria (1999), among others. There have also been important criticisms, including the occasional use of heavy-handed methods in family planning programmes; see e.g. Ramasundaram (1995a), van Hollen (1998), Sundari Ravindran (1999) and Muraleedharan (2001).

TABLE 6.3 *Selected Health-related Indicators, 1998–9*

	India	Tamil Nadu	'Large north Indian states'[a]
Head-count index of poverty, 1993–4			
rural	33	38	35
urban	18	21	22
combined	29	32	32
Death rate, age 0–4, 1996–8			
female	24.7	13.7	32.5
male	21.7	12.3	27.2
Estimated maternal mortality rate, 1987–96 (per 100,000 live births)	479	195	630
Proportion (%) of recent live births preceded by:			
antenatal care	65	99	42
TT vaccine (2 doses)	67	95	54
iron/folic tablets	58	93	34
Proportion of births assisted by health professional	42	84	26
Proportion of children aged 12–23 months 'fully immunized'	42	89	18
Proportion of ever-married women aged 15–49 with knowledge of AIDS	40	87	19

Note: [a] Bihar, Madhya Pradesh, Rajasthan, Uttar Pradesh. The estimates in this column are population-weighted averages of the state-specific figures.

Sources: International Institute for Population Sciences (2000a), pp. 442–3; Government of India (1999a, 2000h); Mari Bhat (2000), Table 3; the poverty estimates are from Deaton and Tarozzi (2000). Unless stated otherwise, the reference year is 1998–9. For further details, see Statistical Appendix.

Tamil Nadu are well supplied with basic drugs; (2) about 40 to 45 per cent of medical officers are women; (3) ANMs meet the medical officer typically six times a month; (4) many primary health centres (more than 250) are open 24 hours a day. In all these respects, the situation in Tamil Nadu contrasts sharply with the situation in most other states.[45] Visaria's qualitative study is corroborated by another, independent study of a more quantitative nature, which investigates the functioning of 'family welfare services' in four Indian states (Tamil Nadu, Karnataka, West Bengal and

[45] See also Visaria (2000b), where the functioning of health services in Tamil Nadu is contrasted with the corresponding situation in Rajasthan.

TABLE 6.4 *Quality of Family Planning Services in Tamil Nadu, 1993*

	Tamil Nadu	Other states[a]
Proportion of interviewed women who were 'visited by ANM [auxiliary nurse midwife] in the last three months'	89	65
Proportion of interviewed women who report that:		
'ANM always discharges duties sincerely'	82	50
'ANM always discusses side effects'	52	28
'clinic staff always cordial'	79	59
'clinic staff gives proper attention'	70	44
'clinic staff also suggest spacing methods [always]'	50	34
'doctors always available [at clinic]'[b]	66	42
'adequate medicines always available [at clinic]'[b]	72	26
Proportion of ANMs who found training to be adequate	98	59
Proportion of ANMS who responded correctly to:		
'when are the chances of conception highest?'	86	52
'what is a tubectomy?'	90	73
Average population served by a Primary Health Centre	30,000	126,000

Notes: [a] Population-weighted average for Bihar, Karnataka and West Bengal (the other three states covered by the same study).
  [b] Based on separate samples of recent users of the Primary Health Centres (529 women in Tamil Nadu and 1,326 in other states).
Sources: Roy and Verma (1999) and Verma and Roy (1999), based on random samples of currently-married women aged 15–49 (about 900 women in each state) in areas served by 18 randomly-selected Primary Health Centres (PHCs) in each state. The second part of the table is based on interviews with 'auxiliary nurse midwives' (ANMs) in the same PHCs (72 ANMs in Tamil Nadu and 220 in other states).

Bihar). This study, too, found remarkable differences between Tamil Nadu and other states in terms of the quality of health services.[46] The findings are illustrated in Table 6.4. It is heartening to find that a vast majority of women in Tamil Nadu consider that 'the ANM always discharges duties sincerely', that 'clinic staff are always cordial' and that 'adequate medicines are always available'. While these findings relate mainly to family planning services, which tend to be in better shape than other aspects of health care (as discussed in the preceding section), Tamil Nadu is one state where the reach of these services is much broader than elsewhere. Auxiliary nurse-midwives, for instance, deliver a wide range of maternal and child health services, instead of concentrating on the promotion of contraception as often happens in other states (Visaria, 2000b).

[46] There were also important contrasts among the other states. Karnataka fared quite well in many respects, while family welfare services in Bihar were least impressive.

These studies also provide interesting clues to the social context that has facilitated Tamil Nadu's achievements in this field. One observation of major interest, for instance, is that the 'social distance' between medical officers and patients is relatively small in Tamil Nadu. This is helped by the fact, noted earlier, that a large proportion (about 40 to 45 per cent) of medical officers in Tamil Nadu are women.[47] In addition, social reform movements and policies of affirmative action have substantially eroded the privileged access of upper castes and classes to the medical profession. As Leela Visaria (2000a) notes (p. 50–1): 'A visit to the primary health centres in the state would convince anybody that many medical officers have non-Brahmanical backgrounds and are very similar to many rural patients in dress, mannerism, language, as well as overall values and attitudes'. Considering that in other parts of India the social distance between doctors and patients contributes substantially to the poor functioning of health institutions, these social factors are no less important than managerial competence or 'political will' in explaining the comparative efficiency of health services in Tamil Nadu.[48]

The foundation of Tamil Nadu's success also draws on a widely accepted recognition of the centrality of public involvement in health care, and along with that, a sustained presence of health matters in the rhetoric as well as reality of local state politics. This, in turn, can be plausibly related to broader features of democratic politics in this state. Tamil Nadu politics have often been described as 'populism', and while that label is not particularly helpful on its own (populism of one sort or another is an intrinsic feature of electoral politics), insightful attempts have been made at understanding the specific features of Tamil Nadu populism, including, for instance, responsiveness to the political assertion of disadvantaged groups.[49] It is also worth noting that women's votes have tended to matter a great deal in Tamil Nadu politics, in a way that does not apply in (say) north India, where women's electoral choices are typically determined by male members of the family. These features of Tamil Nadu politics help to explain why social programmes (varying from mid-day meals at school to social-security schemes and public health services) have figured quite prominently in public debates and electoral competition for many years.

[47] Visaria (2000a), p. 51. This is an informal estimate, attributed to senior health administrators in Chennai (Madras).

[48] There is an interesting parallel here with the role of comparatively narrow social distance between parents and teachers in facilitating the 'schooling revolution in Himachal Pradesh'; see chapter 5.

[49] Subramanian (1999) regards 'assertive populism' as a crucial feature of Tamil Nadu politics. For different perspectives on these matters, see also Swamy (1996, 1998) and Harriss (2000).

Through a changed focus of public discussion, these social issues have received more attention and support, while at the same time helping their political sponsors to benefit from the growing public concern. The mid-day meal programme, for instance, has contributed to the long wave of popularity enjoyed by its promoter, former Chief Minister M.G. Ramachandran ('MGR').

Health matters, too, have been a focus of political competition.[50] In this respect, there is a crucial similarity between Tamil Nadu and Kerala, where health has been an active political issue for a long time. There are reasons to reaffirm the thesis that democratic practice and political empowerment hold the key to the transformation of the lives of people and ultimately to the much needed broadening of social progress in India—as elsewhere.

6.7. ENVIRONMENT AND DEVELOPMENT

We turn now to environmental issues. As we saw in chapter 3, the record of economic and social development in India since independence, though highly uneven and far from exemplary, includes substantial overall progress in many fields. The same period, however, has also been one of formidable environmental plunder. Forests have been decimated, groundwater tables have fallen, rivers and ponds are massively polluted, and the air that city dwellers breathe has grown increasingly noxious and foul.[51]

In view of these contrary trends, there has been a temptation in public discussions to think of 'development' and 'environment' in antagonistic terms. Plausibility is given to this diagnosis of contrariness by the further recognition of the causal connections involved, particularly the fact that many of these deteriorating environmental trends are clearly linked with heightened economic activity, e.g., industrial growth, increased energy consumption, more intensive irrigation, commercial felling of trees, and other such activities that tend to be linked with economic expansion. 'Development' is, thus, held responsible, with some immediate plausibility,

---

[50] In a revealing anecdote, Visaria (2000a, p. 53) reports how the state government in Tamil Nadu recently sold an aircraft used by a former chief minister to purchase ambulances. 'Successive governments', the author adds, 'have shown a knack for impressing the people of the state through such pro-people gestures'.

[51] Environmental degradation in India is extensively documented in the Centre for Science and Environment's *State of India's Environment* reports (e.g. Centre for Science and Environment, 1982, 1999). For further reviews, see also Tata Energy Research Institute (1996, 1998a, 1998b), The Hindu (1999, 2000), Cassen (2000), Gupta (2000).

for the damage. On the other side, environmental activists are often accused of being 'anti-development', since the advocates of accelerated growth often see environmentalists as being unwelcoming (if not obstructive) of economic progress for fear of its adverse environmental impact. The sense of tension is hard to avoid.

That confrontational view, which places development and environment on a collisional path, does not at all fit in with the approach of this book, and it is useful to begin this section by discussing why that is the case. We have seen development as enhancement of human freedom, involving diverse concerns, but incorporating expansion of social opportunities and the quality of life. Since many human freedoms and components of the quality of life are dependent on the integrity of the environment (involving the air we breathe, the water we drink, the epidemiological surroundings in which we live, and so on), development cannot but be sensitive to the quality of the environment. The opportunity to live the kind of lives that people value—and have reason to value—depends inter alia on the nature and robustness of the environment. In this sense, development has to be environment-inclusive.[52] The thesis that development and environment are on a collision course cannot sit comfortably with the recognition of manifest complementarity between the two.

In fact, focusing on the quality of life can help to generate an adequate understanding not only of development, but also of the environment and the central role it plays in our lives. Environment is often understood to refer simply to the state of 'nature', e.g. the extent of forest cover, the depth of the groundwater table, the number of living species, and so on. In so far as it is assumed that this pre-existing nature will stay intact unless we add impurities and pollutants to it, it might appear superficially plausible that the environment is best protected if we interfere with it as little as possible. This understanding is, however, misleading and defective for three distinct reasons.

First, even though the human perspective on the environment is not the only one (the country of Gautama Buddha and Mahaveera does not need to be reminded that animals count—and not just for their contribution

---

[52] The argument that development has to be environment-inclusive has, it appears, been sometimes confused with the altogether contrary view that the environment does not deserve serious attention in development analysis. Since the latter view has on occasion been, somewhat mysteriously, attributed to us (individually or jointly), we should reiterate the obvious point (to avoid any possible confusion) that an environment-inclusive view of development makes it obligatory to consider environmental issues in development analysis, rather than suggesting that they be neglected. See also Drèze and Sen (1989) and Sen (1995a, 1995b).

to the living standards of human beings), the impact of the environment on human lives must inter alia be among the relevant considerations in assessing the richness of the environment. In understanding why the eradication of smallpox is not viewed as an impoverishment of nature in the way, say, the destruction of lovely forests would be, the connection with human lives has to be brought into the explanation. Given that inescapable connection, the assessment of the environment cannot but be dependent on many other features of human lives that are directly—and often constructively—dependent on the process of development.

It is, therefore, not surprising that environmental sustainability has typically been defined in terms of the prospects of preserving and enhancing the quality of human lives. The Brundtland Report, published in 1987, defined 'sustainable development' as 'development that meets the needs of the present without compromising the ability of future generations to meet their own needs'.[53] This rather general formulation has been sharpened by Robert Solow as the requirement that the next generation must be left with 'whatever it takes to achieve a standard of living at least as good as our own and to look after their next generation similarly'.[54] The thing to note immediately is the extent to which sustainability is seen here in terms of the impact of the environment on human living standards.

We can, in fact, make the formulation of sustainability less narrowly anchored to the idea of standard of living of people and broaden the criterion to include what we *value* (and feel committed to), rather than only what we *enjoy* as a part of our living standards.[55] This gives more explicit room for considering what we may be committed to preserve, including aspects of the environment that do not influence our own standard of living. For example the preservation of some animal species may be valued as being important in itself, even if the continuation of that species does not add to our enjoyment or to our living standards in any particular way.

But no matter whether the anchoring is done to our living standards or to our values and commitments, there is an inescapable human connection in assessing the environment, in the light of our values and priorities. What we value, and the reasons that we have for valuing one thing or another, are not independent of the process of development. Social valuation, as we have discussed, is influenced by public discussion, social interactions, and of course, by educational opportunities. Valuation is, among other things, a developmental process.

---

[53] World Commission on Environment and Development (1987), p. 43.
[54] Solow (1992), p. 15.
[55] On this see Sen (1977, 1995a).

Second, while human activities that accompany the process of development may have destructive consequences, it is also within human power to enhance and improve the environment in which we live. Even when we think about the steps that may be taken to halt environmental destruction, we search for constructive human intervention. Our power to intervene and to do it with effectiveness and reasoning may be substantially enhanced by the process of development itself. For example, as was discussed earlier, greater female education and women's employment can help to reduce population growth and the pressure on environmental resources.[56] Similarly, the spread of school education and improvements in its quality can make us more environment conscious. Better communication and a richer media can also make us more aware of the need for environment-oriented thinking. It is easy to find many other examples of such interconnections. In general, seeing development in terms of increasing the effective freedom of human beings brings the constructive agency of people in environment-friendly activities directly within the domain of developmental achievements. Development is empowering and that power can be used to preserve and enrich the environment, and not just to decimate it.

Third, even though it is tempting to think of the environment exclusively in terms of pre-existing natural conditions, our idea of the environment does, in fact, encompass aspects of human creation. For example, the purification of water is a means of improving the environment, at least in an acceptably broad sense. Elimination of epidemics, on which we commented earlier (in relation to the relevance of the human perspective in evaluation), is another good illustration of the created component of the benign nature in which we would like to be engulfed.

It is perhaps also worth remarking here that development is not a new process, and in examining the effects of development on the environment, we must not presume that the entire mechanism has only just been initiated. Some of the environmental effects of changes that have occurred over the last thousands of years are strong enough on their own. Consider, for example, the fact that air pollution in urban India is a major problem today, which can be seen as a by-product of modern development. It is interesting to note, in this context, that according to recent studies, even the hapless commuters in the most congested parts of Delhi breathe a healthier air today than the average village woman, who is exposed to staggering levels of 'indoor pollution' from kitchen smoke.[57] While the

[56] On this see also Sen (1999a, 2000d).
[57] See Centre for Science and Environment (1999), chapter 8, and the literature cited there.

rural environment may seem pre-developmental, and may also evoke romanticism about the charms of 'unspoilt nature', it can, in fact, incorporate a heavy dose of man-made pollution of traditional varieties. This recognition must not, of course, detract attention from the importance, indeed urgency, of tackling pollution in Delhi, which is one of the most polluted mega-cities in the world. But it does suggest that the solution to environmental problems has to be sought in a constructive and forward-looking way, rather than seeking salvation in 'returning' to 'the world we have lost'. We need a better integration of environmental concerns with other development concerns, rather than looking for ways and means of returning to the supposedly healthier lifestyles of the past.

These are some of the reasons for questioning the view of the environment as (1) composed of pre-existing nature, (2) valued for its own sake, and (3) only worsenable—not improvable—through development. We have to move away from that limited vision, and that reexamination makes the environmental issue inseparably linked with the demands of development. Not only must the assessment of development be inclusive of environmental concerns, we must also take note of the various ways in which the process of development may influence the nature of the environment and the values that are invoked in assessing it. This recognition does not, in any way, change the basic fact that the process of economic development can also have very destructive environmental consequences, sometimes even swamping the constructive perspective. But it is important to see the relationship between development and the environment in an adequately broad way, taking note of the constructive prospects as well as destructive possibilities.

6.8. CONSEQUENCES OF ENVIRONMENTAL PLUNDER

What, then, are the main reasons for being concerned about environmental degradation in India and its relation with current patterns of development? Are there real reasons for disquiet? There certainly are overwhelming reasons for this concern.

First, environmental degradation has compromised or 'undone' many of the improvements that were otherwise made possible by greater economic prosperity. For instance, it is arguable that, due to rising congestion and pollution, the quality of life in some of India's larger cities is lower today than it was twenty years ago, in spite of a large increase in per-capita incomes. In rural areas, too, environmental degradation has often considerably diluted if not defeated the gains of economic development. In districts such as Kalahandi in Orissa, for instance, the collapse of the environmental base—especially forests—has undermined people's traditional livelihoods and forced a large proportion of the workforce into seasonal or permanent migration (Drèze, 2001d). While Kalahandi occasionally makes headlines for extreme cases of starvation (if not 'famine'), there is a much larger story behind the headlines, in which environmental degradation plays a major role as a causal antecedent of chronic hunger and deprivation (in addition to being important in its own right).

Second, the present trends of environmental decline are not only intolerable already, they are also incompatible with the basic requirements of sustainable development. To illustrate, air pollution levels in Delhi are already much above WHO standards (e.g. about four times above the safe limit for 'total suspended particles'), yet the number of motorized vehicles—which account for the bulk of the problem—continues to grow at more than 10 per cent per year (Table 6.5).[58] Clearly, something needs to be done, and has to be done soon, given the cumulative effects of this growth. Similarly, present trends of rapid decline of groundwater tables in large parts of the country are utterly unsustainable, and call for urgent attention.

Third, in many cases environmental plunder is an infringement of distributive justice and the basic rights of the underprivileged. In urban areas, for instance, a minority of car owners cause massive pollution, congestion, noise, tension and accidents—all at the expense of the public at large. The people whose lives are impoverished and shattered in this way are often among the poorest in the society, from street vendors to pavement dwellers. There is an aspect of what may be called 'disguised violence'—or even perhaps 'disguised manslaughter'—in the hidden processes that make the fortunes of some dependent on the sufferings and perils of others. Similarly, in rural areas, intensive groundwater exploitation on the part of privileged farmers has often deprived others of access to irrigation and even (in some cases) to drinking water.[59] It is perhaps worth remarking here that even the heated and protracted disputes surrounding the construction of the Narmada dam are, to a great extent, about distributional issues. Indeed, the main concern raised by this project is its adverse impact on the lives of those who are being displaced without consent and without adequate compensation, many of whom also happen to belong to some of the most deprived sections of Indian society.[60]

[58] For further details, see Centre for Science and Environment (1996) and Government of India (1997d).

[59] See e.g. Bhatia (1992); also Cassen (2000) and the literature cited there.

[60] See various contributions in Drèze, Samson and Singh (1997), and the literature cited there; also Roy (1999).

TABLE 6.5 *Selected Indicators of India's Urban Environment*

	Delhi	India (major cities)
Proportion of households living in slums, 1991 (%)	27	27
Proportion of households with access to safe drinking water, 1991	96	81
Proportion of households using 'open spaces' as toilets, 1990[a] (%)	41	61
Proportion of households disposing of garbage 'on the street' or 'outside the house', 1990[a] (%)	67	68
Proportion of population served by a sewage system, 1986-7 (%)	n/a	46
Annual growth of vehicle population, 1983-95 (%)	11	10[b]

Notes: [a] Based on an all-India sample survey of 23,263 households in urban areas (including 4,073 households in Delhi).
[b] Bangalore, Calcutta, Chennai, Delhi, Hyderabad, Mumbai combined.
Source: Centre for Science and Environment (1999), vol. II, pp. 113, 115, 121, 124, 125, 127.

The distributive aspects of environmental plunder have a gender dimension, too. The well-being and freedom of many rural Indian women depend vitally on environmental resources, including convenient access to water, fodder, and fuel, and this connection is often far closer than those that link men to these environmental resources. As a result, women frequently suffer disproportionately from environmental degradation.[61] When different types of disadvantage (such as poverty, gender and location) compound each other, their overall effect can be quite devastating, as is indeed the case for many rural women from poorer families and lower castes. While environmental degradation may affect the lives of all, some lives are much more severely harmed than others.

It is worth considering whether the distributional features of environmental destruction have made it receive less attention than it would have if the main sufferers were among the politically powerful and the socially mighty.[62] No matter how that question is answered,

[61] See e.g. Agarwal (1997a, 1997b, 1998).

[62] This hypothesis, plausible enough in general, receives further support from the fact that one of the few environmental issues to have received serious attention from policy-makers in recent years is urban pollution in Delhi—a problem that happens to have a strong bearing on the quality of life of many people who are in positions of influence and power. In this case, public pressure has even led to fairly drastic action (with help from the Supreme Court), such as the introduction of strict standards on vehicular emissions and the large-scale relocation of polluting industries (with some

there can be little doubt that state intervention to halt environmental degradation in India has been so far rather feeble in comparison with the magnitude of the problem. In fact, not only has public policy tolerated environmental plunder for a long time, it has even, in many cases, actively encouraged it. For one thing, government projects (from dams and mines to firing ranges and nuclear tests) are themselves a major cause of environmental damage. For another, public policy has often subsidized or otherwise encouraged the destruction of the environment by private parties. For instance, the depletion of groundwater resources (especially by large farmers) has been accelerated by electricity subsidies, sugarcane subsidies, and plentiful credit for energized water extraction devices.

Environmental irresponsibility in public policy has both political and ideological roots. To start with, environmental irresponsibility frequently draws on the often-repeated prejudice that a little bit of environmental vandalism is the price to pay for economic development, at least in its early stages. Some have even argued that environmental protection is a 'bourgeois' or 'western' concern, best addressed after economic prosperity has been achieved. This carries with it the suggestion that meanwhile environmental degradation should be tolerated. As D.K. Biswas, director of the Central Pollution Control Board, candidly reports in a recent interview, 'earlier when we talked about the environment, people used to laugh at us'.[63]

More importantly perhaps, public policy in India has tended to be heavily influenced by powerful lobbies that thrive on the private appropriation of environmental resources: mining companies, timber contractors, sugarcane mills, car manufacturers, the plastic industry, to name a few. Sugarcane subsidies, for instance, have far more to do with the political influence of large farmers and mill owners than with the merits of the case. Similarly, public regulation of the infamous 'polybag' has been fiercely opposed by the plastic industry.[64] The need to overcome the damaging influence of class and stratification applies not only to development in general, but also to environmental matters in particular.

---

adverse effects, unfortunately, on employment opportunities for the urban poor). These experiences give a useful glimpse of what could be achieved if similar attention were paid, say, to problems of drinking-water pollution or groundwater depletion in rural areas.

[63] Quoted in Centre for Science and Environment (1996), p. 127.

[64] Polythene bags have become a major environmental hazard in urban India in the nineties, causing widespread clogging of drains, retention of stagnant water, accumulation of non-biodegradable waste, suffocation of wandering animals, etc. For further discussion, see Chaturvedi (1999).

6.9. ENVIRONMENT AND THE CONSTRUCTIVE PERSPECTIVE

Against this background of irresponsibility and apathy, environmental activists have tended to seek help from the judiciary. The nineties have seen an unprecedented wave of 'public interest litigations' on environmental matters. In some cases (e.g. relating to pollution in Delhi), judgements favourable to the environmental cause have been obtained. 'Judicial activism', however, has important limitations as a means of environmental protection.

First, court proceedings are expensive and often drag on for years. The speed of reaction can be spectacularly out of line with the urgency of the problems to be dealt with.

Second, public interest litigations typically arise in response to a crisis. A sound environmental policy, in contrast, needs forward-looking policies and foresight, and even pro-active intervention before an emergency occurs, rather than sequential crisis management, which is often ineffective and inefficient.

Third, judges are not always adequately prepared to handle the highly technical matters arising in environment-related cases. Also, many of the important means of halting environmental plunder, such as variations in taxes and subsidies (including the possible introduction of 'green taxes'), are difficult to explore within the framework of court proceedings.

Fourth, courts tend to deliver sweeping judgements, based on specific petitions, with relatively little scope for exploring alternatives or negotiating agreements. The uncompromising 1996 ban on aquaculture, for instance, caused havoc among shrimp farmers, leading to a series of attempts and counter-attempts to reverse the court's order. Similar controversies have followed the more recent Supreme Court judgement on vehicular standards in Delhi (including the compulsory use of 'compressed natural gas' by city buses).

Finally, while the judicial process is an integral part of India's democratic framework, individual proceedings are often far from democratic. The standard procedures of litigation can be sufficiently expensive or impenetrable to exclude many victims of environmental regress. And while judges undoubtedly try to understand the situation as fully as possible in many cases, they are often remote from the people whose lives are battered and ruined. The handicap of social distance is as real in this field as it is in many other areas of public policy.

All this does not, of course, provide adequate reason for dismissing the importance of the judicial route, which is one of the important avenues to be pursued. Judicial activism has played a fruitful role in generating public awareness of, and media interest in, environmental problems, and in giving some strength (indeed a much needed strength) to environmental pressure groups. The value of judicial involvement in environmental matters must not be lightly dismissed, but the nature of the problem calls for more than that. What is clear enough is that judicial activism on its own is not an adequate and sustainable basis for environmental protection. A more comprehensive approach is needed, which must also incorporate other ways of giving environmental problems the attention they deserve.

When it comes to remedying the environmental dangers, it is necessary to consider the different means that can be used to address the problem adequately. There is, for example, some choice between the route of value formation and that of institutional reform. If people were to care spontaneously about the effects of their actions on the environment (and through that, about their effects on others), then the need for institutional reform would be, to that extent, reduced. On the other side, if institutions could be effectively reshaped (for example, through regulations prohibiting the discharge of effluents, or through 'green taxes', or through appropriate changes in property rights), so that environmental effects are better reflected in private costs and benefits, then the necessity for value formation would, to that extent, decrease. To prevent the poisoning of our water, the fouling of our air, and other calamities, we can get help *both* (1) from value formation that makes us more sensitive to this damage, and (2) from changed institutional arrangements that reduce private incentives to destroy the environment and provide contrary incentives to preserve it.

There is also a third route, which shares some characteristics of each of the other two. This takes the form of social movements that can be translated into community management. There have been notable successes along this route in different parts of India, especially in relatively egalitarian social settings.[65] Such community activities call both for a different outlook on environmental issues (for which appropriate social values can be quite crucial) and for the formation of specific community-based organizations (requiring additional institutional structures). While value formation and institutional reform can, to some extent, be seen as alternative approaches to the environmental problem, there is an opportunity of drawing simultaneously on both, to pursue those changes that require a different outlook and norm as well as new institutions.[66]

[65] See the literature cited in chapter 2 (pp. 60–1)
[66] On the underlying need for valuational and institutional response to the problems of environmental externalities, see Papandreou (1994), and also the literature surveyed there.

There is a strong case for more systematic examination of these issues in contemporary India. Public discussion can play an important part both in encouraging helpful formation of values and in useful exploration of institutional changes. What is needed is not so much the adoption of certain general remedies or mechanical formulas that are frequently championed by one side or the other, but probing scrutiny of the available options in the light of particular challenges. India's democratic framework gives room to such constructive moves, and the opportunities can be more adequately seized than they have been so far. Greater public awareness of these issues and more active public interest in seeking workable solutions can themselves help to advance the prospects of a solution. There is still a long way to go, but environmental activism has gained some considerable ground in India today, and shows promise of advancing more. There are reasons for hope in this, and perhaps even for qualified confidence.

7

Gender Inequality and Women's Agency

7.1. FEMALE DEPRIVATION AND MISSING WOMEN

Inequality between men and women is one of the crucial disparities in many societies, and this is particularly so in India. Differences in schooling opportunities between boys and girls, discussed in chapter 5, illustrate one aspect of this broader phenomenon of gender-based inequality in India. In much of the country, women tend in general to fare quite badly in relative terms compared with men, even within the same families. This is reflected not only in such matters as education and opportunity to develop talents, but also in the more elementary fields of nutrition, health, and survival. Indeed, the mortality rates of females tend to exceed those of males until the late twenties, and this—as we know from the experiences of other countries—is very much in contrast with what tends to happen when men and women receive similar nutritional and health care.[1] One result is a remarkably low ratio of females to males in the Indian population compared with the corresponding ratio not only in Europe and North America, but also in sub-Saharan Africa. The problem is not, of course, unique to India, but it is particularly serious in this country, and certainly deserves public attention as a matter of major priority.

There are, in fact, striking variations in the ratio of females to males in the population (hereafter 'female-male ratio', or FMR for short) in different regions of the world. While there are important social and

[1] See Sen (1992c), and the literature cited there; see also Kynch (1985). For detailed information on age- and sex-specific mortality rates in India, see Government of India (1999a).

cultural influences on survival rates,[2] there is fairly strong medical evidence to the effect that—given similar care—women tend to have lower age-specific mortality rates than men (indeed, even female foetuses are relatively less prone to miscarriage than their male counterparts). Even though males outnumber females at birth (and even more at conception), women tend to outnumber men substantially in Europe and North America, with average ratios of around 1.05.[3] While that includes some remnant effects of greater male mortality in past wars, the ratio would still be substantially above unity after adjusting for that. In contrast, many parts of the developing world have female-male ratios well below unity, for example, 0.98 in north Africa, 0.95 in west Asia, 0.95 in Bangladesh, 0.94 in China. In India and Pakistan, the female-male ratio is among the lowest in the world—about 0.93 in both cases.[4] There is much direct evidence, in India and in many other countries with a sharp 'deficit' of women, of relative neglect of the health and well-being of women (particularly young girls including female infants), resulting in a survival disadvantage of females vis-à-vis males over long periods.

It is easily calculated that no matter what female-male ratio we use as a benchmark for comparison (whether the FMR in contemporary Europe, or in sub-Saharan Africa, or one based on the historical experience of parts of Europe), we would find that there are many millions of 'missing women' in India. The sub-Saharan African ratio had yielded the colossal number of 37 million missing women in 1986 (Drèze and Sen 1989, Table 4.1, p. 52).[5] Stephan Klasen's history-based calculation suggests figures closer to 35 million. These are gigantic figures—and there is no consolation here in the fact that the absolute number of missing women

2 On this see particularly Johansson (1991) and Alaka Basu (1992). See also Sopher (1980b) and Dyson and Moore (1983).

3 The international female-male ratios cited in this section are calculated from United Nations Population Division (1999); the reference year is 1995, the latest year for which 'estimated' (rather than 'projected') figures are available.

4 On south Asia's low female-male ratio, see Bardhan (1974, 1984a, 1988), Mitra (1979), Miller (1981), Kynch and Sen (1983), Kynch (1985), Sen (1984, 1985c, 1989, 1992c), Mazumdar (1985), Drèze and Sen (1989), Coale (1991), Klasen (1994), among others; also Klasen and Wink (2001), and recent studies cited there.

5 It was on the basis of the sub-Saharan African FMR that the figure of 'more than a hundred million missing women' was presented for Asia and north Africa as a whole in Drèze and Sen (1989) and Sen (1989). Coale (1991) suggested a number closer to 60 million, on the basis of the historical experience of Europe, whereas Klasen (1994) arrives at around 90 million missing women based on a different reading of the European experience. While refinements of the exact numbers can certainly continue, it is important to emphasize that no matter which standard FMR we use, we do get very large numbers of missing women.

(though not its ratio to the population) in China is estimated to be even higher—between 38 and 40 million. We do have a problem of basic inequality here of extraordinary proportions.

7.2. ON THE FEMALE-MALE RATIO

We have noted in the preceding section that India as a whole has an exceptionally low female-male ratio. This problem, is not, of course, equally serious in every region of India. As we saw in chapter 3, there are large variations in the female-male ratio between different states. The female-male ratio is particularly low in large parts of north India, especially the north-western states (e.g. 0.86 in Haryana and 0.87 in Punjab), and comparatively high in the south (e.g. 0.99 in Tamil Nadu, 0.98 in Andhra Pradesh, 0.96 in Karnataka).[6] In Kerala, the female-male ratio is well above unity; in fact, it is as high as 1.06, that is, higher than in any of the world's major regions except Eastern Europe.[7]

These regional patterns of female-male ratios are consistent with what is known of the character of gender relations in different parts of the country. The north-western states, for instance, are notorious for highly unequal gender relations, some symptoms of which include the continued practice of female seclusion, low female labour-force participation rates, a large gender gap in literacy rates, extremely restricted female property rights, strong boy preference in fertility decisions, widespread neglect of female children, and drastic separation of a married woman from her natal family. In all these respects, the social standing of women is relatively better in south India (and also in much of the eastern region).[8] Kerala, for its part, has a distinguished history of a more liberated position of

[6] See Table 3.3 in chapter 3. Wherever possible, the Indian female-male ratios cited in this chapter are based on the early results of the 2001 census (Government of India, 2001b). In cases where the relevant data are not available for 2001 (e.g. for age-specific FMRs), we have used the 1991 census (Nanda, 1992). The FMR for India as a whole was very similar in both census years (0.927 in 1991 and 0.933 in 2001).

[7] Kerala's high female-male ratio is partly due to high levels of male outmigration, but even the migration-adjusted FMR is above unity (see e.g. Agnihotri, 1995).

[8] On these regional contrasts in gender relations, see Karve (1965), Bardhan (1974, 1984a), Sopher (1980a, 1980b), Miller (1981), Dyson and Moore (1983), Kolenda (1984), Jain and Banerjee (1985), Caldwell and Caldwell (1987), Mandelbaum (1988), Alaka Basu (1992), Kishor (1993), Agarwal (1994), Uberoi (1994), Kapadia (1995), Malhotra et al. (1995), Murthi, Guio and Drèze (1995), Raju et al. (1999), Dube (2001), among others. As these studies make clear, analyses of gender relations in India need to go beyond the basic north-south dichotomy and explore finer regional contrasts; on the latter, see Malhotra et al. (1995) and Agnihotri (2000).

women in society.[9] Important aspects of this history include a major success in the expansion of female literacy, considerable prominence of women in influential social and professional activities, and a tradition of matriliny for an important section of the population.[10]

These regional contrasts, and also changes in the female-male ratio over time, provide a useful opportunity to investigate different aspects of the problem of low female-male ratios in India. This investigation will be pursued a little further in this section and the next one. The motivation for focusing on the female-male ratio is partly that this indicator of gender inequality is important in its own right, and partly that it sheds some interesting light on other aspects of gender relations, and through that on a number of interlinked features of Indian society.

Two Misconceptions

To begin with, we should deal with two misunderstandings that arise from time to time in popular discussions of the issue of low female-male ratios in India.

First, it is sometimes thought that the main cause of the problem is some phenomenon of hidden female infanticide, not captured in reported death statistics. In fact, census figures on female-male ratios are quite consistent with what one would predict based on (1) a standard female-male ratio at birth of about 0.95, and (2) independently recorded age- and sex-specific mortality rates.[11] To illustrate, the predicted female-male ratio at age 5 in India in 1991, using information on age-specific mortality rates from the Sample Registration System, is 0.94. The *actual* female-male ratio at age 5 for that year, obtained from the 1991 census, is 0.93—quite close to the predicted value.[12]

---

[9] See e.g. Robin Jeffrey (1992).

[10] There are, however, other fields of gender relations where Kerala has a long way to go in removing gender inequality and women's subordination. For instance, the political representation of women is quite poor in Kerala, even today, as can be seen for instance from the low proportion of women in the State Assembly. In this as in other contexts, the misguided temptation to treat Kerala as a 'model' (discussed in chapter 3) must be resisted.

[11] On this point, see also Sudha and Rajan (1999).

[12] The predicted female-male ratio is calculated using the simple formula FMR = $(0.95)(1-q^f)/(1-q^m)$, where q^f and q^m are, respectively, the female and male probability of dying before the fifth birthday. The estimates of q^f and q^m for 1991 (0.101 and 0.091, respectively) are taken from Government of India (1997a). The 'actual' female-male ratio at age 5 is a smoothed value (based on population totals in the 4–6 age group), calculated from Government of India (2000d), p.226.

It is possible, of course, that recorded child deaths include some female infant deaths due to infanticide, which are reported by the parents as due to some other cause. But the anthropological evidence suggests that female infanticide, when it does occur, takes place very soon after birth.[13] The bulk of excess female mortality in childhood, on the other hand, occurs after the age of one, with a less unequal pattern in the first year. In fact, at the all-India level neo-natal and infant mortality rates, in particular, are much the same for males and females, and it is among older children that a pronounced anti-female bias in mortality rates is found.[14] The force of excess female mortality, therefore, is concentrated in age groups beyond that of female infanticide. The female disadvantage in these age groups is itself due to a well-documented practice of preferential treatment of boys and neglect of female children in intra-household allocation. There is, indeed, considerable direct evidence of neglect of female children in terms of health care, nutrition, and related needs, particularly in north India.[15]

It may be argued that the deliberate neglect of female children ought to come under the label of infanticide. There might be a case for this, but the point to recognize is that the social practices that lead to excess female mortality are far more subtle and widespread than the graphic stories of drowning, poisoning, or asphyxiation of female infants that periodically make headlines in the newspapers. This is not to deny that female infanticide, strictly defined, does indeed occur in India today and has done so in the past.[16]

The second misinterpretation concerns some alleged 'Muslim influence'. The reasoning, in so far as there is any, is that female-male ratios in India tend to be particularly low in the north-west of the country, which

[13] See e.g. Panigrahi (1972), Miller (1981), George et al. (1992), and Venkatachalam and Srinivasan (1993).

[14] In 1996, for instance, the infant mortality rate was virtually the same for males and females, but in the 1–4 age group, female mortality was 63 per cent higher than male mortality (Government of India, 1998a, p. 171). In several states, the mortality rate in the 1–4 age group is about twice as high for girls as for boys.

[15] See e.g. Chen, Huq, and D'souza (1981), Miller (1981), Kynch and Sen (1983), Sen and Sengupta (1983), Das Gupta (1987, 1995b), Alaka Basu (1989, 1992), M.E. Khan et al. (1989), Chatterjee (1990), Harriss (1990), B. Agarwal (1991), Deolalikar and Vashishta (1992), Kishor (1994a), among other studies.

[16] Female infanticide has a long history in north India, and remains quite common in particular areas or communities; see e.g. Panigrahi (1972) and Miller (1981). See also George et al. (1992), Venkatachalam and Srinivasan (1993) and Chunkath and Athreya (1997) on the current practice of female infanticide in parts of south India.

is geographically close to Muslim-dominated countries, has been under Muslim influence for a long time and, even now, has a large Muslim population.[17] But a glance at the figures immediately exposes the fragility of this hypothesis. The state of Kerala, which has the highest female-male ratio among Indian states (1.06 in 2001), also has a higher proportion of Muslims in the population than any other state except Jammu and Kashmir, Assam and West Bengal. The state with the lowest proportion of Muslims in the population (1 per cent in 1991) is Punjab, which has had the lowest female-male ratio among all Indian states until it was overtaken by Haryana in 1981. Haryana itself has an extremely small Muslim population (4 per cent of the total population in 1991).

We can take a closer look at this whole issue by examining the extent of gender bias in child mortality rates among Hindus and Muslims in different parts of India. The evidence is summarized in Figure 7.1. This diagram shows the ratio of female child mortality to male child mortality in different states, both for the Hindu population (on the horizontal axis) and for the Muslim population (on the vertical axis). The point representing a particular state lies to the right of the point marked '1' on the horizontal axis if and only if female mortality is higher than male mortality among Hindus, and above the point marked '1' on the vertical axis if the same statement applies for Muslims. Further, a state lies above the diagonal if and only if the ratio of female to male child mortality (which can be interpreted as a measure of anti-female bias in child survival) is *higher* among Muslims than among Hindus.[18]

This figure highlights two points. First, *regional* contrasts in the extent of gender bias in child survival are far more striking than the contrast relating to *religious identity*. Specifically, the relative survival chances of girls are low in large parts of north India (including Haryana, Punjab, Uttar Pradesh, Bihar, and Rajasthan), and this applies whether they are Hindus or Muslims. Second, there is no evidence of any overall tendency for the female disadvantage to be larger among Muslims.

[17] The political value of this kind of argument has not been lost on either side of the north-western border, judging from a recent report of the Pakistan Institute of Development Economics on the condition of women in Pakistan (Shah, 1986). In its analysis of the 'roots of the Pakistani woman's status' (pp. 19–21), this report primarily blames the historical influence of the 'traditions of the Hindu majority in undivided India' for the deprived condition of women in contemporary Pakistan.

[18] The mortality estimates on which Figure 7.1 is based are indirect estimates grounded on census information, and the individual numbers are subject to some margin of error. The purpose of Figure 7.1 is to highlight a broad pattern, rather than to convey precise estimates for particular states.

FIGURE 7.1 *Ratio of Female to Male Child Mortality Among Hindus and Muslims in Different States, 1981–91*

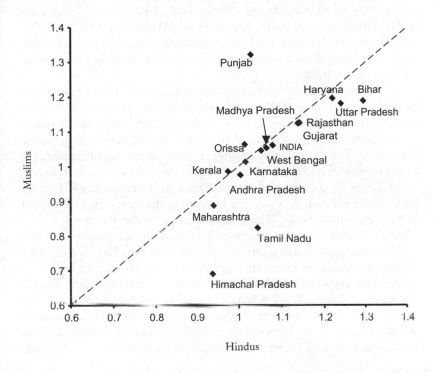

Notes: (1) The horizontal axis indicates the ratio of female child mortality to male child mortality among Hindus; similarly with Muslims on the vertical axis. (2) The child mortality measure used is 'q^5', the probability of dying before age 5. (3) Due to small sample sizes, the estimates for Muslims in Punjab and Himachal Pradesh involve a large margin of error.

Source: Calculated from Government of India (1988a) and Rajan and Mohanachandran (2000). The mortality ratios displayed here are unweighted averages of the 1981 and 1991 ratios.

Time trends

It is well-known that the female-male ratio in India has declined through much of the twentieth century. More precisely, India's female-male ratio declined almost monotonically from 0.97 to 0.93 between 1901 and 1971, and has remained close to 0.93 since 1971, reaching its nadir of 0.927 in 1991. Since then there has been some increase: the latest figure, from the 2001 census, is 0.933.

At the state level, twentieth-century trends in female-male ratios exhibit diverse patterns: since 1901, the female-male ratio has steadily declined in some states (e.g. Bihar, Orissa, Tamil Nadu), steadily increased in others (mainly Kerala and Himachal Pradesh), and followed intermediate patterns elsewhere.[19] Broadly speaking, changes in state-specific female-male ratios in the twentieth century have partly taken the form of a 'convergence' effect, involving a particularly large decline in states starting off with a high female-male ratio, and some increase in the states with the lowest initial female-male ratios. The main exception to this pattern is Kerala, where the female-male ratio increased from a high initial value. In addition to this convergence pattern, however, there has been a fairly broad-based decline of the female-male ratio, not confined to any specific region.

The root causes of the all-India decline are far from obvious.[20] The fall cannot be explained by sex-selective migration, enumeration biases, or a change in the sex ratio at birth.[21] Nor can it be attributed to a change in the age composition of the population (e.g. due to fertility decline). Indeed, if we combine 1991 age-specific female-male ratios with the 1901 age

[19] State-specific female-male ratios since 1901 are given in Nanda (1992), pp. 102–3, and Government of India (2001b), pp. 88–9. For further discussion of these patterns, see Drèze and Sen (1995a), pp. 147–54. On the remarkable increase in the female-male ratio in Himachal Pradesh in the twentieth century, see also Cohen (2000).

[20] Important contributions on this subject include P. Visaria (1967, 1971), Mitra (1979), Miller (1981, 1989), Bardhan (1984a, 1988), I. Sen (1986), Karkal (1987), Dyson (1987), Rajan et al. (1991, 1992), Nanda (1992), Kishor (1993), Agnihotri (1995), Mayer (1999). For a recent review, see Krishnaji (2000).

[21] See P. Visaria (1971) and Nanda (1992), pp. 9–14. The female-male ratio at birth has been declining in recent years, possibly due to sex-selective abortion (see section 7.5). But this a relatively new phenomenon, which cannot explain the sustained decline of the female-male ratio since 1901. A large-scale survey carried out in the nineteen-fifties found a female-male ratio at birth of 942 (Nanda, 1992, p.11), which is quite standard, and the National Family Health Survey 1992–3 found a similar value for the 1970s and 1980s (International Institute for Population Sciences, 1995a, pp. 106–7). On the demographic consequences of sex-selective abortion in India, see Das Gupta and Mari Bhat (1997) and Sudha and Rajan (1999).

distribution of the population, we obtain an overall female-male ratio of 928, very close to the actual female-male ratio of 927 in 1991. And similarly, combining the 1901 age-specific female-male ratios with the 1991 age distribution of the population, we find an overall female-male ratio of 977, very close to the actual 1901 female-male ratio of 972.[22] The decline of India's female-male ratio over time is overwhelmingly due to the decline of *age-specific* female-male ratios, rather than to changes in the age distribution of the population.

All this points to the possibility that the decline of India's female-male ratio in the twentieth century relates to differential changes in male and female mortality rates. In this connection, it is useful to distinguish between two possible causes of major change in the female-male ratio (other than the effects already mentioned). First, the ratio can change in response to a gender-neutral change in the mortality *level* in a particular age group, without there being any change in the *ratio* of female to male mortality in that age group. Since we are looking at a period over which mortality levels have declined in all age groups, this may be referred to as the 'mortality decline effect'. Second, the female-male ratio can change in response to a change in the *ratio* of female to male mortality in a particular age group. This may be called the 'changing mortality bias effect'.

It is possible, in some circumstances, for the mortality decline effect to pull down the female-male ratio. For instance, if the infant mortality rate is lower among females than among males (as is often the case, even in India), then an equi-proportionate decline of male and female infant mortality rates would generally lead to some decline in the female-male ratio. This, and other aspects of the mortality decline effect, may well be a part of the explanation for India's declining female-male ratio in the twentieth century.[23]

This, however, does not mean that the decline in the female-male ratio in India is some kind of 'natural' phenomenon, reflecting little more than the decline of mortality. Indeed, in other regions of the world, the decline of mortality in the twentieth century has usually gone hand in hand with an *increase* in the female-male ratio, reflecting a sustained improvement in the survival chances of females relative to males.[24] Even in Kerala, Sri Lanka, and Himachal Pradesh (three regions of south Asia where gender

---

[22] Calculated from S.B. Mukherjee (1976) and Government of India (1996), p. 19. The age distribution of the 2001 population is not available at the time of writing.
[23] For further discussion, see Drèze and Sen (1995a), pp. 150–3.
[24] See e.g. Preston (1976), chapter 6, and Lopez and Ruzicka (1983).

discrimination is comparatively limited), recent demographic trends have followed this typical pattern.[25] The all-India FMR decline seems to reflect a combination of the 'mortality decline effect' with an adverse 'changing mortality bias effect', or, at the very least, a *failure to remove* the anti-female bias in survival. This applies particularly in the younger age groups, where the anti-female bias remains very strong. As was mentioned earlier, in countries where young males and females receive similar treatment in terms of food, health care, and related necessities, females have substantial survival advantages. India's persistently low female-male ratio suggests some considerable anti-female discrimination, which—in contrast with many other countries—has not gone away with the decline of mortality.[26]

This failure to remove the female disadvantage in survival chances in the younger age groups persists today, and that is one major reason why the female-male ratio remains low, despite improved survival chances of women vis-à-vis men in the older age groups. The point can be seen from data on age-specific mortality rates, which are available from 1971 onwards from India's Sample Registration System.[27] Since then, as Figure 7.2 illustrates, there has been a significant improvement in the survival chances of women vis-à-vis men in the older age groups. This pattern is particularly pronounced in the child-bearing years, mainly due to declining maternal mortality.[28] However, there has been no improvement whatsoever in the relative survival chances of girls vis-à-vis boys in the youngest age groups. If anything, the female disadvantage in early childhood may have risen since 1971, as Figure 7.3 further illustrates. Given that early childhood is also a period of relatively high mortality, this persistent survival disadvantage of young girls is bound to exert a major downward effect on the overall female-male ratio.

Taking all age groups together, the overall survival chances of Indian women are now a little higher than those of Indian men, as can be seen from the recent overtaking of male life expectancy by female life expectancy (the gap between the two is around 2 years, in favour of females, according

[25] As noted earlier, the female-male ratio in Kerala and Himachal Pradesh has steadily increased since 1901. Similarly, mortality decline in Sri Lanka has gone hand in hand with a major improvement in the relative survival chances of females vis-à-vis males; see Nadarajah (1983), Langford (1984, 1994), and Langford and Storey (1993).

[26] For further discussion, based on scrutinizing FMR trends in different age groups, see Drèze and Sen (1995a). On the gender bias in child mortality in India, see Kishor (1994a) and Sudha and Rajan (1999), and the literature cited there.

[27] See Government of India (1999a).

[28] On this, see Mari Bhat (2001).

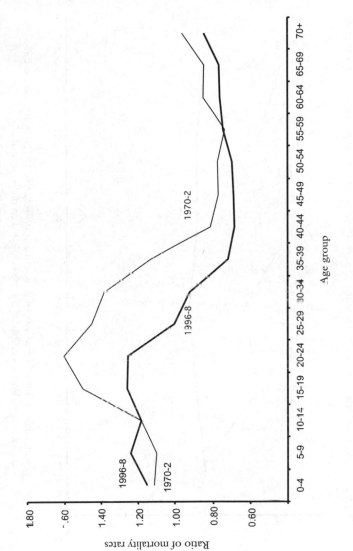

FIGURE 7.2 *Ratio of Female to Male Age-specific Mortality Rates (India), 1970–2 and 1996–8*

Age group

Ratio of mortality rates

1970-2

1996-8

1996-8

1970-2

Source: Calculated from *Sample Registration System*, various annual issues.

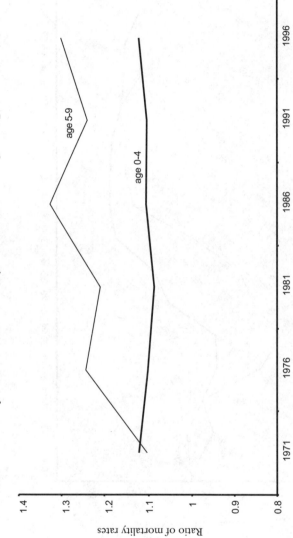

FIGURE 7.3 *Ratio of Female to Male Mortality in the 0–4 and 5–9 Age Groups (India), 1971 to 1996*

Source: Calculated from various annual issues of *Sample Registration System*. The ratios are based on three-year averages of mortality rates centred at the years indicated on the horizontal axis.

to recent estimates). One would normally expect this to be reflected, in due course, in a rising female-male ratio. Meanwhile, however, another downward influence on the female-male ratio has emerged: the steady decline of female-male ratios at birth in many parts of the country, largely due to sex-selective abortion. We shall return to this issue further in this chapter.

Aside from this failure to remove the survival disadvantages of young girls, it is possible that declining relative survival chances of women vis-à-vis men in other age groups have also played a role in the decline of India's female-male ratio in the twentieth century. As Figure 7.2 indicates, there is no evidence of this having happened after 1971, but this does not rule out the possibility of adverse 'changing mortality bias effects' among adults in earlier periods. This might have happened, for instance, because adult men benefited more than adult women from improvements in living conditions and medical care. A further possibility is that more basic changes in gender relations have taken place, leading to a shift in the distribution of resources in favour of men. An example of this possibility is considered presently.

Gender and Caste

The decline of the female-male ratio in India has not been at all even between different castes and communities. Specifically, the decline appears to have been sharper among disadvantaged castes.[29]

Many census reports of the pre-Independence period have noted that the female-male ratio tends to be considerably higher among the 'lower' castes than in the population as a whole.[30] This is no longer the case: in 1991, the female-male ratio among scheduled castes was 922 per thousand, compared with 927 in the population as a whole.[31] As far as the female-male ratio is concerned, the scheduled castes are now much like the rest of the population, in contrast with the earlier pattern.

A detailed examination of this development is complicated by the fact that pre-independence and post-independence census reports use different caste classifications. Pre-independence census reports give caste-

---

[29] For a pioneering discussion of this issue with reference to the post-independence period, see Agnihotri (1995, 2000).

[30] See e.g. Census of India 1931, United Provinces of Agra and Oudh, vol. XVIII, part I, p. 278.

[31] Nanda (1993), p.12, based on 1991 census data. The female-male ratio remains higher among scheduled tribes (972 per thousand in 1991) than in the population as a whole, but that gap too is narrowing over time (Agnihotri, 1995).

specific population totals (for males and females), but post-independence reports do not provide a caste breakdown, except among the scheduled castes. A further difficulty is that the official names of different castes have sometimes changed with 'reclassification'.

To pursue the issues involved in greater detail, we shall scrutinize the relationship between female-male ratios and caste specifically in the state of Uttar Pradesh (which accounts for a large part of the all-India decline in the female-male ratio since 1901). For this state, the 1981 census lists 66 'scheduled castes', of which 47 can be readily identified in the 1901 census volumes. Assuming that these 47 castes are more or less representative of the whole group of scheduled castes, we can reconstruct the 1901 female-male ratio for this group. The results are presented in Table 7.1.[32]

As the table indicates, castes that are now classified as scheduled castes (previously referred to simply as 'untouchables') had much above average female-male ratios in 1901. The Chamars, for instance, who are by far the largest scheduled caste in Uttar Pradesh, had a female-male ratio of 986 in 1901, compared with 937 for the state population as a whole. By 1981, however, the female-male ratio among scheduled castes (including the Chamars) was very close to the state average. This is one indication that, as far as gender relations are concerned, the scheduled castes in Uttar Pradesh are now a little more like the 'higher' castes than they used to be.[33]

The contrast between the scheduled castes and the so-called martial castes (Kshatriya et al.) is particularly interesting. The martial castes, which have a high rank in the caste hierarchy, and an important place in the history and culture of large parts of north India (including Uttar Pradesh), have a long tradition of fierce patriarchy. In fact, the martial castes in north India have played a leading role in the history of female infanticide, child marriage, seclusion, dowry, *sati, johar*, levirate, polygamy, and related patriarchal practices.[34] Among these castes, in Uttar Pradesh, the female-male ratio was already very low at the beginning of the period under consideration (887 in 1901). Further, it has changed little over the years, at least during the pre-independence period (the relevant caste-specific figures are not available for the post-independence period). This is an

[32] Corresponding information for the 1991 and 2001 censuses is not available at the time of writing.

[33] The female-male ratio among Muslims in Uttar Pradesh has also declined a good deal since the beginning of the century (from 957 in 1901 to 903 in 1981), but it remains higher than the female-male ratio for the Hindu population in that state.

[34] See e.g. Tod (1929), Altekar (1956), Karve (1965), Panigrahi (1972), Hitchcock (1975), Bahadur (1978), Miller (1981), Kolenda (1984), Singh (1988).

TABLE 7.1 *Female-Male Ratio and Caste in Uttar Pradesh, 1901 and 1981*

	Total population, 1901 (thousands)	Female-male ratio, 1901	Female-male ratio, 1981
(a) Scheduled castes (SC)			
Chamar	5,891	986	880
All SCs[a]	9,821	970	892
(b) Kshatriya, Rajput, Thakur	3,354	887 ⎤	878[b]
(c) Other Hindu	27,517	929 ⎦	
Hindu (a+b+c)	40,692	935	881
Muslim	6,731	957	903
Other	269	783	884
Total	47,692	937	885

Notes: [a] Only 47 of the 66 castes listed as 'scheduled castes' in the 1981 census could be confidently identified in the 1901 census; the 1901 figures in this row apply to these 47 castes. The 1981 figure includes a tiny proportion (about 1 per cent) of scheduled-caste persons who were *not* counted as 'Hindus' in that census.
[b] Female-male ratio for all Hindus not belonging to a scheduled caste (post-independence censuses provide no information on the caste composition of the population outside the scheduled castes).

Sources: Calculated from Census of India 1901, North-West Provinces and Oudh (Allahabad, 1902), volume 16A; Census of India 1981, Series 22, Uttar Pradesh, Parts IX–i and IX–vii; Census of India 1981, Series 22, Uttar Pradesh, Paper 1 of 1985. The list of scheduled castes is from Census of India 1981, Series 22, Uttar Pradesh, Paper 2 of 1982.

important indication, suggesting that whatever factors led to a decline in the female-male ratio among other castes did not operate among the martial castes over this period—or had already operated earlier. These patterns are consistent with the hypothesis, widely discussed in the literature on social anthropology, that the patriarchal norms of the higher castes are gradually spreading to other castes. The most common interpretation of this phenomenon is that it reflects a process of emulation of the higher castes by the lower castes, with the lifestyle of women playing a central role in this process as a symbol of social status.[35] This process is likely to be particularly strong when the disadvantaged castes experience

[35] The notion of 'Sanskritization' was developed by M.N. Srinivas (1962, 1965, 1967, 1989); see also Berreman (1993), and the more recent studies cited there. Increased resistance to widow remarriage among upwardly-mobile castes (the prohibition of widow remarriage being widely perceived as an upper-caste norm) is a well-documented example of how restrictions on the lifestyle of women often play an important role in the Sanskritization process. On this, see Kolenda (1983), Drèze (1990c), Chen and Drèze (1994), Chen (2000), and the literature cited there.

upward economic mobility. That the norms of the martial castes should often have been taken as the 'model' in Uttar Pradesh is not surprising, given the dominant position which these castes have occupied in that region for a long time.[36]

The observed convergence of female-male ratios among scheduled castes and higher castes may have causes other than this process of emulation. It has often been suggested, for instance, that gender inequality in India tends to be relatively low among poorer households.[37] In the cross-section analysis of district female-male ratios discussed further in this chapter, it is also found that higher levels of poverty tend to go with higher female-male ratios, for a *given* composition of the population in terms of the proportion of scheduled castes and scheduled tribes. It is, in fact, plausible that the partnership aspect of gender relations is stronger in poorer households, where survival depends on effective cooperation, than among privileged households, where women tend to have a more dependent and symbolic position. And this feature of gender relations within the household, in turn, may affect the general status of women in different classes. If there is a causal association of this kind between poverty and gender inequality, then poverty reduction may, in some respects at least, be a source of intensified female disadvantage. The sharp decline of female-male ratios among scheduled castes may be a manifestation of this economic process, rather than being directly related to caste as such.

What is not in doubt is that the convergence effect has taken place (not only in Uttar Pradesh but also in India as a whole), and that it has made some contribution to the overall decline of the female-male ratio in India since 1901.[38] The time pattern of this convergence is also interesting. Specifically, the decline of the female-male ratio among scheduled

---

[36] On the long-standing dominance of martial castes in rural Uttar Pradesh, see Drèze and Gazdar (1996), and the literature cited there. It should be mentioned that the dominant position of these castes in the rural society of Uttar Pradesh derives less from their martial activities as such (which are now largely confined to local feuds and fist fights) than from their temporal power as traditional landowners.

[37] For some relevant studies, see Miller (1981, 1993a), Das Gupta (1987), Krishnaji (1987), Alaka Basu (1992), P. Dasgupta (1993), Rogaly (1994), and Murthi, Guio and Drèze (1995).

[38] The FMR decline among scheduled castes, on its own, must have made a relatively modest contribution to the overall FMR decline in India, given the small share of this group in the total population (about 16 per cent in 1991). But the process of diffusion of the patriarchal culture of the higher castes, and related causal antecedents of the convergence effect, may have affected a broader section of the population. The widespread transition from bride-price to dowry among large parts of the population in south India illustrates this possibility.

castes seems to have been particularly sharp after 1961. In Uttar Pradesh, for instance, the female-male ratio in 1961 was not yet terribly low (comparatively speaking) for the scheduled castes—941 to be exact, compared with 909 for the population as a whole. Thirty years later, the corresponding values were 877 and 879, indicating a massive decline of the female-male ratio among scheduled castes after 1961.[39] A similar pattern applies in India as a whole, with the female-male ratio among scheduled castes falling from 957 in 1961 (compared with 941 for the population as a whole) to 922 in 1991 (compared with 927 for the whole population). It is quite possible that the problem of continued low FMR in India as a whole in recent decades, analysed earlier in this section, relates at least partly to the convergence effects we have just discussed.

All this is a useful reminder of the fact that economic progress on its own may not do very much to reduce gender inequalities. In fact, in so far as the convergent decline of the female-male ratio among scheduled castes is due to some process of emulation linked with their upward economic mobility, or to some other causal process related to the expansion of the economy, this seems to be a case where economic growth leads to some *intensification* of gender bias. The fact that lower levels of poverty are associated with lower female-male ratios in cross-section analysis reinforces these observations based on time trends. Clearly, the removal of gender inequalities cannot be based on some presumption that the problem will resolve itself on its own in the process of economic expansion. Punjab and Haryana are good illustrations of this point: both states have experienced rapid economic growth since independence, and are now far ahead of other Indian states in terms of per-capita income, but they still have the lowest female-male ratios. Achieving greater gender equality involves a process of active social change which is not automatically linked with economic growth.

7.3. WOMEN'S AGENCY AND CHILD SURVIVAL

A number of empirical studies indicate that the extent of anti-female bias in survival is substantially reduced by various influences that give women more voice and agency within the family. One of these influences is female education, and this consideration adds to those already presented in earlier chapters on the crucial role of basic education in general and

---

[39] See Agnihotri (1995), who also presents an insightful analysis of the phenomenon of accelerated FMR decline, after 1961, among the scheduled castes in many Indian states.

female education in particular. Another factor of importance is women's ability to earn an independent income through paid employment.[40] This opportunity tends to enhance the social standing of a woman in the household and the society. Her contribution to the prosperity of the family is, then, more visible, and she also has more voice, because of being less dependent on others. Further, outside employment often has useful 'educational' effects, in terms of exposure to the world outside the family. These positive links between gainful female employment and the status of women are also relevant to the female child, in so far as they affect the importance that is attached to her development and well-being.[41]

It is worth examining more closely how these and other aspects of female agency influence male and female mortality rates, and the extent of gender bias in survival. The age patterns of male and female mortality are complex (Kynch and Sen, 1983), and the discussion in this section will be confined to mortality in the 0–4 age group—hereafter 'under-five mortality'. Countries with basic gender inequality—including India, Pakistan, Bangladesh, China, west Asia, and so on—tend to have a higher ratio of female to male mortality even in this age group, in contrast with the situation in Europe or America or sub-Saharan Africa, where female children typically have a substantial survival advantage. In India itself, as noted earlier, female mortality is considerably higher than male mortality in the 0–4 age group. The female disadvantage is particularly strong in regions of pronounced gender inequality in general.[42]

In a recent study, Murthi, Guio and Drèze (1995) present an analysis of variations in under-five mortality rates between different districts of India in 1981. One aspect of this analysis is an examination of the

---

[40] A higher participation rate of women in so-called 'gainful' activities in sub-Saharan Africa seems to play a major role in placing women there at a less disadvantaged position compared with their counterparts in north Africa and Asia. On this see Boserup (1970), Kynch and Sen (1983), Bardhan (1984a, 1988), and Sen (1984, 1989). Within India, high rates of female labour-force participation among tribal communities, and in the Himalayan region, also help to explain the comparatively favourable status of women (and relatively high female-male ratio) in these societies.

[41] See Miller (1981), Rosenzweig and Schultz (1982), Kynch and Sen (1983), Sen (1985c, 1990), Alaka Basu (1992), Guio (1994), Murthi, Guio and Drèze (1995); also Kishor (1993, 1994a), and the literature cited there. The strength of these relations, however, depends on the nature of women's employment, its social standing, and economic rewards. For further discussion of this issue, see Ursula Sharma (1980, 1986), Kalpana Bardhan (1985), Bina Agarwal (1986), Desai and Jain (1992), among others, and also Nirmala Banerjee's (1982) illuminating study of the condition of 'unorganized women workers' in Calcutta.

[42] See section 7.5; also Statistical Appendix, Table A.3, Part 2.

relationship between an index of female disadvantage in child survival (reflecting the ratio of female to male mortality in the 0–4 age group at the district level) and a number of other district-level variables such as the female literacy rate, female labour-force participation, the incidence of poverty, the level of urbanization, the availability of medical facilities, and the proportion of scheduled castes and scheduled tribes in the population. The basic results are presented in the first column of Table 7.2.[43]

As discussed in Murthi, Guio and Drèze (1995), what is rather striking is that variables directly relating to women's agency (in particular, the female labour-force participation rate and the female literacy rate) appear to have strong effects on the extent of female disadvantage in child survival, and work in the expected direction, i.e. higher levels of female literacy and labour- force participation are associated with lower levels of female disadvantage in child survival. By contrast, variables that relate to the *general* level of development and modernization either turn out to have no statistically significant effect, or suggest that modernization, if anything, *amplifies* the gender bias in child survival. This applies inter alia to urbanization, male literacy, the availability of medical facilities, and the level of poverty (with lower levels of poverty being associated with a *larger* female disadvantage). These results, based on cross-section evidence, reinforce an observation made earlier in connection with the decline of the female-male ratio over time: on their own, the forces of development and modernization do not necessarily lead to a rapid reduction in gender inequalities. In so far as a positive connection does exist in India between the level of development and reduced gender bias in survival, it seems to work *through* variables that are directly related to women's agency, such as female literacy and female labour-force participation.[44]

The analysis also includes dummy variables for different regions, and

[43] For a detailed assessment of these results, see Murthi, Guio and Drèze (1995) and Drèze, Guio and Murthi (1996). The coefficients reported in Table 7.3 are best interpreted, in the first instance, as statistical associations (in line with the 'statistical approach' to regression analysis, on which see Deaton, 1997, pp. 63–4). The underlying causal connections often call for careful evaluation in the light of economic reasoning as well as corroborative evidence. For further discussion and evidence, with special focus on the link between education and fertility, see Drèze and Murthi (2001).

[44] There is also some evidence, from the same study, of high fertility rates being associated with low survival chances of female children vis-à-vis male children (see also Drèze and Murthi, 2001). This is consistent with the fact that the survival disadvantages of female children progressively worsen as we consider children of higher 'parity', that is, the second girl in a family tends to do worse than the first, and so on. On this, see particularly Das Gupta's (1987) pioneering work on rural Punjab; also M.E. Khan et al. (1989) on rural Uttar Pradesh.

TABLE 7.2 *Basic Results of a Cross-section Analysis of the Determinants of Child Mortality, Fertility and Gender Bias in Indian Districts (1981)*

Independent variables	Dependent variable		
	Female disadvantage in child survival (FD)	*Under-five mortality rate, male and female combined (Q5)*	*Total fertility rate (TFR)*
constant	0.86	205.82	6.60
	(3.00)*	(14.37)*	(23.10)*
Female labour-force participation (proportion of 'main workers' in the female population)	−0.02 (−3.85)*	0.44 (1.82)	−0.02 (−3.57)*
Female literacy rate (proportion of literate women in the female population)	−0.04 (−4.46)*	−0.87 (−2.45)*	−0.03 (−4.28)*
Male literacy rate (proportion of literate men in the male population)	0.015 (1.97)*	−0.49 (−1.40)	−0.005 (−0.70)
Level of urbanization (proportion of the population living in urban areas)	0.005 (1.73)	−0.31 (−2.40)*	−0.0004 (−0.15)
Availability of medical facilities (proportion of villages with some medical facilities)	0.005 (1.84)	−0.25 (−2.23)*	−0.002 (−1.04)
Level of rural poverty ('Sen index')	−0.02 (−3.13)*	0.53 (1.76)	0.007 (1.14)
Scheduled castes (proportion of scheduled-caste persons in the population)	−0.01 (−1.13)	0.55 (1.89)	−0.01 (−1.23)
Scheduled tribes (proportion of scheduled-tribe persons in the population)	−0.01 (−3.96)*	−0.60 (−3.57)*	−0.01 (−3.40)*
Dummy variables for different regions[a]			
South	−0.82 (−4.91)*	−41.50 (−3.85)*	−0.55 (2.60)*
East	0.15 (0.81)	−38.08 (−2.91)*	−0.25 (−0.99)
West	−0.15 (−0.87)	−12.35 (−1.32)	−0.38 (−2.06)*

Notes: [a] The different regions are defined as follows: South = Andhra Pradesh, Karnataka, Kerala and Tamil Nadu; East = Bihar, Orissa and West Bengal; West = Gujarat and Maharashtra. The 'default region', for which no dummy variable is included, consists of the northern and central states of Haryana, Madhya Pradesh, Punjab, Rajasthan, and Uttar Pradesh.

* Significant at 5% level (asymptotic t-ratios in brackets).

Source: Murthi, Guio and Drèze (1995), p. 762.

Explanatory Note: The observations on which these regressions are based consist of 296 districts for which the relevant data are available. All the variables relate to 1981, and are based on the 1981 census, except for the 'poverty' indicator. The poverty indicator used for each district is the Sen index of rural poverty in 1972–3 for the National Sample Survey 'region' in which the district in question is situated (the 296 districts are located in 51 different NSS regions). The regressions are based on maximum-likelihood estimation, in a model which takes into account spatial correlation in the error terms. These regressions can be interpreted as the 'reduced form' of a system of simultaneous equations which determines three endogenous variables: the total fertility rate (TFR), the level of child mortality for both sexes combined (Q5), and the extent of female disadvantage in child survival (FD). The latter is measured by the proportionate difference between female and male child mortality (more precisely, by $FD \equiv [Q5_f - Q5_m]/Q5_f$ where $Q5_f$ and $Q5_m$ are the levels of female and male child mortality, respectively). For further details on definitions, sources, estimation, diagnostics, and related issues, and further discussion of the results, see Murthi, Guio and Drèze (1995).

it turns out that at least some of these regional dummies (particularly the 'south India' dummy) are statistically significant even after the other variables are included. In other words, the sharp contrasts that are observed between different regions of India, in terms of the relative survival chances of male and female children, are only partly explained by differences in female literacy, female labour-force participation, and other variables included in this analysis. This suggests that other variables, which may well be hard to quantify, also have an important influence. Women's property rights, cultural or ideological influences, and some aspects of the kinship system (e.g. the rules of exogamy and patrilocality) are plausible examples of such variables.[45]

A similar analysis can be used to examine the effects of different variables on the *level* of under-five mortality for males and females combined. We have already noted that higher female labour-force participation improves

---

[45] On these different influences, see the studies cited in Drèze and Sen (1989), D.B. Gupta et al. (1993) and Dasgupta (1993); also Das Gupta (1990, 1995), Alaka Basu (1992), Sunita Kishor (1993), Bina Agarwal (1994), Malhotra et al. (1995) and Satish Agnihotri (2000), among other recent contributions. The persistence of regional influences on relative survival chances even after controlling for a wide range of district characteristics on which quantitative data are available, has been noted earlier by Sunita Kishor (1993).

the *relative* survival chances of girls vis-à-vis boys. But this does not tell us how female labour-force participation affects the absolute levels of under-five mortality. It is, in fact, difficult to predict whether the effect of higher female labour-force participation on child survival is positive or negative.[46] There are at least two important effects to consider, working in opposite directions. First, as was discussed earlier, involvement in gainful employment has many positive effects on a woman's agency roles, which often include child care. Second, the 'double burden' of household work and outside employment can impair women's ability to ensure the good health of their children, if only by reducing the time available for child-care activities (since men typically show great reluctance to share the domestic chores).[47] In the case of girls, a third consideration is that higher levels of female labour-force participation in the society may enhance the importance attached to the survival of a female child. The net result of these different effects is a matter of empirical investigation. The analysis of district-level data summarized in Table 7.2 (second column) suggests a positive association between female labour-force participation and under-five mortality, but this association is not statistically significant.[48]

Female literacy, on the other hand, is unambiguously found to have a negative and statistically significant impact on under-five mortality, even after controlling for male literacy. This is consistent with extensive evidence of a close relationship between female literacy and child survival

[46] The variable used here to measure female labour-force participation is the ratio of female 'main workers' (women engaged in 'economically productive work' for at least 183 days in the year) to the total female population. The instructions to census investigators make it clear that unpaid 'household duties' are not to be counted as economically productive work (Government of India, 1981, pp. 106–7). The census definition of 'economically productive work' is questionable, but it serves our purpose, since we are interested in the relationship between child survival and women's independent income-earning opportunities (rather than their economic contribution generally—whether or not rewarded).

[47] For useful empirical analyses of this 'maternal dilemma' in the Indian context, see Alaka Basu (1992) and Gillespie and McNeill (1992). On the related issue of the relationship between maternal labour-force participation and child nutrition, see Leslie (1988), Leslie and Paolisso (1989), and the literature cited there.

[48] As discussed in Murthi, Guio and Drèze (1995), it is quite possible that this positive association would vanish altogether after controlling more carefully for the economic and social disadvantages that often motivate Indian women to seek paid employment. That possibility is consistent with international evidence on the relationship between female employment and child nutrition. Based on a review of 50 studies, for instance, Joanne Leslie (1988) concludes that 'overall there is little evidence of a negative effect of maternal employment on child nutrition' (p.1341).

in many countries, including India.[49] Further, the authors find that female literacy has a larger effect on female under-five mortality than on male under-five mortality; this is why the *ratio* of female to male mortality (i.e. the 'female disadvantage' in child survival) is lower at higher levels of female literacy, even though mortality rates fall for both male and female children as female literacy increases.

It is worth adding that, in quantitative terms, the effect of female literacy on child mortality is quite large. This point is illustrated in Table 7.3, which shows how the predicted values of the 'dependent variables' in this analysis (the extent of female disadvantage in child survival, the level of under-five mortality, and the total fertility rate) respond to changes in female literacy when the *other* independent variables are kept at their mean value, and similarly with male literacy and poverty. For instance, keeping other variables constant, an increase in the crude female literacy rate from, say, 22 per cent (the actual 1981 figure) to 75 per cent reduces the predicted value of under-five mortality for males and females combined from 156 per thousand (again, the actual 1981 figure) to 110 per thousand. The powerful effect of female literacy contrasts with the comparatively ineffective roles of, say, male literacy or general poverty reduction as instruments of child mortality reduction. An increase in male literacy over the same range (from 22 to 75 per cent) only reduces under-five mortality from 167 per thousand to 141 per thousand. And a 50 per cent reduction in the incidence of poverty (from the actual 1981 level) only reduces the predicted value of under-five mortality from 156 per thousand to 153 per thousand.

Here again, the message seems to be that some variables relating to women's agency (in this case, female literacy) often play a much more important role in promoting social well-being (in particular, child survival) than variables relating to the general level of opulence or overall economic growth in the society. These findings have important practical implications, given that both types of variables can be influenced through public action, but require very different priorities of intervention.

[49] See J.C. Caldwell (1979, 1986), Behrman and Wolfe (1984, 1987), Ware (1984), A.K. Jain (1985), Cleland and van Ginneken (1988, 1989), Nag (1989), Beenstock and Sturdy (1990), Cleland (1990), Das Gupta (1990), Bhuiya and Streatfield (1991), Bourne and Walker (1991), Thomas et al. (1991), Alaka Basu (1992), Barro and Lee (1993, 1994), International Institute for Population Sciences (1995a), Subbarao and Raney (1995), Pieris and Caldwell (1996), Govindaswamy and Ramesh (1997), Jeffery and Jeffery (1997), Bhargava (1998), Pandey et al. (1998), Ray (1998), Borooah (2000), Mahajan (2001), among others.

TABLE 7.3 *Effects of Selected Independent Variables (Female Literacy, Male Literacy and Poverty) on Child Mortality (Q5), Female Disadvantage (FD) and Fertility (TFR)*

Assumed level of the independent variable (%)	Predicted values of Q5, FD and TFR when the *female literacy rate* takes the value indicated in the first column			Predicted values of Q5, FD and TFR when the *male literacy rate* takes the value indicated in the first column			Predicted values of Q5, FD and TFR when the *proportion of the population below the poverty line* takes the value indicated in the first column[a]		
	Q5	FD	TFR	Q5	FD	TFR	Q5	FD	TFR
10	166.4	10.7	5.38	172.9	-2.0	5.18	151.5	9.8	4.79
20	157.7	5.9	5.07	168.0	-0.1	5.13	152.7	8.5	4.85
30	149.0	1.1	4.76	163.1	1.8	5.08	153.8	7.1	4.91
40	140.2	-3.3	4.45	158.2	3.9	5.03	154.9	5.8	4.97
50	131.5	-7.1	4.15	153.3	5.9	4.98	156.0	4.4	5.03
60	122.8	-10.3	3.84	148.4	8.0	4.93	157.2	3.1	5.09
70	114.0	-12.8	3.53	143.5	10.1	4.88	158.3	1.8	5.15
80	105.3	-14.8	3.22	138.7	12.2	4.83	159.5	0.5	5.21

Notes: [a] For convenience of interpretation, the 'Sen index' has been replaced, in this table, by the 'head-count ratio' (ie. the proportion of the population below the poverty line). The figures presented in the last three columns are based on the same regressions as in Table 7.2, with the Sen index replaced by the head-count ratio.

Source: Murthi, Guio and Drèze (1995), p. 771, based on the regressions presented in Table 7.2. The variables Q5, FD and TFR are defined as in that table.

7.4. FERTILITY AND WOMEN'S EMANCIPATION

As discussed in the preceding chapter, the agency of women is also particularly important for achievements in population policy. The serious adverse effects of high birth rates include their impact on the lives women can lead, and the drudgery of continuous child bearing and rearing, which is routinely imposed on many Asian and African women. There is, as a result, a close connection between women's *well-being* and women's *agency* in bringing about a change in the fertility pattern. Women in India have to face the lack of freedom to do other things that goes with a high frequency of births, not to mention the dangers of repeated pregnancy and high maternal mortality. It is, thus, understandable that reductions in birth rates have often been associated with enhancement of women's status and voice.

These connections are indeed reflected in inter-district variations of the total fertility rate, as Tables 7.2 and 7.3 indicate. In fact, among all the variables included in the analysis, other than regional dummies and the proportion of 'scheduled tribes', the only ones that have a statistically significant association with fertility are female literacy and female labour-force participation. Here again, statistical analysis is consistent with a causal understanding of the importance of women's agency, especially in comparison with the weaker effects of variables relating to general economic progress.

The link between female literacy and fertility is particularly clear. This connection has been widely observed in other countries, and it is not surprising that it should emerge in India too.[50] The unwillingness of educated women to be shackled to continuous child-rearing clearly plays a role in bringing about this change. Education also makes the horizon of vision wider, and, at a more mundane level, helps to disseminate the knowledge of family planning.

As we discussed in chapter 4, Kerala's particular experience of fertility reduction based on women's agency is quite remarkable, and has extremely important lessons for the rest of India. While the total fertility rate for India as a whole is still around 3, that rate in Kerala has now fallen below

[50] For recent empirical analyses of this connection at the international level, see Barro and Lee (1993, 1994), Cassen (1994), Subbarao and Raney (1995) and Schultz (1997). On the connection between fertility and female education in India, see Vlassoff (1980), Jain and Nag (1986), J.C. Caldwell et al.(1989), Satia and Jejeebhoy (1991), Das Gupta (1994), Egerö et al. (1994), Visaria and Visaria (1994), Murthi, Guio and Drèze (1995), Jejeebhoy (1996), Gandotra et al. (1998), Parasuraman et al. (1999), Arokiasamy (2000a, 2000b), and Drèze and Murthi (2001).

the 'replacement level' of 2.1 to 1.8. Kerala's high level of female education has been particularly influential in bringing about this decline in birth rate.[51]

There is also much demographic evidence to indicate that birth rates tend to go down following the decline of death rates.[52] This is partly because the need for having many children to ensure some survivors goes down with lower mortality rates, but also because of the complementarity between the respective means of birth control and death control (giving people access to contraception can be effectively combined with delivery of medical attention and health care). In Kerala, the sharp reduction of death rates has been followed by a rapid decline of fertility, with the birth rate falling from 44 per thousand in 1951–61 to 18 by 1991. Since female agency and literacy are important in the reduction of mortality rates (as was discussed in the last section), that is another—more indirect—route through which women's agency, in general, and female literacy, in particu-lar, can reduce birth rates (in addition to the direct impacts mentioned earlier).

Recently, there has been a good deal of discussion of the imperative need to reduce birth rates in the world, and those in India in particular. China's achievement in cutting down birth rates over a short period through rather draconian measures has suggested to many the need for India to emulate China in this respect. As was discussed in chapter 4, however, the coercive methods do involve many social costs, including the direct one of reduced effective freedom of people—in particular, women—to decide themselves on matters that are clearly rather personal. That aspect of the problem is often dismissed, especially in the West, on the grounds that cultural differences between Asia and the West make such policies acceptable in the Third World in a way they would not be in the West.[53] Cultural relativism is a tricky terrain, and while it is easy enough to refer to 'despotic Oriental traditions', that line of reasoning would be no more convincing than making judgements on what to do in the Western societies today on the basis of the history of Spanish inquisitions or Nazi concentration camps.

It is not clear how the acceptability of coercion can be tested except

[51] See particularly Krishnan (1976, 1991, 1997), Mari Bhat and Rajan (1990, 1992), Zachariah et al. (1994), Kabir and Krishnan (1996).

[52] This is one of the major lessons of research on the 'demographic transition'; see e.g. Kirk (1996) and the literature cited there. The crucial link between mortality and fertility is implicit in the 'reduced form' regressions presented in Table 7.2. For an explicit examination of this relationship, see Drèze and Murthi (2001).

[53] See, for example, Hardin (1993).

through democratic confrontation. While that testing has not occurred in China, it was indeed attempted in India during the Emergency period in the seventies when compulsory birth control was tried by Mrs Gandhi's government, along with suspending various legal rights and civil liberties. The policy of coercion in general—including that in birth control—was overwhelmingly defeated in the general elections that followed. Furthermore, family-planning experts have noted how voluntary birth-control programmes received a severe set-back from that brief programme of compulsory sterilization, as people had become deeply suspicious of the entire movement. The coercive measures of the Emergency period, in fact, aside from having little immediate impact on fertility rates, were followed by a long period of *stagnation* in the birth rate, which ended only in 1985.[54]

There is evidence that some forms of compulsion or forceful pressure to accept birth control (especially sterilization) continue to be used in some Indian states, particularly in the north, where fertility rates tend to be high. Even when coercion is not part of official policy, the government's firm insistence on 'meeting the family-planning targets' has often led administrators and health-care personnel at different levels to resort to pressure tactics that come close to compulsion.[55] Examples of such tactics include verbal threats, making sterilization a condition of eligibility for anti-poverty programmes, depriving mothers of more than two children from maternity benefits, reserving certain kinds of health care services to persons who have been sterilized, and forbidding persons who have more than two children from contesting panchayat elections.[56] The long-run consequences of these practices can be quite disastrous both for health care and for the consensual emergence of social norms.

[54] See e.g. Bose (1991), pp.67–8, and Government of India (1999a), p. 3. The Emergency period also caused a substantial *decline* in medical attendance at birth, and a large *increase* in neo-natal mortality rates, and it took five years for the pre-Emergency levels of these variables to be restored; on this, see Tulasidhar and Sarma (1993).

[55] See the literature cited in chapter 6, p. 210. As mentioned there, the situation appears to have improved in this respect after the recent introduction of the 'target-free approach'. However, forceful calls for the continuation or adoption of heavy-handed methods in this field continue to be made at regular intervals.

[56] The last measure, which is part of official policy in five states at this time, involves a strong violation not only of personal liberty but also of basic democratic norms. It is encouraging to note that an early proposal to extend this measure at the all-India level, incorporated in the government's draft National Population Policy (Government of India, 1994c, p.40), was withdrawn in response to sustained opposition from organizations concerned with women's rights and civil liberties. Nevertheless, bills to introduce, extend or enforce this anti-democratic measure are pending in parliament as well as in several state assemblies.

What also has to be borne in mind is the fact, discussed in chapter 4, that compulsion has not produced a lower birth rate in China compared with what Kerala has already achieved entirely through voluntary channels, relying on the educated agency of women. In fact, it is not at all clear (for reasons discussed earlier) exactly how much of *extra* reduction in birth rate China has been able to achieve by resorting to coercive methods. What must be taken into account in trying to assess the contribution of compulsion is that China has had many social and economic attainments that are favourable to fertility reduction, including expansion of education in general and female education in particular, augmentation of health care, enhancement of employment opportunities for women, and, recently, rapid economic development. These factors would themselves have reduced the birth rates (well below the Indian average, for example). While China seems to get too much credit for its authoritarian measures, it gets far too little credit for other—supportive—policies that have helped to cut down the birth rate. Kerala's low birth rate—lower than China's— also suggests that these supportive influences may be effective enough to render compulsion largely redundant, even if it were acceptable otherwise.

It might also be mentioned here, in passing, that the increasing popularity of sex-selective abortion of female foetuses in China, as well as in parts of India, contrasts sharply with the absence of such a practice in Kerala. As was noted in chapter 4 with reference to China, authoritarian family-planning programmes involve a great danger of contributing to the spread of sex-selective abortion. Indeed, in societies where male children are valued more highly than female children, and where it is considered essential to have (say) at least one male child and preferably two, external pressure to limit births can sharply enhance the temptation to abort female foetuses. This is, in all likelihood, what has happened in China on a fairly large scale in recent years.

As we saw in chapters 4 and 6, Kerala is not alone in having achieved a rapid reduction of the birth rate without compulsion. A similar—if not equally rapid—success has also occurred in Tamil Nadu, where the total fertility rate is now just below the replacement level of 2.1, and also in Himachal Pradesh and Andhra Pradesh, which are expected to reach this level within two years or so. A significant acceleration of fertility decline has also occurred in a number of other states in recent years.[57] Further, what is rather striking is that the states where fertility decline remains slow (including Uttar Pradesh, Bihar, Rajasthan, and Madhya Pradesh)

[57] See Visaria and Visaria (1994) and Natarajan and Jayachandran (2001).

are precisely those where heavy-handed methods have been most extensively used, often to the detriment of positive interventions.

These diverse experiences reinforce the general arguments presented earlier in favour of a collaborative approach to fertility reduction, based on due recognition of the agency of women in bringing down fertility and mortality rates. An unequivocal rejection of all coercive and heavy-handed methods (including those that are currently being used) is essential from many points of view, including those of fertility reduction, mortality reduction, women's well-being and elementary freedom.

7.5. GENDER BIAS IN NATALITY

The demographic correlates of gender inequality include not only sex differentials in mortality (along with overall rates of fertility and child mortality), but also sex differentials in natality. Given a preference for boys over girls that exists in many male-dominated societies, gender inequality can manifest itself in the form of the parents' wanting the new born to be a boy rather than a girl. There was a time when this could be no more than a wish, but with the availability of modern techniques to determine the gender of the foetus, sex-selective abortion has become common in many countries. It is particularly prevalent in east Asia, in China and South Korea in particular, but also in Singapore and Taiwan. It appears that this manifestation of 'high-tech sexism' is now emerging as a statistically significant phenomenon in India as well.

Indeed, at the risk of some oversimplification, it can be argued that the demographic features of gender inequality are beginning to undergo a basic shift in India. There has been some reduction of overall gender bias in mortality rates, and even though the progress is very uneven between the different regions in India, nevertheless the average female life expectancy at birth is now about two years longer than the corresponding male life expectancy. There has been also some increase in the overall female-male ratio in the total population between 1991 and 2001, but this has been restrained by a sharp decline in the female-male ratio among young children. For India as a whole, the female-male ratio of the population in the 0–6 age group has fallen from 94.5 girls per hundred boys in 1991 to 92.7 girls per hundred boys in 2001. While there has been no such decline in some parts of the country (including Kerala), the ratio has fallen very sharply in others, such as Punjab, Haryana, Gujarat, and Maharashtra, which are among the richer Indian states.

Taking together all the evidence that exists, it is clear that this change reflects not a rise in female vis-à-vis male child mortality, but a fall in female births as compared with male births, and is almost certainly connected with the spread of sex-selective abortion. In response to the early manifestations of this phenomenon, the Indian parliament had some years ago banned the use of sex determination techniques for foetuses (except when it is a by-product of other necessary medical investigation). But it appears that the enforcement of this law has been comprehensively neglected, and when questioned by Celia Dugger, the energetic correspondent of *The New York Times*, civil servants cited the reluctance of mothers to give evidence of the use of such techniques as one of the difficulties involved in achieving successful prosecution.[58]

The reluctance of the mothers to give evidence brings out perhaps the most disturbing aspect of this natality inequality, to wit, the 'son preference' that many Indian mothers themselves seem to have. This type of gender inequality cannot be removed, at least in the short run, by the enhancement of women's empowerment and agency, since that agency is itself an integral part of the cause of natality inequality. This recognition demands an important modification—and indeed an extension—of our understanding of the role of women's agency in eliminating gender inequality in India. The enhancement of women's agency which does so much to eliminate sex differentials in mortality rates (and also in reducing fertility and mortality rates in general) cannot be expected, *on its own*, to produce a similar elimination of sex differentials at birth and abortion, and correspondingly in the population of children. What is needed is not merely freedom and power to act, but also freedom and power to question and reassess the prevailing norms and values. The pivotal issue is critical agency.

This problem is not confined to India, and is well illustrated by the experience of countries in east Asia. These countries all have relatively high levels of female education and economic participation, but despite that, in contrast with the biologically common ratio across the world of about 95 girls being born per hundred boys, Singapore and Taiwan have 92 girls, South Korea only 88, and China a mere 86. In fact, the female-male ratio for children is also as low as 88 girls per 100 boys in South Korea and 85 girls per 100 boys in China. Sharp declines in the female-male ratio among children, related largely to sex-selective abortion, have occurred in these countries, taking the proportion of females much below normal, despite relatively high levels of women's education and gainful employment. Strengthening women's agency will not, by itself, solve the problem of 'son preference' when that works through the desires of the mothers themselves. There are apparently some hardy cultural barriers here.

In comparison with female-male ratios among Chinese or South Korean children, the Indian ratio of 92.7 girls for 100 boys (though lower than the previous Indian figure of 94.5) still looks far less unfavourable.[59] But we have to ask whether sex-selective abortion may spread in India as it has in China and South Korea. Indeed, there is strong evidence that this is happening in a big way in parts of the country, such as Punjab and Gujarat.[60] There is, however, something of a social and cultural divide across the country in the extent to which facilities of sex-selective abortion have been seized and put into practice to discriminate against female foetuses.

In fact, the regional division across India in female-male ratio of children seems to split the country into two nearly contiguous halves. As a classificatory device, we can take as a benchmark the female-male ratio among children in advanced industrial countries. That female-male ratio for the 0–5 age group tends to be around 95 per 100 in the industrially advanced countries, e.g., 95.7 in the USA and 94.8 in Germany, and perhaps we can pick the lower of the two (94.8) as a benchmark to judge the normality of the female-male ratio of children in India.

The use of this dividing line produces a remarkable geographical split in the country (see Figure 7.4).[61] There are the states in the north and the west where the female-male ratio of children is consistently *below* the benchmark figure, led by the richest states: Punjab (79.3), Haryana (82.0), and Delhi (86.5), followed by Gujarat (87.8), Himachal Pradesh (89.7), Madhya Pradesh (90.5), Uttaranchal (90.6), Rajasthan (90.9), Uttar

[59]Note that the Chinese and Korean figures apply to children aged between 0 and 4, whereas the Indian figures relate to children between 0 and 6. Nevertheless, even with appropriate age adjustment, the general comparison of female-male ratios holds in much the same way.

[60]The association of sex-selective abortion with fertility decline raises important issues, discussed by Das Gupta and Mari Bhat (1997), Das Gupta and Shuzuo (1999), Drèze and Murthi (2001), Mari Bhat and Zavier (2001). It is particularly important to note that the promotion of fertility decline through coercive methods is likely to fuel the spread of sex-selective abortion. Indeed, as noted earlier, when parents have a strong preference for boys, external pressures to reduce the number of births are likely to enhance the temptation to avoid female children. This consideration adds to the other arguments put forward earlier against the use of coercive methods.

[61]The list of Indian states that figure in this map (and the corresponding comments in the text) is the post-2000 list, with Chattisgarh, Jharkhand and Uttaranchal appearing as separate states (in contrast with the rest of the book, where we follow the pre-2000 state classification).

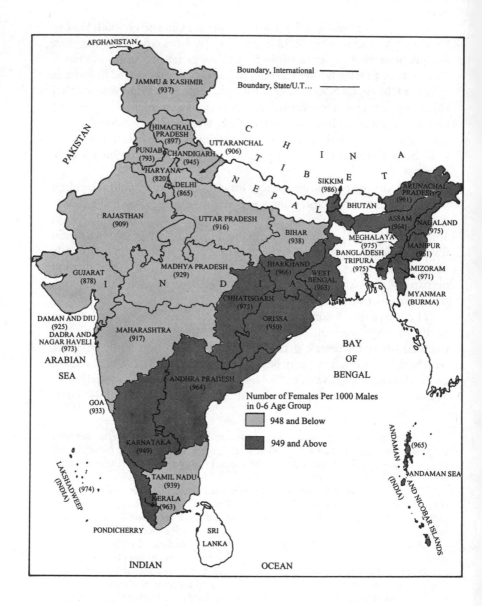

FIGURE 7.4 *Female-Male Ratio in 0–6 Age Group, 2001*

Pradesh (91.6), Maharashtra (91.7), Goa (93.3), Jammu and Kashmir (93.7), and Bihar (93.8). On the other side of the divide, the states in the east and the south tend to have female-male ratios that are *above* the benchmark (94.8 girls per 100 boys): Kerala, Andhra Pradesh, Jharkhand, West Bengal and Assam (each between 96.3 and 96.6), Orissa and Karnataka (around 95.0), and the northeastern states with high ratios (Meghalaya, Mizoram, Manipur, Nagaland, Arunachal Pradesh, Sikkim). The one exception to this adjoining division is Tamil Nadu, where the female-male ratio among children is 93.9, which is higher than the ratio of any state in the deficit list, but still just below the cut-off line used for the partitioning. The astonishing finding is not that one particular state seems to provide a marginal misfit, but how the vast majority of the Indian states fall firmly into two contiguous halves, classified broadly into the north and the west, on one side, and the south and the east, on the other.[62] Indeed, every state in the north and west has a strictly lower female-male ratio of children than every state in the south and east—even Tamil Nadu fits into this classification.

This contrast does not have any obvious economic explanation. The states with anti-female bias include rich states (Punjab and Haryana) as well as poor ones (Madhya Pradesh and Uttar Pradesh), and fast-growing states (Gujarat and Maharashtra) as well as growth failures (Bihar and Uttar Pradesh). There are similar economic variations on the other side, in the states that meet the benchmark. Also, the incidence of sex-specific abortions cannot be explained by the availability of medical resources for determining the sex of the foetus: Kerala and West Bengal in the non-deficit list have at least as much— indeed considerably more—medical facilities than do the deficit states of Madhya Pradesh, Bihar or Rajasthan. If sex determination and abortion centres are less common in Kerala or West Bengal, it is because of a low demand for those specific services, rather than any supply–side difficulty.

This suggests that we have to look beyond economic resources or prosperity or growth into broadly cultural and social influences. It is not unnatural to invoke cultural and social traditions in explaining this

[62]There is considerable affinity between this partitioning and that based on the female-male ratio of *mortality rates of children* (say aged 0–4), varying between 0.91 in West Bengal and 0.93 in Kerala, on one side, in the southern and eastern group, and 1.30 in Punjab, Haryana, and Uttar Pradesh (with high ratios also in Gujarat, Bihar and Rajasthan) in the northern and western group; see Statistical Appendix, Table A.3, Part 5, and also the map presented in Murthi, Guio and Drèze (1995), p. 751. However, the regional division emerging from the classification based on the female-male ratio of children is somewhat sharper.

remarkable division. The invoking of culture has indeed been a productive line of investigation in the literature on regional patterns of gender inequality in India, which points to broad regional divisions similar to (though not exactly the same as) that obtained here on the basis of female-male ratios among children.[63] Political commentators have also noted the fact that the states in the north and west have, by and large, given much more room to religion-based sectional politics than have the east and south. It is not clear whether any causal connection is involved here, but nevertheless, the association between gender inequality on the one hand, and cultural and political distinctions (such as the scope for religion-based politics) is an observed pattern of some interest.

The causal antecedents underlying these associative findings call for further social, anthropological and cultural investigations. We shall not attempt this here, and will not try to go beyond identifying a remarkable geographical division that does currently exist in the field of gender inequality in natality. This phenomenon cries for some firm explanation, going beyond the suggestive linkages that have been briefly noted. It would also be important to keep a close watch on whether the incidence of sex-specific abortions will significantly increase in states in which they are quite uncommon (taking India more in the direction of China and South Korea). Remedial influences must also be considered. Economic growth will clearly not do very much here (as we have noted also for various aspects of gender inequality, as well as other critically important social phenomena). In so far as cultural and political factors appear to be at work, some acknowledgement must also be given to the case for cultivating non-sexist values and egalitarian politics (and the role of feminist activism and of women's organizations). Participation can be critically important in this field as well, in addition to the others we have already identified.

7.6. WIDOWHOOD AND GENDER RELATIONS

One consequence of the low participation of Indian women in public life and political activity is that many social issues relating to women and gender relations receive far too little attention. In recent years, there has been improved awareness of some specific aspects of gender inequality and female deprivation, such as the problem of low female-male ratios and the anti-female bias in child survival. But many other issues continue to get low social recognition from the male-dominated society. Examples

[63]See section 7.2, and the literature cited there.

include the widespread violation of women's legal property rights (aside from the persistence of anti-female biases in the law itself), endemic violence against women, the economic and social rights of sex workers, and the institutional and social requirements of better political representation of women.

Another striking example concerns the well-being of widows.[64] In India, widows represent about 6.5 per cent of the total female population, or more than 30 million women in absolute terms at the time of writing.[65] Further, there is a good deal of evidence of the deprived condition of many widows in India. A recent demographic study, for instance, concludes that mortality rates are, on average, 86 per cent higher among elderly widows than among married women of the same age.[66] Similarly, economic surveys indicate that the loss of one's husband often leads to a sharp decline of household income. Anthropological studies have also highlighted the fact that many widows suffer from social marginalization and psychological hardship, in addition to being particularly vulnerable to poverty.[67]

It should be added that the *prospect* of widowhood reduces the quality of life of most Indian women, even if only a minority of them are actually widowed at any particular point in time. The proportion of widows in the female population rises sharply with age, reaching well over half among women aged 60 and above, and more than two thirds among women aged 70 and above. Thus, an Indian woman who survives to old age is most likely to become a widow. The prospect of losing their husband at some stage cannot but affect the lives of Indian women even before that event. For instance, there is a close relationship between widowhood, old-age insecurity, and fertility decisions in the early stages of married life.

In spite of their magnitude and significance, the deprivations of widows rarely feature in public debates, in the media, or even in social

---

[64] On this, see Drèze (1990c), Chen and Drèze (1994, 1995), Drèze and Srinivasan (1997), Chen (1998, 2000), and the literature cited there. This section draws extensively on these studies. It should be mentioned that, while widows represent the vast majority of single adult women in India, other single women (e.g. those who are divorced or separated) also tend to experience major social disadvantages. On this, see Krishnakumari (1987) and Dandavate et al. (1989), among others.

[65] See Census of India 1991, Series 1 (India), Part IV–A, C Series, *Socio-Cultural Tables*, Vol. 1, pp. 22–3. Sample Registration System data (quoted in the first edition of this book) suggest an even higher proportion of widows in the female population.

[66] See Mari Bhat (1998). These results corroborate earlier findings for Bangladesh (see Rahman et al., 1992).

[67] Marty Chen (2000) has provided a far-reaching study of the different aspects of the deprivation of widows in India.

science research, except when—in a minute number of cases—they take a sensational form, such as *sati*. This fact relates to the general point (further discussed in chapter 10) that endemic but quiet deprivations are often much harder to bring to public attention than sensational events such as a famine or natural disaster, or isolated incidents of grotesque barbarity. A similar point can be made in relation to other aspects of women's deprivation. The frequent media focus on rape, for instance, contrasts with the quiet acceptance of widespread domestic violence against women.

If widowhood is such a neglected social issue, it is partly because the vulnerability associated with losing one's spouse is, overwhelmingly, a woman's experience. Only 1.9 per cent of all Indian men are widowed, compared with 6.5 per cent of women.[68] Further, the consequences of losing one's spouse are very different for men and women. A widower not only has much greater freedom to remarry than his female counterpart, he also has more extensive property rights, wider opportunities for remunerative employment, and a more authoritative claim on economic support from his children. Had the living conditions of widowers been as precarious as those of widows, it is likely that widowed persons would have attracted far more attention.

The circumstances of widows vary a great deal between different regions, communities, classes, and age groups. Nevertheless, it is possible to identify some basic factors of disadvantage and insecurity experienced by many Indian widows. The following considerations emerge with particular force from recent surveys carried out in north India.[69]

First, a strong tradition of patrilineal ownership, which modern legislation has only begun to challenge, makes it hard for many widows to defend their legal inheritance rights. Formally, according to contemporary Indian law, a widow has an unequivocal right to a share of her husband's property, including his land.[70] This is in addition to the legal rights she has—irrespective of her marital status—to a share of her parents' property. Field studies, however, indicate that these legal rights are very often violated, and that a large majority of widows have

[68] Calculated from 1991 census data (see footnote 65). This large gender gap primarily reflects a high incidence of remarriage among widowers.

[69] For the evidence, and further discussion, see Drèze (1990c), Chen and Drèze (1994, 1995), and Chen (1998, 2000).

[70] According to the Hindu Succession Act of 1956, for instance, a widow is entitled to the same share of her husband's land as other 'Class 1' heirs (these also include the deceased person's children and widowed mother, if alive). On the general issue of women's land rights in India, see Bina Agarwal (1994).

limited and insecure property rights. This deprivation of property rights not only represents the loss of a possible source of independent income, but also diminishes the bargaining power of a widow vis-à-vis her in-laws, sons, and other potential supporters.

Second, the norms of patrilocal residence are an important cause of social isolation. In north India, widows are expected to remain in their husband's village, and most of them do so. At the same time, they are unlikely to receive much support from their in-laws. In fact, the relations between a widow and her in-laws are typically quite tense (property rights being one of the most common sources of tension). Widows are thus denied both the freedom to leave their husband's village, and the support they need to live there happily.

Third, widows have a limited freedom to remarry. In some communities, particularly in north-west India, ascriptive leviratic unions (e.g. between a widow and her brother-in-law) remain relatively common. Elsewhere, the dominant pattern is that most childless widows remarry, but only a small proportion of widowed mothers do so.

Fourth, the gender division of labour severely restricts employment opportunities for widows. Census data indicate that age-specific labour-force participation rates are a little higher for widows than for married women. But the low involvement of north Indian women in gainful employment—irrespective of marital status—is a basic problem. Further, because widows tend to be concentrated in the older age groups, their average labour-force participation rate is lower than that of married women.

Fifth, most widows can expect little economic support from their family or community, except possibly in the form of co-residence with one of their adult sons. In particular, the notion that the joint family provides economic security to widows in rural India is little more than a myth. Most surveys find that co-residence of a widow with her in-laws is rare in north India (except in cases of leviratic unions), and that the relationship between a widow and her deceased husband's family is often far from harmonious. An overwhelming majority of widows live on their own, with their unmarried children, or as a dependent in the household of one of their adult sons.[71]

As these observations illustrate, there are close links between the position of widows in society and a whole range of patriarchal institutions such as patrilineal inheritance, patrilocal residence, remarriage norms, and

[71] In south India, a widow without adult sons often lives with the family of one of her married daughters, if she has any. In north India, however, this residence pattern is rare, as it goes against prevailing social norms.

the gender division of labour. The cause of widows must be seen as an integral part of the larger battle against gender inequalities.

Taking effective action (e.g. aimed at more secure land rights for women and better social security arrangements) requires a combination of public pressure and state response. The first task is to bring the issue closer to the centre of public attention. The agency of the women's movement is central to this challenge, in addition to that of widows themselves.[72]

7.7. CRIMINAL VIOLENCE: POVERTY VS PATRIARCHY

As things stand, levels of criminal violence in India appear to be relatively moderate in international perspective. For instance, among 98 developing countries for which comparable data are available from the United Nations World Crime Surveys, India ranks 55th in descending order of the homicide rate.[73] However, homicide rates in India have risen significantly in recent decades, and it is important to be alert to the danger of growing violence in the future. Indeed, the spread of violence is often difficult to reverse. Countries such as Colombia and South Africa seem to be trapped in an unending cycle of endemic violence, involving homicide rates above 200 per million persons per year. A similar danger threatens the most violent parts of India, such as Patna, where the recorded homicide rate is of a similar order of magnitude—194 per million in 1998.[74] Whether we look at trends over time in India, or at regional or international comparisons, there are grounds for concern about the possibility of criminal violence in India rising well above its present level.

Some basic features of homicide in India can be tentatively gleaned from case studies, police reports and related sources.[75] Offenders are

---

[72] Many Indian widows—and other single women—have shown that they are not just victims of the existing social order, but also spirited agents of change; see e.g. Bhatia (1998a), Chen (1998), and Omvedt (1989). The last author, in an enlightening account of collective action by single women in Sangli district (Maharashtra), emphasizes 'the militancy of these women, who tend to provide the vanguard of toiling women's struggles everywhere' (p. 911). It is, in fact, not surprising that single women have often been found at the forefront of social and political movements. Indeed, freedom from conjugal control and the need to earn an independent living often lead single women to adopt a more autonomous and assertive lifestyle than their married sisters.

[73] Fajnzylber, Lederman and Loayza (1998). The main focus of this section is on homicides. On homicide rates in different Indian states, see Statistical Appendix, Table A.3, Part 11.

[74] Government of India (2000g), p. 49.

[75] Useful studies include Kerawalla (1959), Driver (1961), Bayley (1963), Ahuja (1969), Unnathan and Ahuja (1988), Das and Chattopadhyay (1991), Dube (1996a,

mainly young men. Murders by women are extremely rare, and are usually committed in response to provocations such as harassment or infidelity. In the case of murders committed by men, folklore has it that the main motives are '*zan, zar,* and *zamin*' (women, gold, and land).[76] There is obviously an element of stereotype here, but the general notion that disputes relating to property and women account for a substantial proportion of murders is consistent with the evidence (such as it is) from police records and court proceedings.[77] Altercations and vendettas are other common antecedents. Scattered evidence suggests that perpetrator and victim often belong to the same family, caste, community or peer group. For instance, in an insightful case study of 144 convictions for murder in central India, Driver (1961) found that victim and offender belonged to the same caste in 84 per cent of the cases. The main motives were disputes over property, living arrangements or sexual matters, and also transgressions of social norms.

Violent crime is often thought of as a feature of 'modern society', and contrasted with the supposedly peaceful atmosphere of 'traditional communities'. The fact that homicide rates have risen in India since the mid-1970s may appear to corroborate this view. The historical evidence as a whole, however, does not support the hypothesis that violent crime typically rises with the level of development.[78] In western Europe, the incidence of violent crime *declined* steadily during the eighteenth and nineteenth centuries.[79] In developing countries, too, improved living standards are often associated with a decline in the level of violent crime. In India, contrary to popular belief, homicide rates are not higher in urban areas than in rural areas. The notion that Indian villages are havens of peace bears little relation to reality.

Another common view, of opposite inspiration, is that violent crime

---

1996b), among others. For further discussion, see Drèze and Khera (2000); this section draws extensively on that study.

[76] Edwardes (1924) even asserts that 'most of the murders committed in districts as widely separated as the Panjab, Bombay, and Burma' relate to these 'three powerful stimuli' (p.18). The evidential basis of this generalization, however, is not clear from the text.

[77] See e.g. Driver (1961), Table 4, Unnathan and Ahuja (1988), p. 65, and Government of India (1997g), pp. 290–1.

[78] See e.g. Rogers (1989), and the literature cited there.

[79] See Chesnais (1981). As the author notes, the reduction of violent crime in Europe went hand in hand with a steady increase in the *overall* level of crime in conventional terms (e.g. assessed as an unweighted sum of numbers of different crimes such as murder, theft, forgery, arson, etc.).

is an affliction of poverty. This view was particularly influential during the pre-independence period, consistent as it was with colonial prejudices. As one eminent scholar put it, 'hunger and starvation tempt them [the destitute] to tread the easy and devious path of crime'.[80] A similar prediction arises from Gary Becker's influential economic model of crime, with its focus on the opportunity cost of time (Glaeser, 1999). The poor, so goes the argument, face lower economic returns from legitimate occupations, and have a lower opportunity cost of jail time, both of which raise the incentive to commit crimes. It is not difficult to see that this argument, on its own, is far from convincing, especially in the contemporary Indian context. For one thing, poverty is associated not only with low wages but also with high levels of risk aversion. For another, the risk of being caught and convicted in the event of committing a murder tends to be much higher among the poor than among the rich. Indeed, as discussed in chapter 10, the Indian judicial system is effectively far from impartial between different classes. While it is not uncommon for a privileged and influential person to 'get away with murder', the poor live in terror of the police and the courts.

There is little empirical support for the hypothesis that criminal violence is a consequence of poverty. Even though, as mentioned earlier, criminal violence often declines in the process of development and modernization, this is unlikely to be due to a simple 'income effect' (rather than, say, to the effect of rising education levels or improved public measures for the prevention of violent crime). After controlling for education and other relevant variables, cross-country variations in homicide rates appear to bear no significant association with the level of per-capita income (Fajnzylber et al., 1998), and the same applies to inter-regional variations within India (Drèze and Khera, 2000).

In short, it would be misleading to think of criminal violence as a simple by-product of the level of economic development. In order to understand variations in levels of violent crime between different societies, we have to take a more inclusive view of the relevant social and economic influences. There is some evidence, for instance, that *inequality* tends to be associated with high levels of violent crime (Fajnzylber et al., 1998). Many examples of high-crime countries seem to fit into this pattern, including South Africa, several Latin American countries (e.g. Brazil,

---

[80] Haikerwal (1934), p. 64. This conclusion was based on a detailed study of the relation between economic conditions and crime, which also '[proved] beyond doubt the effect of the rains on crime' (p.52). It is possible, of course, that the link between poverty and crime was stronger in those days than it is today.

Colombia, El Salvador, Guatemala), and also, among high-income countries, the United States.

For lack of suitable data, it is difficult to verify whether a similar relationship holds within India. However, a related pattern of much interest has recently come to light: district-specific homicide rates are highly correlated (inversely) with the female-male ratio in the population.[81] This correlation is very robust (e.g. it holds even after controlling for a wide range of other variables), and much stronger than that between the homicide rate and other socio-economic variables for which district-level data are available.

This finding points to a close association between gender inequality (of which low female-male ratios are one manifestation) and criminal violence (specifically, the homicide rate). It is important to note that what is at issue here is not violence *against women*, but the overall homicide rate in the society. Regions with relatively low levels of gender inequality, such as Kerala and Himachal Pradesh (both of which have high female-male ratios) tend to have low levels of criminal violence (in fact those two states have the lowest homicide rates among all major Indian states), and conversely with regions of high gender inequality.

There are several possible interpretations of this association between gender inequality and criminal violence. It can be read, for instance, as one manifestation of a general connection between violence and patriarchy. In so far as patriarchy (in the broad sense of the subjugation of women) is ultimately based on the threat of violence, it is perhaps not surprising that areas of high violence are associated with sharp gender inequalities.

A related version of the argument focuses on the historical role of violence in the emergence of patriarchal norms and institutions. Marvin Harris, among others, has stressed 'the importance of warfare in shaping gender hierarchies'; specifically, the author notes that 'wherever conditions favored the development of warfare among bands and villages, the political and domestic subordination of women increased'.[82] It is possible that the history of warfare in specific parts of India, such as the Gangetic plain, has

---

[81] See Drèze and Khera (2000), where various interpretations of this finding are also discussed. A similar pattern had been noticed earlier, for Uttar Pradesh specifically, by Philip Oldenburg (1992).

[82] Harris (1993), p. 61. The author also makes an important distinction between internal and distant warfare. The latter 'enhances rather than worsens the status of women since it results in avunculocal or matrilocal domestic organizations' (p.66). Harris gives the example of the matrilineal Iroquois, but the observation is also relevant to the Nairs of Kerala (who, like the Iroquois, have a tradition of distant warfare as well as of matriliny).

left a legacy of continuing violence as well as of sharp gender inequality and male preference. This line of analysis is also consistent with the fact, noted earlier, that within north India patriarchal norms tend to be particularly strong among the so-called 'martial castes'.[83]

Another possible aspect of the nexus between violence and patriarchy relates to land ownership. In India, both regional contrasts and comparisons between different communities suggest a close relation between gender inequality and land property. For instance, female-male ratios tend to be particularly low among the property-owning castes (Miller, 1981). Similarly, areas of densely-populated fertile land, with a long history of settled agriculture and private land ownership (e.g. the western part of the Gangetic plain), tend to be associated with low levels of female labour force participation, an emphasis on the joint family, patrilocal post-marital residence, the practice of dowry, and related patriarchal norms.[84] All these, in turn, lead to a devaluation of female children relative to male children, and to low female-male ratios. These particular communities and regions are also likely to be prone to property-related conflicts and violence. Given that a substantial proportion of all homicides are property-related, we might expect a negative association between female-male ratios and murder rates, mediated by property relations.

There are other possible interpretations of the statistical association between female-male ratios and homicide rates in India, and further research is needed to clarify this matter. Meanwhile, these findings reinforce a general theme of this chapter, namely that the social ramifications of gender inequality are potentially very wide. Some manifestations of gender inequality, such as the survival disadvantages of young girls and gender biases in school attendance, are relatively well known. However, the social implications of the subordination of women go much beyond these elementary and glaring inequalities. The association between patriarchy and criminal violence (not just against women) is one example of the less obvious facets of gender inequality. While gender inequality is often thought

[83] There is some tentative evidence (and not just from Hindi films) that even today homicide rates are relatively high in those communities. In a study of village Palanpur (western Uttar Pradesh) spanning five decades, Drèze and Sharma (1998) note that most murders over this period were committed by Thakurs. The authors also mention various other indicators of the continuing influence of militaristic values among the Thakurs: they have the monopoly of guns in the village, spend time in body-building, strive to get jobs in the army and the police, etc.

[84] These associations need not apply if land inheritance is matrilineal; this is one possible reason why they have limited relevance in Kerala, which has a tradition of matrilineal inheritance for a substantial section of the population.

of as a well-understood feature of society, the truth is that we are only beginning to understand its wide-ranging manifestations and implications.

7.8. GENDER EQUALITY AND SOCIAL PROGRESS

Earlier in this chapter, we have had several occasions to note the role of women's agency in social progress. In particular, we have discussed the connections between women's agency and child survival, and also between women's agency and fertility, based on an analysis of inter-district variations in demographic indicators. These connections also show up in more aggregative comparisons of different regions in India. In fact, it is rather striking that the demographically 'backward' regions of India (where mortality, and also fertility, are particularly high) tend also to have highly unequal gender relations. This applies particularly to the large north Indian states (Uttar Pradesh, Bihar, Madhya Pradesh, and Rajasthan). Even in Punjab and Haryana, child mortality and fertility rates are higher than the corresponding averages for south India, despite much higher levels of per-capita income, and this may have something to do with the comprehensive subordination of women in these two states.[85]

Conversely, states which have experienced rapid progress in improving health and reducing mortality and fertility are often those where women play an important social or economic role. Striking examples (from very diverse regions of India) include Kerala, Himachal Pradesh and Manipur.[86] The empowerment of women has had a different basis in each case, involving for instance the early promotion of female literacy, the influence of matrilineal communities, the economic roles of women, and other sources of female emancipation. But the common feature is that women have ended up with a far more equal and active role in the society than their sisters in, say, the large north Indian states. And, correspondingly, there has been far more progress in the fields of health and mortality reduction, not just in terms of reducing the female disadvantage in survival, but also in improving survival chances for *everyone*.

There is a sense in which this connection is fairly obvious. Given the gender division of labour that prevails in most of India, nutrition, child health, and related matters typically depend primarily on women's

---

[85] For details, see Statistical Appendix, Table A.3, Part 2.

[86] On Kerala, see the case study by V.K. Ramachandran (1996) in the companion volume, and the literature cited there. On Himachal Pradesh, see chapters 3 and 5. The case of Manipur, where birth and death rates are comparable to those of Kerala, is examined in A.K. Shiva Kumar (1992, 1994).

decisions and actions. It is, therefore, perhaps unsurprising that social achievements in this domain are more impressive where women are better educated, more resourceful, more valued, more influential, and generally more equal agents in the household and society.

The importance of women's agency, of course, is not confined to the field of demographic change. When the creative abilities and personal contributions of one half of the society are stifled by constant subjugation, in addition to the drudgery of constant domestic work and child-bearing, social opportunities are suppressed in a wide range of domains. Even the level of economic production is likely to be higher, other things being equal, in a society where women are able to engage in a diverse range of activities than in a society where their life is confined to domestic work.[87] The realms of politics and social reform can also be considerably enriched by the active participation of women.

This general connection, too, emerges from broad inter-regional comparisons. Kerala not only has much lower levels of mortality and fertility than, say, Uttar Pradesh or Rajasthan, it has also made far more progress in removing traditional social inequalities, in using public services as a basis for enhancing the quality of life, and in evolving a vigorous civil society. By comparison, the large north Indian states are notorious for the persistence of feudal agrarian relations, for the continued oppression of disadvantaged castes, for chaotic or delinquent public services, and for the comprehensive corruption of political institutions. Even in comparison with south India as a whole (not just Kerala), these north Indian states present a picture of resilient social backwardness. If one were to look for the deep historical roots of these broad regional contrasts in the nature of society and politics, the position of women in society is certainly one of the influences that would command attention.

What is also striking is how the gender factor can overpower many other influences that often receive more attention, such as religious identity and national boundaries. We have already seen that the extent of anti-female bias in child survival does not vary much, if at all, between Hindus and Muslims in north India. Nor does it vary much between north India and Pakistan. The entire region is one where the agency of women has been comprehensively repressed, among Hindus as much as among Muslims or Sikhs, leading not only to this female disadvantage in

---

[87] Drèze and Srinivasan (1996) find that poverty reduction in India between 1972–3 and 1987–8 was more rapid in regions with higher initial levels of female labour force participation. The contrast between south Asia and east Asia (including China) points in the same direction.

child survival but also to the persistence of high levels of mortality and fertility. Similarly, it is remarkable that Kerala and Sri Lanka have so much in common in terms of social achievements, cutting across the religious, cultural, and national boundaries.[88] Here again, the common heritage of less unequal gender relations (which includes less patriarchal kinship systems, less male-dominated property rights, and a greater prominence of women in influential economic, social, and political activities) appears to be a causal factor of major importance.

By way of conclusion, we would like to focus on five elementary points. First, the persistence of extraordinarily high levels of gender inequality and female deprivation is one of India's most serious social failures. Few other regions in the world have achieved so little in promoting gender justice.

Second, gender inequality does not decline automatically with the process of economic growth (at least not at an early stage of development). In fact, we have seen that some important forces operate in the opposite direction (e.g. the tendency of upwardly-mobile castes to impose new restrictions on the lifestyle of women in order to achieve a higher social status). Even where economic growth has a positive influence on the status of women, e.g. by expanding female employment opportunities or literacy rates, this influence tends to be slow and indirect. It is important to aim at more radical and effective social change based on public action.

Third, gender inequality is not only a social failure in itself, it also contributes to other social failures. We have illustrated this link in some detail with particular reference to child mortality and related demographic achievements, but have also pointed to similar links that apply in other fields where the agency of women is important.

Fourth, the agency of women as a force for change is one of the most neglected aspects of the development literature, and this neglect applies as much to India as elsewhere. There has, happily, been a growing awareness in recent years of the disadvantaged predicament of women in Indian society. That understanding of the victimization of women has to be supplemented by a recognition of women as agents of social change. It is not merely that more justice must be received by women, but also that social justice can be achieved only through the active agency of women. The suppression of women from participation in social, political

[88] There are, in particular, striking parallels between the experiences of mortality decline in Kerala and Sri Lanka, including the crucial role, in both cases, of basic education (especially female literacy), health services, and women's agency. On the importance of these enabling factors in Sri Lanka, see Pieris and Caldwell (1996) and Alailima and Sanderatne (1997).

and economic life hurts the people as a whole, not just women. The emancipation of women is an integral part of social progress, not just a 'women's issue'.

Finally, the agency of women is effective in promoting those goals which women tend to value. When those values are distorted by centuries of inequality, for example yielding the perception that boys are to be welcomed more than girls, then the empowerment of women can go hand in hand with persistent inequality and discrimination in some fields, in particular 'boy preference' in births (with possibly brutal results in the form of sex-specific abortions). Indeed, the agency of women can never be adequately free if traditionally discriminatory values remain unexamined and unscrutinized. While values may be culturally influenced (we have provided some evidence corroborating this presumption), it is possible to overcome the barriers of inequality imposed by tradition through greater freedom to question, doubt, and—if convinced—reject. An adequate realization of women's agency relates not only to the freedom to act but also to the freedom to question and reassess. Critical agency is a great ally of development.

8

Security and Democracy in a Nuclear India

8.1. THE WAGES OF WAR

A little over a century ago, a world peace conference was convened at The
Hague at the initiative of Czar Nicholas II. The Czar was perhaps an
unlikely fighter for peace, but he did have a vested interest in avoiding
wars and in limiting the development of armaments in Europe. These
armaments were indeed frightening, especially France and Germany's
latest 'field artillery capable of firing six rounds a minute'.[1] The object
of the conference, as described in the Czar's invitation, was to seek 'the
most effective means of ensuring to all peoples the benefits of a real and
lasting peace, and above all of limiting the progressive development of
existing armaments'.[2]

The Czar's appeal was, on the whole, well received by the European
public, including millions of women from eighteen countries who signed
a petition for peace. The reactions of rulers of states and other political
leaders in positions of real influence were less enthusiastic. In Britain, the
Prince of Wales described the Czar's appeal as 'the greatest rubbish and
nonsense I have heard of'. In Germany, the Kaiser paid something of a
tribute to the proposal in public ('the most interesting and surprising of
this century'), but was reported to have been very critical in private.

The conference was held nevertheless, in October 1899, with the
usual suspects showing up in their most peacable attire. Not surprisingly

---

[1] See Warth (1997), pp. 51–3. On related aspects of the peace conference, see also
Davis (1962) and Tuchman (1966).
[2] Count Mouravieff (1898), p.1.

it was viewed with bewildered suspicion by some of the other participants, one of whom described it as 'a thieves' supper'.[3] Fifteen years later, the 'thieves' were not engaged in supping with each other, but locked in mortal combat, with their respective gigantic armies. The plea for peace had received its formal honour, and now received a decent burial.

The human toll of wars in the twentieth century surpasses the darkest predictions. Even the deeply pessimistic prognostications in Ivan Bloch's *The Future of War*, published in 1899, and which had a role in prompting Nicholas II to convene the peace conference, pale in comparison with the actual events of the twentieth century. Since then, at least 250 wars have been fought (including of course two 'World Wars'), causing more than 100 million deaths.[4]

It is important to reflect on these facts as we enter a new millennium, which some expect, not without reason, to be 'a short millennium'. Though the Cold War has famously come to an end, the astonishing nuclear arsenal of the established powers (which can destroy the world many times over, rather more effectively than the 'six rounds a minute' that had so terrified Nicholas II) is still in place, under varying political arrangements, some of them rather unpredictable. New entrants are continuing to add to the stock of nuclear weapons, which are, to use that oddly peaceful expression, 'ready for delivery', controlled by triggers that are spread more widely than ever before. Also, the ravages of smaller wars and the trail of destruction in one country after another continue forcefully. From the uncontrolled barbarity of 'collateral casualties' to the precisely aimed savagery of 'ethnic cleansing', the march of killing and genocide is unstopped and unrestrained.

All this is much in contrast with the hopes that the end of the Cold War had aroused. There has been a 'peace dividend' of sorts, in the form of a significant decline in world-wide military expenditure in the 1990s. But this has failed to translate into a reduction of the incidence of violent conflicts (a fact that has received considerable notice), and also failed to lead to a commensurate expansion of social expenditures for peaceful development (a fact that deserves much greater attention than it has so far received).

The continuation (if not intensification) of violence across the world in the 1990s is indeed rather striking. On average, about *one third* of the world population lived in a country at war during this period.[5] The

---

[3] Tuchman (1966), p. 447. The participant in question was expelled for his impertinence.

[4] See Sivard (1996), p.7.

[5] The list of countries at war is taken from Dan Smith's (1997) highly informative 'war and peace atlas', pp. 90–6 (the reference period is 1990–5). For further discussion, see Drèze (2000a).

wars in question, moreover, are nasty and vicious. Indeed, contemporary wars are remarkable not only for their widespread incidence, but also for their exceptional ruthlessness. Civilians are typically the main target, accounting for over 80 per cent of war casualties.[6] Aside from violent and grisly deaths, a deluge of ghastly maiming, mutilation and dismemberment fills the history of our times. The quality of brutality, it appears, is not strained.

The human toll of militarism also includes its adverse long-term effects on development and the quality of life. There is, in fact, a real tension here, in terms of contemporary records of development. Leaving out the wages of war and military conflicts, development trends in the second half of the twentieth century include a sustained improvement in living conditions in many countries, discernible for instance in declining mortality rates, rising per-capita incomes, better nutrition, improved education levels and an expansion of civil liberties.[7] But aside from putting some countries out of reach of these achievements, armed conflicts have also imposed intermittent—but recurrent—devastations on many others, which had been otherwise on the road to some real progress. There have been havocs or serious downturns, in various forms, in Afghanistan, Angola, Cambodia, Congo, El Salvador, Eritrea, Ethiopia, Guatemala, Iraq, Lebanon, Mozambique Sierra Leone, Somalia, Sri Lanka, Vietnam, and former Yugoslavia, to mention a few of the victims of war and violence around the world.

Why note the grimness of the world in a book that is specifically on India? The chief reason is that India is a part of this world, and there are lessons—cautionary as well as chilling—for India to learn from the predicament that has overwhelmed many other countries. Indeed, India has been relatively fortunate so far in avoiding the ravages of war. Yet the dangers are strongly present. As India went to war in mid-1999 after nearly thirty years of peace (since the 'eastern' war of 1971 that led to the independence of Bangladesh), the country has reason to ask what had gone wrong. It is a particularly appropriate question to ask since the latest war, with intruders from Pakistan (in the Kargil district of Kashmir), occurred hot on the heels of the tit-for-tat nuclear blasts of May 1998, which many nuclear strategists (not least in India) had predicted would make war 'impossible' between the two neighbours.[8] The results seem to

---

[6] See Drèze (2000a), Figure 2, based on Sivard (1991, 1996).

[7] The spread of AIDS has recently reversed the trend of mortality decline in a number of countries. Unfortunately, that dreadful phenomenon is still in its infancy.

[8] Right up to the Kargil crisis, for instance, simplistic deterrence arguments (such as Kenneth Waltz's 'theory of nuclear weapons being a stabilising factor, especially in adversarial situations') were confidently invoked as proof that 'war between India

have been just the contrary. What, we cannot fail to ask, has gone wrong with that 'theory', or was it not a good theory anyway?

The cautionary lessons emerging from the experiences of other countries around the world pertain not only to the consequences of war, but also to the penalties of military over-activism. These have at least three aspects. First, militarism (in the broad sense of a tendency to use military power, or the threat of it, for political settlements) is a factor of collective insecurity. Second, military preoccupations make exacting demands on a country's resources (financial, human, scientific and other), very often at the expense of development purposes. Third, military imperatives are frequently at odds with democratic values.

We shall return to these distinct issues in due course. Before that, it is worth reexamining the nature and sources of strength in the contemporary world. In particular, we need a clearer understanding of the connections between the moral and the pragmatic, on the one hand, and between civilian strength and military security, on the other.

8.2. The Moral and the Pragmatic

There are extremely important issues of ethics in deciding on military policies, and in particular serious questions about the rightness or wrongness of nuclear policies. Nevertheless, our primary focus of attention in this work is not on the moral questions seen on their own. But we cannot, for good scientific reasons, take the moral and the pragmatic issues to be altogether disparate and totally delinked from each other. The connections between the two include the fact that our behaviour towards each other and how we view each other cannot be divorced from what we make of the ethics of one another's pursuits. For this reason, considerations of morality can have prudential importance as well, and those connections must figure even in our primarily prudential investigation.[9]

It must also be recognized that whether—or to what extent—powerful weapons empower a nation is not a new question. Indeed, well before the age of nuclear armament began, Rabindranath Tagore had expressed a general doubt about the fortifying effects of military strength. Tagore was not as uncompromisingly a pacifist as Mahatma Gandhi was, and his

---

and Pakistan is now simply impossible' (K. Shankar Bajpai, *Times of India*, 27 April 1999).

[9] The connections between the two sets of questions in the analysis of economic problems (and the possibilities of missing the links on the part of the systematic but narrowly circumscribed reasoner—the 'rational fool') were discussed in Sen (1977, 1987a).

warning against the dangers of alleged strength through more and bigger weapons related to the need for critically scrutinizing the exact uses of these weapons as well as the practical importance of the reactions and counteractions of others. Tagore gave cogent expression to the interdependence between the moral and the pragmatic in his lectures on *Nationalism* published in 1917. In criticizing a shift in the policy of Japan (of which he had been a great admirer) towards more militarism, Tagore had argued that if 'in his eagerness for power', a nation 'multiplies his weapons at the cost of his soul, then it is he who is in much greater danger than his enemies' (Tagore, 1917). Tagore was concerned not merely with the morality of the shift in Japanese policies, but also with the responses from others that would be generated by Japan's pursuit of military might.

The 'soul' to which Tagore referred included, as he explained, the need for humanity, and for mutual concern and understanding in international relations. The heavy sacrifices that were forced on Japan later on, through military defeat and nuclear devastation, Tagore did not live to see (he died in 1941), but they would have only added to Tagore's intense sorrow. The conundrum that Tagore invoked, about the weakening effects of military power in a world of reactions and counteractions, has remained active in the writings of contemporary Japanese writers, perhaps mostly notably Kenzaburo Oe (1995). These considerations are relevant in India as well.

Despite the inescapable moral questions involved in nuclear policy, the prudential issues tend to get priority in public discussions. This is perhaps because moral differences are sometimes harder to reconcile. But more immediately, it so happens that some highly influential and assertively 'practical' thinkers are inclined to dismiss moral principles as being quite 'beside the point' (the less inhibited critics call it 'a load of rubbish'). We do not ourselves take that dismissive view of the relevance of morals, but nevertheless we shall concentrate in this book primarily on practical matters—not ethical issues as such.[10] However, for reasons already discussed, moral issues have pragmatic and practical relevance as well.[11] In a world of interaction between different parties who judge each other in deciding on their reactions and counteractions, our individual

---

[10] See, however, our own essays elsewhere, which combine the moral issues with prudential ones: Drèze (2000a) and Sen (2000c). See also the well reasoned study of Bidwai and Vanaik (1999) and the stirring analysis of Roy (1998).

[11] It is also worth noting that our moral differences can become less pronounced when there are fuller agreements on the facts of the case. Many of our moral judgments are 'non-basic' in the sense of being conditional on our contingent factual beliefs. On this see Sen (1967, 1970b: chapter 5).

conduct as well as our international standing are as much under scrutiny as the cunning we respectively display. The analysis of strength and national security in the contemporary world (on which more in the next section) cannot overlook these important connections.

8.3. SOURCES OF STRENGTH AND DANGERS OF UNDERESTIMATION

Military confrontation has often arisen in the past from an overestimation of a country's strength. Many countries that have declared war on others with the firm confidence that they would 'win' have ended up being defeated and sometimes devastated. Examples of this can be found plentifully in the gigantic battles of the World Wars as well as in the smaller wars of the present times. Overestimation of one's powers can lead to counterproductive bellicosity.

But so can an *underestimation* of one's strength. Fear of the enemy—or enemies—can lead to precipitate and ill-thought-out actions, provoking reactions from others and a chain reaction of escalation. To underestimate oneself can be a source of unsettling panic, and can lead to alarmed—and alarming—overreaction. It can be argued that there is an element of just this type of overreach in the contemporary military developments in the subcontinent.

An interesting side light that emerges from a scrutiny of Indian official perceptions associated with recent military escalation in general and nuclear adventures in particular is the extent to which India's own government underestimates her importance as a major country with a democratic polity, a rich multireligious civilization, a well-established tradition in science and technology (including the cutting edge of information technology), and a relatively fast-growing economy. The overestimation of the persuasive power of the bomb goes with an underestimation of the political, cultural, scientific and economic strengths of the country. It also leads to a diversion of resources away from economic development as well as from the pursuit of enriching and empowering progress in scientific and technological fields.

India is not, of course, the only country to have been caught in the web of self-created weakness through ill-considered priorities masquerading as empowerment. To choose an analogy from a very different country, a similar indictment would apply to Britain's involvement with nuclear weapons. The point was put sharply by Sir Michael Atiyah, as the President of the Royal Society, in his 'Anniversary Address' to the Society in 1995:

I believe history will show that the insistence on a UK nuclear capability was fundamentally misguided, a total waste of resources and a significant factor in our relative economic decline over the past 50 years.

The facts are easy to come by. Comparisons with Germany will show that both countries have devoted approximately the same fraction of their resources to Research and Development. However the division between civil and military R & D in the two countries is very different. Given this discrepancy, and the acknowledged importance of science and technology for modern industry, it would have required gross incompetence on the part of our German competitors if they had not derived a major economic benefit from this additional investment. Very similar remarks apply to Japan.

The need for rigorous scrutiny of the priorities of public policy in India has never been stronger. This is not only because of the necessity of keeping firmly in view the crucial demands of well-being and freedom of Indian citizens (many of them poor, illiterate and hungry), but also because the sources of a country's strength—even military strength—demand a more exacting scrutiny than they tend to get. Japan's and Germany's security does not rest primarily on their arsenal, nor mainly on whatever practical advantage they may get from the formal promise of 'protection' from the United States; rather, it derives from the fact that they are economically successful and scientifically advanced, and have standings and a voice that are widely respected across the world. Even China's powerful position and high standing in the international setting is only marginally related to its nuclear capability, and much more influenced by its extraordinary success as an emergent economic giant and a much admired achiever of a social revolution.

The overestimation by Indian political leaders of the empowering effects of India's further pursuit of nuclear weapons goes hand in hand with an astonishing underestimation of India's real sources of strength. This psychology came to light very clearly in the aftermath of the nuclear blasts of May 1998. From George Fernandes' triumphant statement that 'India is not a pushover' to Bal Thackeray's more graphic 'we are not eunuchs any longer', jubilation at India's allegedly new-found power was the order of the day.[12] Implicit in these statements is the notion that *without* nuclear weapons, India would be a 'pushover'. This is making rather short shrift of India's other sources of strength, including its large

---

[12] Bal Thackeray's statement belongs to a long tradition of sexual imagery around nuclear weapons, which goes back at least to Herman Kahn's (1962) vision of nuclear conflict as 'wargasm'; for an illuminating analysis of this phenomenon, see Carol Cohn (1987).

size, democratic politics, multicultural pluralism, fast-growing economy, and scientific and technological capabilities. The overconcentration on military strength in general, and the belief in the persuasive powers of nuclear adventures in particular, are accompanied by a vast underestimation of India's real strengths.

Beyond this general need to understand better the sources of strength and security in the contemporary world, there is need even for a more exacting scrutiny of the mechanics of military power itself. It is frequently claimed that the nuclear blasts that India conducted in May 1998 have made India stronger. In fact, there are good reasons to argue that exactly the opposite has occurred as a result of those tests and the tit-for-tat retaliations by Pakistan.[13] Scoring off against Pakistan is not a good way of thinking about subcontinental coexistence, but since that is the metric in which India's military strength is often judged, let us at least be accurate in doing that rather chilling accounting.

First, India has—and has had—a massive superiority over Pakistan in conventional military strength, but that strategic advantage has become far less significant as a result of the new nuclear balance. Indeed, since Pakistan has explicitly refused to accept a 'no first use' agreement, India's ability to count on conventional superiority is now much reduced.

Second, the fact that India can make nuclear weapons was well established before the matching nuclear tests of May 1998 were conducted. Pokhran-I in 1974 had already established the point, and India's restraint in not going further along the way was the source of some international respect.[14] After the recent set of tests, not only is that appreciation replaced by castigation of India's role in initiating the tit-for-tat blasts by the two neighbours, it is also the case that India and Pakistan are now viewed, after these tests, in much more even terms.

Third, aside from perceptions, Pakistan clearly had a greater technical need for testing, never having conducted a nuclear test before 1998. While Pakistan feared the condemnation of the world community by testing on its own, the Indian blasts in May 1998 created a situation in which Pakistan could go in that direction without being blamed for starting any nuclear adventure.

---

[13] This book, obviously, is not the right vehicle for presenting anything like a comprehensive assessment of the military and civil situation that has been brought about by the Pokhran tests in May 1998 and the Pakistani nuclear blasts that followed a month later in the Chagai Hills. We have written elsewhere on these subjects; see Drèze (2000a) and Sen (2000c). The discussions that follow draw on the analyses presented in those works.

[14] On this and related matters, see Michael Foot's (1999) insightful analysis of the nuclear dilemmas of the contemporary world and India's own position in it.

Fourth, nor was there much success in getting recognition for India as being in the same league as China, or for its grumble that the world pays inadequate attention to the dangers India is supposed to face from China. In fact, as a result of the matching nuclear tests by India and Pakistan, China could stand well above India's little grumbles, gently admonishing it for its criticism of China, and placing itself in the statesman-like position of being a subcontinental peace-maker. As Mark Frazier puts it: 'Had it been India's intention to alert the world to its security concerns about China as a dangerous rising power, the tests managed to do just the opposite—they gave the Chinese officials the opportunity to present China as a cooperative member of the international community seeking to curb nuclear weapons proliferation'.[15]

Security, standing and strength in the contemporary world have demands that seem to be rather dimly perceived in the official policies that have been followed in recent years in India. The underestimation of India's real strengths and their vast potentialities has not served the country well. The mistaken belief in the empowering effects of nuclear weaponization has compounded that error. India does not need being put on the crutches of nuclear weapons to stand firm. Nothing is more important at this time than to bring these issues more clearly and more engagingly within the realm of public scrutiny. That would also be a way of making good use of one of India's exceptional sources of strength, namely its democratic polity.

8.4. DETERRENCE AND SECURITY

Does nuclear deterrence work? It is supposed to have worked very well in keeping the global powers away from war during the long period of the Cold War. It is, thus, legitimate to ask why the allegedly proven effectiveness of nuclear deterrence should not apply in the subcontinent as well. Should Indians and Pakistanis not sleep more peacefully now that nuclear weapons are a guarantee of peace in the subcontinent? There are several distinct reasons for thinking that this is not the case.[16]

---

[15] Frazier (2000), p. 10.

[16] This is aside from the fact that the stability of peace under nuclear deterrence is far from convincing even in the most optimistic of game-theoretic scenarios that have been invoked in the literature. The idea of 'credible threat' itself is full of internal tension, including the fact that once there is no further negotiation to be made, there may be no particular prudential case for a threat of devastation of the enemy to be put into practice (since its main usefulness is in securing a better deal). On these issues see Schelling (1960), Rapoport (1964), Ellsberg (1981), Hardin et al. (1985), Shubik (1987), Freedman (1989), Jervis (1989), Powell (1990), among other contributions.

First, even if it were the case that the nuclearization of India and Pakistan reduces the probability of war between the two, there would be a trade off here between a lower chance of conventional war against some chance of a nuclear holocaust. No sensible decision making can concentrate only on the probability of war without taking note of the consequences of war should it occur.

Second, there is nothing to indicate that the likelihood of conventional war is, in fact, reduced by the nuclearization of India and Pakistan. Indeed, shortly following the nuclear blasts, the two countries did experience a major military confrontation in the Kargil district of Kashmir. The Kargil conflict, as was mentioned earlier, was the first serious 'war' between the two in nearly thirty years. There is some evidence that the confrontation, which was provoked by intrusion across the line of control from Pakistan, was aided and abetted by Pakistan's understanding that India would not be able to retaliate with the full might of its superior conventional forces, precisely because it would fear a nuclear holocaust. Whether or not this analysis is right, there is clearly substance in the general reasoning that the enemy's fear of nuclear annihilation can be an argument in favour of military adventurism. Be that as it may, the proof of the pudding is in the eating, and no matter what the explanation, nuclearization evidently has not prevented non-nuclear conflicts between India and Pakistan. In fact, just the contrary.

Third, the danger of accidental nuclear war is much greater in the subcontinent than it was in the Cold War itself.[17] This is not only because the checks and controls are much looser, but also because the distances involved are so small that there would be little time for negotiation in a crisis or if a first strike were feared. The much discussed hold of fundamentalist 'jehadists' within the Pakistan military and the absence of democratic control over that military add to the fear of a sudden flash point. Even on the Indian side, there has been no dearth of nuclear bravado and thinly-veiled nuclear threats, and while the democratic setting offers some protection against these tendencies, many of the threats have come from people who are dangerously close to the levers of power.

Fourth, there is a need also to assess whether the peace that the global powers enjoyed with nuclear deterrence during the global Cold War was, in fact, predictable and causally robust. The argument for the balance of

---

[17] On this, see also Krepon (2000). Even during the Cold War, the dangers of accidental nuclear war were disturbingly high. One expert estimates that the probability of accidental nuclear war within ten years hovered around 0.05 during that period (Bracken, 1985, p. 50). On these matters, see also Blair (1993, 1997), Butler (1997), and Schell (1998).

terror has commanded much appeal for a long time, and was most eloquently put by Winston Churchill in his last speech to the House of Commons on the 1st of March 1955. His ringing words on this ('safety will be the sturdy child of terror, and survival the twin brother of annihilation') have a mesmerizing effect, but Churchill himself did make exceptions to his rule, when he said that the logic of deterrence 'does not cover the case of lunatics or dictators in the mood of Hitler when he found himself in his final dug-out'.[18]

Dictators or zealots are not unknown in the subcontinent, but perhaps more importantly, we have reason to note that risks have been taken also by people with impeccable credentials of sanity and lucidity. To give just one example, in choosing the path of confrontation in what has come to be called the 'Cuban missile crisis' of 1962, President Kennedy evidently took some significant risks of annihilation on behalf of humanity. Indeed, Theodore C. Sorensen, Special Counsel to President Kennedy, put the facts thus (in a generally admiring passage):

John Kennedy never lost sight of what either war or surrender would do to the whole human race. His UN Mission was preparing for a negotiated peace and his Joint Chiefs of Staff were preparing for war, and he intended to keep both on rein. ... He could not afford to be hasty or hesitant, reckless or afraid. The odds that the Soviets would go all the way to war, he later said, seemed to him then 'somewhere between one out of three and even.'[19]

Well, a chance of annihilation between one-third and one-half is not an easy decision to be taken on behalf of the human race.

When invoking the much eulogized argument that nuclear deterrence makes war less likely, there is a need to recognize that the world was rather lucky to escape annihilation exactly when the deterrence argument was allegedly in full force. The peace of nuclear confrontation in the Cold War was to a great extent due to luck, and the view that this episode establishes the effectiveness of nuclear deterrence is no more convincing than the

---

[18] James (1974), pp. 8629-30. There is considerable evidence that Churchill was, by then, rather doubtful about the security provided by nuclear deterrence, and keen (though hampered by failing health) on taking a more positive step towards mutual denuclearization; on this see Michael Foot (1999), pp. 16–7.

[19] Sorensen (1965), p. 705. General George Lee Butler, former commander in chief of the US Strategic Air Command, goes further, and argues that the world 'survived the Cuban Missile Crisis, not thanks to deterrence, but only by the grace of God' (Butler, 1997). Similarly Robert McNamara, who played a key role in the crisis as one of Kennedy's close advisers, believes that it brought the world 'within a hairbreadth of nuclear war' (quoted in Schell, 1998, p. 47). For further evidence, see also the 'Kennedy Tapes' (May and Zelikow, 1997).

argument that playing Russian roulette is safe because one has survived the first round. To take *post hoc* to be *propter hoc* is always misleading, and in this case, it may be highly dangerous as well. We have to recognize not only that circumstances are rather different in the subcontinent compared with what obtained during the nuclear confrontation in the global Cold War, but also that the world was actually rather fortunate to escape annihilation even in the Cold War itself. And the dangers of extermination did not come only from 'lunatics or dictators', to whom Churchill referred.

There is, thus, little reason to be convinced that nuclearization of the subcontinental confrontations has reduced the risk of war. On the other hand, it certainly has dramatically escalated the penalty of war. Indeed, the consequences of a nuclear war in the subcontinent would be so catastrophic that they would amount to 'the end of imagination', to borrow Arundhati Roy's (1999) arresting expression.

8.5. THE NUCLEAR DEBATE

If the foregoing analysis is right, then India has achieved rather little and lost much from its recent nuclear escalation. The loss is not just in terms of development opportunities, but also, as argued, in the form of a weakening of the country's strength and security, including inter alia its military safety. There is, minimally, an urgent need to debate these issues more fully than has occurred so far. The voice of the pro-nuclear lobby and the short sight of the political nationalist have both been rather dominant in the field, and there is a great necessity to bring the critical arguments to wider public attention and engagement. Happily, there is an impressive and growing literature on this subject, with substance as well as well-informed analyses.[20]

India's own interest is not, however, the only issue to be considered in this context. There is also the broader question of subcontinental peace and security (already considered in the preceding section), which must interest the different countries involved. There is, furthermore, the issue of the injustice and precariousness of the present 'nuclear world order'.

---

[20] See particularly Ramdas (1998), Bidwai and Vanaik (1999), Ghosh (1999), Ram (1999), Reddy (2000); also Abraham (1998, 1999), Kishwar (1998), Jayaraman (1998, 1999), and various contributions in Gardezi and Sharma (1999), Kothari and Zia Mian (2001), and Ramana and Reddy (forthcoming). For defences of Indian nuclearization policy, see Jaswant Singh (1999), Iyengar (2000), Menon (2000), Subrahmanyam (2001), and various contributors in Jasjit Singh (1998), Sondhi (2000), Thomas and Gupta (2000).

Nuclear expansionists in India—and in Pakistan too—have tended to be deeply resentful of the international condemnation of recent nuclear tests in the subcontinent, which—they contend—takes inadequate note of the precarious nuclear situation in the world as a whole, and also the injustice of it. They are surely justified in this resentment, and also right to question the censoriousness of the established nuclear powers which is accompanied by little self-examination of the ethics of their own nuclear policies, including the preservation of a massively unequal nuclear hegemony. As India's Defence Minister, George Fernandes, told Amitav Ghosh: 'Why should the five nations that have nuclear weapons tell us how to behave and what weapons we should have?'[21]

These thoughts are easy to understand and even to sympathize with, viewed on their own. The question remains whether the placing of the subcontinental substory within the broader world context really diminishes the dubiousness of the current nuclear policies of India and Pakistan. Indeed, justified resentment at the smugness of the dominant global powers is not an argument for undertaking policies that make the subcontinent itself a much more dangerous place, without making any serious dent on that smugness.

Two distinct issues need to be carefully distinguished here:

Insecurity and unfairness of the world nuclear order. The prevailing balance of nuclear arrangements and military power in the world remains highly inequitable and insecure. There are excellent reasons for India (and for other countries, including Pakistan) to complain about the military policies of the major powers, particularly the big five that have a monopoly over official nuclear status as well as over permanent membership in the Security Council of the United Nations. The international balance of power that the world establishment seems keen on maintaining, with or without further developments (such as the proposed 'nuclear shield' for the United States), is precarious as well as unfair. There is also an inadequate appreciation in the West of the extent to which the role of the big five arouses suspicion and resentment among the developing countries. This applies not only to the monopoly over nuclear armament, but also to the 'pushing' of conventional armaments in the world market.

---

[21] This was matched by the remark of Qazi Hussain Ahmed, the leader of Jamaat-e-Islami (Pakistan's principal religious party), to Ghosh: '....we don't accept that five nations should have nuclear weapons and others shouldn't. We say, "Let the five also disarm".' See Ghosh (1999), pp. 190 and 197. For an eloquent defence of India's recent nuclear tests in the light of the injustice of the world nuclear order, see the 'postscript' in Jaswant Singh (1999).

For example, as the *Human Development Report 1994*, prepared under the leadership of that visionary Pakistani economist Mahbub ul Haq, pointed out, the top five arms-exporting countries in the world are precisely the five permanent members of the Security Council, responsible for as much as 86 per cent of all the conventional weapons exported in the years preceding the report.[22] Not surprisingly, the Security Council has not been able to take any serious initiative that would really restrain the merchants of death. It is not hard to understand the scepticism in India and Pakistan (and elsewhere) about the quality of leadership—and the sense of responsibility—of the established nuclear powers.

Insecurity and escalation in the subcontinent: The second issue concerns the choices that India—and also Pakistan—actually have, and the criteria that may be intelligently employed to make as good and as safe a choice as is possible. In this calculation the security and insecurity of the subcontinent itself must loom large, since that is what is most influenced by the choices made by India and by Pakistan. In deciding on whether or not to produce or deploy nuclear weapons, India as well as Pakistan must scrutinize not only the alleged gains that motivate these decisions, but also the economic, social and political costs that would result and the increased human insecurity that may be generated.

Since both issues are important, India and also Pakistan may well address each question with adequate seriousness, and not simply forget about the first, on the grounds of the importance of the second (as some international commentators seem to argue). But at the same time, it must also be recognized that the importance of the first does not provide any justification for escalation in the subcontinent itself. In fact, there is nothing to indicate that the nuclear blasts by India and Pakistan have helped to foster more responsible nuclear policies on the part of the big five. If anything, it is quite possible that they have played a part in the further entrenchment of the established nuclear powers in recent years, seen for instance in the US rejection of the 'comprehensive test ban treaty'. India's drive to enter the so-called 'nuclear club' has also undermined her ability to challenge this club from outside, as the Indian government had often done in the past.[23]

[22] *Human Development Report 1994*, pp. 54–5 and Table 3.6.

[23] The Indian government's submissions in international fora (from the United Nations General Assembly to the International Court of Justice) over the years include many eloquent arguments against nuclear weapons. To illustrate: 'We do not believe that the acquisition of nuclear weapons is essential for national security, and… we are also convinced that the existence of nuclear weapons diminishes international security. We, therefore, seek their complete elimination' (India's Foreign Secretary Salman Haider,

The overwhelming consideration, then, is that (as argued in the preceding section) the tit-fot-tat nuclear tests have heightened rather than reduced insecurity in the subcontinent. The unjust nature of world military balance does not change this crucial pragmatic recognition. Indeed, moral resentment of the world cannot possibly justify a prudential blunder at home. The people whose lives are made much less secure as a result of the nuclearization of India and Pakistan are primarily the residents of the subcontinent themselves. Resenting the smugness and unfairness of the global nuclear establishment is not a good reason for shooting oneself in the foot.

8.6. THE SOCIAL COSTS OF MILITARISM

The events that have followed nuclear tests in India and Pakistan in May 1998 provide a stark illustration of the high social costs of militarism. These costs come from different directions—from resource deflection on one side to the undermining of democracy on the other. The problem applies to the escalation of military activities and expenditures in general, but they have a special relevance to the recent expansion of nuclear weaponry.

First and perhaps most important, the biggest cost of nuclear escalation is the uncertainty and insecurity it generates. Ultimately, it is the dramatically increased insecurity of human lives that constitutes the biggest penalty of the subcontinental nuclear adventures. We have already discussed that issue. Bangladesh may now be, by wisdom or by good fortune, the safest place in the subcontinent.

Second, there has been a large increase in military expenditure in India in recent years, with prospects of a further boost in the near future. This is bound to reduce the scope for an expansion of public expenditure on basic services such as health and education. Today, defence spending in India is more than three times as high as the combined expenditure of central and state governments on health. This is not to say that every rupee not spent on defence is likely to be spent on health. But this gaping disproportion does illustrate the fact that the opportunity costs of military expenditure are far from negligible.

Third, the nuclear tests have led to the intensification of a costly and

at the Conference on Disarmament, March 1996). The government's sincerity in issuing these earlier official statements is debatable, since they often went hand in hand with a secret quest for the development of nuclear weapons, but nevertheless, India's abstention from active nuclear blasts after 1974 gave these statements a wider hearing than they could possibly receive today (if they were to be made in the first place).

dangerous arms race in the region. This arms race holds the prospect of a further diversion of scarce resources in the future. The logic of escalation involves a major risk of explosive expansion of military costs, even when each 'player' makes moves that are—within the logic of that 'game'— entirely rational and cogent, seen step by step. Since escalation is a general problem, we shall discuss it further in section 8.8 of this chapter. The escalation risks associated with a nuclear arms race are particularly large and potentially ruinous, even though precise assessments of likely scenarios are hard to make at this time.

Fourth, the diversion of resources involved in military pursuits is not confined to their economic burden. No less important are the demands made on the time and energy of political leaders and government officials, as well as on the attention of the public at large. These resources, too, come partly at the expense of development concerns—an issue to which we shall pay further attention presently.

Fifth, the social costs of military expansion and nuclear ventures include the deflection of India's scientific talents to military-related research, away from more productive lines of research and also from actual economic production. India's scientific establishment is among the most militarized in the world. The Defence Research and Development Organisation alone absorbs more than 30 per cent of government expenditure on scientific research and development (R&D). If one adds R&D expenditure by the Department of Atomic Energy and the Department of Space, the bulk of which is of a quasi-military nature, the proportion rises to an astonishing 64 per cent.[24] To regret this diversion of scientific talents and resources is not, of course, the same as disparaging the achievements of India's scientific community even in these fields. The talents of Indian scientists have been amply demonstrated in many different areas, including military research and development.[25] However, the dedication of scarce and highly skilled talents in these ultimately destructive pursuits involves foregoing tremendous opportunities to use scientific talent for better purposes, related to the

[24] Calculated from Government of India (1999e), Table 4, p. 64. The reference period is 1994–7 (the latest years for which published data are available).
[25] It is, however, hard to judge the exact scientific achievements in the military field, given the veil of secrecy; see e.g. Gopalakrishnan (1998) and Jayaraman (1998), with reference to the 1998 nuclear tests. Even in non-nuclear fields, there are debates as to how much exactly has been achieved in defence-related Indian scientific work (on this, see Smith 1994, Thomas 1997, Arnett 1998, among others). The central issue, however, is not what has been achieved in defence-related Indian science, but what has been lost as a result, in terms of civilian uses of scientific talent.

well-being and quality of life of people. Indeed, there is much further scope for useful scientific research in fields such as public health, environmental protection, agricultural technology, urban transport, and renewable energy. In fact, the antiquated nature of civilian technology in India is rather striking, especially in contrast with supersonic fighter-bombers and ballistic missiles. The task of developing appropriate civilian technology (efficient transport systems, sustainable irrigation devices, drought-resistant crops, etc.) is no less challenging than that of exploding nuclear bombs, and it is a penalty of India's military priorities that these challenges receive much less engagement than they deserve.

This is not, of course, an exhaustive list of the social costs of military expansionism in general, and of nuclear ambitions in particular. The safety of India's nuclear reactors, for instance, is another major concern, hidden behind the veil of secrecy that surrounds all defence-related projects.[26] The role of military contracts in spreading corruption is another aspect of the wide-ranging social costs of militarism, highlighted in recent months by the so-called 'Tehelka exposé'.[27] Going beyond this, there is a larger issue of anti-democratic influences of the military establishment, which has various aspects, ranging from the pernicious effects of defence-related lobbying on public priorities and greater tolerance of human rights violations to the use of propaganda for the purpose of 'tutoring' public opinion. We shall return to this issue in the concluding section of this chapter.

It is, thus, important to take an inclusive view of the social costs of military expansion, going well beyond the 'guns versus butter' issue (important as the latter might be in its own right). Further, it is worth noting that the costs in question tend to be borne by the public at large, and are not always clearly perceived or strongly felt. The hazards of nuclear adventurism, for instance, are fairly remote from the daily lives of its potential victims. By contrast, military expansionism generates substantial and tangible gains for specific constituencies (such as strategic think-tanks and defence research institutions) which also happen to be highly resourceful, cohesive and organized. This asymmetry, which feeds the disproportionate power and influence of pro-military lobbies, is a crucial aspect of the political economy of military expansionism in India as elsewhere.

[26] According to Dr. A. Gopalakrishnan, former director of the Atomic Energy Regulatory Board, India's nuclear reactors are a 'powder keg', and the regulatory process intended to ensure their safety is a 'total farce' (quoted in Chanda, 1999, and Subbarao, 1998, respectively). For further details, see Gopalakrishnan (1999).

[27] See tehelka.com. This problem is of course not specific to India; on world-wide corruption associated with military contracts, see Sampson (1991).

8.7 DEFENCE EXPENDITURE AND SOCIAL NEEDS

This financial year (2001–2), the Indian government is planning to spend Rs 62,000 crore on 'defence' (i.e. about US $ 13 billion at official exchange rates, or a little over US $ 100 billion at 'purchasing power parity' exchange rates). This is the official 'budget estimate' of anticipated expenditure, which has often, in the past, turned out to be an underestimate of actual expenditure. The budget estimate also underestimates the military burden in another sense: it is based on a restritive definition of 'defence expenditure'. For instance, a large proportion of government funding for scientific research in India is allocated to defence-related projects (e.g. space research and nuclear technology), yet this is not counted as 'defence expenditure'.[28] Even the budget estimate of Rs 62,000 crore, however, represents a colossal burden. As mentioned earlier, India's defence budget is about *three* times as large as the combined expenditure of central and state governments on health.

This high level of military expenditure reflects a pattern of accelerated increase in defence budgets in recent years. During the first half of the nineties, India's defence budget increased at a modest rate of about 1.5 per cent per year in real terms. However, the defence budget has increased by leaps and bounds from 1996–7 onwards (starting well before the Kargil confrontation). During the last five years, it has more than doubled in nominal terms, which corresponds to an annual increase of about 10 per cent per year in real terms.[29] As mentioned in chapter 1, this pattern of accelerated increase in India stands in sharp contrast with the worldwide *decline* in military expenditure in the nineties.

The social costs of military expenditure are often downplayed on the grounds that it generates many positive externalities (or 'spillovers'). Examples of spillover effects include civilian applications of military research, public uses of military infrastructure (e.g. roads and satellites), and the involvement of the army in disaster relief. The spillover effects,

[28] Navlakha (1999, 2000) presents alternative estimates, based on the Stockholm International Peace Research Institute's more inclusive definition of 'military spending' (which also includes the cost of para-military forces). Adding the 2000–1 'budget estimates' of anticipated expenditure under relevant heads, he argues that military spending in India is as high as 3.7 per cent of GDP—about 35 per cent higher than the official figure for 'defence expenditure'.

[29] Calculated from official 'revised estimates' of defence expenditure (1996–7 to 2000–1) published in annual budget documents available on the Ministry of Finance website (http://finmin.nic.in), using the Wholesale Price Index as deflator. The estimate for the first half of the nineties is calculated from *SIPRI Yearbook 2000*, p. 273. The SIPRI figures are consistent with India's official budget documents. See also Figure 8.1.

however, are often far from cost-effective, in the light of the large size of total expenditures. It may well be true, for instance, that 'some developments in metallurgy, originally for the LCA [Light Combat Aircraft], have been transferred to the articificial limb centres, because of their strength and light weight' (Ludra, 2000). But it is hard to believe that producing high-tech combat aircrafts is an efficient way of promoting research on artificial limbs. While it is heartening to think that the LCA project has been of some help to those in need of artificial limbs, this fringe benefit does very little to alter the fundamentally wasteful nature of this project.[30]

In other cases, the spillover effects may be more substantial, as with the role of the army in disaster relief. However, positive externalities are not an exclusive feature of military expenditure. Just as soldiers can be mobilized to rescue flood victims, teachers are often deployed (on a much larger scale) to conduct census operations or to help with vaccination campaigns. Further, the possibility of *negative* spillovers from defence spending also needs to be considered. Examples include military uses of civilian facilities (e.g. roads and railways), human rights violations by military personnel, and the environmental destruction caused by a variety of activities, from firing exercises to nuclear tests. In terms of net spillovers, there is little evidence that military expenditure stands out as a particularly beneficial form of public spending—to the extent of putting the cost allocation in a radically different light.

As against these uncertain and limited benefits, there is much evidence that military expenditure adversely affects economic performance by 'crowding out' other uses of scarce resources, such as private investment and social spending.[31] In the case of India, recent increases in military expenditure are bound to affect prospects for a much-needed expansion of public expenditure on health, education, social security and related matters. Indeed, given that the bulk of public revenue is pre-committed in the form of public sector salaries and interest payments, mobilizing

---

[30] The Light Combat Aircraft project, one of the showpieces of the Defence Research and Development Organisation (DRDO), was initiated in 1983 for completion by 1990 at a cost of Rs 560 crore. The project was nowhere near completion in 1999, when the Comptroller and Auditor General noted that the project had already cost Rs 2,000 crore. The report further notes that the project 'is still at the development stage and is facing many uncertainties', and that 'as per present indications and the ministry's optimism, the LCA cannot be expected to be inducted, if at all, before 2005' (Joseph, 1999). Meanwhile, another Rs 2,135 crore is being spent to make up for the shortfall by upgrading older aircraft. For further details, see Government of India (1999b).

[31] See e.g. Deger (1992) and Knight et al. (1996); also Drèze (2000c) and the literature cited there. The 'crowding out' effect is not the only social cost of military expenditure. The diverse social costs discussed in the preceding section are also relevant.

additional resources for the social sectors is a major challenge. Restraining military expenditure is among the few available options (others include discarding wasteful subsidies and expanding the tax base), and in that sense the trade-off between military and social expenditure is quite sharp.[32]

To illustrate, consider the proposal to make elementary education a fundamental right, introduced in the Rajya Sabha in July 1997. Two independent committees appointed by the Department of Education have estimated that implementing this proposal would involve raising annual public expenditure on elementary education by about 0.5 per cent of GDP. The difficulty of mobilizing additional resources on this scale is one major reason why the government has not, so far, endorsed the proposal.[33] Meanwhile, the hike in military expenditure since 1997 has been much larger than the required 0.5 per cent of GDP (about *twice* as large). Even though education expenditure is not the only alternative use of military spending, it is sobering to think that the additional resources allocated to defence in recent years *could* have been used to implement the right to education. Going beyond this specific example, the current preoccupation with military power has been a significant spanner in the wheel of much-needed expansions of public expenditure in India's social sectors.

The most disturbing aspect of recent increases in defence expenditure is that they have not been the object of much dissent or even debate in political circles. Opposition parties, for instance, seem to have taken little interest in this matter. The mainstream media have also been rather uncritical on these issues—unusually so for a press that has such a fine tradition of challenging the establishment. The need for creative questioning has never been stronger.

8.8. ESCALATION: COSTS AND RISKS

We mentioned earlier how the relentless logic of escalation can produce a dangerous confrontation as well as tremendous wastage of resources and opportunities. The subject deserves a closer look since it is so important in understanding recent (and possibly future) developments in India's security environment, especially in relation to Pakistan.

---

[32] In India, defence spending is part of the central government budget, while social spending belongs mainly to state government budgets. However, this does not preclude a trade-off between military and social spending, mediated for instance by centre-state transfers or centrally-sponsored programmes in fields such as health and education.

[33] See chapter 5, and Probe Team (1999), pp. 133–5, for further details. The situation today remains much as described there. The original estimates are presented in Government of India (1997c, 1998b).

The basic irrationality—no less—of escalation has been well discussed by Martin Shubik, the distinguished game theorist. In his 'dollar auction game', two players bid for a dollar in fixed increments of, say, ten cents. The highest bidder gets the dollar, and *both* pay their bids. Experiments with the dollar auction game show that people often bid well beyond one dollar, essentially because at each stage it seems worth bidding a little more to get the dollar.[34] While for the game as a whole it is clearly irrational to offer more than one dollar for a dollar, once the parties are engaged in this game, there is something of a case at each step for going a bit further and committing a little more. The basic problem arises because escalation proceeds in steps, and the narrow logic of each move leads to an irrational outcome for the game as a whole.[35]

There is a reasonably close analogy here with incidents of intensifying military engagement between India and Pakistan. Fighting between India and Pakistan on the Siachen glacier provides a good illustration of step-by-step escalation. Indeed, the history of this interactive episode bears some uncanny resemblance to the dollar auction game. The Siachen glacier is a barren piece of ice, lost at a height of some 18,000 feet, and is of no particular strategic or economic value. The surrounding terrain is so inaccessible and inhospitable that the Simla Agreement of 1972 did not bother to specify precisely where the 'Line of Control' ran in that area. Yet, since 1984 (when the Indian Army made a 'pre-emptive' move into the glacier), thousands of Indian and Pakistani soldiers have been sent there, in a gradually deepening confrontation, to engage in fairly random shelling across the glacier. The financial and human costs have been staggering. India alone is estimated to be spending around Rs 7 crores *every day* (i.e. more than Rs 2,500 crores a year) defending its position on this fairly insignificant spot (Nayar, 2000a). And there is, of course, in addition to financial costs, also the human toll in the form of suffering and death from accidents, frostbite and mountain sickness. The initial move may have been motivated by what one General has described as reasons of 'ego and prestige', but the escalating price of those peculiar objects cannot but outweigh whatever value even inveterate prestige seekers may place on that elusive merchandise.[36]

[34] See Shubik (1971) and Teger (1980).
[35] This is one example of the general phenomenon of 'social traps' of which the 'prisoner's dilemma' is another crucial (and perhaps better-known) illustration. The logic of social traps, and their pervasive role in the genesis of violence and armed conflicts, has been illuminatingly discussed by Anatol Rapoport (1964, 1992, 1995, 1998, 2000).
[36] And this is without taking note of the wisdom of the old Bengali saying that you 'cannot wash and eat' prestige.

Spiralling costs are only one aspect of the penalties of escalation, especially when two nuclear-armed and suspicious neighbours confront each other. There can also be increasing risks of a fuller war, and even some possibility of a nuclear exchange, if the belligerent drills cross— accidentally or by escalating design—the fragile line of restraint. We have already discussed the unreliability of the security allegedly provided by nuclear deterrence, and need only add here that the logic of escalation can make the uneasy equilibrium of restraint all the more fragile, even immensely precarious.

The paradoxes of escalation also apply to arms races in general and to competing military expenditures. Aside from the danger of an accelerated arms race between India and Pakistan in the future, an escalation syndrome is already noticeable in their respective military budgets. As it happens, in terms of the sheer size of military expenditure, this is more clearly observable in Indian budgets than in those of Pakistan. To illustrate, Figure 8.1 presents the size of the defence budgets of the two neighbours since 1991. Indian defence expenditures have gone up rather dramatically. This happened even before the Kargil incident of mid-1999, and the steep rise has continued since then.

On the Pakistani side, military expenditure has stagnated in real terms over the same period, according to official figures.[37] This comparative moderation is undoubtedly influenced by the troubled state of the economy. Indeed, Pakistan has been on the brink of bankruptcy for a few years now, and financial constraints have made it extremely difficult to entertain any major expansion of the military budget. However, these official figures may not reveal the full extent of Pakistan's escalatory responses. To start with, there is greater scope for covert military expenditure in Pakistan than in India, since the former is comparatively free from the supervisory discipline of a parliament and its watch-dog committees. Indeed, there is quite strong evidence that the Kargil operation itself, which certainly represented some radical escalation, did involve covert support provided to the intruders by the Government of Pakistan.

There is another sense in which the expenditure figures may understate Pakistan's escalatory responses. If the stagnation of military expenditure is due to financial bankruptcy, rather than to any freely chosen restraint

[37] There was, in fact, some increase in Pakistan's defence budget in 2000. This is 'hidden' in Figure 8.1 by the transfer of military pensions from the defence budget to the civil administration budget in that year (see *SIPRI Yearbook 2001*, p. 254). Note that, in India, military pensions have been part of the civil administration budget for many years. For further discussion, see Chari (2001b).

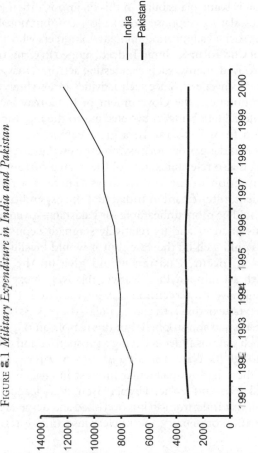

FIGURE 8.1 *Military Expenditure in India and Pakistan*

Sources: *SIPRI Yearbook 2001*, p. 280. The data given there are consistent with official budget documents of India and Pakistan.

(and there is certainly some plausibility in this diagnosis), then we would expect Pakistan's escalatory responses to take low-cost but possibly more provocative forms, such as supporting militant volunteers who are willing to cross the Line of Control in Kashmir. Indeed, judged in terms of causing trouble to the perceived enemy, such clandestine activities may well have considerable 'cost-effectiveness'. Since such activities are also highly irksome to the 'enemy' in question, the Government of India may increasingly justify its escalating military budgets by referring to the intensification of covert intervention from Pakistan. To a great extent, this has already happened, but there is danger of more asymmetric escalation of this kind.

This reasoning is also relevant to one of the strategic issues that have received some attention in the Indian press. There is a remarkably dangerous argument, often heard in India, that the expenditure burden of an arms race would be more unbearable for Pakistan—given its smaller size, its precarious finances and its relatively stagnant economy—than for India.[38] This could well be the case, but it would be silly to expect that if that were to occur, Pakistan would give up the escalating confrontation with a whimper. Provocative, relatively inexpensive but highly troublesome covert interventions can get escalated (Kargil might well have been a foretaste of things to come), unless the process of escalation on both sides is restrained and stopped. For this reason, among others, no country has as much stake as India in having a prosperous and democratic Pakistan. Even though the Nawaz Sharif government was clearly corrupt in specific ways, India had no particular interest in civilian rule being undermined in Pakistan, and replaced by activist military leaders. Indeed, the penalty that can visit India from an impoverished and desperate Pakistan in the present situation of military and nuclear insecurity is terrifying to contemplate.

Escalation is a highly dangerous process in military confrontation, no matter what form it takes. India's swelling military budgets not only entail massive and rapidly increasing resource diversions and other costs (which we have already discussed), they also augment the danger of inducing further bellicose and unsettling responses from Pakistan. Indeed,

---

[38] As Jairam Ramesh (1999) notes: 'There are many in India who believe we *must escalate* defence spending because this will then cause Pakistan to do likewise—and forcing it into the same trap that the erstwhile Soviet Union fell into *vis-à-vis* the US' (Ramesh, 1999, emphasis added). This line of reasoning is apparently so widespread that it has been described as a 'school' (the so-called 'smash them' school) by P.R. Chari, former director of the Institute for Defence Studies and Analyses; see Chari (2001b).

India's and Pakistan's tit-for-tat nuclear blasts fit well into that pattern of interaction.

On a more positive note, escalation has one redeeming feature of great importance, namely that it can proceed 'downward' as well as 'upward'. To illustrate, if two countries are locked in a reciprocal process of arms race, they may be able, by the same logic, to achieve rapid disarmament. The tit-for-tat process, indeed, can work both ways. The same applies to other forms of escalation, including the escalation of hostility. This is one reason why countries with a long record of antagonism sometimes succeed in escaping from the confrontationist trap at astonishing speed. The recent normalization of relations between North Korea and South Korea, though far from secure yet, is one example. In the light of this and other experiences of rapid détente, there are reasons to hope that India and Pakistan, too, will be able to break out of the vicious cycle of escalating confrontation.

8.9. MILITARISM AND DEMOCRACY

Militarism, as was argued in chapter 1, has an oddly dialectical relation with democracy. On one side, expansion of military activities as well as the advocacy of military escalation tends to weaken democracy, by deflecting and distorting public debates, by distracting attention from more constructive concerns of a democratic polity, by encouraging secrecy and censorship, and by nurturing authoritarian tendencies. And at the same time, democratic criticism and protest are also among the most effective ways of countering the excesses of militarism and the insecurity it generates. Both the processes can be observed in India today.

The displacement of development concerns by security concerns reached an unusual level during the latest parliamentary elections (in September 1999) and the campaign that preceded them. The election campaign was dominated by the Kargil crisis (rivalled only by the more esoteric issue of Sonia Gandhi's foreign nationality). Development issues, for their part, received very little attention. The contrast was remarkable. In the previous general elections, during the campaign of early 1998, the main slogan of the Bharatiya Janata Party (which led the winning coalition, both in 1998 and 1999) was '*swasthya, shiksha aur suraksha*' (education, health and security). The future Prime Minister, Mr. Vajpayee, even described the universalization of elementary education as 'the one crucial issue before the country', and Mr. Advani, perhaps the most powerful figure in the BJP other than Vajpayee, was also most supportive of this priority. Eighteen months later, the focus had radically changed: a particular understanding of *suraksha* dominated the agenda, while *swasthya* and *shiksha* were not much to be seen.

The Kargil crisis was, of course, a serious matter, and a legitimate electoral issue. The point that is being made is not that this issue should not have been prominently discussed during the electoral campaign, but rather that because of its understandable prominence, development issues were crowded out. That loss of public attention for vitally important problems is a particularly significant loss for a democratic country, and it is, in fact, a big part of the social cost of military escalation.

In the case of Kargil, the crisis was, to a great extent, imposed on India (even though, as we have argued, the Pokhran-II nuclear blasts made that scenario more likely). The same cannot be said, however, of other diversions of political energies associated with the current climate of preoccupation with military matters. The nuclear tests of May 1998 and their offshoots (economic sanctions, heightened tensions with Pakistan, intensified controversies over the Comprehensive Test Ban Treaty, and so on) have certainly diverted attention from development issues in a dramatic way.

The displacement of development concerns by security concerns can also be seen in the coverage of different news items in the media. To illustrate, Table 8.1 presents a simple count of defence-related and development-related articles published on the front page of one of the finest Indian newspapers, viz. *The Hindu*, from 1996 onwards. Note that 'development' is interpreted here in a very broad sense, and by choosing an inclusive definition, we have made room for public finance, inflation, banking and related matters *within* the category of 'development'. Development issues in that broad sense had received roughly as much front-page coverage as defence issues before the nuclear tests (in 1996 and 1997). In 1998, the share of defence-related articles increased by about 40 per cent (from 15 to 21 per cent of total front-page coverage), and the share of development-related articles declined by the same amount, appearing to reflect almost a one-to-one displacement effect. In 1999, the share of defence-related articles rose by more than another quarter (from 21 to 27 per cent). By then defence matters were getting nearly four times as much coverage as development-related articles. This certainly is a sea change from the rough parity in the years preceding the nuclear blasts.

The imbalance in question is not confined to front-page 'news'. Table 8.2 presents a similar count of 'opinion' articles published on the editorial page of *The Hindu* between January and June 2000. Note that the reference period begins almost two years after the nuclear tests, and also well after the Kargil crisis. Even during this relatively incident-free period,

TABLE 8.1 *Defence vs Development in the Media:*
Front-page Coverage in The Hindu

	1996	1997	1998	1999
(1) Number of front-page articles posted on The Hindu website:	508	556	543	699
(2) Number of defence-related articles:	77	81	115	189
Nuclear weapons	16	0	21	17
Pakistan-related	24	36	50	60
Kashmir-related	28	26	18	105
China-related	4	0	6	9
Other[a]	5	19	20	5
(3) Number of development-related articles:	82	82	48	53
Health and education	0	3	2	0
Development programmes	5	3	0	1
Infrastructural projects	19	14	10	3
Public finance	17	21	9	19
Economic policy	20	16	8	10
Other[b]	21	25	19	20
(4) Share (%) of all front-page articles:				
Defence-related articles	15	15	21	27
Development-related articles	16	15	9	8
Ratio of defence-related to development-related articles	0.9	1.0	2.4	3.6

Notes: [a] Military hardware, defence policy, etc. 'Kashmir-related' includes articles on the Kargil conflict (in 1999).
[b] Economic growth, inflation, banking, disasters, etc.
Source: Compiled from archives posted on *The Hindu* website (*www.hinduonnet.com*). The figures refer to the combined numbers of articles published in February, June and October of the relevant year.

security-related issues captured much more attention than issues of social development. For instance, opinion articles focusing on nuclear weapons and nuclear strategy alone received as much space as all opinion articles on education, health, poverty, unemployment, gender, environmental issues and human rights *together*. Even the severe drought that affected large parts of the country over this period, threatening the livelihoods of millions of people, attracted less comment than, say, the specific question of whether India should sign the Comprehensive Test Ban Treaty (CTBT).

The point here is not that it is necessarily bad for military and nuclear matters to receive such attention, given the substantive developments that occurred over this period. Indeed, the other side of the dialectical relation mentioned earlier—the possible role of democratic opposition in restraining militarism—is substantially dependent on bringing the costs and

TABLE 8.2 *Subjectwise Number of Opinion Articles Published in the Editorial Page of* The Hindu, *January-June 2000*

NATIONAL SECURITY AND RELATED MATTERS	78
Nuclear weapons and nuclear strategy	20
National security: Pakistan-focused	13
National security: Other	10
Terrorism	11
'Kashmir Problem'	7
'North-East Problem'	5
Conflict in Sri Lanka	12
POLITICS AND ECONOMY	108
Domestic economic policy	29
Comment on domestic politics	26
Comment on politics abroad	15
Foreign policy	17
Trade and globalization	9
Information technology	5
Other	7
SOCIAL ISSUES	34
Drought	5
Dams	5
Environment	4
Gender issues	4
Higher education	3
Elementary education	3
Poverty	2
Human Rights	1
Health	0
Other	7
OTHER ISSUES[a]	90

Notes: [a] Communalism (19), constitutional reform (16), Clinton's visit (9), reservation (5), biotechnology (3), corruption (2), nuclear power (2), miscellaneous (27), unidentified (7).

Source: Compiled from archives posted on *The Hindu* website (*www.hinduonnet.com*).

consequences of military escalation firmly into public discussion. There is, thus, much merit in these problems being the subject of wide and open debate.[39] In view of the seriousness of recent military developments, the reporting of these events and the debating of prevailing policies are certainly needed. And yet the need to be preoccupied with these adversities (a 'regrettable necessity', as the term used to be employed in the older literature on national accounting) has the effect of pushing out development matters from the agenda of public discussion. This is an important part of the social costs of military escalation.[40] The loss of focus from development issues is especially significant because public discussion is one of the major ways of bringing about social change in the democratic polity of India.

The displacement of development concerns by security concerns is one aspect of the adverse impact of militarism on the quality of democracy. In addition, there has been a more direct consolidation of anti-democratic tendencies in both India and Pakistan during the last few years. This is, of course, extremely transparent in the case of Pakistan, where democracy collapsed as a fairly direct consequence of the Kargil conflict in 1999. In India, in comparison, democracy is alive and well, and yet the tensions with Pakistan tend to play into the hands of authoritarian and chauvinist activists. The Kargil conflict, for instance, was a period of sustained nationalist propaganda.[41] Similarly, alleged threats to national security

[39] The wide media coverage of defence-related issues reflects, in fact, various endeavours. In India, as in other countries, the pro-military establishment (including the nuclear lobby) has been actively involved in shaping public perceptions of 'security threats' and how they should be dealt with. As one commentator on military intelligence aptly notes, 'media management has been the buzzword in the army in recent years' (Bhatia, 1999). On the other hand, criticisms of military and nuclear adventures are also a part of the newspaper coverage. Given the democratic nature of India, discussions from different perspectives must be seen as inescapable parts of focusing on these issues. But no matter in which direction they argue, the large coverage of military matters does reduce the space available for development issues.

[40] There is an analogy here with the coverage of incidents of communal (or inter-community) violence and tension. The fact that newspapers have paid serious attention to these events (and have often been at the forefront of criticizing the instigators) is certainly a welcome characteristic of the Indian press. And yet it also reflects the seriousness of the communal situation and represents a diversion of attention from other—more constructive—programmes. The acknowledgment that there is something very positive in the fact that these ominous trends are the subject of wide debate and criticism does not obliterate the regrettable nature of the substantive situation which led to the need for such a focus (including the diversion of attention from other, more productive concerns).

[41] On this see Centre for Monitoring the Media (1999) (summarised in Seshu, 1999); also Sainath (1999), Varadarajan (1999), Drèze (2000a).

are frequently invoked to justify repressive measures (such as the revamping of the Terrorism and Disruptive Activities Act) in the country as a whole. These trends are part of the undermining of democracy to which military expansionism contributes.

The prominence of defence-related research and development (R&D) in India also raises some troubling questions about the nature and influence of some of the leading scientific institutions associated with defence research, such as the Defence Research and Development Organisation (DRDO), the Department of Atomic Energy (DAE) and the Department of Space (DOS). The scientific credentials of the highly able scientists involved are not, of course, in doubt. What is less clear is the legitimacy of their being so prominent in the advocacy of nuclear and military expansion. The power of that particular branch of the scientific establishment is a product of public policy, mediated by ample public funding for military R&D, and by the high priority assigned to 'national security' matters, including the imposition of a protective veil of secrecy from behind which experts speak with authority. As the power of the scientific establishment has grown, public priorities themselves have come under its advocacy and influence. Naturally enough, much of this influence has been used to induce continued funding for defence-related scientific research. That is itself a subject of some concern, but in addition this same establishment has also acquired a very strong voice on military matters and on issues of life and death of the citizens. The nuclear tests of May 1998, for instance, were the culmination of years of intensive lobbying by leading scientists.[42]

These are problems that a democratic system, even if somewhat weakened, has to take on board. Parallels to these problems can be found in other democratic countries as well, including the United States, where the military-industrial-scientific complex has been pro-active for a long time. The remedy of these biases must also be sought in more active use of public debates and critical scrutiny. The biases of Indian democracy primarily take the form of giving disproportionate voice and opportunity to some commentators compared with others (we shall return to this issue in chapter 10). Happily, they do not, to any significant extent, take the form of prohibiting the publication or dissemination of rejoinders to these advocacies, nor do they involve disallowing public opposition to governmental policies (including those of nuclear and other military

---

[42] On this see Jayaraman (1998), Arnett (1999), Perkovich (1999), Chengappa (2000). Similarly, the scientific establishment has played a major role in the pre-1998 crusade against India's acceptance of the Comprehensive Test Ban Treaty; see e.g. Deshingkar (1998).

escalation). Thus, there are considerable opportunities of greater public involvement in assessing and appraising established policies.

Given the web of military escalation in which governmental policies seem currently caught, the need for such democratic scrutiny cannot be overemphasized. We have tried to identify the ways in which recent military and nuclear escalations have made the subcontinent a much less secure— indeed greatly more precarious—place, and also generated massive economic, political and social costs, in terms both of resource use and of other consequences. We have also discussed the unfavourable developmental implications of this escalation. The need for democratic scrutiny cannot but be crucial at this time.[43]

[43] This book was completed before the international 'crisis' that began on 11 September 2001 with the terrorist attacks on the World Trade Center in New York. Subsequent events provide many further illustrations of the basic themes of this chapter, concerning the adverse effects of militarism on development, democracy and security. Since 11 September 2001, India's electronic and print media 'have been devoting more than half their time and space to the coverage of the war', according to the Centre for Media Studies (*The Hindu*, 2001). A national debate on chronic hunger and starvation deaths, which received prominent media coverage right up to 10 September, was instantly eclipsed by the 'security' issues (Reddy, 2001b). The crisis was also the occasion for moves towards a restriction of civil liberties, involving for instance the hasty introduction of draconian legislation (such as the 'Prevention of Terrorism Ordinance', known as POTO), ostensibly aimed at terrorist organizations but potentially usable in other contexts as well. Last but not least, the subcontinent entered a new phase of extreme insecurity, marked by heightened tensions between India and Pakistan and even occasional, thinly-veiled nuclear threats.

9

Well Beyond Liberalization

9.1. What Is the Cage?

A tiger in a cage adorned the cover of the informative survey of the Indian economy that *The Economist* published on 4 May 1991.[1] The Indian economy was then in deep trouble, and the special report began with a crisp diagnosis: 'The future of India looks more threatened than for many years'. The analysis put much of the blame for India's economic predicament on its 'ever-proliferating bureaucracy' and its 'licence raj', and expressed the dialectic hope that with the election then due, 'the new government will immediately face a fiscal crisis' and as a consequence it 'might—just might—start a reappraisal of the economic role of government that is so long overdue'. The events that ushered in the economic reforms after the new elections did not depart very far from that dialectical scenario.

The analogy of the caged tiger was an appropriate one in many ways (even if *The Economist* might have been over-kind in referring to 'India's boundless potential'). India does have a long history of commerce, trade, and sophisticated industrial production; even at the time of the industrial revolution, Lancashire had to resort to rather wily tactics to compete with India's unpowered but refined cotton textile industry. It has had a labour force of talent which has shown the ability to adapt to new technical challenges given the opportunity to do so. And Indian entrepreneurs and professionals have been remarkably successful in a variety of economic operations outside

[1] 'A Survey of India', *The Economist*, 4 May 1991. The report was prepared by Clive Crook.

India, varying from running neighbourhood grocery stores (outdoing, for example, 'the nation of shopkeepers' in efficient shopkeeping) to making industrial and trading fortunes (taking an ell whenever they have been given an inch) and, more recently, storming software-related services around the world. There certainly is some animal in the cage.

The reforms that were introduced by the end of 1991 have indeed concentrated on removing the 'licence raj' and the 'ever-proliferating bureaucracy'. While the reforms have not moved as fast as was anticipated, there have been serious steps in that general direction. The liberalization programme has led to a considerable expansion of exports in some sectors and a substantial improvement in the foreign exchange balance. It has also led to a vibrant international response, involving renewed interest in the possibilities of the Indian economy. Three years after the reforms began, the *Forbes* magazine even pictured India on the cover (23 May 1994), with the declaration: 'India may be the best emerging market of all.'

Yet India's development performance in the 1990s has remained quite moderate. As far as overall economic growth is concerned, there has been a significant acceleration compared with the 1980s. The annual growth rate of per-capita GDP, for instance, rose from about 3 per cent per year in the 1980s to 4 per cent per year or so in the 1990s.[2] This was creditable enough, but not quite the spectacular take-off that had been anticipated by market enthusiasts when the reforms were initiated. The 'uncaging of the tiger' has not—at least not yet—led to any tiger-like sprint. Nevertheless, the fact that the reasonable growth rates of the 1980s have been sustained and surpassed in the 1990s is a noteworthy achievement. This is all the more so in international perspective, considering that the 1990s have been a period of relatively slow economic growth in many other countries. In the international comparative league, India has recently been among the 'fast growers'—not an accustomed position for India.

The central issue, however, is not the overall growth rate of the economy. Rather, it is a question of achieving widely-shared development, of a kind that has not really happened in the 1990s (or for that matter earlier). Indeed, there are many reasons for concern about growth patterns in the 1990s, ranging from the near-stagnation of agriculture in per-capita terms to the dismal growth performance of some of the poorer states (e.g. Bihar and Uttar Pradesh). Further, the acceleration of overall economic growth in the 1990s, such as it is, does not appear to have led to a corresponding transformation of living conditions for the poor. In

---

[2] See Table 9.1 in section 9.3; also Statistical Appendix, Table A.2.

fact, as discussed in section 9.3 below, in some important respects the progress of social indicators has slowed down in the 1990s, compared with the 1980s. The picture is not uniformly disappointing: the 1990s, for instance, have been a period of comparatively rapid improvement in literacy rates and school attendance. Nevertheless, as things stand the overall picture is one of relatively limited achievements in the 1990s in terms of poverty reduction and social progress.

These observations reinforce the case, already made in the first edition of this book, for focusing on India's lack of preparedness for *participatory growth*, an issue to which we shall return presently. The growth rates of GNP and GDP can, quite possibly, increase further than they have already done in the 1990s, but the country remains handicapped economically and socially by its overwhelming illiteracy, backwardness in health, debilitating social inequalities, and other crucial failures. These limitations also continue to restrain the participatory possibilities of the growth process. As was argued earlier, the cage that keeps the Indian economy well tamed is not only that of bureaucracy and governmental overactivity, but also that of illiteracy, undernourishment, ill health, and social inequalities, and their causal antecedents: governmental neglect and public inertia.

This recognition does not entail a dismissal of the diagnosis of bureaucratic overactivity, or a disputation of the need for basic economic reforms. In this monograph we have tried to argue for a broader view of economic development, which has to be seen in terms of expanding social opportunities. While the removal of barriers to using markets can significantly enhance such opportunities, the practical usability of these opportunities requires the sharing of certain basic capabilities—including those associated particularly with literacy and education (and also those connected with basic health, social security, gender equality, land rights, local democracy). The rapid expansion of these capabilities depends crucially on public action of a kind that has been severely neglected in India—both before and after the recent reforms. The real issue in 'uncaging' the tiger is the need to go *well beyond* liberalization.

In principle, the social role of the government seems to be widely accepted by all. In particular, the rhetoric of every Indian government—without exception—has included handsome tribute to the importance of basic education. The real issue is not rhetorical acceptability, but the willingness to put actual—not imagined—emphasis on this particular requirement for the transformation of the Indian economy. This simply has not happened. While India has a highly developed—if overextended—

higher education sector, it remains one of the most backward countries in the world in terms of elementary education.[3]

With about 40 per cent of all Indian adults still illiterate, the transformation of the economy is no easy task. Even an efficient utilization of the world market requires production to specification, needs quality control, and depends on an informed consciousness of the economic tasks involved. As discussed in chapter 3, the economic success of the east Asian 'tigers', and more recently of China, has been based on a much higher level of literacy and basic education than India has. This is one aspect of the 'cage' that incarcerates the Indian economy and society.

This diagnosis is not concerned primarily with the overall rate of growth of GNP per head, even though it is hard to assume that illiteracy and ill health are not barriers to achieving high economic performance. India has had comparatively high rates of growth of per capita GNP in the eighties and nineties, and can achieve more in the future. The overall growth rate can be pushed up by rapid expansion of some favourably placed sectors. Some sectors of the economy, especially those that rely on high skills of the kind that India already has plentifully (such as basic computer proficiency), have been growing fast in recent years and can expand even further. However, to have an impact on India's widespread poverty, what is needed is an expansion on a much broader and more equitable basis (as has happened in, say, South Korea or China), and this would be extremely difficult to achieve without giving much greater priority to the removal of illiteracy, undernutrition, ill health, economic insecurity and other barriers to participatory growth.

The central issue, as was already stated, is not just the overall growth rate, which may well go up even further in the near future. We have particularly emphasized the need for participatory growth, which is not the same as high achievement in some particular sectors (oriented to more specialized—and more middle-class—skills), nor the same as a high rate of growth of aggregate GNP per head.[4] For example, in the sixties and seventies, the Brazilian economy grew very fast but achieved rather little reduction of poverty, particularly in terms of social backwardness and sectional deprivation. The lack of participatory nature of that growth

---

[3] This was already beginning to be the case in 1970 when one of the authors of this monograph gave the Lal Bahadur Shastri Memorial Lectures on this subject, under the title 'The Crisis in Indian Education' (Sen 1970a), but all the basic criticisms then made continue to apply today—thirty years further on.

[4] On this see also Drèze and Sen (1989), Part iii, particularly the analysis of what was called 'unaimed opulence'.

was extremely important in that outcome. Comparing Brazil's problems with patterns of more inclusive growth processes in east Asia tends to bring out the big difference made by widely-shared, participatory growth, and the specific role of widespread basic education in fostering growth of this kind.[5] There is something quite important in this choice.[6] India stands in some danger of going Brazil's way, rather than South Korea's.

This does not affect in any way the diagnosis that India offers great investment opportunities in particular sectors even without any further expansion of basic education and health care. The *Forbes* magazine could well be exactly right in seeing India, in the long run, as 'the best emerging market of all' (India's middle class is probably larger than that of any other country), and yet this does not entail—and *Forbes* had not suggested it would—that this is a big force in eliminating poverty and deprivation of the Indian masses. The lesson of East Asia and China (and to some extent also of the more successful states within India) is not just about growth, but about widely-shared growth, assisted by positive state initiatives.

9.2. RADICAL NEEDS AND MODERATE REFORMS

The concentration on participatory growth calls for an integrated view of the process of economic expansion—focusing on the significance of economic growth, on the one hand, and on the importance of the participatory character of that growth, on the other. The crucial role of wide participation is central to this approach, and in so far as this requirement is missed out in policy discussions, that omission calls for rectification. At the same time, we must not confound that requirement with a rejection of the importance of economic growth itself. There has to be growth for it to be participatory.

While the neglect of social opportunities through the lack of adequate progress in basic education, health care, social security, land reforms, and similar fields has been detrimental to economic and social development

---

[5] See particularly Birdsall and Sabot (1993) and Birdsall, Ross and Sabot (1995). On aspects of the Brazilian experience, see also Sachs (1990). On Korean economic development, see the literature cited in chapters 2 and 3, and also the earlier studies of Hong and Krueger (1975), Adelman and Robinson (1978), Datta-Chaudhuri (1979), and Westphal et al. (1985, 1988).

[6] On the contrast between growth in Brazil and South Korea, and more generally between Latin American and east Asian patterns of economic expansion, see also McGuire (1994). The divergence has diminished a little in the 1990s, with South Korea going through a major economic crisis (in 1997–8), and Brazil, on the other hand, adopting more active social policies. The basic contrast, however, remains.

in India, so has been the neglect of appropriate incentives for economic efficiency and expansion. In pointing to the part of the 'cage' that the reformers often tend to ignore, we have no intention of dismissing the other part of the 'cage' that does motivate them. We are arguing for a more complete view of the difficulties that the Indian economy faces, not for shifting our diagnosis from one lopsided view to another. The fact that the boat of Indian officialdom has managed, in the past, to crash on both Scylla and Charybdis at the same time (a feat unknown to Ulysses) does not tell us to avoid only one of these dangers, overlooking the other.

There is scope for serious debate about many aspects of the economic reforms that are currently being introduced in India, and specific arguments have been presented in different directions.[7] Both the exact content of the reforms, and the policy approach in which they are embedded, call for much scrutiny. But these questions do not undermine the general necessity and desirability of removing counterproductive regulations and restrictions, nor of allowing greater use of the opportunities of international exchange. India has paid a heavy price for its overregulated and dysfunctional rules of economic governance, and there is a clear case for removing that handicap.[8]

The counterproductive effects of many governmental restrictions, controls, and regulations in India have been clear for a long time, and have indeed been denounced by scholars and observers of many different persuasions. This problem has not been confined to India only, and has been a general feature of a number of developing countries, including India's neighbours in south Asia.[9] But the limitations have been particularly strong and resilient in India, and have survived many other changes of

[7] For some important contributions to this debate, on different sides, see Rudra (1991), Desai (1993), Patel (1992), Ravallion and Subbarao (1992), Bhagwati (1993), Bhagwati and Srinivasan (1993), Bhattacharya and Mitra (1993), Bagchi (1994), Desai (1994), Eswaran and Kotwal (1994), Ghosh (1994), Joshi and Little (1994, 1996), Mundle (1994), Patnaik (1994), S.L. Rao (1994), Bajpai and Sachs (1996), K. Basu (1996), Bhaduri and Nayyar (1996), World Bank (1997d), Lal (1999), Prabhu (1999), M. Ahluwalia (2000), G. Das (2000), Nagaraj (2000), Saxena (2000), Srinivasan (2000), Swamy (2000), among others; also various contributions in Nayyar (1994), Cassen and Joshi (1995), Ahluwalia and Little (1998), Sachs et al. (1999), Kahkonen and Lanyi (2000), Parikh (2000).

[8] Considering that many of these rules go back to the colonial period, and have clearly outlived whatever usefulness they might have had at that time, there is something peculiar in the fact that there has been so much resistance to their removal, coming from 'nationalist' circles, whether of the left or of the right.

[9] For an early analysis of the negative role of counterproductive regulations in a number of developing countries, see Little, Scitovsky, and Scott (1970). See also

economic policies. The rhetoric of 'equity' has often been invoked to justify governmental interventions without any scrutinized assessment of how those powers will be exercised and what actual effects they will have. In practice, these ill-directed regulations have not only interfered often enough with the efficiency of economic operations (especially of modern industries), they have also failed fairly comprehensively to promote any kind of real equity in distributional matters. Typically, the bureaucracy's rewards from being able to control economic operations, distribute favours, or cause (or threaten to cause) obstructions, have been exploited by those who were already in privileged positions. While a lot of all this was done in the name of the Indian poor, that hapless creature has got very little from it.[10]

Similar remarks apply to the need for making better use of the opportunities offered by international trade. Many countries have made excellent use of these opportunities, and India too can reap much more fully the benefits of economies of scale and efficient division of labour. While greater involvement in trade is sometimes seen as something that compromises the country's economic independence, or that jeopardizes India's sovereignty, there is little objective basis for such fears. Given the diversity of trading partners, the worry that India would be an economic prisoner in the international world of open exchange is quite unfounded. This does not deny the importance of getting the terms and conditions of trade right, or of obtaining a fair deal from the World Trade Organization and other international institutions, which have often been far from even-handed. But in general there is little reason for fearfully abstaining from the benefits offered by international trade and exchange.

In fact, it is worth recalling that India's share of international trade used to be about three times as high, fifty years ago, as it is now, so that an expansion of India's involvement in international trade, far from putting the country in a new and uncertain position, would merely help to restore its position prior to decades of spiralling decline in the world economy.[11] On this whole issue, India has much to learn from China, which has boldly

---

Corden (1974), Krueger (1974), and Bhagwati and Srinivasan (1975), among other contributions.

[10] Recent 'public hearings' in Delhi and elsewhere have highlighted the fact that disadvantaged sections of the population (e.g. hawkers, rickshaw-pullers and the homeless) are often at the receiving end of the arbitrary powers associated with bureaucratic over-regulation. On this, see particularly Kishwar (2001a, 2001b) and Nayar (2001).

[11] On 'India's regression in the world economy', see S.J. Patel (1985, 1994).

seized the opportunities of international trade in recent years, with remarkable results in terms of broad-based expansion of living standards, and without much sign of its economic or political sovereignty being compromised.

While much energy has been spent on sorting out these issues, too little attention has been paid to what is *lacking* in the current orientation of economic policy in India. The removal of counterproductive regulations on domestic production and international trade can form a helpful *part* of a programme of participatory and widely-shared growth, but it may achieve little in the absence of more active public policy aimed at removing the other social handicaps that shackle the Indian economy and reduce the well-being of the population. That, indeed, is one of the main lessons of India's development experience in the 1990s.

The continued neglect of basic education is one telling illustration of the general lack of interest in this broader agenda. There has been much talk, in recent years, about the importance of basic education and the need to give it a 'high priority'. As we saw in chapter 5, however, this rhetoric has not been matched by decisive action on the ground. While there have been significant achievements in specific states in the 1990s, and also some acceleration in the overall rate of school participation (partly due to the rising tide of parental motivation for education), the overall picture of elementary education in India remains dismal. In particular, schooling facilities remain completely out of line with the constitutional goal of universal education to the age of fourteen.

In the field of health care, there are even fewer signs of any determination to address the tragic inadequacies of current policy. As we noted in chapter 6, public expenditure on health care is lower in India than in most other countries (as a proportion of GDP). Further, public health services in rural India have often been extensively displaced by family planning programmes (mainly based on female sterilization). For other services, most citizens are compelled to turn to the private sector, with its high costs and pervasive hazards. These patterns continue in the 1990s. In fact, the share of public expenditure on health as a proportion of GDP has, if anything, declined during this period. This inertia contributes to the persistence of high levels of morbidity and mortality, and has quite possibly played a part in the slowdown of infant mortality decline in the nineties. Endemic undernutrition also continues, with only Bangladesh faring worse than India in that respect, among all countries for which relevant data are available. These failures in a crucially important field of government action receive extraordinarily little attention in current debates.

The limited and lop-sided nature of the current reform programme is also evident from the content of parliamentary proceedings and the news media. While legislative amendments relating to deregulation and privatization are often rushed through parliament and the Cabinet, crucial proposals relating to the fundamental right to education, the people's right to information, the political representation of women, the de-criminalization of politics and related issues have been languishing for years. Similarly, the intensive focus on finance, investment and trade in the mainstream news media sharply contrasts with the scant attention being paid to social matters such as education, health, nutrition, poverty, human rights, and the environment. To illustrate, according to a recent count of newspaper articles published in 17 major English-medium dailies in 1997–8, only 232 articles on elementary education were published over that entire period (roughly one article per newspaper per month), compared with 3,431 articles on international trade and 8,549 articles on foreign investment.[12]

The absence of any real commitment to social reform fits into these general patterns. We have discussed, in chapter 7, how the persistence of extraordinary gender inequalities in India is a major obstacle to social progress. There has been no decisive attempt on the part of the government, before or after the reforms, to challenge these inequalities. The general attitude of the administration, the police, other government institutions and even the courts has rather been to endorse and enforce the traditional view of Indian women as subordinate members of society. Similarly, there has been little real challenge to caste-based inequalities, and the reluctant continuation of reservation policies for disadvantaged castes has gone hand in hand with a tacit acceptance of a caste hierarchy in the Indian society. As we saw earlier, these and other traditional inequalities are resilient factors of economic and social backwardness in India, particularly in rural areas. The persistence of widespread illiteracy, for instance, has much to do with social divisions in education opportunities based on gender, caste and class.

In earlier chapters of this book, we have discussed how policy developments in India, including those since the 'reforms', have continued the tradition of neglecting the fundamental importance of basic capabilities in economic development, and of the positive role of the state in promoting these capabilities. Judged in that perspective, the current reorientation of economic policy is much less of a radical departure from the past than it is often considered to be, and perpetuates some of the most debilitating

---

[12] Probe Team (1999), p. 139. On the elitist biases of the mainstream Indian media, see particularly Sainath (1996); also Tables 8.1 and 8.2 in chapter 8.

biases of earlier regimes. Correcting these biases—not just in political rhetoric but in practical action—calls for a major shift of emphasis in policy-making. There is also an acute need to pay more attention to these issues in public debates and social and political movements, involving the opposition as well as the government.

9.3. Growth and Development in the Nineties

The diagnosis presented so far in this chapter is associated with a particular reading of economic trends in the 1990s, based on the general approach developed in this book. In this context, it is worth taking a closer look at the growth performance of the Indian economy in the 1990s, and also at the relation between economic growth and social achievements. A related reason for doing so is that the Indian economy is often described (particularly in international financial journals) as going through some kind of unprecedented 'boom', unleashed by the reforms initiated in 1991.[13] Some studies also claim that the 1990s have been a period of unprecedented poverty reduction. Following on this, there is a temptation to question the importance of social opportunities for participatory growth. India's performance in the 1990s, it might appear, shows not only that economic growth is the best route to poverty removal, but also that greater attention to social opportunities is not essential for a broad-based economic take-off.

The literature—journalistic as well as academic—on these issues has given room both to myth and to reality (with some even-handedness), and some critical scrutiny is desperately needed here. It is useful to distinguish between three different questions in this context.

1. How much progress has in fact been made in raising the overall rate of economic growth since the move towards liberalization?
2. Does India's recent growth record show that social opportunities are not important for economic success?
3. Is economic growth adequate for poverty removal? Can it obviate the need for efforts at enhancing social opportunities as an essential part of the process of development?

We take up these questions in turn.

---

[13] To illustrate: 'Since the reforms of the early 1990s, the pace of economic growth [in India] has nearly doubled' (International Herald Tribune, 14 September 2000). Unsuspecting western readers have been exposed to many exaggerated statements of this kind in recent years.

TABLE 9.1 *Economic Growth in Recent Decades*

	Average annual growth rates (%)			
	Primary sector (agriculture and related activities)	Secondary sector (manufacturing and related activities)	Tertiary sector (services)	GDP[a]
1950–1 to 1960–1	2.8	6.2	4.2	3.7 (1.7)
1960–1 to 1970–1	2.1	5.4	4.5	3.4 (1.2)
1970–1 to 1980–1	1.9	4.3	4.5	3.4 (1.1)
1980–1 to 1990–1	3.4	6.6	6.7	5.4 (3.3)
1990–1 to 1999–2000	3.3	6.5	7.7	6.0 (4.1)

Notes: [a] In brackets, growth rates of *per-capita* GDP.
Source: Calculated (by semi-log regression) from annual CSO data on 'gross domestic product at factor cost by industry of origin', published in Government of India (2001c), Table 1.3, p. S-5.

Recent Growth Performance

As was mentioned earlier, there is indeed evidence that the overall rate of growth of the gross domestic product of the country as a whole has somewhat speeded up in the 1990s in comparison with the 1980s. This is certainly a positive development, given that the decade of the 1980s itself constituted a period of fairly rapid growth, at least by the standards of India's past. In per-capita terms, the annual growth rate of GDP rose from 3.3 per cent in the 1980s to 4.1 per cent in the 1990s (see Table 9.1). This is a fine enough achievement, even if not quite world shattering, or comparable to the east Asian 'tigers' of yester years, or to China today.

It is, however, important to go beyond this aggregative picture. There is, in particular, the issue of sectoral composition. As Table 9.1 indicates, the growth rates of agricultural and industrial production have not increased at all in the nineties, compared with the eighties. Even during the period *beyond* the initial decline that occurred immediately after the reforms were initiated, the growth rates of the primary and secondary sectors (3.3 and 7.1 per cent per year, respectively, between 1992–3 and 1999–2000) were almost the same as those achieved in the 1980s.[14] The increase in overall

---

[14] The growth rates presented in Table 9.1 involve quantity as well as price effects. The growth rate of the quantity index of agricultural production was actually *lower* in the 1990s than in the 1980s (see Table 9.3 below), but this was 'made up' by price increases in the agricultural sector. It is important to note that the rise of agricultural prices (especially food prices, which rose sharply vis-à-vis other commodity prices in the late 1990s) can be quite harmful for the poor, most of whom buy much of their food on the market. We shall return to this issue in section 9.5.

growth in the 1990s is overwhelmingly driven by accelerated growth of the 'service' sector.

This is not in itself a dismal finding, both because world experience shows that the service sector tends to grow faster with modernization of the economy, and because that sector includes some very dynamic fields, such as uses of information technology and eletronic servicing, in both of which India has made remarkable progress. It is also worth noting that the unprecedented dynamism of some parts of the service sector, such as 'communications' (the fastest-growing sector in the 1990s), can be plausibly linked with the liberalization programme introduced in 1991. For instance, the mushroom growth of long-distance telephone services ('STD booths') all over the country in the 1990s is a prime case of fast expansion through private enterprise, even though state initiative (e.g. in the form of a simplifying and streamlining regulatory framework) has also played a role. Similar comments apply to the phenomenal expansion of software-related export services.[15] What is less clear, however, is the extent to which the rapid growth of the service sector as a whole contributes to the generation of widely-shared employment, the elimination of poverty, and the enhancement of the quality of life. For one thing, the nature of the 'services' in question, and their contribution to better living conditions, call for some scrutiny. Just to give one illustration, when more police are hired in response to a surge in violent crime (related, say, to rising economic disparities), the production of 'services' (in this case policing activities) increases, but this expansion is associated with a *deterioration* of an important aspect of the quality of life.[16] For another, employment in the service sector is often inaccessible to those who lack the required skills or education. The current restructuring of the Indian economy towards this skill and education-intensive sector reinforces what has been said elsewhere in this book about the importance of creating conditions (such as widespread elementary education and good health) that enable people to participate in the process of economic growth.[17]

[15] In 1999–2000, India exported US\$ 2.6 billion of 'software services' (Government of India, 2001c, p. 105). According to the same source, software exports have been growing at 50 per cent per year during the last five years, with a little help from the Y2K bug. It seems to be on the basis of a cheerful extrapolation of these growth rates that a central government minister recently predicted that Indian software exports would reach US\$ 3,000 billion (sic) by 2,010 or so.

[16] A similar issue arises in interpreting the rapid growth of 'public administration', which is officially classified under 'services'. While an expansion of public administration may well be needed, in many cases administrative services are best seen as an 'intermediate input' (with instrumental value in promoting *other* activities) rather than as 'consumption goods' in their own right.

[17] In this connection, it is also worth noting that there has been little reduction

Credit must be given where it is due, but there is really little merit in the often-repeated jubilant assertion that economic reforms have ushered an economic boom in India. That simply is not the case. There is reason for hope in the industrial prospects that are being opened up by the rapid technological transformation that is occurring in some 'high tech' fields (information technology in particular). As things stand, however, there is no clear sign of any acceleration of economic growth in the industrial sector, and the performance of the agricultural sector in the 1990s has been even less impressive. Triumphalism in terms of general productive activity simply cannot be vindicated by the current statistics.

Perhaps the important pattern to recognize is not so much the acceleration of economic growth in the 1990s, compared with the 1980s (that acceleration is quite marginal), but the respectable rates of growth of the Indian economy, by international standards, in *both decades combined*. Indeed, few countries have such a good record of sustained rapid growth over that combined period. Looking at the average annual growth of per-capita GDP in the 1980s and 1990s together, India ranks among the ten fastest-growing countries in the world, along with China, Vietnam, South Korea, Malaysia, Thailand, and Singapore, among others.[18] This achievement is primarily a reflection of the fundamental growth potential of the Indian economy. The economic reforms undertaken so far have helped to enhance that potential in some sectors, but they have not—at least not yet—radically altered it.

Social Opportunity and Economic Growth

We turn now to the second question. Does the accelerated growth of the Indian economy show the irrelevance of the economic role of social opportunities? Does not the fact that liberalization has brought about this change—to the extent that it has—even in the absence of great progress in social opportunities indicate that it is a mistake to emphasize the importance of social change for economic development?

There is a preliminary distinction to be made here. Our emphasis on the importance of social opportunities is not primarily about the overall growth rate, but especially about the removal of poverty and deprivation.

---

of unemployment in India in the nineties. If anything, it appears that unemployment rates have marginally risen, judging from National Sample Survey data; see Reddy (2001a) and Sundaram (2001a).

[18] See e.g. *World Development Indicators 2001*, Table 4.1.

TABLE 9.2 *State-specific Growth Rates of Per-capita 'Gross Domestic Product'*

State	Annual growth rate of per-capita GDP (%)		
	In the 1980s	In the 1990s	
	1980–1 to 1990–1 (Ahluwalia's estimates)	1990–1 to 1998–9 (our estimates)	1991–2 to 1997–8 (Ahluwalia's estimates)
Gujarat	3.2	6.2	7.6
Tamil Nadu	4.0	5.8	5.1
Karnataka	3.4	5.7	3.7
Maharashtra	3.7	5.4	6.0
Kerala	2.3	5.1	4.9
West Bengal	2.5	4.7	5.3
Andhra Pradesh	3.5	3.5	3.7
Orissa	2.5	3.0	1.8
Punjab	3.4	2.8	2.9
Madhya Pradesh	2.2	2.7	4.2
Rajasthan	4.1	2.5	4.0
Haryana	4.0	2.2	2.5
Uttar Pradesh	2.8	1.6	1.3
Bihar	2.6	0.0	0.3
India[a]	3.3	4.0	4.5
Coefficient of variation (of growth rates)	0.20	0.51	0.51

Notes: [a] Our estimates, based on CSO data presented in Government of India (2001c), p. S-5 (see also Table 9.1).

Sources: Calculated from unpublished data kindly supplied by the Central Statistical Organisation; Ahluwalia (2000), also based on CSO data (Ahluwalia's estimates of growth rates of total GDP have been converted in per-capita terms using recent census data on population growth rates). Our own estimates for the 1980–91 and 1991–8 periods (not reported in this table) are consistent with Ahluwalia's estimates for the same periods. The states are ranked in descending order of growth rates in the 1990s. Estimates for the states of Assam, Himachal Pradesh and Jammu and Kashmir are not available.

We shall return presently to the interrelation between economic growth and the removal of economic poverty, but for the moment we just recall the distinction, without denying that it is legitimate enough to ask whether or not the quickening of economic growth since the reforms shows that preparedness in terms of social opportunity is quite irrelevant at least to the genesis of economic growth.

One way of scrutinizing this issue is to look at the regional contrasts within India, since—as discussed earlier in this book—social opportunities are extremely diversely developed in different parts of the country. Table

9.2 presents state-specific estimates of the growth of per-capita gross domestic product (also known, in this context, as 'state domestic product' or SDP). It is interesting to note that despite the general quickening of economic growth in India as a whole, growth did not go up—in fact it fell—in several states between the 1980s and 1990s. Further, the big declines have tended to occur in states that are notorious for their backwardness in terms of social opportunities, such as Bihar, Uttar Pradesh, and Rajasthan. An extreme case is Bihar, where economic growth apparently came to a halt in the decade of liberalization. On the other side, the states that did best in improving their growth performance between the 1980s and the 1990s have tended to be those with a better record (both before and after the reforms) in terms of the promotion of social opportunities, including Gujarat, Maharashtra, the four southern states, and also West Bengal.

This picture is broadly suggestive, rather than statistically decisive. However, two broad patterns emerge with reasonable clarity. First, as Montek Ahluwalia (2000) has noted, the 1990s have witnessed a marked increase in inter-state economic disparities.[19] This finding (illustrated in Figure 9.1) is another cause for concern about growth patterns in the 1990s, in addition to the issue of sectoral composition discussed in the preceding section. In both respects (inter-state disparities and sectoral composition), growth patterns in the 1990s have not been particularly favourable to poverty reduction. It is also worth noting that the sectoral and regional imbalances have often compounded each other in this respect. Indeed, aside from having comparatively low sector-specific growth rates, the poorer states are typically more dependent on agriculture, which has grown particularly slowly in the 1990s. To illlustrate, while it is worrying enough to note that in the 1990s Bihar's economy has not grown at all in per-capita terms, it is even more alarming to find that Bihar's agricultural sector has stagnated in *absolute* terms during that period (i.e. it has *declined* at about 2 per cent per year in per-capita terms). Given the overwhelming dependence of the poor in Bihar on the agricultural sector, this compounding of regional and sectoral disadvantages has seriously affected the prospects of rapid poverty reduction in that state.

Second, there is some evidence that the increase in regional disparities is connected with the role of social opportunities in fostering economic growth. The regional patterns mentioned earlier, for instance, point in that direction. It is also worth noting that there is a significant statistical

[19] On this issue, see also Kurian (2000), Nagaraj (2000), Bandhyopadhyay (2001), and Sarma (2001).

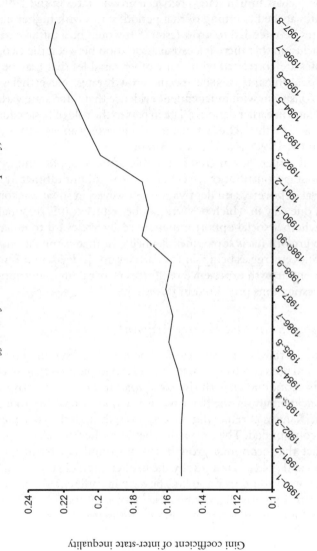

FIGURE 9.1 *Gini Coefficient of Inter-state Economic Inequality, 1980–1 to 1997–8*

Source: Ahluwalia (2000), p. 1639. The Gini coefficient measures inter-state disparities in per-capita 'state domestic product'.

correlation (across Indian states) between growth rates in the 1990s and literacy rates at the beginning of that period: states with higher baseline literacy rates have tended to grow faster.[20] It would be a mistake to jump to the conclusion that there is a causal association between the two, since literacy rates are correlated with many other variables that may be more powerful determinants of state-specific growth rates. Nevertheless, this pattern is consistent with independent evidence that inter-state variations in growth rates in earlier periods relate in part to the role of basic education in economic growth.[21] The fact that the same pattern appears to continue to apply in the 1990s is a matter of interest.

As stated earlier, our interest in the role of social opportunities is not mainly about its contribution to economic growth but ultimately about the removal of poverty and deprivation. However, in so far as economic growth is one way in which poverty can be reduced, it is reasonable to examine whether social opportunities are really irrelevant to enhancing economic growth (as is sometimes claimed). In that examination, social opportunities emerge as being far from irrelevant. Indeed, in this respect India's recent growth experience reinforces rather than undermines the earlier investigations presented in this book.

Social Opportunity and Poverty Removal

Turning to the third issue listed earlier, there is a long-standing debate— an intense and heated debate—on the role of economic growth in removing poverty. Is economic growth the royal road to poverty removal? This enquiry, incidentally, is not the same as the question of the role of the market mechanism in removing poverty, even though the two questions are often confounded. The distinction between the two relates to, both: (1) the fact that economic growth can be stimulated by non-market institutions and policies (not just by the market), and (2) the fact that the market can contribute to removing poverty in different ways—not just through increasing overall growth rates.[22] However, the role of economic growth in removing poverty is an important issue in itself.

[20] The correlation coefficient between the 1991 literacy rate (male and female combined) and the growth rate of per-capita SDP (1990–1 to 1998–9) is 0.62, and is statistically significant at the 1% level.

[21] See e.g. Loh (1997) and Bandhyopadhyay (2001); for related evidence, see also Datt and Ravallion (1998) and Wood and Calandrino (2000).

[22] To illustrate, the use of wage employment to generate income for the deprived can be an efficient means of famine prevention (see chapter 2). Generating an income for the potential destitutes to enable them to compete in the food market

It should be obvious enough that economic growth can be extremely helpful in removing poverty. This is both because the poor can directly share in the increased wealth and income generated by economic growth, and also because the overall increase in national prosperity can help in the financing of public services (including health care and education), which in turn can be particularly useful for the poor and the deprived.[23] This does not, however, make economic growth the only means—not necessarily even the principal means—of poverty removal. This is so for at least three reasons.

First, poverty need not take the form only of low income; there are other kinds of deprivation which we have already discussed, reflecting various 'unfreedoms,' varying from prevalence of preventable or curable illness to social exclusion and the denial of political liberty. How much income the poor get is only one determining influence among many others in dealing with deprivation and poverty, in an adequately broad sense.

Second, even in so far as we concentrate on income poverty only, the ability of the poor to participate in economic growth depends on a variety of enabling social conditions. We have already commented on this in various contexts, and stressed in particular the enabling roles of basic education, good health, microcredit facilities, land reforms, social security arrangements, environmental sustainability, legal provisions, and related factors.

Third, the fruits of economic growth may not be automatically utilized to expand basic social services. There is an inescapable political process involved here. Furthermore, different kinds of public arrangements may receive very different priorities. For example, South Korea did much better in channelling resources to education and health care than, say, Brazil did, which too had fast economic growth, and this greatly helped South Korea to better pursue growth with equity, compared with the-then Brazil. However, South Korea too continued to neglect arrangements for social security, thereby remaining vulnerable to downside risks, and in fact paid a heavy price for this when the economic crisis of 1997 came. Since recessions do occur from time to time, provisions are needed for 'downturn with security' as well as for 'growth with equity.' Removal of poverty and deprivation requires a great deal more than relying on one simple associative connection between economic growth and the incomes of the poor.

---

with other consumers, along with giving the market an incentive to deliver food to the potential victims, does certainly use the market mechanism; but it does not work through economic growth.

[23] On these connections, see Drèze and Sen (1989), chapter 10.

India's Experience of Growth and Poverty Removal

What can we say about this on the basis on India's own recent experience? Before answering this question, a brief discussion of poverty trends in the nineties is in order. As it happens, the evidence is far from clear, and has indeed given room for much controversy.[24]

As a starting point, Figure 9.2 presents recent estimates of the 'headcount index' of poverty based on National Sample Survey (NSS) data—the most widely-used source in the literature on poverty in India. Prior to 1999–2000 (the '55th round'), the estimates are based on a fairly consistent methodology. The corresponding series suggest that there has been no significant decline in rural poverty in the nineties, and that even urban poverty has declined quite slowly during that period. This applies whether one looks at estimates based on the standard '30–day recall' method, or at those based on the experimental '7-day recall' method introduced in the mid-nineties.

At first glance, the 1999–2000 estimates appear to alter this conclusion, in that they indicate a significant decline in poverty in the nineties (at least on the basis of the standard '30-day recall' method). However, these estimates are *not comparable* with the pre-1999 estimates, due to methodological differences between the 55th round and earlier rounds (hence the 'broken' lines in Figure 9.2).[25] In the case of '30-day recall', the methodological changes introduced in 1999–2000 unambiguously 'pull down' the poverty estimates. In the case of '7-day recall', it is not clear whether the 1999–2000 poverty estimates are biased upward or downward, compared with what would have been obtained on the basis of the earlier methodology. As discussed by Angus Deaton (2001) in a detailed assessment of the evidence, 'the 55th round is not very useful for assessing the trend in poverty'.[26]

The non-comparability problem is duly noted in official publications, including the government's latest 'economic survey'.[27] However, these

---

[24] See Datt (1997, 1999a), Gupta (1999), Aiyar (2000), Bhalla (2000a, 2000b), Deaton and Tarozzi (2000), Drèze (2000c), Lal, Mohan and Natarajan (2000), Nagaraj (2000), Ravallion (2000b), Abhijit Sen (2000), Suryanarayana (2000), Sundaram and Tendulkar (2000), P. Visaria (2000), Reddy (2001), among others. For a clear and succinct assessment of many of the issues, see Deaton (2001).

[25] A detailed account of this issue is beyond the scope of this section. For further comments, see the 'explanatory note' in the Statistical Appendix.

[26] Deaton (2001), p. 4. On this point, see also Abhijit Sen (2000).

[27] Government of India (2001c), p. 13: 'The 1999–2000 estimates may not be strictly comparable to the earlier estimates of poverty because of some changes in the methodology of data collection'. The point is reiterated and elaborated on pp. 193–4.

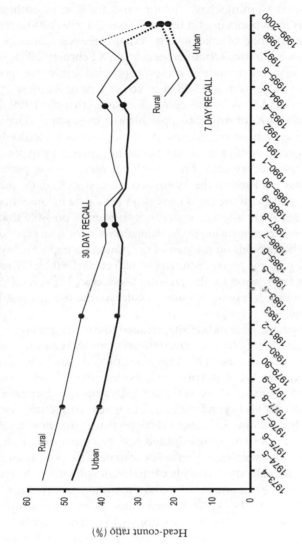

FIGURE 9.2 *Head-count Index of Poverty (India), 1973–4 to 1999–2000*

Sources: See Statistical Appendix, pp. 387–8. The bold-face dots indicate 'quinquennial rounds' of the National Sample Survey

and other expert warnings have not prevented a host of enthusiastic commentators from pouncing on the 'redesigned' 1999–2000 estimates as a long-awaited 'proof' of rapid poverty decline in the post-reform period. Even the Finance Minister's 'budget speech' of 28 February 2001, which drew on the very same economic survey, concluded firmly that 'poverty has fallen from 36 per cent in 1993–4 to 26 per cent or less now'.[28]

There is no solid basis for this conclusion, given that the 1999–2000 poverty estimates are not strictly comparable with earlier ones. This is not the end of the story, however, because there are also reasons to doubt the accuracy of poverty trends for the nineties as they emerge from pre-1999 National Sample Survey data. For one thing, even *average* per-capita expenditure has not risen in the 1990s according to NSS data, and this is hard to reconcile with the rapid increase in per-capita incomes implicit in the GDP and other aggregate statistics. It is quite possible that this inconsistency relates to growing underestimation of per-capita expenditure among richer households on the part of the National Sample Survey, and if this were the case, the *poverty* estimates would remain credible. However, this particular explanation for the growing discrepancy between NSS and 'national accounts' data remains quite speculative, and the jury is still out on this dispute.

Furthermore, the price indices that are used to convert nominal figures into 'real' expenditures seem to overestimate true increases in the cost of living, as has been discussed by Angus Deaton and Alessandro Tarozzi (2000) in particular. When the price indices are corrected, achievements in poverty reduction are more substantial. Deaton and Tarozzi's own adjustments do not go beyond 1993–4, but similar corrections for later years are likely to go in the same direction (that is, to show a greater reduction of poverty than the unadjusted NSS-based estimates indicate).

There is also a possible issue of reliability of some of the poverty estimates based on the annual, 'thin' rounds of the National Sample Survey, as opposed to the larger quinquennial rounds (in the nineties, the latter took place in 1993–4 and 1999–2000). Even the so-called 'thin' samples are in fact fairly large (about 50,000 households), so that the standard errors of the corresponding all-India poverty estimates are very small. However, the effects of non-sampling errors may differ across the thin samples, due to differences in sampling design.[29]

Further work is required to bring the different sources of information more fully in line with each other. There is clearly some uncertainty in the available poverty estimates, and the contrary indications await resolution

[28] See e.g. *http://indiabudget.nic.in/ub2001–02/bs/economic.htm*.
[29] Gaurav Datt and Angus Deaton, personal communications.

on the basis of further investigation. There is, of course, a real possibility that refinements and corrections of the estimates will reveal, in due course, that income poverty has in fact substantially decreased in the nineties.[30] But it is worth noting that even if one were to endorse the official 1999–2000 head-count ratio of 26 per cent, which is known to be biased downward, one would find that poverty reduction in the nineties has proceeded at a similar rate as in earlier decades, in spite of a significant acceleration of aggregate economic growth (see Figure 9.2). As things stand, this is the most optimistic reading of the available evidence.[31]

Pending further evidence on these matters, it is useful to move away from the narrow focus on head-count ratios of income poverty that has dominated this debate, and to consider a broader range of social indicators. Indeed, as discussed earlier, the standard focus on income or expenditure does not do justice to the variety of deprivations we are concerned with, and furthermore, within that narrow approach, the head-count ratio has particularly limited informational value.[32] Looking at the broader evidence of social indicators in the nineties, a somewhat different picture emerges, with areas of accelerated progress as well as indications of slowdown in some fields.

The point is illustrated in Table 9.3, which presents a sample of basic social indicators (see also Figure 9.3). Starting with areas of concern, the decline of infant mortality appears to have slowed down in recent years. During the eighties, India achieved a reduction of 30 per cent in the infant mortality rate—from 114 to 80 between 1980 and 1990. During the nineties, however, the infant mortality rate declined by only 12.5 per cent—from 80 to 70.[33]

[30] Some work-in-progress, aimed at 'correcting' the biases of the 55th round to enable comparisons with earlier rounds (particularly 1993–4, the previous 'quinquennial' round), suggests that head-count ratios have unambiguously declined in the nineties, though not as much as the uncorrected 55th-round estimates indicate (Angus Deaton and K. Sundaram, personal communications; see also Sundaram, 2001b).

[31] The claimed reduction of the head-count ratio (rural and urban areas combined) from 36 to 26 per cent between 1993–4 and 1999–2000 also has to be read in the light of the fact that, in 1993–4, 'poor' households were heavily concentrated near the poverty line, making it possible for many of them to subsequently 'cross the poverty line' on the basis of small increases in per-capita expenditure. Indeed, the decline from 36 to 26 per cent (if real) corresponds to an increase of only 10 per cent or so in average per-capita expenditure, with relatively little change in distribution. Seen from that angle, the claimed reduction of poverty between 1993–4 and 1999–2000 is not particularly implausible, but nor is it a spectacular achievement.

[32] See also pp. 35–6, 86–7, 123–4.

[33] See Government of India (1999a), Table 1, and *Sample Registration Bulletin*,

TABLE 9.3 *India: Development Trends in the 1980s and 1990s*

	Annual rate of change (%)	
	1980s (1980–90)	1990s (1990–2000[a])
Gross domestic product	5.4	6.0
Index of agricultural production	3.4	2.2
Real agricultural wages	5.5	2.5
Head-count index of poverty	–2.6	n/a
Infant mortality rate	–2.9	–1.5
Total fertility rate	–1.7	–1.8
Illiteracy rate (age 7+)	–1.5	–2.8

Note: [a] For mortality and fertility, the reference period ends in 1999 and 1998 respectively (the latest years for which the relevant estimates are available).

Sources: Production indicators: Calculated from Government of India (2001c), pp. S-1 and S-5, and Government of India (2000i), p. 140–1. *Demographic indicators:* Sample Registration System data presented in Government of India (1999a), Table 1, Government of India (2000h), pp. xiv–xv, and *Sample Registration Bulletin,* April 2001, p. 1. *Literacy rates:* Census data presented in Government of India (2001b), p. 115. *Poverty:* Calculated from Datt (1999a). *Agricultural wages:* Calculated from data collected by the Department of Economics and Statistics, partly published in *Agricultural Wages in India* (various years); see also Government of India (2000a), p. 167, and Government of India (2001c), p. 193. All rates of change are calculated by semi-log regression based on annual data (there are no 'gaps' in the annual data series, except for poverty and literacy). For further details, see Statistical Appendix.

Similarly, the growth rate of real agricultural wages fell from over 5 per cent per year in the 1980s to 2.5 per cent or so in the 1990s.[34] Given the close (inverse) association between real agricultural wages and rural poverty, this pattern is consistent with the belief that poverty has continued to decline in the nineties, but perhaps at a slower rate than in the eighties. Incidentally, the regional patterns of growth rates in agricultural wages

---

April 2001; also Statistical Appendix, Table A.6. The problem appears to have been particularly serious during the second half of the nineties, when India's infant mortality rate remained virtually unchanged. Recent research sponsored by UNICEF points to a number of possible causes of this problem, many of them related to the dismal and sometimes even deteriorating condition of basic health services in many states (A.K. Shiva Kumar, personal communication).

[34] See Table 9.3. Sundaram (2001a) presents independent estimates of the growth rates of real wages and earnings, based on comparable NSS data for 1993–4 and 1999–2000. His work suggests that the yearly 'wage earnings' of casual agricultural labourers have grown at 2.5 per cent per year in real terms over that period. This conclusion is highly consistent with our own estimates, presented in Table 9.3. On the slowdown in the rate of growth of real agricultural wages in the 1990s, see also Sarma (2000, 2001).

tend to strengthen our earlier observations relating to regional disparities. Real wages have grown quite fast in most of the western and southern states (especially Gujarat, Tamil Nadu and Kerala—more than 5 per cent per year in each case), but rather slowly in much of the northern region, especially the poorest states (e.g. 0.3 per cent per year in Bihar and 0.7 per cent per year in Orissa).[35]

Note should also be taken of the related issue of rising economic inequalities in the nineties. There is much anecdotal evidence of this problem, and while statistical confirmation of it awaits adequate data, two aspects of the problem are fairly well established. First, as noted earlier, inter-state economic disparities have risen in the nineties, when states that were already comparatively advanced (notably in the western and southern regions) grew particularly fast. Second, there is also strong evidence of rising rural-urban disparities in the nineties, as one might have expected given the sectoral imbalances discussed earlier.[36] Given the adverse social consequences of economic inequality (ranging from elitist biases in public policy to the perpetuation or reinforcement of other types of inequality), this accentuation of economic disparities, from an already high base, is not a trivial matter.

None of this implies that the nineties have been a period of 'impoverishment', as is sometimes claimed. Clearly, there has been continued if uneven progress in terms of most basic indicators of living conditions. As we saw in chapter 5 (see also Table 9.3), there has even been accelerated progress in the specific field of elementary education. But while the impoverishment thesis does not survive close scrutiny, nor does the claim (often made by enthusiastic advocates of the current brand of economic reforms) that the nineties have been a period of unprecedented, broad-based improvement in living conditions. If anything, the overall progress of social indicators was somewhat more impressive in the 1980s, a period of steady improvement on most fronts (see Table 9.3). The potential benefits of accelerated economic growth appear to have been diluted by severe imbalances in growth patterns, growing inequalities, and continued state inertia in crucial social fields.

This broader picture of social progress also contains a useful reminder that eliminating deprivation is as much a matter of public action as one merely of economic growth. Indeed, if there is one area where a 'take-

[35] See Statistical Appendix, Table A.2, Part 11.
[36] On rising rural-urban disparities, see particularly Ravallion (2000b). The fact that real agricultural wages have been rising more slowly than per-capita GDP, and also more slowly than (say) public-sector salaries, can also be read as tentative evidence of increasing economic inequality between occupation groups in the nineties.

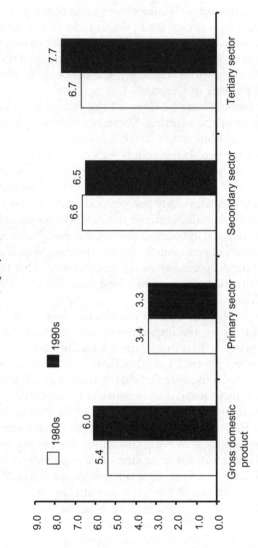

FIGURE 9.3 *India: Development Trends in the 1980s and 1990s*

Part 1. Growth of production
(% per year)

Source: See Table 9.1.

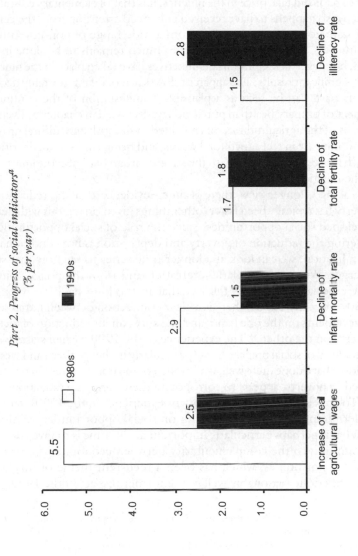

FIGURE 9.3: *India: Development Trends in the 1980s and 1990s*

Part 2. Progress of social indicators[a]
(% per year)

Note: [a]Annual rate of *increase*, for agricultural wages; annual rate of *decline*, for mortality, fertility and illiteracy.
Source: See Table 9.3.

off' of sorts did take place in the nineties, it is that of elementary education, which also happens to have received enhanced attention from the central and state governments as well as from a wide range of non-government institutions. As discussed in chapter 5, much remains to be done in this field, but nevertheless, important initiatives have taken place in the nineties, with significant results. The apparent slowdown of infant mortality decline, for its part, can be seen as a plausible manifestation of the continuing neglect of primary health in public policy, discussed in chapter 6. Even the travails of the agricultural sector (reflected in sluggish agricultural growth, a slow increase in real agricultural wages, and rising rural-urban disparities) may have something to do with the strong 'urban bias' of economic policy in the nineties.[37]

Taking a longer view, there is much evidence that the reduction of poverty has typically been faster (other things given) in regions with better-developed social opportunities. Since the role of social opportunities in fostering the reduction of poverty and deprivation is not conditional on liberalization, we can look at a longer time series to see how that story emerges. What is particularly interesting and from the policy point of view especially relevant is the fact that in the long haul (between the 1950s and early 1990s) there is a clear connection between initial social achievements on the one hand, and the subsequent reduction of income poverty on the other.[38] The experience of the 1990s, when states with a better level of social preparedness (particularly in the southern and western regions) have done quite well, while much of the northern region remained mired in poverty, appears to corroborate these earlier investigations.

To conclude, India's development experience in the 1990s, far from undermining the case for focusing on social opportunities, reinforces it. What is perhaps particularly important at this time is to give adequate recognition to the complementarity between economic progress and social opportunities, which has been a recurrent theme of this book. India has done reasonably well in the former respect in the 1990s, but

---

[37] Public support for agriculture in the nineties has focused mainly on raising 'minimum support prices' (MSPs), with comparatively little investment in rural infrastructure, agricultural research and related inputs (see e.g. Abhijit Sen, 2001). As discussed in section 9.5, raising MSPs is a rather defective way of helping poor farmers, and even ends up hurting them in many cases.

[38] Datt and Ravallion (1998) put their econometric findings thus: 'states starting with better infrastructure and human resources saw significantly higher long-term rates of poverty reduction' (p. 17). The human resources in question were captured, in this study, by the initial levels of literacy and infant mortality.

the continued neglect of the latter (despite some positive change in the specific field of elementary education) has seriously compromised the gains that might otherwise have been derived from the country's renewed economic dynamism. The course of Indian development in the coming decade depends a great deal on the extent to which this imbalance is corrected in the near future.

9.4. Economic Reform and Social Policy

The neglect of social opportunities in India in the nineties is primarily a continuation of earlier distortions of public priorities. These biases, in turn, relate to long-standing inequalities of political power, and in particular to the political marginalization of the poor. We shall come back to these issues in the next chapter. Meanwhile, it is worth asking whether social policy has also been significantly affected (positively or negatively) by the programme of economic reforms initiated in 1991.

In many countries, 'structural adjustment' programmes and related economic reforms have been associated with serious setbacks for the social sectors.[39] Sometimes this is attributed to a conspiracy against the social sectors on the part of the World Bank or the International Monetary Fund, but the real reasons are better sought in the political economy of economic reform and the social sectors. First, fiscal austerity is one of the key ingredients of structural adjustment programmes. In the absence of strong political lobbies to protect them, social expenditures are often 'soft targets' for the financial axe. Second, market-oriented economic reforms tend to be associated with a changing ideological climate, possibly involving deep suspicion of state intervention of every kind. 'Downsizing government' is often assumed to be an intrinsic part of the reform agenda, even though, as argued in chapter 2, liberalization per se need not reduce the role of the state in the economy. Third, policy priorities and political preoccupations also tend to change in periods of market-oriented economic reform, and this too can have the effect of marginalizing the social sectors. When policy-makers and politicians are busy wooing private investors and watching the stock market, social matters sometimes take the back seat. Finally, the expansion of market institutions alters incentive patterns, sometimes to the detriment of social-sector activities. For instance, the expansion of private income-earning opportunities for the well-educated

---

[39] See e.g. Cornia et al. (1987), UNICEF (1993), Ellman (1994), Witter (1996), Mehrotra and Jolly (1997).

often makes it harder to retain skilled personnel in the public sector without major salary increases.[40]

As we saw in chapter 4, the severe decline of publicly-provided health care services in post-reform China had much to do with these processes. A similar— indeed more emphatic—analysis also applies to other countries that have gone through over-enthusiastic market-oriented reforms, such as Russia and Vietnam.[41]

To varying extents, these adverse effects of market-oriented reform on social policy have also been at work in India in the 1990s. However, the damage has been comparatively limited, and there has also been room for new initiatives, as noted in chapter 5 with reference to education. One reason for this is that attempts to impose fiscal discipline have been relatively unsuccessful. In this connection, it should be remembered that India's economic reforms differ from externally-imposed 'structural adjustment programmes'. Unlike many countries subjected to such programmes in recent years, India has not been compelled by international financial institutions to radically scale down public spending.[42] For better or worse, fiscal permissiveness has continued in the 1990s, and this has made it easier to sustain social expenditures (temporarily at least). Public expenditure on health and education, in particular, has expanded rather than declined in real per-capita terms: as noted earlier, the *share* of these expenditures in GDP has declined somewhat in the 1990s, but this has been more than compensated by the healthy growth of GDP itself.[43]

Another reason why India avoided a drastic setback in social policies in the 1990s relates to democratic politics. The role of political opposition

---

[40] This is one reason, among others, why the 'Fifth Pay Commission' in India recommended large salary increases for public sector employees, particularly on the higher rungs of the ladder. As we saw in chapters 5 and 6, these salary increases tend to have an adverse effect on non-salary expenditure (e.g. purchase of medicines, in the case of the health sector), and have also drastically raised the cost of hiring doctors, school teachers, etc.

[41] See Ellman (1994) and Witter (1996), respectively.

[42] In the case of China, the financial constraints on the social sectors in the post-reform period did not arise so much from international pressures as from the erosion of local fund-raising capabilities associated with the transition to the household responsibility system; see chapter 4.

[43] Recent trends in public expenditure on the social sectors in India are reviewed in Pradhan et al. (2000). The dominant pattern is one of fairly stable public expenditure on education, health, and social security, as a *share* of GDP, though some decline did occur in the initial years of economic reform. See also Jalan and Subbarao (1995), Prabhu and Sarker (1998), and Prabhu (1999, 2001).

in preventing a retreat of government involvement in the social sectors clearly emerged at the very beginning of the reform period. Indeed, the first post-reform budget, for 1991–2, involved wide-ranging cuts in government spending, including public expenditure on health and education.[44] This unifocal approach, however, had to be reversed the following year, partly due to the pressure from the opposition. Electoral politics have also played a part in the positive initiatives adopted by some state governments in the 1990s, such as the 'education guarantee scheme' in Madhya Pradesh. As these initiatives illustrate, economic reform is not incompatible with an expansion of state activities in fields such as health and education.

Having said this, there are reasons for concern about the adverse pressures (financial as well as ideological) that have come to bear on the social sectors in recent years, in association with the reorientation of economic policy. While there have been no cuts in real public expenditure per capita on education, health and related sectors, the declining *share* of these expenditures in GDP (especially in the first half of the 1990s) is a serious issue. Also, expenditure increases have been overwhelmingly absorbed in salary increases, reflecting, inter alia, the growing aspirations and demands of the middle classes as well as the need for public-sector salaries at the top to keep up with the growth of income-earning opportunities in the liberalized private sector. As a result, there has often been little improvement in the delivery of actual services. In some states, the problem has been exacerbated by an erosion of public commitment to the widespread and equitable provision of basic public services. In the field of education, these developments have led to a growing reliance on second-track, low-cost schooling facilities, as noted in chapter 5, where we have also discussed some important concerns associated with that approach. Similar remarks apply in the field of health, especially public health.[45]

Another telling illustration of the danger of financial and political marginalization of the social sectors in a period of market-oriented economic reform concerns official response to the recent drought. In comparison with public responses to other recent droughts of comparable severity (e.g. in 1972–3, 1979–80, or 1987–8), this year's relief measures in the drought-affected states have been quite limited. For instance, draconian

---

[44] See Pradhan et al. (2000), Table 4. As the authors show, 1991–2 was an unusual case of *absolute decline* in real public expenditure on the social sectors in India. In per-capita terms, public expenditure on education declined by nearly 5 per cent.

[45] On this, see also various contributions in Qadeer, Sen and Nayar (2001).

ceilings have been imposed on the numbers of labourers to be employed on relief programmes, and public assistance through the public distribution system has also been very meagre. This state of affairs relates, in part, to the difficulty of mobilizing financial resources for drought relief at a time when concerns about the fiscal deficit and its effect on the stock market have more influence on budget allocations than the needs of drought-affected people.[46] It also reflects the difficulty of focusing the attention and commitment of policy-makers on the plight of drought-affected people, at a time when economic policy is overwhelmingly oriented towards the (so-called) 'middle classes'.

The preceding observations reinforce what was said earlier in this chapter about the need to go beyond the present reform agenda, with its narrow focus on liberalization, towards a broader agenda of participatory growth. It is possible, in principle, to combine greater room for economic incentives with a stronger commitment to social policy. This, however, would require some fairly radical departures from the perspective and priorities that have dominated India's economic reforms so far.

9.5 HUNGER AMIDST PLENTY

One specific field where a reorientation of priorities is (we would argue) much needed at this time is that of food policy. Of particular concern is the scandalous phenomenon of mounting food stocks against a background of widespread hunger. We take up this question here because, in addition to the basic importance of this subject, it connects with a number of issues discussed in this chapter and also elsewhere in the book, including the need for equity-oriented reform in the Indian economy, the critical importance of addressing nutritional problems, and the role of democratic practice in giving voice to the underprivileged.

As we saw in chapter 3, nutritional achievements in India are among the lowest in the world. About half of all Indian children are estimated to be undernourished, and more than half of all adult women suffer from anaemia. Low birthweights (themselves reflecting the poor nutritional status of adult women) play a major role in the perpetuation of undernutrition and poor health, and also connect these problems with issues of gender inequality and intra-household discrimination.

---

[46] A personal communication from a senior member of the Finance Ministry clearly indicates that concerns about the fiscal deficit, and its possible effect on India's 'credit rating' (sic), are a major obstacle against the expansion of drought relief programmes at this time. For further discussion of state responses to the recent drought, see Drèze (2001a, 2001b, 2001c) and Drèze and Khera (2001).

There is some evidence of heightened nutritional deprivation during the last two or three years, a period of severe drought in large parts of the country.[47] Over the same period, there has been an unprecedented accumulation of foodgrain stocks on the part of the central government—from about 18 million tonnes in early 1998 (close to the official 'buffer stock' norms) to well over 50 million tonnes as this book goes to press.[48] To put these staggering numbers in perspective, it may help to think of the current stock as the equivalent of about one tonne of food for *each* household below the poverty line. If all the sacks of grain lying in state warehouses were lined up in a row, the line would stretch for one million kilometres or so—more than twice the distance from the earth to the moon.

While these massive food stocks are meant to contribute to the country's 'food security', that objective is clearly not well served when the stocks are built by *depriving* hungry people of much needed food during drought years. Further, the current stocks are more than three times as large as the official buffer stock norms. This huge surplus is, to a great extent, explained by the fact that the government is committed to unrealistically high 'minimum support prices' (MSPs) for foodgrains (wheat and rice in particular). This has boosted production, lowered consumer demand, and forced the government to buy the difference in order to sustain these artificially high prices. Indeed, foodgrain procurement has risen from an average of 22.5 million tonnes per year in 1991–7 to 26 million tonnes in 1998, 31 million tonnes in 1999, and 36 million tonnes in 2000.[49]

[47] See e.g. Drèze (2001b, 2001c, 2001d), Drèze and Khera (2001), Mishra (2001), P. Das (2001), Raval (2001), Sainath (2001a, 2001b), T. Singh (2001), among others. One survey of 105 drought-affected hamlets in Rajasthan found that most families had virtually stopped eating vegetables, pulses, milk products, and related items, and that even foodgrain consumption had been reduced in about a quarter of all households (Drèze and Khera, 2001).

[48] For these and related figures, see Government of India (2001c) and the website of the Food Corporation of India (http://fciweb.nic.in).

[49] Government of India (2001c), Table 1.19. Two further points to note are the following. First, the effectiveness of procurement operations in sustaining the official MSPs varies a great deal between different states and regions, depending inter alia on the procurement infrastructure as well as the bargaining power of local farmers' organizations. In states such as Bihar, where little procurement is taking place, farmers remain vulnerable to localized gluts and price crashes. Second, stock accumulation during the last few years has been further enhanced by a reduction in the 'offtake' from the public distribution system (the main channel through which food stocks are released). This reduction in offtake is linked with the introduction of 'targeting' in 1997, through which the public distribution system was effectively restricted, in many states, to households below the official 'poverty line'. On these and related aspects of India's public distribution system, see Mooij (1999), Krishnaji and Krishnan (2000), Swaminathan (2000), among others.

The distributional effects of high support prices are not entirely clear. There is a widespread conviction that high food prices help the poor, because it is a form of subsidy to the agricultural sector, which is the main source of livelihood of a large number of poor households. But this reasoning is at best incomplete, since it is also the case that many more poor people in India buy much of their food on the market, and tend to be adversely affected when food prices go up. For casual labourers, migrant workers, slum dwellers, rickshaw pullers, rural artisans, and many other deprived sections of the population, cheaper food would be a blessing. It is very important to consider the adverse effects of high food prices on the entitlements of vulnerable groups, along with any gains that might be enjoyed by those who depend (directly or indirectly) on the sale of food for their livelihood.

As it happens, even poor *farmers* are unlikely to benefit much, if at all, from price-support operations. Consider for instance small farmers in, say, Orissa or Jharkhand or Chattisgarh. These farmers typically sell little grain, if any, on the market; instead, they tend to combine subsistence farming with labour migration and other income-earning activities that allow them to buy non-food commodities. Hence, higher food prices would be of little help to them. This is particularly so in drought years, when small farmers typically join the ranks of those who are constrained to buy most of their food on the market (by selling assets or taking loans if need be), and who tend to be hurt by higher food prices.

The overall distributional effects of higher food prices can, thus, be quite adverse. A related issue is that it is not *possible* to sustain artificially high prices, short of destroying or exporting the surplus food.[50] Storing surplus food only postpones the problem. In fact, it *aggravates* the problem, by giving farmers misleading signals to the effect that they should continue growing more foodgrains instead of diversifying their crops. Sooner or later, this is bound to lead to a glut in the foodgrain market and a collapse of market prices, defeating the price-support policy, unless the intention is to accumulate larger and larger stocks indefinitely.

In short, temporarily keeping prices up by storing food at massive public expense is not an effective way of helping needy farmers. This is particularly so during drought years, when 'supporting' food prices by storing large amounts of food carries a serious danger of undermining the food entitlements of large sections of the population.

---

[50] Strenuous efforts have been made, in recent months, to sell part of the surplus food stocks on the world market. This, however, is very difficult, because (1) world prices are much below domestic prices, (2) subsidizing exports would violate WTO rules, and (3) Indian stocks often do not meet world quality standards.

Indeed, it is rather disturbing that massive procurement operations continued and even intensified right through the recent drought. At a time of widespread hunger in drought-affected areas, the government was busy hoarding food on an unprecedented scale and striving to keep prices *up*, making it that much harder for drought-affected people to buy food on the market. It is also the case, of course, that employment programmes and other relief measures were organized in the drought-affected states, averting a famine. But the income-generation effects of these relief programmes were to some extent undone by the policy of high food prices. Even the relief programmes were quite limited in comparison with earlier droughts, in spite of the fact that the availability of gigantic food stocks presented a unique opportunity to expand employment generation programmes at relatively little further cost.

Similar opportunities exist today to make constructive use of the available food stocks. In particular, these resources could be used to implement social security programmes such as employment schemes, school meals, in-kind transfers to the destitute, and an expansion of the public distribution system.[51] These possibilities have received scant attention in recent policy debates, and there is little indication that the government has anything like a coherent plan for the constructive utilization of the country's food stocks. Instead, official policy seems to consist of postponing the problem of ballooning food stocks as long as possible.

This situation of 'hunger amidst plenty' is an extreme case of lopsided priorities, related in turn to sharp inequalities of political power. The government has been quite responsive to the demands of privileged farmers (the main beneficiaries of procurement operations), even boosting minimum support prices against expert recommendations.[52] By contrast, the needs of the hungry millions have counted for very little in the formulation

---

[51] The case for bold state involvement in social security programmes at an early stage of development is discussed in Drèze and Sen (1989, 1991, 1999). In India, Maharashtra's 'employment guarantee scheme' is a particularly significant experience in this respect; see e.g. Mahendra Dev and Ranade (2001), and earlier contributions cited there. There have also been important initiatives in states such as Tamil Nadu (Guhan, 1992b) and Kerala (Kannan and Francis, 2001). In general, however, social security arrangements in India are extremely limited as thing stand, and there is an urgent need for greater activism in this field. On different aspects of this issue, see also Guhan (1992a, 1993, 1995), van Ginneken (1998), Mahendra Dev et al. (2001), and the literature cited there.

[52] Earlier this year, just before the rabi harvest, the Cabinet raised the minimum support price for wheat *against* the recommendations of the Commission for Agricultural Costs and Prices (CACP). Much as predicted by the CACP, wheat procurement in April-May 2001 shot up to an unprecedented 20 million tonnes.

of recent food policies. The answer to this problem is not so much to undermine farmers' organizations, which have every reason to defend the interests of their members.[53] The need, rather, is to build countervailing power through better political organization of underprivileged groups. We shall return to this general issue in the next chapter.

9.6. GLOBALIZATION AND INEQUALITY

Given the growing openness of the Indian economy, this chapter would be incomplete without a few comments on the thorny issue of 'globalization', which (like 'liberalization') has received staunch support as well as comprehensive denunciation from different quarters. There is a crucial need for balance here, and for avoiding the 'dialogue of the deaf' that characterizes many exchanges on this subject, which have the features not of engagement and encounter, but of ships passing at night, throwing invectives at each other. It is important to go beyond that impasse, since the basic attitude to globalization can be crucially significant for the future of India.

Since the confusion relates partly to different perceptions of the term 'globalization', a preliminary clarification on this may be helpful. In recent debates, globalization has often acquired a narrow connotation, associated primarily with the liberalization of international trade and investment. Sometimes the interpretation is even narrower, and focuses on the particular institutional framework within which that expansion is taking place today, involving the World Trade Organization and related bodies. This narrow interpretation does not do justice to the significance of the growing global connectedness and interdependence of societies. It is also making a big concession to those who want to put this growing interdependence primarily at the service of corporate profit and privileged interests. Globalization, in the broad sense of growing interdependence, can also be harnessed for other goals, including those of world peace, environmental sustainability, human rights, democracy and of course shared economic prosperity. The fact that these opportunities have tended to be seriously neglected, and that the 'globalization agenda' is often reduced to the expansion of international trade and investment, should not prevent us from thinking about globalization in adequately broader terms.

[53] As mentioned earlier, however, the present approach of sustaining artificially high food prices is objectively unsustainable. Assessed in that light, the persistent demands of farmers' organizations for high support prices (irrespective of demand conditions and export opportunities) are somewhat short-sighted, if not self-defeating.

The Need for Openness

Turning to more specific questions, we may begin with the view, on one side, that globalization is ruining the world, and is making developing countries in particular succumb to exploitation and destruction by the prosperous 'West'.[54] Take the thesis—often articulated explicitly or by implication—that globalization is a new folly. Is that the case? It can be argued, on the contrary, that globalization (in the broad sense used here) is neither particularly new, nor in general, a folly. The historical perspective is quite relevant here. Indeed, it is instructive to look a little further back in history, say to the beginning of the last millennium rather than at its end. Around 1000 A.D., the global spread of science, technology and mathematics was changing the nature of the old world, though the dissemination then was, to a great extent, in the opposite direction to what we see today. For example, the high technology in the world of 1000 A.D. included paper and printing, the kite and the magnetic compass, the wheel barrow and the rotary fan, the crossbow and gunpowder, the clock and the iron chain suspension bridge. Each one of these examples of high technology of the world a millennium ago was well-established and extensively used in China, and was practically unknown elsewhere. It is globalization that spread them across the world, including Europe.

There is a similar pattern in the spread of eastern influence on western mathematics. The now-standard decimal system, with its place value notation, emerged and became well developed in India between the second and the sixth century, and was thereafter used extensively also by Arab mathematicians. But these procedures reached Europe mainly in the last quarter of the tenth century, and began having their major impact in the early years of the last millennium, playing a major part in the mathematical and scientific revolution that helped to transform Europe. Both the Renaissance, and later the European Enlightenment, were strongly influenced by the currents that had come from outside Europe in the preceding centuries. Indeed, almost certainly Europe would have been a lot

---

[54] The description of the richer countries as 'West' follows the pattern of British imperialism more closely (Britain and India constitute a good 'couple' here) than does the competing term 'North', which is more loyal to the history of French and Portuguese imperialism (primarily in Africa vis-à-vis Europe). The international official community—including the United Nations—seems to have adopted 'North' as the generic term for use, but with an Indian focus, the term 'West' probably captures the nuances better (informed by imperialist writings of James Mill or Thomas Babington Macaulay or Rudyard Kipling).

poorer—intellectually as well as materially—had it resisted the globalization of mathematics, science and technology at that time.

A similar remark can be made about global movements—in the reverse direction—today. The spread of new technology and new methods of production can make a major contribution to economic and social progress in many developing countries—not least in India. To identify this phenomenon with the imperialism of ideas and beliefs would be a serious error. We must not, of course, overlook the fact that there are issues related to globalization that do connect with imperialism. For example, many of the dependent economies remain underdeveloped precisely as a result of the neglect—or worse—implicit in imperialist policies in the past, and this applies no less to India than to any other country. However, it would be a great mistake to see contemporary globalization primarily in terms of a simple analogy with historical imperialism.

Over thousands of years, globalization has shaped the progress of the world, through trade, travel, migration, and dissemination of knowledge. The polar opposite of globalization can be seen as persistent separatism and relentless autarky. There is a worrying image of seclusion that has been invoked in many old Sanskrit texts in India (in *Hitopadesh, Ganapath, Prasannaraghava, Bhattikavya,* among others). This is the story of a frog that lives its whole life within a well and is suspicious of everything outside it. This 'kupamanduka'—the well-frog—has a world view, but it is a world view that is entirely confined to that well. The scientific, cultural and economic history of the world would have been very limited had we lived like well-frogs. This remains an important issue, since there are plenty of well-frogs around today—and also, of course, many solicitors of well-frogs.

The importance of global contact and interaction applies to economic matters among others. Indeed, there is much evidence that global economic relations have fostered prosperity in many different areas on the globe. Pervasive poverty and 'nasty, brutish and short' lives dominated the world a few centuries ago, with only a few pockets of rare affluence. In overcoming that penury, modern technology as well as economic interrelations have been influential, and they remain important today. The economic predicament of the poor across the world cannot be reversed by withholding from them the great advantages of contemporary technology, the economic opportunities associated with international trade and exchange, and the social as well as economic merits of living in open rather than closed societies. Rather, the main issue is how to make good use of the remarkable potential of economic intercourse and technological progress in a way that pays adequate attention to the interests of the deprived and the underdog. This is the challenge that India has to address.

Inequality and Institutions

Thus, the real problems raised by globalization do not, in fact, lie in globalization *per se*, but relate in one way or another to inequality—to disparities in affluence and in political, social and economic power. This issue relates to globalization in three distinct ways. First, as with economic growth, there is a crucial question of participation of poor countries, and of the underprivileged within particular countries, in the new opportunities associated with globalization. Second, aside from the distribution of new benefits, the demands of justice cannot ignore the overwhelming presence of antecedent inequality that characterizes the world. Third, there is an issue of equity of the processes and institutions that currently shape the course of globalization.

For all these reasons, the issue of inequality has to be addressed along with acknowledging the enormous potentialities of international exchange and interaction (economic as well as non-economic). Perhaps the most important connection to appreciate is how far-reaching the role of non-market institutions is in dealing with inequality—even in making good use of the market mechanism in an equitable manner. The insistence on a broader view of economic development and on the importance of social opportunities (including political as well as sociological concerns), which is part of the basic approach of this book, fits with this focus on globalization as an opportunity to be harnessed, rather than either as an evil to be shunned, or as a panacea to be grabbed.

As with inequality *within* nations, addressing inequalities *between* nations also requires the development of non-market institutions. There is, first of all, a strong need for a global commitment to democracy and to other instruments of social equity. There is, of course, no basic conflict between promoting economic interrelations and supporting democratic and social rights. However, as George Soros (among others) has pointed out, international business concerns often prefer to work in orderly autocracies rather than in activist democracies, and may also have a preference for public money being spent to promote the safety and comfort of the upper classes rather than to remove the deprivation of the underdogs.[55] These are not, of course, insurmountable barriers, but it is important that the surmountable barriers be actually surmounted. India would be right to make it easier for international economic interactions to occur and flourish, but this is not at all a reason for neglecting those essential steps that can prevent the benefits from such interactions (and from other economic expansions) from being usurped by those who are already privileged.

[55] See Soros (2000).

Furthermore, the distribution of the benefits of international relations depends also on a variety of international social arrangements, including trade agreements, patent laws, global health initiatives, international educational provisions, facilities for technological dissemination, ecological and environmental conventions, fair treatment of accumulated debts (often incurred by irresponsible military rulers of the past), conflict resolution procedures, and control of the arms trade. The financial architecture of the world that we have inherited from the past includes institutions such as the World Bank, the IMF, the WTO, and other organizations. This institutional architecture was largely set up in the mid-forties, following the Bretton Woods conference held just as the second world war was coming to an end. The framework reflected the prevailing international power structure, and responded to what world leaders saw at that time as the big global problems. But the world was very different then from what it is now, with the bulk of Asia and Africa still under imperialist dominance of one kind or another. It was also a time when the tolerance of insecurity, poverty and inequality was very much greater than it is today. The world of Bretton Woods is not the world of today, and there is every reason to demand radical changes in the institutional framework that governs international economic relations.

Bringing about these changes, however, calls for initiatives and movements that are themselves part of 'globalization' in the broad sense, whether they take the form of creating new international institutions and conventions (from the Kyoto Protocol to the World Commission on Dams), or of the growth of global NGOs (from Amnesty International to Médecins Sans Frontières), or of the expansion of worldwide associative networks (geared, say, to the abolition of Third World debt or to the protection of indigenous rights). Even the mass protests that have taken place at recent 'summits' (from Seattle to Genoa), and which are often simplistically described as 'anti-globalization', can be seen to belong to these global initiatives. These initiatives have already done a great deal to alter the 'globalization agenda' and its institutional foundations, and there is scope for going much further in that direction.

Addressing the issue of inequality (both *between* and *within* nations) is essential for the potentialities of globalization to be realised. At the same time, it is also important to reject the invitation to become *kupamandukas*—or well-frogs. Indeed, introversion and isolationism are no answer to the problem of global inequalities. On the contrary, they tend to play into the hands of chauvinist movements that have no commitment whatsoever to social equality. This is especially so in India, where there is often a dangerously thin line between committed anti-imperialism and reactionary nationalism.[56] The real answer to global inequality lies in the growing possibilities of solidarity across the world, which are part of 'globalization' in the broad sense.

9.7. A CONCLUDING REMARK

Economic policies in India have undergone much change over the last decade, and more changes are in the process of being implemented. The debate surrounding these reforms has mobilized enormous attention and energy, and the arguments presented on each side have been quite forceful and firm, even acrimonious.

In this monograph, we have emphasized the need to take the debates on economic policy well *beyond* the issue of economic reforms in their present form. This is not so much because we see great merit in avoiding acrimonious debates (a bit of healthy mud-slinging might indeed have something to commend it in making people take an interest in complex and apparently dull problems), but because we believe that the concentration on attacking or defending liberalization as the central policy issue distracts attention from a broader understanding of social opportunities of which the use of the market can be *an important yet quite incomplete* part. The economic reforms do constitute a significant departure, but there are many other issues of great importance which have been thoroughly overshadowed by the focus on arguments—both *for* and *against*—the reforms. This has also led to summary assessments—both championing and dismissal—of economic policies that cannot really be judged adequately without placing them in a much wider context.

We have argued for the necessity of asking—and addressing—a very different set of questions, rather than confining the analysis to examining different answers to the old familiar questions. The central issue, we have argued, is to expand the social opportunities open to the people. In so far as these opportunities are compromised—directly or indirectly—by counterproductive regulations and controls, by restrictions on economic initiatives, by the stifling of competition and its efficiency-generating advantages, and so on, the removal of these hindrances must be seen as extremely important. But we have also discussed why the creation and use of social opportunities for all require much more than the 'freeing'

---

[56] On the related intimacy and tensions between 'green' and 'saffron' politics in India, see Mukul Sharma (forthcoming).

of markets. While the case for economic reforms may take good note of the diagnosis that India has too much government in some areas, it ignores the fact that India also has insufficient and ineffective government activity in many other areas, including school education, health care, social security, land reform, environmental protection, and the promotion of social change. This inertia, too, contributes to the persistence of widespread deprivation and social inequality.

What needs curing is not just 'too little market'—nor of course is it 'too much market' (each seen on its own). The expansion of markets is *among* the instruments that can help to promote human capabilities. Given the imperative need for rapid elimination of endemic deprivation in India, it would be irresponsible to ignore that opportunity. But much more is involved in freeing the Indian economy from the cage in which it has been confined, and many of the relevant tasks call for more—not less—government activity and public action. There is need for radical change in the terms of the debate.

10

The Practice of Democracy

10.1. IDEALS, INSTITUTIONS AND PRACTICE

In assessing the past achievements and future potential of Indian democracy, it is useful to distinguish between democratic *ideals*, democratic *institutions* and democratic *practice*. Democratic ideals represent various aspects of the broad idea of 'government of the people, by the people and for the people.' They include political characteristics that can be seen to be intrinsically important in terms of the objective of democratic social living, such as freedom of expression, participation of the people in deciding on the factors governing their lives, public accountability of leaders, and an equitable distribution of power. Democratic institutions go beyond these basic intents, and include such instrumental arrangements as constitutional rights, effective courts, responsive electoral systems, functioning parliaments and assemblies, open and free media, and participatory institutions of local governance (such as panchayats and gram sabhas).

While democratic institutions provide opportunities for achieving democratic ideals, how these opportunities are realized is a matter of democratic practice. The latter depends inter alia on the extent of political participation, the awareness of the public, the vigour of the opposition, the nature of political parties and popular organizations, and various determinants of the distribution of power. Both democratic institutions and democratic practice are important in achieving democracy in the fuller sense, but the presence of the former does not guarantee the latter.

In terms of democratic institutions, India has done reasonably well, and this may look particularly impressive in the international perspective, given the failure of many countries to secure even the most elementary constituents of a democratic institutional structure. Earlier democratic institutions in India—often stretching back in history—were decisively consolidated within the constitutional framework of an independent India.[1] It is often forgotten how radical the constitution was in those days, especially in light of the limited reach of democracy elsewhere in the world. It is not just that most other developing countries were still under the yoke of colonialism and authoritarianism at that time. Even economically advanced countries still lacked the political freedoms guaranteed by the Indian constitution in many cases. In 1947, when India achieved independence, women were still deprived of universal and equal voting rights in many 'developed' countries (Belgium, Canada, Switzerland, and the United States, among others).[2] In Switzerland, women were twenty-four years away from the right to vote. In the United States, African Americans too were effectively deprived of equal voting rights (through systematic denial of the opportunity to register and vote), and state-sponsored racial discrimination (e.g. the prohibition of inter-racial marriages as well as racial segregation in public places) was widespread; it took a protracted civil rights movement, lasting until the late 1960s, to overcome these suppressions of basic democratic freedoms. In other countries of western Europe and north America, elected parliaments often coexisted uncomfortably with lingering monarchies and also conceded temporal powers to church authorities. These 'irregularities' (in terms of

---

[1] How this institutional success relates to the history of Indian society is a valuable subject for research. It is possibly significant that even before independence, some democratic principles had a long tradition in particular regions and within constrained but not negligible domains. There was, for instance, much support for the toleration of heterodoxy, as well as experience of consensus decision-making in village assemblies (or caste panchayats) in some communities. Also, the old classic writings in support of pluralism, toleration and participation (from Ashoka's writings in the third century before Christ to Akbar's pronouncements at the end of the sixteenth century), despite their uneven hold in Indian practice, identified institutional demands that could be invoked in support of the building of democratic institutions in post-independence India, without inviting the suspicion that this was an alien import into Indian society. Indeed, the nationalist movement in India often summoned these historical traditions and memories to use the past to build the future in a skilful way, and Mahatma Gandhi himself was particularly visionary in this constructive exercise. However, to what extent India's past is really a part of the explanation of its greater success with democratic institutions today, compared with other developing countries, is not entirely clear, and the thrust of the explanation may well lie in the nature of contemporary politics, rather than in the specifics of Indian history.

[2] See the comparative international data on 'women's political participation' presented in *Human Development Report 2001*, pp. 226–9.

democratic norms) continue to this day in many cases, in contrast to India where the constitution made a clean sweep of feudalism and laid solid foundations for a modern secular democracy.

India was also among the first countries to include legislation aimed at affirmative action to combat the lasting influence of past social inequalities. The 'reservations' and other priorities for scheduled castes (formerly, the 'untouchables') and scheduled tribes expanded the horizon of legal support for social equity, no matter how we judge the exact achievements and failures of this very early departure. Affirmative action would not become a serious possibility in the United States for many years after the Indian constitution (which had many affirmative provisions) came into effect in 1950.

What is more, India's democratic institutions have—on the whole—stood the test of time and popular support. In the early stages of Indian independence, there was widespread scepticism about the ability of democratic institutions to survive, let alone flourish, in a poverty-stricken and inequality-ridden country.[3] There was also much pessimism about the potential for democracy in the 'third world' as a whole. In both respects, the outlook is much brighter today. India's democratic institutions have proved quite robust (even surviving major challenges such as the imposition of 'emergency' in 1975–7, which was reversed by a popular electoral vote), and enjoy wide legitimacy among most sections of the population.[4] The healthy survival of Indian democracy has also given a major boost to the spread of democracy elsewhere in the world.

Furthermore, the institutional basis of democracy in India has retained some dynamism, particularly reflected in the fact that emendations and extensions have been instituted with some regularity. Since the constitution came into effect in 1950, various constitutional amendments have further enlarged the scope of democratic freedoms. For instance, the 73rd and 74th constitutional amendments (the 'panchayati raj' amendments), which came into effect in 1993, have consolidated the foundations for local democracy.

Much, of course, remains to be done, and there is scope for further institutional democratization in the future. The right to information, for instance, remains severely restricted, and greater accessibility of official records is a needed step for fuller public accountability. Similarly, provisions

---

[3] Even today, there is some perplexity about Indian democracy among political scientists, as can be seen for instance from recent writings on the 'paradoxes' and 'puzzles' associated with the survival of democracy in India; see e.g. Dahl (1989), Weiner (1989), Lijphart (1996), Varshney (1998), Blomkvist (2000b).

[4] On the latter point, see Yadav and Singh (1997) and Pushpendra (1999).

for a better political representation of women are needed to address today's blatant male domination of many democratic institutions, from parliament to panchayat.[5] There is also much scope for more equitable electoral rules, better safeguards against human rights violations, more decentralized governance, and so on.

The *main* limitations of Indian democracy do not, however, relate so much to democratic institutions as to democratic practice. The performance of democratic institutions is contingent on a wide range of social conditions, from educational levels and political traditions to the nature of social inequalities and popular organizations. In many cases, democratic practice in India has been deeply compromised by a variety of social limitations inherited from the past. To illustrate, consider one of the most basic democratic freedoms—the right to vote. India has an impressive electoral system (monitored by an independent Election Commission), which has proved its credibility and resilience on numerous occasions since independence. Voter turnouts in India are also quite respectable by international standards, especially among underprivileged groups.[6] However, the right to vote is not a momentous freedom when voters are so poorly informed that they are unable to distinguish between different political parties, as is still the case in some areas today.[7] Similarly, while Indian elections are formally 'free and fair' in most cases, their effective fairness has been compromised by nepotism, the criminalization of politics, and pervasive inequalities in electoral opportunities as a result of disparities in economic wealth and social privileges.

Another example concerns the legal system. An impartial and efficient judiciary is indispensable for genuine democracy. India's legal system has sound institutional foundations, which incorporate basic democratic

---

[5] How this is best brought about is a subject of active debate at this time in India. See e.g. Kishwar (1996) and Omvedt (2000); also N. Menon(2000) and earlier contributions cited there.

[6] The average voter turnout for nation-wide parliamentary elections in the 1945–97 period was about 60 per cent. This is around the world average for democratic countries with non-compulsory voting, which are mostly much richer than India (see International Institute for Democracy and Electoral Assistance, 1997). For related information, see also Statistical Appendix, Table A.3, Part 10.

[7] See e.g. Bhatia (2000). The author describes the predicament of Dalit women during the 1995 Assembly elections in central Bihar as follows (p. 120): 'Most of the women I interviewed had never voted before, nor did they understand the meaning or significance of *chunav* (elections), vote or parties. While some of them were able to recognize some party symbols, they were often unable to relate the symbol to the party, and none of them could relate it to a particular candidate or programme.'

principles such as impartiality, secularism and equality before the law. In practice, however, its functioning is, in many ways, at variance with democratic ideals. For one thing, the legal system is virtually paralysed by a backlog of millions of 'pending cases'—about 30 million according to one estimate.[8] Legal proceedings can take years (if not decades) to be completed, and are often far from intelligible for the average citizen. For this and other reasons, legal protection tends to remain beyond the effective reach of most, especially the poor. In fact, the legal system can also be used as an instrument of harassment (rather than as an efficient means of dispensing justice).[9] Those at the receiving end of the system can end up suffering terrible injustice. For instance, undertrial prisoners (there are some 250,000 of them in India at this time, according to the Home Ministry) often languish in prison for years without any legal recourse.

Similar points can be made about many other components of the democratic institutional structure.[10] The Indian press has much to offer in terms of quality and pluralism, but with less than 10 per cent of all households subscribing to a daily newspaper (see Statistical Appendix), its contribution to political awareness and public debate remains much below potential. In some states, the legislatures are packed with criminals.[11] Village panchayats are often controlled by the local elite. There are many other failures of democratic practice.

On the positive side, it can indeed be said that there is enormous scope for improving the quality of democracy in India through better democratic practice (and also, to some extent, through expanding democratic institutions). Indeed, democratic practice constantly evolves, as new constituencies are mobilized, new issues come under public scrutiny,

---

[8] Debroy (2000), p. 201. The author adds: 'On an average, it takes twenty years for a dispute to be resolved, unless real estate or land is involved, in which case it takes longer. The Thorat case in Pune took 761 years to be settled, it was started in 1205 and ended in 1966. If present rates of disposal continue and there are absolutely no new cases, it will take 324 years for us to clear the present backlog. The conviction rate is only around 6 per cent.'

[9] For a telling account of what happens when 'a Dalit goes to court', see Sainath (1999). As one Dalit told the author, 'all vakils [lawyers] are dangerous'.

[10] For diverse assessments of the nature, achievements and limitations of Indian democracy, see Committee of Concerned Citizens (1998), Jayal (1999a), Blomkvist (2000a), Frankel et al. (2000), Heller (2000a), Varshney (2000), and the earlier literature cited in these studies.

[11] In Uttar Pradesh, for instance, almost half of the 425 Members of Legislative Assembly (MLAs) were known to have a criminal record in 1994 (T.N. Seshan, Chief Election Commissioner, quoted in Hindustan Times, 16 October 1994).

and new organizational skills are developed. To illustrate, until recently corruption was not much of a political issue in India. It was accepted as a familiar feature of public life, about which little could be done. In the 1990s, however, corruption became a matter of widespread concern and discussion after a wave of high-profile scams were exposed. Innovative campaigns for public accountability and the right to information sprung up in various parts of the country (Rajasthan, Maharashtra, Kerala, Madhya Pradesh, Orissa, among others), and have gradually developed into a major social movement.

This has not, of course, led to an automatic eradication of corruption (far from it), but the issue is at least on the political agenda and there is much scope for securing practical results through harnessing this process. These campaigns, with their innovative focus and techniques (from public hearing to social audit), also signal a transformation of political culture, with much potential in other contexts as well. These developments would have seemed quite unlikely even ten years ago. The nineties have witnessed many other political developments of a similar nature, from pioneering experiments with decentralized planning in Kerala to the growing participation of women in local politics across the country.

As the recent developments show, in various ways, the reach of democratic practice can be radically enhanced in India. But the first step is to see the need for democratic practice as a distinct issue from the existence of democratic institutions. The sense of satisfaction at securing democratic institutions—justified within its context—must not be an excuse for failing to pursue vigorously the strengthening of democratic practice. The great accomplishments in the former do not obviate the need for vigilant pursuit of the latter. There is much scope for making institutionally democratic India more effectively democratic.

10.2. INEQUALITY AND EMPOWERMENT

It is useful to distinguish between different causes of the limitation of democratic practice. Given the democratic institutions, the practice of democracy may be limited for at least three distinct reasons. First, democratic institutions may become dysfunctional due to, say, inefficiency or corruption. Examples include electoral fraud and the paralysis of the legal system through case overload. Second, there may be inadequate use of functional democratic institutions on the part of the concerned persons or groups, often due to limited understanding or skill, and sometimes even limited motivation, given the tradition of unquestioning acceptance. Low electoral participation, and the powerlessness of the public in the face of complex legal proceedings, are some illustrations, among many others.

We have already commented briefly on these two deficiencies. We have also touched on the third reason for the failure of democratic practice, viz. the reach and power of antecedent social inequalities, but we must discuss it more. Democratic practice may indeed be thoroughly undermined by social inequalities, even when democratic institutions are all in place. For instance, even if elections are technically free and fair, their effective fairness may be compromised by the role of money and influence in the electoral process. This also applies to the legal system, which is often far from impartial between different classes (even in the absence of any corruption), if only because richer people can afford better lawyers.

At the risk of some over-simplification, the foundations of democratic practice may, thus, be described as *facility* (functional democratic institutions), *involvement* (informed public engagement with these institutions), and *equity* (a fair distribution of power). The central relevance of equity arises from the fact that a fair distribution of power is a basic—indeed fundamental—requirement of democracy. A government 'by the people' must ultimately include all the people in a symmetric way, and this is essential also to enable the government to become 'of the people and for the people'. This is not, of course, a question of the 'yes or no' type. In most societies, it is the case that a person's ability to use electoral rights, to obtain legal protection, to express oneself in public, and to take advantage of democratic institutions in general tends to vary with class, education, gender and related characteristics. In striving for democratic ideals, reducing the asymmetries of power associated with these social inequalities is one of the central challenges of democratic practice in every institutionally democratic country in the world. That challenge is particularly exacting in India, given its historical economic and social inequalities.

It is, however, important to see the reach of inequality in adequately broad terms. The relevant inequalities can be of very different types. In economic analysis, the lion's share of attention tends to go to the inequality of individual income levels. This is indeed an important part of economic inequality. However, economic inequality is a more inclusive—far larger—concept than mere income inequality, and inequality in the fuller sense goes even beyond economic inequality, no matter how broadly the latter may be defined. There are many economic determinants, other than income, of well-being, freedom and power, and there are social factors—distinct from purely economic ones—that influence inequality between persons and groups.[12]

[12] These distinctions have been discussed further in Sen (1992a). Also important in some contexts is the question of how different types of inequality relate to each other, e.g. how gender or class inequalities interact with the caste hierarchy. For instance,

There has been much discussion in recent years on the discrepancy between measures of income inequality and a broader understanding of the multidimensional nature of economic and social inequality.[13] The contrast can be illustrated through inter-regional comparisons of social inequality in India. For example, the Gini coefficient of the distribution of per-capita expenditures indicates that there is *more* inequality in Kerala than in, say, Bihar or Uttar Pradesh. In fact, Kerala turns out to be one of the most unequal states in this respect, while Bihar is one of the least unequal.[14] The figures may well be correct as far as they go (though many conceptual and practical difficulties arise in the computation of these coefficients). But if we were to rely on them for an overall assessment of social disparities in different states, we would be deeply misled. The broader picture of social and economic inequality must also note, inter alia, the fact that Kerala has (1) comparatively low levels of basic gender inequality (reflected, for instance, in a high female-male ratio), (2) relatively equitable educational opportunities (indeed near-universal literacy, especially among the young), (3) extensive social security arrangements (e.g. broad-based entitlements to homestead land, old-age pensions and the public distribution system), (4) limited incidence of caste oppression (e.g. few violent crimes against scheduled castes), and (5) low rural-urban disparities.[15] In all these respects, Kerala does radically better than Bihar and Uttar Pradesh, which are ridden with inequalities between women and men, between child labourers and school-going children, between low castes and high castes, and so on. And yet these states do better than Kerala in terms of indicators of income inequality seen as a factor on its own. The same point would apply in a comparison with Himachal Pradesh, where (as we saw in chapter 3) social disparities are comparatively limited in many important respects, and yet the Gini coefficient of per-capita expenditure is not particularly low. As these examples illustrate, there is much need for a broad understanding of economic and social inequality.

These distinctions are particularly important in understanding the

in understanding the historical roots of social oppression in north India, it is important to note the particularly powerful way in which caste and class inequalities have tended to reinforce each other in that region; on this see Drèze and Gazdar (1996).

[13] See e.g. Sen (1992a, 1997, 2000a), and the literature cited there.

[14] See Statistical Appendix, Table A.3, Part 1. Note that the available Gini coefficients are sector-specific (i.e. rural or urban); rural-urban disparities, for their part, are comparatively low in Kerala.

[15] Relevant indicators are presented in the Statistical Appendix, Table A.3. On violent crimes against scheduled castes, see Government of India (1999c), chapter 7.

nature of inequality and also the problems of democratic practice in India. Indeed, indicators of income inequality, seen on their own, can be a very deceptive basis for grasping the far-reaching consequences of inequality on Indian lives and democratic practice. They can also hide the diverse ways in which greater equity can be pursued through state policy and public action.

Consider, for instance, the pattern of inequality in Indian society during the last forty years or so. Judging from standard indices of income distribution, there has been little change. The Gini coefficient of per-capita expenditure, for instance, has remained fairly close to 0.30 in rural areas and 0.35 in urban areas throughout that period.[16] This is, however, deceptive as a guide to inequality for two distinct reasons.

First, it overlooks the new developments of inequality that have added to the burden of the older, pre-existing ones. For example, the hold of the newly prosperous and socially influential middle classes escapes notice in the constancy of the Gini coefficient of income distribution. Through dominance over the media, political pressure groups and even instruments of knowledge, this flourishing, vocal and (in absolute numbers) fairly large class enjoys new powers that very few groups could have had in the past, in using the levers of democratic politics. The world has been changing, even if the Gini has not.

Second, the remarkable stickiness of the measures of income inequality over a long period suggests a kind of inescapable immutability of inequality which hides the possibility of change and progress through public policy and social action. Indeed, the stationarity of income inequality is often invoked to argue that attempts to achieve greater equality are likely to be futile, and that economic growth (increasing the size of the pie, rather than altering the shares) is the only effective way of raising living standards. But neither the pessimism about altering inequality, nor the faith in economic growth as the only effective means of improving the lot of the deprived, is entailed by the empirical picture of income distribution.

Indeed, even in terms of India's actual experience, the constancy of income inequality indicators during the post-independence period has gone hand in hand with some fairly major changes—often with much

---

[16] See Datt (1999a, 1999b); also Statistical Appendix, Table A.6. As mentioned in the preceding chapter, there is some evidence of a departure from this pattern in the 1990s, in the form of rising economic inequality; on this see also Ravallion (2000b).

positive achievement—in other kinds of economic and social disparities. For instance, upper-caste dominance in the rural economy and society has been decisively challenged with the abolition of zamindari, the introduction of adult franchise, economic progress among the cultivating castes, and various political movements. Correspondingly, there has been a major rise in the economic and political power of the so-called 'backward castes' (and, to a lesser extent, of scheduled castes).[17] Similarly, the slow but steady march towards universal elementary education has eroded one of the crucial bases of social stratification in India, namely the exclusion of disadvantaged classes and castes from the schooling system. Even in terms of gender relations (perhaps one of the more resilient domains of social inequality in India), there have been some major developments in recent years, involving for instance the emergence of a female advantage in life expectancy (overturning a long history of superior male longevity), a radical diminution of oppressive practices such as child marriage, and growing participation of women in local politics.[18] Other ongoing changes, such as the steady decline of fertility, the accelerated increase in female literacy, and new constitutional provisions for the political representation of women, are likely to facilitate further progress towards more equal gender relations.

No less eminent a sociologist as M.N. Srinivas has even suggested that we are 'living in a revolution' (Srinivas, 1992). Even if we do not accept such optimism about the recent changes (there are fields of stationarity as well as transformation), the last fifty years have certainly been a time of significant change in India's social structure. There is nothing in the record of India's last half a century that would vindicate the thesis of the futility of changing the hold of antecedent economic and social inequalities in India.[19] The rejection of social fatalism and the cynicism that it generates can be extremely important for motivating attempts to work against pre-existing inequalities and for the enhancement of democratic practice.

One crucial implication of this broader perspective on economic and

[17] See Drèze (1997) and Jayaraman and Lanjouw (1999), and the literature cited there.

[18] There have also been some adverse trends, such as the spread of the practice of dowry, which tends to cause daughters to be seen as an economic burden, and also, in the 1990s, the spread of sex-selective abortion (see chapter 7). Here as with other aspects of social inequality, the possibility of negative as well as positive change has to be borne in mind.

[19] On 'futility' arguments as an aspect of the 'rhetoric of reaction', see Hirschman (1991).

social inequality is that it points to many different ways of countering inequalities in Indian society. The reduction of income inequality is a difficult challenge in India as elsewhere, partly due to incentive problems (e.g. the possible need for a link between productivity and reward), and partly because of the resistance of privileged classes. But there is no corresponding reason to tolerate widespread gender discrimination, the continued oppression of disadvantaged castes, the persistent divide between the literates and the non-literates, and other destructive economic and social inequalities. Indeed, the dilemmas that arise in reducing economic inequality (in particular, possible conflicts between efficiency and equity) often have little force in addressing these inequalities. In fact, in many circumstances, distributional concerns are highly *congruent* with other social objectives, including economic efficiency.[20] Reduced gender discrimination, for instance, expands the scope of women's agency, which (as discussed in chapter 7) is an important factor of social change and economic success. Similarly, the universalization of elementary education in India would not only reduce educational disparities (and other social inequalities associated with these disparities) but also contribute to a wide range of other economic and social objectives, given the diverse personal and social roles of education (discussed in chapter 2).

Achieving greater equity in Indian society depends crucially on political action and the practice of democracy. Indeed, a reduction of inequality both contributes to democratic practice and is strengthened by successful practice of democratic freedoms. There is, in fact, a 'virtuous circle' here the nature of which has to be more adequately reflected in policy analysis and social action in India. There have been, as was noted earlier, significant gains in that respect during the last fifty years, and while reductions of inequality have strengthened the reach of democratic practice, they have often been achieved through determined use of the democratic opportunities that were already available. Indeed, the achievements discussed earlier were often the result, at least in part, of democratic political action.

In some cases, these achievements have been facilitated by economic change. For instance, the rise of the 'backward castes' has something to

---

[20] Even in the case of income inequality, there is an important area of congruence between equity and efficiency concerns. For instance, while income redistribution may well raise incentive problems in many cases, asset redistribution (e.g. land reform) is often conducive not only to equity but also to efficiency. On these issues, see Bardhan, Bowles and Gintis (2000), and the literature cited there; also Sen (1992a).

do with their growing economic prosperity, linked inter alia with the 'green revolution' (and, before that, the abolition of zamindari).[21] But even here, political action has played an important role, for instance through farmers' movements as well as direct political participation.

In other cases, political action has succeeded in empowering disadvantaged social groups even in the absence of any significant economic improvement (sometimes even in the face of growing impoverishment). Not so long ago, for instance, tribal communities were routinely displaced by dams and other large projects without any compensation. The situation has radically changed over time, as displaced tribal communities learnt to organize against forced displacement (even though they have not invariably succeeded in changing public policy). Today, this movement is among the most politically active and best organized in India, and is also a source of much inspiration elsewhere in the world. Whatever position one may take on the projects in question, the force of this movement cannot leave any impartial observer without a major recognition of the power and vigour of organized popular resistance.

10.3. DECENTRALIZATION AND LOCAL DEMOCRACY

The interconnections between democratic practice and social equity have a strong bearing on recent initiatives to promote local democracy in India. These initiatives have taken place in the framework of the 73rd and 74th constitutional amendments (the 'Panchayati Raj' amendments), which require all the state governments to introduce certain legislative measures geared to the revitalization of local representative institutions. These measures include mandatory elections at regular intervals, reservation of seats in village panchayats for women and members of scheduled castes or tribes, and substantial devolution of government responsibilities to local authorities. The panchayati raj amendments, which took effect in 1993, have led to a range of interesting initiatives in different parts of the country, undertaken not only by state governments but also by political parties, NGOs, grassroots organizations, women's groups, and other activist formations. There is a great deal to learn from recent developments associated with these initiatives.

Achieving greater democracy at the local level must be a crucial component of the broader task of transforming the practice and quality

---

[21] In some cases, economic empowerment has also contributed to the emancipation of the 'scheduled castes'; see e.g. Sudha Pai's (2001) analysis of the economic antecedents of 'Dalit assertion' in Uttar Pradesh.

of democracy in India. Indeed, local democracy represents one means of participation in the larger democratic system, which is relatively accessible to the disadvantaged, and can be potentially a stepping stone towards other forms of democratic participation. Local democracy can also directly be an important force towards social change. In particular, it has much to contribute to social equity, and can help to transform the relation, at the local level, between employers and employees, between men and women, between high-caste and low-caste people, and so on.

Local democracy is also essential as a basis of public accountability, particularly in the context of the need for effective and equitable management of local public services. These services—from schools and health centres to fair price shops and drinking-water facilities—are often crucial for the quality of life. Their effective functioning, however, depends a great deal on the responsiveness of the concerned authorities to popular demands. To illustrate, it is difficult to see how the endemic problem of teacher absenteeism in rural India can be successfully tackled without involving the proximate and informed agency of village communities in general and parental groups in particular. As things stand, there is no mechanism to ensure any kind of accountability of village teachers to the local community or to the parents in large parts of India, and this is an important factor in the persistence of endemic dereliction of duty.

The importance of local democracy is not confined, of course, to these and other instrumental roles of participatory politics. Participation can also be seen to have intrinsic value for the quality of life. Indeed, being able to do something through political action—for oneself and for others— is one of the elementary freedoms that people have reason to value. The popular appeal of many social movements in India confirms that this basic capability is highly valued even among people who lead very deprived lives in material terms.[22]

Local democracy is sometimes treated as synonymous with 'decentralization', but the two are in fact quite distinct. In particular, decentralization is not necessarily conducive to local democracy. In fact, in situations of sharp local inequalities, decentralization sometimes heightens the concentration of power, and discourages rather than fosters participation among the underprivileged. To illustrate, in some tribal areas where upper-caste landlords and traders dominate village affairs, the devolution of

---

[22] One reason for this is that political action contributes to dignity and self-respect. Many field studies indicate that these sentiments are highly valued by the underprivileged; see e.g. Jodha (1988), Roy (1993), Beck (1994), Mukherjee (1992), Chen and Drèze (1995), Ramachandran (1999), Bhatia (2000).

power associated with the panchayati raj amendments has consolidated their hold and reinforced existing biases in the local power structure.[23]

Similarly, top-down decentralization sometimes undermines local democracy by destabilizing traditional institutions of governance and fostering corruption. An interesting example comes from a recent case study of two villages of Uttarakhand, the hill region of Uttar Pradesh (now Uttaranchal, a separate state), discussed by Niraja Jayal (1999b). The study villages earlier had fairly democratic traditional institutions of local governance, based among other things on consensus decision-making and egalitarian contributions to village funds. Then came state-sponsored panchayat elections and 'decentralized' development programmes, one effect of which was the integration of these villages into a wider system of prevailing corruption, in which these programmes are embedded. This process undermined local democracy and also created sharp social divisions in the villages studied.

Recognition of these dangers should not be seen as an overall indictment of decentralization. There is undoubtedly much need for decentralized governance in India, especially in relation to the management of local public services, where responsiveness to local conditions is paramount. But we must also recognize that the effects of decentralization are highly context-dependent and circumstance-specific, and that its success depends on decentralization being integrated with other aspects of local democracy. A similar observation applies to the panchayati raj amendments. These amendments, like other democratic institutions, have provided a great opportunity to expand the scope of democracy in Indian society, but their practical results have varied a great deal depending on the extent to which institutional reform has been combined with other types of public action.

Recent studies of the developments associated with the panchayati raj amendments in different parts of the country throw much light on these and related issues.[24] It is, first and foremost, very encouraging to find plentiful evidence of active engagement with the new possibilities

___

[23] See e.g. Shah et al. (1998). The recent Panchayati Raj (Extension to Scheduled Areas) Act, which combines further devolution of power with provisions for the empowerment of tribal communities, was introduced partly to address this problem.
[24] A wealth of field-based studies are available; see Omvedt (1990), Lieten (1996a, 1996b), Mathew and Nayak (1996), Mayaram and Pal (1996), Bhatia and Drèze (1998), Crook and Manor (1998), Pai (1998, 2001), Pal (1998), Raj and Mathias (1998), Institute of Social Sciences (1999), Lieten and Srivastava (1999), Mohanty (1999), Vyasulu and Vyasulu (1999), Ghatak and Ghatak (2000), P. Menon (2000), Gaiha and Kulkarni (2001), Mander (2001), Sinha (2001), Mullen (forthcoming), among many others; also the monthly *Panchayati Raj Update* published by the Institute of Social Sciences (New Delhi), and the periodical *Grassroots*.

of local democracy on the part of the Indian public. By all accounts, panchayat elections elicit keen public interest. Voter turnout rates have been high in most states (even higher than in parliamentary or assembly elections), including among underprivileged groups. This is a sea change from the days when members of the lower castes were prevented from voting, or when women were not expected to cast an independent vote. Beyond electoral participation, public interest and involvement in local governance have surged during the last few years, even in areas where apathy used to be widespread.

However, the experience so far confirms that the results of state initiatives to promote local democracy are highly contingent on the social context. Indeed, the reforms associated with the panchayati raj amendments have followed very different courses in different states. At one extreme, Bihar has barely reached the stage of organizing panchayat elections. Kerala, on the other hand, has gone far beyond the constitutional requirements and initiated a visionary campaign of 'decentralized planning' through panchayati raj institutions.[25] Even among states that have followed a similar course in terms of legislative reform, the practical results have varied a great deal depending on the extent of social preparedness in terms of educational levels, political mobilization and social equity. The issue of social preparedness has emerged quite clearly in states like Madhya Pradesh, where (unlike Bihar) the state has been constructively active in legislative reforms (indeed Madhya Pradesh was the first state to implement the panchayati raj amendments), yet the practical results have been held back by the antecedent social inequalities, educational backwardness and other barriers inherited from the past.[26]

The panchayati raj experience highlights the importance of social equity for local democracy, and also the interactive relationship between the two. This can be seen particularly clearly in connection with the issue of political representation of women and disadvantaged castes at the panchayat level. The 73rd amendment stipulates that one third of all panchayat seats are 'reserved' for women, with a similar (overlapping) provision for scheduled castes and tribes.[27] In north India, where caste

[25] On this see e.g. Isaac and Harilal (1997), Powis (1999), Heller (2000b). West Bengal has also been active, for a long time, in making constructive use of local democracy to raise the political profile of the underprivileged, and to carry out economic and social reforms, including land redistribution. For different perspectives on West Bengal's experience, see Kohli (1987), Lieten (1996a), Sengupta and Gazdar (1996), Ghatak and Ghatak (2000), Mullen (forthcoming), among others.

[26] For insightful case studies of the subversion of local democracy by dominant classes and castes in Madhya Pradesh, see Mathew and Nayak (1996).

[27] As mentioned earlier, separate legislation was introduced later for the 'scheduled

and gender inequalities are particularly resilient, the local elites have tended to adapt to this requirement by putting up 'proxy' candidates from the required group, and continuing to wield power through them.[28] The submissive female sarpanch, sitting quietly in a corner while her husband (often initially mistaken for the sarpanch) answers the researcher's questions, is a familiar figure in the critical literature on panchayati raj in north India. In south and western India, the overall picture is quite different in this respect, with greater success in terms of independent political representation of women and scheduled castes. It must, however, be noted that even in north India, there is considerable evidence that the prevailing patterns of social discrimination and political marginalization are far from immutable. Local politics, and the different forms of political mobilization and social activism associated with panchayati raj (for example, training programmes for female candidates and political assertion of the scheduled castes), have provided new avenues through which traditional inequalities can be challenged. The fact that these challenges have often been met with violent repression (including even cases of rape of assertive female sarpanchs) is both a telling reminder of the survival of extreme inequality and oppression in Indian society, and an indication that the politics of panchayati raj are perceived as a serious threat by dominant groups. Over time, the forces of repression seem to be losing some ground, with good prospects of further advance in the direction of both greater social equity and more vibrant local democracy in the near future.[29]

These developments illustrate a crucial feature of local democracy—indeed of democracy in general—namely that it involves a certain amount of 'learning by doing'.[30] Other aspects of this process include the influence of role models (for example, of a successful female sarpanch), the spread of various skills involved in local governance (e.g., the ability to hold orderly meetings or to deal with the state bureaucracy), the evolution

---

areas', with further provisions for the representation and empowerment of disadvantaged groups (especially the 'scheduled tribes').

[28] For a striking case study of this process, see Mander (2001), pp. 137–48. For other examples, see Lieten (1996b), Mathew and Nayak (1996), Drèze and Sharma (1998), Pai (1998), Weaver (2000), among others.

[29] The use of 'proxy candidates', for one, seems to be declining with each panchayat election, and today there are even cases of members of 'reserved' categories contesting non-reserved seats (see e.g. Mishra, 1998, and P. Menon, 2000). The formation of all-women panchayats, initially in Maharashtra (Omvedt, 1990, Gala, 1997), and more recently in several other states (Mishra, 1998, Vyasulu and Vyasulu, 1999), is another interesting example of transformation of village politics based on effective use of the possibilities of local democracy.

[30] On this point, see particularly Mullen (forthcoming); also Mayaram and Pal (1996), especially with reference to the participation of women in panchayat institutions.

of a culture of political participation, the creation of new forms of social mobilization, and even changes in public perceptions of the need for as well as scope for foundational change.[31] Given the dynamism of learning by doing, it is important to resist the pessimism arising from observing particular limitations in the current practice of local democracy. The constructive possibilities over time have to be recognized.

The practice of local democracy is also a form of wider political education. In the context of village politics, people are learning (if only at a varying speed) to organize, to question established patterns of authority, to demand their rights, to resist corruption, and so on. This learning process enhances their preparedness not only for local democracy alone, but also for political participation in general.

In the light of these learning possibilities, the first wave of social change associated with the panchayati raj amendments warrants cautious optimism about the potential for local democracy in India. There are, of course, also matters of concern. These include the frequent derailing of local democracy by social inequality, the limited participation of the public in local governance on a day-to-day basis, the dormant condition of 'gram sabhas' (village assemblies) in many states, the lack of significant devolution of powers in many fields, and—last but not least—the widespread embezzlement of public resources associated with local development programmes under panchayat auspices. Nevertheless, there are clear signs of a sustained expansion of democratic space at the local level, and also of local politics being an important arena of positive social change. The limitations are best addressed through democratic practice itself, and as far as the potential for the latter is concerned, there is much ground for hope.

10.4. Transparency and Corruption

One of the major challenges that democratic practice has to face in India is to eradicate corruption in different fields of civic administration and public life. Among its many terrible consequences, rampant corruption erodes and undermines democratic institutions. And yet democracy itself can be seen as a possible means to fight corruption that can be—and must be—used more effectively. Democratic ideals include the need for transparency and accountability, which are ultimately the principal methods

---

[31] To illustrate, until recently it was extremely rare for an elected sarpanch to be 'recalled' by the local public on grounds of corruption or poor performance, but this practice (which contributes to greater accountability) appears to be increasingly common in many states. For many examples, see the Institute of Social Sciences's monthly *Panchayati Raj Update*.

of restraining and dislodging corrupt practices. There is, thus, a two-way relationship between the practice of democracy and the eradication of corruption. The former can help the latter, but the latter, in its turn, can be of great value in extending the force and effectiveness of the former.

What, we may ask, is so wrong with corruption? There are several reasons for concern, aside from the purely moral criticisms that can be directed at corrupt behaviour, particularly in deontological ethics. First, the efficiency costs of corruption can indeed be very high. In particular, corruption generates additional transaction costs that increase the expensiveness of exchange and production, and also the distortionary effects associated with rent-seeking activities.[32] An Indian readership may not have to be reminded that the need for bribery and oiling many palms can add very substantially to the costs of commerce. The fact that rent-seeking activities can also draw investment and entrepreneurship away from more productive activities into the immediacy of corrupt profits is also quite well-known in India, as it is elsewhere.[33]

Second, corruption can have deeply adverse effects on equity. When citizens have to 'buy' their way through government offices, public hospitals, booking offices, recruitment centres, and police stations, the ones who have the gold tend to rule, no matter how intensely these services may be needed by the less affluent. The power of bribery is the *reductio ad absurdum* of respecting the 'willingness to pay' (a rather overrated signifier of quality in the literature on cost-benefit analysis).[34]

Third, corruption is, as we noted earlier, a major threat to democracy. Indeed, democratic institutions cannot perform their role adequately if the actions of political leaders, civil servants, police officers, judges and others can be mobilized in defence of private and special interests through

[32] The efficiency costs can sometimes be so high as to destroy the fabric of economic activity and exchange. For some interesting historical examples, and further discussion, see Stanislav Andreski's essay on 'the parasitic involution of capitalism' in Andreski (1964). For an insightful survey of the economics of corruption, see Bardhan (1997a).

[33] Corruption can also disable transparency in business matters, and lead firms to take undue risks and make dubious investments of a kind that make them deeply vulnerable, especially from the point of view of workers or shareholders (even when the management does well enough from these opaque decisions). The 'Asian economic crisis' of 1997–8 provides plentiful illustrations of this point. Lack of transparency generates fragility, which may not be adequately noticed until the fragile actually breaks, as it did with remarkable fury in many Asian economies that had a reputation of robustness. On this, see Sen (1999a).

[34] For a critique of traditional methods of cost-benefit analysis, see Sen (2000b); also Drèze (1998c).

illegal inducements. The effect of corruption on ethical codes and social norms also tends to be antithetical to democratic values.

In India, the adverse effects of corruption on democracy have come into sharp focus in recent years in connection with issues of local governance and village politics. While there have been promising steps towards local democracy in the nineties (as discussed in the preceding section), one of the major barriers against further progress has been the prevalence of widespread corruption, particularly related to development programmes and electoral processes. To illustrate, consider the issue of panchayat elections. In most states, the main responsibility of a 'sarpanch' (village head) is to oversee various development programmes, such as the Jawahar Rozgar Yojana (local public works) and the Indira Awas Yojana (a subsidized housing scheme). Attached to these schemes, in many cases, is an organized system of loot of public resources, which requires the sarpanch to 'redistribute' some of the development funds to various officials, varying from the 'gram sevak' to the Junior Engineer, Block Development Officer, and others at different steps of the ladder. Often the shares are pre-specified.[35] The sarpanch himself or herself, of course, tends to be one of the principal beneficiaries. The post of village head can be, under these circumstances, highly lucrative. This is one reason why large sums of money are spent in panchayat election campaigns. Where these patterns apply, local electoral politics are thus integrally linked with various development rackets, and can even generate what might be called 'competitive corruption'.

This nexus undermines local democracy in several ways. First, it raises the up-front cost of election campaigns, making it much harder for poor candidates to participate. Second, this situation can make it very difficult for an honest person motivated by social concerns to contest panchayat elections. Indeed, unlike candidates geared to corruption, an aspiring candidate who wants to forgo the opportunity of replenishing his or her coffers after a successful election is financially at a disadvantage in the electoral competition. In addition, honest candidates often face the prospect

---

[35] See e.g. Jayal (1999b), who reports that in Uttar Pradesh 'the percentages due to various officials and elected representatives are fixed ... the commission amounts are openly announced in the panchayat meetings, and rarely provoke any protest' (p. 25). Even the simple virtue of honesty has come to acquire unsuspected sophistication in being redefined for a world that takes corruption to be the normal state of affairs. One private contractor in Orissa, upon being asked what would happen if the local BDO were honest, exclaimed 'if he is honest, he will stick to his prescribed share' (Drèze, 2000b).

of official harassment for refusing to cooperate with the system of corruption. Third, the task of plundering public resources, distributing commissions and avoiding scrutiny distracts the panchayats from their primary purpose of working for the public good in the area under their jurisdiction. A sarpanch, for example, often has far more to gain from awarding Indira Awas Yojana subsidies to the highest bidders than from responding to the social need for an electricity connection for the village, or from organizing a school enrolment drive.

The 'systemic' nature of the corrupt practices associated with local development is one reason why they are difficult to eradicate: even if one individual culprit is caught and punished, another tends to step into his or her shoes. Another obstacle arises from the fact that the embezzlers (e.g. the sarpanch and private contractor who collude to build a school at half the official cost and pocket the difference) tend to gain at the expense of the public at large. It has been argued, not without reason, that in such situations (known in the economic literature by the somewhat puzzling name of 'corruption with theft') corruption may be particularly hard to eradicate.[36] Indeed, since the losing group consists of a diffuse and typically unorganized collectivity, the losers may find it difficult to take joint action with adequate effectiveness. Vigilance may, of course, be entrusted to a public agency, on the basis of crosschecks, inspections, audits, and so on. However, that supervising agency may often have little incentive to dig deep, which can be bothersome and even dangerous, given the power of the private gainers, compared with the often-inert mass of public losers.

But this is exactly where the remedial use of democracy can be important. The losers may be inactive and hard to mobilize, but once mobilized, the

---

[36] See Shleifer and Vishny (1993), where corruption with theft is contrasted with other situations ('corruption without theft') where one person gains at the expense of some other private individual, as when a railway employee over-charges a passenger for a ticket. In such cases, the loser (e.g. the fleeced passenger) has an incentive to blow the whistle, and sometimes this feature can be used to discourage corruption. To illustrate, it is a remarkable fact that train stations in India still have different queues for different destinations (as opposed to a single queue leading to multiple windows, each serving all destinations). Aside from causing much inconvenience for travellers (because multiple queues raise the variance of waiting time), this queuing system facilitates corruption, since the traveller is a sitting duck for a corrupt employee with a monopoly of the tickets for a particular destination. In a single-queue system, by contrast, travellers who are asked for an extra-legal payment can decline and move to the next counter. This an example of a simple measure that could help to reduce this type of corruption. A long conversation with the station master at Delhi railway station uncovers no specific reason for persisting with multiple queues. 'This is the way it has always been', we were told.

weight of numbers as well as the force of public opinion and open criticism can be quite effective. The practical possibility of such mobilization has been demonstrated in many actual cases. A good illustration comes from the work of such organizations as Mazdoor Kisan Shakti Sangathan (MKSS) in Rajasthan.[37] The movement began in 1987 by organizing underpaid labourers working on drought relief programmes (who can be seen as victims of 'corruption without theft', and were to that extent comparatively easy to mobilize). Following this early success, MKSS started mobilizing village communities against the private appropriation of local development funds (corruption with theft), using means such as public hearings and social audits. The organization has considerable popular support and has achieved some striking successes, involving for instance the restitution of embezzled funds. Over time, it has inspired many similar initiatives elsewhere, from a campaign to expose corruption in the public distribution system in Surguja (Madhya Pradesh) to recent protests against police harassment of rickshaw-pullers and hawkers in Indian cities. A nation-wide 'campaign for the people's right to information', which includes lobbying for adequate legislative reform in this field, has also emerged from these initiatives.

The significance of such movements goes well beyond specific victories such as the restitution of embezzled funds in a particular village, or the introduction of new legislation in a specific state. The demonstration effects can have a much wider reach. Even in areas where no such organizations existed earlier, public initiatives to expose corruption have begun to spread in recent years, with significant results. It has been noted, for instance, that drought relief programmes in Rajasthan in 2000–1 have been remarkably 'corruption-free' (at least in comparison with the situation that prevailed in earlier droughts), largely due to greater public vigilance as well as to the improved accessibility of official records—both of which are closely related to the 'right to information' movement.[38] This is a major achievement, especially in the light of widespread scepticism about the possibility of eradicating corruption in India, and there is a major lesson here about the possibility of achieving wider changes in social

---

[37] There have been earlier initiatives of similar inspiration elsewhere (notably the anti-corruption movement initiated by Anna Hazare in Maharashtra), as well as many new offshoots of these pioneering movements in recent years. On the work of MKSS (which involves a great deal more than corruption-related campaigns), see Roy, Dey and Singh (1993) and Dey and Roy (2000); also Bhatia and Drèze (1998) and Goetz and Jenkins (1999).

[38] See Drèze (2001e).

norms through local action. Similarly, as noted earlier, collective demands for the dismissal of a corrupt sarpanch have become quite common in rural India, and this too is likely to have wider effects on the incidence of corruption at the local level. In all this, there is reason for hope, since there is some prospect that public vigilance may become an integral part of the political culture in many Indian villages.[39]

This is not to say that public vigilance at the village level, on its own, is an adequate means of reducing local corruption, let alone corruption in high places. Other means of action (better incentives, stronger accountability mechanisms, more vigorous sanctions, etc.) also have to be harnessed, involving state intervention as well as cooperative action. Here again, the complementarity between the two—discussed in chapter 2—is of crucial importance. Indeed, grassroots initiatives to eradicate corruption could achieve a great deal more if they were supplemented with a positive response from the state. Instead, state authorities have typically resisted public pressure for greater accountability, not least because most political parties depend heavily on embezzled funds for their survival. Even basic public demands, e.g. for the dismissal of a corrupt sarpanch, have encountered tremendous resistance from state authorities, as they threaten the whole edifice of corruption and the culture of acceptance on which it is based. Overcoming this resistance is another ongoing challenge for democratic practice.

10.5. ACCOUNTABILITY AND COUNTERVAILING POWER

The importance of public vigilance at the village level in curbing corruption, discussed in the last section, is just one example of the general role of vigilance, which can operate at different levels (not just related to local governance), and can be aimed at many different objectives (not just the prevention of corruption). Vigilance is crucial to accountability, which in its turn is central to efficiency and equity of public policies in different spheres.

Earlier in this book, we have stressed the importance of constructive public policies in various fields (basic education, health care, social security,

---

[39] Kerala has gone further than most other states in developing what Patrick Heller aptly calls a 'culture of whistle-blowing' (Heller, 1999, p. 128). In this connection, it is interesting to note that Kerala was ranked as the least corrupt Indian state in a recent opinion poll (*India Today*, 24 November 1997, based on interviews with 1,743 residents of 16 major state capitals). This finding is far from definitive, given the subjective nature of the responses and the ad hoc nature of the sample. Nevertheless, it does point to an interesting pattern that deserves further investigation.

nutritional support, environmental protection, gender equality, among others). And yet there are well recognized inadequacies from which state actions tend systematically to suffer, as has been noted widely across the world. One problem is, often enough, the presence of persistent inefficiency, reflected in such phenomena as bureaucratic delay, breakdown of public services, lack of timeliness and certainty of delivery, and unusually high costs of operation. Inefficiency, in turn, has much to do with the lack of accountability in the public sector. In the private sector, an enterprise that does not deliver the goods is unlikely to survive. Even though market-driven accountability can have a limited reach (especially when there is a lack of competition) and may give unequal power to different consumers (given the differences in their purchasing powers), there is a basic dependence of private firms on the approval of users of their services. This is frequently absent in the case of public services.

If, for example, a public health centre is closed on a work day, the patients may not have any simple means of taking remedial action. Of course, instruments of protest and censure do exist, at least in principle, such as sending a complaint to the local newspaper, or organizing a demonstration, or voting for a rival political party to the one in office, or perhaps even seeking redress from the courts. These means can be widely used, as they indeed are in some parts of India, for example in states such as Kerala (with high levels of education and a long tradition of public activism). But traditions are not easy to establish when they are not already there, and they certainly require a good deal of initiative and acumen. Also, the effectiveness of initiatives in one field may be compromised by a complementary lack of accountability in other fields (for instance, the local administration may or may not be responsive to complaints against particular public institutions).

We have already discussed, earlier on in this book (and even in this chapter), many examples of such problems of accountability in the public sector, and also have had the opportunity of discussing how they can deeply undermine the positive prospects of constructive action by the state. In the absence of adequate public accountability in many parts of the country, teaching standards in government schools have remained abysmally low, health centres have continued to provide dismal services, environmental plunder has gone on unchecked, the public distribution system has been extensively looted, and resettlement programmes have routinely failed. On the other side, we have also had the chance to discuss various efforts that have been undertaken to enhance public accountability, varying from environment-related judicial activism and public audits of local development works to greater recognition and invoking of economic and social rights (e.g. the right to elementary education or the right to food).

The need for accountability has tended to be substantially ignored in Indian institutional reforms. Indeed, the debates on the pros and cons of 'liberalization' have tended to add, to some extent, to the neglect of this problem. There is, in fact, an odd meeting ground here between the advocates and opponents of liberalization. The *advocates* of liberalization have tended to concentrate on privatization, and correspondingly, they have taken little interest in the possibility of improving the performance of the public sector. The *opponents* of liberalization, on the other side, have tended to downplay the inefficiencies of the public sector, in their effort to resist privatization. In the process, the crucial issues of accountability and public sector reform have tended to be highly neglected.

There is perhaps something curious in the fact that accountability levels are so low in India, despite the country's strong democratic tradition. Indeed, democracy is intrinsically concerned with the accountability of political leaders and government officials to the general public. In principle, the contestability of public office in a democracy provides a potential basis for accountability in the public sector. If, for example, plague breaks out somewhere in India, the health officials involved may have to face severe censure and even the Health Minister may have to resign, and these punitive possibilities give those in charge a strong incentive to prevent disasters of this kind. But accountability is much easier to guarantee in cases of this kind (such as an outbreak of plague), in which a sensational failure receives widespread attention, and where large sections of the population (including privileged classes) have a combined stake in seeking effective action. In many other situations, however, the accountability mechanisms are likely to be much weaker, and this is especially so when the failures harm only small groups of less vocal people and those affected happen to be politically marginalized or powerless.

Further, in some cases, other institutions that are themselves part of the democratic system may actually contribute to sheltering the government officers and employees from public scrutiny and censure. For instance, some trade unions in the public sector have tended to block pressures for public scrutiny and sometimes have even helped to dismantle whatever little mechanisms of accountability were in place earlier. We have discussed this in chapter 5 with reference to the issue of low accountability in the schooling system, which has played a major part in depriving millions of children of basic education. In other spheres of the public sector, too, low standards are often blamed on the fact that government employees have permanent jobs and earn salaries unrelated to performance, and have been comfortably sheltered from any pressure to work, no matter how dissatisfied the public might be.

The solution of this problem cannot, obviously, lie in the dismantling— or even undermining—of trade unions, since they have their legitimate functions as well. Indeed, trade unions constitute a necessary part of a decent society, as the dreadful work conditions of non-unionized workers in India bring out. Rather, the remedy must lie in developing and reinforcing the countervailing institutions that can give greater 'voice' to those who have a stake in the efficient provision of public services.

The importance of countervailing power has been particularly emphasized by John Kenneth Galbraith in a classic work in institutional economics (Galbraith, 1952). The effectiveness of institutions has to be assessed in terms of the power they have over each other to moderate their respective influences. Asymmetric power in one domain can be checked by a different configuration of forces in another domain. For example, applying this institutional logic to the regressive influence of teachers' unions on the management of schools, we have argued that the effective way of altering this handicap may have to lie in the development of other—countervailing—institutions, such as parental organizations and gram sabhas, which have a natural interest in enhancing the efficiency of schools.

Similar countervailing institutions can be built up in other fields involving, for instance, the users of particular public services (such as health centres or ration shops) and even the public at large (based for instance on a general need for protection from police harassment or abuses of power). It is important to note that this need not be done on a case by case basis, as if (say) every individual school or health centre needed its own 'watchdog' in order to function effectively. In fact, as mentioned earlier with reference to the eradication of corruption, local demonstrations of vigilance can have wider effects, inter alia by influencing social norms and the political culture. This link between local action and social norms is one important basis for confidence in the possibility of radical change through democratic practice.

10.6. HUMAN RIGHTS AND DEMOCRACY

The effective practice of democracy also involves the acknowledgement and use of the rights of citizens. The rhetoric of rights is omnipresent in the contemporary world. The concept is persistently invoked in many different contexts: political rights in demanding basic participatory freedoms, personal rights to privacy and liberty in defending elementary autonomies in private life, civil rights in protesting against authoritarianism, gay and lesbian rights to safeguard freedoms to pursue minority life styles, and so on. While many of these rights have legal recognition, others—even some extremely important ones—are not matters of legal rights at all. If a government is accused of violating some 'human right' such as the right of free speech, that accusation cannot really be answered simply by pointing out that there is no legal entitlement to free speech in that country. What may be at issue in such cases is not whether the established legal rights have been violated, but (1) whether the scope of these established legal rights should be extended to encompass the demands in question, and (2) whether the claim of people to have those freedoms (such as free speech) should be accepted even in the absence of legal entitlements.

Human rights are rights that relate not to citizenship, but to what is taken to be the entitlement of any human being, no matter of which country he or she is a citizen and no matter what the legal system of that country does or does not guarantee. In fact, it may not even be appropriate to define human rights simply as rights that ideally should be legally recognized. A human right can be invoked in many contexts even when its *legal* enforcement—as opposed to giving it general support—would be inappropriate and unhelpful. For example, the human right of a wife to participate fully, as an equal, in serious family decisions (no matter how chauvinist her husband is) may be widely acknowledged as a human right even by many people who would nevertheless not want this requirement to be legalized and enforced by the police. Similarly, the 'right to respect' is another example where legalization and attempted enforcement would be problematic, even bewilderingly so. Human rights have their own domain, and while their legalizable components can be sensibly used for fresh legislation (or judicial reinterpretation), these rights may also be seen, in other cases, as general demands on individuals and institutions.

Reasoning based on human rights has been used quite effectively in many countries, and this applies to India as well, as we have already discussed in various contexts. Such reasoning can be particularly effective in dealing with violations of political liberties and autonomies, even when the legal rights are somewhat ambiguous. It can also be used to demand public action in support of such rudimentary necessities as elementary school education, basic health care, and so on. Indeed, the trend towards acknowledging the right to elementary education as a 'fundamental right' in India has closely followed the human-rights-based defence of that putative right (as something that children *should* have).

It must, however, be acknowledged that there is still quite a distance to go in the general acceptance in India of a broad band of human rights, including personal liberties and basic civil rights. India is not ordinarily thought of as a major perpetrator of human rights violations, and its international rating in that respect is by no means dismal. Yet major human rights violations do take place in various forms, deeply compromising the integrity of Indian democracy. This applies first and foremost in areas of violent conflict such as Kashmir, the North-East, and parts of Bihar and Andhra Pradesh, where human rights have been extensively abused by military and para-military forces as well as by insurgent groups. In addition, human rights violations of a more 'routine' nature do take place on a substantial scale in other areas as well. Torture in police custody, for instance, is 'pervasive and a daily routine in every one of India's 25 states', according to Amnesty International.[40] Rape and death in custody have also occurred with distressing frequency, as we know even from the published statistics which the Government of India has been persuaded to supply on these issues.[41] Aside from these instances of brutality on the part of state authorities, there are also other human rights violations to consider, ranging from the practice of bonded labour to the victimization of AIDS patients.

The protection of human rights is a prime example of a cause on which democratic 'practice' has a major bearing. This is because formal legal protection and the related constitutional rights are largely in place, and they can be put more into practice, along with broadening their domain through wider recognition of basic human rights. While there is also much scope for better legal safeguards (especially in relation to human rights violations by the Armed Forces, which are sheltered by extensive provisions of immunity)[42], much can be done even within the existing legal framework.

Unfortunately, the protection of human rights in India has been a much neglected field of public activism. Indeed, it is sobering to find that,

---

[40] Amnesty International (1992), p. 1.

[41] See Government of India (1998), chapter 13. While the publication of these figures is a positive step towards transparency and accountability, the figures themselves are gross underestimates. The annual reports of the National Human Rights Commission give much higher figures (e.g. 1,012 custodial deaths in 1997–8 alone), and even the latter are very much on the low side, since they pertain only to cases of custodial death or rape that happened to be reported to the Commission.

[42] Under section 197 of the Code of Criminal Procedure, 'no Court shall take cognizance of any offence alleged to have been committed by any member of the Armed Forces of the Union while acting or purporting to act in the discharge of his official duty, except with the previous sanction of the Central Government'. Even the police enjoy a good deal of effective immunity; see e.g. Varadarajan (1999).

until recently, comprehensive reports on human rights violations in India were compiled mainly by foreign or international agencies (from Amnesty International to the US Embassy). Domestic efforts tended to be confined to relatively unambitious 'fact-finding reports' on specific cases of human rights violations. The mainstream press, for its part, has paid very little attention to these matters (on this, see also Table 8.2 in chapter 8). This is a field where there is enormous scope for more active and ambitious campaigning and organizing, drawing on India's strong tradition and culture of investigative reporting. There have indeed been important initiatives in that direction in recent years.[43]

There are at least three plausible reasons why violations of basic civil liberties have tended to remain out of focus for a long time. First, the tolerance of human rights violations is often assumed to be an essential (if 'regrettable') condition of effective 'counter-insurgency' operations in border areas (mainly in Kashmir, Punjab, and the North-East). Criticism of these operations, no matter how brutal or illegal, tends to be branded as 'anti-national'.[44] This, combined with lack of public awareness of the facts in many cases (itself related to failures of transparency and accountability), has led to a remarkable tolerance for the infringement of human rights not only in those areas but also—through emulation—in other parts of the country.

Second, the Indian military seems to have a large domain of license in violating the rights of citizens on grounds of security. We have already commented, in chapter 8, on the adverse effects of militarism on democracy, relating in particular to (1) displacement of developmental concerns by security concerns, (2) concealment of military activities behind a veil of secrecy, (3) the use of propaganda to rally the public behind prevailing security policies and programmes, (4) the powerful lobbying activities of military commanders, arms dealers, strategic think-tanks, scientific organizations involved in defence-oriented research, and other parts (or close correlates) of the military establishment, and (5) the consolidation of authoritarian tendencies in the society at large, particularly (but not only) during periods of active conflict. Each of these adverse influences

---

[43] See e.g. Committee of Concerned Citizens (1998), Indian Social Institute (2000), People's Union for Democratic Rights (2001). The work of the National Human Rights Commission (set up in 1993), despite its limited mandate and powers, has also made a significant contribution to the cause of human rights in India, and to better public awareness of the issues.

[44] As Kuldip Nayar (one of the courageous journalists who have braved these criticisms over the years) puts it, 'when it comes to Kashmir or the Northeast, the conscience of most in the country becomes dead' (Nayar, 2000b).

of militarism has tended to undermine the guaranteeing of civil and human rights in the democratic polity of India.

Third, human rights violations have a strong class dimension. A well-educated, middle-class person in India does not have much to fear by way of physical harassment from the police or para-military forces. By contrast, underprivileged sections of the population often live in terror of arbitrary repression.[45] The class differentials also make it more difficult to bring human rights issues within the scope of mainstream politics. These perceptions are in need of drastic change, since the Indian public at large has a stake in the integrity of democracy, which can be deeply threatened by widespread human rights violations.

10.7. DEMOCRACY AND PARTICIPATION

Nehru's visionary speech, with which this book began, was addressed to the Constituent Assembly that was making the constitution of the new Republic of India. The assembly's work ended in 1950—half a century ago—when the Indian constitution came into effect. Aside from laying the foundations of India's democratic institutions, the constitution addressed the need to promote social opportunities. In particular, it defined the 'fundamental rights' of all citizens, which include equality before the law, freedom of speech and association, the right to personal liberty, and protection against exploitation. In fact, the 'directive principles of state policy', which supplement hard legislation, go much further than the strict legal provisions. For instance, they urge the state 'to secure a social order for the promotion of welfare of the people' as well as to uphold a range of more specific entitlements, from 'the right to an adequate means of livelihood' and 'free legal aid' to 'free and compulsory education for all children' and 'the right to work'.

However, Dr. Ambedkar, the chairman of the Constituent Assembly's Drafting Committee and essentially the 'author' of the Indian constitution, concluded his work with a profound warning:

On the 26th January 1950, we are going to enter into a life of contradictions. In politics we will have equality and in social and economic life we will have inequality.

---

[45] The Dalit respondent quoted earlier in this chapter (footnote 9) on the intimidating aspects of India's legal system had an even more apprehensive view of the police: 'All the judges of the Supreme Court do not have the power of a single police constable ... The judges can't rewrite the laws and have to listen to arguments of learned lawyers on both sides. A constable here simply makes his own laws. He can do almost anything.' (Sainath, 1999)

This basic tension lives with us to this day, and recognizing the tensions involved is, in fact, quite central in understanding the nature of contemporary India.

The contrast at which Dr. Ambedkar pointed could be expected to have one of two possible consequences. The first possibility was that the inequalities of social and economic opportunities could undermine democracy altogether, and thus leave India with no political equality either. The second possibility was the continuation of the sharp dichotomy, with the survival of democracy, but also of the manifest economic and social inequalities, in an uneasy equilibrium. Dr. Ambedkar's immediate preoccupation was with the first possibility, and he feared that the 'contradiction' that he had identified would undermine democracy itself: 'We must remove this contradiction at the earliest possible moment or else those who suffer from inequality will blow up the structure of political democracy which this Assembly has so laboriously built up.' Fifty years after Dr. Ambedkar's warning, Indian democracy is alive and—on the whole—well. It is the second scenario that we see in India today, with a surviving democracy which is deeply compromised by the tension highlighted by Dr. Ambedkar.

As was discussed earlier in the book (and in this chapter), not only there remain remarkable economic and social inequalities, but also as a consequence there are major asymmetries in the opportunities that different sections of the population have even to participate in democratic institutions. Corresponding to this uneven distribution of power and influence are systematic biases in public priorities and policy. Elitist biases can be found, for instance, in the orientation of the news media (dominated by middle class concerns), parliamentary debates (now heavily geared to business-oriented legislative reforms), the legal system (far from impartial between different classes), foreign policy (strongly influenced by the superpower aspirations of the Indian elite), and so on.

The low priority attached to basic needs fits into this general pattern. While 'lack of political will' is often invoked in this context, it is important to go beyond this black box and to relate policy priorities to the political practice of India's democracy. As we noted in chapter 5, India has world-class institutions of higher education (especially in fields such as management and engineering) side by side with ramshackle primary schools in disadvantaged areas. This contrasting pattern has much to do with the disproportionate influence of privileged classes on public policy. Similarly, the fact that the government spends about three times as much on 'defence' as on health care is not unrelated to the lobbying powers of the military establishment, especially in comparison with those of under-privileged hospital patients.

The limitations of India's democracy sometimes provoke calls for a more authoritarian system of governance, insulated from pressure-group politics. Development, so goes the argument, requires order and discipline. The fact that trains (supposedly) ran on time during the Emergency, in 1975–7, is seen by some as a definitive proof of this proposition. On a less superficial note, authoritarianism is often said to have contributed to rapid development in various countries of east Asia as well as China.

These examples, however, are highly selective. An impartial comparison of development in democratic and authoritarian countries should not be restricted to the more successful countries in the latter group, which also includes Afghanistan, Congo, pre-Aristide Haiti, and North Korea, to cite a few cases where the blessings of authoritarianism have been less transparent. Even in the more successful countries in the authoritarian group, such as China, the suppression of political freedoms has often exacted a heavy price, as we saw in chapter 4. Taking the world picture as a whole, there is no evidence of a positive association between authoritarianism and development, even if development is narrowly interpreted in terms of economic growth.[46] Furthermore, a broader understanding of development, incorporating the expansion of freedom and social opportunities, points to wide-ranging complementarities between development and democracy.[47]

As far as India is concerned, the basic problem of political marginalization of the underprivileged can hardly be solved by marginalizing them *even more* by further concentration of political power. The challenge, rather, is to expand the scope of democracy and address the tension identified by Ambedkar through political action and democratic practice.

In some respects, the challenge of expanding democracy has grown taller in the 1990s. The economic reforms, focused as they are on the promotion of private enterprise and foreign investment, have consolidated the elitist mindset in economic policy and the political influence of the corporate sector. The nuclear tests of May 1998 and the Kargil conflict in 1999 have strengthened the influence of the security establishment, with its considerable demands on public resources and political energies. There has also been an ominous expansion of communal and authoritarian tendencies, marked for instance by the demolition of the Babri Masjid

[46] See, among other comparative studies, Przeworski (1995) and Barro (1996).
[47] On these and related issues, see Sen (1999a).

in December 1992 and the recent wave of violent attacks on Christian 'missionaries'.

The picture is not, however, uniformly bleak. The eighties and nineties have also seen some decisive expansion of the practice of democracy. The decentralized planning experiment in Kerala, the participatory successes of the Bargadar movement and other advancements of land reform in West Bengal, the anti-arrack campaign in Andhra Pradesh, the schooling revolution in Himachal Pradesh, the right to information movement in Rajasthan, and the gradual expansion of the reach of local democracy in many parts of India, are some striking illustrations—among others—of the possibility of defeating the elitist biases of public policy and expanding the horizons of democracy in India. There are no particular reasons for smugness in recording and appreciating these achievements, but they also indicate that things can change and that the practice of democracy is not necessarily doomed in India. Since democracy has been one of the central concerns in the approach developed in this book, there are reasons for hope and optimism in this general recognition.

It has sometimes been claimed that democracy being a majoritarian system cannot really provide an effective voice to the underdogs of society when they happen to be a minority (as for example is the case with those in extreme poverty).[48] It is easy to see why this scepticism about the reach of democracy would appear to be plausible. How, it is asked, can the power of the majority protect the interests of a minority (perhaps even a relatively small minority)? This is a good line of challenge, but it is ultimately too mechanical a line of reasoning and significantly negligent of the participatory basis of the practice of democracy. For one thing, democracy is not the same thing as majority rule, since democratic rights include the protection of freedom of speech and other forms of participation as well as the safeguarding of minority rights. But going beyond that, it is worth noting that the process of public discussion and participatory interaction can make citizens take an interest in the lives of each other.

Indeed, even the fact that democracies tend to be very effective in preventing famines cannot be explained by any mechanical application of majority rule, since the proportion of people who are threatened by a famine is never very large (in fact, typically far less than ten per cent of the population and most often less than five per cent).[49] Similarly, it is hard to explain how cases of rape or torture, when publicized, can become politically explosive issues, even when the number of victims—actual or

[48] See e.g. Nandy (2000).
[49] See Drèze and Sen (1989).

potential—is relatively small. As has been said, democracy is 'government by discussion' and the political salience of selective misery depends not only on the specific number of sufferers, but also on the effectiveness of public discussions that politicize the sufferings involved.

It is for these reasons that further progress of democratic practice in India must crucially depend on enriching the participatory processes. We have identified some successes as well as some failures in the participatory basis of Indian democracy. Much will depend on the possibility of enhancing public participation more widely in India. In the multi-institutional format of the process of development (incorporating markets as well as the government, the media, popular organizations, and other enabling institutions), public participation has a crucial role to play in the expansion of the reach and effectiveness of each of these institutions as well as in the integration of their joint functions. India's record in all this is one of limited success, but a critical examination of this record also indicates how the limitations can be overcome and the successes enhanced and secured. We have tried to clarify how the further advancement of development and democracy in India can most effectively proceed. There are reasons here for hopeful engagement.

Statistical Appendix

Explanatory Note

This Appendix presents statistical information on aspects of Indian economic and social development. Table A.1 focuses on international comparisons of development indicators for selected Asian countries. Table A.2 attempts to integrate some of these comparisons with a consideration of internal contrasts within India. The Indian states appearing in this table are those for which case studies are presented in the 'companion volume' (Drèze and Sen, 1996). Table A.3 presents a broad range of economic and social indicators for India's major states (those with a population of at least 5 million in 1991). Table A.4 gives summary indicators for the seven states of the north-eastern region, and Table A.5 presents similar information for the three 'new' states of Chattisgarh, Jharkhand and Uttaranchal (formerly part of Madhya Pradesh, Bihar, and Uttar Pradesh, respectively). Finally, Table A.6 provides some information relating to trends over time.

1. SOURCES

In constructing the tables included in this appendix as well as in the text, we have tried to concentrate on indicators for which the informational basis is relatively reliable. Even for these indicators, there are occasional difficulties, including minor discrepancies between different statistical sources. For the purpose of international comparisons (such as those presented in Table A.1), we have typically used *World Development Indicators 2001*.[1] In a few cases where the relevant indicators were not available in

[1] *World Development Indicators 2001* is available both in printed form (World Bank,

that publication, we have used *Human Development Report 2001* (United Nations Development Programme, 2001). For state-specific indicators within India, we have relied, in each case, on the most appropriate national statistical source, e.g. the Sample Registration System for mortality and fertility rates, the decennial censuses for literacy rates, the National Sample Survey for per-capita expenditure, and so on. In some tables (e.g. Table A.3), we have also made use of the all-India figure from the same source. It is worth mentioning that, in most cases, these all-India figures from national statistical sources are consistent with the corresponding figures given in *World Development Indicators 2001*, which are used here for the purpose of international comparisons.[2]

Some figures are quite sensitive to the choice of reference year. Generally, we have used the most recent year for which the relevant information is available as the reference year, unless there were specific reasons to use some other year (and these have been explicitly noted). For demographic indicators, such as mortality and fertility rates, we have often used three-year averages to enhance the reliability of the estimates.

2. COMMENTS ON SPECIFIC INDICATORS

Literacy Rates

In India, the standard source for literacy rates is the country-wide census conducted every ten years. The last census took place in early 2001. As things stand, literacy rates derived from the 2001 census are available only for the age group of 7 years and above. For other age groups (e.g. age 15 and above, or age 15–19), literacy rates are available from the National Family Health Survey 1998–9, also known as NFHS-II. Fortunately, the two sources (2001 census and NFHS-II) appear to be quite consistent. Since the National Family Health Survey provides more detailed information, and since 1999 is the 'standard' reference year for international comparisons in this book, we have made extensive use of NFHS-II literacy rates. The

---

2001b) and in electronic form (CD-ROM). Unless stated otherwise, references to *World Development Indicators 2001* should be understood to mean the printed version.

[2] In the first edition of this book, we had to deal with significant discrepancies between national statistical sources (e.g. Sample Registration System data) and international publications such as the World Bank's annual *World Development Report*, largely reflecting the 'lags' involved in incorporating the latest data in international databases (see Drèze and Sen, 1995a, pp. 208–10). This problem appears to be much less serious today.

census-based literacy rates for the 7+ age group in 2001 are presented in Table A.3 in this appendix (and also in Table 3.3, chapter 3). For international comparisons of literacy rates (e.g. in Table A.1 in this appendix), we have normally used the figures given in *World Development Indicators 2001*. These are broadly consistent with the above-mentioned sources for India, though there are minor discrepancies. For instance, India's 'adult male literacy rate' (age 15 and above) in 1999 was 68 per cent according to *World Development Indicators 2001* and 72 per cent according to NFHS-II.[3] Whenever such discrepancies arose, we have tended to opt for the NFHS-II figures, which appear to be comparatively accurate, or to mention the figures from *both* sources.

In section 4.2 (chapter 4), we have made extensive use of literacy rates derived from India's 1981 and 1991 censuses and China's 1982 and 1990 censuses. For further discussion of the relevant sources, and of the methodological issues arising in comparisons of literacy rates in India and China, see Drèze and Loh (1995).

China's Per-capita GDP

The level of China's real per-capita income in comparison with other countries (India in particular) has been a matter of much debate. World Bank estimates have been the object of frequent and substantial revision, leading to a certain amount of confusion.[4] For instance, according to World Bank estimates published in successive *World Development Reports*, China has been growing much faster than India in the 1990s, yet the proportionate gap between the two countries, in terms of real per-capita income (evaluated on the basis of 'purchasing power parity' exchange rates), has remained more or less constant. This internal inconsistency is

---

[3] The NFHS-II estimate is consistent with the 2001 census figure of 76 per cent for male literacy in the age group of *7 years and above*, bearing in mind that 7+ literacy rates in India tend to be significantly higher than 15+ literacy rates. In the case of female literacy, there is no discrepancy between the different sources mentioned here.

[4] As Harry Wu (2000) puts it in a recent review of the evidence, 'the World Bank [purchasing power parity] estimates for China have been very different from other [PPP] estimates and so inconsistent over time that it is difficult to reconcile later revised estimates with early ones' (p. 486). In some cases, 'adjustments' of the World Bank estimates of China's per-capita income were made in response to political pressure from the Chinese government, aimed for instance at ensuring that China continues to be classified as a 'low-income country' (see Garnaut and Ma, 1993, p. 122).

largely removed in recent time-series data presented in CD-ROM versions of *World Development Indicators*, but the consistency appears to be achieved in part by implausible downward adjustments of China's per-capita income in earlier years.[5] This continuing tension suggests that World Bank estimates of the level of real per-capita income in China today may call for substantial upward adjustment. There is, indeed, much independent evidence in favour of such adjustments.[6] Meanwhile, given the evident unreliability of available estimates of China's real per-capita income, we have made little use of these estimates.

'State Domestic Product' for Indian States

India's Central Statistical Organisation publishes estimates of each state's gross domestic product, also known as 'state domestic product' (SDP). We have avoided inter-state comparisons of SDP *levels*, as the state-specific estimates are not strictly comparable, due to differences in methodology. However, SDP data have been used to calculate the *growth rate* of the economy in each state (see Table A.3, Part 1). This is legitimate, since the methodology is broadly consistent over time, even though it varies between states.

State-specific Poverty Indices

Poverty indices in India are usually calculated from National Sample Survey (NSS) data on consumer expenditure. For state-specific indices, it is advisable to use the larger quinquennial surveys, rather than the 'thin' annual surveys. The latest quinquennial survey (the '55th round') pertains to 1999–2000, but state-specific poverty estimates based on this recent survey are not available at the time of writing (except for provisional and somewhat controversial Planning Commission figures). Hence, we have used poverty estimates for the preceding quinquennial round (the 50th round), which relates to 1993–4. The estimates are

---

[5] The problem can be seen from Table 4.1 in chapter 4: the latest World Bank estimates of *levels* and *growth rates* of real per-capita income in China and India have the implausible implication that China's real per-capita income around 1980 was only about half as high as India's.

[6] See Wu (2000), Table 2, and the literature cited there; also Keidel (1992), Garnaut and Ma (1993), and Maddison (1998), pp. 152–3. To quote Wu (2000) again, 'almost all empirical results have supported the downward-bias hypothesis for China's GDP level' (p. 475). He attributes this bias to a combination of 'undercoverage effect' and 'price distortion effect'.

due to Angus Deaton and Alessandro Tarozzi (2000). In addition to the standard 'head-count ratio' (i.e. the proportion of the population below the poverty line), Table A.3 presents estimates of the 'poverty-gap index' for the major Indian states.[7] We are most grateful to Angus Deaton for these additional, unpublished estimates.

It should be mentioned that inter-state comparisons of poverty indices can be quite sensitive to differences in methodology and assumptions between different studies. For 1993–4, several sets of estimates are available, and the rankings of Indian states in terms of poverty levels vary significantly between the different series.[8] To illustrate, Rajasthan's rank in the (descending) scale of head-count ratios, among 16 major states for which the relevant 1993–4 estimates are available, varies from third to fifteenth between different sources. We have opted for Deaton and Tarozzi's estimates because they involve particularly careful corrections for inter-state as well as rural-urban price differences.[9] Even these skilful estimates, however, should be interpreted with caution, bearing in mind the inherent conceptual and practical difficulties involved in inter-state poverty comparisons (even within the standard expenditure-based approach).

Poverty Trends

While inter-state comparisons of poverty levels based on expenditure data are inherently difficult, poverty indices have been effectively utilized to assess poverty trends over time. For purposes of poverty comparisons

---

[7] The 'poverty gap' is the difference between a person's expenditure and the 'poverty line'. The 'poverty-gap index' is essentially the aggregate poverty gap (obtained as an unweighted sum of poverty gaps among persons below the poverty line), suitably normalized. Unlike the head-count ratio, the poverty-gap index takes into account the *extent* to which poor people's incomes or expenditures fall short of the poverty line. However, both the head-count ratio and the poverty-gap index are insensitive to the interpersonal distribution of incomes or expenditures below the poverty line. For lack of adequate data, state-specific 'distribution-sensitive' poverty indices (such as the 'squared poverty gap' index or the 'Sen index') are not given in this appendix. For all-India 'squared poverty gap' indices, see Table A.6.

[8] For alternative 1993–4 estimates (all based on the 50th round of the National Sample Survey), see Datt (1998, 1999b), Dubey and Gangopadhyay (1998), Deaton and Tarozzi (2000).

[9] Note that the Deaton and Tarozzi (2000) poverty estimates for 1993–4 presented in Table A.1 are not directly comparable to the corresponding 1993–4 estimates from the time-series of poverty indices given in Table A.6 and Figure 9.2 (chapter 9). This is because the 1993–4 poverty line used by Deaton and Tarozzi is adjusted to 'correct' for upward biases in standard price indices (arising from the failure to update commodity 'weights' over time). See also p. 326.

over time (e.g. in Table A.6), we have relied mainly on Gaurav Datt's internally consistent series of poverty indices for India and Indian states from 1951 onwards.[10] This is the most complete source, and it is broadly consistent with other series of poverty estimates over time, e.g. those due to Sundaram and Tendulkar (2000) or to the Planning Commission (Gupta, 1999).[11]

Datt's estimates end in 1997. In Figure 9.2, which goes beyond 1997, we have combined Datt's estimates with unpublished estimates from 1993–4 onwards due to Angus Deaton, which also include head-count ratios based on the experimental '7-day recall' schedule. The 'link' year used in splicing the two series (which give similar poverty estimates for all years between 1993–4 and 1997) is 1993–4, when a 'quinquennial' survey took place.

For 1999–2000, Deaton's series (used in Figure 9.2) simply incorporates the 'official' Planning Commission figures (see e.g. Government of India, 2001c, p. 13). As mentioned in the text (p. 324), these 1999–2000 head-count ratios are not strictly comparable with the earlier estimates, due to significant methodological changes introduced in the 55th round of the National Sample Survey. Briefly, the problem is as follows.[12] Prior to 1999–2000, the standard '30-day recall' schedule and the experimental '7-day recall' schedule were administered to *different* (and independent) samples of households. These alternative schedules produced two series of independent poverty estimates, with a fairly stable 'gap' between the head-count ratios based on 30-day and 7-day recall (see Figure 9.2), essentially reflecting the better coverage of '7-day recall' expenditure data. In 1999–2000, 30-day recall and 7-day recall data were collected for the *same* households, in two adjacent columns on the same pages of a single questionnaire. This led to a sudden 'reconciliation' of the 30-day recall and 7-day recall data (see Figure 9.2), presumably reflecting efforts to achieve 'consistency' on the part of investigators and/or respondents. This reconciliation is likely to produce a downward bias in the '30-day recall' head-count ratios, and an upward bias in the '7-day recall' head-count ratios (compared with what would have been obtained on the basis of the earlier approach), in so far as the two series are 'pulled' towards each other.[13]

[10] See Datt (1997, 1998, 1999a, 1999b).

[11] See the comparative summary of longitudinal poverty estimates in Abhijit Sen (2000), Table 1.

[12] For further details, see Abhijit Sen (2000) and Angus Deaton (2001).

[13] In principle, however, the upward bias in the '7-day recall' head-count ratios could be compensated by an improved overall coverage of the expenditure data arising from the combined use of the two approaches.

3. Sources Used in Table A.3

For convenience, the sources used in Table A.3 (which provides state-specific information on a range of social and economic indicators), along with brief explanatory remarks, are listed in a chart at the end of this appendix.

TABLE A.1 *Economic and Social Indicators in India and Selected Asian Countries, 1999*

	India	Bangladesh	Nepal	Pakistan	Sri Lanka	China	South Korea	Indonesia	Thailand
POPULATION (millions)	998	128	23	135	19	1,254	47	207	60
PER-CAPITA INCOME AND RELATED INDICATORS									
GNP per capita (US $)	440	370	220	470	820	780[a]	8,490	600	2,010
PPP estimates of GNP per capita (1999 international dollars)	2,149	1,475	1,219	1,757	3,056	3,291[a]	14,637	2,439	5,599
PPP estimates of GNP per capita (USA=100)	7.0	4.8	4.0	5.8	10.1	11.1[a]	48.7	8.3	18.6
Average annual growth rate of per-capita GNP, 1965–98 (%)	2.7	1.4	1.1	2.7	3.0	6.8	6.6	4.7	5.0
Average annual growth rate of per-capita GDP (%)									
1980–90	3.7	1.9	2.0	3.6	2.8	8.6	8.4	4.4	6.4
1990–99	4.1	3.1	2.5	1.3	4.1	9.6	4.7	3.0	3.5
Estimated proportion of the population below international poverty line of US $1/day, 1995–8[b] (%)	44	29	38	31	7	19	<2	7.7	<2
LONGEVITY, MORTALITY AND FERTILITY									
Life expectancy at birth (years)									
Female	64	61	58	64	76	72	77	68	71
Male	62	60	58	62	71	68	69	64	67
Persons	63	61	58	63	73	70	73	66	69
Crude death rate (per 1,000)	9	9	10	8	6	7	6	7	7
Infant mortality rate (per 1,000 live births)	71	61	75	90	15	30	8	42	28
Proportion of low-birthweight babies, 1995–9[b] (%)	33	30	n/a	25	25	6	9	8	6

Table A.1 (contd.)

	India	Bangladesh	Nepal	Pakistan	Sri Lanka	China	South Korea	Indonesia	Thailand
Maternal mortality rate, 1990–99[b] (per 100,000 live births)	410	440	n/a	n/a	60	55	20	450	44
Crude birth rate (per 1,000)	26	28	34	34	17	16	14	22	17
Total fertility rate	3.1	3.2	4.3	4.8	2.1	1.9	1.6	2.6	1.9
LITERACY AND EDUCATION									
Adult literacy rate (age 15+) (%)									
Female	44[c]	29	23	30	89	75	96	81	93
Male	72[c]	52	58	59	94	91	99	91	97
Estimated 'net enrolment ratio' at the primary level, 1997 (% of relevant age group)	77	75	78	n/a	100	100	100	99	88
Estimated mean years of schooling (age 25+), 1992	2.4	2	2.1	1.9	7.2	5	9.3	4.1	3.9
Pupil-teacher ratio at primary level, 1997 (pupils per teacher)	62	n/a	39	40	28	24	31	22	n/a
OTHER GENDER-RELATED INDICATORS									
Female-male ratio (women per 100 men)	93	95	98	93	101	94	99	100	100
Female share of the labour force (%)	32	42	41	28	36	45	41	41	46
Estimated prevalence of anaemia among pregnant women, 1985–99[b] (%)	88	53	65	37	39	52	n/a	64	57
SAVINGS, INVESTMENT AND TRADE									
Gross domestic savings as proportion of GDP (%)	20	17	13	10	20	40	34	32	33

Table A.1 (contd.)

	India	Bangladesh	Nepal	Pakistan	Sri Lanka	China	South Korea	Indonesia	Thailand
Gross domestic investment as proportion of GDP (%)	24	20	19	15	25	40	27	14	21
Gross foreign direct investment as proportion of PPP GDP (%)	0.1	0.1	0.0	0.3	0.4	1.0	2.1	0.9	1.8
Exports of goods and non-factor services as proportion of GDP (%)	11	14	22	15	36	22	42	54	57
Trade in goods as a proportion of PPP GDP (%)	3.6	6.8	6.8	8.0	16.9	8.0	35.9	12.3	29.4
Average annual growth rate of value of exports (%)									
1980–90	7.3	7.6	8.1	8.1	5.5	12.9	15.0	-0.3	14.0
1990–99	10.4	12.3	8.2	6.6	12.9	15.8	10.9	9.4	12.5
Total debt service as proportion of exports of goods and services (%)	15	10	8	31	8	9	25	30	22

Notes: [a] Subject to a substantial margin of error (see Explanatory Note).
[b] Data refer to the most recent year for which data are available within the specified period.
[c] Based on the National Family Health Survey 1998–9; the corresponding World Bank estimates are 44 and 68, respectively.

Sources: World Development Indicators 2001, Tables 1.1, 1.2, 1.3, 2.1, 2.2, 2.6, 2.11, 2.13, 2.14, 2.17, 2.18, 2.19, 3.11, 3.15, 4.4, 4.9, 4.17 and 6.1; United Nations Population Division (1999); *Human Development Report 1994,* p. 146; *Human Development Indicators 2000,* Tables 1.4 and 2.10; *Human Development Report 2001,* Table 7; *World Development Report 2000–1,* Tables 1, 3, 11 and 13. Unless stated otherwise, the reference year is 1999.

TABLE A.2 India in Comparative Perspective, 1999

Country/ state	Population (millions)	Growth rate of per-capita GDP (% per year)		Adult literacy rate (age 15+) (%)		Life expectancy at birth (years)		Crude death rate (per 1,000)	Infant mortality rate (per 1,000 live births)	Total fertility rate	Female-male ratio (women per 100 men)
		1980–90	1990–9	Female	Male	Female	Male				
Bangladesh	128	1.9	3.1	29	52	61	60	9	61	3.2	95
Pakistan	135	3.6	1.3	30	50	64	62	8	90	4.8	93
Sri Lanka	19	2.8	4.1	89	94	76	71	6	15	2.1	101
Kerala	31	2.3	5.1	83	93	76[a]	70[a]	6[b]	14[b]	1.8[c]	106
West Bengal	78	2.5	4.7	52	75	64[a]	62[a]	7[b]	53[b]	2.5[c]	93
Uttar Pradesh	169	2.8	1.6	34	60	57[a]	58[a]	10[b]	84[b]	4.8[c]	90
INDIA	998	3.7	4.1	44	72	64	62	9	71	3.1	93
China	1,254	8.6	9.6	75	91	72	68	7	30	1.9	94
South Korea	47	8.4	4.7	96	99	77	69	6	8	1.6	99
Thailand	60	6.4	3.5	93	95	71	67	7	28	1.9	100

Notes: [a] 1993–7.   [b] 1997–9.   [c] 1996–8.

Sources: For countries (including India): see Table A.1. For Indian states: see Table A.3 and the Explanatory Note. Unless stated otherwise, the reference year is 1999.

Table A.3 Selected Indicators for Major Indian States

PART 1: Income-related Indicators

State	Population, 2001 (millions)	Average household expenditure per capita, 1999–2000[a] (Rs/month)	Growth rate of real per-capita 'state domestic product' (% per year)		Poverty indices, 1993–4					Gini coefficient of per-capita expenditure, 1993–4		Proportion (%) of 'asset-poor' households, 1992–3[c]
					Head-count ratio (%)			Poverty-gap index				
			1980s[b]	1990s[b]	Rural	Urban	Combined	Rural	Urban	Rural	Urban	
Andhra Pradesh	76	541	3.5	3.5 (3.9)	29	18	26	5.8	3.4	28.9	32.3	39
Assam	27	475	n/a	1.0 (1.0)	35	13	33	5.7	2.0	n/a	n/a	58
Bihar	110	414	2.6	0.0 (1.6)	49	27	46	10.7	5.6	22.5	30.9	62
Gujarat	51	678	3.2	6.2 (5.3)	32	15	26	6.8	2.6	24.0	29.1	27
Haryana	21	771	4.0	2.2 (3.1)	17	11	15	3.0	1.9	n/a	n/a	11
Himachal Pradesh	6	740	n/a	4.0 (4.6)	17	4	16	3.0	0.5	n/a	n/a	7
Jammu & Kashmir	10	745	n/a	n/a (n/a)	10	3	8	1.6	0.5	n/a	n/a	n/a
Karnataka	53	640	3.4	5.7 (6.1)	38	21	33	8.6	4.5	27.0	31.9	28
Kerala	32	810	2.3	5.1 (5.0)	19	14	18	3.9	2.7	30.1	34.3	15
Madhya Pradesh	81	475	2.4	2.7 (2.6)	37	19	32	8.2	3.5	28.0	33.0	49
Maharashtra	97	699	3.7	5.4 (5.1)	43	18	33	11.2	4.6	30.7	35.7	27
Orissa	37	410	2.5	3.0 (3.1)	44	15	40	9.7	3.0	24.6	30.7	54
Punjab	24	795	3.4	2.8 (2.8)	6	8	7	1.0	1.1	n/a	n/a	8
Rajasthan	56	607	4.1	2.5 (2.9)	23	18	22	4.4	3.2	26.5	29.4	40
Tamil Nadu	62	715	4.0	5.8 (6.0)	38	21	32	9.1	4.5	31.2	34.8	33
Uttar Pradesh	175	514	2.8	1.6 (2.1)	29	22	27	5.8	4.6	28.1	32.3	49
West Bengal	80	571	2.5	4.7 (5.0)	25	16	23	4.2	2.9	25.4	33.8	44
INDIA	1,027	589	3.3	4.0 (4.4)	33	18	29	7.0	3.7	28.6	34.3	40

Notes: [a] At current prices, without adjustments for inter-state price differentials.   [b] 1980–1 to 1990–1 (for 1980s) and 1990–1 to 1998–9 (for 1990s). In brackets, growth rates for the period 1992–3 to 1998–9.   [c] Based on an index of ownership of durables (see 'sources').

Table A.3 (contd.)

PART 2: Mortality and Fertility

State	Life expectancy at birth, 1993–7 (years)		Infant mortality rate, 1997–9 (per 1,000 live births)	Death rate, age 0–4, 1996–8 (per 1,000)		Estimated maternal mortality rate, 1987–96 (per 100,000 live births)	Death rate, 1997–9 (per 1,000)	Birth rate, 1997–9 (per 1,000)	Total fertility rate, 1996–8
	Female	Male		Female	Male				
Andhra Pradesh	63.5	61.2	65	17.5	17.6	283	8.4	22.2	2.5
Assam	57.1	56.6	76	26.3	26.0	984	9.9	27.7	3.2
Bihar	58.4	60.4	68	27.7	23.7	513	9.4	31.0	4.4
Gujarat	62.9	60.9	63	22.2	18.6	596	7.8	25.5	3.0
Haryana	64.6	63.7	69	26.0	19.9	472	8.0	27.6	3.4
Himachal Pradesh	65.2	64.6	63	17[a]	17[a]	n/a	7.7	23.0	2.4
Jammu & Kashmir	n/a	n/a	45[b]	n/a	n/a	n/a	5.4[b]	19.8[b]	n/a
Karnataka	64.9	51.6	56	17.2	15.9	480	7.7	22.3	2.5
Kerala	75.9	70.4	14	3.4	3.7	n/a	6.3	18.1	1.8
Madhya Pradesh	55.2	55.6	93	33.8	31.9	700	10.8	30.9	4.0
Maharashtra	66.6	64.1	48	13.2	12.2	380	7.5	22.2	2.7
Orissa	57.0	57.1	97	28.9	29.5	597	10.9	25.4	3.0
Punjab	68.3	66.7	53	17.9	13.8	n/a	7.5	22.4	2.7
Rajasthan	60.1	59.1	83	31.9	27.5	580	8.7	31.6	4.2
Tamil Nadu	65.1	63.2	53	13.7	12.3	195	8.2	19.2	2.0
Uttar Pradesh	56.0	58.1	84	34.9	26.9	737	10.4	32.7	4.8
West Bengal	63.6	62.2	53	15.8	17.4	458	7.4	21.5	2.5
INDIA	61.8	60.4	71	24.7	21.7	479	8.9	26.6	3.3

Notes: [a] 1991–8.   [b] 1998 (provisional figures).

Table A.3 (contd.)

State	Literacy rate, age 7+, 2001 (%)		Literacy rate, age 15–19, 1998–9 (%)		Proportion of persons aged 15–19 who have attained a specific grade, 1992–3 (%)			
					Grade 5		Grade 8	
	Female	Male	Female	Male	Female	Male	Female	Male
Andhra Pradesh	51	71	64	80	47	68	33	52
Assam	56	72	73	82	51	65	37	47
Bihar	35	62	49	73	34	67	26	52
Gujarat	59	81	73	88	63	77	43	58
Haryana	56	79	83	92	61	82	38	56
Himachal Pradesh	68	86	95	97	78	91	51	63
Jammu & Kashmir	42	66	63	85	68[a]	88[a]	46[a]	62[a]
Karnataka	57	76	72	82	53	70	36	55
Kerala	88	94	98	99	93	95	77	73
Madhya Pradesh	51	77	62	85	44	73	25	47
Maharashtra	68	86	82	91	67	84	49	67
Orissa	51	76	69	87	45	69	30	50
Punjab	64	76	86	89	74	77	57	57
Rajasthan	44	76	51	86	32	70	19	47
Tamil Nadu	65	82	82	94	67	81	45	59
Uttar Pradesh	44	71	58	84	41	72	30	55
West Bengal	60	78	72	84	51	62	28	39
INDIA	54	76	68	85	51	73	36	54

Notes: [a] Jammu region only.

Table A.3 (contd.)

State	Proportion of children aged 5–14 attending school (%)				Proportion of never-enrolled children in 10–12 age group, 1992–3[a] (%)			
	Female		Male		Rural		Urban	
	1992–3	1998–9	1992–3	1998–9	Female	Male	Female	Male
Andhra Pradesh	55	71	72	81	43	23	14	8
Assam	66	75	74	80	25	19	21	11
Bihar	38	54	64	71	63	32	31	12
Gujarat	68	73	82	84	25	9	10	5
Haryana	75	86	87	91	19	5	5	5
Himachal Pradesh	88	97	94	99	7	3	6	1
Jammu & Kashmir	80[b]	78	91[b]	90	19[b]	4[b]	1[b]	3[b]
Karnataka	64	78	76	82	35	19	17	10
Kerala	95	97	95	97	1	1	1	2
Madhya Pradesh	55	71	69	81	42	21	11	9
Maharashtra	77	87	86	90	26	9	5	4
Orissa	62	75	77	83	34	18	19	6
Punjab	78	90	83	92	21	12	9	7
Rajasthan	41	63	74	86	60	19	22	9
Tamil Nadu	79	89	86	91	14	7	6	3
Uttar Pradesh	48	69	73	83	50	20	23	17
West Bengal	63	77	73	80	29	25	18	9
INDIA	59	74	76	83	40	19	14	9

Notes: [a] Unweighted average of the figures for ages 10, 11 and 12.   [b] Jammu region only.

Table A.3 (contd.)

PART 5: Other Gender-related Indicators

State	Female-male ratio, 2001 (women per 1,000 men)	Ratio of female to male death rate, age 0–4, 1996–8 (%)	Proportion of women aged 20–24 married before age 18, 1998–9 (%)	Female labour force participation rate, 1991 (%)	Percentage of ever-married women aged 15–49 (1998–9) who:				Share of female employment in total public-sector employment, 1989 (%)
					work outside the household	have access to money	do not need permission to: go to the market	do not need permission to: visit relatives	
Andhra Pradesh	978	99	64	34	41	58	20	15	10
Assam	932	101	41	22	15	35	13	14	n/a
Bihar	926	117	71	15	17	67	22	21	7
Gujarat	921	119	41	26	27	74	55	51	14
Haryana	861	131	42	11	9	71	37	21	13
Himachal Pradesh	970	100[a]	11	35	9	80	33	31	11
Jammu & Kashmir	900	n/a	22	n/a	12	58	12	8	10
Karnataka	964	108	46	29	35	67	43	34	15
Kerala	1,058	92	17	16	23	66	48	38	30
Madhya Pradesh	937	106	65	33	31	49	21	20	10
Maharashtra	922	108	48	33	35	64	49	32	13
Orissa	972	98	38	21	23	46	18	15	7
Punjab	874	130	12	4	9	78	50	28	15
Rajasthan	922	116	68	27	13	41	19	17	11
Tamil Nadu	986	111	25	30	43	79	79	56	19
Uttar Pradesh	902	130	62	12	11	52	17	12	8
West Bengal	934	91	46	11	23	51	18	14	10
INDIA	933	114	50	22	25	60	32	24	n/a

Notes: [a] 1991–8.

Table A.3 (contd.)

PART 6: Reproductive Health and Related Matters

State	Contraceptive prevalence, 1998-9[a] (%)			Proportion of births attended by health professional, 1998-9	Proportion of recent births preceded by specific types of maternal care, 1998-9 (%)			Proportion of ever-married women aged 15-49 with knowledge of AIDS, 1998-9 (%)
	All methods	Modern permanent methods	Modern temporary methods		Antenatal care	Tetanus vaccine (2 doses)	IFA[b] for 3 or more months	
Andhra Pradesh	60	57	2	65	93	82	71	55
Assam	43	17	10	21	60	52	45	34
Bihar	25	20	2	23	36	58	20	12
Gujarat	59	45	8	54	86	73	67	30
Haryana	62	41	12	42	58	80	53	44
Himachal Pradesh	68	52	8	40	87	66	71	61
Jammu & Kashmir	49	31	11	42	83	78	56	32
Karnataka	58	52	4	59	86	75	74	58
Kerala	64	51	5	94	99	86	89	87
Madhya Pradesh	44	38	5	30	61	55	38	23
Maharashtra	61	52	8	59	90	75	72	61
Orissa	47	36	5	33	80	74	62	39
Punjab	67	31	23	63	74	90	64	55
Rajasthan	40	32	6	36	48	52	31	21
Tamil Nadu	52	46	4	84	99	95	84	87
Uttar Pradesh	28	16	6	22	35	51	21	20
West Bengal	67	34	14	44	90	82	56	26
INDIA	48	36	7	42	65	67	48	40

Notes: [a] Proportion of currently-married women aged 15-49 who are practising contraception.   [b] Iron and folic acid (tablets or syrup).

Table A.3 (contd.)

PART 7: Health Care and Related Matters

State	Proportion (%) of mothers who know about ORS[a] packets, 1998-9	Proportion (%) of children with diarrhoea who were treated with oral rehydration therapy, 1998-9	Share of the public sector in the provision of:[b]		Proportion (%) of children aged 12-23 months (1998-9) who have received:		Proportion (%) of children aged 12-35 months who have received at least one dose of vitamin A, 1998-9
			Vaccination	Contraception	Full immunization[c]	No immunization	
Andhra Pradesh	73	55	74	79	59	5	25
Assam	43	54	n/a	64	17	33	15
Bihar	38	41	87	77	11	17	10
Gujarat	62	42	83	72	53	7	52
Haryana	72	58	93	80	63	10	45
Himachal Pradesh	93	68	n/a	92	83	3	71
Jammu & Kashmir	73	67	n/a	69	57	10	36
Karnataka	79	58	n/a	85	60	8	48
Kerala	89	90	71	66	80	2	44
Madhya Pradesh	56	46	92	87	22	14	24
Maharashtra	65	51	64	75	78	2	65
Orissa	73	67	97	90	44	9	42
Punjab	82	65	88	64	72	9	57
Rajasthan	45	34	88	86	17	23	18
Tamil Nadu	83	45	78	74	89	0.3	16
Uttar Pradesh	59	36	82	71	21	30	14
West Bengal	76	73	88	70	44	14	43
INDIA	62	48	82	76	42	14	30

Notes: [a] Oral rehydration salts. [b] Proportion of vaccinated children and current users of modern contraception who obtained vaccination/contraception from the public medical sector.
[c] Tuberculosis, polio, diptheria, pertussis, tetanus and measles.

Table A.3 (contd.)

PART 8: *Nutrition-related Indicators*

State	Proportion (%) of adult women[a] with body mass index below 18.5 kg/m², 1998-9	Proportion adult of women[a] with any anaemia, 1998-9 (%)	Proportion (%) of severely undernourished children below age 3 1998-9			Proportion (%) of persons with moderate or severe anaemia, 1998-9		Proportion (%) of households using adequately iodized salt, 1998-9
			Weight-for-age	Height-for-age	Weight-for-height	Adult women[a]	Children aged 6-35 months	
Andhra Pradesh	37	50	10	14	1.6	17	49	27
Assam	27	70	13	34	3.3	27	32	80
Bihar	39	63	26	34	5.5	21	54	47
Gujarat	37	46	16	23	2.4	17	50	56
Haryana	26	47	10	24	0.8	16	66	71
Himachal Pradesh	30	41	12	18	3.3	9	41	91
Jammu & Kashmir	26	59	8	17	1.2	20	42	53
Karnataka	39	42	17	16	3.9	16	51	43
Kerala	19	23	5	7	0.7	3	19	39
Madhya Pradesh	38	54	24	28	4.3	17	53	57
Maharashtra	40	49	18	14	2.5	17	52	60
Orissa	48	63	21	18	3.9	18	46	35
Punjab	17	41	9	17	0.8	13	63	75
Rajasthan	36	49	21	29	1.9	16	62	46
Tamil Nadu	29	57	11	12	3.8	20	47	21
Uttar Pradesh	36	49	22	31	2.1	15	55	49
West Bengal	44	63	16	19	1.6	17	52	62
INDIA	36	52	18	23	2.8	17	51	49

Notes: [a] Ever-married women aged 15-49.

Table A.3 (contd.)

PART 9: *Other Public Services*

State	*Proportion of villages with medical facilities, 1981 (%)*	*Number of hospital beds per million persons, 1991–8[a]*	*Proportion of the population receiving subsidized foodgrains from the public distribution system, 1993–4 (%)*		*Per-capita consumption of foodgrains obtained through the public distribution system, 1993–4 [kg/year]*		*Proportion of households having access to safe drinking water, 1991 (%)*		*Proportion of households with electricity connection, 1998–9 (%)*
			Rural	*Urban*	*Rural*	*Urban*	*Rural*	*Urban*	
Andhra Pradesh	23	1,034	63	42	30.7	20.6	57	87	74
Assam	n/a	727	20	26	5.7	13.4	61	88	26
Bihar	14	507	4	4	1.4	1.8	62	86	18
Gujarat	26	1,769	42	24	13.0	9.8	67	93	84
Haryana	57	600	5	5	1.4	1.6	68	95	89
Himachal Pradesh	13	1,663	45	32	31.8	30.0	77	94	97
Jammu & Kashmir	18	1,184	8	54	7.1	53.3	n/a	n/a	90
Karnataka	11	1,124	56	52	12.0	18.4	73	90	81
Kerala	96	3,463	80	74	54.1	51.7	71	85	72
Madhya Pradesh	6	427	11	14	4.4	5.6	54	87	68
Maharashtra	18	1,538	38	24	8.7	9.8	62	95	82
Orissa	11	473	5	17	1.8	5.6	47	81	34
Punjab	24	1,106	2	2	0.9	1.0	94	98	96
Rajasthan	13	716	16	10	13.3	10.9	53	91	64
Tamil Nadu	23	1,101	69	60	24.5	23.3	68	88	79
Uttar Pradesh	10	601	4	5	3.8	3.1	60	91	37
West Bengal	13	909	10	32	2.8	19.3	84	95	37
INDIA	14	926	27	29	10.6	13.7	64	91	60

Notes: [a] Latest year for which data are available within 1991–8 period.

Table A.3 (contd.)

PART 10: Media and Politics

State	Proportion (%) of households subscribing to a daily newspaper, 1998[a]		Proportion (%) of households that have ever made use of a telephone, 1998		Proportion (%) of ever-married women aged 15–49 exposed to any media, 1998–9	Voter turnout, 1999 (%)		
	Rural	Urban	Rural	Urban		Female	Male	Persons
Andhra Pradesh	2	17	29	68	76	66	72	69
Assam	10	46	24	71	53	70	73	71
Bihar	2	13	21	54	27	53	69	62
Gujarat	5	27	54	85	66	41	53	47
Haryana	3	24	46	75	67	58	68	64
Himachal Pradesh	n/a	n/a	n/a	n/a	84	54	59	57
Jammu & Kashmir	n/a	n/a	n/a	n/a	74	29	36	32
Karnataka	3	25	39	77	79	65	70	68
Kerala	26	51	81	83	89	70	71	70
Madhya Pradesh	1	19	15	64	55	46	63	55
Maharashtra	5	36	32	82	70	58	64	61
Orissa	1	17	12	60	44	50	61	56
Punjab	5	18	54	72	82	55	58	56
Rajasthan	3	29	35	73	37	46	61	54
Tamil Nadu	3	19	37	70	80	55	61	58
Uttar Pradesh	1	17	20	57	45	48	58	54
West Bengal	3	20	17	63	61	73	77	75
INDIA	4	25	29	71	60	56	64	60

Notes: [a] Daily purchase is counted as 'subscribing'.

Table A.3 (contd.)

State	Proportion (%) of rural households not owning any agricultural land, 1992–3	Proportion (%) of agricultural labourers in rural population, 1991	Average wage rate of casual agricultural labourers, 1997–9 (Rs/day at 1960–1 prices)	Growth rate of real agricultural wages, 1990–2000	Murder rate, 1998 (murders per million persons)	Suicide rate, 1997 (suicides per million persons)
Andhra Pradesh	45	23	2.90	1.3	40	116
Assam	42	4	2.63	-0.7	65	119
Bihar	41	12	2.24	0.3	55	14
Gujarat	39	11	3.71	5.1	30	85
Haryana	43	7	4.87	2.7	43	84
Himachal Pradesh	16	1	n/a	n/a	21	51
Jammu & Kashmir	20	n/a	n/a	n/a	70	11
Karnataka	32	15	2.23	3.2	33	203
Kerala	63	9	6.78	7.9	14	285
Madhya Pradesh	30	11	2.33	1.8	42	99
Maharashtra	30	16	2.71	1.6	34	143
Orissa	36	11	1.85	0.7	28	92
Punjab	49	9	3.96	-0.8	33	27
Rajasthan	16	4	3.48	2.8	29	62
Tamil Nadu	59	20	3.13	6.7	32	153
Uttar Pradesh	22	7	2.73	2.5	51	27
West Bengal	42	10	3.55	1.6	27	185
INDIA	36	11	2.97	2.5	40	100

TABLE A.4 *Selected Development Indicators for the North-Eastern States* PART 1

| | Population, 2001 (millions) | Female-male ratio, 2001 (women per 1,000 men) | | Infant mortality rate 1997-9 (per 1000 live births) | Death rate, age 0-4, 1995-7 (per 1,000) | | Total fertility rate, 1995-7 | Literacy rates (%) | | | | Proportion of children aged 6-14 attending school, 1998-9 (%) | |
| | | | | | | | | age 7+, 2001 | | age 15-19, 1998-9 | | | |
		All ages	Age 0-6		Female	Male		Female	Male	Female	Male	Female	Male
Arunachal Pradesh	1.0	901	961	43	15.2	14.9	2.8	44	64	78	86	77	86
Manipur	2.4	978	961	25	10.6	9.4	2.4	60	78	88	92	88	93
Meghalaya	2.3	975	975	56	19.1	25.2	4.0	60	66	82	83	85	81
Mizoram	0.9	938	971	19	n/a	n/a	n/a	86	91	97	98	91	91
Nagaland	2.0	909	975	n/a	4.2	6.0	1.5	62	72	85	91	84	88
Sikkim	0.5	875	986	49	12.6	16.7	2.5	62	77	86	91	89	89
Tripura	3.2	950	975	42	12.6	15.4	2.1	65	82	91	95	88	91
NORTH-EASTERN REGION[a]	12.3	945	971	40	12.3	14.1	2.5	62	75	87	91	86	88
INDIA	1,027.0	933	927	71	25.1	22.4	3.4	54	76	68	85	74	83

Notes: [a] Except for 'population', the figures in this row are population-weighted averages of the state-specific figures.

TABLE A.4 *Selected Development Indicators for the North-Eastern States* PART 2

	Female labour force participation rate, 1991 (%)	Proportion (%) of women aged 20–24 married before age 18, 1998–9	Proportion (%) of adult women who have access to money, 1998–9[a]	Proportion (%) of births attended by health professional, 1998–9	Proportion (%) of children aged 12–23 months (1998–9) who have received		Proportion (%) of severely undernourished children, 1998–9[b]	Voter turnout, 1999 (%)	
					Full immuniz-ation	No immuni-zation		Female	Male
Arunachal Pradesh	38	28	79	32	21	29	8	75	69
Manipur	39	10	77	54	42	17	5	64	67
Meghalaya	35	26	82	21	14	42	11	53	59
Mizoram	44	12	55	68	60	11	5	63	68
Nagaland	38	23	28	33	14	33	7	75	77
Sikkim	30	22	79	35	47	18	4	83	80
Tripura	14	n/a	n/a	n/a	n/a	n/a	n/a	65	71
NORTH-EASTERN REGION[c]	31	20	67	39	29	27	8	66	69
INDIA	22	50	60	42	42	14	18	56	64

Notes: [a] Base: ever-married women aged 15-49.
[b] Weight-for-age criterion (children under age 3).
[c] Population-weighted averages of the state-specific figures.
Sources: See Table A.3.

TABLE A.5 *Development Indicators for the 'New' States*

	Chattisgarh[a]	Jharkhand[a]	Uttaranchal[a]	India
Population, 2001 (millions)	20.8	26.9	8.5	1,027
Female-male ratio,2001 (women per 1,000 men)				
All ages	990	941	964	933
Age 0–6	975	966	906	927
Infant mortality rate, 1999 (per 1,000 live births)	78	71	52	70
Death rate, 1999 (per 1,000)	9.6	8.9	6.5	8.7
Birth rate, 1999 (per 1,000)	26.9	26.3	19.6	26.1
Literacy rate, age 7+, 2001 (%)				
Female	52	39	60	54
Male	78	68	84	76

Notes: [a] Formerly part of Madhya Pradesh, Bihar, and Uttar Pradesh, respectively.
Sources: Government of India (2001b) and *Sample Registration Bulletin*, April 2001.

Table A.6 *India: Trends over Time*

	1950-1	1960-1	1970-1	1973-4	1977-8	1980-1	1983-4	1987-8	1990-1	1993-4	1997-8	1999-2000	Index of annual rate of change, 1970-1 to 1999-2000[a] (%)
Population (millions)	361	439	548	–	–	683	–	–	843	–	–	1,027[b]	2.0
Gross domestic product at constant prices (1950-1 = 100)	100	147	211	222	266	286	335	396	493	556	723	820	4.8
Index of agricultural production (1950-1 = 100)	100	149	186	187	220	221	257	250	321	341	357	383	2.9
Index of industrial production (1950-1 = 100)	100	198	357	395	496	546	655	908	1,160	1,266	1,742	1,956	6.1
Gross domestic capital formation (as % of GDP)	8.7	14.4	15.5	17.4	18.4	20.3	18.7	22.5	26.3	23.1	25.0	23.3	1.7
'Volume index' of foreign trade (1978-9 = 100)													
exports	–	–	59	70	93	108	113	140	194	258	386	n/a	6.7
imports	–	–	67	87	100	138	185	205	238	329	562	n/a	7.8
Employment in organized private sector[c] (1,000 persons)	–	5,040	6,742	6,794	7,043	7,395	7,346	7,392	7,677	7,930	8,748	8,698[d]	0.9
Employment in the public sector (1,000 persons)	–	7,050	10,731	12,486	14,200	15,484	16,869	18,320	19,058	19,445	19,418	19,415[d]	2.1

Table A.6 (contd.)

	1950–1	1960–1	1970–1	1973–4	1977–8	1980–1	1983–4	1987–8	1990–1	1993–4	1997–8	1999–2000	Index of annual rate of change 1970–1 to 1999–2000[a] (%)
Per-capita earnings of public-sector employees (Rs/year at 1960 prices)	–	–	–	2,229	3,101	3,551	3,939	4,421	5,171	5,664	7,187	n/a	3.9
Real wages of agricultural labourers (Rs/day at 1960 prices)	–	–	1.52	1.37	1.74	1.65	1.71	2.36	2.48	2.59	2.99	2.95	2.8
Per-capita net availability of cereals and pulses[e] (grams/day)	397	460	453	426	458	440	457	472	485	477	475	462	0.2
Head-count index of poverty[f] (%)													
rural	45.6	48.1	56.2	55.5	50.6	–	45.3	39.2	35.4	36.7	36.6	n/a	–1.8
urban	36.1	46.9	46.1	46.8	40.5	–	35.7	36.2	33.1	30.5	29.0	n/a	–1.7
'Squared poverty gap' index of poverty[f] (%)													
rural	7.1	5.8	7.3	7.2	6.1	–	4.8	3.0	2.8	2.8	2.7	n/a	–4.2
urban	4.6	6.3	5.6	5.2	4.5	–	3.6	3.1	3.1	2.4	2.5	n/a	–3.1
Gini coefficient of per-capita consumer expenditure													
rural	33.7	32.5	28.8	28.5	30.9	–	30.1	29.4	27.7	28.6	30.6	n/a	0.0
urban	40.0	35.6	34.7	30.3	34.7	–	34.1	34.6	34.0	34.3	36.5	n/a	0.3

Table A.6 (contd.)

	1950–1	1960–1	1970–1	1973–4	1977–8	1980–1	1983–4	1987–8	1990–1	1993–4	1997–8	1999–2000	Index of annual rate of change, 1970–1 to 1999–2000[a] (%)
Literacy rate[g] (%)													
female	9	15	22	–	–	30	–	–	39	–	–	54[b]	3.0
male	27	40	46	–	–	56	–	–	64	–	–	76[b]	1.6
Birth rate[h] (per 1,000)	39.9	41.7	36.9	34.5	33.3	33.9	33.9	31.5	29.5	28.7	26.5	26.1[d]	–1.1
Infant mortality rate (per 1,000 live births)	~180	n/a	129	126	127	110	104	94	80	74	72	70[d]	–2.7
Life expectancy at birth[i] (years)	32.1	41.3	45.6	–	–	53.9	55.5	57.7	59.0	60.5	61.1	63	1.0

Notes: [a] Average annual growth rate, calculated by OLS regression of the logarithm of the relevant variable on time, based on all available observations for the period 1970–1 to 1999–2000 (including observations not reported in the table).
[b] 2001.
[c] Non-agricultural establishments employing ten persons or more.
[d] 1999.
[e] Three-year averages. The figures for '1950–1' and '1999–2000' are three-year averages for 1951–3 and 1998–2000, respectively.
[f] For years other than those corresponding to 'quinquennial' NSS surveys (i.e. years other than 1977–8, 1983–4, 1987–8, 1993–4), the estimate is a two-year average ending in the reference year (e.g. average of 1969–70 and 1970–1, for '1970–1'). The figures for '1950–1' and '1997–8' are two-year averages ending in 1952 and 1997, respectively.
[g] Age 5 and above for 1951, 1961 and 1971; age 7 and above for 1981 onwards.
[h] Data for 1950–1 and 1960–1 relate to the periods 1941–51 and 1951–61, respectively (census estimates).
[i] Data for 1950–1, 1960–1 and 1970–1 relate to the decade preceding the reference year (e.g. 1941–50, for the '1950–1' estimate). The 1980–1 figure is an unweighted average of SRS-based estimates for 1976–80 and 1981–5. The estimation periods associated with other reference years are as follows: 1981–5 (for '1983–4'); 1986–90 (for '1987–8'); unweighted average of 1986–90 and 1991–5 (for '1990–1'); unweighted average of 1991–5 and 1992–6 (for '1993–4'); 1993–7 (for '1997–8'); the last figure, 63 years for '1999–2000', is the 1999 estimate published in World Development Indicators 2001.

Table A.6 (contd.)

Sources: Population: Government of India (2001b), p. 34, based on census data. *Gross domestic product*: Government of India (2001c), p. S-5. *Index of agricultural production*: Government of India (2000i), pp. 140–1. *Index of industrial production*: Calculated from CSO data presented in Government of India (2001a). *Capital formation*: Government of India (2001c), p. S-9. *Foreign trade*: Government of India (2001c), p. S-97. *Employment*: Calculated from Government of India, *Economic Survey 1976–7*, pp. 79–80, *Economic Survey 1985–6*, pp. 142–3, *Economic Survey 1993–4*, pp. S-53 and S-54, *Economic Survey 2000–1*, p. S-53. *Earnings of public-sector employees*: Government of India (2001c), p. S-54. *Agricultural wages*: Calculated from data collected by the Department of Economics and Statistics, partly published in *Agricultural Wages in India* (various years). *Availability of cereals and pulses*: Government of India (2001c), p. S-24. *Poverty and inequality indices*: Datt (1997, 1999a, 1999b), based on National Sample Survey data. *Literacy*: Government of India (2001c), p. S-1, and *Sample Registration Bulletin*, April 2001, Table 1. *Birth and death rates*: Government of India (1999a), Table 1, Government of India (2001c), p. S-1, and *Sample Registration Bulletin*, April 2001, Table 1. *Infant mortality rate*: Government of India (1999a), Table 1, and *Sample Registration Bulletin*, April 2001, Table 1; the 1951 estimate is from Dyson (1997), pp. 111–7. *Life expectancy*: Up to 1970–1: census-based estimates presented in Government of India (2001c), p. S-1; 1980–1 to 1997–8: calculated from SRS-based estimates presented in Government of India (1999a), p. 16; the 1999–2000 figure is from *World Development Indicators 2001*. In cases where the original source gives figures for calendar years, we have placed the figure for a particular year in the column corresponding to the pair of years *ending* in that year (e.g. the 1991 literacy rate appears in the 1990–1 column, etc.)

Sources Used in Tables A.3

Indicator	Source
Part 1	
Population, 2001	Census of India 2001, 'provisional population totals' (Government of India, 2001b, p. 142).
Household expenditure per capita, 1999–2000	Calculated from National Sample Survey Organisation (2000), Statements 3R and 3U; the rural and urban figures have been aggregated using the relevant population weights, from the 2001 census.
Growth rate of real per-capita 'state domestic product'	For the 1980s: Ahluwalia (2000), Table 1 (Ahluwalia's estimates of growth rates of total GDP have been converted in per-capita terms using recent census data on population growth rates). For the 1990s: calculated (by semi-log regression) from unpublished Central Statistical Organisation data supplied by the Planning Commission. Our own estimates for the 1980s, based on CSO data, are consistent with Ahluwalia's.
Poverty indices, 1993–4	Deaton and Tarozzi (2000), Table 10, based on National Sample Survey data; the 'poverty gap' indices are based on further calculations by Angus Deaton, using the same data. The head-count ratios for rural and urban areas 'combined' are population-weighted averages of the rural and urban head-count ratios.
Gini coefficient of per-capita expenditure, 1993–4	Datt (1997, 1999a, 1999b), based on National Sample Survey data.
Proportion (%) of 'asset-poor' households, 1992–3	Filmer and Pritchett (1999), Table 2, based on an index of ownership of durables constructed (using the 'principal components' method) from National Family Health Survey data.
Part 2	
Life expectancy, 1993–7	Unpublished Sample Registration System (SRS) estimates supplied by the Office of the Registrar General, to be published in *Sample Registration System*; partly published in Government of India (2001c), p. S-116.
Infant mortality, 1997–9	Three-year average based on SRS data presented in Government of India (1999a), Table 1, Government of India (2000h), p. 74, and *Sample Registration Bulletin*, April 2001, Table 1.
Death rate, age 0–4, 1996–8	Three-year average based on SRS data presented in Government of India (1999a), Tables 10 and 11, and Government of India (2000h), Table 8.
Estimated maternal mortality rate, 1987–96	Mari Bhat (2001), Table 7.
Death rate and birth rate, 1997–9	Three-year of averages based on SRS data presented in Government of India (1999a), Table 1, Government of India (2000h), pp. 31 and 63, and *Sample Registration Bulletin*, April 2001, Table 1. The figures for Jammu & Kashmir are from *Sample Registration Bulletin*, October 1999, Table 1.

Indicator	Source
Total fertility rate, 1996–8	Three-year average based on SRS data presented in Government of India (1999a), Table 1 and Government of India (2000h), p. 46.

Part 3

Indicator	Source
Literacy rates, age 7 and above, 2001	Census of India 2001, 'provisional population totals' (Government of India, 2001b, p. 143).
Literacy rates, age 15–19, 1998–9	National Family Health Survey 1998-9 (International Institute for Population Sciences, forthcoming).
Proportion of persons aged 15–19 who have attained a specific grade, 1992–3	Calculated from Filmer (1999), based on the National Family Health Survey 1992–3.

Part 4

Indicator	Source
School attendance, 1992–3 and 1998–9	International Institute for Population Sciences (1995b), Table 3.10, p. 56, and International Institute for Population Sciences (forthcoming).
Proportion of never-enrolled children in the 10–12 age group, 1992–3	Calculated from Filmer (1999), based on National Family Health Survey data (unweighted average of the relevant figures for ages 10, 11 and 12).

Part 5

Indicator	Source
Female-male ratio, 2001	Census of India 2001, 'provisional population totals' (Government of India, 2001b, p. 141).
Ratio of female to male death rate, age 0–4, 1996–8	Calculated from SRS data presented in Government of India (1999a), Tables 10 and 11, and Government of India (2000h), Table 8, pp. 169–85.
Proportion of women aged 20–24 married before age 18, 1998–9	International Institute for Population Sciences (2000a), p. 440, based on the National Family Health Survey 1998–9.
Female labour force participation rate, 1991	Census data presented in Government of India (2001c), p. 115.
Indicators of women's autonomy, 1998–9	International Institute for Population Sciences (2000a), Table 3.9, p. 65 and Table 3.12, p. 70, based on the National Family Health Survey 1998–9.
Share of female employment in the public sector, 1989	Nuna (1990), p. 99.

Parts 6–8

Indicator	Source
'Reproductive health and related matters' (Part 6)	International Institute for Population Sciences (2000a), pp. 142, 234, 293, 305, based on the National Family Health Survey 1998–9.
'Health care and related matters' (Part 7)	International Institute for Population Sciences (2000a), pp. 157, 209, 215, 223, 227, and International Institute for Population Sciences (forthcoming), Table 6.9, based on the National Family Health Survey 1998–9.
'Nutrition-related indicators' (Part 8)	International Institute for Population Sciences (2000a), pp. 246, 252, 270, 273, 440, based on the National Family Health Survey 1998–9.

Indicator	Source
Part 9	
Proportion of villages with medical facilities, 1981	Calculated from the *District Census Handbooks* of the 1981 census.
Availability of hospital beds, 1991–8	Calculated from Government of India (2001e), p. 173, and Government of India (2001b), pp. 42–3.
Reach of public distribution system, 1993–4	Special tabulation of National Sample Survey data (50th round) by Alessandro Tarozzi, Princeton University.
Access to safe drinking water, 1991	Sundaram and Tendulkar (1994), based on 1991 census data.
Electrification, 1998–9	International Institute for Population Sciences (2000a), Table 2.12, p. 38, based on the National Family Health Survey 1998–9.
Part 10	
Newspaper subscription, 1998	National Sample Survey Organisation (1999), Report 450, Statement 13.
Use of telephone, 1998	Calculated from National Sample Survey Organisation (1999), Report 450, Statement 11, p. 33.
Media exposure, 1998–9	International Institute for Population Sciences (2000a), Table 3.7, p. 60, based on the National Family Health Survey 1998–9.
Voter turnout, 1999	Calculated from Election Commission of India (2000), pp. 8, 19–24 and 93.
Part 11	
Ownership of agricultural land, 1992–3	International Institute for Population Sciences (1995a), Table 3.13, and International Institute for Population Sciences (1995b), Table 3.9.
Proportion of agricultural labourers in the rural population, 1991	Calculated from 1991 census data presented in Nanda (1992), Tables 3 and 3.1.
Real agricultural wages, 1997–9 .	Data supplied by the Department of Economics and Statistics, partly published in *Agricultural Wages in India* (various years). The all-India figure is a weighted average of the state-specific figures (with weights proportional to the number of agricultural labourers in each state).
Growth rate of real agricultural wages, 1990–2000	Calculated from Department of Economic and Statistics data (see above).
Murder rate, 1998	National Crime Records Bureau data presented in Government of India (2000g), Table 6, p. 49.
Suicide rate, 1997	National Crime Records Bureau data presented in Government of India (1999d), Table 15, p. 134.

References*

Abraham, Itty (1998), *The Making of the Indian Atomic Bomb* (London: Zed)
_____ (1999), 'Nuclear Power and Human Security', *Bulletin of Concerned Asian Scholars*, 31.
Acharya, Poromesh, and associates (1996), 'Educating West Bengal: Problems of Participatory Management', mimeo, Siksha Bhavna, Calcutta.
Acharya, Sarthi (1989), 'Agricultural Wages in India: A Disaggregated Analysis', *Indian Journal of Agricultural Economics*, 44.
Adelman, Irma, and Morris, Cynthia T. (1973), *Economic Growth and Social Equity in Developing Countries* (Stanford: Stanford University Press).
Adelman, Irma, and Robinson, Sherman (1978), *Income Distribution Policy in Developing Countries: A Case Study of Korea* (Oxford: Clarendon Press).
Agarwal, Anil, and Narain, Sunita (1989), *Towards Green Villages* (New Delhi: Centre for Science and Environment).
Agarwal, Bina (1986), 'Women, Poverty and Agricultural Growth in India', *Journal of Peasant Studies*, 13.
_____ (1991), 'Social Security and the Family: Coping with Seasonality and Calamity in Rural India', in Ahmad et al. (1991).
_____ (1994), *A Field of One's Own: Gender and Land Rights in South Asia* (Cambridge: Cambridge University Press).
_____ (1996), 'Tribal Matriliny in Transition: The Garos, Khasis and Lalungs of North-East India', Working Paper 10/WP 50, World Employment Programme, ILO, Geneva.

*This list of references includes a number of articles published in newspapers and magazines not ordinarily available in libraries; most of these articles, however, can be found on the websites of the relevant periodicals (e.g. www.hinduonnet.com for *The Hindu*).

—— (1997a), 'Gender, Environment and Poverty Interlinks: Regional Variations and Temporal Shifts in Rural India, 1971–1991', *World Development*, 25.

—— (1997b), 'Environmental Action, Gender Equity, and Women's Participation', *Development and Change*, 28.

—— (1998), 'Environmental Management, Equity and Ecofeminism: Debating India's Experience', *Journal of Peasant Studies*, 25.

Aggarwal, Yash (2000), *An Assessment of Trends in Access and Retention* (New Delhi: National Institute of Educational Planning and Administration).

Agnihotri, A., and Sivaswamy, G. (1993), *Total Literacy Campaign in the Sundergarh District of Orissa* (New Delhi: Directorate of Adult Education).

Agnihotri, Satish (1995), 'Missing Females: A Disaggregated Analysis', *Economic and Political Weekly*, 19 August.

—— (1996), 'Sex Ratio Variations in India: What Do Languages Tell Us?', paper presented at the annual conference of the Indian Association for the Study of Population, Vadodara.

—— (2000), *Sex Ratio Patterns in the Indian Population: A Fresh Exploration* (New Delhi: Sage).

Ahluwalia, I. J., and Little, I.M.D. (eds.) (1998), *India's Economic Reforms and Development* (New Delhi: Oxford University Press).

Ahluwalia, Montek S. (1978), 'Rural Poverty and Agricultural Performance in India', *Journal of Development Studies*, 14.

—— (2000), 'Economic Performance of States in Post-reforms Period', *Economic and Political Weekly*, 6 May.

Ahmad, E., Drèze, J.P., Hills, J., and Sen, A.K. (eds.) (1991), *Social Security in Developing Countries* (Oxford: Oxford University Press).

Ahuja, Ram (1969), *Female Offenders in India* (Meerut: Meenakshi Prakashan).

Aiyar, Swaminathan S. A. (2000), 'New Light on the Poverty Puzzle', *Economic Times*, 14 June.

Akerlof, George (1970), 'Quality Uncertainty and the Market Mechanism', *Quarterly Journal of Economics*, 84.

AKG Centre for Research and Studies (1994), *International Congress on Kerala Studies: Abstracts*, 5 volumes (Thiruvananthapuram: AKG Centre for Research and Studies).

Alailima, P., and Sanderatne, N. (1997), 'Social Policies in a Slowly Growing Economy: Sri Lanka', in Mehrotra and Jolly (1997).

Alamgir, Mohiuddin (1980), *Famine in South Asia* (Boston: Oelgeschlager, Gunn and Hain).

Alesina, Alberto, and Rodrik, Dani (1994), 'Distributive Politics and Economic Growth', *Quarterly Journal of Economics*, 109.

Altekar, A.S. (1956), *The Position of Women in Hindu Civilization* (Delhi: Motilal Banarsidass).

Amnesty International (1992), *India: Torture, Rape and Deaths in Custody* (New York: Amnesty International).

Amsden, Alice H. (1989), *Asia's Next Giant: Late Industrialization in South Korea* (Oxford: Clarendon Press).

Amsden, Alice H. (1994), 'Why Isn't the Whole World Experimenting with the East Asian Model to Develop?', *World Development*, 22.

Anand, Sudhir (1993), 'Inequality Between and Within Nations', mimeo, Center for Population and Development Studies, Harvard University.

Anand, Sudhir, and Kanbur, S.M. Ravi (1990), 'Public Policy and Basic Needs Provision: Intervention and Achievement in Sri Lanka', in Drèze and Sen (1990), vol. III.

Anand, Sudhir, and Kanbur, S.M. Ravi (1993), 'Inequality and Development: A Critique', *Journal of Development Economics*, 40.

Anand, Sudhir, and Ravallion, Martin (1993), 'Human Development in Poor Countries: On the Role of Private Incomes and Public Services', *Journal of Economic Perspectives*, 7.

Andreski, Stanislav (1964), *Elements of Comparative Sociology* (London: Weidenfeld & Nicolson).

Andreski, Stanislav (1992), *Wars, Revolutions, Dictatorships* (London: Frank Cass).

Anon (2001), 'Growth and Poverty', background paper prepared for Himachal Pradesh's Human Development Report; mimeo, United Nations Development Programme, New Delhi.

Antia, N.H., Dutta, G.P., and Kasbekar, A.B. (2000), *Health and Medical Care: A People's Movement* (Mumbai: Foundation for Research in Community Health).

Antony, T.V. (1992), 'The Family Planning Programme: Lessons from Tamil Nadu's Experience', *Indian Journal of Social Science*, 5.

Anveshi (1993), 'Reworking Gender Relations, Redefining Politics: Nellore Village Women against Arrack', *Economic and Political Weekly*, 16 January.

Archer, David, and Costello, Patrick (1990), *Literacy and Power: The Latin American Battleground* (London: Earthscan Publications).

Arneson, R. (1989), 'Equality and Equality of Opportunity for Welfare', *Philosophical Studies*, 56.

Arnett, Eric (1998), 'Big Science, Small Results', *Bulletin of the Atomic Scientists*, 54.

—— (1999), 'Nuclear Tests by India and Pakistan', in *SIPRI Yearbook 1999* (Oxford: Oxford University Press).

Arokiasamy, P. (2000a), 'Gender Preference, Contraceptive Use and Fertility in India', mimeo, International Institute for Population Sciences, Mumbai.

—— (2000b), 'Gender Bias in Child Health Care and Excess Female Child Mortality in India. The Roles of Culture, Household Economic Status and Women's Position', mimeo, International Institute for Population Sciences, Mumbai.

Arrow, Kenneth J. (1951), 'An Extension of the Basic Theorems of Classical Welfare Economics', in Neyman, J. (ed.) (1951), *Proceedings of the Second Berkeley Symposium on Mathematical Economics* (Berkeley, CA: University of California Press).

—— (1963a), *Social Choice and Individual Values*, second edition (New York: Wiley).

_____ (1963b), 'Uncertainty and the Welfare Economics of Medical Care', *American Economic Review*, 53.

Arrow, Kenneth J., and Hahn, Frank (1971), *General Competitive Analysis* (San Francisco: Hoden-Day).

Arrow, K.J., Sen, A.K., and Suzumura, K. (eds.) (1996–7), *Social Choice Re-examined*, 2 volumes (Basingstoke: Macmillan).

Ashton, B., Hill, K., Piazza, A., and Zeitz, R. (1984), 'Famine in China, 1958–61', *Population and Development Review*, 10.

Ashworth, Tony (1980), *Trench Warfare 1914–1918: The Live and Let Live System* (London: Macmillan).

Athreya, V.B., and Chunkath, S.R. (1996), *Literacy and Empowerment* (New Delhi: Sage).

Atiyah, Sir Michael (1995), Presidential 'Anniversary Address' at the Anniversary Meeting of the Royal Society, 30 November; partly reprinted in *The Guardian*, 1 December 1995.

Atkinson, A.B. (1969), 'Import Strategy and Growth under Conditions of Stagnant Export Earnings', *Oxford Economic Papers*, 21.

_____ (1989), *Poverty and Social Security* (New York: Harvester and Wheatsheaf).

_____ (1995), 'Capabilities, Exclusion, and the Supply of Goods', in Basu et al. (1995).

Azad, K.C., Swarup, R., and Sikka, B.K. (1988), *Horticultural Development in Hill Areas: A Study of Himachal Pradesh* (Delhi: Mittal).

Aziz, Abdul (1994), 'History of Panchayat Reforms in Karnataka', paper presented at a seminar on 'Management of Education under Panchayati Raj' held at the National Institute of Educational Planning and Administration, 27–28 October, New Delhi.

Babu, S.C., and Hallam, J.A. (1989), 'Socioeconomic Impacts of School Feeding Programmes: Empirical Evidence from a South Indian Village', *Food Policy*, 14.

Bagchi, Amiya K. (1994), 'Making Sense of Government's Macroeconomic Stabilization Strategy', *Economic and Political Weekly*, 30 April.

Bahadur, K.P. (1978), *History, Caste and Culture of the Rajputs* (Delhi: Ess Publications).

Bajpai, N., and Sachs, J., (1996), 'India's Economic Reforms: Some Lessons from East Asia', Development Discussion Paper 532a, Harvard Institute for International Development.

Baland, J.M., and Platteau, J.P. (1996), *Halting the Degradation of Natural Resources: Is There a Role for Rural Communities?* (Oxford: Clarendon).

Balassa, Bela (1991), *Economic Policies in the Pacific Area Developing Countries* (New York: New York University Press).

Bandhyopadhyay, Sanghamitra (2001), 'Twin Peaks: Convergence Empirics of Economic Growth across Indian States', paper presented at a conference on 'Growth and Poverty' held at the World Institute for Development Economics Research (WIDER), Helsinki.

Banerjee, A., Gertler, P., and Ghatak, M. (forthcoming), 'Empowerment and Efficiency: The Economics of a Tenancy Reform', to be published in *Journal of Political Economy*.

Banerji, Debabar (1985), *Health and Family Planning Services in India* (New Delhi: Lok Paksh).

_____ (1989), 'Rural Social Transformation and Change in Health Behaviour', *Economic and Political Weekly*, 1 July.

_____ (1996), 'Political Economy of Public Health in India', in Das Gupta, Krishnan and Chen (1996).

_____ (1997), 'India's Forgotten People and the Sickness of the Public Health Services', unpublished study; summarised as a three-part article in *Health for the Millions* (May-June 1997, July-August 1997 and March-April 1998).

Banerjee, Nirmala (1982), *Unorganised Women Workers: The Calcutta Experience* (Calcutta: Centre for Studies in Social Sciences).

Banerji, Rukmini (1997), 'Why Don't Children Complete Primary School? A Case Study of a Low-Income Neighbourhood in Delhi', *Economic and Political Weekly*, 9 August.

Banerjee, Sumanta (1992), ' "Uses of Literacy": Total Literacy Campaign in Three West Bengal Districts', *Economic and Political Weekly*, 29 February.

_____ (1994), 'Obstacles to Change', *Economic and Political Weekly*, 26 March.

Banister, Judith (1987), *China's Changing Population* (Standford: Stanford University Press).

_____ (1992), 'Demographic Aspects of Poverty in China', background paper prepared for the World Bank (1992) report *China: Strategies for Reducing Poverty in the 1990s* (Washington, DC: World Bank).

_____ (1984), 'Recent Data on the Population of China', *Population and Development Review*, 10.

Bara, D., Bhengra, R., and Minz, B. (1991), 'Tribal Female Literacy: Factors in Differentiation among Munda Religious Communities', *Social Action*, 41.

Bardhan, Kalpana (1985), 'Womens' Work, Welfare and Status', *Economic and Political Weekly*, 21 December.

Bardhan, Pranab (1974), 'On Life and Death Questions', *Economic and Political Weekly*, 9 (Special Number).

_____ (1984a), *Land, Labor and Rural Poverty* (New York: Columbia University Press).

_____ (1984b), *The Political Economy of Development in India* (Oxford: Blackwell).

_____ (1988), 'Sex Disparity in Child Survival in Rural India', in Srinivasan and Bardhan (1998).

_____ (1995), 'The Contributions of Endogenous Growth Theory to the Analysis of Development Problems: An Assessment', in Behrman, J., and Srinivasan, T.N. (eds.) (1995), *Handbook of Development Economics*, vol. IIIB (Amsterdam: North Holland).

_____ (1997a), 'Corruption and Development: A Review of the Issues', *Journal of Economic Literature*, 35.

_____ (1997b), 'The State against Society: The Great Divide in Indian Social Science Discourse', in Bose, S., and Jalal, A. (eds.) (1997), *Nationalism, Democracy and Development: State and Politics in India* (New Delhi: Oxford University Press).

Bardhan, P., Bowles, S., and Gintis, H. (2000), 'Wealth Inequality, Credit Constraints, and Economic Performance', in Atkinson, A.B., and Bourguignon, F. (eds.) (2000), *Handbook of Income Distribution* (Amsterdam: North-Holland).

Bardhan, P.K., and Rudra, A. (1975), 'Totems and Taboos of Left Mythology', *Economic and Political Weekly*, 26 April.

Barker, D.J.P. (1998), *Mothers, Babies and Health in Later Life* (Edinburgh: Churchill Livingstone).

Barro, Robert J. (1990a), 'Government Spending in a Simple Model of Endogenous Growth', *Journal of Political Economy*, 98.

—— (1990b), 'Economic Growth in a Cross Section of Countries', *Quarterly Journal of Economics*, 105.

—— (1996), *Getting it Right: Markets and Choices in a Free Society* (Cambridge, MA: MIT Press).

Barro, Robert J., and Lee, Jong-Wha (1993), 'International Comparisons of Educational Attainment', *Journal of Monetary Economics*, 32.

—— (1994), 'Losers and Winners in Economic Growth', *Proceedings of the World Bank Annual Conference on Development Economics 1993*, supplement to the *World Bank Economic Review* and *World Bank Research Observer* (Washington, DC: World Bank).

Bashir, Sajitha (2000), *Government Expenditure on Elementary Education in the Nineties* (New Delhi: The European Commission).

Bashir, Sajitha, and Ayyar, R.V. Vaidyanatha (2001), 'District Primary Education Programme', mimeo, National Council of Educational Research and Training, New Delhi; forthcoming in *Encyclopedia of Indian Education* (New Delhi: NCERT).

Basu, Alaka Malwade (1989), 'Is Discrimination in Food Really Necessary for Explaining Sex Differentials in Childhood Mortality?', *Population Studies*, 43.

—— (1992), *Culture, the Status of Women and Demographic Behaviour* (Oxford: Clarendon Press).

—— (1999), 'Fertility Decline and Increasing Gender Imbalances in India: Including a Possible South Indian Turnaround', *Development and Change*, 30.

Basu, Aparna (1988), 'A Century's Journey: Women's Education in Western India, 1820–1920', in Chanana (1988).

Basu, Kaushik (1996), 'Some Institutional and Legal Prerequisites of Economic Reform in India', in Bakker, H.E., and Schulte Nordholt, N.G. (eds.) (1996), *Corruption and Legitimacy* (Amsterdam: SISWO Publications).

—— (2000), *Prelude to Political Economy: A Study of the Social and Political Foundations of Economics* (Oxford: Oxford University Press).

Basu, K., Pattanaik, P., and Suzumura, K. (eds.)(1995), *Choice, Welfare, and Development* (Oxford: Clarendon).

Bayley, David H. (1963), 'Violent Public Protest in India: 1900–1960', *Indian Journal of Political Science*, 24.

Beck, Tony (1994), *The Experience of Poverty: Fighting for Respect and Resources in Village India* (London: Intermediate Technology Publications).

Beenstock, M., and Sturdy, P. (1990), 'The Determinants of Infant Mortality in Regional India', *World Development*, 18.

Behrman, Jere R. (1987), 'Schooling in Developing Countries: Which Countries Are the Under- and Over-Achievers and What Is the Schooling Impact?', *Economics of Education Review*, 6.

Behrman, Jere R., and Deolalikar, Anil B. (1988), 'Health and Nutrition', in Chenery and Srinivasan (1988).

Behrman, Jere R., and Schneider, Ryan (1994), 'An International Perspective on Schooling Investments in the Last Quarter Century in Some Fast-Growing East and Southeast Asian Countries', *Asian Development Review*, 12.

Behrman, Jere R., and Srinivasan, T.N. (eds.) (1994), *Handbook of Development Economics*, vol. III (Amsterdam: North-Holland).

Behrman, J.R., and Wolfe, B.L. (1984), 'More Evidence on Nutrition Demand: Income Seems Overrated and Women's Schooling Underemphasized', *Journal of Development Economics*, 14.

—— (1987), 'How Does Mother's Schooling Affect Family Health, Nutrition, Medical Care Usage, and Household Sanitation?', *Journal of Econometrics*, 36.

Bello, Walden (1998), 'East Asia: On the Eve of the Great Transformation?', *Review of International Political Economy*, 5.

Bello, Walden, and Rosenfeld, Stephanie (1991), *Dragons in Distress: Asia's Miracle Economies in Crisis* (London: Penguin).

Berlin, I. (1969), *Four Essays on Liberty*, 2nd edition (Oxford: Oxford University Press).

Bernstein, T.P. (1984), 'Stalinism, Famine, and Chinese Peasants', *Theory and Society*, 13.

Berreman, Gerald D. (1962), 'Village Exogamy in Northernmost India', *Southwestern Journal of Anthropology*, 18.

—— (1972), *Hindus of the Himalayas: Ethnography and Change*, second edition (Delhi: Oxford University Press).

—— (1993), 'Sanskritization as Female Oppression in India', in Miller (1993b).

Béteille, André (1999), 'Record of Rights: The Marie-Antoinette Solution', *Times of India*, 28 January.

Bhaduri, A., and Nayyar, D. (1996), *The Intelligent Person's Guide to Liberalization* (New Delhi: Penguin).

Bhagwati, Jagdish (1993), *India in Transition* (Oxford: Clarendon Press).

Bhagwati, Jagdish, and Srinivasan, T.N. (1975), *Foreign Trade Regimes and Economic Development: India* (New York: National Bureau of Economic Research).

—— (1993), *India's Economic Reforms* (New Delhi: Ministry of Finance, Government of India).

Bhalla, A.S. (1992), *Uneven Development in the Third World: A Study of India and China* (London: Macmillan).

Bhalla, Sheila (1995), 'Development, Poverty and Policy: The Haryana Experience', *Economic and Political Weekly*, 14 October.

Bhalla, Surjit (2000a), 'Growth and Poverty in India: Myth and Reality', mimeo, Oxus Research and Investments, New Delhi.

—— (2000b), 'FAQ's on Poverty in India', mimeo, Oxus Research and Investments, New Delhi.

Bhargava, Alok (1998), 'Family Planning, Gender Differences and Infant Mortality: Evidence from Uttar Pradesh (India)', mimeo, Department of Economics, University of Houston.

Bhatia, Bela (1992), 'Lush Fields and Parched Throats', *Economic and Political Weekly*, 19 December.

—— (1998a) 'Social Action with Rural Widows in Gujarat', in Chen (1998).

—— (1998b), 'Rethinking Revolution in Bihar', *Seminar*, 464.

—— (2000), 'The Naxalite Movement in Central Bihar', PhD thesis, University of Cambridge.

Bhatia, Bela, and Drèze, Jean (1998), 'For Democracy and Development', *Frontline*, 6 March.

Bhatia, Bimal (1999), 'The Media's Role in a War', *Hindustan Times*, 3 August.

Bhattacharya, B.B., and Mitra, Arup (1993), 'Employment and Structural Adjustment', *Economic and Political Weekly*, 18 September.

Bhatty, Kiran (1998), 'Educational Deprivation in India: A Survey of Field Investigations', *Economic and Political Weekly*, 4–10 July.

—— (forthcoming), 'Social Capital and the State: Educational Performance in Himachal Pradesh', PhD thesis, London School of Economics.

Bhatty, Zarina (1999), 'Educational Backwardness in Mewat', in Probe Team (1999).

Bhuiya, A., and Streatfield, K.(1991), 'Mothers' Education and Survival of Female Children in a Rural Area of Bangladesh', *Population Studies*, 45.

Bidani, B., and Ravallion, M. (1997), 'Decomposing Social Indicators Using Distributional Data', *Journal of Econometrics*, 77.

Bidwai, P., and Vanaik, A. (1999), *South Asia on a Short Fuse: Nuclear Politics and the Future of Global Disarmament* (New Delhi: Oxford University Press).

Binswanger, Hans, and Rosenzweig, Mark (1984), *Contractual Arrangements, Employment and Wages in Rural Labour Markets in Asia* (New Haven: Yale University Press).

Birdsall, Nancy (1993), 'Social Development Is Economic Development', Policy Research Working Paper 1123, World Bank, Washington, DC.

Birdsall, Nancy, Ross, David, and Sabot, Richard H. (1995), 'Virtuous Circles: Human Capital, Growth and Equity in East Asia', *World Bank Economic Review*, 9.

Birdsall, Nancy, and Sabot, Richard H. (eds.) (1993), *Opportunity Forgone: Education, Growth and Inequality in Brazil* (Washington, DC: World Bank).

Blackorby, Charles, and Donaldson, David (1980), 'Ethical Indices for the Measurement of Poverty', *Econometrica*, 48.

Blair, Bruce G. (1993), *The Logic of Accidental Nuclear War* (Washington, DC: Brookings Institution).

—— (1997), Statement to the House National Security Subcommittee, 13 March; available at www.house.gov/hasc/1997schedule.htm.

Bliss, Christopher, and Stern, Nicholas (1978), 'Productivity, Wages and Nutrition', *Journal of Development Economics*, 5.

_____ (1982), *Palanpur: The Economy of an Indian Village* (Oxford: Oxford University Press).

Bloch, Jan de (1899), *The Future of War*, translated by R.C. Long (Boston: Ginn).

Blomkvist, Hans (2000a), 'Democracy, Social Capital, and Civil Society in India', mimeo, Uppsala University; to be published in Elliott, C. (ed.) (forthcoming), *Civil and Uncivil Society in India* (Delhi: Oxford University Press).

_____ (2000b), 'Traditional Communities, Caste, and Democracy: The Indian Mystery', mimeo, Uppsala University; to be published in Dekker, P., and Uslaner, E. (eds.) (forthcoming), *Social Capital and Politics in Everyday Life* (London: Routledge).

Bloom, Gerald (1998), 'Primary Health Care Meets the Market in China and Vietnam', *Health Policy*, 44.

Bloom, Gerald, and Gu Xingyuan (1997a), 'Introduction to Health Sector Reform in China', *IDS Bulletin*, 28.

Bloom, Gerald, and Gu Xingyuan (1997b), 'Health Sector Reform: Lessons from China', *Social Science and Medicine*, 45.

Bloom, Gerald, and Wilkes, Andreas (eds.) (1997), *Health in Transition: Reforming China's Rural Health Services*, special issue of *IDS Bulletin*, 28.

Bloom, G., Tang Sheng-Lan, and Gu Xingyuan (1995), 'Financing Rural Health Services: Lessons in China in the Context of Economic Reform', *Journal of International Development*, 7.

Bondroit, Marie-Eve (1998), 'Les Déterminants de l'Alphabétisation Féminine: Le Cas de l'Inde', MA thesis, Université de Namur, Belgium.

_____ (1999), 'Gender Relations and Schooling: Himachal Pradesh vs Haryana', in Probe Team (1999).

Borooah, V.K. (2000), 'Do Children in India Benefit from Having Mothers Who Are Literate?', paper prepared for the Programme of Research on Human Development of the National Council of Applied Economic Research, New Delhi.

Bose, Ashish (1991), *Demographic Diversity of India* (Delhi: B.R. Publishing).

Boserup, Ester (1970), *Women's Role in Economic Development* (New York: St Martin's).

Bourne, K., and Walker, G.M.(1991), 'The Differential Effect of Mothers' Education on Mortality of Boys and Girls in India', *Population Studies*, 45.

Bowles, Samuel (1998), 'Endogenous Preferences: The Cultural Consequences of Markets and Other Economic Institutions', *Journal of Economic Literature*, 36.

Bracken, Paul (1985), 'Accidental Nuclear War', in Allison, G.T., Carnesale, A., and Nye, J.S. (eds.) (1985), *Hawks, Doves and Owls: An Agenda for Avoiding Nuclear War* (New York: W.W. Norton).

Bramall, Chris, and Jones, Marion (1993), 'Rural Income Inequality in China since 1978', *Journal of Peasant Studies*, 21.

Breman, Jan (1974), *Patronage and Exploitation* (Berkeley, CA: University of California Press).

Brown, Lester R., and Eckholm, Erik P. (1974), *By Bread Alone* (Oxford: Pergamon).

Brown, Lester R., and Halweil, Brian (1999), 'India Reaching 1 Billion on August 15: No Celebration Planned', *International Herald Tribune*, 11 August.

Bruton, Henry, with Abeyesekara, G., Sanderatne, N., and Yusof, Z.A. (1993), *The Political Economy of Poverty, Equity, and Growth: Sri Lanka and Malaysia* (New York: Oxford University Press).

Buchanan, James M., and Yoon, Yong J. (1994), *The Return to Increasing Returns* (Ann Arbor: University of Michigan Press).

Budakoti, D.K. (1988), 'Study of the Community and Community Health Work in Two Primary Health Centres in Chamoli District of Uttar Pradesh', MPhil dissertation, Centre for Social Medicine and Community Health, Jawaharlal Nehru University, New Delhi.

Bumgarner, R. (1992), 'China: Long-Term Issues and Options for the Health Transition', World Bank Country Study, World Bank, Washington, DC.

Burgess, Robin (2000), 'Land Distribution and Welfare in Rural China', mimeo, STICERD, London School of Economics; forthcoming as a STICERD Working Paper.

Burra, Neera (1988), *Child Labour Health Hazards* (New Delhi: Seminar Publications).

—— (1995), *Born to Work: Child Labour in India* (Delhi: Oxford University Press).

Butler, General George Lee (1997), 'Time to End the Age of Nukes', *Bulletin of Atomic Scientists*, 53.

Byrd, W., and Lin, Q. (eds.) (1990), *China's Rural Industry: Structure, Development, and Reform* (Oxford: Oxford University Press).

Cable, Vincent (1995), 'Indian Liberalisation and the Private Sector', in Cassen and Joshi (1995).

Caldwell, J.C. (1979), 'Education as a Factor in Mortality Decline: An Examination of Nigerian Data', *Population Studies*, 33.

—— (1986), 'Routes to Low Mortality in Poor Countries', *Population and Development Review*, 12.

Caldwell, J.C., Reddy, P.H., and Caldwell, P. (1985), 'Educational Transition in Rural South India', *Population and Development Review*, 11.

Caldwell, J.C., Reddy, P.H., and Caldwell, P. (1989), *The Causes of Demographic Change* (Madison: University of Wisconsin Press).

Caldwell, P., and Caldwell, J.C. (1987), 'Where There is a Narrower Gap between Female and Male Situations: Lessons from South India and Sri Lanka', paper presented at a workshop on 'Differentials in Mortality and Health Care', BAMANEH/SSRC, Dhaka.

Cassen, Robert (2000), 'Population, Development and Environment: India and Beyond', mimeo, London School of Economics.

Cassen, Robert, and Joshi, Vijay (eds.) (1995), *India: The Future of Economic Reform* (Delhi: Oxford University Press).

Cassen, Robert, with contributors (1994), *Population and Development: Old Debates, New Conclusions* (Washington, DC: Transaction Books).

Castaneda, T. (1985), 'Determinantes del Descenso de la Mortalidad Infantil en Chile 1975–1983', *Cuadernos de Economía*, 22.

Central Statistical Organisation (1991a), *Estimates of State Domestic Product and Gross Fixed Capital Formation* (New Delhi: CSO).

—— (1991b), *National Accounts Statistics* (New Delhi: CSO).

—— (1994), *National Accounts Statistics* (New Delhi: CSO).

—— (1999), *National Accounts Statistics* (New Delhi: CSO).

Centre for Monitoring the Indian Economy (1994a), *Basic Statistics Relating to the Indian Economy* (Mumbai: CMIE).

—— (1994b), *Basic Statistics Relating to the States of India* (Mumbai: CMIE).

—— (1999), *Public Finance* (Mumbai: CMIE).

Centre for Monitoring the Media (1999), 'The Media and Kargil: Information War with Dummy Missiles', mimeo, Centre for Monitoring the Media, Mumbai.

Centre for Science and Environment (1982), *State of India's Environment: First Citizens' Report* (New Delhi: CSE).

—— (1996), *Slow Murder: The Deadly Story of Vehicular Pollution in India* (New Delhi: CSE).

—— (1999), *The Citizen's Fifth Report*, State of India's Environment Series, 2 volumes (New Delhi: CSE).

Chakrabarti, Anindita, and Banerjea, Niharika (2000), 'Primary Education in Himachal Pradesh: A Case Study of Kinnaur District', *Journal of Educational Planning and Administration*, 14.

Chakravarti, Anand (2001), *Social Power and Everyday Class Relations: Agrarian Transformation in North Bihar* (New Delhi: Sage).

Chakravarty, Sukhamoy (1969), *Capital and Development Planning* (Cambridge, MA: MIT Press).

—— (1987), *Development Planning: The Indian Experience* (Oxford: Oxford University Press).

Chakravarty-Kaul, Minoti (1996), *Common Lands and Customary Law: Institutional Change in North India over the Past Two Centuries* (Delhi: Oxford University Press).

Chanana, Karuna (1996), 'Educational Attainment, Status Production and Women's Autonomy: A Study of Two Generations of Punjabi Women in New Delhi', in Jeffery and Basu (1996).

—— (ed.) (1988), *Socialisation, Education and Women: Explorations in Gender Identity* (New Delhi: Orient Longman).

Chand, Ramesh (1996), 'Ecological and Economic Impact of Horticultural Development in the Himalayas: Evidence from Himachal Pradesh', *Economic and Political Weekly*, 29 June.

Chanda, Nayan (1999), 'The Perils of Power', *Far Eastern Economic Review*, 4 February.

Chandhok, H.L. (1990), *Indian Database*, vol. II (New Delhi: The Policy Group).

Chari, P.R. (2001a), 'Nuclear Restraint and Risk Reduction in South Asia', transcript of a presentation made on 16 February at the Henry L. Stimson Center; available at www.ceip.org.

—— (2001b), 'The Pakistani Defence Cut', *The Hindu*, 14 July.

Chatterjee, Meera (1990), 'Indian Women: Their Health and Productivity', Discussion Paper 109, World Bank, Washington, DC.

Chattopadhyay, R., and Duflo, E. (2001), 'Women's Leadership and Policy Decisions: Evidence from a Nationwide Randomized Experiment in India', Discussion Paper 114, Institute for Economic Development, Boston University.

Chaturvedi, Bharati (1999), 'Plastic Bags: A Modern-day Blight', *The Hindu*.

Chaudhri, D.P. (1979), *Education, Innovations, and Agricultural Development* (London: Croom Helm).

——(1996), *A Dynamic Profile of Child Labour in India, 1951–1991* (New Delhi: ILO).

Chaudhuri, M. (1993), *Indian Women's Movement* (New Delhi: Radiant).

Chaudhuri, Pramit (ed.) (1971), *Aspects of Indian Economic Development* (London: Allen & Unwin).

Chaudhuri, S., Sundari Ravindran, T.K., Antia, N.H., and Mistry, N. (1996), 'Taking Health to Women: Some NGO Experiments', Monograph 1, Institute of Social Studies Trust, New Delhi.

Chaujar, Paro, and Ateeq, Nasir (2000), 'The Relevance of Education for Child Labour: A Case Study of Agra, U.P.', project report, Centre for Education and Communication, New Delhi.

Chen, K., Jefferson, G.H., and Singh, I. (1992), 'Lessons from China's Economic Reform', *Journal of Comparative Economics*, 16.

Chen, L., Huq, E., and D'Souza, S. (1981), 'Sex Bias in the Family Allocation of Food and Health Care in Rural Bangladesh', *Population and Development Review*, 7.

Chen, Marty (1991), *Coping with Seasonality and Drought* (London: Sage).

——(ed.) (1998), *Widows in India: Social Neglect and Public Action* (New Delhi: Sage).

——(2000), *Perpetual Mourning: Widowhood in Rural India* (Oxford and New Delhi: Oxford University Press).

Chen, Marty, and Drèze, Jean (1994), 'Widowhood and Well-being in Rural North India', in Das Gupta et al. (1994).

Chen, Marty, and Drèze, Jean (1995), 'Recent Research on Widows in India', *Economic and Political Weekly*, 30 September.

Chenery, Hollis, and Srinivasan, T.N. (eds.) (1988), *Handbook of Development Economics*, vol. I (Amsterdam: North-Holland).

Chengappa, Raj (2000), *Weapons of Peace: The Story of India's Quest to be a Nuclear Power* (New Delhi: Harper Collins).

Chesnais, Jean-Claude (1981), *Histoire de la Violence en Occident de 1800 à nos Jours* (Paris: Laffont).

Chichilnisky, Graciella (1983), 'North-South Trade with Export Enclaves: Food Consumption and Food Exports', mimeo, Columbia University.

Chinese Academy of Social Sciences (1987), *Almanac of China's Population 1986* (Beijing:Population Research Centre).

Choudhary, K.M., and Bapat, M.T. (1975), 'A Study of Impact of Famine and Relief Measures in Gujarat and Rajasthan', mimeo, Agricultural Economics Research Centre, Sardar Patel University.

Chunkath, S.R., and Athreya, V.B. (1997), 'Female infanticide in Tamil Nadu: Some Evidence', *Economic and Political Weekly*, 26 April.

CINI-ASHA (1996), 'Our Present Day Understanding of Child Labour Issues', *The Administrator*, 16.

Cleland, J. (1990), 'Maternal Education and Child Survival: Further Evidence and Explanations', in Caldwell, J. et al. (eds.) (1990), *What we Know About Health Transition: The Cultural, Social and Behavioural Determinants of Health* (Canberra: Health Transition Centre, Australian National University).

Cleland, J., and van Ginneken, J. (1988), 'Maternal Education and Child Survival in Developing Countries: The Search for Pathways of Influence', *Social Science and Medicine*, 27.

Cleland, J., and van Ginneken, J. (1989), 'The Effect of Maternal Schooling on Childhood Mortality: The Search for an Explanation', *Journal of Biosocial Science*, 10.

Coale, Ansley J. (1991), 'Excess Female Mortality and the Balance of the Sexes: An Estimate of the Number of "Missing Females"', *Population and Development Review*, 17.

—— (1993), 'Mortality Schedules in China Derived from Data in the 1982 and 1990 Censuses', Working Paper 93-7, Office of Population Research, Princeton University.

Coale, Ansley J., and Banister, Judith (1994), 'Five Decades of Missing Females in China', *Demography*, 31.

Cohen, Alex (2000), 'Excess Female Mortality in India: The Case of Himachal Pradesh', mimeo, Harvard Medical School.

Cohen, G.A. (1990), 'Equality of What? On Welfare, Goods and Capabilities', *Recherches Economiques de Louvain*, 56.

—— (1993), 'Equality of What? On Welfare, Resources and Capabilities', in Nussbaum and Sen (1993).

Cohn, Carol (1987), 'Sex and Death in the Rational World of Defense Intellectuals', *Signs*, 12.

Colclough, Christopher, and Lewin, Keith (1993), *Educating All the Children* (Oxford: Oxford University Press).

Coles, J.L., and Hammond, P.J. (1995), 'Walrasian Equilibrium without Survival: Existence, Efficiency, and Remedial Policy', in Basu et al. (1995).

Committee of Concerned Citizens (1998), *In Search of Democratic Space* (Hyderabad: Committee of Concerned Citizens).

Committee on the Status of Women in India (1974), *Towards Equality* (New Delhi: Ministry of Education and Social Welfare).

Cooper, Charles (1983), 'Extensions of the Raj-Sen Model of Economic Growth', *Oxford Economic Papers*, 35.

Corden, W. Max (1974), *Trade Policy and Economic Welfare* (Oxford: Clarendon Press).

—— (1993), 'Seven Asian Miracle Economies: Overview of Macroeconomic Policies', mimeo, World Bank, Washington, DC.

Cornia, G., Jolly, R., and Stewart, F. (1987), *Adjustment with a Human Face* (Oxford: Clarendon).

Count Mouravieff (1898), 'Message of the Czar', reprinted in Carnegie Endowment for International Peace (1921), *Documents Relating to the Program of the First Hague Peace Conference* (Oxford: Clarendon).

Coutinho, L., Bisht, S., and Raje, G. (2000), 'Numerical Narratives and Documentary Practices: Vaccines, Targets and Reports of Immunisation Programme', *Economic and Political Weekly*, 19 February.

Crocker, D.A. (1991), 'Toward Development Ethics', *World Development*, 19.

_____ (1992), 'Functioning and Capability: The Foundations of Sen's and Nussbaum's Development Ethics', *Political Theory*, 20.

Crook, R.C., and Manor, J. (1998), *Democracy and Decentralisation in South Asia and West Africa: Participation, Accountablity and Performance* (Cambridge: Cambridge University Press).

Currie, Bob (2000), *The Politics of Hunger in India: A Study of Democracy, Governance and Kalahandi's Poverty* (London and Chennai: Macmillan).

Dahl, Robert (1989), *Democracy and its Critics* (New Haven: Yale University Press).

Dandavate, P., Kumari, R., and Verghese, J. (eds.) (1989): *Widows, Abandoned and Destitute Women in India* (New Delhi: Radiant Publishers).

Dandekar, V.M., and Rath, N. (1971), *Poverty in India* (Bombay: Sameeksha Trust).

Das, Gurcharan (2000), *India Unbound* (New Delhi: Penguin).

Das, Prafulla (2001), 'Hunger in a Land of Plenty', *The Hindu*, 9 September.

Das, S., and Chattopadhyay, B. (1991), 'Rural Crime in Police Perception: A Study of Village Crime Notebooks', *Economic and Political Weekly*, 19 January.

Das Gupta, Monica (1987), 'Selective Discrimination against Female Children in Rural Punjab', *Population and Development Review*, 13.

_____ (1990), 'Death Clustering, Mother's Education and the Determinants of Child Mortality in Rural Punjab, India', *Population Studies*, 44.

_____ (1994), 'What Motivates Fertility Decline? Lessons from a Case Study of Punjab, India', in Egerö and Hammarskjöld (1994).

_____ (1995a), 'Fertility Decline in Punjab, India: Parallels with Historical Europe', *Population Studies*, 49.

_____ (1995b), 'Life Course Perspectives on Women's Autonomy and Health Outcomes', *American Anthropologist*, 97.

Das Gupta, Monica, Krishnan, T.N., and Chen, Lincoln (eds.) (1994), *Women's Health in India: Risk and Vulnerability* (Mumbai: Oxford University Press).

Das Gupta, Monica, Krishnan, T.N., and Chen, Lincoln (eds.) (1996) *Health, Poverty and Development in India* (New Delhi: Oxford University Press).

Das Gupta, Monica, and Li Shuzuo (1999), 'Gender Bias in China, South Korea and India: Effects of War, Famine and Fertility Decline', mimeo, forthcoming in *Development and Change*.

Das Gupta, M., and Mari Bhat, P.N. (1997), 'Fertility Decline and Increased Manifestation of Sex Bias in India', *Population Studies*, 51.

Dasgupta, Partha (1993), *An Inquiry into Well-being and Destitution* (Oxford: Clarendon Press).

Dasgupta, Partha, and Ray, Debraj (1986), 'Inequality as a Determinant of Malnutrition and Unemployment: Theory', *Economic Journal*, 96.

Dasgupta, Partha, and Ray, Debraj (1987), 'Inequality as a Determinant of Malnutrition and Unemployment: Policy', *Economic Journal*, 97.

Dasgupta, Partha, and Ray, Debraj (1990), 'Adapting to Undernourishment: The Biological Evidence and Its Implications', in Drèze and Sen (1990), vol. I.

Datt, Gaurav (1997), 'Poverty in India and Indian States', mimeo, International Food Policy Research Institute, Washington, DC.

—— (1998), 'Poverty in India and Indian States: An Update', *Indian Journal of Labour Economics*, 41.

—— (1999a), 'Has Poverty Declined since Economic Reforms?', *Economic and Political Weekly*, 11–17 December.

—— (1999b), 'Poverty in India: Trends and Decompositions', mimeo, World Bank, Washington, DC.

Datt, Gaurav, and Ravallion, Martin (1995), 'Growth and Poverty in Rural India', Policy Research Working Paper 1405, World Bank, Washington, DC.

Datt, Gaurav, and Ravallion, Martin (1998), 'Why Have Some Indian States Done Better than Others at Reducing Rural Poverty?', *Economica*, 65.

Datta, Ramesh C. (2001), 'Public Action, Social Security and Unorganised Sector', in Mahendra Dev et al. (2001).

Datta-Chaudhuri, Mrinal (1979), 'Industrialization and Foreign Trade: An Analysis Based on the Development Experience of the Republic of Korea and the Philippines', Working Paper II–4 , International Labour Organization, Bangkok.

—— (1990), 'Market Failure and Government Failure', *Journal of Economic Perspectives*, 4.

Davis, Calvin DeArmond (1962), *The United States and the First Hague Peace Conference* (Ithaca, NY: Cornell University Press).

Dayaram (2001), 'Para Teachers in Primary Education: A Status Report', mimeo, Ed. CIL, New Delhi.

De, A., Majumdar, M., Samson, M., and Noronha, C. (2000), *Role of Private Schools in Basic Education* (New Delhi: National Institute of Educational Planning and Administration).

De, A., Noronha, C., and Samson, M. (2000), *Primary Education in Himachal Pradesh: Examining a Success Story* (New Delhi: National Institute of Educational Planning and Administration).

Deaton, Angus (1997), *The Analysis of Household Surveys* (Baltimore: Johns Hopkins).

—— (2001), 'Measuring Poverty in India: Where Are We Now?', mimeo, Department of Economics, Princeton University.

Deaton, Angus, and Tarozzi, Alessandro (2000), 'Prices and Poverty in India', Working Paper 196, Research Program in Development Studies, Princeton University.

Debreu, Gérard (1959), *Theory of Value* (New York: Wiley).

Debroy, Bibek (2000), *In the Dock: Absurdities of Indian Law* (Delhi: Konark).

Debroy, B., Bhandari, L., and Banik, J. (2000), 'How Are the States Doing?', mimeo, Rajiv Gandhi Institute for Contemporary Studies, New Delhi.

De Geyndt, W., Xiyan Zhao, and Shunli Liu (1992), 'From Barefoot Doctor to Village Doctor in Rural China', World Bank Technical Paper 187, Asia Technical Department Series, World Bank, Washington, DC.

Deger, Saadet (1992), 'Military Expenditure and Economic Development: Issues and Debates', in Lamb, G., and Kallab, V. (eds.) (1992), 'Military Expenditure and Economic Development', Discussion Paper 185, World Bank, Washington, DC.

Deolalikar, Anil, and Vashishtha, Prem (1992), 'The Utilization of Government and Private Health Services in India', mimeo, National Council of Applied Economic Research, New Delhi.

Deolalikar, Anil, and Vashishtha, Prem (1996), 'The Health and Medical Sector in India: Potential Reforms and Problems', IRIS Working Paper 9, Center for Institutional Reform and the Informal Sector, University of Maryland at College Park.

Desai, Ashok (1994), *My Economic Affair* (New Delhi: Wiley Eastern).

Desai, G.M., Singh, G., and Sah, D.C. (1979), 'Impact of Scarcity on Farm Economy and Significance of Relief Operations', CMA Monograph 84, Indian Institute of Management, Ahmedabad.

Desai, Meghnad (1989), 'Poverty and Capability: Towards an Empirically Implementable Measure', in Bracho, F. (ed.) (1989), *Towards a New Way to Measure Development* (Caracao: Office of the High Commission, Venezuela).

—— (1991), 'Human Development: Concepts and Measurement', *European Economic Review*, 35.

—— (1993), *Capitalism, Socialism and the Indian Economy* (Mumbai: Export-Import Bank of India).

—— (1994), 'The Measurement Problem in Economics', *Scottish Journal of Political Economy*, 41.

Desai, Neera (ed.) (1988), *A Decade of Women's Movement in India* (Mumbai: Himalaya Publishing House).

Desai, Sonalde, and Jain, Devaki (1992), 'Maternal Employment and Changes in Family Dynamics: The Social Context of Women's Work in Rural South India', Working Paper 39, Population council, New York.

Deshingkar, G. (1998), 'Indian Politics and Arms Control', in Arnett, E. (ed.) (1998), *Nuclear Weapons and Arms Control in South Asia after the Test Ban* (Oxford: Oxford University Press).

Deshpande, Rajeshwari (1999), 'Organising the Unorganised: Case of Hamal Panchayat', *Economic and Political Weekly*, 25 September.

Dey, Nikhil, and Roy, Aruna (2000), 'The Right to Information: Facilitating People's Participation and State Accountability', paper presented at a conference on 'Directions of Political Change in India' held at the University of Oxford.

Dietrich, Gabriele (1992), *Reflections on the Women's Movement in India: Religion, Ecology, Development* (New Delhi: Horizon India Books).

Drèze, Jean (1990a), 'Famine Prevention in India', in Drèze and Sen (1990), vol. II.

_____ (1990b), 'Famine Prevention in Africa', in Drèze and Sen (1990), vol. II.

_____ (1990c), 'Widows in Rural India', Discussion Paper 26, Development Economics Research Programme, STICERD, London School of Economics.

_____ (1990d), 'Poverty in India and the IRDP Delusion', *Economic and Political Weekly*, 29 September.

_____ (1997), 'Palanpur 1957-93: Occupational Change, Land Ownership and Social Inequality', in Breman, J., Kloos, P., and Saith, A. (eds.) (1997), *The Village in Asia Revisited* (New Delhi: Oxford University Press).

_____ (1998a), 'Patterns of Literacy and their Social Context', mimeo, Delhi School of Economics; to be published in Das, V. et al. (eds.) (forthcoming) *Encyclopaedia of Sociology and Social Anthropology* (New Delhi: Oxford University Press).

_____ (1998b), 'The Fundamental Right to Education: Squaring the Circle', *Seminar*, No. 464 (April).

_____ (1998c), 'Distribution Matters in Cost-Benefit Analysis', *Journal of Public Economics*, 70.

_____ (1999), 'Himachal's Success in Promoting Female Education', *Manushi*, 112.

_____ (2000a), 'Militarism, Development and Democracy', *Economic and Political Weekly*, 1 April.

_____ (2000b), 'Comments', in Dethier, J.J. (ed.) (2000), *Governance, Decentralisation and Reform in China, India and Russia* (Boston: Kluwer).

_____ (2000c), 'Poverty: Beyond Head-count Ratios', *The Hindu*, 9 September.

_____ (2001a), 'Starving the Poor', *The Hindu*, 26 and 27 February.

_____ (2001b), 'Wake Up and Take Charge', *Hindustan Times*, 29 April.

_____ (2001c), 'From Food-for-work to Fight-for-work', *The Hindu*, 14 June.

_____ (2001d), 'No More Lifelines: Political Economy of Hunger in Orissa', *Times of India*, 17 September.

_____ (2001e), 'Upholding the Right to Food', *The Hindu*, 27 June.

Drèze, Jean, and Gazdar, Haris (1996), 'Uttar Pradesh: The Burden of Inertia', in Drèze and Sen (1996).

Drèze, Jean, Guio, Anne-Catherine, and Murthi, Mamta (1996), 'Demographic Outcomes, Economic Development and Women's Agency', *Economic and Political Weekly*, 6 July.

Drèze, Jean, and Khera, Reetika (2000), 'Crime, Gender and Society in India: Insights from Homicide Data', *Population and Development Review*, 26.

Drèze, Jean, and Khera, Reetika (2001), 'Poverty of Policy, Scarcity of Will', *Times of India*, 18 May.

Drèze, Jean, and Kingdon, Geeta Gandhi (2001), 'School Participation in Rural India', *Review of Development Economics*, 5.

Drèze, J.P., Lanjouw, P., and Sharma, N. (1998), 'Economic Development in Palanpur, 1957–93', in Lanjouw and Stern (1998).

Drèze, Jean, and Loh, Jackie (1995), 'Literacy in India and China', *Economic and Political Weekly*, 11 November.

Drèze, Jean, and Mukherjee, Anindita (1989), 'Labour Contracts in Rural India: Theories and Evidence', in Chakravarty, S. (ed.) (1989), *The Balance between Industry and Agriculture in Economic Development*, vol. III (London: Macmillan).

Drèze, Jean, and Murthi, Mamta (2001), 'Fertility, Education, and Development: Evidence from India', *Population and Development Review*, 27.

Drèze, J.P., Samson, M., and Singh, S. (eds.) (1997), *The Dam and the Nation: Displacement and Resettlement in the Narmada Valley* (New Delhi: Oxford University Press).

Drèze, Jean, and Saran, Mrinalini (1995), 'Primary Education and Economic Development in China and India: Overview and Two Case Studies', in Basu et al. (1995).

Drèze, Jean, and Sen, Amartya (1989), *Hunger and Public Action* (Oxford: Clarendon Press).

Drèze, Jean, and Sen, Amartya (eds.) (1990), *The Political Economy of Hunger*, 3 volumes (Oxford: Clarendon Press).

Drèze, Jean, and Sen, Amartya (1991), 'Public Action for Social Security', in Ahmad et al. (1991).

Drèze, Jean, and Sen, Amartya (1995a), *India: Economic Development and Social Opportunity* (Oxford and New Delhi: Oxford University Press); reprinted in *The Amartya Sen and Jean Drèze Omnibus* (Delhi: Oxford University Press).

Drèze, Jean, and Sen, Amartya (1995b), 'Basic Education as a Political Issue', *Journal of Educational Planning and Administration*, 9.

Drèze, Jean, and Sen, Amartya (eds.) (1996), *Indian Development: Selected Regional Perspectives* (Oxford and Delhi: Oxford University Press).

Drèze, Jean, and Sen, Amartya (1999), 'Public Action and Social Inequality', in Harriss-White and Subramanian (1999).

Drèze, Jean, and Sharma, Naresh (1998), 'Palanpur: Population, Society, Economy', in Lanjouw and Stern (1998).

Drèze, Jean, and Srinivasan, P.V. (1996), 'Poverty in India: Regional Estimates, 1987-8', Discussion Paper 70, Development Economics Research Programme, STICERD, London School of Economics; forthcoming (revised) in *Journal of Quantitative Economics*.

Drèze, Jean, and Srinivasan, P.V. (1997), 'Widowhood and Poverty in Rural India', *Journal of Development Economics*, 54; reprinted in Chen (1998).

Driver, Edwin D. (1961), 'Interaction and Criminal Homicide in India', *Social Forces*, 40.

Dube, Leela (1988), 'On the Construction of Gender: Hindu Girls in Patrilineal India', in Chanana (1998).

—— (2001), *Anthropological Explorations of Gender* (New Delhi: Sage).

Dube, Saurabh (1996a), 'Telling Tales and Trying Truths: Transgressions, Entitlements and Legalities in Village Disputes, Late Colonial Central India', *Studies in History*, 12.

—— (1996b), 'Village Disputes and Colonial Law: Two Cases from Chattisgarh', in Jayaram, N., and Saberwal, S. (eds.) (1996), *Social Conflict* (Delhi: Oxford University Press).

Dubey, A., and Gangopadhyay, S. (1998), 'Counting the Poor: Where are the

Poor in India?', Sarvekshana Analytical Report 1, Department of Statistics, New Delhi.

Duggal, Ravi (2000a), *The Private Health Sector in India: Nature, Trends, and a Critique* (New Delhi: Voluntary Health Association of India).

Duggal, Ravi (2000b), 'Where Are We Today?', *Seminar*, No. 489.

Dugger, Celia (2001), 'Abortion in India is Tipping Scales Sharply Against Girls', New York Times, 22 April.

Duraisamy, Malathy (2000), 'Child Schooling and Child Work in India', mimeo, Programme of Research on Human Development, National Council of Applied Economic Research, New Delhi.

Duraisamy, P. (2000), 'Health Status and Health Care in Rural India', mimeo, Department of Econometrics, University of Madras, Chennai.

Dutta, Bhaskar (1994), 'Poverty in India: Trends, Determinants and Policy Issues', mimeo, Indian Statistical Institute, New Delhi.

Dutta, B., Panda, M., and Wadhwa, W. (1997), 'Human Development in India', in Subramanian, S. (ed.) (1997), *Measurement of Inequality and Poverty* (New Delhi: Oxford University Press).

Duvvury, Nata (1989), 'Women in Agriculture: A Review of the Indian Literature', *Economic and Political Weekly*, 28 October.

Dworkin, Ronald (1978), *Taking Rights Seriously*, 2nd edition (London: Duckworth).

——— (1981), 'What Is Equality? Part 1: Equality of Welfare', and 'What is Equality? Part 2: Equality of Resources', *Philosophy and Public Affairs*, 10.

Dyson, Tim (1987), 'Excess Female Mortality in India: Uncertain Evidence on a Narrowing Differential', in Srinivasan, K., and Mukerji, S. (eds.) (1987), *Dynamics of Population and Family Welfare 1987* (Mumbai: Himalaya).

——— (1997), 'Infant and Child Mortality in the Indian Subcontinent, 1881–1947', in Bideau, A., Desjardins, B., and Brignoli, H.P. (eds.) (1997), *Infant and Child Mortality in the Past* (Oxford: Clarendon).

Dyson, Tim, and Moore, Mick (1983), 'On Kinship Structure, Female Autonomy, and Demographic Behavior in India', *Population and Development Review*, 9.

Easterly, W., Kremer, M., Pritchett, L., and Summers, L. (1993), 'Good Policy or Good Luck? Country Growth Performance and Temporary Shocks', mimeo, World Bank, Washington, DC.

Edwardes, S.M. (1924), *Crime in India*, reprinted 1988 (Jaipur: Printwell Publishers).

Egerö, B., and Hammarskjöld, M. (eds.) (1994), *Understanding Reproductive Change: Kenya, Tamil Nadu, Punjab, Costa Rica* (Cambridge, MA: Harvard Series on Population and International Health).

Ehrlich, Paul (1968), *The Population Bomb* (New York: Ballantine Books).

Ehrlich, P., and Ehrlich, A. (1990), *The Population Explosion* (New York: Simon and Schuster).

Election Commission of India (2000), *Statistical Report on General Elections, 1999 to the 13th Lok Sabha. Vol. 1: National and State Abstracts and Detailed Results* (New Delhi: ECI).

Ellman, Michael (1994), 'The Increase in Death and Disease under "Katastroika"', *Cambridge Journal of Economics*, 18.

Ellsberg, Daniel (1981), 'Call to Mutiny', in Thompson, E.P., and Smith, D. (eds.) (1981), *Protest and Survive* (New York: Monthly Review Press).

Elster, J. (1989), 'Social Norms and Economic Theory', *Journal of Economic Perspectives*, 3.

EPW Research Foundation (1993), 'Poverty Levels in India: Norms, Estimates and Trends', *Economic and Political Weekly*, 21 August.

Eswaran, Mukesh, and Kotwal, Ashok (1994), *Why Poverty Persists in India* (New Delhi: Oxford University Press).

Ethier, W., Helpman, E., and Neary, P. (1993), *Theory, Policy, and Dynamics in International Trade: Essays in Honor of Ronald W. Jones* (New York: Cambridge University Press).

Fajnzylber, P., Lederman, D., and Loayza, N. (1998), 'What Causes Violent Crime?', mimeo, World Bank, Washington, DC.

Fallows, James (1994), *Looking at the Sun: The Rise of the New East Asian Economic and Political System* (New York: Pantheon).

Fernandes, W., and Thukral, E. (eds.)(1989), *Development, Displacement and Rehabilitation* (New Delhi: Indian Social Institute).

Filmer, Deon (1999), 'Educational Attainment and Enrollment Profiles: A Resource Book Based on an Analysis of Demographic and Health Survey Data', mimeo, World Bank, Washington, DC (partly available on the World Bank's website).

Filmer, Deon, and Pritchett, Lant (1999), 'Educational Enrollment and Attainment in India: Household Wealth, Gender, Village, and State Effects', *Journal of Educational Planning and Administration* 13.

Findlay, Ronald (1993), *Trade, Development, and Political Economy: Selected Essays of Ronald Findlay* (Brookfield, VT: Aldershot, Hants).

Fishlow, A., Gwin, C., Haggarad, S., Rodrik, D., and Wade, R. (1994), *Miracle or Design? Lessons from the East Asian Experience* (Washington, DC: Overseas Development Council).

Foot, Michael (1999), *Dr. Strangelove, I Presume* (London: Victor Gollancz).

Foster, James (1984), 'On Economic Poverty: A Survey of Aggregate Measures', *Advances in Econometrics*, 3.

Foster, J., Greer, J., and Thorbecke, E. (1984), 'A Class of Decomposable Poverty Measures', *Econometrica*, 52.

Frank, Robert H. (1984), *Choosing the Right Pond: Human Behavior and the Quest for Status* (New York: Oxford University Press).

Franke, Richard, and Chasin, Barbara (1989), *Kerala: Radical Reform as Development in an Indian State* (San Francisco: Institute for Food and Development Policy).

Frankel, F., Hasan, Z., Bhargava, R., and Arora, B. (eds.) (2000), *Transforming India: Social and Political Dynamics of Democracy* (Oxford: Oxford University Press).

Frazier, Mark W. (2000), 'China-India Relations since Pokhran II: Assessing Sources of Conflict and Cooperation', *Access Asia Review*, National Bureau of Asian Research, 3 July.

Freedman, Lawrence (1989), *The Evolution of Nuclear Strategy*, second edition (London: Macmillan).

Fuchs, Victor (1986), *The Health Economy* (Cambridge: Harvard University Press).
Gadgil, M., and Guha, R. (1995), *Ecology and Equity: The Uses and Abuse of Nature in Contemporary India* (London: Routledge).
Gaiha, Raghav (1993), *Design of Poverty Alleviation Strategy in Rural Areas* (Rome: Food and Agriculture Organization).
Gaiha, R., and Kulkarni, V. (2001), 'Panchayats, Communities and Rural Poor in India', mimeo, Faculty of Management Studies, University of Delhi.
Gala, Chetna (1997), 'Empowering Women in Villages: All Women Village Councils in Maharashtra, India', *Bulletin of Concerned Asian Scholars*, 29.
Galbraith, John Kenneth (1952), *American Capitalism: The Concept of Countervailing Power* (Boston: Houghton Mifflin).
Galenson, Walter (ed.) (1979), *Economic Growth and Structural Change in Taiwan* (Ithaca: Cornell University Press).
Gandotra, M.M., Retherford, R.D., Pandey, A., Luther, N.Y., and Mishra, V.K. (1998), 'Fertility in India', NFHS Subject Reports 9, International Institute for Population Sciences, Mumbai.
Gardezi, H., and Sharma, H. (eds.) (1999), 'The South Asian Bomb: Reality and Illusion', special issue of *Bulletin of Concerned Asian Scholars*.
Garnaut, R., and Guonan Ma (1993), 'How Rich is China?: Evidence from the Food Economy', *Australian Journal of Chinese Affairs*, 30.
Garnaut, R., and Yiping Huang (eds.) (2001), *Growth without Miracles: Readings on the Chinese Economy in the Era of Reforms* (Oxford: Oxford University Press).
Gaul, Karen (1994), 'Exploding Myths: Women, Men and Work in a Himachal Village', *Manushi*, No. 81.
Gazdar, Haris, and Sengupta, Sunil (1999), 'Agricultural Growth and Recent Trends in Well-being in Rural West Bengal', in Rogaly et al. (1999).
George, P.S. (1994), 'Management of Education in Kerala', paper presented at a seminar on 'Management of Education under Panchayati Raj' held at the National Institute of Educational Planning and Administration, 27–28 October.
George, S., Abel, R., and Miller, B.D. (1992), 'Female infanticide in Rural South India', *Economic and Political Weekly*, 30 May.
Ghatak, Maitreya, and Ghatak, Maitreesh (2000), 'Grassroots Democracy: A Study of the Panchayat System in West Bengal', paper presented at a conference on 'Experiments in Empowered Deliberative Democracy', Madison (Wisconsin), January.
Ghate, Prabhu (1984), *Direct Attacks on Rural Poverty* (New Delhi: Concept).
Ghosh, Amitav (1999), *Countdown* (New Delhi: Ravi Dayal).
Ghosh, Arun (1994), 'Structural Adjustment and Industrial and Environmental Concerns', *Economic and Political Weekly*, 19 February.
Ghosh, A., Ananthamurthy, U.R., Béteille, A., Kansal, S.M., Mazumdar, V., and Vanaik, A. (1994), 'Evaluation of Literacy Campaigns in India', report of an independent expert group appointed by the Ministry of Human Resource Development (New Delhi: Ministry of Human Resource Development).
Gillespie, S.R., and McNeill, G. (1992), *Food, Health and Survival in India and Developing Countries* (New Delhi: Oxford University Press).

Glaeser, Edward L. (1999), 'An Overview of Crime and Punishment', mimeo, National Bureau of Economic Research, Cambridge, MA.

Goetz, A.M., and Jenkins, R. (1999), 'Accounts and Accountability: Theoretical Implications of the Right to Information Campaign Movement in India', *Third World Quarterly*, 20.

Gopal, Sarvepalli (ed.) (1983), *Jawaharlal Nehru: An Anthology* (Oxford and Delhi: Oxford University Press).

Gopalakrishnan, A. (1998), 'Margins of Error: Verifying Claims on Nuclear Tests', *Times of India*, 20 November.

Gopalakrishnan, A. (1999), 'Issues of Nuclear Safety', *Frontline*, 13 March.

Gopalan, C. (1994), 'Low Birth Weights: Significance and Implications', in Sachdev, H.P.S., and Choudhury, P. (eds.) (1994), *Nutrition in Children: Developing Country Concerns* (New Delhi: Cambridge Press).

Government of India (1955), *Report of the States Reorganization Commission* (New Delhi: Ministry of Home Affairs).

—— (1979), *Report of the Committee on Child Labour* (New Delhi: Ministry of Labour).

—— (1981), *Census of India 1981: Series I (India), Part II-A(i), General Population Tables, Tables A-1 to A-3* (New Delhi: Office of the Registrar General).

—— (1982), *Sample Registration System 1979–80* (New Delhi: Office of the Registrar General).

—— (1982b), *Statement on National Health Policy* (New Delhi: Ministry of Health and Family Welfare).

—— (1985), *National Health Policy* (New Delhi: Lok Sabha Secretariat).

—— (1988a), ' Child Mortality Estimates of India', Occasional Paper 5 of 1988, Demography Division, Office of the Registrar General, New Delhi.

—— (1988b), 'Fertility in India: An Analysis of 1981 Census Data', Occasional Paper 13 of 1988, Demography Division, Office of the Registrar General, New Delhi.

—— (1989a), 'Child Mortality, Age at Marriage and Fertility in India', Occasional Paper 2 of 1989, Demography Division, Office of the Registrar General, New Delhi.

—— (1989b), *The Drought of 1989: Response and Management* (New Delhi: Ministry of Agriculture).

—— (1991), *Family Welfare Programme in India: Yearbook 1989–90* (New Delhi: Ministry of Health and Family Welfare).

—— (1992a), *Sample Registration System 1989* (New Delhi: Office of the Registrar General).

—— (1992b), *Annual Report 1991–92 (Part I) of the Department of Education* (New Delhi: Ministry of Human Resource Development).

—— (1992c), *National Policy on Education 1986 (With Modifications Undertaken in 1992)* (New Delhi: Ministry of Human Resource Development).

—— (1992d), *National Policy on Education 1986: Programme of Action 1992* (New Delhi: Ministry of Human Resource Development).

—— (1992e), *Health Information of India: 1991* (New Delhi: Central Bureau of Health Intelligence, Ministry of Health and Family Welfare).

_____ (1993a), *Sample Registration System: Fertility and Mortality Indicators 1990* (New Delhi: Office of the Registrar General).

_____ (1993b), *Sample Registration System: Fertility and Mortality Indicators 1991* (New Delhi: Office of the Registrar General).

_____ (1993c), *Education for All: The Indian Scene* (New Delhi: Ministry of Human Resource Development).

_____ (1993d), *Education for All, The Indian Scene: Widening Horizons* (New Delhi: Ministry of Human Resource Development).

_____ (1993e), 'Housing and Amenities: A Brief Analysis of the Housing Tables of 1991 Census', Census of India 1991, Paper 2 of 1993, Office of the Registrar General, New Delhi.

_____ (1994a), *Economic Survey 1993–94* (New Delhi: Ministry of Finance).

_____ (1994b), *Status Report of Literacy and Post Literacy Campaigns* (New Delhi: Directorate of Adult Education).

_____ (1994c), 'National Population Policy', draft report of the Committee on Population appointed by the National Development Council.

_____ (1994d), 'Poverty Eradication through Growth, Employment and Social Development', Planning Commission, New Delhi.

_____ (1994e), *Learning without Burden: Report of the National Advisory Committee Appointed by the Ministry of Human Resource Development* (New Delhi: Ministry of Human Resource Development).

_____ (1994f), *Annual Report 1993–94 (Part I) of the Department of Education* (New Delhi: Ministry of Human Resource Development).

_____ (1995), *Economic Survey 1994–95* (New Delhi: Ministry of Finance).

_____ (1996), *Census of India 1991: Population Projections for India and States, 1996–2016* (New Delhi: Office of the Registrar General).

_____ (1997a), 'District Level Estimates of Fertility and Child Mortality for 1991 and their Relations with Other Variables', Occasional Paper 1 of 1997, Office of the Registrar General, New Delhi.

_____ (1997b), *Availability of Infrastructural Facilities in Rural Areas of India: An Analysis of Village Directory* (New Delhi: Office of the Registrar General).

_____ (1997c), 'Report of the Committee of State Education Ministers on Implications of the Proposal to Make Elementary Education a Fundamental Right', mimeo, Department of Education, New Delhi.

_____ (1997d), *White Paper on Pollution in Delhi* (New Delhi: Ministry of Environment and Forests).

_____ (1997e), *Annual Report 1990–7* (New Delhi: Department of Education, Ministry of Human Resource Development).

_____ (1997f), *Sample Registration System: Fertility and Mortality Indicators 1994* (New Delhi: Office of the Registrar General).

_____ (1997g), *Crime in India 1995* (New Delhi: National Crime Records Bureau).

_____ (1998a), *Sample Registration System: Statistical Report 1996* (New Delhi: Office of the Registrar General).

_____ (1998b), 'Draft Report of the Group of Experts on the Financial Resource Requirements for Operationalising the Proposed 83rd Constitutional Amendment Bill Making the Right to Free and Compulsory Education upto

14 Years of Age a Fundamental Right', mimeo, Department of Education, New Delhi.

—— (1998c), *Annual Report 1997–98* (New Delhi: Department of Education).

—— (1998d), *Sample Registration System: Statistical Report 1995* (New Delhi: Office of the Registrar General).

—— (1999a), *Compendium of India's Fertility and Mortality Indicators 1971–1997* (New Delhi: Office of the Registrar General).

—— (1999b), *Report of the CAG on Ministry of Defence* (New Delhi: Office of the Comptroller and Auditor General).

—— (1999c), *Crime in India 1997* (New Delhi: National Crime Records Bureau).

—— (1999d), *Accidental Deaths and Suicides in India 1997* (New Delhi: National Crime Records Bureau)

—— (1999e), *Research and Development Statistics 1996–97* (New Delhi: Department of Science and Technology).

—— (2000a), *Economic Survey 1999–2000* (New Delhi: Ministry of Finance).

—— (2000b), 'Census Data Online', *www.censusindia.net.*

—— (2000c), *National Population Policy 2000* (New Delhi: Ministry of Health and Family Welfare).

—— (2000d), *Selected Educational Statistics 1998–99* (New Delhi: Ministry of Human Resource Development).

—— (2000e), *Expenditure Budget 2000–2001* (New Delhi: Ministry of Finance).

—— (2000f), *State Finances: A Study of Budgets 1999–2000* (New Delhi: Reserve Bank of India).

—— (2000g), *Crime in India 1998* (New Delhi: National Crime Records Bureau).

—— (2000h), *Sample Registration System 1998* (New Delhi: Office of the Registrar General).

—— (2000i), *Agricultural Statistics at a Glance* (New Delhi: Ministry of Agriculture).

—— (2001a), *Handbook of Industrial Policy and Statistics* (New Delhi: Ministry of Commerce and Industry).

Government of India (2001b), 'Provisional Population Totals', Census of India 2001, Series 1 (India), Paper 1 of 2001, Office of the Registrar General, New Delhi.

—— (2001c), *Economic Survey 2000–2001* (New Delhi: Ministry of Finance).

—— (2001d), 'Poverty Estimates for 1999-2000', mimeo, Press Information Bureau.

—— (2001e), *Health Information of India 1997 & 1998* (New Delhi: Ministry of Health and Family Welfare).

Government of Madhya Pradesh (2000), *From Your School to Our School* (Bhopal: Rajiv Gandhi Shiksha Mission).

Govinda, R., and Varghese, N.V. (1993), 'Quality of Primary Schooling: An Empirical Study', *Journal of Educational Planning and Administration*, 6.

Govindaswamy, P., and Ramesh, B.M. (1997), 'Maternal Education and the Utilization of Maternal and Child Health Services in India', NFHS Subject Report 5, International Institute for Population Sciences, Mumbai.

Grant, James P. (1978), *Disparity Reduction Rates in Social Indicators* (Washington, DC: Overseas Development Council).

Greenhalgh, S., Zhu, Chuzhu and Li, Nan (1995), 'Restraining Population Growth in Three Chinese Villages: 1988–93', *Population and Development Review*, 20.

Griffin, Keith, and Knight, John (eds.) (1990), *Human Development and the International Development Strategy for the 1990s* (London: Macmillan).

Griffin, Keith, and Zhao, Renwei (eds.) (1993), *The Distribution of Income in China* (London: Macmillan).

Griffith-Jones, S., and Kimmis, J. (eds.) (1999), *East Asia: What Happened to the Development Miracle?*, special issue of *IDS Bulletin*, 30.

Grossman, Gene M., and Helpman, Elhanan (1990), 'Comparative Advantage and Long-run Growth', *American Economic Review*, 80.

Grossman, Gene M., and Helpman, Elhanan (1991a), 'Quality Ladders and Product Cycles', *Quarterly Journal of Economics*, 106.

Grossman, Gene M., and Helpman, Elhanan (1991b), *Innovation and Growth in the Global Economy* (Cambridge, MA: MIT Press).

Guha, Ramachandra (1989), *The Unquiet Woods: Ecological Change and Peasant Resistance in the Himalaya* (New Delhi: Oxford University Press).

Guhan, S. (1992a), 'Social Security in India: Looking One Step Ahead', in Harriss et al. (1992).

—— (1992b), 'Social Security Initiatives in Tamil Nadu 1989', in Subramanian, S. (ed.) (1992), *Themes in Development Economics* (New Delhi: Oxford University Press).

—— (1993), 'Social Security for the Unorganised Poor: A Feasible Blueprint for India', mimeo, Madras Institute of Development Studies, Chennai.

—— (1995), 'Social Security Options for Developing Countries', in Gigueiredo, J.B., and Shaheed, Z. (eds.) (1995), *New Approaches to Poverty Analysis and Policy* (Geneva: International Institute of Labour Studies).

Guio, Anne-Catherine (1994), 'Aspects du Sex Ratio en Inde', MSc thesis, Université de Namur, Belgium.

Gupta, D.B., Basu, A., and Asthana, R. (1993), 'Population Change, Women's Role and Status, and Development in India: A Review', mimeo, Institute of Economic Growth, Delhi University.

Gupta, N., Pal, P., Bhargava, M., and Daga, M. (1992), 'Health of Women and Children in Rajasthan', *Economic and Political Weekly*, 17 October.

Gupta, S.P. (1999), 'Tricle Down Theory Revisited: The Role of Employment and Poverty', V.B. Singh Memorial Lecture, 41st Annual Conference of the Indian Society of Labour Economics, 18–20 November, Mumbai.

Gupta, Shreekant (2000), *India: Mainstreaming the Environment for Sustainable Development* (Manila: Asian Development Bank).

Haikerwal, Bejoy Shanker (1934), *Economic and Social Aspects of Crime in India* (London: Allen & Unwin).

Halliburton, Murphy (1998), 'Suicide: A Paradox of Development in Kerala', *Economic and Political Weekly*, 5–12 September.

Halstead, S.B., Walsh, J., and Warren, K. (1985), *Good Health at Low Cost* (New York: Rockefeller Foundation).

Hamlin, A., and Pettit, P. (eds.) (1989), *The Good Polity: Normative Analysis of the State* (Oxford: Blackwell).

Hanchate, A., and Dyson, T. (2000), 'Trends in the Composition of Food Consumption and their Impact on Nutrition and Poverty in Rural India', mimeo, London School of Economics.

Hardin, Garrett (1993), *Living Within Limits* (New York: Oxford University Press).

Hardin, R., Mearsheimer, J., Dworkin, G., and Goodin, R. (eds.) (1985), *Nuclear Deterrence: Ethics and Strategy* (Chicago: University of Chicago Press).

Harris, Marvin (1993), 'The Evolution of Human Gender Hierarchies: A Trial Formulation', in Miller (1993b).

Harriss, Barbara (1990), 'The Intrafamily Distribution of Hunger in South Asia', in Drèze and Sen (1990), vol. I.

Harriss, B., Guhan, S., and Cassen, R. (eds.) (1992), *Poverty in India: Research and Policy* (New Delhi: Oxford University Press).

Harriss, John (1993), 'What is Happening in Rural West Bengal? Agrarian Reform, Growth and Distribution', *Economic and Political Weekly*, 12 June.

—— (2000), 'Populism, Tamil Style: Is It Really a Success?', *Review of Development and Change*, 5.

Harriss-White, B., and Subramanian, S. (eds.) (1999), *Illfare in India: Essays on India's Social Sector in Honour of S. Guhan* (New Delhi: Sage).

Hayami, Yujiro (1997), *Development Economics: From the Poverty to the Wealth of Nations* (Oxford: Clarendon).

Hayami, Yujiro, and Aoki, Masahiko (eds.) (1998), *The Institutional Foundations of East Asian Economic Development* (Basingstoke: Macmillan).

Hayami, Y., and Otsuka, K. (1993), *The Economics of Contract Choice* (Oxford: Clarendon).

HealthWatch Trust (1999), *The Community-based Reproductive and Child Health in India: Progress and Constraints* (Jaipur: HealthWatch Trust).

Helleiner, G.K. (ed.) (1992), *Trade Policy, Industrialization, and Development* (Oxford: Clarendon).

Heller, Patrick (1999), *The Labor of Development: Workers and the Transformation of Capitalism in Kerala, India* (Ithaca, NY: Cornell University Press).

—— (2000a), 'Degrees of Democracy: Some Comparative Lessons from India', *World Politics*, 52.

—— (2000b), 'Moving the State: The Politics of Democratic Decentralization in Kerala, South Africa and Porto Alegre', paper presented at an international conference on 'Democratic Decentralisation' held in Thiruvananthapuram, 23–27 May.

Helpman, Elhanan, and Krugman, Paul R. (1990), *Market Structure and Foreign Trade* (Cambridge, MA: MIT Press).

Helpman, Elhanan, and Razin, Assad (eds.) (1991), *International Trade and Trade Policy* (Cambridge: MIT Press).

Hillier, S., and Shen, J. (1996), 'Health Care Systems in Transition: People's Republic of China. Part I: An Overview of China's Health Care system', *Journal of Public Health Medicine*, 18.

Hinton, William (1983), *Shenfan* (New York: Random Press).

—— (1990), *The Great Reversal: The Privatization of China, 1978–1989* (New York: Monthly Review Press).

Hirschman, Albert O. (1970), *Exit, Voice and Loyalty* (Cambridge, MA: Harvard University Press).

—— (1991), *The Rhetoric of Reaction: Perversity, Futility, Jeopardy* (Cambridge, MA: Belknap Press).

Hirschman, Albert O. (1992), *Rival Views of Market Society and Other Recent Essays* (Cambridge, MA: Harvard University Press).

Hitchcock, John T. (1975), 'The Idea of the Martial Rajput', in Singer, M. (ed.) (1975), *Traditional India: Structure and Change* (Jaipur: Rawat Publications).

Hong, W., and Krueger, Anne O. (eds.) (1975), *Trade and Development in Korea* (Seoul: Korea Development Institute).

Hopper, Gordon R. (1999), 'Changing Food Production and Quality of Diet in India', *Population and Development Review*, 25.

Howes, Stephen (1992), 'Purchasing Power, Infant Mortality and Literacy in China and India: An Inter-provincial Analysis', Discussion Paper 19, Research Programme on the Chinese Economy, STICERD, London School of Economics.

Howes, Stephen, and Hussain, Athar (1994), 'Regional Growth and Inequality in Rural China', Discussion Paper 11, Series on Economic Transformation and Public Finance, STICERD, London School of Economics.

Hubbard, Michael (1988), 'Drought Relief and Drought-Proofing in the State of Gujarat, India', in Curtis, D., Hubbard, M., and Shepherd, A. (eds.) (1988), *Preventing Famine: Policies and Prospects for Africa* (New York and London: Routledge).

Hull, Terence (1990), 'Recent Trends in Sex Ratios at Birth in China', *Population and Development Review*, 16.

Hussain, Athar (ed.) (1989), *China and the World Economy* (London: STICERD, London School of Economics).

Indian Council of Medical Research (1989), *Evaluation of Quality of Maternal and Child Health and Family Planning Services* (New Delhi: ICMR).

Indian Institute of Health Management Research (1999), *Facility Survey (1999) under Reproductive and Child Health Project: Rajasthan* (Jaipur: IIHMR).

Indian Institute of Management (1985), *Study of Facility Utilization and Programme Management in Family Welfare* (Ahmedabad: Public Systems Group, Indian Institute of Management).

—— (2000), *A Review of Primary Education Packages in Madhya Pradesh* (Ahmedabad: IIM).

Indian Social Institute (2000), *State of Human Rights in India 1999* (New Delhi: Indian Social Institute).

Institute of Social Sciences (1999), *Panchayati Raj Update*, vol. vi (New Delhi: Institute of Social Sciences).

International Institute for Democracy and Electoral Assistance (1997), *Voter Turnout from 1945 to 1997: A Global Report on Political Participation* (Stockholm: IDEA).

International Institute for Population Sciences (1994), *National Family Health Survey 1992–93: Uttar Pradesh* (Mumbai: IIPS).

―――― (1995a), *National Family Health Survey 1992–93: India* (Mumbai: IIPS).

―――― (1995b), *National Family Health Survey 1992–93,* state volumes (Mumbai: IIPS).

―――― (1995c), *National Family Health Survey 1992–93: Kerala* (Mumbai: IIPS).

―――― (1999), 'National Family Health Survey 1998–9: Preliminary State Reports', mimeo, IIPS, Mumbai.

―――― (2000a), *National Family Health Survey 1998–99 (NFHS-2): India* (Mumbai: IIPS).

―――― (2000b), 'National Family Health Survey (NFHS-2)', wallchart with summary results of the second National Family Health Survey, 1998–9.

―――― (forthcoming), *National Family Health Survey 1998–9,* state volumes (Mumbai: IIPS).

Isaac, T., and Harilal, K.N. (1997), 'Planning for Empowerment: People's Campaign for Decentralised Planning in Kerala', *Economic and Political Weekly,* 4 January.

Iyengar, P.K. (2000), 'Imperatives before India', *Frontline,* 22 July.

Iyengar, Sudarshan, and Bhargava, Ashok (1987), 'Primary Health Care and Family Welfare Programme in Rural Gujarat', *Economic and Political Weekly,* 4 July.

Iyer, A., and Jesani, A. (1999), 'Barriers to the Quality of Care: The Experience of Auxiliary Nurse-Midwives in Rural Maharashtra', in Koenig and Khan (1999).

Jain, A.K. (1985), 'Determinants of Regional Variations in Infant Mortality in Rural India', *Population Studies,* 39.

Jain, A.K., and Nag, M. (1986), 'Importance of Female Primary Education for Fertility Reduction in India', *Economic and Political Weekly,* 6 September.

Jain, Devaki, and Banerjee, Nirmala (eds.) (1985), *Tyranny of the Household: Investigative Essays in Women's Work* (New Delhi: Vikas).

Jain, L.R., Sundaram, K., and Tendulkar, S.D. (1988), 'Dimensions of Rural Poverty: An Inter-Regional Profile', *Economic and Political Weekly,* November (special issue); reprinted in Krishnaswamy (1990).

Jalan, Bimal (1991), *India's Economic Crisis* (Delhi: Oxford University Press).

―――― (ed.) (1992), *The Indian Economy: Problems and Prospects* (New Delhi: Viking).

Jalan, J., and Subbarao, K. (1995), 'Adjustment and Social Sectors in India', in Cassen and Joshi (1995).

James, Robert Rhodes (1974), *Winston S. Churchill: His Complete Speeches 1897– 1963* (New York: R.R. Bowker).

Jayachandran, Usha (1997), 'The Determinants of Primary Education in India', MSc thesis, Department of Economics, Delhi School of Economics.

―――― (2001), 'School Attendance in India', mimeo; forthcoming as a Working Paper of the Centre for Development Economics at the Delhi School of Economics.

Jayal, Niraja Gopal (1999a), *Democracy and the State: Welfare, Secularism and Development in Contemporary India* (Oxford: Oxford University Press).

—— (1999b), 'Democracy and Social Capital in the Central Himalaya: A Tale of Two Villages', paper presented at a conference on Democracy and Social Capital in Segmented Societies, Uppsala University, June 1999.

Jayaraman, R., and Lanjouw, P. (1999), 'The Evolution of Poverty and Inequality in Indian Villages', *World Bank Research Observer*, 14.

Jayaraman, T. (1998), 'Indian Science after Pokhran-II', *Seminar*, 468.

—— (1999), 'Science, Politics, and the Indian Bomb: Some Preliminary Considerations', *Bulletin of Concerned Asian Scholars*, 31.

Jeffery, Patricia, and Jeffery, Roger (1998), 'Silver Bullet or Passing Fancy? Girls' Schooling and Population Policy', in Jackson, C., and Pearson, C. (eds.) (1998), *Feminist Visions of Development* (London: Routledge).

Jeffery, P., Jeffery, R., and Lyon, P. (1989), *Labour Pains and Labour Power: Women and Child-bearing in India* (London: Zed).

Jeffery, Roger (1988), *The Politics of Health in India* (Berkeley: University of California Press).

Jeffery, Roger, and Basu, Alaka (eds.) (1996), *Girls' Schooling, Women's Autonomy and Fertility Change in South Asia* (New Delhi: Sage).

Jeffery, R., and Jeffery, P. (1997), *Population, Gender and Politics: Demographic Change in Rural North India* (Cambridge: Cambridge University Press).

Jeffrey, Robin (1987), 'Culture and Governments: How Women Made Kerala Literate', *Pacific Affairs*, 60.

—— (1992), *Politics, Women and Well-Being: How Kerala Became 'A Model'* (Cambridge: Cambridge University Press).

Jejeebhoy, Shireen (1996), *Women's Education, Autonomy, and Reproductive Behaviour: Experience from Developing Countries* (Oxford: Oxford University Press).

Jena, B., and Pati, R.N. (eds.) (1989), *Health and Family Welfare Services in India* (New Delhi: Ashish).

Jervis, Robert (1989), *The Meaning of the Nuclear Revolution* (Ithaca: Cornell University Press).

Jesani, Amar (1990), 'Limits of Empowerment: Women in Rural Health Care', *Economic and Political Weekly*, 19 May.

Jha, Jyotsna (2000), 'Education Guarantee Scheme and Alternative Schooling: Community-based Initiatives in Primary Education in Madhya Pradesh', in Government of Madhya Pradesh (2000).

Jodha, N.S. (1988), 'Poverty Debate in India: A Minority View', *Economic and Political Weekly*, special number.

Johansen, Frida (1993), 'Poverty Reduction in East Asia: The Silent Revolution', Discussion Paper 203, East Asia and Pacific Region Series, World Bank, Washington, DC.

Johansson, Sheila R. (1991), 'Welfare, Mortality and Gender: Continuity and Change in Explanations for Male/Female Mortality Differences over Three Centuries', *Continuity and Change*, 6.

Johansson, S., and Nygren, O. (1991), 'The Missing Girls of China: A New Demographic Account', *Population and Development Review*, 17.

Joseph, Josy (1999), 'CAG Drops a Bombshell on DRDO', news report, Rediff On the Net (*www.rediff.com/news/1999/dec/17drdo.htm*).

Joshi, V., and Little, I.M.D. (1994), *India: Macroeconomics and Political Economy 1964–91* (Washington, DC: World Bank).

Joshi, V., and Little, I.M.D. (1996), *India's Economic Reforms, 1991–2001* (Oxford: Clarendon).

Kabeer, Naila (2001), 'Deprivation, Discrimination and Delivery: Competing Explanations for Child Labour and Educational Failure in South Asia', Working Paper 135, Institute of Development Studies, Sussex.

Kabir, M., and Krishnan, T.N. (1996), 'Social Intermediation and Health Changes: Lessons from Kerala', in Das Gupta et al. (1996).

Kahn, Herman (1962), *Thinking the Unthinkable* (New York: Horizon Press).

Kahkonen, S., and Lanyi, A. (eds.) (2000), *Institutions, Incentives and Economic Reforms in India* (New Delhi: Sage).

Kakar, Sudhir (1979), 'Childhood in India', *International Social Science Journal*, 31.

Kakwani, Nanak (1986), *Analyzing Redistribution Policies* (Cambridge: Cambridge University Press).

—— (1993), 'Peformance in Living Standards: An International Comparison', *Journal of Development Economics*, 41.

Kakwani, Nanak, and Subbarao, K. (1990), 'Rural Poverty and its Alleviation in India', *Economic and Political Weekly*, 3 June.

Kanbargi, R. (ed.) (1991), *Child Labour in the Indian Subcontinent* (New Delhi: Sage).

Kane, Penny (1988), *Famine in China, 1959–61: Demographic and Social Implications* (New York: St. Martin's Press).

Kannan, K.P. (1995), 'Public Intervention and Poverty Alleviation: A Study of the Declining Incidence of Rural Poverty in Kerala', *Development and Change*, 26.

Kannan, K.P., and Francis, S.F. (2001), 'State-assisted Social Security for Poverty Alleviation and Human Development: Kerala's Record and its Lessons', in Mahendra Dev et al. (2001).

Kannan, K.P., Thankappan, K.R., Raman Kutty, V., and Aravindan, K.P. (1991), *Health and Development in Rural Kerala* (Trivandrum: Kerala Sastra Sahitya Parishad).

Kapadia, Karin (1995), *Siva and Her Sisters: Gender, Caste, and Class in Rural South India* (Boulder, CO: Westview Press).

—— (1997), 'Emancipatory Processes in Rural Tamil Nadu Today: An Anthropological Study of Discourse and Practice Relating to Rights', research proposal, International Institute of Asian Studies, Amsterdam.

Kaplan, Robert D. (1994), 'The Coming Anarchy', *Atlantic Monthly*, 273 (2 February).

Karkal, Malini (1987), 'Differentials in Mortality by Sex', *Economic and Political Weekly*, 8 August.

Karlekar, Malavika (1988), 'Woman's Nature and the Access to Education', in Chanana (1988).

Karve, Irawati (1965), *Kinship Organisation in India* (Mumbai: Asia Publishing House).

Keen, David (1998), *The Economic Functions of Violence in Civil Wars*, Adelphi Papers, No. 320, International Institute for Strategic Studies.

Keidel, A. (1992), 'How Badly do China's National Accounts Underestimate China's GNP?', Paper E 8042, Rock Creek Research Inc.

Keith-Krelik, Yasmin (1995), 'Development, for Better or Worse: A Case Study on the Effects of Development on the Social and Cultural Environment of Spiti', unpublished dissertation, Department of Politics, University of Newcastle-upon-Tyne.

Kerawalla, Perin C. (1959), *A Study in Indian Crime* (Mumbai: Popular Book Depot).

Khan, A.R., Griffin, K., Riskin, C., and Zhao Renwei (1992), 'Household Income and its Distribution in China', *China Quarterly*, No. 132.

Khan, A.R., and Riskin, C. (2001), *Inequality and Poverty in China in the Age of Globalization* (New York: Oxford University Press).

Khan, M.E., Anker, R., Ghosh Dastidar, S.K., and Bairathi, S. (1989), 'Inequalities between Men and Women in Nutrition and Family Welfare Services: An In-depth Enquiry in an Indian Village', in Caldwell, J.C., and Santow, G. (eds.) (1989), *Selected Readings in the Cultural, Social and Behavioral Determinants of Health*, Health Transition Series No.1 (Canberra: Health Transition Centre, Australian National University).

Khan, M.E., Ghosh Dastidar, S.K., and Singh, R. (1986), 'Nutrition and Health Practices among the Rural Women: A Case Study of Uttar Pradesh', *Journal of Family Welfare*, 33.

Khan, M.E., Gupta, R.B., Prasad, C.V.S., and Ghosh Dastidar, S.K. (1988), *Performance of Health and Family Welfare Programme in India* (Mumbai: Himalaya Publishing House).

Khan, M.E., Gupta, R.B., Prasad, C.V.S., and Ghosh Dastidar, S.K. (eds.) (1987), *Performance of Family Planning in India: Observations from Bihar, Uttar Pradesh, Rajasthan and Madhya Pradesh* (New Delhi: Himalaya Publishing House).

Khan, M.E., and Prasad, C.V.S. (1983), *Under-Utilization of Health Services in Rural India: A Comparative Study of Bihar, Gujarat and Karnataka* (Baroda: Operations Research Group).

Khan, M.E., Prasad, C.V.S., and Majumdar, A. (1980), *People's Perceptions about Family Planning in India* (New Delhi: Concept).

Khan, M.E., Prasad, C.V.S., and Qaiser, N. (1987), 'Reasons for Under-utilization of Health Services: Case Study of a PHC in a Tribal Area of Bihar', *Demography India*, 16.

Khatu, K.K., Tamang, A.K., and Rao, C.R. (1983), *Working Children in India* (Baroda: Operations Research Group).

Kim, Kiwan, and Leipziger, Danny (1997), 'Korea: A Case of Government-Led Development', in Leipziger, D. (ed.) (1997), *Lessons from East Asia* (Ann Arbor: University of Michigan Press).

Kingdon, Geeta Gandhi (1994), 'An Economic Evaluation of School Management-Types in Urban India: A Case Study of Uttar Pradesh,' PhD thesis, University of Oxford.

—— (1996), 'Private Schooling in India: Size, Nature and Equity-effects', Discussion Paper 72, Development Economics Research Programme, STICERD, London School of Economics.

Kingdon, G.G., and Drèze, J.P. (1998), 'Biases in Educational Statistics', *The Hindu*, 6 March.

Kingdon, G.G., and Muzammil, Mohd (2001), 'A Political Economy of Education in India: The Case of UP', *Economic and Political Weekly*, 11 and 18 August.

Kirk, D. (1996), 'Demographic Transition Theory', *Population Studies*, 50.

Kishor, Sunita (1993), ' "May God Give Sons to All": Gender and Child Mortality in India', *American Sociological Review*, 58.

—— (1994a), 'Gender Differentials in Child Mortality: A Review of the Evidence', in Das Gupta et al. (1994).

—— (1994b), 'Fertility Decline in Tamil Nadu, India', in Egerö and Hammarskjöld (1994).

Kishwar, Madhu (1996), 'Women's Marginal Role in Politics', *Manushi*, 97.

—— (1998), 'BJP's Wargasm', *Manushi*, 106.

—— (2001a), 'Blackmail, Bribes and Beatings', *Manushi*, 124.

—— (2001b), 'License-Quota-Raid Raj: Economic Warfare Against Rickshaw Owners and Pullers', *Manushi*, 125.

Kishwar, Madhu, and Vanita, Ruth (eds.) (1991), *In Search of Answers*, second revised edition (New Delhi: Horizon India).

Klasen, Stephan (1994), ' "Missing Women" Reconsidered', *World Development*, 22.

Klasen, Stephan, and Wink, Claudia (2001), 'Missing Women: Currents Trends in Gender Bias in Mortality', mimeo, University of Munich.

Knight, John, and Song, Lina (1993), 'The Spatial Contribution to Income Inequality in Rural China', *Cambridge Journal of Economics*, 17.

Knight, M., Loayza, N., and Villanueva, D. (1996), 'The Peace Dividend: Military Spending Cuts and Economic Growth', *IMF Staff Papers*, 43.

Koenig, M.A., and Khan, M.E. (eds.) (1999), *Improving Quality of Care in India's Family Welfare Programme* (New York: Population Council).

Kohli, Atul (1987), *The State and Poverty in India: The Politics of Reform* (Cambridge: Cambridge University Press).

Kolenda, Pauline (1983), 'Widowhood among "Untouchable" Chuhras', in Ostor, A., Fruzzetti, L., and Barnett, S. (eds.) (1983), *Concepts of Person: Kinship, Caste and Marriage in India* (Delhi: Oxford Univerity Press).

—— (1984), 'Woman as Tribute, Woman as Flower: Images of "Woman" in Weddings in North and South India', *American Ethnologist*, 11.

Koopmans, T. (1957), *Three Essays on the State of Economic Science* (New Haven: Yale University Press).

Kothari, Smitu (2000), 'A Million Mutinies Now: Lesser-known Environmental Movements in India', *Humanscape*, October.

Kothari, Smitu, and Zia Mian (eds.) (2001), *Out of the Nuclear Shadow* (New Delhi: Rainbow Publishers).

Krepon, Michael (2000), 'Some Cold War Lessons', *Outlook*, 31 July.

Krishnaji, N. (1987), 'Poverty and Sex Ratio: Some Data and Speculations', *Economic and Political Weekly*, 6 June.

—— (1992), *Pauperising Agriculture: Studies in Agrarian Change and Demographic Structure* (Delhi: Oxford University Press).

—— (2000), 'Trends in Sex Ratio: A Review in Tribute to Asok Mitra', *Economic and Political Weekly*, 1 April.

Krishnaji, N., and Krishnan, T.N. (eds.) (2000), *Public Support for Food Security: The Public Distribution System in India* (New Delhi: Sage).

Krishnakumari, N.S. (1987), *Status of Single Women in India* (Delhi: Uppal).

Krishnamoorty, S., Kulkarni, P.M., and Audinarayana, N. (1996), 'Causes of Fertility Transition in Tamil Nadu: Observations from a Field Study', mimeo, Project on Strategies and Financing for Human Development, UNDP, New Delhi.

Krishnan, T.N. (1976), 'Demographic Transition in Kerala: Facts and Factors', *Economic and Political Weekly*, 11 (31–33), special number.

—— (1991), 'Kerala's Health Transition: Facts and Factors', mimes, Center for Population and Development Studies, Harvard University.

—— (1997), 'The Route to Social Development in Kerala: Social Intermediation and Public Action', in Mehrotra and Jolly (1997).

Krishnaraj, M., Sudarshan, R., and Shariff, A. (eds.) (1998), *Gender, Population and Development* (New Delhi: Oxford University Press).

Krishnaswamy, K.S. (ed.) (1990), *Poverty and Income Distribution* (Delhi: Oxford University Press).

Krueger, Anne O. (1974), 'The Political Economy of the Rent-Seeking Society', *American Economic Review*, 64.

Krugman, Paul R. (1979), 'Increasing Returns, Monopolistic Competition, and International Trade', *Journal of International Economics*, 9.

—— (1986), *Strategic Trade Policy and the New International Economics* (Cambridge, MA: MIT Press).

—— (1987), 'The Narrow Moving Band, the Dutch Disease, and the Consequences of Mrs. Thatcher: Notes on Trade in the Presence of Scale Economies', *Journal of Development Economics*, 27.

Krugman, Paul R., and Smith, Alisdair (eds.) (1994), *Empirical Studies of Strategic Trade Policy* (Chicago: University of Chicago Press).

Kulkarni, P.M., Krishnamoorty, S., and Audinarayana N. (1996), 'Review of Research on Fertility in Tamil Nadu', mimeo, Project on Strategies and Financing for Human Development, UNDP, New Delhi.

Kumar, A.K. Shiva (1991), 'UNDP's Human Development Index: A Computation for Indian States', *Economic and Political Weekly*, 12 October.

_____ (1992), 'Maternal Capabilities and Child Survival in Low Income Regions: An Economic Analysis of Infant Mortality in India', PhD thesis, Harvard University.

_____ (1994), 'Women's Capabilities and Infant Mortality: Lessons from Manipur', in Das Gupta et al. (1994).

Kumar, Krishna (1986), 'Education: Towards a Policy', *Economic and Political Weekly*, 5 April.

_____ (1991), *The Political Agenda of Education* (New Delhi: Sage).

Kumar, K., Priyam, M., and Saxena, S. (2001), 'Beyond the Smokescreen: DPEP and Primary Education in India', *Economic and Political Weekly*, 17 February.

Kung, J.K., and Liu, S. (1997), 'Farmers' Preferences Regarding Ownership and Land Tenure in Post-Mao China: Unexpected Evidence from Eight Counties', *China Journal*, 38.

Kuo, S. (1983), *The Taiwan Economy in Transition* (Boulder, CO: Westview).

Kurian, N.J. (1989), 'Anti-Poverty Programmes: A Reappraisal', *Economic and Political Weekly*, 25 March.

_____ (2000), 'Widening Regional Disparities in India: Some Indicators', *Economic and Political Weekly*, 12 February.

Kurrien, John (1983), *Elementary Education in India: Myth, Reality, Alternative* (New Delhi: Vikas).

Kynch, Jocelyn (1985), 'How Many Women Are Enough?', in *Third World Affairs 1985* (London: Third World Foundation).

Kynch, Jocelyn, and Sen, Amartya (1983), 'Indian Women: Well-being and Survival', *Cambridge Journal of Economics*, 7.

Labenne, Sophie (1995), 'Analyse Econométrique du Travail des Enfants en Inde', MSc thesis, Department of Economics, Université de Namur, Belgium.

Lal, Deepak (1995), 'India and China: Contrasts in Economic Liberalization?', *World Development*, 23.

Lal, Deepak (1999), *Unfinished Business: India in the World Economy* (New Delhi: Oxford University Press).

Lal, D., Mohan, R., and Natarajan, I. (2001), 'Economic Reform and Poverty Alleviation: A Tale of Two Surveys', *Economic and Political Weekly*, 24 March.

Lane, Robert E. (1991), *The Market Experience* (Cambridge: Cambridge University Press).

_____ (1994), 'Quality of Life and Quality of Persons: A New Role for Government', *Political Theory*, 22.

Langford, Christopher (1984), 'Sex Differentials in Mortality in Sri Lanka: Changes since the 1920s', *Journal of Bio-social Science*, 16.

_____ (1994), 'Sex Differentials in Mortality in Sri Lanka: Past Trends and the Situation Recently', *Scientific Yearbook*, Volume A, Economics Department, The Aristotle University of Thessaloniki.

Langford, Christopher, and Storey, Pamela (1993), 'Sex Differentials in Mortality Early in the Twentieth Century: Sri Lanka and India Compared', *Population and Development Review*, 19.

Lanjouw, P., and Stern, N.H. (1998), *Economic Development in Palanpur over Five Decades* (New Delhi and Oxford: Oxford University Press).

Leclercq, François (2001a), 'Patterns and Determinants of Elementary School Enrollment in Rural North India', mimeo, Centre de Sciences Humaines, New Delhi, and Université de Paris.

_____ (2001b), 'Child Work, Schooling, and Household Resources in Rural North India', in Massun, L., and Ramachandran, N. (eds.), (2001), *Coming to Grips with Rural Child Work: The Food Security Approach* (New Delhi: Institute for Human Development).

_____ (2001c), 'Towards an Assessment of the Education Guarantee Scheme in Madhya Pradesh', mimeo, Centre de Sciences Humaines, New Delhi.

Leslie, Joanne (1988), 'Women's Work and Child Nutrition in the Third World', *World Development*, 16.

Leslie, J., and Paolisso, M. (eds.) (1989), *Women, Work and Child Welfare in the Third World* (Boulder, CO: Westview).

Lewis, John (1995), *India's Political Economy: Governance and Reform* (Delhi: Oxford University Press).

Lewis, W. Arthur (1955), *The Theory of Economic Growth* (London: Allen & Unwin).

Li Chengrui (1992), *A Study of China's Population* (Beijing: Foreign Languages Press).

Lieten, G.K. (1993), *Continuity and Change in Rural West Bengal* (London: Sage).

_____ (1996a), *Development, Devolution and Democracy: Village Discourse in West Bengal* (New Delhi: Sage).

_____ (1996b), 'Panchayats in Western Uttar Pradesh: "Namesake" Members', *Economic and Political Weekly*, 28 September.

_____ (2000), 'Children, Work and Education', *Economic and Political Weekly*, 10–17 June.

Lieten, G.K., and Srivastava, R. (1999), *Unequal Partners: Power Relations, Devolution and Development in Uttar Pradesh* (New Delhi: Sage).

Lijphart, Arend (1996), 'The Puzzle of Indian Democracy: A Consociational Interpretation', *American Political Science Review*, 90.

Lin, Justin Yifu (1992), 'Rural Reforms and Agricultural Growth in China', *American Economic Review*, 82.

Lindblom, Charles (1982), 'The Market as a Prison', *Journal of Politics*, 44.

Lipton, Michael, and Ravallion, Martin (1994), 'Poverty and Policy', in Behrman and Srinivasan (1994).

Little, Ian M.D. (1977), 'Development Economics', in Bullock, A., Stallybrass, O., and Trombley, S. (eds.) (1977), *The Fontana Dictionary of Modern Thought*, 2nd edition (London: Fontana Press).

_____ (1982), *Economic Development* (New York: Basic Books).

Little, Ian M.D., Scitovsky, Tibor, and Scott, Maurice Fg. (1970), *Industry and Trade in Some Developing Countries* (Oxford: Clarendon).

Loh, Jackie (1993), 'A Summary of Literacy in China', mimeo, STICERD, London School of Economics.

_____ (1997), 'Education and Economic Growth in India: An Aggregate Production Function Approach', in National Council of Educational Research and Training (1997), *School Effectiveness and Learning Achievement at Primary Stage, International Perspective* (New Delhi: National Council for Educational Research and Training).

Lokshala Team (1996), *Shala Se Lokshala Ki Or* (New Delhi: Bharat Jan Vigyan Jatha).

Lopez, Alan D., and Ruzicka, Lado T. (eds.) (1983), *Sex Differentials in Mortality: Trends, Determinants and Consequences*, Miscellaneous Series 4, Department of Demography, Australian National University, Canberra.

Lucas, Robert E. (1988), 'On the Mechanics of Economic Development', *Journal of Monetary Economics*, 22.

_____ (1993), 'Making a Miracle', *Econometrica*, 63.

Ludra, T.K.S. (2000), 'Guns v/s Butter Syndrome: War Economics as a Tool of Development', *www.indiavotes.com/columns1/y2kmay4-tksludra.html*, 24 May.

Maddison, Angus (1998), *Chinese Economic Performance in the Long Run* (Paris: Organization for Economic Cooperation and Development).

Mahajan, Aprajit (2001), 'A Note on Prenatal Care, Immunization and Birth Order in India', mimeo, Princeton University.

Maharatna, Arup (1997), 'Children's Work Activities, Surplus Labour and Fertility: Case Study of Six Villages in Birbhum', *Economic and Political Weekly*, 15 February.

Mahendra Dev, S. (1994), 'Social Security in the Unorganized Sector: Lessons from the Experiences of Kerala and Tamil Nadu', *Indian Journal of Labour Economics*, 37.

Mahendra Dev, S., Antony, P., Gayathri, V., and Mamgain, R.P. (eds.) (2001), *Social and Economic Security in India* (New Delhi: Institute for Human Development).

Mahendra Dev, S., and Ranade, A. (2001), 'Employment Guarantee Scheme and Employment Security', in Mahendra Dev et al. (2001).

Majumdar, Manabi (1997), 'Rural Literacy Scene in Tamil Nadu and Rajasthan', Discussion Paper 23, Studies on Human Development in India, UNDP, New Delhi; to be published in Vaidyanathan and Nair (forthcoming).

_____ (1998), 'Child Labor as a Human Security Problem: Evidence From India', mimeo, Harvard Center for Population and Development Studies, Harvard University.

_____ (2000), 'Classes for the Masses? Social Capital, Social Distance and the Quality of the Government School System', mimeo, Madras Institute of Development Studies, Chennai.

Majumdar, Tapas (1983), *Investment in Education and Social Choice* (Cambridge: Cambridge University Press).

_____ (1993), 'The Relation between Educational Attainment and Ability to Obtain Social Security in the States of India', mimeo, World Institute for Development Economics Research, Helsinki.

Malenbaum, W. (1956), 'India and China: Development Contrasts', *Journal of Political Economy*, 64.

_____ (1959), 'India and China: Contrasts in Development Performance', *American Economic Review*, 49.

_____ (1982), 'Modern Economic Growth in India and China: The Comparison Revisited, 1950–1980', *Economic Development and Cultural Change*, 30.

Malhotra, A., Vanneman, R., and Kishor, S. (1995), 'Fertility, Dimensions of Patriarchy, and Development in India', *Population and Development Review*, 21.

Malinvaud, E., et al. (1997), *Development Strategy and Management of the Market Economy* (Oxford: Clarendon).

Mandelbaum, David G. (1988), *Women's Seclusion and Men's Honor: Sex Roles in North India* (Tucson: University of Arizona Press).

Mander, Harsh (2001), *Unheard Voices: Stories of Forgotten Lives* (New Delhi: Penguin).

Mander, Harsh, and Rao, Vidya (1996), *An Agenda for Caring: Interventions for Marginalised Groups* (New Delhi: Voluntary Health Association of India).

Mankiw, N. G., Romer, D., and Weil, D. (1992), 'A Contribution to the Empirics of Economic Growth', *Quarterly Journal of Economics*, 107.

Mari Bhat, P.N. (1989), 'Mortality and Fertility in India, 1881–1961: A Reassessment', in Dyson, T. (ed.) (1989), *India's Historical Demography* (London: Curzon Press)

_____ (1998), ' Widowhood and Mortality in India', in Chen (1998).

_____ (2000), 'Maternal Mortality in India', mimeo, Institute of Economic Growth, Delhi University.

_____ (2001), 'Maternal Mortality in India: An Update', mimeo, Institute of Economic Growth, New Delhi.

Mari Bhat, P.N. and Rajan, S.I. (1990), 'Demographic Transition in Kerala Revisited', *Economic and Political Weekly*, 1–8 September.

Mari Bhat, P.N. and Rajan, S.I. (1992), 'Demographic Transition in Kerala: A Reply', *Economic and Political Weekly*, 6 June.

Mari Bhat, P.N., and Zavier, A.J. Francis (2001), 'Fertility Decline and Gender Bias in North India', mimeo, Institute of Economic Growth, Delhi University.

Marx, Karl (1857–8), *Grundrisse: Foundations of the Critique of Political Economy*, English translation, Nicolaus, M. (Harmondsworth: Penguin Books, 1973).

_____ (1887), *Capital*, vol. I (London: Sonnenschein).

Mata, L., and Rosero, L. (1988), 'National Health and Social Development in Costa Rica: A Case Study of Intersectoral Action', Technical Paper 13, Pan American Health Organization, Washington, DC.

Mathew, E.T. (1999), 'Growth of Literacy in Kerala: State Intervention, Missionary Initiatives and Social Movements', *Economic and Political Weekly*, 25 September.

Mathew, George, and Nayak, Ramesh (1996), 'Panchayats at Work: What it Means for the Oppressed', *Economic and Political Weekly*, 16 July.

Mathur, K., and Bhattacharya, M. (1975), *Administrative Response to Emergency: A Study of Scarcity Administration in Maharashtra* (New Delhi: Concept).

Matson, Jim, and Selden, Mark (1992), 'Poverty and Inequality in China and India', *Economic and Political Weekly*, 4 April.

Matsuyama, Kiminori (1991), 'Increasing Returns, Industrialization and Indeterminacy of Equilibrium', *Quarterly Journal of Economics*, 106.

Maurya, K.N. (1989), 'An Analysis of Causative Factors Responsible for Low Utilisation of Health and Family Welfare Services', in Jena and Pati (1989).

Mavalankar, Dileep (2000), 'Paradigm Shift in India's Family Welfare Programme: A Review of Target-free Approach in Family Planning', mimeo, Public Systems Group, Indian Institute of Management, Ahmedabad.

May, E. R., and Zelikow, P.D. (1997), *The Kennedy Tapes* (Cambridge, MA: Harvard University Press).

Mayaram, Shail, and Pal, Pritam (1996), 'The politics of Women's Reservation: Women Panchayat Representatives in Rajasthan, Performance, Problems and Potential', Working Paper 74, Institute of Development Studies, Jaipur.

Mayer, Peter (1999), 'India's Falling Sex Ratios', *Population and Development Review*, 25.

Mazumdar, Vina (1985), *Emergence of Women's Question in India and the Role of Women's Studies* (New Delhi: Centre for Women's Development Studies).

McGuire, James W. (1994), 'Development Policy and its Determinants in East Asia and Latin America', *Journal of Public Policy*, 14.

McKenzie, Lionel (1959), 'On the Existence of General Equilibrium for a Competitive Market', *Econometrica*, 27.

Mehrotra, Nidhi (1999), 'Primary Schooling in Rural India: Determinants of Demand', PhD thesis, University of Chicago.

Mehrotra, Santosh (2001a), 'Financing Elementary Education in India: Summary Findings and Policy Recommendations of a UNICEF Study', draft report, UNICEF, New Delhi; to be published in UNICEF (forthcoming), *Uncaging the Tiger Economy: Financing Elementary Education in India* (New Delhi: UNICEF).

—— (2001b), 'Potential for New Reforms', mimeo, UNICEF, New Delhi; to be published in UNICEF (forthcoming), *Uncaging the Tiger Economy: Financing Elementary Education in India* (New Delhi: UNICEF).

Mehrotra, S., and Buckland, P. (2001), 'Managing Schoolteacher Costs for Access and Quality in Developing Countries: A Comparative Analysis', mimeo, UNICEF, New York; forthcoming in *Economic and Political Weekly*.

Mehrotra, S., and Jolly, R. (eds.) (1997), *Development with a Human Face: Experiences in Social Achievement and Economic Growth* (Oxford: Clarendon).

Mencher, Joan (1980), 'The Lessons and Non-Lessons from Kerala', *Economic and Political Weekly*, special number: 1781-1802.

Meng Lian and Wang Xiaolu (2000), 'Estimation of the Reliability of Statistical Data on China's Economic Growth' (in Chinese), *Jingji Yanjiu* (*Economic Research*), 10.

Menon, Nivedita (2000), 'Elusive "Woman": Feminism and Women's Reservation Bill', *Economic and Political Weekly*, 28 October.

Menon, Parvati (2000), 'The Woman's Place', *Frontline*, 18 March.

Menon, Raja (2000), *A Nuclear Strategy for India* (New Delhi: Sage).

Mill, John Stuart (1848), *Principles of Political Economy* (London: Parker; republished, Fairfield: Augustus Kelley, 1976).

_____ (1859), *On Liberty* (republished, Harmondsworth: Penguin, 1954).

_____ (1861), *Utilitarianism* (republished, London: Dent, 1929).

_____ (1869), *The Subjection of Women*, London; republished in Alice S. Rossi (ed.) (1970), *Essays on Sex Equality* (Chicago: University of Chicago Press).

Miller, Barbara (1981), *The Endangered Sex* (Ithaca: Cornell University Press).

_____ (1989), 'Changing Patterns of Juvenile Sex Ratios in Rural India, 1961 to 1971', *Economic and Political Weekly*, 3 June.

_____ (1993a), 'On Poverty, Child Survival and Gender: Models and Misperceptions', *Third World Planning Review*, 15.

_____ (ed.) (1993b), *Sex and Gender Hierarchies* (Cambridge: Cambridge University Press).

Minhas, B. (1992), 'Educational Deprivation and its Role as a Spoiler of Access to Better Life in India', in Dutta, A., and Agrawal, M.M. (eds.) (1992), *The Quality of Life* (Delhi: B.R. Publishing).

Minhas, B.S., Jain, L.R., and Tendulkar, S.D. (1991), 'Declining Incidence of Poverty in India in the 1980s', *Economic and Political Weekly*, 6–13 July.

Minturn, Leigh (1993), *Sita's Daughters: Coming Out of Purdah, The Rajput Women of Khalapur Revisited* (New York: Oxford University Press).

Mishra, Neelabh (2001), 'Post-mortem of Hunger', *Hindustan Times*, 4 April.

Mishra, Sweta (1998), 'Women and the 73rd Constitutional Amendment Act: A Critical Appraisal', in Raj and Mathias (1998).

Misra, Rajeev L. (2001), 'Preface', in Misra et al. (2001).

Misra, R., Chatterjee, R., and Rao, S. (eds.) (2001), 'Changing the Indian Health System: Current Issues, Future Directions', draft report of the India Health Study commissioned by the WHO Commission on Macroeconomics and Health; mimeo, Indian Council for Research on International Economic Relations, New Delhi.

Mitra, Ashok (1979), *Implications of Declining Sex Ratio in India's Population* (Mumbai: Allied Publishers).

Mohanty, Bidyut (1999), 'Panchayati Raj Institutions and Women', in Ray and Basu (1999).

Moller, Joanne (1993), 'Inside and Outside: Conceptual Continuities from Household to Region in Kumaon, North India', PhD thesis, London School of Economics.

Mooij, Jos (1999), *Food Policy and the Indian State: The Public Distribution System in South India* (New Delhi: Oxford University Press).

Morris, Morris D. (1979), *Measuring the Condition of the World's Poor* (Oxford. Pergamon Press).

Mukherjee, Neela (1992), 'Rural Communities' Perceptions of Poverty and Well Being: Some Case Studies in a Participatory Framework', paper presented at a workshop on 'Meanings of Agriculture' held at the School of Oriental and African Studies, London, 13–15 July.

Mukherjee, Sudhansu Bhusan (1976), *The Age Distribution of the Indian Population: A Reconstruction for the States and Territories, 1881–1961* (Honolulu: East-West Centre).

Mukhopadhyay, Alok (1997), 'Foreword', in Voluntary Health Association of India (1997).

Mukhopadhyay, Swapna (ed.) (1998), *Women's Health, Public Policy and Community Action* (New Delhi: Manohar).

Mullen, Rani (forthcoming), 'Does Local Governance Matter? The Relationship between Village Government and Social Welfare in Selected Indian States', PhD thesis, Princeton University.

Mundle, Sudipto (1994), 'Deprivation and Public Policy: Redefining the Developmental State', The Wertheim Lecture 1994, Centre for Asian Studies Amsterdam (CASA), Amsterdam.

Munshi, Kaivan (2000), 'Social Change and Individual Decisions: With an Application to the Demographic Transition', mimeo, University of Pennsylvania.

Muraleedharan, V.R. (2001), 'Public Health Care System in Tamil Nadu: A Critical Overview of its Strengths and Weaknesses', background paper prepared for the WHO Commission on Macroeconomics and Health; mimeo, Indian Institute of Technology, Chennai.

Murray, C.J.L., and Lopez, A.D. (eds.) (1996), *The Global Burden of Disease* (Cambridge, MA: Harvard University Press).

Murthi, M., Guio, A.C., and Drèze, J.P. (1995), 'Mortality, Fertility and Gender Bias in India', *Population and Development Review*, 21; reprinted in Drèze and Sen (1996).

Muzammil, Mohd., and Kingdon, Geeta Gandhi (2001), 'Teachers, Politics, and Education in India: A Political Economy Analysis', mimeo, University of Oxford; to be published as a monograph.

Myrdal, Gunnar (1968), *Asian Drama* (New York: Pantheon).

Nadarajah, T. (1983), 'The Transition from Higher Female to Higher Male Mortality in Sri Lanka', *Population and Development Review*, 9.

Nag, Moni (1983), 'Impact of Social Development and Economic Development on Mortality: Comparative Study of Kerala and West Bengal', *Economic and Political Weekly*, 28 (annual number, May).

—— (1989) 'Political Awareness as a Factor in Accesibility of Health Services: A Case Study of Rural Kerala and West Bengal', *Economic and Political Weekly*, 25 February.

Nagaraj, R. (2000), 'Indian Economy since 1980: Virtuous Growth or Polarisation?', *Economic and Political Weekly*, 5 August.

Nagarajan, R. (1997), 'Landholding, Child Labour and Schooling', *Journal of Rural Development*, 16.

Naik, J.P. (1975a), *Elementary Education in India: A Promise to Keep* (Mumbai: Allied).

—— (1975b), *Equity, Quality and Quantity: The Elusive Triangle in India* (Mumbai: Allied).

—— (1982), *The Education Commission and After* (New Delhi: Allied).

Nair, K.N., Sivanandan, P., and Retnam, V.C.V. (1984), 'Education, Employment and Landholding Pattern in a Tamil Village', *Economic and Political Weekly*, 16–23 June.

Nair, P.R.G. (1981), *Primary Education, Population Growth and Socio-Economic Change: A Comparative Study with Particular Reference to Kerala* (New Delhi: Allied).

Nambissan, Geetha B. (1996), 'Equity in Education: The Schooling of Dalit Children', Discussion Paper 15, Studies on Human Development in India, UNDP, New Delhi.

—— (1997), 'Schooling of Children in Rural Rajasthan: A Study of Jhadol and Alwar Tehsil', mimeo, Project on Strategies and Financing for Human Development, UNDP, New Delhi; to be published in Vaidyanathan and Nair (forthcoming).

Nanda, A.R. (1991), 'Provisional Population Totals: Workers and their Distribution', Census of India 1991, Series 1, Paper 3 of 1991, Office of the Registrar General, New Delhi.

—— (1992), 'Final Population Totals: Brief Analysis of Primary Census Abstract', Census of India 1991, Series 1, Paper 2 of 1992, Office of the Registrar General, New Delhi.

—— (1993), 'Union Primary Census Abstract for Scheduled Castes and Scheduled Tribes', Census of India 1991, Series 1, Paper 1 of 1993, Office of the Registrar General, New Delhi.

Nandraj, Sunil (1994), 'Beyond the Law and the Lord: Quality of Private Health Care', *Economic and Political Weekly*, 2 July.

—— (1997), 'Unhealthy Prescriptions: The Need for Health Sector Reform in India', in *Informing and Reforming*, Newsletter of the International Clearinghouse of Health System Reform Initiatives, No. 2.

Nandy, Ashis (2000), 'Why Development and Prosperity will not Remove Poverty', *Humanscape*, November.

Narain, I. (1972), 'Rural Local Politics and Primary School Management', in Rudolph and Rudolph (1972).

Natarajan, K.S., and Jayachandran, V. (2001), 'Population Growth in 21st Century India', in Srinivasan, K., and Vlassoff, M. (eds.) (2001), *Population-Development Nexus in India: Challenges for the New Millenium* (New Delhi: Tata McGraw Hill).

National Academy of Sciences (1971), *Rapid Population Growth: Consequences and Policy Implications*, vol. I (Baltimore, MD: Johns Hopkins University Press).

National Council of Applied Economic Research (1996), *Human Development Profile of India. Volume II: Statistical Tables* (New Delhi: NCAER).

—— (1997), 'Time Utilization of Children', provisional tables, MIMAP project, NCAER, New Delhi.

—— (2000), 'Who Benefits from Public Health Spending in India?', mimeo, NCAER, New Delhi.

National Council of Educational Research and Training (1992), *Fifth All-India Educational Survey*, 2 volumes (New Delhi: NCERT).

—— (1997), *Sixth All-India Educational Survey, National Tables, Volume 1* (New Delhi: NCERT).

National Institute of Public Cooperation and Child Development (1992), *Statistics on Children in India: Pocket Book 1992* (New Delhi: NIPCCD).

National Sample Survey Organisation (1997), 'Economic Activities and School Attendance by Children in India', Revised Report 412, NSSO, New Delhi.

—— (1999), 'Travel and Use of Mass Media and Financial Services by Indian Households', Report 450, NSSO, New Delhi.

—— (2000), 'Household Consumer Expenditure in India 1999-2000: Key Results', Report 454, NSSO, New Delhi.

—— (2001), 'Level and Pattern of Consumer Expenditure in India 1999-2000', Report 457, NSSO, New Delhi.

Naughton, Barry (1999), 'Causes et Conséquences des Disparités dans la Croissance Economique des Provinces Chinoises', *Revue d'Economie du Développement*, June.

Nautiyal, K.C. (1989), *Education and Rural Poor* (New Delhi: Commonwealth Publishers).

Navlakha, Gautam (1999), 'Defence Spending: Cost of Fighting Imaginary Enemies', *Economic and Political Weekly*, 7 May.

Navlakha, Gautam (2000), 'Downsizing "National Security"', *Economic and Political Weekly*, 13 May.

Nayar, Kuldip (2000a), 'Accountability in J&K', *The Hindu*, 7 January.

—— (2000b), 'Double Standards', *The Hindu*, 18 November.

—— (2001), 'Hounded and Harassed', *The Hindu*, 8 October.

Nayyar, Deepak (ed.) (1994), *Industrial Growth and Stagnation: The Debate in India* (Oxford: Oxford University Press).

Nayyar, Rohini (1991), *Rural Poverty in India: An Analysis of Inter-state Differences* (New York: Oxford University Press).

Nieuwenhuys, Olga (1994), *Children's Lifeworlds: Gender, Welfare and Labour in the Developing World* (London: Routledge).

Ninan, K. (1994), 'Poverty and Income Distribution in India', *Economic and Political Weekly*, 18 June.

Nozick, Robert (1974), *Anarchy, State and Utopia* (Oxford: Blackwell).

Nuna, Sheel C. (1990), *Women and Development* (New Delhi: National Institute of Educational Planning and Administration).

Nussbaum, Martha (1992), 'Human Functioning and Social Justice', *Political Theory*, 20.

—— (1993), 'Non-relative Virtues: An Aristotelian Approach', in Nussbaum and Sen (1993).

Nussbaum, Martha, and Sen, Amartya (eds.) (1993), *The Quality of Life* (Oxford: Clarendon Press).

Oe, Kenzaburo (1995), *Japan, the Ambiguous, and Myself* (Tokyo and New York: Kodansha International).

Oldenburg, Philip (1992), 'Sex Ratio, Son Preference and Violence in India: A Research Note', *Economic and Political Weekly*, 5–12 December.

Omvedt, Gail (1980), *We Will Smash this Prison! Indian Women in Struggle* (London: Zed).

—— (1989), 'Rural Women Fight for Independence', *Economic and Political Weekly*, 29 April.

—— (1990), 'Women, Zilla Parishads and Panchayati Raj: Chandwad to Vitner', *Economic and Political Weekly*, 4 August.

—— (1993), *Reinventing Revolution: New Social Movements and the Socialist Tradition in India* (London: M.E. Sharpe).

—— (2000), 'Women and PR', *The Hindu*, 11 September.

Oommen, M.A. (ed.) (1999), *Kerala's Development Experience*, 2 volumes (New Delhi: Concept).

Operations Research Group (1999), 'Evaluation Study to Assess the Efficiency and Effectiveness of the National Programme for Nutritional Support to Primary Education in Ten States of India', report submitted to UNICEF, New Delhi.

Osmani, Siddiq R. (1997), 'Poverty and Nutrition in South Asia', in UN Sub-Committee on Nutrition (1997), *Nutrition and Poverty* (Geneva: WHO).

—— (1990), 'Nutrition and the Economics of Food: Implications of Some Recent Controversies', in Drèze and Sen (1990), vol. I.

—— (1991), 'Social Security in South Asia', in Ahmad, Drèze, Hills, and Sen (1991).

—— (ed.) (1992), *Nutrition and Poverty* (Oxford: Clarendon Press).

Osmani, S.R., and Sen, A.K. (2001), 'The Hidden Penalties of Gender Inequality: Fetal Origins of Adult Diseases', paper presented at the First World Congress on the Fetal Origins of Adult Disease, Mumbai, 2–4 February.

Ota, Masako (forthcoming), 'Between Work and School: Rural Children in Andhra Pradesh, India', PhD thesis, University of East Anglia.

Otsuka, K., et al. (1992), 'Land and Labor Contracts in Agrarian Economies: Theories and Facts', *Journal of Economic Literature*, 30.

Otsuka, K., and Hayami, Y. (1988), 'Theories of Share Tenancy: A Critical Survey', *Economic Development and Cultural Change*, 36.

Pachauri, S., and Subramanian, S. (1999), *Implementing a Reproductive Health Agenda in India: The Beginning* (New Delhi: Population Council).

Paddock, William, and Paddock, Paul (1968), *Famine—1975!* (London: Weidenfeld and Nicolson).

Pai, Sudha (1998), 'Pradhanis in New Panchayats: Field Notes from Meerut District', *Economic and Political Weekly*, 2 May.

—— (2001), 'Social Capital, Panchayats and Grassroots Democracy: Politics of Dalit Assertion in Two Districts of Uttar Pradesh', *Economic and Political Weekly*, 24 February.

Pal, Mahi (1998), 'Woman in Panchayat: Experiences of a Training Camp', *Economic and Political Weekly*, 24 January.

Pal, Sarmistha (1994), 'Choice of Casual and Regular Labour Contracts in Indian Agriculture: A Theoretical and Empirical Analysis', PhD thesis, London School of Economics.

Pandey, A., Choe, M.K., Luther, N.Y., Sahu, D., and Chand, J. (1998), 'Infant and Child Mortality in India', NFHS Subject Report 11, International Institute for Population Sciences, Mumbai.

Panigrahi, Lalita (1972), *British Social Policy and Female Infanticide in India* (New Delhi: Munshiram Manoharlal).

Panikar, P.G.K., and Soman, C.R. (1984), *Health Status of Kerala: The Paradox of Economic Backwardness and Health Development* (Thiruvananthapuram: Centre for Development Studies).

Panikar, P.G.K., and Soman, C.R. (1985), *Status of Women and Children in Kerala* (Thiruvananthapuram: Centre for Development Studies).

Papandreou, Andreas (1994), *Externality and Institutions* (Oxford: Clarendon Press).

Parasuraman, S., Roy, T.K., Radha Devi, D., Paswan, B., Arokiasamy, P., and Unisa, S. (1999), *Role of Women's Education in Shaping Fertility in India: Evidences from National Family Health Survey* (Mumbai: Himalaya).

Parayil, Govindan (ed.) (2000), *Kerala: The Development Experience—Reflections on Sustainability and Replicability* (London: Zed).

Parikh, Kirit (1994), 'Who Gets How Much from PDS—How Effectively Does It Reach the Poor?', *Sarvekshana*, January-March.

—— (ed.) (2000), *India Development Report 1999–2000* (New Delhi: Oxford University Press).

Parikh, Kirit, and Sudarshan, R. (eds.) (1993), *Human Development and Structural Adjustment* (Madras: Macmillan).

Parmar, H.S. (1979), 'Subsistence Economy of Rural Himachal Pradesh: A Case Study of Three Small Villages', *Economic Affairs*, 24.

Patel, I.G. (1992), 'New Economic Policies: A Historical Perspective', *Economic and Political Weekly*, 4–11 January.

Patel, Surendra J. (1985), 'India's Regression in the World Economy', *Economic and Political Weekly*, 28 September.

—— (1994), *Indian Economy Towards the 21st Century* (Mumbai: Orient Longman).

Pathak, Shekhar (1997), 'State, Society and Natural Resources in Himalaya', *Economic and Political Weekly*, 26 April.

Patnaik, Prabhat (1994), 'International Capital and National Economic Policy: A Critique of India's Economic Reforms', *Economic and Political Weekly*, 19 March.

Peng, Xizhe (1987), 'Demographic Consequences of the Great Leap Forward in China's Provinces', *Population and Development Review*, 13.

—— (1991), *Demographic Transition in China: Fertility Trends since the 1950s* (Oxford: Clarendon).

Peng, X., and Huang, J. (1999), 'Chinese Traditional Medicine and Abnormal Sex Ratio at Birth in China', *Journal of Biosocial Science*, 31.

Peoples Union for Democratic Rights (2001), *Grim Realities of Life, Death and Survival in Jammu and Kashmir*, report of a joint fact-finding team of civil liberties, democratic rights and human rights organizations (New Delhi: PUDR).

Perkins, Dwight (1983), 'Research on the Economy of the People's Republic of China: A Survey of the Field', *Journal of Asian Studies*, 42.

_____(1988), 'Reforming China's Economic System', *Journal of Economic Literature*, 26.

Perkovich, George (1999), *India's Nuclear Bomb: The Impact of Global Proliferation* (Berkeley: University of California Press).

Persson, Torsten, and Tabellini, Guido (1994), 'Is Inequality Harmful to Growth? Theory and Evidence', *American Economic Review*, 84.

Pieris, I., and Caldwell, B. (1996), 'Gender and Health in Sri Lanka', paper presented at a workshop on 'Gender Perspectives in Population, Health and Development', National Council of Applied Economic Research, New Delhi, January.

Platteau, Jean-Philippe (1995), 'A Broad Framework for Analysis of Evolving Patron-Client Ties in Agrarian Economies', *World Development*, 23.

Pojda, J., and Kelley, L. (2000), 'Low Birthweight', ACC/SCN Nutrition Policy Paper 18, UN ACC Sub-Committee on Nutrition, Geneva.

Poitevin, Guy, and Rairkar, Hema (1985), *Inde: Village au Féminin* (Paris: L'Harmattan).

Powell, Robert (1990), *Nuclear Deterrence Theory: The Search for Credibility* (Cambridge: Cambridge University Press).

Powis, Benjamin (1999), 'Bottom-up Approaches to Decentralisation: The People's Planning Campaign in Kerala', MSc dissertation, University of Sussex.

Prabhu, K. Seeta (1999), 'Social Sectors During Economic Reforms: The Indian Experience', *Oxford Development Studies*, 27.

_____ (2001), *Economic Reform and Social Sector Development: A Study of Two Indian States* (New Delhi and London: Sage).

Prabhu, K. Seeta, and Sarker, P.C. (1998), 'Financing Human Development in Indian States: Trends and Implications (1974–75 to 1995–96)', mimeo, Department of Economics, University of Mumbai.

Pradhan, B.K., and Subramanian, A. (2000), 'Education, Openness and the Poor', Discussion Paper 14, National Council of Applied Economic Research, New Delhi.

Pradhan, B.K., Tripathy, K.K., and Rajan, R. (2000), 'Public Spending and Outcome of Social Service in India: A Review during the Regime of Policy Reforms', Discussion Paper 15, National Council of Applied Economic Research, New Delhi.

Prakasamma, M. (1989), 'Analysis of Factors Influencing Performance of Auxiliary Nurse Midwives in Nizamabad District', PhD thesis, Centre for Social Medicine and Community Health, Jawaharlal Nehru University, New Delhi.

Prakash, B.A. (ed.) (1999), *Kerala's Economic Development: Issues and Problems* (New Delhi: Sage).

Prasad, K.V. Eswara (1987), *Wastage, Stagnation and Inequality of Opportunity in Rural Primary Education: A Case Study of Andhra Pradesh* (New Delhi: Ministy of Human Resource Development).

Preston, Samuel H. (1976), *Mortality Patterns in National Populations* (New York: Academic Press).

Pritchett, Lant, and Summers, Lawrence (1996), 'Wealthier is Healthier', *Journal of Human Resources*, 31.

Priya, Ritu (1987), 'Family Planning and Health Care: A Case Study from Rajasthan', paper presented at the 12th Annual Meeting of Medico Friends Circle.

—— (1990), 'Dubious Package Deal: Health Care in Eighth Plan', *Economic and Political Weekly*, 18 August.

PROBE Team (1999). *Public Report on Basic Education in India* (New Delhi: Oxford University Press).

Przeworski, Adam (ed.) (1995), *Sustainable Democracy* (Cambridge: Cambridge University Press).

Psacharopoulos, George (1988): 'Education and Development: A Review', *World Bank Research Observer*, 3.

—— (1994), 'Returns to Investment in Education: A Global Update', *World Development*, 22.

Pushpendra (1999), 'Dalit Assertion through Electoral Politics', *Economic and Political Weekly*, 4 September.

Qadeer, I., Sen, K., and Nayar, K.R. (eds.) (2001), *Public Health and the Poverty of Reforms* (New Delhi: Sage).

Quibria, M.G., and Rashid, S. (1984), 'The Puzzle of Sharecropping: A Survey of Theories', *World Development*, 12.

Raghunandan, D., Baru, R., Lakshmi, G., and Sengupta, A. (1987), 'Health Seeking Behaviour and the Primary Health Care System: Case Study of a Backward Village in Andhra Pradesh', report submitted to the United Nations University, Tokyo; mimeo, Society for Economic and Social Studies, New Delhi.

Rahman, O., Foster, A., and Menken, J. (1992) 'Older Widow Mortality in Rural Bangladesh', *Social Science and Medicine*, 34.

Raj, K.N., and Sen, A.K. (1961), 'Alternative Patterns of Growth under Conditions of Stagnant Export Earnings', *Oxford Economic Papers*, 13.

Raj, K.N., and Tharakan, M. (1983), 'Agrarian Reform in Kerala and Its Impact on the Rural Economy', in Ghose, A. (ed.) (1983), *Agrarian Reform in Contemporary Developing Countries* (London: Croom Helm).

Raj, Sebasti L., and Mathias, E. (eds.) (1998), *People's Power and Panchayati Raj: Theory and Practice* (New Delhi: Indian Social Institute).

Rajan, S., and Jayakumar, A. (1992), 'Impact of Noon-Meal Programme on Education: An Exploratory Study in Tamil Nadu', *Economic and Political Weekly*, 24 October.

Rajan, S.I., Mishra, U.S., and Navaneetham, K. (1991), 'Decline in Sex Ratio: An Alternative Explanation?', *Economic and Political Weekly*, 21 December.

Rajan, S.I., Mishra, U.S., and Navaneetham, K. (1992), 'Decline in Sex Ratio: Alternative Explanation Revisited', *Economic and Political Weekly*, 14 November.

Rajan, S.I., and Mohanachandran, P. (2000), 'Infant and Child Mortality Estimates, 1991 Census', *Economic and Political Weekly*, 16 December.

Rajivan, Anuradha K. (1991), 'Weight Variations among Preschoolers: An Analysis of Evidence from Rural Tamil Nadu', PhD thesis, University of Southern California.

Rajivan, A.K. (2001), 'Nutrition Security in Tamil Nadu', in Mahendra Dev et al. (2001).

Raju, S., Atkins, P.J., Kumar, N., and Townsend, J. (1999), *Atlas of Women and Men in India* (New Delhi: Kali for Women).

Ram, Atma (2000), 'Education', background paper prepared for Himachal Pradesh's Human Development Report; mimeo, UNDP, New Delhi.

Ram, N. (1990), 'An Independent Press and Anti-Hunger Strategies: The Indian Experience', in Drèze and Sen (1990), vol. I.

—— (1999), *Riding the Nuclear Tiger* (New Delhi: Leftword Books).

Ramachandran, V.K. (1990), *Wage Labour and Unfreedom in Agriculture: An Indian Case Study* (Oxford: Clarendon Press).

—— (1996), 'Kerala's Development Achievements', in Drèze and Sen (1996).

Ramachandran, V.K., and Swaminathan, M. (1999), 'New Data on Calorie Intakes', *Frontline*, 12 March.

Ramachandran, Vimala (1999), 'Needed: A Life of Dignity', *The Hindu*, 7 October.

Ramachandran, Vimala, and Visaria, Leela (1997), 'Emerging Issues in Reproductive Health', *Economic and Political Weekly*, 6 September.

Ramalingaswami, V., Deo, M.G., Guleria, J.S., Malhotra, K.K., Sood, S.K., Om, P., and Sinha, R.V.N. (1971), 'Studies of the Bihar Famine of 1966–1967', in Blix, G., et al. (eds.) (1971), *Famine: Nutrition and Relief Operations in Times of Disaster* (Uppsala: Swedish Nutrition Foundation).

Ramana, M.V., and Reddy, C. Rammanohar (forthcoming), *Prisoners of the Nuclear Dream* (New Delhi: Orient Longman).

Ramasundaram, S. (1995a), 'Implementation of Family Welfare Programme: An Overview', mimeo, Health and Welfare Department, Government of Tamil Nadu.

—— (1995b), 'Causes for the Rapid Fertility Decline in Tamil Nadu: A Policy Planner's Perspective', *Demography India*, 24.

Ramasundaram, S., Rangarajan, T., and Muthuramalingam, S. (1997), 'The Role of Political Will and Official Commitment in Tamil Nadu's Fertility Decline', Studies of Human Development in India Discussion Paper 24, Centre for Development Studies, Thiruvananthapuram.

Ramdas, L. (1998), 'Pokhran-II and its Fallout', *Frontline*, 4 July.

Ramesh, Jairam (1999), 'War and Costs', *India Today*, 28 June.

Rana, Kumar, et al. (2001), 'Reach and Governance of Primary Education in India: A Study in Three Districts of West Bengal', mimeo, Pratichi (India) Trust, Delhi.

Rao, Nitya (1993), 'Total Literacy Campaigns: A Field Report', *Economic and Political Weekly*, 8 May.

Rao, S.L. (1994), 'Labour Adjustment as Part of Industrial Restructuring', *Economic and Political Weekly*, 5 February.

Rapoport, Anatol (1964), *Strategy and Conscience* (New York: Schocken).

—— (1992), *Peace: An Idea Whose Time has Come* (Ann Arbor: University of Michigan Press).

—— (1995), *The Origins of Violence* (New Brunswick: Transaction Publishers).

—— (1998), *Decision Theory and Decision Behaviour*, second edition (London: Macmillan).

—— (2000), *Certainties and Doubts: A Philosophy of Life* (Montréal: Black Rose).

Raval, Sheela (2001), 'Consumed by Hunger', *India Today*, 21 May.

Ravallion, Martin (1987), *Markets and Famines* (Oxford: Clarendon Press).

—— (1994), *Poverty Comparisons* (Chur, Switzerland: Harwood Academic Press).

—— (2000a), 'On the Conditions for Pro-poor Economic Growth in India', mimeo, ARQADE, Univerty of Toulouse.

—— (2000b), 'Should Poverty Measures be Anchored to the National Accounts', mimeo, ARQADE, Univerty of Toulouse.

Ravallion, M., and Subbarao, K. (1992), 'Adjustment and Human Development in India', *Journal of the Indian School of Political Economy*, January-March.

Rawal, V., and Swaminathan, M. (1998), 'Changing Trajectories: Agricultural Growth in West Bengal, 1950 to 1996', *Economic and Political Weekly*, 3 October.

Rawski, Thomas G. (1999), 'China's Economy After Fifty Years: Retrospect and Prospect', mimeo, University of Pittsburgh.

Rawski, Thomas G. (2001), 'China's GDP Statistics: A Case of Caveat Lector?', mimeo, University of Pittsburgh.

Ray, B., and Basu, A. (eds.) (1999), *From Independence Towards Freedom: Indian Women since 1947* (New Delhi: Oxford University Press).

Ray, Rabindra (1992), *The Naxalites and their Ideology* (New Delhi: Oxford University Press).

Ray, Ranjan (1998), 'Child Health and its Determinants in Developing Countries: A Cross Country Comparison', mimeo, School of Economics, University of Tasmania.

Raz, J. (1986), *The Morality of Freedom* (Oxford: Clarendon Press).

Raza, M. (1990), *Education, Development and Society* (New Delhi: Vikas Publishing House).

Raza, M., and Ramachandaran, H. (1990), 'Responsiveness to Educational Inputs: A Study of Rural Households', *Indian Journal of Social Science*, 3.

Reddy, C. Rammanohar (2000), 'Estimating the Cost of Nuclear Weaponisation in India', paper presented at a workshop on 'Economic Aspects of National Security' held at the Delhi School of Economics, March 2000; to be published in Ramana and Reddy (forthcoming).

—— (2001a), 'Poverty and Unemployment in the 1990s', *The Hindu*, 20 January.

—— (2001b), 'Whatever Happened to the 60 Million Tonnes?', *The Hindu*, 28 October.

Reddy, Sanjay (1988), 'An Independent Press Working Against Famine: The Nigerian Experience', *Journal of Modern African Studies*, 26.

Riskin, Carl (1987), *China's Political Economy: The Quest for Development since 1949* (Oxford: Oxford University Press).

—— (1990), 'Feeding China', in Drèze and Sen (1990), vol. III.

—— (1993), 'Income Distribution and Poverty in Rural China', in Griffin and Zhao Renwei (1993).

—— (1998), 'Seven Questions about the Chinese Famine of 1959–61', *China Economic Review*, 9.

Rodrik, Dani (1994), 'King Kong Meets Godzilla: The World Bank and *The East Asian Miracle*', Discussion Paper 944, Centre for Economic Policy Research, London.

Roemer, John (1982), *A General Theory of Exploitation and Class* (Cambridge, MA: Harvard Univserty Press).

Rogaly, Ben (1994), 'Rural Labour Arrangements in West Bengal, India', PhD thesis, University of Oxford.

Rogaly, B., Harriss-White, B., and Bose, S. (eds.) (1999) *Sonar Bangla? Agricultural Growth and Agrarian Change in West Bengal and Bangladesh* (New Delhi: Sage).

Rogers, John D. (1989), 'Theories of Crime and Development: An Historical Perspective', *Journal of Development Studies*, 25.

Romer, Paul M. (1986), 'Increasing Returns and Long-Run Growth', *Journal of Political Economy*, 94.

—— (1987a), 'Growth Based on Increasing Returns Due to Specialization', *American Economic Review*, 77.

—— (1987b), 'Two Strategies for Economic Development: Using Ideas and Producing Ideas', in *Proceedings of the World Bank Annual Conference on Development Economics 1992* (Washington, DC: World Bank).

—— (1990), 'Endogenous Technical Change', *Journal of Political Economy*, 98.

Romer, Paul M. (1993), 'Idea Gaps and Object Gaps in Economic Development', *Journal of Monetary Economics*, 32.

Rose, Kalima (1992), *Where Women are Leaders: The SEWA Movement in India* (London: Zed Books).

Rosen, George (1992), *Contrasting Styles of Industrial Reform: China and India in the 1980s* (Chicago: University of Chicago Press).

Rosenzweig, Mark R., and Schultz, T. Paul (1982), 'Market Opportunities, Genetic Endowments, and Intrafamily Resource Distribution: Child Survival in Rural India', *American Economic Review*, 72.

Rothschild, Emma (2001), *Economic Sentiments: Adam Smith, Condorcet, and the Enlightenment* (Cambridge, MA: Harvard University Press).

Rothschild, M., and Stiglitz, J. (1976), 'Equilibrium in Competitive Insurance Markets', *Quarterly Journal of Economics*, 90.

Roy, Aruna, Dey, Nikhil and Singh, Shanker (1993), 'Living with Dignity and Social Justice: Rural Workers Rights to Creative Development', mimeo, Mazdoor Kisan Shakti Sangathan, Devdungri.

Roy, Arundhati (1998), 'The End of Imagination', *Frontline*, 27 July; reprinted in Roy (1999).

—— (1999), *The Cost of Living* (London: Flamingo).

Roy, D.K.S. (1992), *Women in Peasant Movements: Tebhaga, Naxalite and After* (New Delhi: Manohar Publications).

Roy, S.B. (1992), 'Forest Protection Committees in West Bengal', *Economic and Political Weekly*, 18 July.

Roy, T.K., and Verma, R.K. (1999), 'Women's Perceptions of the Quality of Family Welfare Services in Four Indian States', in Koenig and Khan (1999).

Rudolph, S.H., and Rudolph, L.I. (eds.) (1972), *Education and Politics in India: Studies in Organization, Society, and Policy* (Cambridge, MA: Harvard University Press).

Rudra, Ashok (1988), 'Emerging Class Structure in Rural India', in Srinivasan and Bardhan (1988).

—— (1991), 'Privatisation and Deregulation', *Economic and Political Weekly*, 21 December.

Rummel, R.J. (1994), *Death by Government: Genocide and Mass Murder in the Twentieth Century* (New Jersey: Transaction Publishers).

—— (1998), *Statistics of Democide: Genocide and Mass Murder since 1900* (Munster: Lit Verlag).

Rustagi, Preet (1996), 'The Structure and Dynamics of Indian Rural Labour Market', PhD thesis, Centre for Economic Studies and Planning, Jawaharlal Nehru University.

Ruud, Arild Engelsen (1994), 'Land and Power: The Marxist Conquest of West Bengal', *Modern Asian Studies*, 28.

—— (1999), 'From Untouchable to Communist: Wealth, Power and Status among Supporters of the Communist Party (Marxist) in Rural West Bengal', in Rogaly et al. (1999).

Sachau, E.C. (ed.) (1992), *Alberuni's India*, originally published in 1910 (New Delhi: Munshiram Manoharlal Publishers).

Sachs, I. (1990), 'Growth and Poverty: Some Lessons from Brazil', in Drèze and Sen (1990), vol. III.

Sachs, J.D., Varshney, A., and Bajpai, N. (eds.) (1999), *India in the Era of Economic Reforms* (New Delhi: Oxford University Press).

Saha, Anamitra, and Swaminathan, Madhura (1994), 'Agricultural Growth in West Bengal in the 1980s: A Disaggregation by Districts and Crops', *Economic and Political Weekly*, 26 March.

Sahn, David, and Alderman, Harold (1988), 'The Effects of Human Capital on Wages, and the Determinants of Labor Supply in a Developing Country', *Journal of Development Economics*, 29.

Sainath, P. (1996), *Everybody Loves a Good Drought* (New Delhi: Penguin).

—— (1999), 'A Dalit Goes to Court', *The Hindu*, 13 June and 11 July.

—— (2001a), 'Rajasthan's Drought: Abundance of Food, Scarcity of Vision', *The Hindu*, 18 March and 25 March.

—— (2001b), 'More Hunger Deaths in Maharashtra than in Orissa', *Times of India*, 9 September.

—— (2001c), 'Hero by Name and Deed', *The Hindu*, 21 January.

Saith, Ashwani (1990), 'Development Strategies and the Rural Poor', *Journal of Development Studies*, 17.

Saldanha, Denzil (1994), 'Report on the Total Literacy Campaign', mimeo, Tata Institute of Social Sciences, Bombay.

Salim, A. Abdul, and Nair, P.R. Gopinathan (1997), 'Education System in Kerala:

An Enquiry into Social Intervention, Financing and Regional Policies', mimeo, Project on Strategies and Financing for Human Development, UNDP, New Delhi.

Sampson, Anthony (1991), *The Arms Bazaar* (London: Hodder and Stoughton).

Sangwan, N., and Maru, R.M. (1999), 'The Target-free Approach: An Overview', *Journal of Health Management*, 1.

Sanshodhan (2000), *A Matter of Quality* (Mussoorie: Society for Integrated Development of Himalayas).

Saraswat, S.P., and Sikka, B.K. (1990), *Socio-economic Survey of an Affluent Village in Himachal Pradesh (A Study of Village Kiari in District Shimla)* (Shimla: Agro-Economic Research Centre, Himachal Pradesh University).

Sarkar, Rinki (1999), 'Poverty, Governance and Reliance on Local Forest Resources', draft report of a pilot survey of the Bharmour region of Chamba district, Centre for Development Economics at the Delhi School of Economics.

Sarma, Sasanka (2000), 'Agricultural Wages: Trends and Determinants', MPhil thesis, Delhi School of Economics.

—— (2001), 'Agricultural Wages in India: An Analysis of Regions and States', mimeo, Centre for Development Economics at the Delhi School of Economics; forthcoming in *Indian Journal of Labour Economics*.

Satia, J.K., and Jejeebhoy, S.J.(eds) (1991), *The Demographic Challenge: A Study of Four Large Indian States* (Delhi: Oxford University Press).

Sax, W. (1991), *Mountain Goddess: Gender and Politics in a Himalayan Pilgrimage* (New York: Oxford University Press).

Saxena, N.C. (1996), 'Instances of Some Anti-poor Government Policies in India', mimeo, Lal Bahadur Shastri National Academy of Administration, Mussoorie.

—— (2000), 'How Have the Poor Done?', *Economic and Political Weekly*, 7 October.

Schell, Jonathan (1998), *The Gift of Time: The Case for Abolishing Nuclear Weapons Now* (London: Granta).

Schelling, Thomas (1960), *The Strategy of Conflict* (Cambridge, MA: Harvard University Press).

Schultz, T. Paul (1988), 'Education Investments and Returns', in Chenery and Srinivasan (1988).

—— (1997), 'Demand for Children in Low Income Countries', in Rosenzweig, M.R., and Stark, O. (eds.) (1997), *Handbook of Population and Family Economics* (Amsterdam: Elsevier Science B V).

Schultz, Theodore W. (1962), 'Reflections on Investment in Man', *Journal of Political Economy*, 70.

—— (1963), *The Economic Value of Education* (New York: Columbia University Press).

—— (1971), *Investment in Human Capital* (New York: Free Press and Macmillan).

—— (1980), *Investing in People* (San Francisco: University of California Press).

Scrimshaw, Nevin (1997), 'The Lasting Damage of Early Malnutrition', mimeo, World Food Programme, 31 May.

Seetharamu, A.S. (1994), 'Structure and Management of Education in Karnataka

State', paper presented as a seminar on 'Management of Education under Panchayati Raj' held at the National Institute of Educational Planning and Administration, 27–28 October.

Sen, Abhijit (2000), 'Estimates of Consumer Expenditure and its Distribution', *Economic and Political Weekly*, 16 December.

—— (2001), 'The Farming Crisis: A Whole Crop of Uncertainties', *Frontline*, 2 February.

Sen, Amartya (1967), 'The Nature and Classes of Prescriptive Judgements', *Philosophical Quarterly*, 17.

—— (1970a), 'Aspects of Indian Education', Lal Bahadur Shastri Memorial Lecture at the Institute of Public Enterprise, Hyderabad; reprinted in Malik, S.C. (ed), *Management and Organization of Indian Universities* (Shimla: Institute of Advanced Study), and partly reprinted in Chaudhuri, P. (ed.) (1971), *Aspects of Indian Economic Development* (London: Allen and Unwin).

—— (1970b), *Collective Choice and Social Welfare* (San Francisco: Holden-Day); republished 1979 (Amsterdam: North-Holland).

—— (1973), 'On the Development of Basic Income Indicators to Supplement GNP Measures', *Economic Bulletin for Asia and the Far East*, United Nations, 24.

—— (1976a), 'Real National Income', *Review of Economic Studies*, 43.

—— (1976b), 'Poverty: An Ordinal Approach to Measurement', *Econometrica*, 44.

—— (1977), 'Rational Fools: A Critique of the Behavioural Foundations of Economic Theory', *Philosophy and Public Affairs*, 6.

—— (1980), 'Equality of What?', in McMurrin, S. (ed.) (1980), *Tanner Lectures on Human Values*, vol. I (Cambridge: Cambridge University Press).

—— (1981), *Poverty and Famines* (Oxford: Clarendon Press).

—— (1982), 'How Is India Doing?', *New York Review of Books*, 29.

—— (1983a), 'Development: Which Way Now?', *Economic Journal*, 93.

—— (1983b), 'Poor, Relatively Spekaing', *Oxford Economic Papers*, 35.

—— (1984), *Resources, Values and Development* (Oxford: Blackwell, and Cambridge, MA: Harvard University Press).

—— (1985a), *Commodities and Capabilities* (Amsterdam: North-Holland).

—— (1985b), 'Well-being, Agency and Freedom: The Dewey Lectures 1984', *Journal of Philosophy*, 82.

—— (1985c), 'Women, Technology and Sexual Divisions', *Trade and Development* (United Nations Conference on Trade and Development UNCTAD), 6.

—— (1987a), *The Standard of Living*, Tanner Lectures with discussion by J. Muellbauer and others, ed. G. Hawthorn (Cambridge: Cambridge University Press).

—— (1987b), *On Ethics and Economics* (Oxford: Blackwell).

—— (1988), 'India and Africa: What Do We Have to Learn from Each Other?', in Arrow, K.I. (ed.) (1988), *The Balance between Industry and Agriculture in Economic Development*, vol. I (London: Macmillan).

_____ (1989), 'Women's Survival as a Development Problem', *Bulletin of the American Academy of Arts and Sciences*, 43; shortened version published in *New York Review of Books*, Christmas number (20 December), 1993.

_____ (1990), 'Gender and Cooperative Conflict', in Tinker (1990).

_____ (1992a), *Inequality Reexamined* (Oxford: Clarendon Press, and Cambridge, MA: Harvard University Press).

_____ (1992b), 'Life and Death in China: A Reply', *World Development*, 20.

_____ (1992c), 'Missing Women', *British Medical Journal*, 304 (March).

_____ (1993a), 'Markets and Freedoms', *Oxford Economic Papers*, 45.

_____ (1993b), 'Markets and the Freedom to Choose', paper presented at the Kiel Institute of World Economics; to be published in a volume on 'The Ethical Foundations of the Market Economy'.

_____ (1994a), 'Population and Reasoned Agency', in Lindahl-Kiessling, K., and Landberg, H. (eds.) (1994), *Population, Economic Development, and the Environment* (Oxford: Oxford University Press).

_____ (1994b), 'Population: Delusion and Reality', *New York Review of Books*, 22 September.

_____ (1995a), 'Environmental Evaluation and Social Choice: Contingent Valuation and the Market Analogy', *Japanese Economic Review*, 46.

_____ (1995b), 'Environmental Values and Economic Reasoning', Nexus lecture published in Dutch, *Nexus*, 13.

_____ (1997), 'From Income Inequality to Economic Inequality', *Southern Economic Journal*, 64.

_____ (1999a), *Development as Freedom* (Oxford: Oxford University Press).

_____ (1999b), 'The Possibility of Social Choice', Nobel Lecture, *American Economic Review*, 89.

_____ (1999c), 'Democracy as a Universal Value', *Journal of Democracy*, 34.

_____ (2000a), 'Social Justice and the Distribution of Income', in Atkinson, A.B., and Bourguignon, F. (eds.) (2000), *Handbook of Income Distribution* (Amsterdam: Elsevier).

_____ (2000b), 'The Discipline of Cost-benefit Analysis', *Journal of Legal Studies*, 29.

_____ (2000c), 'India and the Bomb', *The New Republic*, 25 September; also published in *Frontline*, 29 September.

_____ (2000d), 'Population and Gender Equity', *The Nation*, 24 July; reprinted (as 'Gender Equity and the Population Problem') in *International Journal of Health Services*, 31 (2001).

Sen, Amartya, and Sengupta, Sunil (1983), 'Malnutrition of Rural Children and the Sex Bias', *Economic and Political Weekly*, 19 (annual number).

Sen, Binayak (2001), 'People's Health Care Initiatives in Chhattisgarh District, Madhya Pradesh', in Qadeer et al. (2001).

Sen, G., Germain, A., and Chen, L. (eds.) (1994), *Population Policies Reconsidered: Health, Empowerment, and Rights* (Harvard Series on Population and International Health).

Sen, Ilina (1986), 'Geography of Secular Change in Sex Ratio in 1981: How Much Room for Optimism?', *Economic and Political Weekly*, 22 March.

—— (ed.) (1990), *A Space within the Struggle: Women's Participation in People's Movements* (New Delhi: Kali for Women).

Senapaty, Manju (1997), 'Gender Implications of Economic Reforms in the Education Sector in India: Case of Haryana and Madhya Pradesh', PhD thesis, University of Manchester.

Sengupta, Sohini (2000), 'Political Economy of Irrigation: Tanks in Orissa, 1850–1996', *Economic and Political Weekly*, 30 December.

Sengupta, Sunil, and Gazdar, Haris (1996), 'Agrarian Politics and Rural Development in West Bengal', in Drèze and Sen (1996).

Seshu, Geeta (1999), 'Media and Kargil: Information Blitz with Dummy Missiles', *Economic and Political Weekly*, 9 October.

Sethi, R., and Somanathan, E. (1996), 'The Evolution of Social Norms in Common Property Resource Use', *American Economic Review*, 86.

Shah, M., Banerji, D., Vijayshankar, P.S., and Ambasta, P. (1998), *India's Drylands: Tribal Societies and Development through Environmental Regeneration* (New Delhi: Oxford University Press).

Shah, M.H. (1989), 'Factors Responsible for Low Performance of Family Welfare Programme', in Jena and Pati (1989).

Shah, Nasra M. (ed.) (1986), *Pakistani Women: A Socioeconomic and Demographic Profile* (Islamabad: Pakistan Institute of Development Economics).

Shah, Tushaar (1987), 'Gains from Social Forestry: Lessons from West Bengal', mimeo, Institute of Rural Management, Anand.

Shariff, Abusaleh (1999), *India: Human Development Report* (New Delhi: Oxford University Press).

Sharma, L.R. (1987), *The Economy of Himachal Pradesh* (Delhi: Mittal).

Sharma, Mukul (forthcoming), *Green and Saffron: Environment and the Hindu Right in India*, to be published as a monograph.

Sharma, Ursula (1980), *Women, Work and Property in North-West India* (London: Tavistock).

—— (1986), *Women's Work, Class, and the Urban Household: A Study of Shimla, North India* (New York: Tavistock).

Shiva, Meera (1996), 'Health', contribution to the *Alternative Economic Survey 1995–96* of the Alternative Survey Group (New Delhi: Delhi Science Forum).

Shleifer, A., and Vishny, R. (1993), 'Corruption', *Quarterly Journal of Economics*, 108.

Shubik, Martin (1971), 'The Dollar Auction Game: A Paradox in Non-cooperative Behavior and Escalation', *Journal of Conflict Resolution*, 15.

—— (1987), 'Game Theory Models of Strategic Behavior and Nuclear Deterrence', Cowles Foundation Discussion Paper 829, Cowles Foundation for Research in Economics, Yale University.

Shukla, A., and Phadke, A. (2000), 'Putting Health on People's Agenda', *Economic and Political Weekly*, 12 August.

Sikka, B.K., and Singh, D.V. (1992), 'Malana: An Oldest Democracy Sustainability

Issues in Village Economy (Himachal Pradesh)', mimeo, Agro-Economic Research Centre, Himachal Pradesh University, Shimla.

Sikshasandhan (2000), 'Draft Report on Evaluation of Secondary Schools under ST & SC Development Department, Government of Orissa', mimeo, Sikshasandhan, Bhubaneswar.

Singh, Chetan (1998), *Natural Premises: Ecology and Peasant Life in the Western Himalaya 1800–1950* (New Delhi: Oxford University Press).

Singh, Inderjit (1990), *The Great Ascent: The Rural Poor in South Asia* (Baltimore: Johns Hopkins).

Singh, Jasjit (ed.)(1998), *Nuclear India* (New Delhi: Knowledge World).

Singh, Jaswant (1999), *Defending India* (New York: St Martin's Press).

Singh, K.B.K. (1988), *Marriage and Family System of Rajputs* (New Delhi: Wisdom Press).

Singh, K.S. (1975), *The Indian Famine, 1967* (New Delhi: People's Publishing House).

Singh, M.G. (1985), *Social, Cultural and Economic Survey of Himachal Pradesh* (Shimla: Minerva Book House).

—— (1992), *Himachal Pradesh: History, Culture and Economy* (Shimla: Minerva Book House).

Singh, Tavleen (2001), 'Grain of Untruth', *India Today*, 28 May.

Sinha, Amarjeet (2001), 'Political Mobilisation, Human Development and Poverty Elimination: Some Lessons from Indian States', paper prepared for an International Conference on Education, University of Oxford.

Sinha, Amarjeet, and Sinha, Ajay (1995), 'Primary Schooling in Northern India: A Field Investigation', mimeo, Centre for Sustainable Development, Lal Bahadur Shastri National Academy of Administration, Mussoorie.

Sinha, Shantha (1995), 'Child Labour and Education Policy in India', CSD Papers, Series 1, Centre for Sustainable Development, Lal Bahadur Shastri National Academy of Administration, Mussoorie.

Sipahimalani, Vandana (1998), 'Education in the Rural Indian Household: A Gender Based Perspective', mimeo, Department of Economics, Yale University.

Sivard, Ruth (1991), *World Military and Social Expenditures 1991* (Washington, DC: World Priorities).

—— (1996), *World Military and Social Expenditures 1996* (Washington, DC: World Priorities).

Sivasubramonian, S. (2000), *The National Income of India in the Twentieth Century* (New Delhi: Oxford University Press).

Smith, Adam (1776), *An Inquiry into the Nature and Causes of The Wealth of Nations*, republished in Campbell, R.H., and Skinner, A.S. (eds.) (1976), *Adam Smith: An Inquiry into the Nature and Causes of The Wealth of Nations* (Oxford: Clarendon).

—— (1790), *The Theory of Moral Sentiments*, revised edition (republished, Oxford: Clarendon Press, 1975).

Smith, Chris (1994), *India's Ad Hoc Arsenal: Direction or Drift in Defence Policy?* (Oxford: Oxford University Press for SIPRI).

Smith, Dan (1997), *The State of War and Peace Atlas* (London: Penguin Reference).

Solow, Robert M. (1956), 'A Contribution to the Theory of Economic Growth', *Quarterly Journal of Economics*, 70.

——— (1957), 'Technical Change and Aggregate Production Function', *Review of Economics and Statistics*, 39.

——— (1992), *An Almost Practical Step toward Sustainability* (Washington, DC: Resources for the Future).

Somanathan, E. (1991), 'Deforestation, Property Rights and Incentives in Central Himalaya', *Economic and Political Weekly*, 26 January.

Sondhi, M.L. (ed.) (2000), *Nuclear Weapons and India's National Security* (New Delhi: Har-Anand).

Sopher, David (1980a), 'The Geographical Patterning of Culture in India', in Sopher (1980b).

——— (ed.) (1980b), *An Exploration of India: Geographical Perspectives on Society and Culture* (Ithaca, NY: Cornell University Press).

Sorensen, Theodore C. (1965), *Kennedy* (London: Hodder and Stoughton).

Soros, George (2000), *Open Society: Reforming Global Capitalism* (New York: Public Affairs).

Srinivas, M.N. (1962), *Caste in Modern India and Other Essays* (Mumbai: Allied).

——— (1965), *Religion and Society among the Coorgs of South India* (Mumbai: Asia Publishing House).

——— (1967), 'The Cohesive Role of Sanskritization', in Mason, P. (ed.) (1967), *India and Ceylon: Unity and Diversity* (London: Oxford University Press).

——— (1989), *The Cohesive Role of Sanskritization and Other Essays* (New Delhi: Oxford University Press).

——— (1992), *On Living in a Revolution and Other Essays* (New Delhi: Oxford University Press).

Srinivasan, K. (1995), 'Lessons from Goa, Kerala and Tamil Nadu: The Three Successful Fertility Transition States in India', *Demography India*, 24.

Srinivasan, T.N. (ed.) (1994), *Agriculture and Foreign Trade in China and India since 1950* (San Francisco: International Center for Economic Growth).

——— (2000), *Eight Lectures on India's Economic Reforms* (New Delhi: Oxford University Press).

Srinivasan, T.N., and Bardhan, Pranab (eds.) (1974), *Poverty and Income Distribution in India* (Calcutta: Statistical Publishing Society).

Srinivasan, T.N., and Bardhan, Pranab (eds.) (1988), *Rural Poverty in South Asia* (New York: Columbia University Press).

Srivastava, Ranjana (2000), 'Evaluation of Community-based Primary Schooling Initiatives in Madhya Pradesh: Education Guarantee Scheme and Alternative School', in Government of Madhya Pradesh (2000).

Srivastava, Ravi (1997), 'Access to Basic Education in Uttar Pradesh: Results from Field Survey', mimeo, Project on Strategies and Financing for Human Development, UNDP, New Delhi; to be published in Vaidyanathan and Nair (forthcoming).

—— (2001a), 'Inequality and Education Security', in Mahendra Dev et al. (2001).

—— (2001b), 'Access to Basic Education in Rural Uttar Pradesh', in Vaidyanathan and Nair (2001).

State Statistical Bureau of the People's Republic of China (1985), *1981 Population Census of China*, Chinese edition (Beijing: Population Census Office).

—— (1992), *China Population Statistics Yearbook 1992* (Beijing: Population Census Office).

—— (1993a), *Tabulation of the 1990 Census of the People's Republic of China*, vol. II, Chinese edition (Beijing: China Statistical Information and Consultancy Service Center).

—— (1993b), *China Statistical Yearbook 1993* (Beijing: China Statistical Information and Consultancy Service Center).

—— (1999), *China Population Statistics Yearbook 1999* (Beijing: Population Census Office).

Stevenson, H., and Stigler, J. (1992), *The Learning Gap* (New York: Summit).

Stewart, Frances (1985), *Basic Needs in Developing Countries* (Baltimore: Johns Hopkins).

Stiglitz, Joseph (1996), 'Some Lessons from the East Asian Miracle', *World Bank Research Observer*, 11.

—— (1998), 'The East Asian Crisis and its Implications for India', mimeo, World Bank, Washington, DC.

Stockholm International Peace Research Institute (1999), *SIPRI Yearbook 1999* (Oxford: Oxford University Press).

—— (2000), *SIPRI Yearbook 2000* (Oxford: Oxford University Press).

—— (2001), *SIPRI Yearbook 2001* (Oxford: Oxford University Press).

Stokey, Nancy L. (1988), 'Learning by Doing and the Introduction of New Goods', *Journal of Political Economy*, 96.

Stokey, Nancy L. (1991), 'Human Capital, Product Quality and Growth', *Quarterly Journal of Economics*, 106.

Stree Shakti Sanghatana (1989), *'We Were Making History': Women and the Telangana Uprising* (London: Zed Books).

Streeten, Paul, Burki, S.J., Mahbub ul Haq, Hick, N., and Stewart, F. (1981), *First Things First: Meeting Basic Needs in Developing Countries* (New York: Oxford University Press).

Subbarao, B.K. (1998), 'India's Nuclear Prowess: False Claims and Tragic Truths', *Manushi*, 109.

Subbarao, K., and Raney, L. (1995), 'Social Gains from Female Education: A Cross-National Study', *Economic Development and Cultural Change*, 44.

Subrahmanyam, K. (2001), 'Nuclear Doctrine for India', in Sharma, Rajeev (ed.) (2001), *The Pakistan Trap* (New Delhi: UBS Publishers).

Subramaniam, V. (1975), *Parched Earth: The Maharashtra Drought 1970–73* (Mumbai: Orient Longmans).

Subramanian, Narendra (1999), *Ethnicity and Populist Mobilization: Political Parties, Citizens and Democracy in South India* (New Delhi: Oxford University Press).

Sudha, S., and Rajan, S.I. (1999), 'Female Demographic Disadvantage in India 1981–1991: Sex-selective Abortions and Female Infanticide', *Development and Change*, 30.

Summers, Lawrence H. (1992), 'Investing in All the People: Educating Women in Developing Countries', Working Paper, World Bank, Washington, DC.

Sundaram, K. (2001a), 'Employment-Unemployment Situation in Nineties: Some Results from NSS 55th Round Survey', *Economic and Political Weekly*, 17 March.

—— (2001b), 'Employment and Poverty in India in the Nineteen Nineties: Further Results from NSS 55th Round Employment-Unemployment Survey, 1999-2000', Working Paper 95, Centre for Development Economics at the Delhi School of Economics.

Sundaram, K., and Tendulkar, S. (1994), 'On Measuring Shelter Deprivation in India', Working Paper 23, Centre for Development Economics at the Delhi School of Economics.

Sundaram, K., and Tendulkar, S. (2000), 'Poverty in India: An Assessment and Analysis', mimeo, Delhi School of Economics.

Sundararaman, Sudha (1996), 'Literacy Campaigns: Lessons for Women's Movement', *Economic and Political Weekly*, 18 May.

Sundari Ravindran, T.K. (1993), 'Women and the Politics of Development in India', *Reproductive Health Matters*, 1.

—— (1999), 'Rural Women's Experiences with Family Welfare Services in Tamil Nadu', in Koenig and Khan (1999).

Suryanarayana, M.H. (2000), 'How Real Is the Secular Decline in Rural Poverty?', *Economic and Political Weekly*, 17 June.

Svedberg, Peter (2000), *Poverty and Undernutrition: Theory, Measurement, and Policy* (Oxford: Oxford University Press).

Swaminathan, Madhura (1990), 'Village Level Implementation of IRDP: Comparison of West Bengal and Tamil Nadu', *Economic and Political Weekly*, 31 March.

—— (2000), *Weakening Welfare: The Public Distribution of Food in India* (New Delhi: LeftWord Books).

Swaminathan, Mina (1991), 'Child Care Services in Tamil Nadu', *Economic and Political Weekly*, 28 December.

Swamy, Arun (1996), 'The Nation, the People and the Poor: Sandwich Tactics in Party Competition and Policy Formation, India 1933–1996', PhD thesis, University of California, Berkeley.

—— (1998), 'Parties, Political Identities and the Absence of Mass Political Violence in South India', in Basu, A., and Kohli, A. (eds.) (1998), *Community Conflicts and the State in India* (New Delhi: Oxford University Press).

Swamy, G.V. (1991), 'Common Property Resources and Tribal Economy', paper presented at the Ninth Annual Conference of the Andhra Pradesh Economic Association, Vijaywada; published in the proceedings of the conference.

Swamy, Subramanian (2000), *India's Economic Performance and Reforms: A Perspective for the New Millenium* (New Delhi: Konark).

Tagore, Rabindranath (1991 [1917]), *Nationalism*, new edition with an introduction by E.P. Thompson (London: Macmillan).

Talib, Mohammad (1999), 'Social Class in the Classroom', mimeo, reprinted in abridged form in Probe Team (1999).

Tarozzi, Alessandro (2000), 'India's Public Distribution System and its Efficacy as a Poverty Alleviation Program', PhD thesis (in progress), Princeton University.

Tata Energy Research Institute (1996), *State of India's Environment (A Quantitative Analysis)*, Project Report No. 95EE52 (New Delhi: TERI).

____ (1998a), *Looking Back to Thinking Ahead* (New Delhi: TERI).

____ (1998b), *India's Environment Pollution and Protection*, Project Report No. 97ED57 (New Delhi: TERI).

Teger, Allan I. (1980), *Too Much Invested to Quit* (Oxford: Pergamon).

Tendulkar, S.D., Sundaram, K., and Jain, L.R. (1993), 'Poverty in India, 1970–71 to 1988–89', Working Paper, ILO-ARTEP, New Delhi.

Tharamangalam, Joseph (1998), 'The Perils of Social Development without Economic Growth: The Development Debacle of Kerala, India', *Bulletin of Concerned Asian Scholars*, 30.

Tharu, S., and Lalita., K. (eds.) (1991), *Women Writing in India*, 2 volumes (New Delhi: Oxford University Press).

The Hindu (1999), *Survey of the Environment '99* (Chennai: The Hindu).

____ (2000), *Survey of the Environment 2000* (Chennai: The Hindu).

____ (2001), 'Media Goes Overboard over Afghan Coverage', *The Hindu*, 24 October.

Thirlwall, A.P. (1994), *Growth and Development*, fifth edition (London: Macmillan).

Thomas, D., Strauss, J., and Henriques, M.H. (1991), 'How Does Mother's Education Affect Child Height?', *Journal of Human Resources*, 26.

Thomas, Raju G.C. (1997), 'Arms Procurement in India: Military Self-reliance versus Technological Self-sufficiency', in Arnett, E. (ed.) (1997), *Military Capacity and the Risk of War: China, India, Pakistan and Iran* (Oxford: Oxford University Press).

Thomas, R.G.C., and Gupta, A. (eds.) (2000), *India's Nuclear Security* (Boulder, CO: Lynne Reiner).

Tilak, J.B.G. (1995), 'Costs and Financing of Education in India: A Review of Issues, Problems and Prospects', Discussion Paper 5, Studies on Human Development in India, United Nations Development Programme, New Delhi..

____ (1996), 'How Free is Free Primary Education in India?', *Economic and Political Weekly*, 3 February.

____ (2000a), 'Household Expenditure on Education in India: A Preliminary Examination of the 52nd Round of the National Sample Survey', mimeo, National Institute of Educational Planning and Administration, New Delhi.

____ (2000b), 'Determinants of Household Expenditure on Education in Rural India: A Study Based on the NCAER Survey on Human Development in India', mimeo, National Institute of Educational Planning and Administration, New Delhi.

Tilak, J.B.G., and Sudarshan, R.M. (2000), 'Private Schooling in Rural India', mimeo, Programme of Research in Human Development, National Council of Applied Economic Research, New Delhi.

Tinker, Irene (ed.) (1990), *Persistent Inequalities* (New York: Oxford University Press).

Tod, James (1929), *Annals and Antiquities of Rajasthan*, 2 volumes, reprinted 1972 (London: Routledge and Kegan Paul).

Tomkins, Andrew, and Watson, Fiona (1989), *Malnutrition and Infection: A Review* (London: London School of Hygiene and Tropical Medicine).

Toye, John (1993), *Dilemmas of Development*, second edition (Oxford: Blackwell).

Tuchman, Barbara (1966), *The Proud Tower: A Portrait of the World Before the War 1890–1914* (London: Macmillan).

Tulasidhar, V.B., and Sarma, J.V.M. (1993), 'Public Expenditure, Medical Care at Birth and Infant Mortality: A Comparative Study of States in India', in Berman, P., and Khan, M.E. (eds.) (1993), *Paying for India's Health Care* (New Delhi: Sage).

Tyagi, P.N. (1993), *Education for All: A Graphic Presentation*, second edition (New Delhi: National Institute of Educational Planning and Administration).

Uberoi, Patricia (ed.) (1994), *Family, Kinship and Marriage in India* (New Delhi: Oxford University Press).

Unnathan, T.K.N., and Ahuja, R. (1988), 'Sub-culture of Violence: The Indian Context', in Rao, S. Venugopal (ed.) (1988), *Perspectives in Criminology* (Delhi: Vikas).

UNICEF (1993), 'Central and Eastern Europe in Transition: Public Policy and Social Conditions', Regional Monitoring Report No. 1, UNICEF, New York.

—— (1994), *The State of the World's Children 1994* (New York: UNICEF).

—— (1996), *The Progress of Nations* (New York: UNICEF).

United Nations Development Programme (1990), *Human Development Report 1990* (New York: Oxford University Press).

—— (1999), *The China Human Development Report* (New York: Oxford University Press).

—— (2001), *Human Development Report 2001* (New York: Oxford University Press).

—— (forthcoming), *Human Development Report: Himachal Pradesh* (New Delhi: UNDP).

United Nations Population Division (1997), *The Age and Sex Distribution of the World Populations: The 1996 Revision* (New York: UN Population Division).

—— (1999), *World Population Prospects: The 1998 Revision. Vol II: The Sex and Age Distribution of the World Population* (New York: UNPD).

—— (forthcoming), *World Population Prospects: The 2000 Revision* (New York: UNDP).

Vaidyanathan, A. (1997), 'Studies on Health and Health Care: A Review of Findings', mimeo, Madras Institute of Development Studies, Chennai.

Vaidyanathan, A., and Nair, P.R. Gopinathan (eds.) (forthcoming), *Elementary Education in Rural India* (New Delhi: Sage).

van Creveld, Martin (1991), *The Transformation of War* (New York: Free Press).

van Ginneken, Wouter (ed.) (1998), *Social Security for All Indians* (New Delhi: Oxford University Press).

van Hollen, C. (1998), 'Moving Targets: Routine IUD Insertion in Maternity Wards in Tamil Nadu, India', *Reproductive Health Matters*, 6.

Varadarajan, Siddharth (1999), 'Truth About Torture: Saga of the Lonely Indian Prisoner', *Times of India*, 26 June.

Varshney, Ashutosh (1998), 'Why Democracy Survives', *Journal of Democracy*, 9.

—— (2000), 'Is India Becoming More Democratic?', *Journal of Asian Studies*, 59.

Vasavi, A.R. (2000), 'Exclusion, Elimination and Opportunity: Primary Schools and Schooling in Selected Regions of India', draft report, National Institute of Advanced Studies, Bangalore.

Venkatachalam, R., and Srinivasan, V. (1993), *Female Infanticide* (New Delhi: Har-Anand).

Verma, Jyoti (1989), 'Women Education: A Media of Social Change', *Social Change*, 19.

Verma, R.K., and Roy, T.K. (1999), 'Assessing the Quality of Family Planning Service Providers in Four Indian States', in Koenig and Khan (1999).

Verma, V.S. (1988), *A Handbook of Population Statistics* (New Delhi: Office of the Registrar General).

Vijaychandran, V. (2001), 'Health Empowerment of the People: The Kerala Experience', in Misra et al. (2001).

Visaria, Leela (2000a), 'Innovations in Tamil Nadu', *Seminar*, No. 489.

—— (2000b), 'From Contraceptive Targets to Reproductive Health: Evolution of India's Policies and Programmes', mimeo, New Delhi.

Visaria, Leela, and Visaria, Pravin (1998), *Reproductive Health in Policy and Practice* (Washington, DC: Population Reference Bureau).

Visaria, Leela, and Visaria, Pravin (1999), 'Rajasthan and Tamil Nadu', in Health Watch Trust (1999).

Visaria, Pravin (1967), 'The Sex Ratio of the Population of India and Pakistan and Regional Variations during 1901–1961', in Bose, Ashish (ed.) (1967), *Pattern of Population Change in India 1951–1961* (Mumbai: Allied Publishers).

—— (1971), *The Sex Ratio of the Population of India*, Monograph 10, Census of India 1961, Office of the Registrar General, New Delhi.

—— (2000), 'Alternative Estimates of Poverty in India', *Economic Times*, 27 June.

Visaria, P., Gumber, A., and Visaria, L. (1993), 'Literacy and Primary Education in India, 1980–81 to 1991', *Journal of Educational Planning and Administration*, 7.

Visaria, Pravin, and Visaria, Leela (1994), 'Demographic Transition: Accelerating Fertility Decline in 1980s', *Economic and Political Weekly*, 17–24 December.

Vlassoff, Carol (1980), 'Unmarried Adolescent Females in Rural India: A Study of the Social Impact of Education', *Journal of Marriage and the Family*, 42.

—— (1996), 'Against the Odds: The Changing Impact of Schooling on Female Autonomy and Fertility in an Indian Village', in Jeffery and Basu (1996).

Voluntary Health Association of India (1997), *Report of the Independent Commission on Health in India* (New Delhi: VHAI).

Vyas, V.S., and Bhargava, P. (1995), 'Public Intervention for Poverty Alleviation: An Overview', *Economic and Political Weekly*, 14–21 October.

Vyasulu, Poornima, and Vyasulu, Vinod (1999), 'Women in Panchayati Raj: Grass Roots Democracy in Malgudi', *Economic and Political Weeekly*, 25 December.

Vyasulu, Vinod (1995), 'Management of Poverty Alleviation Programmes in Karnataka: An Overview', *Economic and Political Weekly*, 14–21 October.

―― (1998), 'In the Wonderland of Primary Education', report submitted to the Rajiv Gandhi Prathmik Siksha Mission, Bhopal; reprinted in Government of Madhya Pradesh (2000).

Wade, Robert (1988), *Village Republics: Economic Conditions for Collective Action in South India* (Cambridge: Cambridge University Press).

―― (1990), *Governing the Market: Economic Theory and the Role of the Government in East Asian Industrialization* (Princeton: Princeton University Press).

―― (1999), 'Gestalt Shift: From 'Miracle' to 'Cronyism' in the Asian Crisis', *IDS Bulletin*, 30.

Wadley, S., and Derr, B. (1989), 'Karimpur 1925-1984: Understanding Rural India Through Restudies', in Bardhan, P.K. (ed.) (1989), *Conversations between Economists and Anthropologists* (New Delhi: Oxford University Press).

Ware, H. (1984), 'Effects of Maternal Education, Women's Roles, and Child Care on Child Mortality', in Mosley, W.H. and Chen, L.C. (eds.) (1984), *Child Survival: Strategies for Research* (New York: Population Council).

Warth, Robert D. (1997), *Nicholas II* (London: Praeger).

Weaver, Mary Anne (2000), 'Gandhi's Daughters', *The New Yorker*, February.

Weiner, Myron (1989), *The Indian Paradox: Essays in Indian Politics*, edited by Ashutosh Varshney (New Delhi: Sage).

Weiner, Myron (1991), *The Child and the State in India: Child Labor and Education Policy in Comparative Perspective* (Princeton: Princeton University Press).

Weitzmann, Martin L., and Chenggang Xu (1993), 'Chinese Township Village Enterprises as Vaguely Defined Cooperatives', Discussion Paper 26, Research Programme on the Chinese Economy, STICERD, London School of Economics.

Westphal, L.E., Kim, L., and Dahlman, C. (1985), 'Reflections on Korea's Acquisition of Technological Capability', in Rosenberg, N. et al. (eds.) (1985), *International Technology Transfer: Concepts, Measures and Comparisons* (New York: Praeger).

Westphal, Larry E., Rhee, Yung Whee, and Pursell, Garry (1988), *Korean Industrial Competence: Where It Came From* (Washington, DC: World Bank)

White, Gordon (ed.) (1988), *Developmental States in East Asia* (New York: St Martin's Press).

White, Sydney (1998), 'From "Barefoot Doctor" to "Village Doctor" in Tiger Springs Village: A Case Study of Rural Health Care Transformation in Socialist China', *Human Organization*, 57.

Witter, Sophie (1996), ' "Doi-Moi" and Health: The Effect of Economic Reforms on the Health System in Vietnam', *International Journal of Health Planning and Management*, 11.

Wong, L. (1994), 'Privatization of Social Welfare in Post-Mao China', *Asian Survey*, 34.

Wood, Adrian (1991), 'China's Economic System: A Brief Description, with Some Suggestions for Further Reform', Discussion Paper 29, Research Programme on the Chinese Economy, STICERD, London School of Economics.

Wood, A., and Calandrino, M. (2000), 'When Other Giant Awakens: Trade and Human Resources in India', *Economic and Political Weekly*, 30 December.

World Bank (1983), *China: Socialist Economic Development* (Washington, DC: World Bank).

____ (1989), *India: Poverty, Employment, and Social Services* (Washington, DC: World Bank).

____ (1992), *China: Strategies for Reducing Poverty in the 1990s* (Washington, DC: World Bank).

____ (1993a), *The World Food Outlook* (Washington, DC: World Bank).

____ (1993b), *World Development Report 1993* (New York: Oxford University Press).

____ (1993c), *The East Asian Miracle* (New York: Oxford University Press).

____ (1994a), 'India: Policy and Finance Strategies for Strengthening Primary Health Care Services', mimeo, World Bank, Washington, DC.

____ (1994b), *World Development Report 1994* (New York: Oxford University Press).

____ (1997a), *India: Achievements and Challenges in Reducing Poverty* (Washington, DC: World Bank).

____ (1997b), *Development in Practice: Primary Education in India* (New Delhi: Allied Publishing).

____ (1997c), *Financing Health Care: Issues and Options for China* (Washington, DC: World Bank).

____ (1997d), *India: Five Years of Stabilization and Reform and the Challenges Ahead* (Washington, DC: World Bank).

____ (1999), *A Fine Balance: Some Options for Private and Public Health Care in Urban India* (World Bank: Washington, DC).

____ (2000a), *World Development Indicators 2000* (Washington, DC: World Bank).

____ (2000b), *India: Reducing Poverty, Accelerating Development* (New Delhi: Oxford University Press).

____ (2000c), *World Development Report 2000/2001* (New York: Oxford University Press).

____ (2001a), 'India's Future Health Systems: Issues and Options', draft report, World Bank, New Delhi.

____ (2001b), *World Development Indicators 2001* (Washington, DC: World Bank).

World Commission on Environment and Development (1987), *Our Common Future* (New York: Oxford University Press).

World Health Organisation (2000), *World Health Report 2000* (Geneva: WHO).

Wu, Harry X. (2000), 'China's GDP Level and Growth Performance: Alternative Estimates and the Implications', *Review of Income and Wealth*, 46.

Yadav, Y., and Singh, V.B. (1997), 'The Maturing of a Democracy', *India Today*, 31 August.

Yang, Dali L., and Su, Fubing (1998), 'The Politics of Famine and Reform in Rural China', *China Economic Review*, 9.

Yao Shujie (1999), 'Economic Growth, Income Inequality and Poverty in China under Economic Reforms', *Journal of Development Studies*, 35.

Young, Alwyn (1992), 'A Tale of Two Cities: Factor Accumulation and Technical Change in Hong Kong and Singapore', NBER *Macroeconomics Annual 1992*.

Yu Dezhi (1992), 'Changes in Health Care Financing and Health Status: The Case of China in the 1980s', Innocenti Occasional Papers, Economic Policy Series, No. 34, International Child Development Centre, Florence.

Zachariah, K. C. (1997), 'Demographic Transition: A Response to Official Policies and Programmes', in Zachariah and Rajan (1997).

Zachariah, K.C., and Rajan, S.I. (eds.) (1997), *Kerala's Demographic Transition: Determinants and Consequences* (New Delhi: Sage).

Zachariah, K.C., Rajan, S.I., Sarma, P.S., Navaneetham, K., Nair, P.S.G., and Misra, U.S. (1994), *Demographic Transition in Kerala in the 1980s* (Thiruvananthapuram: Centre for Development Studies).

Zeng Yi, Tu Ping, Gu Baochang, Xu Yi, Li Bohua, and Li Yongping (1993), 'Causes and Implications of the Recent Increase in the Reported Sex Ratio at Birth in China', *Population and Development Review*, 19.

Zhang, J. (1998), 'The Imbalance of Sex Ratio at Birth, and Its Causes and Countermeasures in China', *China Population Research Newsletter*, June.

Zweifel, P., and Breyer, F. (1997), *Health Economics* (Oxford: Oxford University Press).

Subject Index

accountability 39, 58, 108, 132–4, 142, 304–5, 349, 352, 358–71, 373–5
  and countervailing power 368–71
  and public vigilance 92, 108, 175–6, 183, 213, 352, 363–71
  in the public sector 31, 213, 368–71
  in the schooling system 31, 108, 158, 171, 172–6, 181, 183, 187, 359, 368–71
  see also corruption, democracy, public vigilance, voice
Afghanistan 65, 277, 377
Africa 4, 11, 46, 64n, 190, 196, 203, 253, 341
  north 79, 136, 204, 230
  sub-Saharan 51, 65, 66, 67, 68, 69, 86, 149, 160, 196, 204, 229, 230, 246
agricultural growth 95, 122, 307, 316–8, 320, 330, 332, 408
agricultural labourers 30, 55, 94, 107, 145, 338, 404
agricultural wages, growth of 328–9, 331–2, 404, 409
AIDS 39, 43, 66, 215, 277, 373, 399
America, north 27n, 43, 229, 348
  see also United States

anaemia 67–70, 336
Andaman and Nicobar Islands 160
Andhra Pradesh 20, 84, 96, 106, 111, 169, 182n, 186, 194, 210, 231, 235, 249n, 256, 261, 319, 373, 394, 395, 396, 397, 398, 399, 400, 401, 402, 403, 404
Angola 277
anti-arrack campaign in Andhra Pradesh 20, 378
Argentina 65
armed conflicts, see war
Armenia 86
arms races see military expansion
arms trade 287–8, 291, 344
  dominated by members of the Security Council 288
Arunachal Pradesh 26, 405, 406
Assam 84, 88, 169, 234, 261, 319n, 394, 395, 396, 397, 398, 399, 400, 401, 402, 403, 404
authoritarianism vii-viii, 9, 39, 44–45, 132–40, 142, 291, 299, 303–5, 343, 348, 373–5, 377–8
  attractions of 142, 343, 377
  and famines 4, 24, 132–4, 142, 264, 378
  and population policy 134–40, 142, 210–12, 214, 254–7, 259

in China 14–15, 44, 120, 132–42, 253–7, 377
see also democracy, freedom

Bangalore 56, 77, 224n
Bangladesh 12, 46, 67, 230, 246, 263n, 277, 313, 391, 392
Belgium 348
Bhutan 69n
Bihar 15, 19, 84, 86, 87, 88, 95, 96, 98n, 102, 103, 111, 139, 145n, 149, 151, 152, 154n, 160, 166, 167n, 169, 178n, 183, 209n, 215n, 216n, 234, 235, 236, 249n, 256, 261, 271, 307, 319, 320, 329, 337n, 350n, 354, 361, 373, 388, 394, 395, 396, 397, 398, 399, 400, 401, 402, 403, 404
birthweights, low 68–70, 115–6, 336
see also hunger and undernourishment
Botswana 66
Brazil 72, 73, 268, 309, 310, 323
Britain 44, 51n, 64, 194, 204, 275, 280, 281, 341n
bureaucracy 37, 40–1, 52–6, 175–6, 203, 306–8, 310–2, 362, 369
and arbitrary power 55, 312
see also regulation
Burma 267n
Burundi 202

Cambodia 44, 45, 65, 202, 277
Canada 97, 348
capabilities xiii–xv, 3–4, 6–8, 34–41, 86, 90, 314–5, 345–6, 359
instrumental and intrinsic importance of 34–41, 52–3, 81–3
and economic growth 34–8, 306–15
and poverty 34–8, 86, 123–4, 323
see also freedom, social opportunities
caste 10–11, 28, 30, 55, 62, 69, 100, 107, 109, 111, 143–50, 202, 217, 272, 314, 349, 351, 352–63

and education 85, 100, 143–50, 155, 179–81, 217
and gender 241–5
see also inequality
Chattisgarh ix-x, 15, 259, 338, 383, 407
see also Madhya Pradesh
child labour 16, 39, 72, 155–9, 177, 182, 184–5, 354
see also school attendance
child mortality 11, 64–70, 83–9, 124–8, 136–9, 213–5, 254, 271–3, 313, 327–32
gender bias in 68–70, 84–6, 105–6, 136–7, 157, 229–252, 257–62, 272–3
and education 18–19, 87–89, 91, 102, 137–9, 183–4, 198–200, 245–54, 271–3
and women's agency 18–19, 87–9, 91, 137–40, 213–5, 245–54, 257–62, 271–3
see also mortality
China xiv, 112–42, 341, 384–6, 390–3
complementarity between pre-reform achievements and post-reform performance of xiv, 14–15, 76–79, 112–4, 130–1, 140–2
economic growth in 47, 70–1, 115, 120–3, 309–10, 316, 318, 385–6, 390
economic reforms in 13–15, 44, 53, 55, 70–1, 112–4, 122–30, 140–2, 309–10, 312–3, 334
famine in 14, 127, 131–4, 142
food and nutrition in 115–6, 121, 123, 132–4
gender issues in 14, 117, 134–40, 141, 230–1, 246, 257–9, 262, 272
health care in 14, 43–4, 79, 113, 121–2, 128–30, 141–2, 203, 334
land ownership in 14, 79–80, 113, 141
lessons from xiv, 70–1, 112–4, 140–2, 309–10, 312–3

literacy and education in xiv, 12–15,
43–4, 76–8, 113–20, 122, 130–
1, 149, 151, 160–1
mortality and fertility in 44, 114–6,
121–2, 124–8, 141–2, 191, 194
perceptions of 112–14, 281, 283,
301
political system of 14–15, 44, 120,
132–40, 142, 377
population policy in 14, 128, 134–
40, 254–6
post-reform performance of 44, 47,
71, 77–8, 115, 122–30, 140–2,
312–3
poverty in 114–5, 122–4
pre-reform achievements of xiv, 14,
76, 79, 116–22
public services in 44, 114–31
and India xiv, 12–15, 70–1, 76–8,
101, 112–42, 283, 309–10,
312–3, 316
Cochin 94n, 99, 100, 160
Colombia 266, 269
Congo 66, 277, 377
class 3, 11, 22, 28–32, 94–97, 145,
172, 201–2, 217, 225, 268,
310, 314, 335–6, 343, 352–8,
375–6
see also inequality
class structure 28–32
Cold War 276, 283–6
common property resources 60–1,
107–8
communalism vii, 96, 262, 302–3, 345,
377
comparative international perspectives*
xiv, 11–5, 27, 64–83, 189–91,
266, 340–5, 347–50, 390–3
Bangladesh and India 12–13, 67,
289, 313, 390–3
China and India xiv, 12–15, 70–1,
76–8, 101, 112–42, 283, 309–
10, 312–3, 316, 390–3
east Asia and India xiv, 13–14, 70–

81, 130–1, 149, 161, 309–10,
316, 318, 390–3
India and sub-Saharan Africa 11,
65–70, 149, 160, 196, 229–31,
246
India and the United States 348–9
India and the world 11–15, 64–73,
79, 149, 160–1, 189–96, 201–
4, 246, 229–31, 275–8, 340–5,
390–3
Kerala and China 15, 115–20, 124–
8, 137–40, 142
on democracy 4, 43–5, 132–42,
277, 342–3, 347–50, 377–8
on economic growth 47, 49, 70–3,
82–3, 120–3, 130–1, 307, 309–
10, 316–8
on economic reform xiv, 53, 55, 70–
81, 112–42, 309–10, 333–4
on gender inequality 68–70, 134–
40, 229–31, 257–9, 272–3
on health and health care 43–4, 64,
70, 79, 82–3, 128–30, 141–2,
201–4, 229–31
on hunger and undernourishment
67–70, 115–6, 196
on literacy and education xiv, 12, 15,
43–44, 64–70, 75–81, 114–20,
122, 130–1, 149, 160–1
on mortality and fertility 11, 64–
70, 114–6, 124–8, 134–42,
190–1, 229–31, 250–1, 253–7
on poverty 114–5, 122–4, 342,
344
on public expenditure 43–44, 203–
4
on social policy xiv, 12, 43–4, 70–
81, 82–3, 112–42, 201–4, 309–
10, 333–4
on the social costs of militarism
275–8, 279–80, 294–99, 344
see also regional comparisons
compulsory schooling 41, 144, 154–5,
164–5, 375

* See also Statistical Appendix.

and the right to education 184–6,
375
cooperative action xiv, 17, 33, 56–63,
107–110, 227–8, 344–5, 347–
79
and competition 58–9
and development 56–8, 107–10
and economic reform 62–3
and environmental protection 56–
7, 60–1, 63, 227–8
and social context 56–61, 107–110,
179–84, 217, 227, 360
and state intervention 56–61, 109,
176, 179–84, 368
and the market mechanism 56–61
and the schooling system 59–60,
108
in Himachal Pradesh 59, 105, 107–
10, 179–84
Coorg 160
corporate power 28, 203, 225, 340,
343, 377
corruption 53, 62–3, 111, 174–5, 206,
272, 291, 302, 351–3, 360,
363–8, 371
what is wrong with it 206, 363–6
and democracy 352, 363–6
see also accountability, democracy
Costa Rica 12, 65, 71, 97
credit facilities 10, 22, 109, 199, 225,
323, 336
criminal violence 29–30, 72, 103, 111,
266–71, 317, 351, 354
poverty versus patriarchy 266–71
and gender inequality 269–71
see also violence, war
criminalization of politics 62, 314,
350–1, 365–6
Cuba 12, 43, 65, 203, 285
Cuban missile crisis 285

dams 223, 225, 302, 344, 358
decentralization 111, 175–6, 349–50,
358–63
see also local democracy
defence, see security

defence expenditure, see military expenditure
deforestation 25, 197, 218, 220
Delhi 55n, 105n, 221, 222, 223, 224n,
226, 259, 312n
democracy vii-viii, xv, 1–11, 14–15, 20,
23–33, 42–6, 57–8, 91–4, 132–
40, 142, 280–2, 298–305, 340,
342–5, 347–79
ideals, institutions and practice 347–
53
constructive importance of 10–11,
24–8, 32–3, 220, 226–8, 347–
79
instrumental role of viii, 25–8, 32–
3, 42–5, 91–4, 132–40, 142,
186–8, 212–3, 217–8, 226–8
intrinsic value of 24–5, 32–3, 57–8,
359
local 19–21, 60–61, 94–7, 105,
107–111, 179–81, 308, 347,
358–68
and economic development 4, 24,
377
and elections 24, 45, 93, 217–8,
255, 299–300, 347–8, 365–6,
378
and famine prevention 4, 24, 132–
4, 142, 378
and militarism viii, 26–28, 277–8,
280–3, 284, 286, 289, 291,
296, 298–305, 372–5
and minority interests 28–32, 378–
9
in Indian history 348, 360
in international perspective 4, 43–
45, 132–42, 277, 342–3, 347–
50, 377–8
see also democratic practice, local
democracy, participation
democratic ideals 347, 353
democratic institutions viii, 1–8, 20,
23–5, 28, 44–5, 94, 133–4,
226–8, 299–305, 347–53, 358–
71, 375–9
see also institutions

democratic practice viii, xv, 23–5, 43, 91–4, 186–8, 217–8, 226–8, 263–4, 283, 286, 299, 304–5, 334–5, 336, 339–40, 344–5, 347–79
  foundations of 39, 352–3
  and social inequality 8–11, 24, 28–32, 91–4, 217–8, 271–4, 347, 350–63, 368–71, 375–9
  see also democracy, empowerment, inequality, local democracy, political action, rights
democratic rights 3–4, 24–5, 44–5, 132–4, 142, 210–1, 254–7, 277, 291, 299–305, 340, 343, 347–79
  see also rights
demographic transition 84–9, 101–2, 110–1, 134–40, 189–96, 198–200, 254–7
  and gender equity 17–20, 107, 137–40, 198–200, 245–57, 271–4
  in Himachal Pradesh 20, 101–102, 107, 183–4, 199
  in Tamil Nadu 17, 19, 84–9, 109, 111, 138–40, 199, 213–8, 256
  in China, see China
  see also fertility, health, mortality, population
Denmark 65, 98n
deregulation 40, 53–4, 61–3, 311–2, 314, 345–6
  see also liberalization, regulation
development economics, priorities in vii–viii, 34–8, 42
dignity and self-respect 95–6, 359, 372
discouragement effect 154–9
displacement, see involuntary displacement
drought and drought relief 291, 302, 335–40, 367–8
  see also famine

east Asia xiv, 13–4, 70–81, 113, 130–1, 190, 309–10, 364, 390–3
  democracy in 4, 377
  economic crisis in 4, 80–1, 122, 310, 323, 364
  economic success of xiv, 13–14, 47, 70–81, 309–10, 316, 318
  education in 13–14, 70–81, 130, 149, 161, 309–10, 323
  gender inequality in 78–79, 257–9, 272
  participatory growth in xiv, 13–14, 70–81, 309–10, 323
  role of the state in xiv, 13–14, 47, 70–81, 130–1, 204, 309–10, 323
East Timor 45n
economic growth vi, 3, 34–38, 48–9, 70–81, 99, 280, 282, 306–33, 334, 385–6, 390, 393, 394
  sector-specific 77–8, 307, 309, 315–22, 328, 330, 332
  and human capital 75–9, 81–3, 179, 306–15, 320–22
  and participation, see participatory growth
  and population growth 134–6, 197–8
  and poverty 34–36, 38, 87, 105, 122–8, 307–10, 315–33, 355
  and social opportunities vi, 12–14, 16, 34–38, 70–3, 78, 81–3, 105, 179, 306–33
  in the nineties vi, 78, 306–10, 315–33
  in Indian states 13, 16, 17, 72–3, 95–6, 98–9, 105, 108–9, 179, 307, 318–22, 386, 393, 394
  in China, see China
  see also growth-mediated progress, participatory growth
economic reform vi–vii, xiv–xv, 14, 20–23, 52–53, 61–63, 130–1, 140–2, 306–33, 345–6, 370, 377
  lopsidedness of 37–38, 61–3, 306–15, 332–6, 370, 377
  need for 20–23, 37–8, 306–8, 310–13, 345–6
  need to go beyond vi, 20–23, 37–8, 61–63, 130–1, 306–36, 345–6

and cooperative action 62–3
and participatory growth 20–3, 37–8, 306–15
and poverty 315–33
and role of the state 20–23, 27–8, 52–3, 61–3, 310–15, 333–6, 370
and social inequality 123, 320–1, 329, 333–6
and social policy 20–23, 38–41, 52–3, 61–3, 122–30, 140–2, 166–72, 310–15, 327–36, 370
in China, *see* China
see also liberalization, participatory growth
economies of scale 47–9, 54, 73–5, 312
education vi–viii, xiii–xv, 2, 4–8, 12–7, 38–44, 64–70, 76–9, 83–94, 99–101, 115–20, 130–1, 143–88, 221, 268, 308–10, 361–3, 368, 391
economic contributions of 13–14, 38–41, 76–9, 81–3, 163–4, 181–2, 308–10, 317, 320, 322, 323
empowerment value of 18, 29, 39–40, 143–6, 273, 350, 353, 356, 361, 369
gender aspects of 18, 39, 68–70, 85, 91, 96, 106–7, 117, 143–64, 177–84
parental motivation for 144, 154–9, 160–4, 185, 313
personal and social roles of 38–41, 87–89, 143–6, 153, 183–4, 199–200, 268, 308–10
politics of xiv–xv, 42–3, 77, 133–4, 144–6, 168–76, 184–8, 201, 299–303, 308–9, 333–4, 368–71
progress in the nineties 148, 151–3, 159, 164, 308, 313, 328–32
public expenditure on 22–23, 96, 166, 168–72, 186, 293–4, 333–6
social dimension of 41–44, 56–7, 59–60, 155, 160–4, 177–86
social disparities in 78, 83–5, 146–53, 179–80
and inequality 18, 41–2, 91–4,

100–1, 146–53, 179–83, 187, 271–4, 314, 353–8
and political action xiv–xv, 39, 58, 91–4, 100–1, 120, 144–5, 174, 186–8, 350, 353, 361, 369
and social change 38–41, 143–6, 177–84, 350, 353, 356, 361, 369
and social movements 77, 91–4, 100–1, 120, 144–5, 186–8
as a fundamental right 41–2, 167, 184–7, 294, 314, 370, 372
as an influence on mortality 18–19, 87–9, 91, 102, 137–9, 183–4, 198–200, 245–54, 271–3
in the media 43, 168, 301–2, 313–4
in China, *see* China
see also female education, human capital, Himachal Pradesh, Kerala, literacy rates, school attendance, schooling system
education policy xiv–xv, 143–88, 183
elitism of 308–9, 376
inadequacy of 12, 21–3, 38, 77, 130–1, 152–3, 164–7, 186–8, 308–9, 313–5, 345–6
inconsistency of ends and means 164–8, 313
in 'market economies' 43–44
in the nineties vi–vii, 21–23, 111, 151–2, 168–72, 329, 332–6
elections 9, 24, 217–8, 255, 299–300, 347–8, 365–6
influence of money power and social privilege in 9, 350, 353, 365–6, 403, 406
participation in 93, 217, 255, 348–50, 352–3, 361, 365–6
and public accountability 133, 217–8, 369–70
see also accountability, democracy, participation
El Salvador 269, 277
employment and unemployment 4, 21–22, 30–31, 37, 50, 56, 77–8, 98–9, 110, 225, 264–5, 301, 308–10, 316–8, 335–6, 339, 409

in the nineties 317–8
see also female labour-force participation, participatory growth
Employment Guarantee Scheme 339
empowerment 1–11, 28–32, 39–40,
70, 91–7, 106, 110, 111, 113–
6, 143–6, 217–8, 198–200, 214,
218, 221, 266, 271–4, 347–79
see also democratic practice, freedom,
inequality
England see Britain
entitlements 24, 31, 41–44, 47, 50, 72,
91, 186, 336–40, 354, 372, 375
see also rights
environment vi-viii, 23–6, 218–28, 302,
314, 323
degradation and destruction of 25,
39, 110–1, 197–8, 218–25,
293,, 369
protection of 2, 21, 25–6, 29, 54,
56–7, 60–3, 95, 218–22, 226–
8, 291, 340, 344, 346, 369
and development 218–23, 323
and population, 25, 135–6, 190–
1, 197–8, 221
and public policy 25–26, 224–8
and social inequality 223–7
and the constructive perspective
25–26, 221–2, 226–8
equity, as a requirement of effective
democracy 353, 375–9
see also democratic practice, inequality
Eritrea 277
escalation 26–27, 280, 285–6, 288–
90, 294–300, 303, 305
irrationality of 290, 295
see also military expansion, military
expenditure, nuclear deterrence
Ethiopia 66, 277
Europe 27n, 43, 47, 65n, 141, 194,
203, 204, 229, 230n, 231, 246,
267, 275, 341, 348

family planning 42, 102, 106–7, 134–
40, 174, 199–200, 207–18,
253–7, 399
coercion versus cooperation 134–

40, 142, 210–12, 214, 254–7,
259
use of targets in 210–12, 255
and health services 137–40, 207–18
in Tamil Nadu 138–40, 213–8
see also fertility, health, population
policy
famine and famine prevention 11, 45–
7, 50–3, 65–7, 131–4, 190, 196,
223, 264, 322–3, 335–40
and democracy 4, 24, 132–4, 142,
264, 378
in China, see China
see also hunger
female education 67–70, 83–5, 101–
10, 115–20, 143–64, 177–84,
221, 229, 231–2, 271–4
and empowerment 17–20, 143–6,
198–200, 273, 356
and fertility 91, 137–40, 198–200,
213–4, 245–57, 271–3
and child mortality 18–9, 70, 87–9,
91, 137–9, 183–4, 198–200,
245–54, 271–3
and gender bias in child survival
245–52
and gender relations 145, 160–4,
181–3, 198–200, 271–4, 356
and natality inequality 257–62, 274
and social change 101–110, 143–
6, 160–4, 271–4, 356
see also education, Himachal Pradesh,
Kerala, women's agency
female labour-force participation xv, 14,
18, 68–69, 78–9, 109, 137–40,
161–2, 177, 181–2, 199, 200,
214, 221, 231, 245–54, 271–4,
391, 398, 406
and child mortality 199–200, 245–
52
and education 181–2
and gender inequality 68–9, 105–7,
161–2, 181–2, 199–200, 214,
231, 245–6, 265, 273
see also employment, women's agency
female-male ratios 18, 66, 68–70, 84–
6, 91, 136–7, 214, 229–46, 257–

62, 354, 391, 393, 398, 405, 407
among scheduled castes 241–5
decline over time of 236–45
regional patterns of 84–6, 105–6, 229–35, 246, 257–62, 354
two misconceptions about 232–5
and mortality decline 236–41
and sex-selective abortion 105–6, 136–7, 241, 257–62
see also gender inequality, mortality
female infanticide 232–3, 242
female teachers 91, 161, 167, 182
see also school teachers
fertility 69–70, 134–40, 189–200, 208–18, 247–9, 253–7, 259, 263, 328, 384, 391, 393, 395, 405
regional contrasts in 84–6, 102, 104, 194–6, 213, 248–9, 253–4
and gender inequality 69–70, 136–40, 213–4, 231, 247, 253–7, 271–4, 356
and women's agency 17, 19, 107, 137–40, 198–200, 213–4, 217, 253–7, 271–4
and mortality, see demographic transition
in China, see China
see also demographic transition, family planning, population
Finland 98n
food vii, 31–2, 50–2, 196–8, 336–40, 409
consumption 95, 121, 123, 132, 196–8, 337, 402
countermovements 51
entitlements 50–2, 132–3, 336–40, 370
prices 31–2, 50–1, 187, 316, 336–40
production 121, 196–8
stocks vii, 31–2, 336–40
trade 50–2, 322–3, 338
see also famine, hunger
France 194, 275, 341n

freedom xiv–xv, 1–8, 14–5, 17–20, 23–5, 34–41, 52–3, 201, 253–7, 271–4, 347–79
as an end and as means xiv–xv, 3–8, 52–3, 81–83
positive and negative 61
relation between different types of 3–6, 20, 38–41
the perspective of 1–8, 32–33, 34–38, 62–3, 219–21, 359, 377
see also democracy, participation, social opportunities, women's agency
gender inequality viii, 10–11, 17–20, 55, 66–70, 78–79, 83–87, 91, 105–7, 196–7, 201–2, 224, 229–74, 302, 314, 353–8, 361–3, 369, 372
in child survival 68–70, 105–6, 136–7, 157, 229–52, 272–3
in natality 105–6, 136–8, 257–62
and birth order 157, 247
and caste 241–5
and criminal violence 266–71
and economic development 18, 78–79, 244–5, 247–8, 251–2, 270–4, 308
and education 18, 39, 69, 85, 96, 106–7, 117–9, 143–64, 179–83, 214, 229, 231, 273
and female labour-force participation 18, 78–79, 106–7, 161–2, 181–2, 245–52, 273
and fertility 69–70, 136–40, 198–200, 213–4, 271–3
and poverty 244–5
and property rights 18, 69, 100, 141, 161–4, 199, 231–2, 249, 262–6, 269–73
see also female-male ratios, inequality, women's agency
gender relations xiii, 17–20, 68–70, 137–40, 160–4, 229–74
regional contrasts in 83–87, 105–

7, 163–4, 181–3, 231–6, 265, 271–4
widowhood and 262–6
in Himachal Pradesh, see Himachal Pradesh
in Kerala, see Kerala
in Tamil Nadu, see Tamil Nadu
in Uttar Pradesh, see Uttar Pradesh
see also gender inequality, women's agency
Georgia 86, 202
Germany 44, 45, 47, 203n, 275, 281
Ghana 12, 66
globalization 32, 302, 340–45
government
distinct from state 44–5
overactivity and underactivity 20–23, 308
positive roles of vi-vii, xiv–xv, 1–11, 15, 20–23, 34–63, 70–83, 41–63, 89, 105, 108–9, 112–4, 120–2, 130–1, 140–2, 183, 202–7, 217–8, 226–8, 308–10, 313–315, 317, 322–3, 333–6, 345–6, 359, 368–9, 375–9
and cooperative action 56–61, 109, 176, 183, 227
and the market mechanism 20–23, 43–56, 140–2, 202–7
see also local governance, public action, public services
gram sabhas 347, 363, 371
Goa 111, 208, 261
Greece 65
groundwater, depletion of 25, 55, 218, 223, 225
growth-mediated success 70–83
Guatemala 45n, 269, 277
Gujarat 17, 57n, 84, 88, 111, 148, 169, 194, 207, 210, 235, 249n, 257, 259, 261, 319, 320, 329, 394, 396, 397, 398, 399, 400, 401, 402, 403, 404

Haiti 65, 377

Haryana 84, 85, 86, 87, 88, 99n, 104, 105, 106, 107, 109, 111, 169, 179, 180, 183, 231, 234, 235, 245, 249n, 255n, 257, 259, 261, 271, 319, 394, 395, 396, 397, 398, 399, 400, 401, 402, 403, 404
hawkers 30, 55, 223, 312, 367
head-count index of poverty 114–5, 122–4, 324–8, 386–8, 390
limitations of 87, 123–4, 327, 386–8
trends over time 122–4, 324–8, 387–8, 409
in China 114–5, 122–4
in Indian states 83–89, 95, 98–99, 104, 386–7
see also poverty
health and health care vi-vii, xiii–xv, 2, 5–8, 30–31, 79, 83–94, 108, 120–30, 137–9, 200, 218, 247–8, 291, 327–8, 333–6, 344, 399–402, 406
as a social responsibility 41–44, 201–7, 372
displaced by family planning 208–13, 313
economic contributions of xv, 38–41, 79, 81–83, 308–10, 317, 323
gender aspects of 69–70, 92, 106, 200, 207–18, 229–254, 271–4, 336
neglected in public policy xiv–xv, 12, 21–23, 28, 38–41, 130–1, 201–13, 308–10, 313–5, 327–33, 335, 345–6, 369
personal and social roles of 38–41
politics of xiv–xv, 42–43, 91–94, 108, 128–30, 133–4, 201, 212–3, 217–8, 299–303, 333–4, 359, 368–72, 376–7
private provision of 129–30, 202, 204, 206, 208–9
public expenditure on 22–23, 129–

30, 202–4, 212, 292, 294, 313, 333–6
social dimension of 41–44, 56–57, 201–7
and inequality 41–42, 201–202, 217
in Rajasthan 206–7, 210, 215
in Tamil Nadu 87–9, 103, 205, 207–9, 213–18
in the media 43, 301–2, 313–4
in 'market economies' 43–44, 202–4
in China, see China
see also mortality
Himachal Pradesh 101–110, 177–184, 393–407
contrasted with Haryana 104–110, 179–80, 182–3
cooperative action in 59, 107–109, 179–84
development experience of 101–110
foundations of rapid progress in 59, 104–110, 177–84
gender relations in 20, 105–107, 181–3, 214, 235–8, 259, 269, 271
local democracy in 107–108, 179–84
mortality and fertility in 84, 88, 102–103, 106, 139, 184, 195, 199, 256, 271
poverty in 84, 88, 99, 102, 104, 179, 184
school attendance in 84–85, 101–110, 120, 154, 163, 173, 177
'schooling revolution' in 17, 20, 59, 102, 176–84, 205, 217, 378
social achievements of 19, 72, 84–5, 101–110, 120, 177, 183–4, 256, 269, 271
social inequality in 107–109, 179–83, 354
state initiatives in 105, 169, 183–4, 205, 208
women's agency in 20, 105–107, 181–3, 271

Himalayan region 101, 163, 179, 246n
homicide, see murder
Hong Kong 47, 64, 71, 76, 113
human capital 73–81, 308–10, 317, 320–22, 332
roles of 38–41, 75
and more basic values 7, 81–83
see also capabilities, education, health, social opportunities
human rights 24–5, 28–29, 62, 134, 136, 211, 254–5, 291, 293, 304–5, 340, 348, 350, 371–5
distinction from legal rights 371–2
in the media 301–2, 314, 374
the notion of 371–2
see also rights
hunger and undernourishment vi-viii, 30, 52, 67–70, 79, 121, 123, 184, 196–8, 201, 222–3, 268, 271–2, 305, 308, 313–4, 336–40
amidst plenty 31–32, 336–40
does it matter 67–69, 79, 308–10
evidence of 67–70, 115–6, 123, 196, 336, 401, 406
and gender inequality 69–70, 336
see also famine, food
Hyderabad 56, 77, 224n

immunization 89, 91–92, 103, 107, 205, 207–18, 293, 400, 406
income and purchasing power 4–5, 8, 28, 34–8, 50–2, 55, 64–65, 68, 71, 82–83, 87, 91, 103–4, 114–5, 122–4, 179, 196–7, 265, 268, 271, 277, 315–333, 336–40, 385–6, 390, 393, 394
see also poverty
Indonesia 4, 12, 202, 391
industrial growth 77–78, 96, 122, 218, 309, 316–8, 330, 408
see also economic growth
inequality vi, viii, xiv–xv, 1–3, 5, 54–6, 69–71, 107–10, 201–2, 329, 343–5, 347–71, 375–9, 387

assessment of 8, 55–56, 353–6, 387, 394, 409
caste-based 10–11, 28, 30, 62, 69, 85, 100, 107, 109, 143–50, 179–81, 202, 217, 241–5, 272, 314, 349, 351, 352–63
economic 8–9, 48, 54–6, 107–8, 123, 179–1, 319–22, 329, 353–8, 394
of educational opportunities 8, 10, 78, 83–85, 96, 143–64, 179–81, 353–8
not immutable 9–11, 110, 353–8
rural-urban 132, 149, 354
and democratic practice viii-ix, 8–11, 24, 28–32, 93–94, 110, 179–81, 224–5, 333, 339–40, 347, 350–63, 368–71, 375–9
and efficiency 71, 78, 108–9, 272, 308–10, 314, 356–7
and criminal violence 268–9
and empowerment 17–20, 28–32, 93–96, 110–1, 143–6, 198–200, 271–4, 347–9, 352–8, 361–3, 366–72, 375–9
and environmental issues 60–61, 223–6
and globalization 340–5
and local democracy 60–61, 107–8, 179–81, 358–68
and participation viii-ix, 8–11, 28–32, 55, 91–4, 217–8, 271–4, 347–79
and policy priorities 8–11, 28–32, 55, 93–4, 143–4, 179–81, 186–8, 217–8, 224–5, 314, 329, 333–6, 339–40, 347–53, 355, 370, 375–9
and public action xiii, 8–11, 28–32, 61, 91–4, 107–10, 217–8, 343–5, 347–79
in the nineties 111, 319–22, 329
see also gender inequality
infant mortality, see child mortality
infanticide, see female infanticide
informal sector 30–32

work conditions in 31, 54, 371, 373
information 132–3
and the market mechanism 41, 54, 206
right to 17, 314, 349, 352, 367, 378
see also media
information technology vii, 2, 11, 56, 77, 280, 302, 309, 317–8
infrastructure 21, 95, 105, 135, 191, 197–8, 213, 292, 332, 337
institutions 6, 20–23, 24, 28, 44–46, 107–8, 227–8, 343–5, 347–79
complementarity of 20, 32–33, 46–53, 56–61, 109, 140–2, 176, 343–5, 368–71, 379
see also democratic institutions
international comparisons, see comparative international perspectives
International Monetary Fund 333, 344
international trade 22, 73–75, 113, 306–7, 312–3, 317, 338, 340–5, 392, 408
and economies of scale 48–49, 73–75, 312
involuntary displacement 28, 223, 358, 369
Iraq 45n, 65, 277
Italy 65

Jamaica 12, 71, 137
Jammu and Kashmir 84, 99n, 102n, 234, 261, 319n, 394, 395, 396, 397, 398, 399, 400, 401, 402, 403, 404
Japan 47, 49, 79, 279
Jharkhand ix-x, 15, 259, 261, 338, 383, 407
see also Bihar

Kalahandi 222, 223
Karnataka 84, 88, 111, 169, 175, 209n, 215, 216n, 231, 235, 249n, 261, 319, 394, 395, 396, 397, 398, 399, 400, 401, 402, 403, 404
Kashmir 45n, 101n, 111, 277, 284, 301, 302, 373, 374

Kenya 12, 65
Kerala x, xvi, 15–17, 83–94, 97–101,
105, 214, 249, 393–407
contrasted with China 15, 115–20,
124–8, 137–40, 142
contrasted with Uttar Pradesh 15–
17, 59, 73, 85, 89–94, 146–9,
187–8
corruption and violence in 93, 269,
368
economic performance of 13, 16,
72–3, 98–99, 115, 319, 329
gender inequality and women's
agency in 84–85, 91, 120, 137–
40, 163, 231–2, 234–8, 253–7,
261, 269–70, 271–3
land reform in 16, 80, 93, 354
literacy and education in 15–17, 19,
59, 84–85, 90–94, 98–102, 115–
120, 143, 146–53, 160–1, 163,
167, 169, 187, 254, 271–3, 369
mortality and fertility in 15–16, 18–
19, 72, 84–88, 90, 101, 115,
124–8, 137–40, 194–5, 199,
213, 271–3
not a 'model' 98, 232
political participation in 91–94,
110, 213, 218, 352, 361, 368–
9, 378
poverty in 84, 90–91, 98–99
public services in 59, 89–94, 167,
205, 207, 208, 213, 218, 272–
3, 339
public vigilance in 91–92, 187, 213,
352
regional disparities within 94, 100–
101
significance of 97–101
social achievements of 15–17, 72,
83–94, 101, 103, 106, 110,
115, 124–8, 137–40, 146–53,
208, 253–4, 269, 271–3, 339,
352, 368
social inequality in 93–94, 110,
272, 354
suicide in 97–99

land ownership 30, 107, 131, 141, 244,
267, 270, 351, 354, 404
role in active economic agency 22,
79–80, 94–5, 131, 141, 308, 323
and economic equity 94–5, 107,
131, 141, 244, 354, 357, 361
as an influence on gender equity 18,
100, 138, 141, 161–4, 199,
231–2, 244, 249, 262–6, 270–1
see also women's property rights
land reform 2, 14, 16, 21–22, 71, 79–
80, 94–7, 107, 111, 131, 141,
308, 310, 323, 346, 357, 361,
378
in China, see China
Lao 65
Latin America 115, 145n, 204, 268,
310n
Lebanon 277
legal rights 10, 24, 46–7, 61, 143–5,
171, 184–6, 226–7, 255, 262–
5, 323, 349, 351, 353, 371–5
see also rights
legal system 10, 24, 46–47, 53–54, 58,
61–2, 184–6, 226–7, 268, 323,
347–53, 369, 371–5, 376
see also democratic institutions
liberalization vi-vii, xiv–xv, 20–23, 32,
40, 47, 53–56, 61–63, 80–81,
113, 130–1, 140–2, 305–336,
340, 345–6
rationale of 20–23, 37–8, 306–8,
310–13, 345–6
need to go beyond vi, xiv–xv, 20–
23, 52–53, 61–63, 130–1, 306–
336, 345–6
and public accountability 370
see also economic reform, participatory growth
life expectancy 15–16, 19, 64–66, 68,
71, 82, 84–85, 101, 114–5, 121–
2, 124–8, 137, 141–2, 238–9,
356, 390, 393, 395, 410
in China 15, 114–5, 121–2, 124–
8, 137, 141–2, 390
see also mortality

literacy, *see* education
literacy rates 12–13, 64–70, 83–85,
    146–53, 160, 177–8, 328–9,
    331, 384–5, 391, 393, 396,
    405, 407, 410
  among disadvantaged groups 85,
    146–53
  in India vis-à-vis China 12–13, 76–
    77, 114–120, 149, 160–1, 384–
    5, 391
  in India vis-à-vis east Asia 13, 76–
    77, 149, 160–1, 391, 393
  in India vis-à-vis sub-Saharan Africa
    67–70, 149, 160, 391, 393
  in Indian states 15, 83–89, 101,
    104, 146–53, 177–8, 393, 396,
    405, 407
  in China, *see* China
  see also education, female education
local democracy 19–21, 60–61, 94–7,
    105, 107–111, 308, 347, 358–
    68
  distinct from decentralization 175–
    6, 359–60
  as a learning process 361–3
  and corruption 360, 363–8
  and social inequality 60–61, 107–
    8, 179–81, 358–68
  and the quality of life 107–110, 359
  see also democracy, panchayats
local governance 14, 60–61, 94–97,
    175–6, 179–81, 187, 347, 358–
    68

Madhya Pradesh 15, 17, 19, 84, 85,
    86, 87, 88, 89, 98n, 102, 111,
    139, 149, 151, 152, 154n, 159,
    160, 166, 167n, 169, 170, 171,
    174, 176, 178n, 215n, 235,
    249n, 256, 259, 261, 271, 319,
    335, 352, 361, 367, 383, 394,
    395, 396, 397, 398, 399, 400,
    401, 402, 403, 404
Maharashtra 20, 94, 106n, 111, 144,
    169, 207, 210, 235, 249n, 257,
    261, 266n, 319, 320, 339n,
    352, 394, 395, 396, 397, 398,
    399, 400, 401, 402, 403, 404
Malabar, insights from 94, 100–1
  see also Kerala
Malawi 65, 69n
Malaysia 97, 318
Manipur 111n, 163, 261, 271, 405,
    406
market mania and market phobia 53–6
markets xiii–xv, 7, 13–4, 20–3, 32–3,
    41, 43–56, 71, 80, 113–4, 202–
    3, 206, 208–9, 306–23, 345–6,
    379
  institutional foundations of 46
  manipulation of 45–6, 50–1
  and cooperative action 56–61
  and education 7, 13–4, 41, 43–4,
    130–1, 333–4
  and famine 45–7, 50–3
  and government 20–3, 32–33, 43–
    56, 71, 80, 130–1, 140–2, 201–
    9, 306–36, 345–6, 379
  and social inequality 10, 48, 54–6,
    343
  and social norms 47, 58–9
  see also institutions, liberalization
market-complementary interventions
    49–53, 345–6
market-excluding interventions 49–53
maternal mortality, *see* mortality
Mauritius 66
media 43, 59, 132–4, 168, 214, 221,
    226–7, 263–4, 300–3, 355, 376
  as a democratic institution 9–10,
    20, 28–29, 132–4, 263–4, 294,
    301–3, 347, 351, 369, 374, 379
  coverage of development *versus*
    security issues 300–3, 305, 374
  social priorities of 9, 28, 43, 190,
    263–4, 294, 300–3, 305, 313–
    4, 376
  see also democracy, propaganda
Meghalaya 163, 261, 405, 406
Mewat 105n
middle classes 22, 172, 310, 335–6,
    355, 375–6

migrant labourers 29, 338
military expansion vii-viii, 2, 23–24, 26–28, 275–305
  danger of escalation 26–7, 280, 285, 288–90, 294–9, 296, 305
  insecurities associated with vii-viii, 2, 23, 26–28, 277–89, 294–9, 296, 305
  need for democratic scrutiny of viii, 26–8, 277–8, 283, 286, 294, 299, 301–5, 373–5
  social costs of vii-viii, 26–8, 44–5, 47, 278, 280–1, 289–92, 305, 345, 373–5, 377
  and corruption 291, 374
  and democracy viii, 23–4, 26–8, 278, 280–3, 284, 286, 289, 291, 296, 298, 299–305, 373–5, 377
  and human rights 291, 293, 304–5, 373–5
  and propaganda 291, 303, 374
  and scientific research 290–2, 304, 374
  and strength 278–83
  as a diversion of development concerns 26–8, 278, 280–1, 290, 299–300, 305, 374
  as a social trap 295
  see also escalation, nuclear deterrence, war
military expenditure viii, 2, 26–8, 187, 276, 289–99
  compared with health expenditure 27, 289, 292, 376
  escalation of 27, 289–90, 292, 296–9
  social costs of 27, 276, 278, 289–94
  trends in 27, 276, 292
  in India and Pakistan 27, 294–9
minimum wages 31, 55, 96, 145
'missing women' 18, 229–31
  see also female-male ratio, gender inequality
Mizoram 163, 261, 405, 406
Moldova 86

morbidity patterns 116, 201, 204
  see also health
mortality 64–70, 83–9, 124–8, 277, 384, 390, 395, 405, 407
  among widows 263
  of children 11, 64–70, 83–9, 124–8, 136–9, 157, 213–5, 229–52, 254, 257–62, 271–3, 313, 327–32, 390, 393, 395, 405, 407, 410
  of females vis-à-vis males 68–70, 84–86, 105–6, 136–7, 157, 229–52, 272–3, 395, 398, 405, 391, 395
  maternal 215
  and education 18–19, 87–9, 91, 102, 137–9, 183–4, 198–200, 245–54, 271–3
  and fertility, see demographic transition
  in Indian states 83–90, 101–4, 106, 115, 213–5, 234–5, 271–2, 395, 405, 407
  in China, see China
  see also child mortality, demographic transition, female-male ratios, health, life expectancy
Mozambique 69n, 277
murder rate 103, 266–71
  see also criminal violence
Myanmar (Burma) 12, 65, 160n, 202, 267

Nagaland 148, 261, 405, 406
Narmada dam 223
natality inequality 105–6, 136–8, 241, 256–62, 274, 356
  see also gender inequality
national security, see security
Naxalite movement 30, 113
Nepal 65, 391
Netherlands 43
Niger 65
North-eastern states 373, 374, 405, 406
North Korea 43, 77
nuclear deterrence 277–8

does it work 277–8, 283–6, 296, 305
moral and pragmatic issues 278–80
risk of escalation 280, 283–6, 288–9, 296, 298–9, 305
and security 277–89, 291, 296
nuclear plants, as a powder keg 291
nuclear tests vii, 26–7, 225, 277–8, 282–3, 289–90, 293, 298–9, 300–2, 304–377
scientific aspects of 282, 290, 304
nuclear weapons 2, 276, 301–2, 304–5
risk of accidental war 284, 296
terms of the debate on 286–9
and strength 276–83
see also military expansion
nutrition, see hunger and undernourishment

Orissa 61n, 84, 86, 88, 96, 102, 106n, 149, 169, 181n, 222, 235, 236, 249n, 261, 319, 329, 338, 365n, 394, 395, 396, 397, 398, 399, 400, 401, 402, 403, 404
ownership xiii, 129–31, 140–1, 357
see also land ownership, property rights

Pakistan 26–7, 390–3
democracy in 298, 303
détente with 299
gender inequality in 69, 230, 234, 246, 272
military expenditure in 27, 296–9
nuclear tests in 26, 277–8, 282–4, 287–9
tensions with 26–7, 277–8, 282, 284, 294–9, 301–3
Palanpur 270
panchayats 19–20, 94–7, 108, 175, 176, 255, 347, 350–1, 358–68
participation viii–ix, xiii–xv, 1–11, 23–8, 28–33, 91–4, 132–4, 143, 271–4, 262, 304–5, 307–15, 347–79
economic, see participatory growth

electoral 93, 217, 255, 348–50, 352–3, 361, 365–6, 403, 406
political 7, 10, 24–25, 28–32, 39–40, 93–4, 143–6, 217–8, 272, 304–5, 347–79
and inequality viii–ix, 8–11, 28–32, 55, 91–4, 217–8, 271–4, 347–79
see also democratic practice, freedom, participatory growth, public action, women's agency
participatory growth vi, xiv–xv, 14, 20–3, 70–81, 108–9, 123, 130–1, 306–33, 336, 345–6
India's lack of preparedness for xiv, 14, 40–1, 52–3, 77–8, 130–1, 308–10, 313–15, 318–22
Philippines 12, 80
political action vi, xiii–xv, 28–32, 93–7, 110, 174, 186–8, 217–8, 304–5, 339 40, 344 5, 355 8, 359, 360–3, 366–8, 368–71, 377–8
see also democratic practice, public action
pollution 25, 218, 221–7
population growth vii, 39, 65, 134–40, 189–200
concerns and scrutiny 134–6, 189–96
India's billionth citizen vii, 189
Malthusian fears and the real issues 65, 134–6, 196–8
and economic growth 134–6, 197–8
and food supply 65, 196 8
and gender equity 17–20, 107, 137–40, 198–200, 245–57, 271–4
and environmental resources 25, 135–6, 190–1, 197–8, 221
and social infrastructure 135, 191, 197–8
in historical perspective 189–91
in India and China 134–40, 191, 194
see also demographic transition, fertility, population policy

population 'bomb' vii, 191–4, 203
population policy vii, 134–40, 189–
200, 208–18, 253–62
coercion versus cooperation 134–
40, 142, 210–12, 214, 254–7,
259
in China, see China
see also demographic transition,
fertility
Portugal 65, 341n
poverty vi, 1–2, 4–5
as capability failure 36, 123–4, 323
levels and trends 83–89, 114–5,
122–4, 324–33, 386–8, 390, 394
measurement of 87, 123–4, 386–8
the concept of 36, 123–4, 323
and child mortality 86–9, 246–52,
332
and criminal violence 266–71
and democracy 349, 378
and economic growth 34–6, 38,
70–3, 87, 122–4, 306–10, 315–
53
and gender inequality 244–5, 247–
52, 273
in Indian states 83, 89, 90–1, 95,
99, 102, 332, 386–8
in the media 302, 314
in the nineties 123, 307–8, 315–
33, 337, 387–8
in China, see China
see also head-count index, social
opportunities
Prevention of Terrorism Ordinance
(POTO) 305
see also human rights, military expansion
privatization xv, 32, 47, 53, 128–30,
140–1, 172, 202, 314, 370
PROBE report on Indian education x,
154–84
propaganda 42, 299–305, 374
property rights 46–48, 54, 140–1, 227,
267, 270, 344
see also ownership, women's property
rights

public action v, viii–ix, xiii, xv, 1–8, 16,
23–33, 41–4, 56–61, 70–83,
89, 91–4, 143–6, 186–8, 212–
3, 343–5, 347–79
and government policy viii, xv, 9,
24–25, 44–5, 58, 91–2, 109,
132–4, 168, 186–8, 212–3, 217–
8, 224–8, 263–4, 230–5, 286,
299–305, 314–5, 334–5, 339–40
and social inequality 8–11, 24–25,
28–32, 91–4, 217–8, 224–5,
271–4, 347–79
see also democratic practice, participation, political action
public distribution system 31, 55, 92,
104, 108, 336, 337, 339, 354,
359, 367, 369, 402
public expenditure 103–4, 293–4, 333–
6, 343
on education 22–3, 96, 166, 168–
72, 186, 293–4, 333–6
on health 22–3, 129–30, 202–4,
212, 292, 294, 313, 333–6, 376
on 'defence' viii, 2, 27, 289, 292–
4, 296–9, 376–7
and economic reform 313, 333–6
in 'market economies' 43–4
public interest litigation 10, 171, 186,
226–7, 369
public services vi, xiii–xv, 22–3, 70–3,
89–94, 14, 105, 108, 128–30,
140–2, 180–1, 201–18, 272,
308–10, 313–5, 322–3, 332–6,
359–60, 364, 368–71, 399, 402
see also government, social policy
public vigilance 62–3, 92, 108, 175–
6, 181, 187, 213, 226–7, 286,
352, 359, 363–71
see also accountability, democratic
practice
Punjab 84, 85, 86, 87, 88, 99n, 102n,
163n, 179, 194, 231, 234, 235,
249n, 257, 259, 261, 267n,
271, 319, 374, 394, 395, 396,
397, 398, 399, 400, 401, 402,
403, 404

Rajasthan 15, 17, 19, 69n, 84, 86, 111,
139, 149, 151, 152, 154n, 160,
164, 166, 167n, 169, 173, 176,
178n, 187n, 206, 207, 210,
215n, 234, 235, 249n, 255n,
256, 259, 261, 271, 272, 319,
320, 337n, 352, 367, 378, 387,
394, 395, 396, 397, 398, 399,
400, 401, 402, 403, 404
regional comparisons within India* x,
xv–xvi, 15–7, 66, 72–3, 83–9,
115–20, 269–71, 318–22, 383–
7, 393–407
Himachal Pradesh vis-à-vis Haryana
104–10, 179–80, 182–3
Himachal Pradesh vis-à-vis Kerala
103, 106, 109–10, 177–8
Kerala vis-à-vis Uttar Pradesh 15–
7, 59, 73, 85–6, 89–94, 139,
146–9, 187–8, 271–2, 354
'north and west' vis à vis 'south and
east' 231, 257–62
Tamil Nadu vis-à-vis other states 13,
87–9, 137–9, 213–8, 256–7
of development indicators 15–7,
66, 83–9, 98, 102–4, 106, 111,
115, 215, 383–7, 393–407
of economic performance 111, 115,
318–22, 329, 332
of educational levels 83–9, 90–1,
96–7, 102–3, 106, 115–20,
146–53, 177–8, 320–2, 384–5
of fertility and mortality 19, 83–9,
102–4, 115, 124–8, 137–40,
194–6, 198–200, 213–5, 231–
6, 245–54, 257–62, 271–3, 384
of female-male ratios 66, 84–86,
105–6, 231–6, 269–71
of gender relations 83–7, 91, 105–
7, 137–40, 161–4, 182–3, 214,
231–6, 245–9, 257–62, 269–
73
of political participation 19–20, 91–
4, 361–2, 368

of poverty indicators 83–9, 95, 104,
215, 329, 332, 386–7
of public services 59, 89–94, 104,
169, 207–8, 210, 214, 272
of school facilities 59, 91–2, 96–7,
104, 167, 183
of social inequality 93–4, 105–8,
110–11, 149–51, 180, 217,
269–72, 354, 361–2
see also comparative international
perspectives
regulation 53–6, xiv–xv
excesses of xiv, 16, 55, 310–12, 345
need for 54, 206, 208–9, 225, 227
see also deregulation, economic
reform, liberalization
rickshaw pullers 55, 312, 338, 367
rights 4, 9, 24–5, 28–32, 41–4, 45, 61–
2, 223, 254–5, 263, 343–4,
369–70, 371–5
to education 41–4, 167, 184–7,
294, 314, 370, 372, 375
to food and health care 41–4, 336–
40, 370, 372
to information 17, 314, 349, 352,
367, 378
to respect 372
to vote 9, 348–50
to work 375
see also democratic rights, entitlements, human rights, legal rights,
property rights
Russia 47, 53, 108n, 334
see also Soviet Union
Rwanda 45n

Sanskritization 243–4
Saudi Arabia 85n
Scandinavia 98
scheduled castes 147–50, 180, 349,
358, 360–3
and gender inequality 241–5
see also caste
scheduled tribes 28, 105, 109, 149,

163, 244, 246–8, 253, 349, 358, 360–3

political marginalization of 28, 109, 358–63

and gender inequality 109, 149, 163, 241, 246–8

and involuntary displacement 28, 358

school attendance 12–3, 39, 84–5, 91–2, 146–53, 366

contrasted with official enrolment figures 146–8

levels and trends 84–5, 92, 96, 103, 106, 146–53, 165, 391, 396–7, 405

myths about 154–9

progress in the nineties 148, 151–3, 159, 164, 173, 308, 313, 329, 332

and child labour 39, 155–9, 177

and the discouragement effect 154–9

in Bangladesh 12–13, 391

in Himachal Pradesh 84–5, 101–10, 120, 177, 396–7

see also education

school meals 159, 164, 185, 214, 217

school quality 152–3, 158–9, 161, 166–7, 170–6, 183, 185, 369

school teachers 31, 92, 97, 108, 159, 166–76, 180–85, 293, 334, 359, 368–71

involvement of women as 91–92, 161, 167, 182

schooling system 59–60, 146–53, 164–72

community monitoring of 59–60, 108, 175–6, 181, 183

growing differentiation of 153, 171–2

improved accessibility of 105, 166, 170–1

need for accountability in 108, 158, 166–7, 172–6, 187, 359, 368–71

social discrimination in 158, 170–2, 181

state of 92, 96–7, 152, 3, 158, 166–7, 172–3, 369

and 'second-track' facilities 168–72

see also education, education policy, school teachers

sectarian divisions, see communalism

security vii-viii, 275–305

compromised by nuclear tests 26–7, 277–89, 296, 305

and strength 278–83

see also military expansion, nuclear deterrence

service sector, growth of 56, 309, 316–8, 330

see also economic growth

sex-selective abortion 105–6, 136–8, 241, 256–62, 274, 356

see also child mortality, gender inequality

sharecropping 30, 79–80, 94

Siachen glacier 295

Sierra Leone 65, 277

Sikkim 163, 261, 405, 406

Singapore 47, 64, 71, 97, 113, 257, 258, 318

smaller Indian states 102, 11

social capital 93, 108

see also cooperative action

social distance 10, 226

and school education 155, 158, 173, 181

and health care 10, 217

see also inequality

social inequality, see inequality

social norms and values 42–3, 47, 58–60, 108, 155, 179–81, 199–200, 362–3, 365, 367–8, 371, 378–9

formation and scrutiny of 10–11, 25, 41–3, 45, 155, 164, 179–81, 184–5, 199–200, 220, 227–8, 258, 262, 274, 278–80, 286, 362–3, 365, 367–8, 371, 378–9

and democracy 10–1, 24–8, 362–3, 365, 367–8, 371
possibility of radical change 370–1
social opportunities ix, xiii–xv, 6–23, 26, 29, 31, 34–44, 56–7, 75–81, 89–111, 131, 140–2, 219, 272, 306–36, 343, 345–6, 375, 377
and economic growth 12–14, 34–8, 75–81, 122–8, 131, 273, 306–33
in the nineties 20–23, 123, 306–36
in China, see China
see also capabilities, comparative international perspectives, freedom, regional comparisons
social policy vi-vii, xiii–xv, 1–8, 12, 20–23, 34–44, 59–63, 70–83, 87–111, 140–2, 293–4, 333–6, 375–9
and economic reform vi vii, xiii xv, 20–3, 38–41, 52–3, 61–3, 122–30, 140–2, 166–72, 310–15, 327–36, 370
in 'market economies' 43–4, 202–4
see also education, environment, government, health, inequality, land reform, social security, women's agency
social security vi, 14, 28, 31, 91, 141, 214, 266, 293, 299–300, 308, 310, 323, 334, 354, 368
a neglected issue in India 21, 31, 345–6
in east Asia 80 1, 323
in 'market economies' 43–4
social traps 295
software production vii, 2, 56, 77, 309
solidarity 28–32, 42, 96, 344–5, 378–9
Somalia 47, 277
South Africa 266, 268
South Korea 4, 12, 13, 47, 49, 65, 70, 71, 72, 73, 75n, 76, 77, 79, 97, 113, 115, 124, 125, 128, 131, 257, 258, 259, 262, 309, 310, 318, 323, 391, 392
Soviet Union 27n, 45n, 64n, 65n, 141
Sri Lanka 12, 13, 66, 71, 97, 124, 125, 128, 237, 238n, 273, 277, 302, 391, 392
structural adjustment 187, 333–6
subsidies 32, 41, 225, 226, 294, 336–40, 365
Sudan 4, 45n, 202
suicide 97–9, 102–3, 404
support-led success 71–3
sustainable development xv, 220, 223
see also environment
Sweden 64
Switzerland 348
Syria 69n

Taiwan 12, 47, 71, 75n, 79, 113, 257, 258
Tamil Nadu 66, 81, 100, 111, 156, 169, 173, 175, 207, 319, 329, 339, 393–407
demographic transition in 17, 19, 84–9, 103, 109, 111, 139, 194–5, 199, 213–8, 256
gender inequality and women's agency in 19, 84, 106, 139, 199, 213 8, 231, 235 6, 261
health and health care in 87–9, 103, 205, 207–9, 213–18
teachers, see school teachers
Thailand 4, 12, 13, 47, 70, 71, 76, 77, 318, 391, 392
Third World debt 57, 344
Tibet 118, 119, 120
Togo 69n
torture 44, 373, 378
Total Literacy Campaign 19, 20, 42, 152, 155, 164, 187–8
trade unions 30–1, 145, 206, 370–1
transparency, see accountability
Travancore 94n, 99, 100, 100n, 160
tribes, see scheduled tribes
Tripura 405, 406

498 / SUBJECT INDEX

Uganda 44, 45
Ukraine 86
unaimed opulence 72–3, 309–10
undernourishment, see hunger
undertrial prisoners 29, 351
unemployment, see employment
United Arab Emirates 85n
United Kingdom see Britain
United States 27n, 54, 65, 85, 137,
    194, 203, 246, 269, 281, 285n,
    348, 349
universal elementary education 144,
    154–5, 159, 171–3, 177, 183,
    299–300, 356–7
  as a constitutional goal 41–2, 144,
    152–5, 164–7, 184–6, 294,
    313, 375
  as a matter of social justice 153
  the shifting goalpost of 164–7,
    299–300
  see also education
urban environment 221–7
  see also environment
Uruguay 65
Uttar Pradesh ix-x, xvi, 66, 83–94, 103,
    105, 108, 110, 154, 249, 256,
    365, 383, 393–407
  contrasted with Kerala 15–17, 59,
    73, 85, 89–94, 139, 146–9,
    187–8, 271–2
  criminal violence in 93, 111, 269–
    70, 351
  economic performance of 307, 319–
    20
  gender inequality in 19, 66, 84–5,
    91, 139, 234–5, 242–5, 247,
    259–61, 371–2, 354
  literacy and education in 59, 84, 90–
    2, 102, 139, 146–54, 156, 158,
    160–1, 166–9, 178, 183, 187–8
  mortality and fertility in 19, 83–9,
    139, 195, 271–2
  political participation in 91–94,
    351, 358, 360
  public services in 59, 89–94, 111,
    139, 210, 215, 272

social achievements of 17, 61, 66,
    83–94, 111, 215, 256, 272
social inequality in 93, 272, 354, 358
Uttaranchal ix-x, 15, 108, 163, 259,
    360, 383, 407
  see also Uttar Pradesh
Uzbekistan 137

values, formation and scrutiny of 10–
    11, 25, 41–3, 45, 155, 164, 179–
    81, 220, 227–8, 258, 262, 274,
    278–80, 286, 362–3, 365, 367–
    8, 371
  see also social norms
Vietnam 12, 53, 277, 318, 334
violence 29–30, 44, 57–58, 72, 93, 96,
    101, 103, 223, 263–4, 266–71,
    275–8, 303, 317, 354, 362
  as a social trap 295
  see also criminal violence, military
    expansion, war
voice and voicelessness 28–32, 172,
    175–6, 187, 200, 246, 304–5,
    336, 339–40, 370, 378
  see also accountability, democratic
    practice, political action
voter turnouts, see elections

wages and salaries 31, 102, 328–9,
    331–2, 333–6, 370, 409
war and warfare 58, 66–7, 269–70
  penalties of 44–5, 47, 57–8, 66–7,
    101, 269–70, 275–8, 279–80,
    286, 295, 305, 344
  in the twentieth century 275–7
  see also military expansion
water, see groundwater
West Bengal x, xvi, 89, 94–7, 209, 215–
    6, 234–5, 261, 393–407
  agricultural growth in 95–6
  economic performance of 86, 95–
    6, 319–20
  land reform in 80, 94–7, 111, 361,
    378
  local democracy in 94–7, 361
  political change in 94–7

poverty in 84, 86, 95
school education in 84, 96–7, 168–9
social achievements of 84, 94–7, 106, 194, 261
widows 29, 145, 157, 200, 214, 243, 262–6
women's agency xiii, 17–20, 91, 105–110, 198–200, 217, 229–74
and balance of power within the family 18, 69, 198–200, 245–6, 253
and child survival 18–19, 87–9, 107, 137–40, 198–200, 245–52, 271–3
and education 18, 91, 108, 138, 160–4, 181–3, 198–200, 271–2
and fertility decline 17, 19, 107, 137–40, 198–200, 213–4, 217, 253–7, 271–3
and gender inequality 18, 91, 198–200, 229–74, 357
and sex-selective abortion 138, 257–62
and social progress xiii, 17–20, 91, 105–110, 161, 270–4, 314, 357
and the power to question prevailing norms 198–200, 257–62, 274

see also female labour-force participation, gender inequality, gender relations, women's political participation
women's education, see female education
women's labour-force participation, see female labour-force participation
women's political participation 18–20, 29, 182, 217–8, 232, 263, 266, 271–4, 275, 314, 348–53, 356, 358, 360–3
women's property rights 18, 69, 100, 138, 141, 143, 161–4, 199, 231–2, 249, 262–6, 269–73
World Bank 121, 187, 333, 344, 384–6
World Trade Center, terrorist attacks on 305
World Trade Organization 312, 338, 340, 344

Yemen 65
Yugoslavia 277

Zaire see Congo
Zambia 12
Zimbabwe 12

Name Index

Abraham, Itty 286n
Acharya, Poromesh 97n
Adelman, Irma 35n, 310n
Advani, L.K. 299
Agarwal, Anil 60n
Agarwal, Bina x, xvi, 36n, 141n, 163n, 224n, 231n, 233n, 246n, 249n, 264n
Aggarwal, Yash 92n, 104n, 166n, 167n
Agnihotri, Anita 164n
Agnihotri, Satish xvi, 85n, 163n, 231n, 236n, 241n, 245n, 249n
Ahluwalia, Isher Judge 311n
Ahluwalia, Montek Singh 36n, 311n, 319n, 320, 321n, 412
Ahmed, Qazi Hussain 287n
Ahuja, Ram 266n, 267n
Aiyar, Swaminathan S.A. 324n
Akbar 348n
Akerlof, George 41n, 42n
Alailima, Patricia 72n, 273n
Alamgir, Mohiuddin 46n
Alberuni 145n
Alderman, Harold 79n
Alesina, Alberto 71n
Ali, Fazl 102n
Altekar, A.S. 242n
Ambatkar, Sanjay xvi
Ambedkar, B.R. 144, 375, 376, 377

Amsden, Alice H. 47n, 80n, 131n
Anand, Sudhir xvi, 35n, 72n, 82, 83
Andreski, Stanislav 58n, 364n
Antia, N.H. 206n
Antony, T.V. 213n
Aoki, Masahiko 47n
Archer, David xvi, 145n
Aristotle 3, 5, 35
Arneson, R. 61n
Arnett, Eric 290n, 304n
Arokiasamy, P. x, 253n
Arrow, Kenneth J. 9n, 41n, 48n
Ashoka 6, 348n
Ashworth, Tony 58n
Asthana, M.D. x
Asthana, Roli xvi
Ateeq, Nasir 157n
Athreya, V.B. 164n, 233n
Atiyah, Michael 280
Atkinson, A.B. 35n, 74n, 124n
Ayyar, Vaidyanatha R.V. xvi
Azad, K.C. 109n
Aziz, Abdul 175n

Babu, S.C. 214n
Bagchi, Amiya K. x, xvi, 311n
Bahadur, K.P. 242n
Bajpai, K. Shankar 278n
Bajpai, N. 311n

Baland, Jean-Marie 60n
Balassa, Bela 47n
Bandhyopadhyay, Sanghamitra 320n, 322n
Banerjea, Niharika 179n
Banerjee, Abhijit 95n
Banerjee, Nirmala 231n, 246n
Banerjee, Sumanta 42n, 94n
Banerji, Debabar 202n, 206n, 210
Banerji, Rukmini 154n, 156n
Banister, Judith 121, 127n, 137n
Banthia, J.K. x
Bapat, M.T. 132n
Bara, D. 144n
Bardhan, Kalpana 18n, 246n
Bardhan, Pranab x, 32n, 36n, 60n, 71n, 75n, 230n, 231n, 236n, 246n, 357n, 364n
Barker, D.J.P. 69n
Barro, Robert J. 75n, 251n, 253n, 377n
Bashir, Sajitha x, 166n, 169n
Basu, Aparna 18n, 144n
Basu, Alaka Malwade 230n, 231n, 233n, 244n, 246n, 249n, 250n, 251n
Basu, Kaushik xvi, 42n, 311n
Bayley, David H. 266n
Beck, Tony 36n, 95n, 359n
Becker, Gary 268
Beenstock, M. 251n
Behrman, Jere R. 40n, 75n, 251n
Bello, Walden 47n, 81n
Berlin, Isaiah 61n
Bernstein, T.P. 133n
Berreman, Gerald D. 108n, 163n, 243n
Béteille, André 184n
Bhaduri, Amit 37n, 311n
Bhagwati, Jagdish 37, 38, 311n, 312n
Bhalla, A.S. 112n, 122n
Bhalla, Sheila 105n
Bhalla, Surjit 324n
Bhargava, Alok 251n
Bhargava, Ashok 210
Bhargava, P. 36n
Bhatia, Bela x, xvi, 30n, 55n, 145n, 223n, 266n, 350n, 359n, 360, 367n
Bhatia, Bimal 303n

Bhattacharya, B.B. 311n
Bhattacharya, M. 132n
Bhatty, Kiran x, 106n, 154n, 156n, 179n 183n
Bhatty, Zarina 105n, 106n
Bhuiya, A. 251n
Bidani, B. 83n
Bidwai, Praful x, 279n, 286n
Binswanger, Hans 79n
Birdsall, Nancy 47n, 72n, 75n, 78n, 310n
Bisht, S. 211n
Biswas, D.K. 225
Blanchflower, David 98n
Blackorby, Charles 124n
Blair, Bruce G. 284n
Bliss, Christopher 79n
Bloch, Ivan 276
Blomkvist, Hans x, 60n, 93n 349n, 351n
Bloom, Gerald 129n, 130n
Bondroit, Marie-Eve 106n, 154n, 179n, 183n
Borooah, V.K. 251n
Bose, Ashish 255n
Bose, Sugata 95n
Boserup, Ester 246n
Bourne, K. 251n
Bowles, Samuel 42n, 71n, 357n
Bracken, Paul 284n
Bramall, Chris 123n
Breman, Jan 55n
Breyer, F. 41n
Brown, Lester R. 64n
Bruton, Henry 72n
Buchanan, James M. 48n, 49
Buckland, P. 169n
Budakoti, D.K. 210
Burgess, Robin x, xvi, 141n
Bumgarner, R. 116n
Burra, Neera 157n
Butler, George Lee 284n, 285n
Byrd, W. 122n, 141n

Cable, Vincent 54n
Calandrino, M. 112n
Caldwell, B. 251n, 273n

Caldwell, J.C. 72n, 89n, 144n, 154n, 161n, 162n, 163n, 231n, 251n, 253n
Caldwell, P. 231n
Cassen, Robert x, xvi, 36n, 37n, 136n, 218n, 223n, 253n, 311n
Castaneda, T. 72n
Chakrabarti, Anindita 179n
Chakravarti, Anand 145n
Chakravarty, Sukhamoy 74n
Chakravarty-Kaul, Minoti 60n
Chanana, Karuna 39n, 144n, 145n, 154n
Chand, Ramesh 110n
Chanda, Nayan 291n
Chander, Subhash x
Chari, P.R. 296n, 298n
Chasin, Barbara 90n
Chatterjee, Meera 233n
Chattopadhyay, B. xvi, 266n
Chattopadhyay, R. 19n
Chaturvedi, Bharati 225n
Chaudhri, D.P. 40n, 154n, 156
Chaudhuri, M. 18n
Chaudhuri, S. 206n
Chaujar, Paro 157n
Chen, K. 122n
Chen, Lincoln xvi, 136n, 233n
Chen, Marty xvi, 132n, 243n, 263n, 264n, 266n, 359n
Chenery, Hollis 35n
Chengappa, Raj 304n
Chenggang Xu 141n
Chesnais, Jean-Claude 267n
Chichilnisky, Graciella 51n
Choudhary, K.M. 132n
Chunkath, S.R. 164n, 233n
Churchill, Winston 190, 285, 286
Cleland, J. 251n
Coale, Ansley J. xvi, 122n, 124n, 125n, 127n, 137n, 230n
Cohen, Alex 236n
Cohen, G.A. 61n
Cohn, Carol 281n
Colclough, Christopher 40n
Coles, J.L. 46n

Corden, W. Max xvi, 47n, 312n
Condorcet, Marquis de 5, 9, 38, 52
Cooper, Charles 74n
Cornia, G. 333n
Costello, Patrick 145n
Coutinho, L. 209n, 210n, 211n
Crook, Clive 306n
Crook, R.C. 175n, 360n
Currie, Bob 132n

Dahl, Robert 349n
Dandavate, P. 263n
Dandekar, V.M. 36n
Das, Gurcharan x, 311n
Das, Prafulla 337n
Das, S. 266n
Das Gupta, Monica x, xvi, 233n, 236n, 244n, 247n, 249n, 251n, 253n, 259n
Dasgupta, Ashim x
Dasgupta, Partha 35n, 40n, 42n, 61n, 69n, 79n, 121n, 136n, 244n, 249n
Datt, Gaurav x, xvi, 36n, 87n, 99n, 322n, 326n, 332n, 324n, 328n, 355n, 387n, 388, 412
Datta, Ramesh C. 32n
Datta-Chaudhuri, Mrinal 80n, 310n
Davis, Calvin De Armond 275n
Dayaram 170n
De, Anuradha x, 153n, 164n, 172n, 179n
Deaton, Angus x, xvi, 35n, 87n, 88n, 99n, 104n, 172n, 179n, 215n, 247n, 324, 326, 327n, 387, 388, 412
Debreu, Gérard 48n
Debroy, Bibek x, 83n, 351n
Deger, Saadet 293n
De Geyndt, W. 129n
Deng Xiao Ping 44
Deolalikar, Anil B. 40n, 202n, 233n
Derr, B. 94n
Desai, G.M. 132n
Desai, Meghnad 35n, 37n, 311n
Desai, Neera 18n
Desai, Sonalde 246n

Deshingkar, G. 304n
Deshpande, Rajeshwari 32n
Dey, Nikhil 32n, 367n
Dietrich, Gabriele 18n
Donaldson, David 124n
Driver, Edwin D. 266n, 267n
D'Souza, S. 233n
Dube, Leela 162n, 231n
Dube, Saurabh 266n
Dubey, Amaresh 124n, 387n
Duflo, Esther 19n
Duggal, Ravi x, 202n, 206n
Dugger, Celia 258
Duraisamy, M. 156n
Duraisamy, P. 201n
Dutta, Bhaskar xvi, 36n, 83n, 124n
Duvvury, Nata 18n
Dyson, Tim x, xvi, 95n, 230n, 231n, 236n
Dworkin, Ronald 9n, 61n

Easterly, W. 75n
Eckholm, Erik P. 64n
Edwards, S.M. 267n
Egerö, B. 253n
Ehrlich, A. 64n
Ehrlich, Paul 64n, 65n
Ellman, Michael 333n, 334n
Ellsberg, Daniel 283n
Elster, Jon 42n
Eswaran, Mukesh 311n
Ethier, W. 74n
Ewell, Raymond 65n

Fajnzylber, P. 266n, 268
Fallows, James 47n
Fernandes, George 281, 287
Fernandes, Walter 28n
Filmer, Deon x, 13n, 92n, 147n, 150n, 412, 413
Findlay, Ronald 74n
Fishlow, A. 47n, 71n, 75n
Fitzgerald, Edward v
Foot, Michael 282n, 285n
Foster, James 124n
Francis, S.F. 339n

Frank, Robert H. 42n
Franke, Richard 90n
Frankel, Francine 351n
Frazier, Mark 283n
Freedman, Lawrence 283n
Fuchs, Victor 40n
Furman, Jason xvii

Gadgil, M. 60n, 95n
Gaiha, Raghav 36n, 360n
Gala, Chetna 362n
Galbraith, John Kenneth 371
Galenson, Walter 79n
Gandhi, Indira 255
Gandhi, Mahatma 144, 146, 278, 348n
Gandhi, Sonia 299
Gandotra, M.M. 253n
Gangopadhyay, S. 124n, 387n
Gardezi, H. 286n
Garenne, Michel xvi
Gargee 160
Garnaut, R. 122n, 123n, 385n, 386n
Gaul, Karen 108n
Gautama Buddha 5, 6, 219
Gazdar, Haris x, xvi, 15, 17n, 66n, 83n, 89, 90n, 93n, 94n, 95n, 109n, 146n, 154n, 158n, 161, 187, 244n, 354n, 361n
George, P.S. 100n
George, S. 233n
Germain, A. 136n
Gertler, P. 95n
Ghatak, Maitreesh 95n, 360n, 361n
Ghatak, Maitreya 360n, 361n
Ghate, Prabhu 36n
Ghosh, Amitav 286n, 287
Ghosh, Arun xvi, 19n, 20n, 144n, 155n, 164n, 188n, 311n
Ghosh, Debasish xvi
Gillespie, S.R. 250n
Gintis, Herbert 71n, 357n
Glaeser, Edward L. 268
Goetz, A.M. 367n
Gokhale, Gopal Krishna 144
Gopal, Sarvepalli 113n
Gopalakrishnan, A. 290n, 291n

Gopalakrishnan, R. x
Gopalan, C. 69n
Goswami, Anomita xvii
Govinda, R. 153n, 154n
Govindaswamy, P. 251n
Grant, James P. 35n
Greenhalgh, S. 137n
Greer, J. 124n
Griffin, Keith 35n, 123n
Griffith-Jones, S. 80n
Grossman, Gene M. 48n, 73n
Gu Xingyuan 129n
Guha, Ramachandra 60n, 95n, 108n
Guhan, S. 36n, 214n, 339n
Guio, Anne-Catherine xvi, 89n, 199n,
 231n, 244n, 246, 247, 249n, 250n,
 252n, 253n, 261n
Gupta, A. 286n
Gupta, D.B 249n
Gupta, N. 210
Gupta, S.P. 324n, 388
Gupta, Shreekant 218n

Hahn, Frank 48n
Haider, Salman 288n
Haikerwal, Bejoy Shanker 268n
Hallam, J.A. 214n
Halliburton, Murphy 98n
Halstead, S.B. 72n
Halweil, Brian 64n
Hamlin, A. 61n
Hammond, P.J. 46n
Hanchate, A. 95n
Haq, Mahbub ul 288
Hardin, Garrett 64n, 254n, 283n
Harilal, K.N. 361n
Harris, Marvin 269n
Harriss, John x, 95n, 217n
Harriss-White, B. 36n, 95n, 233n
Hauser, Philip Moris 190n
Hayami, Yujiro 47n, 80n
Hayek, Friedrich 5
Helleiner, G.K. 74n
Heller, Patrick 90n, 93n, 351n, 361n,
 368n

Helpman, Elhanan 48n, 73n, 74n
Hillier, S. 129n
Hinton, William 55n, 128, 129n
Hirschman, Albert O. 45n, 172n, 356n
Hitchcock, John T. 242n
Hong, W. 310n
Hopper, Gordon R. 197
Hoskote, Arunima xi
Howes, Stephen x, xvi, 112n, 123n
Huang, J. 137n
Hubbard, Michael 132n
Hull, Terence 137n
Huq, E. 233n
Hussain, Athar x, xvi, 122n, 123n

Idi Amin 44, 45
Isaac, Thomas 361n
Iyengar, P.K. 286n
Iyengar, Sudarshan 210
Iyer, A. 210

Jain, A.K. 251n, 253n
Jain, Devaki 231n, 246n
Jain, L.R. 36n, 124n
Jalan, Bimal 37n
Jalan, Jyotsna 334n
James, Robert Rhodes 285n
Jayachandran, Usha x, 154n, 182n
Jayachandran, V. 194n, 256n
Jayakumar, A. 164n, 214n
Jayal, Niraja Gopal 60n, 61n, 108n,
 351n, 360, 365n
Jayaprakash Narayan 144
Jayaraman, Raji 356n
Jayaraman, T. x, 286n, 290n, 304n
Jeffery, Patricia 145n, 210n, 251n
Jeffery, Roger 145n, 210n, 251n
Jeffrey, Robin 90n, 91n, 138n, 144n,
 232n
Jejeebhoy, S.J. 253n
Jenkins, Robert 367n
Jennings, Jackie xvii
Jervis, Robert 283n
Jesani, Amar 210n
Jha, Jyotsna 171n

Jha, Madan Mohan xvi
Jha, Praveen xvi
Jha, Shikha xvi
Jianqun, Fang xvi
Jodha, N.S. 359n
Johansen, Frida 47n
Johansson, Sheila 137n, 230n
Jolly, Richard 72n, 80n, 333n
Jones, Marion 123n
Joseph, Josy 293n
Joshi, Vijay 37n, 311n

Kabeer, Naila 154n
Kabir, M. 90, 100n, 254n
Kahkonen, S. 311n
Kahn, Herman 281n
Kakar, Sudhir 162
Kakwani, Nanak 35n, 36n, 124n
Kanbargi, R. 157n
Kanbur, S.M. Ravi 72n, 82n
Kane, Penny 132n
Kannan, K.P. 90n, 339n
Kant, Immanuel 7
Kapadia, Karin 55n, 156n, 231n
Kaplan, Robert D. 64n
Karkal, Malini 236n
Karlekar, Malavika 144n, 145n
Karve, Irawati 231n, 242n
Karve, Maharshi 144
Katoch, Rajan x
Kaul, Inge xvi
Keen, David 58n
Keidel, A. 386n
Keith-Krelik, Yasmin 108n
Kennedy, John F. 285
Kerawalla, Perin C. 266n
Khan, Abdul Ghaffar 144
Khan, A.R. 122n, 123n
Khan, M.E. 206n, 208n, 210n, 213n, 233n, 247n
Khatu, K.K. 157n
Khayyam, Omar v
Khemani, Stuti xvi
Khera, Reetika xi, 267n, 268, 269n, 336n, 337n

Kim, Kiwan 79n, 80n
Kimmis, J. 80n
Kingdon, Geeta Gandhi x, 54, 59n, 146n, 148n, 154n, 164n, 172n, 179n
Kipling, Rudyard 341n
Kirk, D. 254n
Kishor, Sunita xvi, 162n, 199n, 213n, 231n, 233n, 236n, 246n, 249n
Kishwar, Madhu 18n, 55n, 286n, 312n, 350n
Klasen, Stephan xvi, 230
Knight, Frank 5
Knight, John 35n, 123n
Knight, M. 293n
Kochupillai, N. 205n
Koenig, M.A. 206n, 208n, 210n
Kohli, Atul xvi, 361n
Kolenda, Pauline 231n, 242n, 243n
Koopmans, T. 48n
Kothari, Smitu 32n, 286n
Kotwal, Ashok 311n
Kozel, Valerie x
Krepon, Michael 284n
Krishnaji, N. 36n, 236n, 244n, 337n
Krishnakumari, N.S. 263n
Krishnamoorthy, S. 213n
Krishnan, T.N. 90n, 100n, 254n, 337n
Krishnaswamy, K.S. 36n
Krueger, Anne O. 310n, 312n
Krugman, Paul R. 48n, 73n, 74n, 75n
Kulkarni, P.M. 213n, 360n
Kumar, A.K. Shiva x, xi, xvi, 66n, 111n, 163n, 271n, 328n
Kumar, Krishna 164n, 168n, 172n
Kung, J.K. 141n
Kuo, S. 79n
Kurian, N.J. 36n, 320n
Kurrien, John xvi, 146n, 164n
Kynch, Jocelyn 229n, 230n, 233n, 246

Labenne, Sophie 154n
Lal, Deepak 112n, 311n, 324n
Lalita, K. 160n
Lane, Robert E. 35n, 40n, 45n

Langford, Christopher xvi, 238n
Lanjouw, Peter xvi, 54n, 60n, 109n,
  156n, 356n
Lanyi, A. 311n
Leclercq, François 154n, 156n, 157n,
  170n, 171n
Lederman, D. 266n
Lee, Jong-Wha 75n, 251n, 253n
Leipziger, Danny 79n, 80n
Leslie, Joanne 250n
Lewis, John 37n
Lewis, W.A. 36n, 37n
Li Chengrui 139n
Lieten, G.K. 95n, 144n, 152n, 154n,
  156n, 158n, 360n, 361n, 362n
Lijphart, Arend 349n
Lin, Justin Yifu 122n
Lin, Q. 141n
Lindblom, Charles 45n
Lipton, Michael 36n
Little, Ian M.D. 34, 37n, 311n
Liu, S. 141n
Loayza, N. 266n
Lochan, Rajeev x
Loh, Jackie xvii, 116n, 117n, 118n,
  119n, 322n, 385
Lopez, A.D. 201n, 237n
Lucas, Robert E. 47n, 73n, 75n
Ludra, T.K.S. 293

Ma, Guonan 123n, 385n, 386n
Macaulay, Thomas Babington 341n
Maddison, Angus 121n, 386n
Mahajan, Aprajit 251n
Maharatna, Arup x, 154n, 156n
Mahaveera 219
Mahendra Dev, S. xvi, 90n, 214n, 339n
Maitreyi 160
Majumdar, Manabi x, 154n, 156n,
  172n, 181n
Majumdar, Tapas 40, 92n, 144n
Malaney, Pia xvii
Malenbaum, W. 112n
Malhotra, A. 199n, 231n, 249n
Malinvaud, E. 75n
Mandelbaum, David G. 231n

Mander, Harsh x, 29n, 360n, 362n
Mankiw, N.G. 75n
Manor, James x, xvi, 175n, 360n
Mao Zedong 114
Mari Bhat, P.N. x, 90n, 191n, 215n,
  236n, 238n, 254n, 259n, 263n, 412
Maru, R.M. 211n
Marx, Karl 5, 38, 55n, 145
Mata, L. 72n
Mathew, E.T. 90n
Mathew, George xvi, 360n, 361n, 362n
Mathias, E. 360n
Mathur, K. 132n
Matson, Jim 112n
Matsuyama, Kiminori 75n
Maurya, K.N. 210n
Mavalankar, Dileep 211n
May, E.R. 285n
Mayaram, Shail 360n, 362n
Mayer, Peter 236n
Mazumdar, Vina 230n
McGuire, James W. 310n
McKenzie, Lionel 48n
McNamara, Robert 285n
McNeill, G. 250n
Meenakshisundaram, S.S. xvi
Mehrotra, Harinder x
Mehrotra, Nidhi x, xvi, 154n, 179n
Mehrotra, Santosh 72n, 80n, 169n,
  176n, 333n
Mehta, Aditi xvi
Mehta, Ajay xvi
Mehta, Sumati xvi
Mencher, Joan 90n, 92n, 213n
Meng Lian 121n, 122n
Menon, Meera 206n
Menon, Nivedita 350n
Menon, Parvati 360n, 362n
Menon, Raja 286n
Mill, James 341n
Mill, John Stuart 5, 34, 35, 38
Miller, Barbara 163n, 230n, 231n, 233n,
  236n, 242n, 244n, 246n, 270
Minhas, B.S. 36n, 159n
Minturn, Leigh 152n
Mishra, Neelabh 337n

Mishra, Sweta 362n
Misra, Rajeev 206n
Mitra, Arup 311n
Mitra, Ashok 230n, 236n
Mohan, Rakesh 324n
Mohanachandran, P. 235n
Mohanty, Bidyut 360n
Moller, Joanne 108n
Mooij, Jos 337n
Moore, Mick 230n, 231n
Morris, Cynthia T. 35n
Morris, Morris D. 35n
Mouravieff, Count 275n
Mukherjee, Anindita 55n
Mukherjee, Neela 359n
Mukherjee, Sudhansu B. 237n
Mukhopadhyay, Alok 206n
Mullen, Rani x, 360n, 361n, 362n
Mundle, Sudipto 311n
Munshi, Kaivan xvi, 42n
Muraleedharan, V.R. 214n
Murray, C.J.L. 201n
Murthi, Mamta x, xvi, 89n, 199n, 231n, 244n, 246, 247, 249n, 250n, 252n, 253n, 254, 259n, 261n
Murthy, Nirmala xvi
Muzammil, Mohd. 59n

Nadarajah, T. 238n
Nag, Moni 90n, 92n, 144n, 213n, 251n, 253n
Nagaraj, R. 311n, 320n, 324n
Nagarajan, R. 156n
Naik, J.P. 164n
Nair, K.N. 144n
Nair, P.R.Gopinath 90n, 100n, 144n, 154n
Nambissan, Geetha B. 154n, 158n
Nanda, A.R. xvi, 107n, 231n, 236n, 241n
Nandraj, Sunil 206n
Nandy, Ashis 378n
Narain, I. 187
Narain, Sunita 60n
Natarajan, I. 324n
Natarajan, K.S. xvi, 194n, 256n

Naughton, Barry 123n
Nautiyal, K.C. 144n
Navlakha, Gautam 292n
Nayak, Ramesh 360n, 361n, 362n
Nayar, K.R. 335n
Nayar, Kuldip 55n, 295, 312n, 374n
Nayyar, Deepak 37n, 311n
Nayyar, Rohini 36n
Neary, P. 74n
Nehru, Jawaharlal 1, 2, 4, 5, 6, 8, 35, 38, 113
Nicholas II, Czar 275, 276
Nieuwenhuys, Olga 157n
Ninan, K. 36n
Noronha, Claire x, xi, 172n, 179n
Nozick, Robert 61n
Nussbaum, Martha 3n, 35n
Nygren, O. 137n

Oe, Kenzaburo 279
Oldenburg, Philip 269n
Olson-Lanjouw, Jenny xvi
Omvedt, Gail 18n, 266n, 350n, 360n, 362n
Oommen, M.A. 90n
Osmani, Siddiq R. x, 36n, 40n, 69n, 70n, 79n, 121n
Ota, Masako 154n
Otsuka, K. 80n

Pachauri, S. 211n
Paddock, Paul 64n
Paddock, William 64n
Pai, Sudha 358n, 360n, 362n
Pal, Mahi 360n
Pal, Pritam 360n, 362n
Pal, Sarmistha xvi, 55n
Pandey, A. 251n
Pandita Ramabai 144
Panigrahi, Lalita 233n, 242n
Panikar, P.G.K. 90n
Paolisso, M. 250n
Papandreou, Andreas 227n
Parasuraman, S. 253n
Parayil, Govindan 90n
Parikh, Kirit 36n, 55n, 311n

Parmar, H.S. 108n
Parmar, S.S. xvi, 183
Patel, I.G. 311n
Patel, Surendra J. 112n, 312n
Pathak, Shekhar 110n
Patnaik, Prabhat 311n
Peng, Xizhe xvi, 120n, 132n, 137n, 139n
Perkins, Dwight 121n, 122n
Perkovich, George 304n
Persson, Torsten 71n
Pettit, P. 61n
Phadke, A. 206n
Phule, Jotirao 144
Pieris, I. 251n, 273n
Platteau, Jean-Philippe 55n, 60n
Poitevin, Guy 18n
Pol Pot 45
Powell, Robert 283n
Powis, Benjamin 361n
Prabhu, K. Seeta 311n, 334n
Pradhan, B.K. 159n, 334n, 335n
Prakasamma, M. 210n
Prakash, B.A. 90n
Prasad, C.V.S. 206n, 210n
Prasad, K.V. Eswara 146n, 154n, 174n
Preston, Samuel H. 237n
Pritchett, Lant x, 82n, 412
Priya, Ritu xvi, 210n
Priyam, M. 168n
Przeworski, Adam 377n
Psacharopoulos, George 40n
Pushpendra x, 349n

Qadeer, I. 335n
Qaiser, N. 210n
Quibria, M.G. 79n

Rabindran, Shanti xvii
Raghunandan, D. 210
Rairkar, Hema 18n
Raj, K.N. 74n, 90n
Raj, Sebasti I 360n
Rajan, S. 164n, 214n
Rajan, S.I. 90n, 232n, 235n, 236n, 238n, 254
Raje, G. 211n
Rajivan, A.K. 214n
Raju, S. 231n
Ram, Atma 183n
Ram, N. x, 286n
Ramachandran, H. 163n
Ramachandran, M.G. 218
Ramachandran, V.K. x, xi, xvi, 15n, 16n, 55n, 89, 90, 93n, 95n, 100n, 101n, 120, 125n, 138n, 160nn, 213n, 271n
Ramachandran, Vimala 211n, 359n
Ramana, M.V. 286n
Ramasundaram, S. 210n, 213n, 214n
Ramdas, L. 286n
Ramesh, B.M. 251n
Ramesh, Jairam 298n
Ramlingaswami, V. 132n
Rampal, Anita x
Rana, Kumar 97n
Ranade, Ajit xvi, 339n
Raney, L. 251n, 253n
Ranjan, Sharad xvi
Rao, K.V. x
Rao, Nina xvi
Rao, Nitya 164n
Rao, Sujatha xi
Rao, S.L. 311n
Rapoport, Anatol 283n, 295n
Rashid, S. 79n
Rath, N. 36n
Ravallion, Martin xi, 35n, 36n, 46n, 82, 83, 99n, 124n, 311n, 322n, 324n, 328n, 329n, 332n, 355n
Rawal, V. 95n
Rawski, Thomas G. xi, 122n
Ray, B. 18n
Ray, Debraj 69n, 79n, 121n
Ray, Rabindra 30n
Ray, Ranjan 251n
Raz, J. 61n
Raza, M. 144n, 163n
Razin, Assad 74n
Reagan, Ronald 43

Reddy, C. Rammanohar xi, 286n, 305n, 318n, 324n
Ricardo, David 74
Riskin, Carl xi, xvi, 72n, 121n, 122n, 123n, 132n, 133n
Robinson, Sherman 310n
Rodrik, Dani 47n, 71n, 75n, 80n
Roemer, John 61n
Rogaly, Ben xi, 95n, 244n
Rogers, John D. 267n
Rohde, John xvi
Romer, D. 75n
Romer, Paul M. xvi, 48n, 73n, 75n
Rose, Kalima 18n, 19n, 210n
Rosen, George 112n, 122n
Rosenfeld, Stephanie 81n
Rosenzweig, Mark 79n, 246n
Rosero, L. 72n
Ross, David 3n, 47n, 75n, 78n, 310n
Rothschild, Emma xi, xvi, 52n
Rothschild, M. 41n
Roy, Aruna 32n, 359n, 367n
Roy, Arundhati 28n, 223n, 279n, 286
Roy, D.K.S. 18n
Roy, Rammohan 144
Roy, S.B. 95n
Roy, T.K. x, 209n, 216n, 223n
Rudra, Ashok 30n, 32n, 311n
Rummel, R.J. 45n
Rustagi, Preet 156n
Ruud, Arild Engelsen 95
Ruzicka, Lado T. 237n

Sabot, Richard H. 47n, 72n, 75n, 78n, 310n
Sachs, I. 72n, 310n
Sachs, J.D. 37n, 311n
Saha, Anamitra 95n
Sahn, David 79n
Sainath, P. 158n, 303n, 314n, 337n, 351n, 375n
Saith, Ashwani 36n
Saldanha, Denzil xvi, 164n
Salim, A. Abdul 100n
Sampson, Anthony 291n

Samson, Meera x, xvi, xvii, 28n, 172n, 179n
Sanderatne, N. 72n
Sangwan, N. 211n
Saran, Mrinalini 120, 129n, 144n, 161n, 163n
Sarangi, Sudipta xvi
Saraswat, S.P. 108n
Sarkar, P.C. 334n
Sarkar, Rinki xi, 108n
Sarma, Sasanka xi, 320n, 328n
Satia, J.K. 253n
Sax, W. 108n
Saxena, N.C. x, 55n, 311n
Saxena, S. 168n
Schell, Jonathan 284n, 285n
Schelling, Thomas 283n
Schneider, Ryan 75n
Schultz, T. Paul 38n, 253n, 246n
Schultz, Theodore W. 38n
Scitovsky, Tibor 311n
Scott, Maurice Fg. 311n
Scrimshaw, Nevin 67n, 69n, 196n
Seetharamu, A.S. 175n
Sen, Abhijit xi, 324n, 332n, 388n
Sen, Binayak 206n
Sen, Geeta 136n
Sen, Ilina 18n, 32n, 236n
Sen, K. 335n
Sen, Pronab x
Sen, Somnath xi
Senapaty, Manju 154n
Sengupta, Sunil x, xi, xvi, 15n, 17n, 89, 94n, 95n, 233n, 361n
Seshan, T.N. 351n
Seshu, Geeta 303n
Sethi, R. 42n
Shah, M. 360n
Shah, M.H. 210n
Shah, Nasra M. 234n
Shah, Tushaar 95n
Sharada, A.L. xi
Shariff, Abusaleh 83n, 105n, 107n, 171n, 172n, 177n, 180n, 201n, 205n

510 / NAME INDEX

Sharma, H. 286n
Sharma, L.R. 101, 109
Sharma, Mukul 345n
Sharma, Naresh 54n, 60n, 109n, 156n, 270n, 362n
Sharma, Ursula 163n, 246n
Shen, J. 129n
Shetty, S.K. xvi
Shiva, Meera 210n
Shleifer, A. 366n
Shubik, Martin 283n, 295
Shukla, A. 206n
Shuzuo, Li 259n
Siddiqui, Farooque xi, 174n
Sikka, B.K. 108n, 109n
Singh, Amrit xvi
Singh, Chetan 107n, 108n
Singh, D.V. 108n
Singh, Inderjit 36n
Singh, Jasjit 286n
Singh, Jaswant 286n, 287n
Singh, K.B.K. 242n
Singh, K.S. 132n
Singh, M.G. 101, 102n, 109n
Singh, R.P. x
Singh, Satyajit 28n, 223n
Singh, Shanker 367n
Singh, Tavleen 337n
Singh, V.B. 349n
Singha, H.S. 165
Sinha, Ajay 154n
Sinha, Amarjeet x, xvi, 154n, 168n, 360n
Sinha, Shantha 156n
Sinha, S.K. x
Sipahimalani, Vandana 154n, 164n
Sivard, Ruth 276n, 277n
Sivaswamy, G. 164n
Smith, Adam 5, 34n, 35, 38, 48, 51, 52, 73, 74, 123n
Smith, Chris 74n, 290n
Smith, Dan 276n
Solow, Robert M. 75, 220
Soman, C.R. 90n
Somanathan, E. xvi, 60n, 61n, 108n, 110n

Somanathan, Rohini xvii
Sondhi, M.L. 286n
Song, Lina 123n
Sopher, David 163n, 230n, 231n
Sorensen, Theodore C. 285
Soros, George 343
Srinivas, M.N. 243n, 356
Srinivasan, K. 213n
Srinivasan, P.V. xi, xvii, 109n, 253n, 272n
Srinivasan, T.N. xvii, 35n, 36n, 37, 38, 112n, 311n, 312n
Srinivasan, V. 233n
Srivastava, Ranjana 171n
Srivastava, Ravi 154n, 163n, 181n, 360n
Srivastava, Snigdha xvii
Stern, Nicholas 79n
Stevenson, H. 75n
Stewart, Frances 35n
Stigler, J. 75n
Stiglitz, Joseph 41n, 47n, 80n
Stokey, Nancy L. 73n, 75n
Storey, Pamela 238n
Streatfield, K. 251n
Streeten, Paul 35n
Sturdy, P. 251n
Su, Fubing 132n
Subbarao, K. 36n, 251n, 253n, 311n, 334n
Subrahmanyam, K. xi, 286n
Subramanian, A. 159n
Subramanian, Narendra 217n
Subramanian, S. xi, 211n.
Sudarshan, R. 36n
Sudarshan, R.M. 172n
Sudha, S. 232n, 236n, 238n
Summers, Lawrence H. 40n, 82n
Sundaram, K. xviii, 124n, 318n, 324n, 327n, 328n, 388, 414
Sundararaman, Sudha 20n, 152n, 164n
Sundari Ravindran, T.K. 210n, 214n
Suryanarayana, M.H. 324n
Suzumura, K. 9n
Svedberg, Peter 67n, 196n

Svedrofsky, Anna Marie xvii
Swaminathan, Madhura 95n, 337n
Swaminathan, Mina 175, 214n
Swamy, Arun 217n
Swamy, G.V. 61n
Swarup, R. 109n

Tabellini, Guido 71n
Tagore, Rabindranath 144, 278, 279
Talib, Mohammad 158n
Tharakan, M. 90n
Tarozzi, Alessandro xi, 55n, 87n, 88n,
    92n, 99n, 104n, 215n, 324n, 326,
    387, 412, 414
Teger, Allan I. 295n
Tendulkar, S.D. xvii, 36n, 124n, 324n,
    388, 414
Thackeray, Bal 281
Thakur, Sarojini xvii
Tharamangalam, Joseph 99n
Tharu, S. 160n
Thatcher, Margaret 43, 44
Thirlwall, A.P. 35n
Thomas, D. 251n
Thomas, Raju G.C. 286n, 290n
Thorbecke, E. 124n
Thukral, E. 28n
Tilak, J.B.G. xvii, 157n, 164n, 166n,
    172n
Tod, James 242n
Tomkins, Andrew 121n
Toye, John 35n
Tuchman, Barbara 275n, 276n
Turgot 38

Uberoi, Patricia 231n
Unnathan, T.K.N. 266n, 267n

Vaidyanathan, A. 154n, 201n
Vajpayee, Atal Behari 299
van Creveld, Martin 58n
van Ginneken, J. 251n
van Ginneken, Wouter 339n
van Hollen, C. 214n
Vanaik, Achin xi, 279n, 286n

Vanita, Ruth 18n
Vanneman, R. 199n
Varadarajan, Siddharth 303n, 373n
Varghese, N.V. 153n, 154n
Varshney, Ashutosh 349n, 351n
Vasavi, A.R. 144n, 152n, 153n, 154n,
    158n
Vashishtha, Prem 202n, 233n
Vaughan, Rosie xi
Venkatachalam, R. 233n
Verma, Jyoti 144n
Verma, R.K. 209n, 216n
Vijaychandran, V. 90n
Visaria, Leela 209n, 211n, 214, 215n,
    216n, 217, 218n, 253n, 256n
Visaria, Pravin xi, 165n, 211n, 213n,
    214n, 236n, 253n, 256n, 324n
Vishny, R. 366n
Vivekananda, Swami 144
Vlassoff, Carol 144n, 253n
Voltaire 5
Vyas, V.S. 36n
Vyasulu, Poornima 360n, 362n
Vyasulu, Vinod 152n, 171n, 175n,
    360n, 362n

Wade, Robert 47n, 60n, 80n, 131n
Wadley, S. 94n
Walker, G.M. 251n
Waltz, Kenneth 277n
Wang, Limin xi, xvi
Wang, Xiaolu 121n, 122n
Ware, H. 251n
Warth, Robert D. 275n
Watson, Fiona 121n
Weaver, Mary Anne 362n
Weil, D. 75n
Weiner, Myron 39n, 146n, 157n, 164n,
    184, 349n
Weitzman, Martin L. 141n
Westphal, Larry E. 310n
White, Gordon 47n, 80n, 129n
Wilkes, Andreas 129n
Williamson, John xvii
Wink, Claudia 230n

Witter, Sophie 333n, 334n
Wolfe, B.L. 251n
Wong, L. 129n
Wood, Adrian 112n, 122n
Wu, Harry X. 122n, 385n, 386n

Yadav, Yogendra 349n
Yang, Dali L. 132n
Yao Shujie 123n
Yiping Huang 122n
Yoon, Yong J. 48n, 49
Young, Alwyn 75n

Yu Dezhi 129n

Zachariah, K.C. 90n, 203n, 254n
Zaidi, Lehar xi
Zaidi, Salman xi
Zavier, A.J. Francis 259n
Zelikow, P.D. 285n
Zeng Yi 137n
Zhang, J. 137n
Zhao Renwei 123n
Zia Mian 286n
Zweifel, P. 41n